The Handbook of Forensic Psychopathology and Treatment

The Handbook of Forensic Psychopathology and Treatment explores the relationship between psychopathology and criminal behaviour in juveniles and adults. It provides a detailed explanation of the developmental pathway from the process of increasing criminal behaviour and becoming a forensic patient, to assessment, treatment and rehabilitation.

Incorporating theoretical and scientific research reviews, as well as reviews regarding forensic rehabilitation, the book covers the theory, maintenance and treatment of psychopathology in offenders who have committed a crime.

The Handbook of Forensic Psychopathology and Treatment will be of interest to master's and postgraduate students studying the relationship between psychopathology and crime, as well as researchers and clinicians working in forensic psychiatry institutions or departments.

Dr Maaike Cima works at the Radboud University Nijmegen, the Netherlands, and has been an academic in the field of Forensic Psychiatry since 2001. One of her most important publications is the article 'Psychopaths know right from wrong, but just don't care' (SCAN, 2010). Her current research builds on this study, examining moral cognitions, moral emotions and moral behaviour in (delinquent) juveniles.

The Handbook of Forensic Psychopathology and Treatment

Edited by Maaike Cima

LONDON AND NEW YORK

First published 2016
by Routledge
2 Park Square, Milton Park, Abingdon, Oxon OX14 4RN

and by Routledge
711 Third Avenue, New York, NY 10017

Routledge is an imprint of the Taylor & Francis Group, an informa business

© 2016 selection and editorial matter, Maaike Cima; individual
chapters, the contributors

The right of the editor to be identified as the author of the editorial
material, and of the authors for their individual chapters, has been
asserted in accordance with sections 77 and 78 of the Copyright,
Designs and Patents Act 1988.

All rights reserved. No part of this book may be reprinted or
reproduced or utilised in any form or by any electronic, mechanical,
or other means, now known or hereafter invented, including
photocopying and recording, or in any information storage or
retrieval system, without permission in writing from the publishers.

Trademark notice: Product or corporate names may be trademarks
or registered trademarks, and are used only for identification and
explanation without intent to infringe.

British Library Cataloguing in Publication Data
A catalogue record for this book is available from the British Library

Library of Congress Cataloging in Publication Data
Names: Cima-Knijff, Maaike José, 1973-, editor.
Title: Handbook of forensic psychopathology and treatment /
    edited by Maaike José Cima-Knijff.
Description: Abingdon, Oxon ; New York, NY : Routledge, 2016. |
    Includes bibliographical references.
Identifiers: LCCN 2015045846| ISBN 9780415657747 (hardback) |
    ISBN 9780415657754 (pbk.) | ISBN 9781315637105 (ebook)
Subjects: | MESH: Forensic Psychiatry. | Crime—psychology. |
    Criminals—psychology. | Dangerous Behavior. |
    Mental Disorders—therapy. | Mentally Ill Persons—legislation
    & jurisprudence.
Classification: LCC RA1151 | NLM W 740 | DDC 614/.15—dc23
LC record available at http://lccn.loc.gov/2015045846

ISBN: 978-0-415-65774-7 (hbk)
ISBN: 978-0-415-65775-4 (pbk)
ISBN: 978-1-315-63710-5 (ebk)

Typeset in Bembo
by Swales & Willis Ltd, Exeter, Devon, UK

Contents

List of boxes	vii
List of figures	viii
List of tables	ix
Notes on contributors	x

Introduction: forensic psychopathology and treatment	1
MAAIKE CIMA	

PART I
Theoretical introduction   13

1 Defining forensic psycho(patho)logy	15
ERIC RASSIN	
2 Scientific research in forensic samples	25
SCOTT O. LILIENFELD, ASHLEY L. WATTS, BRITTANY	
A. ROBINSON AND SARAH FRANCIS SMITH	

PART II
Development of antisocial behaviour   53

3 Children at risk for serious conduct problems	55
PAUL J. FRICK AND ELIZABETH A. SHIRTCLIFF	
4 Biological approaches to externalising disorders and juvenile psychopathic traits	74
MORAN D. COHN, ARNE POPMA, ADRIAN RAINE AND MAAIKE CIMA	
5 Juvenile offenders	97
ANDRIES KOREBRITS	
6 Conscience: moral cognitions, moral emotions and moral behaviour	113
MAAIKE CIMA	

vi   *Contents*

PART III
Psychopathology and crime
141

7   Deception: faking good or bad   143
    KIM VAN OORSOUW, MARCO JELICIC AND MAAIKE CIMA

8   Aggression   157
    FRANCA TONNAER, MAAIKE CIMA AND ARNOUD ARNTZ

9   Personality disorders and crime   183
    JILL LOBBESTAEL AND RENÉ CANE

10 Contemporary approaches to psychopathy   206
    INTI A. BRAZIL AND MAAIKE CIMA

11 Violent offenders: neurobiology and crime   227
    ALEXANDRIA K. JOHNSON AND ANDREA L. GLENN

12 Safe community reintegration of sex-offenders through
    Circles of Support and Accountability   242
    MECHTILD HÖING AND BAS VOGELVANG

13 Psychotic disorders and violence: what do we know so far?   255
    MAARTEN PETERS, HENK NIJMAN AND JOOST À. CAMPO

14 Aggressive behaviour in offenders with intellectual disabilities:
    theories and treatment   276
    MARIJE KEULEN-DE VOS AND KARIN FRIJTERS

15 Autism and (violent) offending: an overview of current
    knowledge, risk factors and treatment   307
    LYSANDRA PODESTA AND ANNA M.T. BOSMAN

PART IV
Risk assessment and rehabilitation
335

16 Risk management in forensic psychiatry: integrating a social
    network approach   337
    LYDIA TER HAAR-POMP, STEFAN BOGAERTS AND MARINUS SPREEN

17 Forensic rehabilitation: a phase of transition on a lifelong
    risk (and health) continuum   352
    SANNE VERWAAIJEN AND MARION VAN BINSBERGEN

    Index   374

Boxes

6.1	Example of an impersonal and personal dilemma	128
8.1	Interaction of vulnerability and environmental influences	167
9.1	Cluster A personality disorder	184
9.2	Cluster B personality disorder	186
9.3	Cluster C personality disorder	189
16.1	Forensic Social Network Analysis (FSNA) case study: background information	343
16.2	Forensic Social Network Analysis (FSNA) case study of 'Brian': answering the FSNA main questions based on FSNA (interview) data	344
16.3	Forensic Social Network Analysis (FSNA) case study of 'Brian': analysis and interpretation of the data	346
16.4	Forensic Social Network Analysis (FSNA) case study of 'Brian': risk management implications/interventions	347

Figures

8.1	The General Aggression Model	169
10.1	Location of the orbitofrontal cortex and amygdala	214
12.1	The Circles of Support and Accountability intervention model	249
16.1	Network patterns leading up to and during the offences	347
16.2	Current and return network	347
17.1	Three-component model	362
17.2	Transfer to society and aftercare planning (risk prognosis) on a lifelong continuum	363

Tables

6.1	Development of conscience according to Piaget (1932) versus Kohlberg (1981; 1984) versus Gibbs (2010)	117
12.1	Recidivism studies	246
13.1	Overview of the most important cognitive domains and deficits related to schizophrenia: spectrum	261

Contributors

Arnoud Arntz, PhD, Department of Clinical Psychology, University of Amsterdam (UVA), Amsterdam, the Netherlands.

Stefan Bogaerts, PhD, Department of Developmental Psychology, Tilburg University (UvT), Tilburg, the Netherlands; and FPC De Kijvelanden/Dok, Rotterdam, the Netherlands.

Anna M.T. Bosman, PhD, Department of Special Education, Behavioural Science Institute, Radboud University, Nijmegen, the Netherlands.

Inti A. Brazil, PhD, Department of Neuropsychology and Rehabilitation Psychology, Donders Institute for Brain, Cognition and Behavior, Radboud University, Nijmegen, the Netherlands.

Joost à Campo, MD, PhD, Mondriaan, Mental Health Institute, Heerlen, the Netherlands.

Maaike Cima, PhD, Department of Developmental Psychopathology, Behavioral Science Institute (BSI), Radboud University, Nijmegen, the Netherlands; and CONRISQ Group, the Netherlands.

Moran D. Cohn, MA, Department of Child and Adolescent Psychiatry, VU University Medical Center, Amsterdam, the Netherlands.

René Cane, MSc, Department of Clinical Psychological Science, Maastricht University, the Netherlands.

Paul J. Frick, PhD, Department of Psychology, Louisiana State University, the United States; and Learning Science Institute of Australia, Australian Catholic University, Australia.

Karin Frijters, MSc, Forensic Psychiatric Hospital 'de Beuken', Trajectum, Boschoord, the Netherlands.

Andrea L. Glenn, PhD, Center for the Prevention of Youth Behavior Problems, Department of Psychology, University of Alabama, the United States.

Mechtild Höing, PhD, Avans Center for Safety Policy and Criminal Justice, Avans University of Applied Sciences, the Netherlands.

Notes on contributors xi

Marco Jelicic, PhD, Department of Clinical Psychological Science, Forensic Psychology Section, Maastricht University, the Netherlands.

Alexandria K. Johnson, PhD, Department of Psychology, University of Alabama, the United States.

Marije Keulen–De Vos, PhD, Forensic Psychiatric Centre de Rooyse Wissel (CONRISQ Group), Venray, the Netherlands.

Andries Korebrits, MD, PhD, Department of Child and Adolescent Psychiatry, Psychotherapy and Psychosomatics, Helios Park Hospital/ University of Leipzig, Leipzig, Germany.

Scott O. Lilienfeld, PhD, Department of Psychology, Clinical Psychology, Emory University, Atlanta, the United States.

Jill Lobbestael, PhD, Department of Clinical Psychological Science, Maastricht University, the Netherlands.

Henk Nijman, PhD, Behavioural Science Institute (BSI), Radboud University, Nijmegen, the Netherlands; and Altrecht Aventurijn, Den Dolder, the Netherlands.

Kim van Oorsouw, PhD, Department of Clinical Psychological Science, Forensic Psychology Section, Maastricht University, Maastricht, the Netherlands.

Maarten Peters, PhD, Department of Clinical Psychological Science, Forensic Psychology Section, Maastricht University, Maastricht, the Netherlands; and U–center, Mental Health Clinic, Epen, the Netherlands.

Lysandra Podesta, MSc, Department of Special Education, Radboud University, Nijmegen, the Netherlands.

Arne Popma, PhD, Institute of Law and Criminology, Faculty of Law, Leiden University, Leiden, the Netherlands.

Adrian Raine, PhD, Department of Criminology, Psychology, University of Pennsylvania, Pennsylvania, the United States.

Eric Rassin, PhD, Faculty of Social Sciences and School of Law of Erasmus University Rotterdam, Rotterdam, the Netherlands.

Brittany A. Robinson, MA, Department of Psychology, Clinical Psychology, Emory University, Atlanta, the United States.

Elizabeth A. Shirtcliff, PhD, Department of Human Development and Family Studies, Iowa State University, the United States.

Sarah Francis Smith, MA, Department of Psychology, Clinical Psychology, Emory University, Atlanta, the United States.

Marinus Spreen, PhD, FPC Dr. S. van Mesdag, Groningen, The Netherlands; and Stenden University, Leeuwarden, the Netherlands.

xii *Notes on contributors*

Lydia ter Haar-Pomp, MSc, Stenden University, Leeuwarden, the Netherlands; FPC Dr. S. van Mesdag, Groningen, the Netherlands; and Faculty of Social and Behavioural Sciences, Tilburg University, Tilburg, the Netherlands.

Franca Tonnaer, PhD, Forensic Psychiatric Centre de Rooyse Wissel (CONRISQ Group), Venray, the Netherlands; and Faculty of Psychology and Neuroscience, Department of Clinical Psychological Science, Maastricht University, the Netherlands.

Marion van Binsbergen, PhD, CONRISQ Group, Ottho Gerhard Heldring-stichting, Zetten, the Netherlands.

Sanne Verwaaijen, PhD, CONRISQ Group, Forensic Psychiatric Centre de Rooyse Wissel, Venray, the Netherlands.

Bas Vogelvang, PhD, Avans University of Applied Sciences/Circles NL Research Group, the Netherlands.

Ashley L. Watts, MA, Department of Psychology, Clinical Psychology, Emory University, Atlanta, the United States.

Introduction

Forensic psychopathology and treatment

Maaike Cima

Introduction

Several theories exist regarding the origins of psychopathology. Currently it is thought that many forms of psychopathology are the result of an interaction between a genetic predisposition and a stress-inducing environment. In other words, the interaction of an innate vulnerability and personal circumstances leads to psychopathology, depending on the manner in which an individual has learned to cope with these circumstances. In line with this proposition, psychopathology has been associated with the risk of developing maladaptive patterns of emotion regulation during adolescence (Silvers, Buhle, & Ochsner, 2014). Accordingly, a decreased ability to cope with stress due to maladaptive emotion regulation may lead to all kinds of psychopathology, like depression, anxiety or problems with self-control (Appelo-Wichers, Appelo, & Bos, 2008).

Emotion regulation can be defined as controlling the way in which emotions are experienced and expressed during certain stress-inducing situations. From this perspective, psychopathological disorders can be divided into *externalising* and *internalising* disorders. Externalising disorders relate to under-control or a lack of emotional control, whereas internalising disorders are related to an over-control of emotions. Externalising problems during childhood often result in aggressive, impulsiveness and hyperactivity. In severe cases this results in the diagnosis of conduct disorder, a disorder characterised by aggressive, impulsive and antisocial behaviour. These behavioural problems may in some cases be a risk for the development of later criminal and violent behaviour (Betz, 1995; Farrington, 1989; Moffitt, 1993; Liu, 2004), which is particularly disturbing for the environment. In contrast, internalising problems are troublesome for the person themself (Mervielde, Clerq de, De Fruyt, & Leeuwen, 2005). Internalising problem behaviour relates to the over-control of emotions, in which emotions are often directed inwards, leading to an unbalance in the person themself, often resulting in mood and anxiety disorders, psychosomatic complaints and inhibited behaviour (Muler, ten Kate, & Eurlings-Bontekoe, 2009). Empirical support for the view that externalising and internalising disorders are the result of over- versus under-control of emotions mainly comes from psychophysiological studies. These studies show an association between externalising problems and under-activation of autonomic functioning (e.g. heart rate, startle response and skin conductance), while internalising problems relate to autonomic over-activation (Dietrich et al., 2007).

Although externalising and internalising problems differ in their under-lying aetiology considering emotion regulation, there is also some overlap within and between these dimensions of psychopathology (Zoccolillo, 1992). For instance, within the internalising dimension, there is a strong overlap of depression and anxiety (Verhulst, Ende van der, Ferdinand, & Kasius, 1997; Craske, 2003), while within the externalising dimension there is a strong over-lap between ADHD and conduct problems (Beauchaine, Hinshaw, & Pang, 2010). However, there is also some overlap between the two dimensions, as shown in the association between depression and antisocial conduct problems (Angold, Costello, & Erkanli, 1999). Additionally, externalising problems can cause internalising problems, for instance because of peer rejection. In addi-tion, it has been suggested that certain biological markers may be equivalent for both externalising and internalising psychopathology. Such markers are not specific for internalising or externalising problems, but seem important in both dimensions. These markers include disturbances in certain neurotransmitter systems, such as 5-HIAA metabolism (Goodman, New, & Siever, 2004), but also the distinct activation patterns of the autonomic nervous system, and the hypo- and hyper-arousal of the hypothalamic-pituitary-adrenal (HPA) axis (Ruttle et al., 2011). Additionally, anatomical and structural deviations in brain areas including the orbitofrontal cortex (inhibiting subcortical impulses), cin-gulate cortex (evaluating emotional information) and adjacent ventromedial cortex seem to be related to both externalising and internalising behavioural problems. In 2003, Lilienfeld described the possibility that for both dimen-sions a third common factor may be responsible for the psychopathology, such as temperament (also see De Fruyt, Mervielde, & Leeuwen, 2002; Vasey & Dadds, 2001). Indeed, temperament is not specifically related to externalising or internalising problems, but is non-specifically related to all kinds of psy-chopathology across both dimensions. Biological correlates such as autonomic hypo-arousal (Cornet, de Kogel, Nijman, Raine, & van der Laan, in press), low heart rate (Lorber, 2004), brain damage and hormones influence tempera-ment development, eliciting a certain rearing style. Notably, the neurobiol-ogy of parent–child relationships, or so-called *developmental social neuroscience*, describes how the neurobiology of parenting is concerned with brain processes that support caregiving and emphasise the importance of how early care affects the development of the stress response system that influences emotional regula-tion capabilities through a lifespan (Hughes & Baylin, 2012). The interaction of biological correlates with psychological (development of temperament) and social (rearing style) factors may predispose an individual to the development of both externalising and internalising psychopathology. Therefore, it is essential to begin prevention and intervention programmes as early as possible when the brain is still malleable, to optimise behavioural changes and prevent the start of a developmental route into externalising or internalising problems.

From the few studies available in the literature regarding the development of emotion regulation, controlling one's emotions seems to be a learning process that is associated with the maturation of particular frontal brain regions. This maturation relates to age wherein childhood and adolescence is the most critical period for the development of emotion regulation problems. Individuals learn adequate and successful regulation skills especially during this period that are helpful during the rest of their lives to deal with stress. In some cases, however, this is the beginning of a period of a lifelong battle with emotion regulation problems, and mental and physical health issues. Therefore, adolescence is a sensitive period for the beginning of all kinds of problems (Kessler et al., 2005). This has to do with a variety of maturation mechanisms around this age in the field of psychosocial factors, including school and relationships, but also biological and environmental factors, like puberty hormones. Although adolescence is a period of neurobiological and behavioural changes that normally act in favour of optimising the brain for future challenges, these changes may also represent susceptibility for the development of different types of psychopathology (Paus, Keshavan, & Giedd, 2008). However, psychopathology additionally depends on the historical context. In other words, disorders describe people in need who suffer in a specific time and place, in a unique relationship with certain circumstances This means that an individual who shows signs of restlessness (a symptom of ADHD) in one environment may not show this in another, which suggests that a psychopathology is not a characteristic of an individual but of the relationship between the individual and their environment (Bosman, in press). Accordingly, De Wachter (2008) described how certain historical developments relate to an increase in certain psychopathology diagnoses. For instance, he claims that given the increase of competition and possible choices in current society, certain symptoms of a borderline personality disorder are not as uncommon as they once were.

Although some children and adolescents displaying externalising problem behaviour develop into antisocial adults (approximately 30%–40% of adolescents; Robins & Price, 1991), some develop internalising problems (Kim-Cohen et al., 2003), and a substantial number show no further psychopathology later in life. Within a subgroup of children who start displaying externalising problems at an early age (so-called early starters), biological correlates seem to play a more important role than externalising problems that start later in life (late onset; Hinshaw, Lahey, & Hart, 1993). Perhaps, therefore, externalising problems with an early start are often more persistent, also called life-course persistent type, and have a more difficult prognosis compared with late onset, so-called adolescent-limited type (see also Chapter 5; Angold, & Costello, 2001; Moffitt, 1993). For internalising problems there also seems to be a certain continuity in the way that certain internalising disorders predict the same disorders later (homotypical), as well as certain disorders predicting other disorders (heterotypical; Beauchaine et al., 2010). Interestingly, fear may be a protecting factor as well as a risk factor for the development of psychopathology. For instance, low levels of fear can be a risk factor for developing externalising antisocial behaviour, while high levels of fear may protect a person

4   *Maaike Cima*

from developing antisocial aggressive behaviour, though this is also a risk for developing internalising disorders (Granic, 2014).

Levels of fear are correlated to different levels of the stress hormone cortisol and the regulation of the HPA axis. Children with externalising problems often demonstrate low levels of the stress hormone cortisol, especially when induced into stress (Van Goozen et al., 1998, 2000). Although low levels of cortisol have a genetical component, there are also environmental factors, as for instance demonstrated in a study of Carlson and Earls (1996). They showed a relationship between serious neglect and low levels of cortisol in young children. Correspondingly, fear does not stand on its own, and is often triggered by environmental factors. In this context one might refer to the *Diathesis-Stress model*, which states that biological vulnerability in combination with a negative environment increases the chance of developing negative outcomes. In addition to the *Diathesis-Stress model*, the *Differential Susceptibility Theory* explains the relationship between biological vulnerability and both negative and positive environmental influences in the development of different forms of psychopathology.

For instance, in a study by Bakermans-Kranenburg and Ijzendoorn in 2006, the moderation effect of genes (dopamine receptor D4-7 repeat polymorphism; DRD4-7R) in the relationship between the sensitivity of the mother and externalising behaviour was demonstrated. These researchers found that children with the DRD4-7R allele and an insensitive mother showed significantly more externalising behaviour than children with the same allele but sensitive mothers. Children with the DRD4-7R allele and sensitive mothers showed the least externalising behaviours while the sensitivity of the mother had no effect on children without this DRD4-7R allele. A study by Obradovic, Bush, Stamperdahl, Adler, and Boyce (2010) showed that children of 5 years of age with high cortisol reactivity levels were classified by their teachers as less prosocial in their behaviour when these children were raised in unfavourable circumstances. When these children were raised under benign circumstances they showed the highest levels of prosocial behaviours, even in comparison with children with low cortisol reactivity. These studies demonstrate that more vulnerable individuals are more sensitive to environmental circumstances, for development associated with both negative and positive environments. A similar finding concerns the role of the genotype in cycles of violence and psychological trauma. For example, Caspi and colleagues (2002) showed that abused children with high levels of the neurotransmitter metabolism enzyme monoamine oxidase (MAOA) are less likely to develop antisocial behaviour later on in life, as opposed to abused children with low MAOA levels. As a result, Caspi et al. (2002) propose that stressful experiences are a risk factor in the development of antisocial externalising behaviour, in some but not all cases of victims of abuse (Caspi et al., 2002). Although recently Duncan (Duncan & Keller, 2011; Duncan, Pollastri, & Smoller, 2014) discussed the reliability of this hypothesis given the lack of replication, this theory seems promising in explaining the interaction of predisposition and a stress-increasing environment in socio-psycho-neurobiological determinants of psychopathology.

Focus of the book

This book is written for practitioners in the field of forensic psychopathology as well as for master's degree students studying forensic psychopathology themes. The book will also be of interest for scientists conducting research in forensic psychology and forensic psychopathology. This book will therefore incorporate both theoretical and scientific research overviews, as well as reviews regarding treatment and forensic rehabilitation. The book includes, first, the development of antisocial behaviour (where does it go wrong?); second, psychopathology and crime (psychopathy, personality disorders, violence, psychosis, intellectual disability); and third, risk assessment and rehabilitation (what to do if we treat forensic patients to reintegrate them back into society). In our opinion this structure, from aetiology to psychopathology to rehabilitation, covers the pathway from committing a crime to receiving treatment, and eventually trying to find a way back into society.

Chapters

Part I, Theoretical Introduction, contains two chapters reflecting on the basic theoretical orientations of forensic psychopathology. Chapter 1 explains the differences between forensic psychology, forensic psychopathology, forensic psychiatry and criminology. It will make clear that forensic psychopathology focuses on the relationship between disorders and crime (development of antisocial criminal behaviour, treatment of offenders, neurobiology of crime). Moreover, several contradictions within forensic psychopathology will be discussed, such as the underestimation of science, lab-research versus field-research, the relevance of forensic psychopathology knowledge to the judge, and the mission of a forensic psychologist. Scientific studies in the clinical field often constitute a challenge to researchers. However, scientific studies in the forensic clinical field are even more challenging, given the population being studied as well as the legal context in which the research has to take place. Chapter 2 in this part will therefore explain the central features of science in forensic psychopathology and focus on the difference between scientific studies and pseudoscientific studies within the forensic psychopathological field. In this chapter the question of how science and scientific thinking can inform research and clinical practice in forensic psychopathology will be addressed. In doing so, four major goals are aimed to accomplish: (1) Describe the central features of science for forensic psychologists and forensic psychology students; (2) Outline key differences between scientific and legal thinking; (3) Delineate widespread cognitive obstacles to scientific thinking; (4) Distinguish science from pseudoscience, with illustrations from forensic psychology research. Moreover, the seven deadly sins of pseudoscience will be outlined and several cognitive biases in scientific thinking will be explained. Therefore, this chapter is relevant to both master's and PhD students as well as clinicians working in the field wishing to learn more about evidence-based research and treatment.

Part II, Development of Antisocial Behaviour, includes four chapters summarising research on the origins of criminal pathways and several approaches

6   Maaike Cima

to understand the relationship between emotions, aggression and morality in childhood and adolescence. Chapter 3 gives an overview of several studies demonstrating there is a certain subgroup of children who are at risk of developing very cold-hearted and fearless characteristics, which put them at risk for developing antisocial criminal behaviour. Research is summarized showing behavioral, cognitive-emotional, and biological differences in children with severe conduct problems depending on whether they also show significant levels of callous-unemotional (CU) traits. These differences support a model in which children who show elevated CU traits have a temperament characterized by reduced emotional responsiveness to punishment and distress in others that place them at risk for problems in the development of empathy and guilt. In contrast, other children with severe conduct problems seem to show difficulties regulating their negative emotions leading to conduct problems either directly (e.g. hurting others when angry) or indirectly (e.g. being rejected by peers and missing important socializing experiences). These distinct pathways are being included in new diagnostic criteria for conduct disorders and they are important to consider in both etiological research and when designing prevention and treatment programs for children with severe conduct problems. This chapter will focus on very young children as opposed to Chapter 5, which discusses young adolescents.

The second chapter of this part (Chapter 4) focuses on typical adolescence-related behavioural patterns, especially externalising disorders. This chapter reviews the current neuroimaging literature on atypical neural processes in externalising disorders related to three cognitive functions: inhibition, reward and loss processing, and affective empathy. A dimensional approach of the psychopathy concept is described to explain the heterogeneity among juveniles with externalising disorders. The relationships between certain psychopathy dimensions and the three cognitive functions are discussed in light of their clinical consequences and the operation of the legal system. As in Chapter 3, this chapter emphasises the importance of CU traits. In this respect, emotional hyperreactivity and disinhibition seem to be preferentially associated with impulsive-antisocial traits, while emotional hyporeactivity and empathy deficits are preferentially associated with callous-unemotional traits. There appear to be multiple neural mechanisms underlying the decision-making deficits observed in juveniles with externalised disorders, which are differentially associated with dimensions of psychopathic traits. The consequences of these findings for clinical practice and the operation of the legal system are discussed in this chapter.

In the next chapter of this part (Chapter 5), several risk factors of antisocial behaviour will be identified, putting certain children at risk for embarking on a criminal career. Additionally, this chapter gives an overview of juvenile offender characteristics, in which the model of Moffitt (1993) will be described. This model makes a distinction between life-persistent criminals, often starting their criminal careers early in life (before age 10 years), and adolescent-limited offenders who often start criminal activities around

Introduction 7

puberty. Risk and protective factors in relation to criminal pathways will be presented. Furthermore, the importance of creating treatment protocols intervening at the right time during development integrating several risk factors (biological, psychological, and social) is highlighted.

The final chapter of this part (Chapter 6) provides an overview of theories regarding moral development and conscience. This chapter unravels conscience into three important components: moral cognitions, moral emotions and moral behaviour. This chapter discuses the development of conscience, related concepts of conscience such as temperament, socialisation and attachment, and describes the relationship between moral emotions, moral cognitions, and moral behavior. Finally, it is discussed whether conscience can be adequately measured and whether it is possible to restore conscience in those who seem without conscience.

Part III, Psychopathology and Crime, includes nine chapters summarising research on the relationship between several forms of psychopathology and criminal behaviour. Within the population of forensic psychiatric clinics, several forms of psychopathological behaviours are present. Before summarising these different psychopathological types, the first chapter of this part (Chapter 7) introduces a common but often underestimated construct of malingering and deception. Malingering and deception often occurs as a symptom of an antisocial personality disorder and given the presence of this personality disorder within forensic clinics, one has to be aware of the relationship between psychopathology and 'faking good or bad'. This chapter therefore highlights several psychopathology problems in relation to deception.

In the next chapter (Chapter 8), the concept of aggression is explained and several theories explaining the origin of aggression are described. Given the fact that within forensic psychiatric clinics aggression is a very important treatment focus in light of recidivism estimations, this chapter highlights the importance of the construct of impulsivity in relationship to risk assessment and treatment. In relation to risk assessment within the forensic field, various risk factors relate to aggression and various abnormalities in neurobiology (the frontal lobe, autonomic reactivity, hormones and neurochemical functioning) seem to predispose individuals towards aggressive responses. Furthermore, aggression is frequently associated with personality disorders, especially cluster-B personality disorders, which are overrepresented within forensic psychiatry clinics (Fazel & Danesh, 2002; Ullrich et al., 2008).

Therefore, in the next chapter (Chapter 9), personality disorders and their relationship with crime are outlined. All 10 personality disorders will be summarised and the relationship between an antisocial personality disorder and psychopathy will be explained. Furthermore, the relationship between certain personality types with specific offences will be highlighted. The chapters ends with a critical note on how personality disorders relate to crime. Partly tautological relations between personality disorders and crime, unreliable self-report assessment, gender issues and high comorbidity postulate extra challenges for drawing firm conclusions on how personality disorders and crime intertwine.

8   *Maaike Cima*

A common association of mental illness and crime is the image of a classic psychopath. The concept of psychopathy is not new, but research regarding the origins and treatment of psychopathic individuals is still developing. This chapter reports about the conceptual discussions but also consensus of the conceptualisation of the construct of psychopathy. Although psychopathy is often labelled as a personality disorder, it is still not recognised as such in the current (5th) edition of the Diagnostic and Statistical Manual (DSM). The next chapter (Chapter 10) describes psychopathy as a construct reflecting certain personality traits. Several conceptualisations and measurements of psychopathy will be delineated. In particular, the distinct factor structures describing this disorder are discussed. Furthermore, this chapter highlights cognitive and neurobiological perspectives on psychopathy. Although most models agree that dysfunctional connectivity between the amygdala and orbitofrontal cortex (OFC) is related to psychopathic behaviour, more recent models argue that impairments extend beyond the amygdala and OFC (see Anderson & Kiehl, 2012). Additionally, social cognition relevant to our understanding of psychopathy is discussed.

An in-depth study on the neurobiology mechanism underlying violent criminal behaviour of violent offenders is discussed in the next chapter (Chapter 11). This chapter discusses how deficits in particular brain regions may pave the way for criminal development. Moreover, the contribution of individual differences in the anatomy and function of certain brain regions, hormones and environments and the interrelationship between these factors form an exciting line of research, which will hopefully lead to more promising discoveries regarding the aetiology of violence.

A common difficulty in forensic rehabilitation is the resocialisation of forensic patients into society, especially sex offenders. The next chapter (Chapter 12) introduces the *Circles of Support and Accountability* (COSA) approach that facilitates circles of support and supervision by professionals in the field of sex offender management. Research regarding the effectiveness of this approach as a promising tool in preventing sexual re-offending is discussed.

Besides personality disorders as a common form of psychopathology within the forensic field, psychotic disorders are also highly prevalent. The relationship between psychotic disorders and crime is examined in the next chapter (Chapter 13). The main diagnostic features and theories regarding the aetiology of these disorders are explained. Furthermore, a state-of-the-art perspective on the psychotic-violence link is provided.

The next chapter (Chapter 14) highlights potential causes for aggressive and criminal antisocial behaviour in individuals with intellectual disabilities. Prevalence rates of intellectual disability among forensic psychiatric patients typically vary between 3% and 50% (e.g. Deb, Thomas, & Bright, 2001; Holland, 2004). Therapists are challenged in finding appropriate treatment programmes, since most are not suitable for these types of patients. This chapter discusses several theories regarding the relationship between high levels of aggression and intellectual disability and reviews available treatment options for forensic patients with intellectual disabilities.

Although autism spectrum disorder is a common form of psychopathology within the forensic field, the scientific literature regarding the relationship between this disorder and criminal behaviour is sparse. The next chapter (Chapter 15) summarises several symptoms inherent to the disorder, but also to criminal behaviour such as unemotional behaviour and disturbed empathic ability. In this regard differences between autism spectrum disorder and psychopathy are discussed. Finally, this chapter concludes with treatment options.

Finally, Part IV, Risk Assessment and Rehabilitation, includes two chapters describing risk management in the forensic field and forensic rehabilitation as a lifelong risk continuum. The first chapter of this section (Chapter 16) reviews models of risk assessment and defines a network approach. The effectiveness of these risk management tools is discussed and the *Forensic Social Network Analysis* method is introduced as a practical tool to measure dynamic social network factors on an individual level.

In the final chapter (Chapter 17) it is argued that a criminal act or instance of antisocial conduct is not a single exclusive event, but is often preceded by early factors emerging during childhood and/or adolescence. The treatment model *Risk Needs Responsivity* is emphasised, which proposes that treatment should match the level of risk and criminogenic needs. Since this book is on the theory, maintenance and treatment of psychopathology in criminal offenders, including both juveniles and adults, the artificial division of separate juveniles and adults into legal and practical correctional services is discussed. Additionally, this final chapter addresses the issue of a lifelong vulnerability to violence-related behaviours, and treatment based on the concept of a lifelong risk continuum.

Concluding remarks

This book intends to contribute to knowledge regarding the relation between psychopathology and crime and aims to be an inspiration for researchers and clinicians to promote research and practice in this area.

No one is born a criminal. But some of us are born with a biological predisposition that, in interaction with certain environmental cues, may be a risk for developing psychopathological symptoms, which sometimes escalate into criminal behaviour. Despite such a predisposition, puberty is a vulnerable period. Even with a mature and healthy brain it is often difficult to control one's own behaviour, especially when the stress system is activated. Juveniles are in the process of maturation, where the limbic system dominates, promoting rapid increases in arousal. The decrease in prefrontal emotion regulation abilities makes young people even more vulnerable to develop all kinds of psychopathology and antisocial, criminal behaviours. It is therefore important to guide them in the right direction until they are mature adults.

10   Maaike Cima

Literature

Anderson, N. E., & Kiehl, K. A. (2012). The psychopath magnetized: Insights from brain imaging. *Trends in Cognitive Sciences, 16*(1), 52–60.

Angold, A., Costello, E. J., & Erkanli, A. (1999). Comorbidity. *Journal of Child Psychology and Psychiatry, 40*, 57–87.

Angold, J. E., & Costello, A. (2001). The epidemiology of disorders of conduct: Nosological issues and comorbidity. In J. Hill & B. Maugham (Eds.), *Conduct Disorders in Childhood and Adolescence* (pp. 126–168). Cambridge: Cambridge University Press.

Appelo-Wichers, R., Appelo, M., & Bos, E. (2008). Rationele rehabilitatie bij jongeren met emotieregulatie-problematiek: een pilotstudie. *Kind en Adolescent Praktijk, 7*, 102–110.

Bakermans-Kranenburg, M. J., & IJzendoorn, M. H. (2006). Gene-environment interaction of the dopamine D4 receptor (DRD4) and observed maternal insensitivity predicting externalizing behavior in pre-schoolers. *Developmental Psychobiology, 48*, 406–409.

Beauchaine, T. P., Hinshaw, S. P., & Pang, K. L. (2010). Comorbidity of attention-deficit/hyperactivity disorder and early-onset conduct disorder: Biological, environmental, and developmental mechanisms. *Clinical Psychology, 17*, 327–336.

Betz, C. L. (1995). Childhood violence: A nursing concern. *Issues in Comprehensive Pedriatric Nursing, 18*, 149–161.

Bosman, A. M. T. (in press). Disorders are reduced normativity emerging from the relationship between organisms and their environment. In K. Hens, D. Cutas, & D. Horstkötter (Eds.), *Parental Responsibility in the Context of Neuroscience and Genetics.* Berlin: Springer Verlag.

Carlson, M., & Earls, F. (1996). Psychological and neuroendocrinological sequelae of early social deprivation in institutionalized children in Romania. *Annals of the New York Academy of Science, 807*, 419–428.

Caspi, A., McClay, J., Moffitt, T. E., Mill, J., Martin, J., Craig, I. W., Taylor, A., & Poulton, R. (2002). Role of genotype in the cycle of violence in maltreated children. *Science, 297*, 851–854.

Cornet, L. J., Kogel, C. H. de, Nijman, H. L., Raine, A., & Laan, P. H. van der (in press). Neurobiological factors as predictors of cognitive-behavioral therapy outcome in individuals with antisocial behavior: A review of the literature. *International Journal of Offender Therapy and Comparative Criminology, 58*(11), 1279–1296.

Craske, M. G. (2003). *Origins of Phobias and Anxiety Disorders: Why More Women than Men?* Amsterdam: Elsevier.

Deb, S., Thomas, M., & Bright, C. (2001). Mental disorders in adults with intellectual disability: Part I: Prevalence of functional psychiatric illness among a community-based population aged 16 and 64 years. *Journal of Intellectual Disability Research, 45*(6), 495–505. doi: 10.1046/j.1365-2788.2001.00374.

De Wachter, D. (2008). Borderline-times. *Psyche: Tijdschrift van de VVGG, 20*(3), 8–10.

Dietrich, A., Riese, H., Frouke, E. P. L., Sondeijker, A., Greaves-Lord, K., Roon, A. van Ormel, J., Neeleman, J., & Rosmalen, J. G. M. (2007). Externalizing and internalizing problems in relation to autonomic function: A population-based study in preadolescents. *Journal of the American Academy of Child and Adolescent Psychiatry, 46*, 378–386.

Duncan, L. E., & Keller, M. C. (2011). A critical review of the first 10 years of candidate gene-by-environment interaction research in psychiatry. *American Journal of Psychiatry, 168*, 1041–1049.

Duncan, L. E., Pollastri, A. R., & Smoller, J. W. (2014). Mind the gap: Why many geneticists and psychological scientists have discrepant views about Gene–Environment Interaction (GXE) Research. *American Psychologist, 69*, 249–268.

Farrington, D. P. (1989). Early predictors of adolescent aggression and adult violence. *Violence and Victims, 4*, 79–100.

Fazel, S., & Danesh, J. (2002). Serious mental disorder in 23 000 prisoners: A systematic review of 62 surveys. *The Lancet, 359*, 545–550.

Fruyt, F. de, Mervielde, I., & Leeuwen, K. van (2002). The consistency of personality type classification across samples and five-factor measures. *European Journal of Personality, 16*, 57–72.

Goodman, M., New, A., & Siever, L. (2004). Trauma, genes, and the neurobiology of personality disorders. *Annals New York Academy of Sciences, 1032*, 104–116.

Goozen, S. van, Matthys, W., Cohen-Kettenis, P., Gispen-de Wied, C., Wiegant, V., & Engeland, H. van (1998). Salivary cortisol and cardiovascular activity during stress in oppositional defiant disorder boys and normal controls. *Biological Psychiatry, 53*, 531–539.

Goozen, S. van, Matthys, W., & Engeland, H. van (2000). Antisociaal gedrag van kinderen: Een neurobiologisch perspectief. *Justitiële Verkenningen, 26*, 65–75.

Granic, I. (2014). The role of anxiety in the development, maintenance, and treatment of childhood aggression. *Development and Psychopathology, 26*, 1515–1530.

Gross, J. J., & Thompson, R. A. (2007). Emotion regulation: Conceptual foundation. In J. J. Gross (Ed.), *Handbook of Emotion Regulation* (pp. 3–24). New York: Guilford Press.

Hinshaw, S. P., Lahey, B. B., & Hart, E. L. (1993). Issues of taxonomy and comorbidity in the development of conduct disorder. *Development of Psychopathology, 5*, 31–49.

Holland, A. J. (2004). Criminal behavior and developmental disability: An epidemiological perspective. In W. R. Lindsay, J. L. Taylor, & P. Sturmey (Ed.), *Offenders with Developmental Disabilities* (pp. 23–34). Chichester, UK: Wiley & Sons.

Hughes, D. A., & Baylin, J. (2012). *Brain-Based Parenting: The Neuroscience of Caregiving for Healthy Attachment.* London: Norton & Co.

Kessler, R. C., Berglund, P., Demler, O., Jin, R., Merikangas, K. R., & Walters, E. (2005). Lifetime prevalence and age-of-onset distributions of DSM-IV disorders in the National Comorbidity Survey Replication. *Archives of General Psychiatry, 62*, 593–602.

Kim-Cohen, J., Caspi, A., Moffitt, T. E., Harrington, H., Milne, B. J., & Poulton, R. (2003). Prior juvenile diagnoses in adults with mental disorder: Developmental followback of a prospective-longitudinal cohort. *Archives of General Psychiatry, 60*, 709–717.

Kochanska, G., & Aksan, N. (2006). Children's conscience and self-regulation. *Journal of Personality, 74*, 1587–1618.

Lilienfeld, S. O. (2003). Comorbidity between and within childhood externalizing and internalizing disorders: Reflections and directions. *Journal of Abnormal Child Psychology, 31*, 285–291.

Liu, J. (2004). Childhood externalizing behaviour: Theory and implications. *Journal of Childhood and Adolescent Psychiatry Nursery, 17*, 93–103.

Lorber, M. F. (2004). Psychophysiology of aggression, psychopathy, and conduct problems: A meta-analysis. *Psychological Bulletin, 130*, 531.

Mervielde, I., Clerq, B. de, De Fruyt, F., & Leeuwen, K. van (2005). Temperament, personality, and developmental psychopathology as childhood antecedents of personality disorders, *Journal of Personality Disorders, 19*, 171–201.

12 Maaike Cima

Moffitt, T. E. (1993). Life-course persistent and adolescent-limited antisocial behaviour: A developmental taxonomy. *Psychological Review, 100,* 674–701.

Muler, N., Kate, C. ten, & Eurlings-Bontekoe, L. (2009). Internaliserende problematiek in de kindertijd als risicofactor voor de ontwikkeling van persoonlijkheidspathologie op latere leeftijd. In E. H. M. Eurlings-Bontekoe, R. Verheul, & W. M. Snellen (Eds.), *Handboek persoonlijkheidspathologie* (pp. 63–72). Houten: Bohn Stafleu van Loghum.

Obradovic, J., Bush, N. R., Stamperdahl, J., Adler, N. E., & Boyce, W. T. (2010). Biological sensitivity to context: The interactive effects of stress reactivity and family adversity on socioemotional behavior and school readiness. *Child Development, 81,* 270–289.

Paus, T., Keshavan, M., & Giedd, J. N. (2008). Why do many psychiatric disorders emerge during adolescence? *Nature Reviews Neuroscience, 9,* 947–957.

Robins, L. N., & Price, R. K. (1991). Adult disorders predicted by childhood conduct problems: Results from the NIMH epidemiologic catchment area project. *Psychiatry, 54,* 113–132.

Ruttle, P. L., Shirtcliff, E. A., Serbin, L. A., Fisher, D. B., Stack, D. M., & Schwartzman, A. E. (2011). Disentangling psychobiological mechanisms underlying internalizing and externalizing behaviors in youth: Longitudinal and concurrent associations with cortisol. *Hormones and Behavior, 59,* 123–132.

Silvers, J. A., Buhle, J. T., & Ochsner, K. N. (2014). The neuroscience of emotion regulation: Basic mechanisms and their role in development, aging and psychopathology. In K. Ochsner & S. M. Kosslyn (Eds.), *The Handbook of Cognitive Neuroscience* (Vol. 1; pp. 1–40). New York: Oxford University Press.

Stieben, J., Lewis, M. D., Granic, I., Zelazo, P. D., Segalowitz, S., & Pepler, D. (2007). Neurophysiological mechanisms of emotion regulation for subtypes of externalizing children. *Development and Psychopathology, 19,* 455–480.

Ullrich, S., Deasy, D., Smith, J., Johnson, B., Clarke, M., Broughton, N., & Coid, J. (2008). Detecting personality disorder in the prison population of England and Wales: Comparing case identification using the SCID-II screen and SCID-II clinical interview. *The Journal of Forensic Psychiatry & Psychology, 19*(3), 301–322.

Vasey, M. W., & Dadds, M. R. (2001). *The Developmental Psychopathology of Anxiety.* New York: Oxford University Press.

Verhulst, F. C., Ende, J. van der, Ferdinand, R. F., & Kasius, M. C. (1997). The prevalence of DSM-III-R diagnoses in a national sample of Dutch adolescents. *Archives of General Psychiatry, 54,* 329–336.

Zoccolillo, M. (1992). Co-occurrence of conduct disorder and its adult outcomes with depressive and anxiety disorders: A review. *Journal of the American Academy of Child and Adolescent Psychiatry, 31,* 547–556.

Part I
Theoretical introduction

1 Defining forensic psycho(patho)logy

Eric Rassin

Introduction

Forensic psychology is a popular discipline. For example, of the approximately 13,000 members of the Dutch Psychological Association, 1,400 (i.e. 10%) call themselves forensic psychologists. Typical topics of reports produced by forensic psychologists are criminal responsibility, risk assessment, and competence to stand trial, but also the credibility of eyewitness testimony, confession evidence, and line-up outcomes, as well as child care and custody. The psychopathological consequences of crime, for example the development of post-traumatic stress disorder (PTSD) in victims, also fall within the domain of forensic psychology (see Gudjonsson & Haward, 1998; Sigurdsson & Gudjonsson, 2004). Forensic psychopathology is closely linked to forensic psychiatry, although the latter discipline is medical and hence quite practical, patient-centred, and less focused on psychological theories of mental disorders and crime.

In this chapter, the focus of forensic psychopathology will be discussed. Foremost, problems and challenges will be pinpointed. First, the legal context of forensic psychopathology will be briefly discussed. Next, assumptions underlying forensic psychopathology will be targeted, followed by scientific, legal, and ethical issues.

Crime and punishment

The criminal justice system seeks to sustain societal coherence. Within this main frame, several discrete punishment goals can be distinguished. For example, de Keijser, van der Leeden, and Jackson (2002) discuss no fewer than six effects of punishment. To start with, there is specific (the perpetrator will not engage in criminal activity again) and general (other members will not engage in criminal activities) prevention. Third, there is the immediate protection of society (incapacitation). Fourth, retribution is sought. That is, the perpetrator has to pay for and thus undo his crime. Fifth, and also crucial, is rehabilitation: once the perpetrator has completed his punishment, he can return to society with a clean sheet. Finally, there is the restoration of moral balance as a more abstract goal of punishment. That is, the balance in society is disturbed by the crime, and this disturbance can be resolved by punishing the perpetrator.

16 *Eric Rassin*

It remains to be seen to what extent the specific punishment goals can be achieved. For one thing, incapacitation will be complete by definition if the perpetrator is sentenced to imprisonment and thus removed from society. By contrast, the success of rehabilitation is less clear. Meanwhile, it must be feared that incarceration has some very negative side effects on mental functioning. For example, Pratt, Webb, and Shaw (2006) found that ex-criminals are at increased risk of committing suicide after release from prison. The scientific data on specific prevention (i.e. the reduction of recidivism) are not promising. Particularly, recidivism after incarceration is quite robust, with observed rates as high as 60% (see Wartna, El Harbachi, & van der Knaap, 2005).

The failure to prevent future crime by means of punishment is at odds with the classic behaviouristic notion that humans are sensitive to learning through reward and punishment. However, it must be acknowledged that the way in which offenders are punished in western societies is quite different from what behaviourists do in their animal laboratories. For the reduction of the forbidden behaviour to take place, punishment must be harsh, applied consistently, and applied with high contiguity. In practice, criminal punishment tends to be relatively lenient, applied infrequently (in approximately only 4% of the registered crimes; Rassin, 2009), and applied with considerable delay (see Dickinson, Watt, & Griffiths, 1992). Hence, it is not surprising that the specific preventive effect of criminal punishment is not as strong as would be expected based on scientific research on reward and punishment.

In the Netherlands, like in many other western countries, the criminal code has a clause that enables the judge to sentence mentally disordered offenders, not to regular imprisonment, but to incarceration in a forensic clinic. Forensic treatment can be ordered if the perpetrator has some 'retarded development or disturbance of his mental capacities'. In theory, there can be several reasons to exclude mentally disordered offenders from the standard set of punishments. First, it can be considered immoral to seek retribution if the perpetrator is mentally disordered. Second, it can be argued that disordered offenders are incapable of learning from punishment, because there is something wrong with their behavioural inhibition system (Gray, 1982). Thus, the criminal irresponsibility clause simply assumes that disordered offenders are at increased risk of recidivism, even though the recidivism rates for non-disordered offenders are already considerably high, and with theoretical reason so.

Assumptions underlying the Dutch system of criminal irresponsibility

The mere existence of criminal irresponsibility clauses has several implications. First, as borne out by the considerations above, the legislator seemingly adheres to the punishment goals of retributions (or rather exceptions thereof) and specific prevention. By contrast, if incapacitation were the legislator's primary goal of punishment, all offenders could simply be incarcerated without distinguishing between sane and disordered ones.

A second assumption underlying criminal irresponsibility clauses is that there is, or should be, a clear understanding of what constitutes irresponsibility (in the Dutch system: a retarded development or disturbance of mental capacities). Strikingly, there is little consensus on this matter. Presently, the bulk of forensic patients suffer from antisocial personality disorder, psychotic disorder, and/or paraphilia (Blansjaar, Beukers, & van Kordelaar, 2008). In the past, the distribution of disorders among forensic patients was, however, quite different (e.g. for a period of time there was more emphasis on addiction as a reason for irresponsibility; van der Wolf, 2012). While the psychiatric diagnosis is a major part of the forensic evaluation of offenders, traditionally, scientific forensic psychology has focused primarily on psychological theories of crime. Interestingly, the different psychological schools have produced their own insights (Robins, Gosling, & Craik, 1999). Evidently, behaviourism has produced some classical studies on the development of crime, such as Bandura, Ross, and Ross' (1961) findings of the modelling of aggressive behaviour. However, behaviourism does not elaborate on the link between psychopathology and crime. Notably, the old psychodynamic theories did find their way into forensic psychopathology. For example, many people think that being victimised in childhood results in criminal behaviours in adulthood. Although this causal hypothesis may well be construed as a behaviouristic notion (i.e. seeing crime leads to acting criminally), some forensic psychologists seem to prefer a psychodynamic interpretation of this relationship (but see Rind, Bauserman, & Tromovitch, 1998). For example, Lehnecke (2004) postulates the theory that mentally disordered sex criminals have come to their illness and crime because of a triad of a childhood symbiotic relation with their mother, an absent father, and a psychotraumatic experience (e.g. being the victim of a sex crime). Cognitive psychologists have concentrated on mental deficits in disordered offenders such as a reduced recognition of emotions in others (Montagne et al., 2005), or lack of empathy (Ali, Amorim, & Chamorro-Premuzic, 2009), or even theory of mind (i.e. the attribution of mind to oneself and others; see Baron-Cohen, Leslie, & Frith, 1985). Such general deficits may lead the tenacious offender to behave egocentrically and antisocially. In the last decade, biologically oriented theories have become popular. Such theories can involve neurobiological processes (e.g. changes in hormonal activity as a cause of disinhibition and aggression, see Flinn, Ponzi, & Muehlenbein, 2012). Much attention has also been given to anatomic or functional abnormalities in the offender's brain (Perez, 2012).

Forensic psychological practice has recently begun to focus on offenders' personality traits deemed relevant. As such, the focus has shifted away from classic notions (e.g. the understanding of right and wrong) towards offenders' characteristics that predict recidivism. Psychopathy, as measured with the Psychopathy Checklist Revised (PCL-R; Hare et al., 1990), is currently considered the best predictor of risk of future offending (Hildebrand, de Ruiter, & de Vogel, 2003; van der Wolf, 2012).

Besides the underlying moral theory of justice, and the need for consensus on the nature of criminal irresponsibility, a third assumption is that the relevant concepts can be measured reliably and validly. Mentally disordered offenders cannot be expected to always be frank in discussions with their therapists. It would be naive to lean on self-reports when diagnosing individuals in this population. It is evidently futile to ask an offender: 'are you a psychopath?' Therefore, the use of self-reports can be problematic in forensic psychology (see Cima, van Bergen, & Kremer, 2008). Test subjects may simply not be able to report on variables of interest, or may not wish to do so (see Schwarz, 1999, for self-report issues in general). Instead of self-reports, the primary source of information in forensic psychology is observation ratings. Although in the case of psychopathy, it is understandable that experts prefer to rely on observation scales rather than self-reports, it must be acknowledged that from a psychometric point of view, observation instruments are no less fragile than self-reports. Like the latter, the former ideally have to possess proven internal consistency, factor structure, test-retest reliability, and convergent, divergent, and predictive validity. And whereas self-reports do not need to be interrater-reliable, observation scales do. The list of desired psychometric properties is quite long, and it remains to be seen whether all observation scales relied on in forensic practice adhere to all criteria. As for the PCL-R, the forensic expert has to resist automatic inferences when scoring the test. Imagine a test subject who smiles in a friendly way at the psychologist. Would the psychologist think of this friendliness as superficial charm (one of the criteria for psychopathy) more readily if he knows that the subject is suspected of violent rape? Can it be excluded that the PCL-R score is somewhat artificially elevated because the test subject is generally a suspect of a severe crime, and is thus likely to meet various PCL-R criteria? Interestingly, there is a self-report measure of psychopathy that evades the well-known respondent bias by relying on items that hide their measurement pretence. Even though this Psychopathic Personality Inventory (PPI; Lilienfeld & Andrews, 1996) may be a considerable alternative to the PCL-R, to the best of the author's knowledge, this measure is hardly or not employed in forensic clinics. A more classic example is that in clinical and forensic practice, the Rorschach ink blot test is still used (Koenraadt, Mooij, & van Mulbregt, 2007), even though its psychometric qualities are by and large unproven (Garb et al., 2005; Lilienfeld et al., 2006).

Recently, forensic practice has started to employ brain scans as diagnostic tools. Intuitively, it is appealing to scan the offender's brain, because that yields the opportunity to study 'the source' of the problem. However, there are some flipsides to this development. For one thing, it is unclear to what extent brain abnormalities cause or even correspond with psychopathology or criminal behaviour. Further, the nature of for example fMRI (i.e. a compilation of thousands of statistical tests comparing changes in activity in numerous voxels) invites false positive conclusions (Vul, Harris, Winkielman, & Pashler, 2009). Nonetheless, brain scans are very popular at the moment (Weisberg, Keil, Goodstein, Rawson, & Gray, 2008). Meanwhile, there is some evidence that the inclusion of neuroscientific information in forensic reports influences judges in unexpected ways. For example, judges tend to be more lenient to

Defining forensic psycho(patho)logy 19

psychopaths if the psychopathy is explained in terms of brain abnormalities and processes (Aspinwall, Brown, & Tabery, 2012).

Recently, Fazel, Singh, Doll, and Grann (2012) conducted a meta–analysis on the accuracy of well-known risk assessment instruments, such as the HCR–20, SVR–20, and PCL–R. The authors concluded that 'Although risk assessment tools are widely used in clinical and criminal justice settings, their predictive accuracy varies' and 'their use as sole determinants of detention, sentencing, and release is not supported by the current evidence' (p. 2). Of course, forensic psychologists can be expected to rely on more than one measure to reach their conclusions. However, it is not always so that accumulation of more imperfect diagnostic information increases the accuracy of the ultimate conclusion. By analogy, the soup does not get any better after throwing in more bad ingredients. Lilienfeld, Wood, and Garb (2006) refer to the mistaken idea that the soup should get better as the 'alchemist's fantasy'.

A fourth and final assumption underlying the criminal irresponsibility clause is that forensic treatment must be effective. If not, there would be no reason to treat offenders at all. It is important to note that, currently, forensic therapy does not aim at reducing psychiatric symptoms, but merely at making the patient fit for return to society. Hence, the adage in forensic psychiatry is 'no cure but control'. Although it may be hard to believe, to date, the effects of much of the psychotherapeutic interventions currently practised in the forensic setting are unknown. Only recently has the field begun to develop 'evidence-based' therapies, thereby implicitly and somewhat reluctantly admitting that therapies so far may not have been evidence-based (van der Wolf, 2012). Not only are much of the forensic psychotherapies currently practised of unknown quality, some may even be counterproductive. For example, group therapy and insight-increasing therapies may make psychopaths better able to recruit future victims, and thus make them more dangerous than when they first were admitted to forensic care (Hildebrand, de Ruiter, & de Vogel, 2003). Notwithstanding this critique, looking at recidivism rates, it must be concluded that forensic treatment generally does work. By and large, forensic ex-patients re-offend only half as often as do ex-prisoners (Wartna et al., 2005).

Scientific, legal, and ethical issues

So far, several assumptions and cornerstones of forensic psychopathology have been discussed. In this section, a few more abstract problems concerning criminal irresponsibility will be highlighted. First, it is important to note that the institute of forensic psychopathology is in essence a paradox. It taps into a fundamental difference in legal and psychological reasoning. For the forensic psycho(patho) logist, explaining (criminal) behaviour is a highly interesting effort. However, it must be acknowledged that psychologists tend to continue explaining until there is no room for unpredictable choices of free will. For example, psychodynamics dictate that behaviour is guided by unconscious processes, behaviourism attributes all action to the environment, cognitive psychology attributes it to

20   *Eric Rassin*

existing schemas, and neuroscience holds (neuro)biological processes responsible for our behaviour. Thus, consequent psychological reasoning, regardless of its orientation (see Robins et al., 1999), will readily yield the conclusion that the individual is at least partly irresponsible for his own acts. Such theoretical thinking cannot be indulged by lawyers, however, because for the law, the human individual is and should be the smallest responsible unit. One cannot shift his responsibility away to his arms, legs, brain, or disorder. As such, the question of criminal responsibility is a little odd in the light of legal doctrine (Frenkel, 1989).

Second, the above-mentioned recent shift of focus towards risk assessment deserves some theoretical underpinning. Note that the original reason for excluding disordered offenders from the standard set of punishments was that they cannot be held responsible for their crimes, because of a retarded development or disturbance of their mental capacities. Once the system starts to assess the risk of future crime, at the point where the judge chooses between incarceration and forensic treatment (or a combination thereof), the goal of making the system more humane (e.g. by not exercising retribution) is abandoned in favour of mechanically predicting risk. Disordered offenders are then no longer sentenced to forensic treatment, because the system does not punish those who are irresponsible, but merely those considered dangerous. Hence, the inclusion of risk assessment at the diagnostic phase (as currently practised in the Dutch system) is a fundamental departure from part of the traditional view on irresponsibility.

A similar comment can be made regarding the periodical evaluation of forensic patients. During such an evaluation, forensic psychiatrists and psychologists evaluate to what extent the patient still poses a threat to his environment. If the threat has diminished, the patient can return to society; if not, incarceration in the forensic hospital will be prolonged. This evaluation is a crucial but also potentially problematic challenge for the practising forensic psychologist. For one thing, it is striking that the release from the criminal institution is contingent upon a positive evaluation by experts for disordered offenders, but not for 'normal' prisoners. Legally, this difference between forensic patients and prisoners is warranted, but for the forensic psychologist, this context constitutes an obligation to make decisions about release versus prolongation as flawless as possible. Notably, though, release/prolongation decisions seem to be far from perfectly accurate (Fazel et al., 2012), although the relatively modest recidivism rates for forensic ex-patients compared to ex-prisoners suggest that, at the population level, these decisions are of some validity.

Note that the stakes are unusually high for offenders, environment, and experts. Faulty conclusions can have serious consequences. False negatives (i.e. concluding that the patient is not at risk, whereas in reality he is) result in the release of dangerous individuals. False positives result in the prolonged incarceration of an individual who is in fact ready to return to society. Ironically, it is very hard if not impossible to detect false positive rates associated with the use of specific risk assessment instruments. Imagine a disordered criminal of whom the experts conclude that he is not yet ready for release from the forensic psychiatric hospital.

Defining forensic psycho(patho)logy   21

Imagine further that during his prolonged incarceration, he does not display any signs of aggression or dangerousness. His good behaviour cannot be construed as actual absence of aggression, because he was not exposed to his natural environment. Perhaps he is less likely to be aggressive in the hospital compared to the freedom of society. Thus, false positive rates are hard to determine. Perhaps the best way to detect them is to study the patient's behaviour during leaves from the institution – if any. In an attempt to increase the accuracy of prolongation decisions, some forensic clinics have begun to employ the polygraph, relying on the old control question technique (CQT). However, this development needs careful scrutinising, because the CQT suffers from a high false positive rate (see Gannon, Beech, & Ward, 2008). In effect, prolonging the stay of a forensic patient who is in fact ready to return to society is as unfortunate as a miscarriage of justice. Therefore, the reduction if not elimination of false positives should be a priority of forensic psychology.

Forensic psychopathology as a unique discipline

To date, the majority of forensic psychologists in the field have graduated in clinical psychology and have subsequently received training in a forensic clinic. Specialised undergraduate programmes in forensic psychology are scarce. It can be argued that undergraduate clinical programmes fall short in preparing students for the forensic field. For one thing, such programmes lack legal expertise, and therefore the candidate forensic psychologist is insufficiently aware of the context in which he is to operate. Note that the standard clinical context differs from the forensic context in various ways. To name a few differences: the clinician works for the patient whereas the forensic psychologist works for the judge or hospital; in clinical psychology the patient's privacy is valued much more than in the forensic setting; the regular patient suffers from his complaint and is motivated to cooperate, whereas the typical forensic patient makes others suffer from his disorder and is not necessarily motivated to cooperate. Finally, clinical psychology is client–centred whereas forensic psychology is truth–centred (Greenberg & Shuman, 1997). It is one thing to treat a (forensic) patient, to build up a good working relationship, and to show empathy. It is quite another to act as a distant evaluating professional. Notably, in Dutch forensic practice, the roles of therapist and evaluator are not always separated. One can imagine that the working relationship is tempered if the therapist has recently decided that the patient has not yet improved.

Forensic psychopathology is also unique in that the stakes are extremely high. Misdiagnosing an obsessive-compulsive disorder for a specific phobia is one thing; misdiagnosing a psychopath is quite something else. While the stakes are high, the consumers of forensic psychologists' products (judges) are lays. Thus, compared to the scientist whose every product (i.e. manuscript) is subject to scrutiny in the peer-review process, the forensic psychologist has little opportunity to learn from his peers. At the same time, the sensitive context in which the forensic psychologist has to operate makes transparency difficult.

22   Eric Rassin

Also, forensic clinics are not ideal places to conduct randomised clinical controlled trials. If for no other reason, it would appear strange to appoint part of the new forensic patients to a control condition in which they receive no treatment for the first six months of their stay. According to some authors, that would be unethical (van der Wolf, 2012). Although this may appear so from a practical stance, scientifically, offering patients treatment that may not work, or may even be dangerous (Lilienfeld, 2007), is far worse. All this makes the field of forensic psychology a slightly closed shop. This may potentially hinder scientific progress (Lilienfeld & Landfield, 2008).

Concluding thoughts

Forensic psychopathology is an interesting discipline at the intersection of psychology, psychiatry, and law. It is also a practice that carries great responsibility, because decisions made by forensic psycho(patho)logists have a major impact on other people's lives. Against this background, it is hardly surprising that forensic psychology is popular with students and practising psychologists. Having said that, it must be acknowledged that forensic psychopathology is in fact a very small field. The number of forensic patients is only a small fraction of that of prisoners.

Notwithstanding the modest size of the forensic field, media coverage tends to be disproportionate. That is, recidivism in forensic ex-patients receives ample media attention, whereas crimes committed by ex-prisoners receive far less attention. This skewed media coverage may well lead people (including politicians) to have little faith in forensic treatment. As mentioned before, however, forensic ex-patients return to crime far less often than do ex-prisoners (even when controlling for crime type).

Notwithstanding the success of forensic treatment borne out by reduced recidivism rates, forensic psychopathology is a dynamic discipline facing numerous challenges (e.g. Derks, 2001). To solve some of the problems discussed in this chapter, it could be argued that the differentiation between disordered and non-disordered offenders at the time of sentencing should be abandoned. Instead, legislation might dictate that every prisoner receives some forensic treatment (i.e. a programme that prepares for return to society) in the later years of incarceration.

Finally, the issues discussed in this chapter pertain to the Dutch system of criminal irresponsibility. However, it is to be expected that the topics discussed can, mutatis mutandis, be translated to numerous comparable systems employed in other western countries.

Literature

Ali, F., Amorim, I.S., & Chamorro-Premuzic, T. (2009). Empathy deficits and trait emotional intelligence in psychopathy and Machiavellianism. *Personality and Individual Differences, 47,* 758–762.

Aspinwall, L.G., Brown, T.R., & Tabery, J. (2012). The double-edged sword: Does biomechanism increase or decrease judges' sentencing of psychopaths? *Science, 337,* 846–849.

Bandura, A., Ross, D., & Ross, S.A. (1961). Transmission of aggression through imitation of aggressive models. *Journal of Abnormal and Social Psychology, 63,* 575–582.

Baron-Cohen, S., Leslie, A.M., & Frith, U. (1985). Does the autistic child have a 'theory of mind'? *Cognition, 21,* 37–46.

Blansjaar, B.A., Beukers, M.M., & Van Kordelaar, W.F. (eds.) (2008). *Stoornis en delict: Handboek psychiatrische en psychologische rapportage in strafzaken [Pathology and crime: Handbook of psychiatric and psychological reports in criminal proceedings].* Utrecht: De Tijdstroom.

Cima, M., van Bergen, S., & Kremer, K. (2008). Development of the Supernomality Scale-Revisited and its relationship with psychopathy. *Journal of Forensic Science, 53,* 975–981.

De Keijser, J.M., van der Leeden, R., & Jackson, J.L. (2002). From moral theory to penal attitudes and back: A theoretically integrated modeling approach. *Behavioral Sciences and the Law,* 20, 317–335.

Derks, W. (2001). *Het oordeel van Hippias: Over de deskundigheid van psychiaters en psychologen en hun invloed op de strafrechtspraktijk [Hippias' judgment: On the expertise of psychiatrists and psychologists, and their influence on the criminal justice system].* Amsterdam: De Arbeiderspers.

Dickinson, A., Watt, A., & Griffiths, W.J. (1992). Free-operant acquisition with delayed reinforcement. *Quarterly Journal of Experimental Psychology: Comparative and Physiological Psychology, 45B,* 241–258.

Fazel, S., Singh, J.P., Doll, H., & Grann, M. (2012). Use of risk assessment instruments to predict violence and antisocial behaviour in 73 samples involving 24827 people: Systematic review and meta-analysis. *British Medical Journal.* DOI: 10.1136/bmj.e4692.

Flinn, M.V., Ponzi, D., & Muehlenbein, M.P. (2012). Hormonal mechanisms for regulation of aggression in human coalitions. *Human Nature, 23,* 68–88.

Frenkel, F. (1989). Toerekeningsvatbaarheid: Een schijnprobleem [Criminal irresponsibility: A pseudo problem]. *De Psycholoog, 24,* 499–503.

Gannon, T.A., Beech, A.R., & Ward, T. (2008). Does the polygraph lead to better risk prediction for sexual offenders? *Aggression and Violent Behavior, 13,* 29–44.

Garb, H.N., Wood, J.M., Lilienfeld, S.O., & Nezworski, M.T. (2005). Roots of the Rorschach controversy. *Clinical Psychology Review, 25,* 97–118.

Gray, J.A. (1982). *The neuropsychology of anxiety: An inquiry into the function of the septo-hippocampus system.* New York: Oxford University Press.

Greenberg, S.A., & Shuman, D.W. (1997). Irreconcilable conflict between therapeutic and forensic roles. *Professional Psychology: Research and Practice, 28,* 50–57.

Gudjonsson, G.H., & Haward, L.R.C. (1998). *Forensic psychology: A guide to practice.* London: Routledge.

Hare, R.D., Harpur, T.J., Hakstian, A.R., Forth, A.E., Hart, S.D., & Newman, J.P. (1990). The Revised Psychopathy Checklist: Reliability and factor structure. *Psychological Assessment: A Journal of Clinical and Consulting Psychology, 2,* 338–341.

Hildebrand, M., de Ruiter, C., & de Vogel, V. (2003). Recidive van verkrachters en aanranders na tbs: De relatie met psychopathie en seksuele deviatie [Recidivism in sex offenders after forensic treatment: Relation with psychopathy and sexual deviance]. *De Psycholoog, 38,* 114–124.

24 Eric Rassin

Koenraadt, F., Mooij, A., & Van Mulbregt, J. (eds.) (2007). *The mental condition in criminal law: Forensic psychiatry and psychological assessment in a residential setting.* Amsterdam: Dutch University Press.

Lehnecke, K.M. (2004). *De rol van moeder-zoon symbiose in perversie en zedendelinquentie: Een wetenschappelijke verantwoording over de mogelijke gevolgen van een symbiotische moeder-zoonrelatie die niet door vader wordt beëindigd [The role of mother-son symbiosis in perversion and sex offence: A scientific account of the possible consequences of a symbiotic mother-son relationship that is not terminated by the father].* Nijmegen: Wolf Legal Publishers.

Lilienfeld, S.O. (2007). Psychological treatments that cause harm. *Perspectives on Psychological Science, 2,* 53–70.

Lilienfeld, S.O., & Andrews, B.P. (1996). Development and preliminary validation of a self report measure of psychopathic personality traits in noncriminal populations. *Journal of Personality Assessment, 66,* 488–524.

Lilienfeld, S.O., & Landfield, K. (2008). Science and pseudoscience in law enforcement: A user-friendly primer. *Criminal Justice and Behavior, 35,* 1215–1230.

Lilienfeld, S.O., Wood, J.M., & Garb, H.N. (2006). Why questionable psychological tests remain popular. *The Scientific Review of Alternative Medicine, 10,* 6–15.

Montagne, B., Van Honk, J., Kessels, R.P.C., Frigerio, E., Burt, M., Van Zandvoort, M.J.E., Perrett, D.I., & De Haan, E.H.F. (2005). Reduced efficiency in recognising fear in subjects scoring high on psychopathic personality characteristics. *Personality and Individual Differences, 38,* 5–11.

Perez, P.R. (2012). The etiology of psychopathy: A neuropsychological perspective. *Aggression and Violent Behavior, 17,* 519–522.

Pratt, D., Piper, M., Appleby, L., Webb, R., & Shaw, J. (2006). Suicide in recently released prisoners: A population-based cohort study. *The Lancet, 368,* 119–123.

Rassin, E. (2009). *Tussen sofa en toga: Een inleiding in de rechtspsychologie [Between sofa and toga: An introduction to legal psychology].* Den Haag: Boom juridische uitgevers.

Rind, B., Bauserman, R., & Tromovitch, P. (1998). A meta-analytic examination of assumed properties of child sexual abuse using college samples. *Psychological Bulletin, 124,* 22–53.Robins, R.W., Gosling, S.D., & Craik, K.H. (1999). An empirical analysis of trends in psychology. *American Psychologist, 54,* 117–128.

Schwarz, N. (1999). Self-reports: How the questions shape the answers. *American Psychologist, 54,* 93–105.

Sigurdsson, J.F., & Gudjonsson, G.H. (2004). Forensic psychology in Iceland: A survey of members of the Icelandic Psychological Society. *Scandinavian Journal of Psychology, 45,* 325–329.

van der Wolf, M.J.F. (2012). *TBS: Veroordeeld tot vooroordeel: Een analyse van historische fundamenten van recente knelpunten, het systeem en buitenlandse alternatieven [Forensic treatment: Sentenced to prejudice: An analysis of historical foundations of recent pitfalls, the system, and foreign alternatives].* Oisterwijk: Wolf Legal Publishers.

Vul, E., Harris, C., Winkielman, P., & Pashler, H. (2009). Puzzlingly high correlations in fMRI studies of emotion, personality, and social cognition. *Psychological Science, 4,* 274–290.

Wartna, B.S.J., El Harbachi, S., & Van der Knaap, L.M. (2005). *Buiten behandeling: Een cijfermatig overzicht van de strafrechtelijke recidive van ex-terbeschikkinggestelden [Beyond treatment: A quantitative analysis of recidivism in forensic ex-patients].* Den Haag: WODC.

Weisberg, D.S., Keil, F.C., Goodstein, J., Rawson, E., & Gray, J.R. (2008). The seductive allure of neuroscience explanations. *Journal of Cognitive Neuroscience, 20,* 470–477.

2 Scientific research in forensic samples

Scott O. Lilienfeld, Ashley L. Watts, Brittany A. Robinson and Sarah Francis Smith

Introduction

Revisiting our opening question: the essence of science

Philosophers have long debated the deceptively complex question posed in our opening line, with no definitive resolution in sight. Hence, we make no pretence at offering a conclusive answer here. Nevertheless, most philosophers agree that science is *not* merely a body of knowledge. What makes chemistry, physics, biology or, more controversially (see Berezow & Campbell, 2013; Lilienfeld, 2012, for competing views), psychology sciences is not their substance matter, as one can investigate any of these disciplines either scientifically or nonscientifically. For example, alchemy, cold fusion, creation science and phrenology are subdisciplines housed within the domains of chemistry, physics, biology and psychology, respectively, but they are all decidedly unscientific. Yet what renders them unscientific, and what distinguishes them from scientific subareas within each of these broad fields of study?

Science as an approach to evidence

The answer, we propose, is that the core of science is an *approach* to evidence. Specifically, we contend that science is fundamentally a systematic means of collecting, analysing and interpreting evidence that focuses on rooting out errors in one's web of beliefs (O'Donohue, Fowler, & Lilienfeld, 2007; Popper, 1959). By subjecting our cherished assumptions to careful scrutiny, science aims to align them more closely with external reality. Hence, the essence of science is error reduction and elimination. A core assumption here is *scientific realism*: There is a real world 'out there' to be described and explained, even if we can never apprehend it fully (McMullin, 1984). For example, researchers in forensic psychopathology routinely debate the relative merits of competing approaches to risk prediction, often subjecting widely used actuarial and clinical judgement measures to careful empirical scrutiny (e.g. Singh, Grann, & Fazel, 2011). In this way, they strive to identify drawbacks in extant risk prediction methods, and to learn from these shortcomings to improve our field's capacity to forecast violence in the real world.

26   Scott O. Lilienfeld et al.

Although science relies on *empiricism* – an emphasis on observation – it is not identical to it (Willingham, 2012). As we will discover later (see 'Cognitive impediments to scientific thinking'), science rejects pure empiricism, as it recognises that unguided observations of nature are often fallible. Hence, science mandates that observations be informed and constrained by research methods, which help researchers to (a) select which data to attend to and ignore, and (b) analyse and interpret the data they have collected. Hence, in contrast to *naïve empiricism* (Strong, 1991), which assumes that raw observations of reality are largely unaffected by biases and therefore accurate, science emphasises *systematic empiricism*, which assumes that raw perceptions are often biased by the preconceptions of observers, and must therefore be shaped and refined by research techniques.

Science as akin to natural selection

In Donald Campbell's (1974) influential *evolutionary epistemology*, science is analogous to natural selection in that it ideally discards 'unfit' ideas – those that do not withstand the test of rigorous scrutiny – and ideally leaves more fit ideas in its wake. Much as species that are the best adapted to their environments are the most likely to transmit their genes to subsequent generations, scientific ideas that provide the best fit to extant data are the most likely to survive to influence future generations of researchers. The goal of science, therefore, is to filter out erroneous beliefs and retain those with higher ideological fitness. Of course, science in practice does not always achieve this lofty goal, because it is practised by humans, who are necessarily fallible. Nevertheless, it aspires to the goal of minimising mistakes and thereby arriving at a closer approximation of the truth.

Note that this evolutionary view of knowledge acquisition implies that scientific knowledge is inherently provisional. Just as no species is guaranteed to survive forever (indeed, more than 99% of all species that have ever lived on the Earth have become extinct; Jablonski, 2004), no scientific idea is certain to endure indefinitely. In this regard, Sir Karl Popper (1976) and other postpositivist philosophers of science emphasised that scientific ideas are at best corroborated, never 'confirmed' or 'proven'. Even the best established scientific theories might in principle be overturned by contrary data. In the context of forensic psychopathology research, we should similarly recognise that no measures of psychological disorders, such as psychopathic personality (psychopathy), are strictly 'gold standards' (Skeem & Cooke, 2010); at best, they are 'silver' standards that have survived repeated attempts to disconfirm their construct validity (see Cronbach & Meehl, 1955). Still, some scientific theories, such as Charles Darwin and Albert Russell Wallace's theory of evolution by natural selection, are so extensively corroborated by so many independent lines of evidence (see Coyne, 2009) that we can provisionally christen them as 'true'. Similarly, in the forensic psychopathology literature, we can say with substantial, although by no means absolute, certainty that deficits in emotional processing underlie at least some of the behavioural deficits of psychopathic personality (psychopathy; see Blair & Blair, 2005).

Complementary perspectives on science

Four additional views of science complement and enrich the perspectives we have offered thus far; we describe each in turn. We should bear in mind, however, that these views are prescriptive rather than descriptive. That is, they tell us how science *should* operate, but not always how it *does* operate.

Science is a prescription for humility (McFall, 1996)

Because science forces us to admit that we are all fallible, it is an implicit acknowledgement of epistemic modesty. In the words of the late astronomer Carl Sagan and his wife Anne Druyan (Sagan, 1995), all good scientists have a voice in their heads that quietly but insistently intones, 'You might be mistaken. You've been wrong before.' This point is frequently misunderstood, in part because personality research demonstrates that successful scientists tend to be highly confident and competitive individuals (Feist, 2008), often advocating forcefully and at times dogmatically for their positions. Yet even though many scientists themselves are not especially humble, the scientific community holds their feet to the fire, insisting that they subject their ideas to independent scrutiny. As the sociologist Robert Merton (1973) observed, the scientific community typically insists on certain 'norms'. At least two of Merton's norms seem relevant to the role of humility in science. What Merton termed 'organized skepticism' means that scientists should strive to subject each other's claims to thoughtful scrutiny; what Merton termed 'disinterestedness' means that scientists should strive to put aside their personal biases and allegiances in an effort to get closer to the truth.

Science is the maximisation of informed criticism

This view, propounded by Popper's student William Bartley (1984), highlights the fact that science is a 'contact sport'. It is not for the faint of heart or thin-skinned. As Robert Pirsig (1974) put it in his classic book, *Zen and the Art of Motorcycle Maintenance*, science starts off its examination of questions by alerting us, 'Okay, Nature, that's the end of the nice guy' (p. 111). By subjecting all propositions to intense scrutiny, science aims to weed out errors. Ideas that can pass the test of withering criticism are, all things being equal, more likely to be correct than those that do not. Although criticism is rarely fun for the criticised, it is the lifeblood of science.

Science requires us to bend over backwards to prove ourselves wrong

This view, most often associated with Nobel-prize-winning physicist Richard Feynman (1986), underscores the crucial point that we should design our studies so that they have the best possible chance of proving our beliefs incorrect. Such investigations constitute what Popper (1959) termed 'risky tests' (see also

28   *Scott O. Lilienfeld et al.*

Meehl, 1978), those that stand a fighting chance of demonstrating that the theory that spawned our hypotheses is false.

Indeed, Popper (1959) argued famously that *falsifiability* – the ability to disprove an assertion – is the core criterion demarcating scientific from pseudoscientific knowledge claims. Admittedly, few contemporary philosophers of science are strict Popperians, largely because falsifiability almost surely fails as a necessary and sufficient criterion for scientific status. For example, although astrology is falsifiable (and has essentially been falsified; Dean, Mather, & Kelly, 1996), it is a prototypical example of pseudoscience. At the same time, many philosophers of science share Popper's view that scientists should be striving to prove themselves wrong; only then can they be justified in their confidence (although never with absolute certainty) that their beliefs are likely to be correct. For example, researchers who hold a specific aetiological view of psychopathy, such as the theory that psychopathy stems from deficits in fearlessness (Lykken, 1991) or response modulation (viz., the tendency to neglect extraneous stimuli once presented with a dominant response set; Newman & Kosson, 1986), should be assiduously designing their investigations so that they could refute these models if they are mistaken. Nevertheless, in science, risky tests are often avoided (Meehl, 1978), because for a host of reasons (e.g. fame, money, academic promotion, career advancement, face-saving), investigators are typically reinforced for carrying out weak tests of their preferred theories (Lilienfeld, 2010b; Lykken, 1991). Hence, it is all the more imperative that their scientific peers insist on risky tests. Again, although scientists themselves may not always behave scientifically, the scientific community (largely by means of its peer review process; see 'Distinguishing science from pseudoscience in forensic psychopathology') typically pushes them to do so, even if it occasionally drags them kicking and screaming along the way.

Framing Feynman's and Popper's views in the lingo of modern social cognition, we can say that scientific methodology comprises a set of systematic tools for compensating for *confirmation bias* (Lilienfeld, Ammirati, & David, 2012; Tavris & Aronson, 2007) and allied cognitive biases. Confirmation bias, a concept we will revisit in the forthcoming section (see 'Cognitive impediments to scientific thinking'), is the deeply ingrained propensity to seek out evidence consistent with our hypotheses and to deny, dismiss or distort evidence that is not (Nickerson, 1998). At least some data suggest that scientists are at least as prone to confirmation bias as are nonscientists (Mahoney, 1977). One key difference between good and bad scientists, we propose, is that the former are typically aware that they are susceptible to confirmation bias and make concerted efforts to overcome it, whereas the latter typically believe themselves immune to confirmation bias. Indeed, as we will later discuss, a core feature distinguishing science from pseudoscience may be the failure to institute systematic safeguards against confirmation bias (Herbert et al., 2000; Lilienfeld & Landfield, 2008).

Moreover, because of its relentless efforts to minimise confirmation bias, science at its best tends to be self-correcting over the long haul, even if this

Scientific research in forensic samples   29

process takes longer than most of us would like (Ioannidis, 2005). For example, for decades most psychopathologists viewed schizophrenia as a condition of primarily psychosocial aetiology, largely emanating from inadequate or harsh parenting. Yet eventually, twin and adoption data collected in the 1960s and 1970s put that pernicious idea to rest, firmly establishing that schizophrenia is a moderately to highly heritable condition (Gottesman, 1991).

Science helps us to avoid being fooled

Feynman (1974), ever the fount of delightful phrases describing science, noted that 'the first principle is that you should not fool yourself – and you are the easiest person to fool' (p. 12). By urging us to adopt protections against our own biases and other cognitive errors, science ideally minimises the odds that we will draw erroneous conclusions. As Pirsig (1974) put it, 'The real purpose of the scientific method is to make sure that Nature hasn't misled you into thinking something you don't actually know' (p. 107). With the exception of Pirsig's invocation of 'the' scientific method (see 'Summary'), we concur wholeheartedly.

Science as error reduction and elimination: an example from psychopathy research

One example of this error reduction and elimination process in forensic psychopathology research comes from progress in the assessment of psychopathic personality (psychopathy). Psychopathy has long been one of the most controversial and least understood constructs in psychopathology (Blackburn, 1988; Lewis, 1974; Skeem, Polaschek, Patrick, & Lilienfeld, 2011), despite being the subject of substantial research.

Several methodological obstacles have contributed to this contentious state of affairs. Several decades ago, studies revealed weak or at best modest relations among widely used measures of psychopathy (e.g. Hundleby & Ross, 1977), such as the Minnesota Multiphasic Personality Inventory Psychopathic Deviate scale (MMPI Pd; McKinley & Hathaway, 1944) and the California Psychological Inventory Socialization scale (CPI So; Gough, 1969). Even more troubling, shared method variance (i.e. self-report versus interview method of assessment) appeared to contribute to these unimpressive correlations at least as much as did content overlap across measures. In addition, most self-report psychopathy measures at that time correlated negligibly with the core personality features (e.g. lack of guilt, callousness, narcissism) classically associated with psychopathy (Harpur, Hare, & Hakstian, 1989). Instead, most of these measures correlated moderately or highly with indices of nonspecific behavioural deviance, such as the DSM diagnosis of antisocial personality disorder (ASPD; see Lilienfeld & Fowler, 2006, for a review).

In response to these problems, psychopathy researchers took the initiative to develop better measures. On the forefront of this movement was psychologist Robert D. Hare, who constructed a new psychopathy measure designed to

30   Scott O. Lilienfeld et al.

circumvent the shortcomings of extant instruments (Hare, 1980). Hare noted that the diagnosis of ASPD did not adequately identify individuals who possess the core personality features often associated with psychopathy. Hence, his initial scale rated inmates on a global 7-point scale designed to capture Cleckley's (1941/1988) classic conceptualisation of psychopathy, which describes these personality features. Nevertheless, these ratings, useful as they were, were not as reliable as might have been desired (in psychological science, reliability refers to consistency of measurement, such as consistency in the ratings of different clinicians, whereas in the legal system, reliability more often refers to a theory's scientific support). In response, Hare (1980) refined this measure by developing the Psychopathy Checklist, which asks evaluators to rate 16 Cleckley criteria for psychopathy and six other items on a 0 (not present) to 2 (present) scale on the basis of a clinical interview and review of file data. A final 20-item version, the Psychopathy Checklist – Revised (Hare, 1993/2001), was later developed after removing two psychometrically problematic items from the checklist. Later investigators developed well-validated self-report indices of psychopathy that followed the lead of the PCL and similarly helped to improve upon previous measures of this condition (see Lilienfeld & Fowler, 2006, for a review; see also Chapter 11).

The genesis of the Psychopathy Checklist (and related versions) led to the reduction of a substantial amount of error in the assessment of psychopathy, due largely to (a) greater standardisation of administration and (b) a shift in focus from behaviour-based conceptualisation of psychopathy to more personality-based conceptualisation. As a consequence, it has reinvigorated research on the correlates and aetiology of psychopathy. The PCL-R possesses high interrater reliability and internal consistency; moreover, research supporting its construct validity abounds (Hare, 2003; Hart, Hare, & Harpur, 1992). Nevertheless, as is to be expected in a scientific discipline, healthy debate regarding the meaning of PCL-R scores continues (Skeem & Cooke, 2010; see Hare & Neumann, 2009, for a rebuttal).

At the same time, we do not wish to be pollyannish. Even when errors are corrected in forensic psychology research, poorly supported ideas and methods may persist. For example, although data convincingly demonstrate that the polygraph test is a detector of arousal rather than of lies *per se*, and that it is associated with high levels of false positive errors (in which innocent people are erroneously labelled as guilty; see Iacono & Lykken, 1997), this technique continues to be used widely in some forensic settings (Gannon, Beech, & Ward, 2008). In addition, as we will discuss later (see 'Illusory correlation'), the organised-disorganised crime dichotomy remains popular in the classification of serial killers despite a paucity of supportive evidence (Canter, Alison, Alison, & Wentink, 2004; Sewall, Krupp, & Lalumière, 2013). The march of progress in forensic psychology, as in other branches of applied science, is often gradual and uneven.

In sum, science is not defined solely by a body of knowledge. Nor is it a single method or monolithic truth-generating device, although copious myths regarding the existence of 'the' scientific method persist (Bauer, 1994). Instead, at the core of the engine of science is a systematic approach to evidence that emphasises the necessity of adopting procedural safeguards – termed research methods – against error in the service of aligning our beliefs more closely with external reality. These research methods constitute a toolbox of finely honed techniques that have been found repeatedly to reduce the risk of error. In this respect, science diminishes the odds that we will fool ourselves and fool others (Meehl, 1993). In the long run, although not invariably in the short run, science allows us to develop and test forensic psychology techniques that better identify the guilty and protect the innocent, and that help us to better understand the assessment, correlates, causes, treatment and prevention of psychological disorders linked to an increased risk for crime.

Scientific versus legal reasoning

To grasp the challenges of applying scientific knowledge to forensic psychopathology research, it is essential to recognise that this translation is fraught with conceptual difficulties. In many ways, science and the legal system are alien worlds (Lilienfeld & Byron, 2012). They rarely communicate directly, and when they do, they frequently talk past each other. For example, many novice expert witnesses are surprised to find that opposing attorneys often focus more on their credentials and perceived conflicts of interest than on the scientific merits of their arguments. They may also be surprised to discover that jurors tend to be more persuaded by clinical opinions than by actuarial data, a sobering conclusion underscored by experimental research (Krauss & Sales, 2001). To a large extent, the wide gap in communication between science and the law stems from the vastly differing assumptions and epistemic approaches of these two worlds.

Two views of confirmation bias

As we have seen, sciences share an abiding commitment to combating confirmation bias. For example, rigorous psychological research insists on keeping observers blind as to who is the experimental versus control group, and on sophisticated statistical techniques (e.g. correlational and multiple regression methods) to minimise errors in inference. For instance, the technique of meta-analysis helps to reduce, although by no means eliminate, biases in author judgement and interpretation that render many narrative literature reviews difficult to evaluate (Hunter & Schmidt, 2004; Meehl, 1990). Moreover, much as many scientists detest the often ego-bruising and at times frustrating peer review process, this system helps the scientific community to weed out errors in design, data analysis and interpretation (Stanovich, 2012). Indeed, many an author who has groused about the imperfections in the peer review process ultimately comes to recognise its value. As Benton Underwood (1957) put it over a half-century ago:

> The rejection of my own manuscripts has a sordid aftermath: (a) one day of depression; (b) one day of utter contempt for the editor and his accomplices; (c) one day of decrying the conspiracy against letting Truth be published; (d) one day of fretful ideas about changing my profession; and (e) one day of re-evaluating the manuscript in view of the editor's comments followed by the conclusion that I was lucky it wasn't accepted!
>
> (p. 96)

In its often relentless emphasis on communal 'policing' of claims, science relies largely on an *inquisitorial* model: scientists put forth assertions, and peers subject these claims to meticulous and often ruthless scrutiny in an effort to ensure that these claims pass muster. The sloppy scientist whose work does not incorporate adequate procedural protections against confirmation bias is likely to see his or her manuscript submission shredded mercilessly by unforgiving reviewers.

In contrast, the legal system, at least in the United States, relies on an *adversarial* model. Prosecution and defence each aim to present their best case, rarely if ever acknowledging shortcomings in their positions. In many respects, this system embraces and even encourages confirmation bias. The assumption is that the 'truth will win out' when each side gets the opportunity to play its best hand. Although perhaps not inherently unscientific *per se*, this model may not weed out errors as efficiently or effectively as does science, because its ultimate success rests on who makes a more persuasive argument to jurors rather than on whose hypotheses best comport with data.

The general versus the particular

The differences between the scientific and legal systems hardly end there. As David Faigman (2008) observed, science tends to deal with general principles, the legal system with the particulars of the individual case. For example, a psychologist who studies eyewitness memory (e.g. Loftus, 1996) typically tries to identify overarching principles that govern how all people perceive and recall crimes. In contrast, attorneys are necessarily concerned with the specifics of their client's case: Was she accused unjustly on the basis of a faulty eyewitness report? Bridging the wide chasm between the general, namely the domain of science, and the particular, namely the domain of the law, is a formidable challenge, and it helps to explain why many attorneys are dubious that psychological science can assist them.

In many respects, this distinction parallels the hoary distinction between nomothetic and idiographic approaches to personality and psychopathology (Maher & Gottesman, 2005). This distinction, it is worth noting, may lie at the core of the much-decried gap between research and practice in clinical psychology (Lilienfeld, Ritschel, Lynn, Cautin, & Latzman, 2013). Researchers typically strive to reach nomothetic conclusions that apply to most or all of humanity, whereas clinicians are necessarily forced to deal with the idiographic particulars of the individual client. As a consequence, the latter may be tempted to override empirically derived nomothetic formulas (statistical prediction rules) in the case of individual clients, even though a substantial body of research indicates that doing so is typically ill-advised (Dawes, Faust, & Meehl, 1989; Grove, Zald, Lebow, Snitz, & Nelson, 2000).

Scepticism versus acceptance of common sense wisdom

Finally, perhaps because of its relentless efforts to compensate for human error, science, especially psychological science, tends to be sceptical of common sense views of human nature (Chabris & Simons, 2010; Lilienfeld, Lynn, Ruscio, & Beyerstein, 2010). It recognises that people's intuitions about how their minds work are often woefully mistaken. For example, data show that large proportions, even majorities, of laypersons believe that (a) full moons are linked to heightened rates of odd behaviours and crimes (Russell & Dua, 1983); (b) people with schizophrenia have multiple personalities (Vaughan, 1977); (c) expressing pent-up anger typically reduces people's risk for aggression (Brown, 1983); and (d) we should attach more credence to memories retrieved under hypnosis than to other memories (Green, Page, Rasekhy, Johnson, & Bernhardt, 2006). Yet scientific research roundly disconfirms all of these propositions (Lilienfeld et al., 2013).

In contrast, the legal system tends to be considerably more accepting of common sense psychology (e.g. Redding, 1998). Paul Meehl (1989), probably the most influential clinical psychologist of the 20th century, acknowledged that common sense psychology is at times correct and should not be reflexively discarded in the face of contrary scientific evidence. At the same time, Meehl noted that conventional wisdom regarding human nature is sometimes mistaken: Legislators and judges have relied upon the 'fireside inductions' (common sense, anecdotal, introspective and culturally transmitted beliefs about human behaviour) in making and enforcing law as a mode of social control. The behaviour sciences conflict at times with the fireside inductions (p. 521).

One high-profile example of legal reliance on fireside inductions comes from a widely publicised 2006 case involving then vice-presidential aide, Scooter Libby, who was accused of 'outing' ex-CIA agent Valeria Plame. In that case, U.S. District Judge Reggie Walton refused to admit the expert testimony of University of California at Los Angeles memory researcher and psychology professor Robert Bjork. Libby's defence team had wanted Bjork to present peer-reviewed evidence documenting that the inconsistencies in Libby's story over time did not prove that he had perjured himself, because such discrepancies could just as readily be chalked up to the vicissitudes of memory.

What was Walton's rationale for disqualifying Bjork as an expert? Bjork's testimony, he insisted, could only confirm juror's intuitive beliefs, because laypersons are already well aware of the fallibility of memory. Jurors, he wrote in his summary opinion, 'do not need the guidance of a memory expert to use

34   *Scott O. Lilienfeld et al.*

their "common sense" in the understanding of how memory works' (Chabris & Simons, 2010). Yet Walton's claim runs counter to survey data demonstrating that a staggering 63% of the American public believes that human memory operates like a video camera or DVD accurately recording all of the events we experience (Chabris & Simons, 2011; see also Simons & Chabris, 2012, for a replication; see also McCann, Shindler, & Hammond, 2003, for examples of judges' erroneous reliance on common sense wisdom with respect to eyewitness memory).

As another illustration, in a relatively recent U.S. Supreme Court ruling (Brown v. EMA, 2011), justices cavalierly dismissed findings that exposure to violent video games leads children to complete partial word stems with a letter that lends the word an aggressive meaning. For example, compared with children in a control condition, children who play violent video games are more likely to complete the word stem 'EXPLO_ E' with a 'D' than with an 'R'. Several justices were not impressed: 'The prevention of this phenomenon, which might have been anticipated with common sense, is not a compelling state interest' (Brown v. EMA, 2011, p. 13). The merits of this opinion aside, the justices' invocation of common sense in evaluating the plausibility and importance of a psychological finding again underscores the sharp difference between legal and scientific thinking.

Cognitive impediments to scientific thinking

Following the pioneering work of Keith Stanovich and Richard West (2000), Nobel-prize-winning psychologist Daniel Kahneman (2011) delineated two basic modes of human thinking (see also Evans & Stanovich, 2013). System 1 thinking tends to be rapid, automatic and intuitive; System 2 thinking tends to be deliberate, controlled and analytical. At the risk of reifying and anthropomorphising these two modes of information processing, which may lie on a continuum (Keren & Schul, 2009; Kruglanski, 2013), System 1 initially believes what it hears, and System 2 only later subjects it to critical scrutiny.

Believing first, disbelieving second

In a widely cited illustration of this principle, Daniel Gilbert (1991) presented participants with statements based on a word from the Hopi language (such 'A monischa is an armadillo'); a few seconds later, they discovered whether the assertion was true. On some trials, subjects were distracted in the intervening seconds by a challenging task – hitting a button as soon as they heard a musical tone – intended to prevent them from processing these statements mentally. Later, when Gilbert asked distracted subjects whether each statement was true, they tended to identify statements as true that were actually false – but not vice-versa. At first, we believe; only later do we disbelieve.

The judicial system typically ignores the crucial distinction between System 1 and System 2 reasoning. For example, research using 'mock' (simulated) jurors demonstrates that judges' instructions to jurors to ignore a piece of evidence presented during the trial ('Please strike that from the record') are often ineffective, because this information still exerts a significant influence on their verdicts (Steblay, Besirevic, Fulero, & Jimenez-Lorente, 1999). False beliefs often persist long after they have been discredited, a phenomenon that psychologists term 'belief perseverance' (Ross, Lepper, & Hubbard, 1975).

When viewed in the light of the System 1–System 2 distinction, we can regard scientific methods as formalised techniques for harnessing the power of System 2 thinking to override errors in System 1 thinking (Lilienfeld, Lynn, Namy, & Woolf, 2013). System 1 thinking is generally more consistent with our gut hunches and intuitions, and hence tends to be our 'default' mode of thinking. In contrast, System 2 thinking is almost always more effortful, as it forces us to engage our critical thinking capacities.

This perspective dovetails with the fact that scientific thinking does not come naturally to any of us (Cromer, 1994; McCauley, 2011). Indeed, in many respects, scientific thinking is decidedly unnatural for the human species, as it often requires all of us to think in a manner contrary to our intuitions. It strikes most of us as wildly implausible that in each breath of air we take, we are more than likely inhaling a molecule inhaled by Oliver Cromwell (see Wolpert, 1993), although it is almost certainly true. In the forensic arena, it may similarly strike us as self-evident that people who confess to serious crimes must be guilty of them, although ample data disconfirm this belief (Kassin & Gudjonsson, 2004). Because scientific thinking often contradicts common sense, it must be nurtured and practised regularly.

A bevy of biases

Psychologists have identified a host of cognitive biases that impede our capacity to reason scientifically (see Pohl, 2005). Many of these distortions probably reflect a propensity for System 1 reasoning. Here we review six biases that are especially pertinent to forensic psychopathology (see also Lilienfeld, Ammirati, & David, 2012).

Naïve realism

Naïve realism is the tempting error of assuming that we perceive the world exactly as it is (Ross & Ward, 1996). From the standpoint of the naïve realist, seeing is believing. Yet we know from psychological research that naïve realism is mistaken, because our perceptions of the world are shaped not only by external reality, but also by internal reality – our biases, beliefs and preconceptions. To a substantial extent, believing is seeing (Gilovich, 1991). For example, virtually all of us fall prey to striking visual illusions, and most of us are susceptible to inattentional blindness, the failure to spot obvious new stimuli passing across our visual fields, such as a gorilla cavalierly strolling in front of a group of people rapidly exchanging basketball passes (Chabris & Simons, 2010).

36   *Scott O. Lilienfeld et al.*

Naïve realism bears significant implications for forensic psychology. For example, in a free-response portion of a survey, approximately half of both undergraduates and psychotherapists likened human memory to a precise reproduction of reality, invoking such metaphors as 'videofilm', 'computer' and 'mirror' (Merckelbach & Wessel, 1998, p. 767). The belief that human memory can be trusted to provide a veridical replica of reality may imbue eye-witness memories with an unwarranted cachet of credibility. Indeed, in one survey, 62% of jurors believed – incorrectly – that eyewitnesses who are highly confident in their memories are especially likely to be accurate (Benton, Ross, Bradshaw, Thomas, & Bradshaw, 2005; see also Wise & Safer, 2004).

Confirmation bias

As readers may have already surmised from our foregoing discussion, we can sum up confirmation bias in five words: 'Seek and ye shall find' (Lilienfeld et al., 2013). As noted by Baron (1994), confirmation bias 'makes us into lawyers, hired by our own earlier views to defend them against all accusations rather than detectives seeking the truth itself' (p. 218; see also Watkins, 2009). To a large extent, scientific thinking is designed to minimise confirmation bias, especially the tendency for investigators to find evidence for their favoured hypotheses.

Researchers in forensic psychopathology attempt to compensate for confirmation bias in numerous ways, such as by using blinded observations. Although they often neglect to do so, investigators should also be explicitly stating their hypotheses prior to conducting analyses. Otherwise, they may inadvertently 'cherry-pick' results that support their hypotheses while ignoring or downplaying those that do not. Moreover, because memory biases tend to be self-serving (McDonald & Hirt, 1997), researchers may falsely recall having predicted these positive outcomes before undertaking the analyses. Misrepresenting exploratory research as confirmatory in published articles is arguably the most widespread – and pernicious – questionable research practice in psychology (Fiedler, 2011).

Perhaps all too evident in the legal system, confirmation bias run amok can lead to false accusations, costly trials and wrongful convictions. Beginning in 2006, members of the Duke University lacrosse team were subjects of a confirmation bias-fuelled inquisition led by prosecutor Mike Nifong. Several members of the team were falsely accused of rape by Crystal Gail Magnum, who had been hired by the players as an exotic dancer. Magnum accused the players in the absence of DNA evidence linking any of them to rape. Magnum was eventually discredited as an unreliable witness, with many inconsistencies in her story and a history of similar unfounded accusations (Schorn, 2006). Perhaps driven by a desire to win at all costs, prosecutor Nifong clung to the supposed guilt of the Duke lacrosse players, ignoring clear evidence to the contrary, some of which he withheld. Eventually, the charges against the Duke students were dropped and prosecutor Nifong was disbarred.

Hindsight bias

We all know that hindsight is 20–20, but this truism is easily forgotten by all of us, especially when our findings support our research or clinical hypotheses. Indeed, we are all susceptible to hindsight bias – the 'I knew it all along effect' – which is the error of perceiving events as more predictable after they have occurred compared with before they occurred (Fischoff, 1996; Hawkins & Hastie, 1990). Hindsight bias stems in part from the fact that we are adept at constructing stories to fit data, even when such stories are apocryphal (Shermer, 2011). For example, operating as forensic clinicians, we may commit the error of assuming that because a mentally maladjusted prisoner was sexually abused in childhood, this abuse must have played a key causal role in the prisoner's recent criminal behaviour. Yet this 'deterministic reasoning' (Garb, 1998) may be unwarranted, as the abuse may bear no causal relation to the individual's misbehaviour.

Uncritical use of heuristics

Heuristics are rules of thumb, or mental shortcuts, that often help us to solve problems more quickly and efficiently (Kahneman, 2011). They are generally adaptive, because more often than not, they generate approximately correct answers (Gigerenzer, 2007). Nevertheless, heuristics can at times lead us astray if we apply them uncritically; that is, if we do not systematically evaluate their accuracy using System 2 reasoning.

When using the *availability* heuristic, we gauge the likelihood of an occurrence by the ease with which it comes to mind (Tversky & Kahneman, 1974). For example, imagine that we are working in a prison setting as a forensic psychologist. If someone were to ask us whether there are more people with psychopathy in our low-security prison unit than in a locked psychiatric ward (which has a high base rate of psychotic, but not psychopathic, patients), we would probably get the answer correct just by consulting our memory bank. We recall more individuals with prominent psychopathic traits in the former than in the latter setting, and we rely on availability as a mental shortcut to the right answer. Yet, in other cases, availability can lead us to incorrect answers. For example, imagine that we are working in a forensic setting with a high *base rate*, or prevalence, of patients who have a history of head trauma. When asked to estimate the proportion of forensic patients *in general* who have a history of head trauma, we may provide too high an estimate, because memories of forensic patients with head trauma come readily to our minds.

When using the *representativeness* heuristic, in contrast, we apply the mental shortcut of 'like goes with like'. More formally, this heuristic uses the similarity of an occurrence to a prototype to gauge its likelihood (Gilovich & Savitsky, 1996; Tversky & Kahneman, 1974). Like the availability heuristic, this heuristic typically leads to correct, or at least mostly correct, answers. During an initial interview, we may accurately discern that a prison inmate who is charming

38 Scott O. Lilienfeld et al.

and poised, yet dishonest, grandiose, guiltless and callous, is a classic Cleckley (see Cleckley, 1941/1976) psychopath, because the patient matches our stereotype of Cleckley psychopathy.

Yet this heuristic, like others, can predispose us to erroneous inferences if applied carelessly. While rotating through our university's counselling centre, we might reflexively diagnose a charming and self-centred undergraduate as a psychopath, because he reminds us of prototypical psychopaths we have encountered during our clinical training. In doing so, we might well be mistaken, because we may be falling prey to *base rate neglect*, a frequent casualty of representative thinking (Bar–Hillel, 1980). Base rate neglect is the tendency to accord insufficient weight to the prevalence of a phenomenon in one's sample. Such neglect is especially likely when we become so taken with the patient's match to a prototype ('Wow, he really seems like a textbook psychopath!') that we neglect to assign sufficient weight to the *a priori* likelihood of a diagnosis in the sample (Garb, 1998). In this case, we may be unaware of, or forgetting, the crucial fact that the prevalence of full-blown psychopathy is undergraduate samples is quite low (perhaps about 1%; Forth, Brown, Hart, & Hare, 1996) and considerably lower than that of prison samples. Because base rate information tends to be much less salient than diagnostic information, it frequently fades into our cognitive backgrounds and is readily neglected (Borgida & Nisbett, 1977).

Illusory correlation

None of us is immune to the tendency to see patterns in meaningless stimuli. Many individuals hold strong convictions regarding associations among phenomena, such as rainy weather and joint pain, when in fact no such associations exist (Redelmeier & Tversky, 1990). For example, a staggering 45% of college students (Rotton & Kelly, 1985) believe in the 'lunar lunacy effect', the belief (noted earlier) that individuals are more prone to unusual behaviours (e.g. psychotic symptoms, suicides, violent crimes) during full moons. Nevertheless, research has debunked the existence of this effect (Lilienfeld & Arkowitz, 2009; Rotton & Kelly, 1985).

Illusory correlation, first described by clinical psychologists Chapman and Chapman (1967, 1969), is a mental mirage. It refers to 'the report by observers of a correlation between two classes of events which, in reality, (a) are not correlated, or (b) are correlated to a lesser extent than reported, or (c) are correlated in the opposite direction from that which is reported' (Chapman, 1967, p. 151). Hence, when we fall prey to this error, we perceive a statistical association that is objectively absent, or a statistical association that is considerably weaker in magnitude than objectively exists.

The closely allied 'in my experience' fallacy is especially relevant to forensic settings. Criminal profiling, the practice of predicting (or postdicting) a criminal's personality and behaviours based on crime scene evidence (Douglas, Ressler, Burgess, & Hartman, 1986), may be especially susceptible to pitfalls associated with illusory correlations. This tool is widely used in forensic settings despite a virtually wholesale absence of scientific support (Snook, Cullen, Bennell, Taylor, & Gendreau, 2008). One of the most common FBI typologies, the organised-disorganised distinction noted earlier (Ressler, Burgess, Douglas, Hartman, & D'Agostino, 1986), posits that based on crime scene behaviours, crimes can be subdivided into those that were planned or unplanned. Moreover, this typology assumes that offenders can be classified as high functioning or low functioning based on background characteristics. Nevertheless, this typology has not been supported by research (Canter et al., 2004). Despite this negative evidence, criminal profiling and the organised-disorganised typology remain widely used in forensic settings, presumably because many criminal investigators are convinced that they capture reality.

As with other illusory correlations, such perceived associations between crime scene behaviours and offender characteristics may be perpetuated by an over-attendance to 'hits' rather than 'misses'. This propensity often stems from confirmation bias, because observers may focus selectively on data that support their hunches and hypotheses. For example, criminal profilers probably preferentially recall times when crime scenes supported the organised-disorganised typology and forget those that did not.

Bias blind spot

In contrast to the biases discussed thus far, bias blind spot is a 'meta-bias' – a bias regarding biases. In this respect, we can think of it as the 'mother of all biases'. Bias blind spot, sometimes informally called the 'not me fallacy', is the propensity to regard other people, but not ourselves, as biased (Pronin, Lin, & Ross, 2002). As a consequence, it can predispose us to become overconfident in forensic and other clinical settings. Indeed, clinician overconfidence has been observed on a host of tasks, such as the neuropsychologists' detection of malingerers (Faust, Hart, Guilmette, & Arkes, 1988; Garb, 1998; see also Chapter 8). Research demonstrates that most of us are adept at spotting biases, such as hindsight bias, confirmation bias and self-serving bias (the tendency to attribute our successes to internal sources, but our failures to external sources) in other people, but that we are usually oblivious to the same biases in our own reasoning. Just as few of us believe that we have an accent, largely because we do not notice it, few of us believe that we are less than objective in our reasoning, largely because we carry these biases with us everywhere we go. Research demonstrates that high levels of intelligence offer no immunity to bias blind spot. To the contrary, some evidence suggests that people with high IQs may be especially prone to this meta-bias (West, Meserve, & Stanovich, 2012), perhaps because they are prone to the illusions of omniscience and invulnerability (Sternberg & Jordan, 2005), the mistaken beliefs that they are all-knowing and immune to error, respectively.

Bias blind spot holds important implications for forensic assessment. For example, as a forensic psychologist, we might maintain that we can safely ignore

40   *Scott O. Lilienfeld et al.*

the sizeable accumulated literature on the superiority of actuarial (statistical or mechanical) prediction in violence prediction relative to clinical prediction (Hilton, Harris, & Rice, 2006) and instead rely exclusively on our informal clinical judgement to inform our forecasts of aggression among released prisoners. In doing so, we may assume that this large and well-replicated body of research applies to other clinicians, but not to us, because we are immune to biases in clinical judgement that afflict 'less skilled' or 'less insightful' clinicians. Yet we would almost certainly be wrong, and would almost surely increase our risk of predictive errors (Grove & Meehl, 1996).

Distinguishing science from pseudoscience in forensic psychopathology

Returning full circle to the issues raised at the outset of the chapter, we conclude with a discussion of how to distinguish scientific from pseudoscientific assertions in forensic psychology, including forensic psychopathology. Pseudoscientific claims are imposters of scientific claims; they may appear to be scientific at first blush, but on closer inspection they do not 'play by the rules' of science. Putting it more formally, as noted earlier, pseudosciences tend to lack the systematic safeguards against confirmation bias that characterise mature sciences (Lilienfeld, 2010a).

Admittedly, the distinction between science and pseudoscience is almost surely not clear-cut (Pigliucci & Boudry, 2013). Sciences and pseudosciences almost certainly fall along a continuum, with no bright line demarcating them (cf., Popper, 1959). At the same time, we can identify several helpful indicators or 'warning signs' that distinguish most scientific from pseudoscientific knowledge claims. All things being equal, the more such warning signs displayed by a discipline, the more suspect of it we should become (Lilienfeld et al., 2012). Moreover, the more likely this discipline is to contain doubtful or poorly supported assertions.

Here, we briefly outline seven such warning signs, which we term the 'Seven Deadly Sins' of pseudoscience, and offer one example from forensic psychology to illustrate each. All of these warning signs reflect a partial or complete failure to compensate for confirmation bias, resulting in an inadequate or inefficient process of error elimination (see Lilienfeld & Landfield, 2008; and Lilienfeld et al., 2012, for additional pseudoscience indicators). Although we separate these warning signs for didactic purposes, in practice they often overlap, so that certain dubious claims frequently embody multiple 'sins'.

Deadly Sin #1: *Overuse of ad hoc hypotheses.* As noted earlier, Popper (1959) contended that a theory's falsifiability – the ability to disprove this theory with evidence – decides its placement on the continuum of science versus pseudoscience. A theory or claim that could be supported by any conceivable set of observed evidence is unfalsifiable and therefore unscientific, because no evidence could refute it. Although Popper was probably mistaken that falsifiability is a sufficient condition for distinguishing sciences from pseudosciences (Pigliucci & Boudry, 2013), he was almost certainly correct that a theory that is consistent with every conceivable piece of evidence is not scientific. Scientific theories must predict certain observations while excluding others.

Popper recognised, although perhaps did not emphasise sufficiently (Lakatos, 1975; Meehl, 1978), that even theories that could be considered falsifiable *in principle* may be rendered virtually unfalsifiable *in practice* by the indiscriminate use of *ad hoc hypotheses* – after-the-fact alternative hypotheses designed to explain away negative findings. This practice essentially creates 'loopholes' that preclude the distinction between ideas that withstand repeated challenges and those that do not. For example, in response to a meta-analysis (Wood et al., 2010) that found the Rorschach Inkblot Test to be largely useless for detecting psychopathy, one author team (Cunliffe et al., 2012) responded by maintaining that the results almost surely would have been different had categorical rather than dimensional indices of psychopathy been used. This remarkable *ad hoc* hypothesis runs counter to overwhelming evidence that dimensional measures of psychopathology almost always yield substantially higher correlations than do categorical measures, even for taxonic constructs (Markon, Chmielewski, & Miller, 2011). More broadly, this type of *ad hoc* reasoning exemplifies what Dawes (1994) termed an 'argument from a vacuum' – an assertion that one's hypothesis is supported by evidence that does not exist.

Deadly Sin #2: *Lack of self-correction.* Scientific claims should be self-correcting over time rather than stagnant, so that errors in methodology and reasoning that are not scientifically supported are ultimately discarded from our 'web of beliefs'; that is, our belief system. Pseudosciences, in contrast, tend to show minimal change over time. This stasis enables a culture of continued support of methods and theories in the face of repeated contrary evidence, an ethos that runs counter to the progressive nature of science. For example, despite clear-cut scientific evidence that certain suggestive techniques for memory recovery, such as hypnosis, guided imagery and repeated cueing, are associated with a heightened risk of false memories in many clients, a nontrivial minority of psychotherapists continue to use such methods to excavate purportedly repressed recollections of child sexual abuse (Legault & Laurence, 2007).

Deadly Sin #3: *Emphasis on confirmation.* As we have seen, confirmation bias is one of the hallmarks of pseudoscience. Whereas mature sciences embrace methodological safeguards against error and independent scrutiny, pseudosciences tend to disregard such bulwarks and instead place their bets on the often-unachievable objectivity of researchers. Confirmation bias can also lead to positive results being weighted more heavily than negative results ('cherry-picking'), so that almost any evidence supporting a claim is emphasised. This practice runs afoul of Popper's (1959) sage advice that science typically works best by subjecting claims to the risk of falsification, a nugget of wisdom that even individuals who do not accept all of Popper's writings can wholeheartedly endorse. Indeed, a strictly Popperian view of science requires us to place substantially more weight on negative than on positive findings, with the caveat that the former derive from methodologically sound studies. As Meehl (1978) observed, 'the whole idea of simply counting noses is

42   *Scott O. Lilienfeld et al.*

wrong, because a theory that has seven facts for it and three facts against it is not in good shape, and it would not be considered so in any developed science' (p. 823). One troubling example of confirmation bias in forensic work derives from the continued reliance on highly coercive methods (e.g. false evidence ploys) to elicit confessions from suspects. Such methods at times elicit genuine confessions, which proponents seize upon as evidence for their effectiveness. Yet such selective reasoning neglects the fact that these methods are consistently associated with an increased risk of false confessions in laboratory paradigms (Kassin et al., 2007) and more important, in real-world settings (Kassin, Bogart, & Kerner, 2012).

Deadly Sin #4: *Evasion of peer review*. Although hardly infallible or free of political influence (see Peters & Ceci, 1982, for an old but still relevant critique), the peer review process is a critical phase of quality control for reducing errors (e.g. in data collection, analysis and interpretation) in research before it is disseminated into the public square of knowledge. This process requires that scientific research be submitted to journal editorial boards or grant review committees, allowing colleagues to identify conceptual or methodological flaws in investigators' research. In pseudosciences, in contrast, claims frequently fly 'under the radar' of peer review, so that advocates routinely promote assertions before they have been subjected to independent scrutiny. For example, several companies now use brain-based (e.g. functional magnetic resonance imaging) lie detection techniques in an effort to ferret out deceptive suspects in companies (Satel & Lilienfeld, 2013). Yet many or most of these companies' extravagant claims have never been subjected to rigorous peer review.

Deadly Sin #5: *Overreliance on anecdotal and testimonial evidence*. Perhaps one of the most common errors in pseudosciences is the misidentification of multiple anecdotes as convincing evidence, as exemplified in the aphorism that 'the plural of anecdote is not fact'. Good scientists are aware that anecdotes, such as 'I know a person who' stories (see Stanovich, 2012), are typically limited in their evidentiary warrant because they (1) can be difficult to verify, (2) are of unclear or questionable representativeness and (3) are almost always susceptible to plausible rival explanations. Still, anecdotal reports can sometimes be helpful in generating preliminary ideas that can later be tested in more systematic investigations (Gilovich, 1991). One example of the perils of overreliance on anecdotal evidence can be seen in the legal system's heavy emphasis on eyewitness testimony. Although such testimony is at times reasonably accurate, it is susceptible to a host of biasing factors and therefore must be evaluated with healthy scepticism. For example, all things being equal, eyewitness reports tend to be less accurate when a weapon is used during the crime (the 'weapon focus' effect), when lighting conditions are poor, when the witness is intoxicated and when the witness must identify a suspect of a different race (Wells, Memon, & Penrod, 2006). Yet in part because striking anecdotal reports of correct eyewitness identifications abound in the news and entertainment media, most triers of fact tend to place undue weight on them (Benton et al., 2005).

Scientific research in forensic samples 43

Deadly Sin #6: *Absence of connectivity.* Connectivity, as defined by Stanovich (2012), is the extent to which new scientific knowledge builds on or 'connects up' with extant knowledge. Sciences tend to cultivate connectivity, with novel claims and theories linked to well-established findings from previous research. Conversely, pseudosciences are often more fragmented in nature, proposing entirely new paradigms out of thin air that may not be tied to existing knowledge. Although on rare occasions, successful new paradigms suddenly arise in developed sciences – a phenomenon deemed 'revolutionary science' (Kuhn, 2012) – even these occurrences are almost always inspired by accumulated anomalies in existing scientific models. In forensic psychology, one case of a striking absence of connectivity comes from research on so-called 'truth serum' (Piper, 1993), which is still used in some forensic settings in an attempt to distinguish accurate statements from falsehoods among suspected criminals. In fact, 'truth' serums are nothing of the sort, and in fact are merely medications – almost always barbiturates – designed to sedate the central nervous system. Large bodies of scientific evidence demonstrate that these medications merely lower people's inhibitions, rendering them more likely to admit to just about anything, either true or false (Lynn, Krackow, Loftus, Locke, & Lilienfeld, 2015). Yet an absence of connectivity permits proponents of truth serums to advance claims regarding their effectiveness that go well beyond the data.

Deadly Sin #7: *Extraordinary claims.* Finally, many pseudosciences are marked by a fondness for extraordinary claims. As Truzzi (1978) and later Sagan (1995) argued, extraordinary claims require extraordinary evidence – a standard that is almost never upheld within pseudosciences. This handy maxim reminds us that assertions that overthrow much or all of extant knowledge *might* be correct, but before taking them seriously, we should insist on especially persuasive evidence. Many pseudosciences flout this principle, proposing remarkable claims that are not supported by compelling or even especially suggestive evidence. For example, some advocates of the polygraph or so-called 'lie detector' test insist that this technique boasts accuracy rates as high as 95 or even 99%. Yet laboratory and field data suggest that the standard polygraph test is only slightly better than chance for detecting deception, especially when suspects fail the test (Iacono, 2008).

Concluding thoughts

Some readers may interpret this chapter as an uncritical encomium to science. If so, they would be mistaken. Science is hardly infallible, and even at its best it leaves many errors unearthed (see Ioannidis, 2005, for sobering examples). Furthermore, because science is practised by human beings, it is inevitably subject to sloppiness, biases, political agendas, conflicts of interest and petty personal rivalries. Science is not a panacea for any, let alone all, human frailties.

At the same time, science remains the best tool that the human race has developed for minimising error and for protecting our species from its own propensity towards biases to which we are all susceptible (O'Donohue,

44   *Scott O. Lilienfeld et al.*

Fowler, & Lilienfeld, 2007). As such, it is our best current hope for arriving at reasonable approximations to the truth. Unless and until a better approach appears on the scene, we are well advised to stick with it. Moreover, much of the beauty of science derives from its self-correcting nature. To the extent that some current scientific techniques are less than optimal for rooting out mistakes, science itself can help us to uncover and implement better ones. Such self-correction may occur more slowly than we might like, and it typically unfolds with multiple fits and starts. Nevertheless, the pressures imposed by the broader scientific community on individual scientists to subject their beloved assertions to scrutiny enhance the likelihood that errors in research will be detected and ultimately eradicated.

Fortunately, as the other chapters in this book make clear, science has already paid generous dividends in the arena of forensic psychopathology. It has allowed us to make significant advances in the assessment, diagnosis, correlates, causes and treatment of mental illness in criminal settings, and there is ample reason to believe that this promising track record will continue.

Literature

Bar-Hillel, M. (1980). The base-rate fallacy in probability judgments. *Acta Psychologica, 44*, 211–233. doi:10.1080/13854040903527287

Baron, J. (1994). *Thinking and deciding.* Cambridge: Cambridge University Press.

Bartley, W. W. (1984). *The retreat to commitment.* New York: Open Court.

Bauer, H. H. (1994). *Scientific literacy and the myth of the scientific method.* Champaign, IL: University of Illinois Press.

Benton, T. R., Ross, D. F., Bradshaw, E., & Thomas, W. N. (2005). Eyewitness memory is still not common sense: Comparing jurors, judges and law enforcement to eyewitness expertise. *Applied Cognitive Psychology, 20*(1), 115–129.

Berezow, A., & Campbell, H. (2013). Lefty nonsense: The real war on science. *New Scientist, 217*(2902), 24–25.

Blackburn, R. (1988). On moral judgements and personality disorders. The myth of psychopathic personality revisited. *British Journal of Psychiatry, 153*, 505–512.

Blair, R. J. R., & Blair, K. (2005). *The psychopath: Emotion and the brain.* Oxford: Blackwell.

Borgida, E., & Nisbett, R. E. (1977). The differential impact of abstract vs. concrete information on decisions. *Applied Social Psychology, 7*, 258–271.

Brown, L. T. (1983). Some more misconceptions about psychology among introductory psychology students. *Teaching of Psychology, 10*, 207–210.

Brown v. EMA (2011). Retrieved from: http://www.supremecourt.gov/opinions/10pdf/08- 1448.pdf.

Campbell, D. T. (1974). Evolutionary epistemology. In P. A. Schilpp (Ed.), *The philosophy of Karl Popper* (pp. 413–463). La Salle, IL: Open Court.

Canter, D. V., Alison, L. J., Alison, E., & Wentink, N. (2004). The organized/disorganized typology of serial murder: Myth or model? *Psychology, Public Policy, and Law, 10*(3), 293–320.

Chabris, C. F., & Simons, D. (2010). Would you spot the gorilla? *New Scientist, 206*, 32–33.

Scientific research in forensic samples   45

Chabris, C. F., & Simons, D. (2011). What people believe about how memory works: A representative sample of the U.S. population. *PLoS ONE, 6*(8), 1–7.

Chapman, L. J. (1967). Illusory correlation in observational report. *Journal of Verbal Learning and Verbal Behavior, 6*(1), 151–155.

Chapman, L. J., & Chapman, J. P. (1967). Genesis of popular but erroneous diagnostic observations. *Journal of Abnormal Psychology, 72*, 193–204. doi:10.1037/h0024670

Chapman, L. J., & Chapman, J. P. (1969). Illusory correlation as an obstacle to the use of valid psychodiagnostic signs. *Journal of Abnormal Psychology, 74*, 271–280.

Cleckley, H. (1941/1988). *The mask of sanity: An attempt to reinterpret the so-called psychopathic personality*. Oxford: Mosby.

Cleckley, H. (1976). *The mask of sanity* (5th ed.). St. Louis, MO: CV Mosby.

Coyne, J. A. (2009). *Why evolution is true*. New York: Viking.

Cromer, A. (1994). *Uncommon sense: The heretical nature of science*. New York: Oxford University Press.

Cronbach, L. J., & Meehl, P. E. (1955). Construct validity in psychological tests. *Psychological Bulletin, 52*, 281–302. doi:10.1037/h0040957

Cunliffe, T. B., Gacono, C. B., Meloy, R., Smith, J. M., Taylor, E. E., & Landry, D. (2012). Psychopathy and the Rorschach: A response to Wood et al. (2010). *Archives of Assessment Psychology, 2*(1), 1–31.

Dawes, R. M. (1994). *House of cards: Psychology and psychotherapy built on myth*. New York: Free Press.

Dawes, R. M., Faust, D., & Meehl, P. E. (1989). Clinical versus actuarial judgment. *Science, 243*, 1668–1674.

Dean, G., Mather, A., & Kelly, I. W. (1996). Astrology. In G. Stein (Ed.), *Encyclopedia of the paranormal* (pp. 47–99). New York: Prometheus.

Douglas, J. E., Ressler, R. K., Burgess, A. W., & Hartman, C. R. (1986). Criminal profiling from crime scene analysis. *Behavioral Sciences & The Law, 4*(4), 401–421.

Douglas, K. S., Guy, L. S., & Hart, S. D. (2009). Psychosis as a risk factor for violence to others: A meta-analysis. *Psychological Bulletin, 135*(5), 679–706.

Evans, J. S. B. T., & Stanovich, K. E. (2013). Theory and metatheory in the study of dual processing: Reply to comments. *Perspectives on Psychological Science, 8*, 263–271. doi:10.1177/1745691613483774

Faigman, D. (2008). *Constitutional fictions: A unified theory of constitutional facts*. New York: Oxford University Press.

Faust, D., Hart, K. J., Guilmette, T. J., & Arkes, H. R. (1988). Neuropsychologists' capacity to detect adolescent malingerers. *Professional Psychology: Research and Practice, 19*(5), 508–515.

Feist, G. J. (2008). The psychology of science has arrived. *Journal of the Psychology of Science and Technology, 1*, 2–5.

Feynman, R. P. (1974). Cargo cult science. *Engineering and Science, 37*(7), 10–13.

Feynman, R. P. (1986). *'Surely you're joking, Mr. Feynman!': Adventures of a curious character*. New York: WW Norton & Company.

Fiedler, K. (2011). Voodoo correlations are everywhere – Not only in neuroscience. *Perspectives on Psychological Science, 6*, 163–171.

Fischoff, B. (1996). Hindsight is not equal to foresight: The effect of outcome knowledge on judgment under uncertainty. *Journal of Experimental Psychology, 1*, 288–299.

Forth, A. E., Brown, S. L., Hart, S. D., & Hare, R. D. (1996). The assessment of psychopathy in male and female noncriminals: Reliability and validity. *Personality and Individual Differences, 20*(5), 531–543.

46 *Scott O. Lilienfeld et al.*

Gannon, T. A., Beech, A. R., & Ward, T. (2008). Does the polygraph lead to better risk prediction for sexual offenders? *Aggression and Violent Behavior, 13*(1), 29–44.

Garb, H. N. (1998). *Studying the clinician: Judgment research and psychological assessment.* Washington, DC: American Psychological Association.

Garb, H. N., Wood, J. M., & Nezworski, M. (2000). Projective techniques and the detection of child sexual abuse. *Child Maltreatment, 5,* 161–168.

Gigerenzer, G. (2007). *Gut feelings: The intelligence of the unconscious.* New York: Viking.

Gilbert, D. T. (1991). How mental systems believe. *American Psychologist, 46,* 107–119.

Gilovich, T. (1991). *How we know what isn't so: The fallibility of human reason in everyday life.* New York: Free Press.

Gilovich, T., & Savitsky, K. (1996). Like goes with like: The role of representativeness in erroneous and pseudoscientific beliefs. *Skeptical Inquirer, 20,* 34–40.

Gottesman, I. I. (1991). *Schizophrenia genesis: The origins of madness.* New York: WH Freeman/Times Books/Henry Holt & Co.

Gough, H. G. (1969). *California Psychological Inventory: Manual (rev. ed.).* Palo Alto, CA: Consulting Psychologists Press.

Green, J. P., Page, R. A., Rasekhy, R., Johnson, L. K., & Bernhardt, S. E. (2006). Cultural views and attitudes about hypnosis: A survey of college students across four countries. *International Journal of Clinical and Experimental Hypnosis, 54,* 263–280.

Grove, W. M., & Meehl, P. E. (1996). Comparative efficiency of informal (subjective, impressionistic) and formal (mechanical, algorithmic) prediction procedures: The clinical-statistical controversy. *Psychology, Public Policy, and Law, 2*(2), 293–323.

Grove, W. M., Zald, D. H., Lebow, B. S., Snitz, B. E., & Nelson, C. (2000). Clinical versus mechanical prediction: A meta-analysis. *Psychological Assessment, 1*(1), 19–30.

Hare, R. D. (1980). A research scale for the assessment of psychopathy in criminal populations. *Personality and Individual Differences, 1*(2), 111–119.

Hare, R. D. (1993). *Without conscience: The disturbing world of the psychopaths among us.* New York: Pocket Books.

Hare, R. D. (2003). *Manual for the psychopathy checklist – Revised.* Toronto, CA: Multi-Health Systems.

Hare, R. D., & Neumann, C. S. (2009). Psychopathy: Assessment and forensic implications. *Canadian Journal of Psychiatry, 54,* 791–802.

Harpur, T. J., Hare, R. D., & Hakstian, A. R. (1989). Two-factor conceptualization of psychopathy: Construct validity and assessment implications. *Psychological Assessment: A Journal of Consulting and Clinical Psychology, 1*(1), 6–17. doi:10.1037/1040-3590.1.1.6

Hart, S. D., Hare, R. D., & Harpur, T. J. (1992). The psychopathy checklist – revised (PCL–R): An overview for researchers and clinicians. In J. C. Rosen & P. McReynolds (Eds), *Advances in psychological assessment,* Vol. 8 (pp. 103–130). New York: Plenum Press.

Hawkins, S. A., & Hastie, R. (1990). Hindsight: Biased judgments of past events after the outcomes are known. *Psychological Bulletin, 107,* 311–327.

Herbert, J. D., Lilienfeld, S. O., Lohr, J. M., Montgomery, R. W., O'Donohue, W. T., Rosen, G. M., & Tolin, D. T. (2000). Science and pseudoscience in the development of eye movement desensitization and reprocessing: Implications for clinical psychology. *Clinical Psychology Review, 20*(8), 945–971. doi:10.1016/S0272-7358(99)00017-3

Hilton, N. Z., Harris, G. T., & Rice, M. E. (2006). Sixty-six years of research on the clinical versus actuarial prediction of violence. *The Counseling Psychologist, 34*(3), 400–409.

Hundleby, J. D., & Ross, B. E. (1977). Comparison measures of psychopathy. *Journal of Consulting and Clinical Psychology, 45*(4), 702–703.

Hunter, J. E., & Schmidt, F. L. (2004.). *Methods of meta-analysis: Correcting error and bias in research findings.* Thousand Oaks, CA: Sage Publications, Inc.

Iacono, W. G. (2008). The forensic application of 'brain fingerprinting': Why scientists should encourage the use of P300 memory detection methods. *The American Journal of Bioethics, 8*(1), 30–32.

Iacono, W. G., & Lykken, D. T. (1997). The validity of the lie detector: Two surveys of scientific opinion. *Journal of Applied Psychology, 82,* 426–433.

Ioannidis, J. P. A. (2005). Why most published research findings are false. *PLoS ONE, 2*(8), e124. doi:10.1371/journal.pmed.0020124

Jablonski, N. G. (2004). The evolution of human skin and skin color. *Annual Review of Anthropology,* 585–623.

Kahneman, D. (2011). *Thinking: Fast and slow.* New York: Farrar, Straus and Giroux.

Kassin, S. M., Bogart, D., & Kerner, J. (2012). Confessions that corrupt evidence from the DNA exoneration case files. *Psychological Science, 23*(1), 41–45.

Kassin, S. M., & Gudjonsson, G. H. (2004). The psychology of confessions: A review of the literature and issues. *Psychological Science in the Public Interest, 5*(2), 33–67. doi:10.1111/j.1529-1006.2004.00016.x

Kassin, S. M., Leo, R. A., Meissner, C. A., Richman, K. D., Colwell, L. H., Leach, A.-M., & La Fon, D. (2007). Police interviewing and interrogation: A self-report survey of police practices and beliefs. *Law and Human Behavior, 31*(4), 381–400.

Keren, G., & Schul, Y. (2009). Two is not always better than one: A critical evaluation of two-system theories. *Perspectives on Psychological Science, 4*(6), 533–550.

Krauss, D. A., & Sales, B. D. (2001). The effects of clinical and scientific expert testimony on juror decision making in capital sentencing. *Psychology, Public Policy, and Law 2001, 7*(2), 267–310. doi:10.1037/1076-8971.7.2.267

Kruglanski, A. W. (2013). Only one? The default interventionist perspective as a unimodal – Commentary on Evans & Stanovich. *Perspectives on Psychological Science, 8*(3), 242–247. doi:10.1177/1745691613483477

Kuhn, T. S. (2012). *The structure of scientific revolutions.* Chicago: University of Chicago Press.

Lakatos, I. (1975). Falsification and the methodology of scientific research programmes. In I. Lakatos (Ed), *Can theories be refuted?* (pp. 205–259). Dordrecht, the Netherlands: Springer.

Legault, E., & Laurence, J.-R. (2007). Recovered memories of childhood sexual abuse: Social worker, psychologist, and psychiatrist reports of beliefs, practices and cases. *Australian Journal of Clinical and Experimental Hypnosis, 35*(2), 111–133.

Lewis, A. (1974). Psychopathic personality: A most elusive category. *Psychological Medicine, 4*(2), 133–140.

Lilienfeld, S. O. (2010a). Fudge factor. *Scientific American, 303*(18).

Lilienfeld, S. O. (2010b). Can psychology become a science? *Personality and Individual Differences, 49*(4), 281–288.

Lilienfeld, S. O. (2012). Public skepticism of psychology: Why many people perceive the study of human behavior as unscientific. *American Psychologist, 67*(2), 111–129. doi:10.1037/a0023963

Lilienfeld, S. O., Ammirati, R., & David, M. (2012). Distinguishing science from pseudoscience in school psychology: Science and scientific thinking as safeguards against human error. *Journal of School Psychology, 50*(1), 7–36. doi:10.1016/j.jsp.2011.09.006

48 *Scott O. Lilienfeld et al.*

Lilienfeld, S. O., & Arkowitz, H. (2009). Lunacy and the full moon: Does a full moon really trigger strange behaviour? *Scientific American Mind, 19*(6), 80–81.

Lilienfeld, S. O., & Byron, R. (2012). Your brain on trial. *Scientific American Mind, 23,* 44–53. doi:10.1038/scientificamericanmind0113-44

Lilienfeld, S. O., & Fowler, K. A. (2006). The self-report assessment of psychopathy: Problems, pitfalls, and promises. In C. J. Patrick (Ed.), *Handbook of psychopathy* (pp. 107–132). New York: Guilford Press.

Lilienfeld, S. O., & Landfield, K. (2008). Science and pseudoscience in law enforcement: A user-friendly primer. *Criminal Justice and Behavior, 35,* 1215–1230.

Lilienfeld, S. O., Lynn, S. J., Namy, L., & Woolf, N. (2013). *Psychology: From inquiry to understanding.* Boston, MA: Allyn & Bacon.

Lilienfeld, S. O., Lynn, S. J., Ruscio, J., & Beyerstein, B. L. (2010). *50 great myths of popular psychology: Shattering widespread misconceptions about human behavior.* New York: Wiley-Blackwell.

Lilienfeld, S. O., Ritschel, L. A., Lynn, S. J., Cautin, R. L., & Latzman, R. D. (2013). Why many clinical psychologists are resistant to evidence-based practice: Root causes and constructive remedies. *Clinical Psychology Review, 33,* 883–900.

Loftus, E. F. (1996). *Eyewitness testimony.* Cambridge, MA: Harvard University Press.

Lykken, D. T. (1991). What's wrong with psychology anyway? In D. Cicchetti & W. M. Grove (Eds.), *Thinking clearly about psychology: Matters of public interest* (Vol. 1, pp. 3–39). Minneapolis, MN: University of Minnesota Press.

Lynn, S. J., Krackow, E., Loftus, E. F., Locke, T. G., & Lilienfeld, S. O. (2015). Constructing the past: Problematic memory recovery techniques in psychotherapy. In S. O. Lilienfeld, S. J. Lynn and J. M. Lohr (Eds.), *Science and pseudoscience in clinical psychology* (pp. 210–244). New York: The Guilford Press.

Maher, B. A., & Gottesman, I. I. (2005). Deconstructing, reconstructing, preserving Paul E. Meehl's legacy of construct validity. *Psychological Assessment, 17*(4), 415–422.

Mahoney, M. J. (1977). Publication prejudices: An experimental study of confirmation bias in the peer review system. *Cognitive Therapy and Research, 1,* 161–175.

Markon, K. E., Chmielewski, M., & Miller, C. J. (2011). The reliability and validity of discrete and continuous measures of psychopathology: A quantitative review. *Psychological Bulletin, 137*(5), 856–879. doi:10.1037/a0023678

McCann, J. T., Shindler, K. L., & Hammond, T. R. (2003). The science and pseudoscience of expert testimony. In S. O. Lilienfeld, J. M. Lohr, & S. J. Lynn (Eds.), *Science and pseudoscience in contemporary clinical psychology* (pp. 77–108). New York: Guilford.

McCauley, R. N. (2011). *Why religion is natural and science is not.* New York: Oxford University Press.

McDonald, H. E., & Hirt, E. R. (1997). When expectancy meets desire: Motivational effects in reconstructive memory. *Journal of Personality and Social Psychology, 72*(1), 5–23. doi:10.1037/0022-3514.72.1.5

McFall, R. M. (1996). Making psychology incorruptible. *Applied and Preventive Psychology, 5,* 9–16.

McKinley, J. C., & Hathaway, S. R. (1944). The Minnesota Multiphasic Personality Inventory, V: hysteria, hypomania, and psychopathic deviate. *Journal of Applied Psychology, 28,* 153–174.

McMullin, E. (1984). A case for scientific realism. In J. Leplin (Ed.), *Scientific realism* (pp. 8–40). Berkeley, CA: University of California Press.

Meehl, P. E. (1978). Theoretical risks and tabular asterisks: Sir Karl, Sir Ronald, and the slow progress of soft psychology. *Journal of Consulting and Clinical Psychology, 46*, 806–834.

Meehl, P. E. (1989). Schizotaxia revisited. *Archives of General Psychiatry, 46*(10), 935–944.

Meehl, P. E. (1990). Why summaries of research on psychological theories are often uninterpretable. *Psychological Reports, 66*, 195–244.

Meehl, P. E. (1993). Philosophy of science: Help or hindrance? *Psychological Reports, 72*, 707–733.

Merckelbach, H., & Wessel, I. (1998). Assumptions of students and psychotherapists about memory. *Psychological Reports, 82*(3), 763–770.

Merton, R. K. (1973). *The sociology of science: Theoretical and empirical investigations.* Chicago, IL: University of Chicago Press.

Newman, J. P., & Kosson, D. S. (1986). Passive avoidance learning in psychopathic and nonpsychopathic offenders. *Journal of Abnormal Psychology, 95*(3), 252.

Nickerson, R. S. (1998). Confirmation bias: A ubiquitous phenomenon in many guises. *Review of General Psychology, 2*, 175–220.

O'Donohue, W. T., Fowler, K. A., & Lilienfeld, S. O. (2007). Science is an essential safeguard against human error. In S. O. Lilienfeld & W. T. O'Donohue (Eds.), *The great ideas of clinical science: 17 principles that every mental health professional should understand* (pp. 3–27). New York: Routledge.

Peters, D. P., & Ceci, S. J. (1982). Peer-review practices of psychological journals: The fate of published articles, submitted again. *Behavioral and Brain Sciences, 5*, 187–255.

Pigliucci, M., & Boudry, M. (2013). *Philosophy of pseudoscience: Reconsidering the demarcation problem.* Chicago, IL: University of Chicago Press.

Piper, A. (1993). 'Truth serum' and 'recovered memories' of sexual abuse: A review of the evidence. *Journal of Psychiatry and Law, 21*, 447–471.

Pirsig, R. (1974). *Zen and the art of motorcycle maintenance.* New York: Bantam Books.

Pohl, R. F. (2005). *Cognitive illusions: A handbook of fallacies and biases in thinking, judgment, and reasoning.* Hove, UK: Psychology Press.

Popper, K. R. (1959). *The logic of scientific discovery.* Oxford: Basic Books.

Popper, K. R. (1976). A note on verisimilitude. *The British Journal for the Philosophy of Science, 27*(2), 147–159.

Pronin, E., Lin, D. Y., & Ross, L. (2002). The bias blind spot: Perceptions of bias in self versus others. *Personality and Social Psychology* Bulletin, 28, 369–381.

Redding, R. E. (1998). How common-sense psychology can inform law and psycho-legal research. Roundtable, The University of Chicago Law School, 5, 107–142.

Redelmeier, D., & Tversky, A. (1990). The discrepancy between medical decisions for individual patients and for groups. *New England Journal of Medicine, 273*, 302–305.

Ressler, R. K., Burgess, A. W., Douglas, J. E., Hartman, C. R., & D'Agostino, R. B. (1986). Sexual killers and their victims identifying patterns through crime scene analysis. *Journal of Interpersonal Violence, 1*(3), 288–308.

Ross, L., Lepper, M. R., & Hubbard, M. (1975). Perseverance in self-perception and social perception: Biased attributional processes in the debriefing paradigm. *Journal of Personality and Social Psychology, 32*, 880–892.

Ross, L., & Ward, A. (1996). Naive realism in everyday life: Implications for social conflict and misunderstanding. In E. S. Reed, E. Turiel, T. Brown, E. S. Reed, E. Turiel, & T. Brown (Eds.), *Values and knowledge* (pp. 103–135). Hillsdale, NJ: Erlbaum.

Rotton, J., & Kelly, I. W. (1985). Much ado about the full moon: A meta-analysis of lunar-lunacy research. *Psychological Bulletin, 97*, 286–306.

Russell, G. W., & Dua, M. (1983). Lunar influences on human aggression. *Social Behavior and Personality, 11*, 41–44.

Sagan, C. (1995). *The demon-haunted world: Science as a candle in the dark.* New York: Random House.

Satel, S., & Lilienfeld, S. O. (2013). *Brainwashed: The seductive appeal of mindless neuroscience.* New York: Basic Books.

Schorn, D. (2006). Duke rape suspects speak out. *60 Minutes* (CBS News), 3.

Sewall, L. A., Krupp, D. B., & Lalumière, M. L. (2013). A test of two typologies of sexual homicide. *Sexual Abuse: A Journal of Research and Treatment, 25*(1), 82–100.

Shermer, M. (2011). *The believing brain: From ghosts and gods to politics and conspiracies.* New York: Macmillan.

Simons, D. J., & Chabris, C.F. (2012). Common (mis)beliefs about memory: A replication and comparison of telephone and Mechanical Turk survey methods. *PLoS ONE, 7*, e51876.

Singh, J. P., Grann, M., & Fazel, S. (2011). A comparative study of violence risk assessment tools: A systematic review and metaregression analysis of 68 studies involving 25,980 participants. *Clinical Psychology Review, 31*, 499–513.

Skeem, J. L., & Cooke, D. J. (2010). Is criminal behavior a central component of psychopathy? Conceptual directions for resolving the debate. *Psychological Assessment, 22*, 433–455.

Skeem, J. L., Polaschek, D. L., Patrick, C. J., & Lilienfeld, S. O. (2011). Psychopathic personality bridging the gap between scientific evidence and public policy. *Psychological Science in the Public Interest, 12*(3), 95–162.

Snook, B., Cullen, R. M., Bennell, C., Taylor, P. J., & Gendreau, P. (2008). The criminal profiling illusion: What's behind the smoke and mirrors? *Criminal Justice and Behavior, 35*, 1257–1276.

Stanovich, K. E. (2012). Cumulative progress in understanding our multiple minds thinking twice: Two minds in one brain. *The American Journal of Psychology, 125*, 116–121.

Stanovich, K. E., & West, R. F. (2000). Individual differences in reasoning: Implications for the rationality debate? *Behavioral and Brain Sciences, 23*, 645–665.

Steblay, N. M., Besirevic, J., Fulero, S. M., & Jimenez-Lorente, B. (1999). The effects of pretrial publicity on juror verdicts: A meta-analytic review. *Law and Human Behavior, 23*(2), 219–235.

Sternberg, R. J., & Jordan, J. (Eds.). (2005). *A handbook of wisdom: Psychological perspectives.* New York: Cambridge University Press.

Strong, S. R. (1991). Theory-driven science and naive empiricism in counseling psychology. *Journal of Counseling Psychology, 38*, 204–207.

Tavris, C., & Aronson, E. (2007). *Mistakes were made (but not by me): Why we justify foolish beliefs, bad decisions, and hurtful acts.* Orlando, FL: Harcourt Press.

Truzzi, M. (1978). On the extraordinary: An attempt at clarification. *Zetetic Scholar, 1*, 11–22.

Tversky, A., & Kahneman, D. (1974). Judgment under uncertainty: Heuristics and biases. *Science, 185*, 1124–1131.

Underwood, B. J. (1957). Interference and forgetting. *Psychological Review, 64*(1), 49–60.

Vaughan, E. D. (1977). Misconceptions about psychology among introductory psychology students. *Teaching of Psychology, 4*, 139–141.

Watkins, M. W. (2009). Errors in diagnostic decision making and clinical judgment. In T. B. Gutkin & C. R. Reynolds (Eds.), *Handbook of school psychology* (pp. 210–229). (4th ed.). Hoboken, NJ: Wiley.

Wells, G. L., Memon, A., & Penrod, S. D. (2006). Eyewitness evidence improving its probative value. *Psychological Science in the Public Interest*, 7(2), 45–75.

West, R. F., Meserve, R. J., & Stanovich, K. E. (2012). Cognitive sophistication does not attenuate the bias blind spot. *Journal of Personality and Social Psychology*, 103(3), 506–519.

Willingham, D. T. (2012). *When can you trust the experts: How to tell good science from bad in education*. San Francisco, CA: Wiley.

Wise, R. A., & Safer, M. A. (2004). What US judges know and believe about eyewitness testimony. *Applied Cognitive Psychology*, 18(4), 427–443.

Wolpert, L. (1993). *The unnatural nature of science: Why science does not make (common) sense*. Cambridge, MA: Harvard University Press.

Wood, J. M., Lilienfeld, S. O., Nezworski, M. T., Garb, H. N., Allen, K. H., & Wildermuth, J. L. (2010). Validity of Rorschach inkblot scores for discriminating psychopaths from nonpsychopaths in forensic populations: A meta-analysis. *Psychological Assessment*, 22, 336–349.

Part II

Development of antisocial behaviour

3 Children at risk for serious conduct problems

Paul J. Frick and Elizabeth A. Shirtcliff

Introduction

A consistent finding from research on serious antisocial, aggressive and delinquent behaviour is that early onset of conduct problems (i.e. before the onset of puberty) is one of the best predictors of risk for antisocial outcomes in adolescence and adulthood (Moffitt, 2006). This finding has important implications for causal theories of serious conduct problems because it suggests that problems emerging early in development can set the stage for more serious problems later in life. More importantly, it has implications for prevention as there are a number of interventions that are successful for treating conduct problems in young children and subsequently reducing their risk for various antisocial outcomes (Frick, 2012). As a result, it is imperative to (a) gain a thorough understanding of early risk factors that can influence the development of conduct problems and (b) determine how these risk factors negatively influence the healthy development of the child, placing him or her at risk for serious behaviour problems.

Both parts of this process are critical. For example, it is important to know that exposure to environmental toxins prenatally is a risk factor for later adolescent antisocial behaviour (Brennan, Grekin, & Mednick, 1999) because this finding has led to preventive interventions designed to enhance the health of women during pregnancy and these interventions have resulted in significant reductions in antisocial behaviour when the child is in adolescence and young adulthood (Olds et al., 1998). However, it is also critical to understand *how* prenatal exposure to toxins may influence the developing child because such an understanding could advance theories of the aetiology of serious conduct problems by helping to document some common causal mechanisms that can lead to problem behaviour (Brennan, Grekin, & Mednick, 2003). Further, such an understanding of how risk factors lead to the development of serious conduct problems could advance treatments which seek to help a child overcome early adversity and show healthy emotional and behavioural adjustment despite being exposed to iatrogenic influences early in development.

The current chapter summarises research on risk factors that have been associated with early emerging conduct problems. Rather than attempting to

56   Paul Frick and Elizabeth Shirtcliff

provide an exhaustive review of all of the dispositional and environmental risk factors that have been associated with childhood conduct problems, we focus on a few factors that we feel are particularly important for understanding developmental mechanisms which directly lead to the child's problem behaviour. Specifically, we summarise research on several emotional and cognitive styles (i.e. temperaments) that have been linked to serious conduct problems and which likely mediate the effects of many other risk factors on the developing child. We discuss how these temperaments can place a child at risk for showing serious aggressive and antisocial behaviour beginning in childhood. We review research suggesting that these different temperaments likely lead to different causal pathways in the development of serious conduct problems. We also review research showing how these different temperaments and subsequent problems in development could explain the divergent behavioural, emotional, cognitive and biological characteristics displayed by subgroups of children with serious conduct problems. Finally, we summarise the implications of this developmental model for the diagnosis and treatment of children with serious conduct problems.

Temperamental risk factors for conduct problems

Temperament has been defined as individual differences in emotional reactivity and in the self-regulation of emotion that are influenced over time by genes, maturation and the environment (Rothbart, 2012). The potential role of temperament as a risk factor for the development of conduct problems has long been recognised. Early definitions of temperament used the term 'difficult temperament' to describe children who were irregular in their behaviour and biological functions, were highly active, showed intense reactions to a wide variety of stimuli, had affective states in which irritability and other aspects of negative mood predominate, and adapted poorly to environmental changes (Thomas & Chess, 1977). Children designated with such temperamental characteristics were found to be at risk for conduct problems (Kingston & Priour, 1995). However, the construct of 'difficultness' encompassed many different dimensions of emotionality and behaviour which made it unclear whether there were certain dimensions of the difficult temperament that were most important for predicting conduct problems.

One particular dimension of difficult temperament – reactivity to stimuli designed to elicit negative affect – has emerged as an important risk factor for childhood conduct problems (Frick & Morris, 2004; Frick & Viding, 2009). Emotional reactivity involves the child's latency to respond, response threshold and response intensity to environmental stimuli (Fox & Calkins, 2003). Negative emotional reactivity reflects the ease of eliciting a negative mood such as anger, sadness, fear and frustration and is characterised by the degree of distress in response to real or perceived provocations, novel events or frustrating situations. Individual differences in the tendency to react with strong negative emotions are relatively stable in early childhood and increase in stability

Children at risk for serious conduct problems 57

from adolescence and into adulthood (Deater-Deckard & Wang, 2012). These individual differences in emotional reactivity have been documented as a risk factor for conduct problems in a number of longitudinal studies. For example, children who were highly reactive during observational interactions with mothers at age 2 were rated as having more conduct problems than their peers at school entry (Rubin, Burgess, Dwyer, & Hastings, 2003; Shaw, Owens, Vondra, & Keenan, 1996). These prospective relations have been shown over longer periods, with susceptibility to anger and hostility in infancy and early childhood being linked to conduct problems in elementary school (Lengua, West, & Sandler, 1998), and with antisocial behaviour and delinquency later in adolescence and young adulthood (Caspi, 2000).

Frick and Morris (2004) proposed that emotional reactivity can have direct effects on the child's propensity to display conduct problems and aggressive behaviour. For example, a child who often reacts with strong angry and hostile emotions may act aggressively within the context of these strong emotions without thinking of the potential consequences of these acts. He or she may feel bad and guilty after the emotion subsides but still have problems controlling these emotions in the future. Frick and Morris (2004) also proposed that indirect effects of anger reactivity on the development of conduct problems are possible. For example, aggressive children who show strong emotional reactions tend to selectively attend to hostile cues in peer interactions (Dodge, Pettit, McClaskey, & Brown, 1986), make hostile attributions to the intent of peer behaviours when the intent is not readily apparent (Dodge, Lochman, Harnish, Bates, & Pettit, 1997) and more readily access aggressive responses to peer provocations (Asarnow & Callan, 1985). In addition, a child who responds with intense emotional reactions is more likely to be rejected by peers (Rubin, Bukowski, & Parker, 1998) and such peer rejection can lead a child to miss out on important socialising experiences that take place within the peer group, such as learning effective social skills (Dodge et al., 2003). Finally, poor emotional regulation can affect how a child responds to socialisation attempts by parents by making them more difficult to discipline, leading to hostile and coercive parent-child interactions (Patterson, Reid, & Dishion, 1992).

Thus, a temperamental pattern characterised by high rates of anger, hostility and frustration is an important childhood risk factor for conduct problems and could explain many of the cognitive and social risk factors to conduct problems identified in past research. Research has also documented another temperament characterised by *low* fear which has also been linked to serious conduct problems. Fearless (Rothbart & Bates, 1998) or behaviourally uninhibited (Kagan, 2012) children consistently approach novel and potentially dangerous people, activities and stimuli. They are also less sensitive to cues of punishment and show less physiological arousal to unexpected and unfamiliar events. Research has linked low levels of fear with the development of conduct problems concurrently (Frick, Lilienfeld, Ellis, Loney, & Silverthorn, 1999) and prospectively (Barker, Oliver, Viding, Salekin, & Maughan, 2011;

58   *Paul Frick and Elizabeth Shirtcliff*

Glenn, Raine, Venables, & Mednick, 2007; Shaw, Gilliom, Ingoldsby, & Nagin, 2003). For example, Shaw et al. (2003) reported that, when studied with a number of other known risk factors for conduct problems (e.g. child intelligence, parental adjustment, harsh and rejecting parenting), only fearlessness to a frightening sound at age 2 predicted both initial level of conduct problem severity at age 2 and persistence of conduct problems between the ages of 2 and 8. Similarly, Barker et al. (2011) reported that a fearless temperament at age 2 predicted conduct problems at age 13 in a population-based sample (N = 7,000). Finally, Glenn et al. (2007) found low fearfulness at age 3 predicted antisocial behaviour in adulthood.

A number of reasons have been given to explain this link between low fear and the development of conduct problems. For example, low arousal may be experienced as an aversive state that leads the individual to seek novel and dangerous activities (i.e. fearless behaviours) in an attempt to increase his or her level of arousal. Many antisocial behaviours, especially covert antisocial behaviours, can be viewed as a form of thrill-seeking behaviour (Raine, 2002). Low fear and other associated features of this temperament (e.g. punishment insensitivity; low emotional arousal to negative stimuli) could also have an indirect effect on the development of severe conduct problems by leading to deficits in conscience development. Kochanska (1993) and Dadds and Salmon (2003) independently proposed that discomforting arousal or anxiety that follow wrong-doing and punishment are integral in the development of an internal system that functions to inhibit misbehaviour, even in the absence of the punishing agent. These authors proposed that fearless children with deficits in their emotional responses to punishment may not experience this 'deviation anxiety' which could impede conscience development. Blair and colleagues (Blair, 1995; Blair, Colledge, & Mitchell, 2001) suggest that children who show reduced negative emotional responses to distress cues in others may have problems in the early development of empathic concern and perspective-taking which rely on 'emotional contagion' in which a child becomes emotionally aroused to signs of distress in others (e.g. another child crying).

Thus, there may be at least two distinct temperamental patterns present early in life that predict the onset of severe conduct problems and antisocial behaviour later in development and may explain many of the risk factors frequently associated with childhood conduct problems. Importantly, these two temperaments are associated with different patterns of emotional reactivity and likely lead to conduct problems through very different developmental processes. High rates of negative emotional reactivity likely predispose the child to have problems adequately regulating emotions, leading to conduct problems that are in response to real or perceived provocation and which typically occur in the context of high emotional arousal. Alternatively, a fearless temperament is likely to predispose the child to having problems in the normal development of guilt and empathy that can lead to serious conduct problems due to the failure of the child to respond to typical socialisation practices and to be concerned about the consequences of their behaviour for others. This developmental model leads to the prediction of distinct subgroups of children with severe conduct problems with very different behavioural, emotional, cognitive and biological characteristics. In the following sections, we review research investigating the presence of distinct pathways to the development of severe conduct problems in children which seem to support such a model.

Support for two developmental pathways: behavioural evidence

The first prediction from this dual pathway model is that there should be two distinct groups of children with serious conduct problems who differ behaviourally with respect to problems in guilt and empathy versus emotional reactivity. Consistent with this prediction, about 20–50% of children with serious conduct problems show significant and non-normative levels of callous-unemotional (CU) traits characterised by a lack of guilt, a lack of concern about the feelings of others, a lack of concern about performance in important activities and shallow or deficient affect (Kahn, Frick, Youngstrom, Findling, & Youngstrom, 2012; Pardini, Stepp, Hipwell, Stouthamer-Loeber, & Loeber, 2012; Rowe et al., 2010). These CU traits are negatively correlated with measures of guilt and remorse (Lotze, Ravindran, & Myers, 2010; Pardini & Byrd, 2012) and empathy (Chabrol, Van Leeuwen, Rodgers, & Gibbs, 2011; Dadds et al., 2009; Jones, Happe, Gilbert, Burnett, & Viding, 2010; Kimonis, Frick, Skeem et al., 2008; Pardini & Byrd, 2012). Importantly, children with serious conduct problems and elevated CU traits show deficits in empathy, whereas those with serious conduct problems without CU traits do not (Jones et al., 2010; Schwenck et al., 2012).

Research has also demonstrated that children with CU traits are more likely to score higher on measures of thrill and adventure seeking (Barker et al., 2011; Frick et al., 1999; Pardini, 2006) and lower on measures of anxiety (Frick et al., 1999; Pardini et al., 2012). Again, lower fear and anxiety seem to be specific to children with serious conduct problems with elevated CU traits. Specifically, Pardini et al. (2012) studied a community sample of 1,862 girls aged 6 to 8 and reported that girls with serious conduct problems and elevated CU traits were more aggressive both at baseline and across a 6-year follow-up period, but they showed *lower* levels of anxiety than girls with serious conduct problems and normative levels of CU traits.

In contrast, research suggests that conduct problems in the absence of elevated CU traits are positively correlated with measures of anxiety (Frick et al., 1999; Pardini, Lochman, & Frick, 2003; Pardini et al., 2012). These findings are consistent with the contention that children with serious conduct problems but normative levels of CU traits show problems regulating high negative emotional reactivity. Also supporting this contention, when children with serious conduct problems and normative levels of CU traits act aggressively, it is often confined to reactive forms of aggression in response to real or perceived provocation (Frick, Cornell, Barry, Bodin, & Dane, 2003). Reactive aggression has been specifically associated with problems in anger, hostility, and other

60   *Paul Frick and Elizabeth Shirtcliff*

problems regulating negative emotions (Dodge & Pettit, 2003). Finally, problems in emotional regulation can make a child more likely to evoke harsh and inconsistent parenting, leading to coercive exchanges between the parent and child. Consistent with this contention, conduct problems are more strongly associated with hostile and coercive parenting in children with normative levels of CU traits (Pasalich, Dadds, Hawes, & Brennan, 2012; Wootton, Frick, Shelton, & Silverthorn, 1997).

Support for two developmental pathways: emotional and cognitive evidence

Thus, there is a wealth of behavioural data to support a model of early childhood risk for serious conduct problems that proposes at least two distinct pathways which differ in their temperamental characteristics. A number of recent reviews have shown differences in the emotional and cognitive characteristics of children with severe conduct problems with and without elevated CU traits (Frick & Viding, 2009; Frick & White, 2008). Children with elevated CU traits are more likely to show an insensitivity to punishment cues using tasks in which a reward-dominant response set is primed (Frick et al., 2003), and they respond poorly to gradual punishment schedules (Blair et al., 2001). Adolescents with elevated CU traits underestimate the likelihood that they will be punished for misbehaviour relative to other adolescents with severe behaviour problems (Pardini, Lochman, & Frick, 2003). Several studies have reported that children and adolescents with severe conduct problems and elevated CU traits endorse more deviant values and goals in social situations, such as viewing aggression as a more acceptable means for obtaining goals, blaming others for their misbehaviour and emphasising the importance of dominance and revenge in social conflicts (Chabrol et al., 2011; Pardini, 2011; Pardini et al., 2003; Stickle, Kirkpatrick, & Brush, 2009). In contrast, children with conduct problems but with normative levels of CU traits are more likely to show deficits in verbal intelligence (Loney, Frick, Ellis, & McCoy, 1998; Salekin, Neumann, Leistico, & Zalot, 2004) and are more likely to attribute hostile intent to peer actions (Frick et al., 2003). Importantly, both low verbal abilities and a hostile attributional bias have been associated with emotional regulation problems (Lemerise & Maulden, 2010).

Perhaps the most consistent difference between children with serious conduct problems with and without elevated CU traits is in their pattern of responding to emotional stimuli. Specifically, children and adolescents with elevated CU traits show weaker responses to cues of distress in others than other children and adolescents with severe conduct problems (Blair et al., 2001; Kimonis, Frick, Fazekas, & Loney, 2006; Kimonis, Frick, Muñoz, & Aucoin, 2008; Marsh et al., 2011). Further, children with both serious conduct problems and elevated CU traits show a lower magnitude of heart rate change to emotionally evocative films compared to youth with serious conduct problems but normative CU traits (Anastassiou-Hadjicharalambous & Warden, 2008;

de Wied, van Boxtel, Matthys, & Meeus, 2012). These emotional differences have been documented from very early in childhood. Willoughby, Waschbusch, Moore, and Propper (2011) reported that 5-year-old children with high parent-reported CU traits and Oppositional Defiant Disorder (ODD) symptoms showed less negative reactivity to the still-face paradigm (i.e. parental face showing no emotion or interaction) as infants (6 months) compared to those with ODD symptoms and normative levels of CU traits. In contrast to signs of emotional blunting in children high on CU traits, children or adolescents with severe conduct problems but normative levels of CU traits show no deficits in responsivity and recognition of emotions in others (Blair et al., 2001; Dadds et al., 2006; Dadds, El Masry, Wimalaweera, & Guastella, 2007). Indeed, several studies have shown that this group of children with conduct problems show enhanced emotional responsiveness to negative emotional stimuli, including distress in others (Kimonis et al., 2006; Loney, Frick, Clements, Ellis, & Kerlin, 2003). To illustrate differential patterns of emotional reactivity across groups of children with severe conduct problems, Kimonis et al. (2006) studied non-referred 6–13-year-old children and measured their emotional responses on a dot-probe task, which assesses a child's attentional orienting to pictures of emotional and neutral content. They found an interaction between conduct problems and CU traits in children's emotional responses, such that children with conduct problems high on CU traits showed reduced attentional orienting to pictures of people and animals in pain and distress, whereas children with conduct problems low on CU traits showed enhanced attentional orienting to these pictures.

Support for two developmental pathways: biological evidence

There is also support for two developmental pathways to serious conduct problems from biologically oriented research. For example, a large twin study has suggested that the strength of genetic and environmental influences on conduct problems in young children (ages 7 and 9) differs depending on the presence of elevated CU traits (Viding, Frick, & Plomin, 2007; Viding, Jones, Frick, Moffitt, & Plomin, 2008). Furthermore, functional imaging studies have suggested that children with both conduct problems and elevated CU traits exhibit lower right amygdala activity in response to fearful faces in comparison to normal controls (Jones, Laurens, Herba, Barker, & Viding, 2009; Marsh et al., 2008; White et al., 2012) and lower right amygdala activity during an affective theory of mind task compared to normal controls (Sebastian et al., 2012). Importantly, Sebastian et al. (2012) demonstrated that children with severe conduct problems with normative levels of CU traits showed the opposite pattern of amygdala activity (i.e. increased right amygdala activity). These studies support the presence of biological differences across the two subgroups of children with severe conduct problems and are promising in that they advance our understanding of the biological underpinning of the emotional and cognitive characteristics of children in the two developmental pathways.

Another area of biologically oriented research that could be important for understanding the emotional differences between children with severe conduct problems with and without elevated levels of CU traits involves biomarkers of the stress response system (SRS) (Lupien et al., 2006; Theall, Drury, & Shirtcliff, 2012). These biomarkers are responsive to the environment, capable of changing dramatically to reflect changes in social contextual cues and can influence a wide range of behavioural outcomes. SRS biomarkers enhance the individual's ability to encode or filter salient social contextual cues and thereby increase (or decrease) the likelihood that the individual will behaviourally respond to that social context (Del Giudice, Ellis, & Shirtcliff, 2011). Thus, these biomarkers are critical for defining a child's temperamental style and explaining how that style unfolds across early development. Although research on temperament styles and SRS has largely operated in parallel, these physiological systems of the SRS instantiate behavioural propensities and thus serve as a mechanism underlying temperament and the associated behavioural propensities. In short, the SRS provides a mechanism to understand how temperament contributes to serious conduct problems 'under the skin'.

A recent way to conceptualise the SRS, the adaptive calibration model (ACM), could be particularly helpful for understanding why various biomarkers operate differentially within the different temperamental pathways for severe conduct problems. The ACM describes four prototypical SRS profiles predicted by the degree of environmental stress encountered early in life and throughout childhood (Del Giudice et al., 2011). Two profiles (Sensitive and Buffered) are characteristic of low to moderate stress exposure and do not demonstrate high levels of risk for serious conduct problems. However, two profiles proposed in the ACM (Vigilant and Unemotional) correspond very closely to the two developmental pathways to severe conduct problems.

The Vigilant pattern is expected within social environments that are dangerous, unpredictable and threat-laden where there may be advantages to being highly attuned to cues of danger or threat. SRS activity is generally elevated and is highly responsive to stress, benefiting the individual by allowing him or her to respond quickly and efficiently to threats. However, this vigilance comes at the cost of high trait anxiety and a hostile attribution bias which, as noted above, have been associated with severe conduct problems in children with normative levels of CU traits. By analogy, the Vigilant pattern follows the 'smoke detector' principle in which the cost of frequent, inaccurate responses (i.e. many false alarms) is outweighed by the benefits of a correct alarm. *Low* parasympathetic tone within the Vigilant pattern would be linked with less inhibition of cardiac functioning, and consequently with greater underlying arousal and attention to threat. *High* sympathetic activity within the Vigilant pattern functions to increase heart rate, respiration, blood supply to skeletal muscles and glucose release into the bloodstream which permit greater fight-or-flight responses (Hastings, Zahn-Waxler, & McShane, 2006). Although the Vigilant pattern is dominated by a highly responsive sympathetic nervous system, the Hypothalamic Pituitary Axis (HPA) is also highly reactive in this pattern. If a threat is sufficiently large, the Vigilant pattern will quickly mount an HPA response and recover slowly from the heightened emotional activity after the social challenge terminates. Prolonged heightened HPA activity during stress allows the Vigilant individual to be more 'open' to salient social and emotional cues in their environment, especially threatening or dangerous cues, and to enhance behavioural responses to those cues.

The Unemotional ACM profile is characterised by blunted HPA functioning (van Goozen, Fairchild, Snoek, & Harold, 2007) and low parasympathetic activity (i.e. high immediate autonomic arousal), at least within highly personally relevant contexts (Katz, 2007). The unemotional profile is expected within social environments characterised by traumatic and/or chronic life stress exposure as the HPA axis would not be anticipated to be able to respond to every frequent extreme stressor, but instead would become blunted over time (Miller, Chen, & Zhou, 2007; Weems & Carrion, 2007) through (in part) altered negative feedback (Yehuda, 1998). These patterns of HPA and autonomic activity could explain a number of the characteristics of children with elevated CU traits. Specifically, rapid and early parasympathic arousal is specifically expected during agonistic social contexts (e.g. peer provocation), permitting the individual to mount an early fight-or-flight response. The sympathetic activity, consequently, is generally low in basal settings but can appear more normal during agonistic confrontations (van Goozen, Matthys, Cohen-Kettenis, Buitelaar, & van Engeland, 2000; Waschbusch et al., 2002). This may provide a physiological profile for the instrumental aggression in children with elevated CU traits because low basal autonomic activity permits calm planning, and then a brief fight-or-flight response enhances performance during confrontation or social situations in which dominance is the goal. What distinguishes the unemotional profile is that this sympathetic activation does not cross the higher threshold of an HPA response. Low basal and reactive HPA activity allow the individual to ignore social evaluative or judgement and function efficiently during extremely unpredictable situations in which others would feel anxious (Shirtcliff, Granger, Booth, & Johnson, 2005; Shirtcliff et al., 2009). This has many advantages, as it allows the individual to be shielded from the full impact of traumatic, chronic stressors, filtering out the vast majority of social and emotional information from their environment. Yet there are also costs, most of which stem from the function of the HPA to enhance emotional learning and memory (Pilgrim, Marin, & Lupien, 2010; Preuss & Wolf, 2009; Stark et al., 2006). These costs may underlie a number of the characteristics of children with CU traits.

First, HPA functioning is implicated during positive emotional states (Bateup, Booth, Shirtcliff, & Granger, 2002; Berk et al., 1989), so blunted HPA activity in general might require the individual to seek more intense positive emotional settings and lead to the thrill-seeking behaviours of youth with elevated CU traits. For example, blunted basal HPA activity is a risk factor for relapse and initiation of drug abuse (Dawes et al., 1999; Lovallo, Dickensheets, Myers, Thomas, & Nixon, 2000; Sorocco, Lovallo, Vincent, & Collins, 2006),

64   *Paul Frick and Elizabeth Shirtcliff*

and the rise in HPA activity following use (Lovallo, 2006) is one proposed mechanism for why use is likely to persist into addiction (Koob & Le Moal, 2001, 2008). Further, HPA activity is implicated broadly across social settings which may call for the individual to share in the emotions and stressors of another (Buchanan, Bagley, Stansfield, & Preston, 2012; Ruttle, Serbin, Stack, Schwartzman, & Shirtcliff, 2011) which forms the basis of empathy and social connection. Individuals with low HPA may generally feel less social connection to others (Shirtcliff et al., 2009) and this may manifest as uncaring or callous affect and lack of prosocial behavioural responses to others' distress. Third, blunted HPA activity would allow individuals to be insulated from recognising distressing cues in another individual and diminish the process of emotional learning by shielding the individual from social rejection, disapproval and shame (Del Giudice et al., 2011; Lewis & Ramsay, 2002). Such filtering of distress cues, even if that distress were caused by the individual, could contribute to the callous use of aggression and violence in children high on CU traits. Fourth, low HPA activity allows the individual to filter emotional cues within him or herself as well (Bugental, Martorell, & Barraza, 2003; van Honk, Schutter, Hermans, & Putman, 2003). As a result, punishment will not be distressing (as compared to other individuals) because low HPA activity will allow them to filter punishment cues, pain or distress information. Exacting greater and greater punishments would serve to entrench the unemotional pattern further (Koob & Le Moal, 2001, 2008).

Thus, these two profiles of the ACM, Vigilant and Unemotional, appear to correspond conceptually to the two developmental pathways to serious conduct problems. The ACM emphasises that these biological patterns influence behavioural outcomes and reflect a propensity to respond to a context in a particular way. The SRS provides a mechanism for how temperament operates to increase or decrease an individual's propensity for serious conduct problems. Direct tests of the ACM profiles and their association with conduct problems have not been conducted. However, research that finds both low and high SRS activity as a risk factor for conduct problems is supportive of the link (Essex et al., 2011; Ruttle et al., 2011; Skinner, Shirtcliff, Haggerty, Coe, & Catalano, 2011). An important implication of both the ACM view of stress reactivity and more traditional views of temperamental risk is that the risk profiles unfold over time as the individual learns to increase or decrease their behaviour, depending on feedback within the environment. The SRS changes over development, enhancing or diminishing learning and memory for salient information. The implication for prevention or intervention efforts is that this learning process can change based on the individual's proximate social context, and that learning will be reflected in upregulation or downregulation of the SRS which further influences learning and memory for salient social information. Prevention or intervention efforts can change the SRS to be more normative (Cicchetti, Rogosch, Toth, & Sturge-Apple, 2011; Fisher, Gunnar, Chamberlain, & Reid, 2000) and thus potentially diminish the child's risk for conduct problems (Shirtcliff, Skinner, Obasi, & Haggerty, under review).

Implications for research, diagnosis and treatment

Taken together, there appear to be at least two developmental pathways to serious conduct problem in childhood with distinct cognitive, emotional and biological risk factors. Implications for research are clear: research should no longer focus simply on documenting what risk factors are associated with serious conduct problems or which risk factors account for the most unique variance in conduct problems and aggression measures. Such methods ignore the possibility that serious conduct problems may have different causes across different groups of children. This is illustrated best by the findings reviewed previously showing that children high on conduct problems exhibit very different emotional profiles and differences in the corresponding neural activity depending on the presence of elevated CU traits.

Given these differences in risk factors, it will be important for CU traits to be included in the diagnostic criteria for conduct disorders in young children to guide aetiological research. Including CU traits in diagnostic criteria is also supported by research indicating that CU traits designate a more severe and stable pattern of problem behaviour within children who show severe conduct problems. For example, Kahn et al. (2012) provided data from both community (n = 1,136) and clinic-referred (n = 566) samples and reported that children with a diagnosis of conduct disorder (CD) who also exhibited elevated CU traits were more severe than those with a diagnosis of CD only, especially by being more aggressive and cruel (see also Pardini et al., 2012; Rowe et al., 2010). Research has also indicated that children with CU traits and severe conduct problems are at risk for more severe antisocial outcomes even controlling for their more severe behaviour problems. Byrd, Loeber, and Pardini (2012) reported that parent and teacher-rated CU traits at age 7 predicted criminal behaviour at age 25 among a sample of boys (n = 503), even when controlling for childhood CD, ADHD and ODD. McMahon et al. (2010) reported that CU traits in 7th grade predicted adult antisocial outcomes (e.g. adult arrests, adult antisocial personality symptoms) even when controlling for ADHD, ODD, CD and childhood-onset of CD in a high-risk community sample (n = 754).

Based on this research, the 5th edition of the *Diagnostic and Statistical Manual of Mental Disorders* (DSM-5; American Psychiatric Association, 2013) has added to the diagnosis of CD a specifier to designate those youth with serious conduct problems who also show elevated rates of CU traits (Frick & Nigg, 2012). For children who meet criteria for CD, the specifier would be given if the child shows two or more of the following characteristics persistently over at least 12 months and in more than one relationship or setting: lack of remorse or guilt, callous-lack of empathy, unconcern about performance in important activities, and shallow or deficient affect. Importantly, in an attempt to minimise the potential for iatrogenic effects of the label 'callous-unemotional', the name for the specifier is 'with Limited Prosocial Emotions' which is consistent with the association between CU traits and empathy and guilt (i.e. prosocial emotions).

Finally, and potentially most importantly, using CU traits to designate distinct subgroups of children and adolescents with serious conduct problems has important implications for prevention and treatment. By recognising the unique causal processes leading to the severe conduct problems of children with and without elevated CU traits, intensive and comprehensive interventions can be tailored to the unique characteristics of the different groups (Frick, 2012). For example, interventions that focus on teaching skills needed to regulate anger and other negative emotions (Larson & Lochman, 2003) or that focus on reducing harsh and ineffective parenting (McMahon & Forehand, 2003) may be more effective for children with serious conduct problems without elevated CU traits who are more likely to show problems with emotional regulation and who are more like to experience harsh, inconsistent and coercive parenting. In contrast, interventions which teach emotional recognition skills and other skills related to empathic concern or which focus on finding unique ways to motivate the child with CU traits that do not rely solely on punishment may be more effective for children who show elevated levels of CU traits (Dadds et al., 2012; Hawes & Dadds, 2005).

In summary, the different developmental pathways to severe conduct problems are not only important for guiding aetiological research on the distinct causal processes leading to the behaviour problems across different subgroups of children with conduct problems, but they are also important for guiding comprehensive and individualised approaches to treatment. As a result, as research advances our understanding of the causal mechanisms underlying the conduct problems in the different pathways, this understanding can guide treatments to more directly target these mechanisms (Frick, 2012). Both of these interrelated endeavours (i.e. understanding causal factors and testing tailored treatments) will likely be enhanced by upcoming changes in the diagnostic classification of children with severe conduct problems by explicitly recognising the importance of CU traits in designating important and distinct developmental pathways to severe conduct problems in children.

Literature

American Psychiatric Association (2013). *The diagnostic and statistical manual of mental disorders – 5th edition.* Washington, DC: American Psychiatric Association.

Anastassiou-Hadjicharalambous, X., & Warden, D. (2008). Physiologically-indexed and self-perceived affective empathy in conduct-disordered children high and low on callous–unemotional traits. *Child Psychiatry and Human Development, 39,* 503–517.

Asarnow, J. R., & Callan, J. W. (1985). Boys with peer adjustment problems: Social cognitive processes. *Journal of Consulting and Clinical Psychology, 53,* 80–87.

Barker, E. D., Oliver, B. R., Viding, E., Salekin, R. T., & Maughan, B. (2011). The impact of prenatal maternal risk, fearless temperament, and early parenting on adolescent callous-unemotional traits: A 14-year longitudinal investigation. *Journal of Child Psychology and Psychiatry, 52,* 878–888.

Bateup, H. S., Booth, A., Shirtcliff, E. A., & Granger, D. A. (2002). Testosterone, cortisol, and women's competition. *Evolution and Human Behaviour, 23,* 181–192.

Berk, L. S., Tan, S. A., Fry, W. F., Napier, B. J., Lee, J. W., & Hubbard, R. W. (1989). Neuroendocrine and stress hormone changes during mirthful laughter. *Journal of the American Medical Society*, *298*, 390–396.

Blair, R. J. R. (1995). A cognitive developmental approach to morality: Investigating the psychopath. *Cognition*, *57*, 1–29.

Blair, R. J. R., Colledge, E., & Mitchell, D. G. V. (2001). Somatic markers and response reversal: Is there orbitofrontal cortex dysfunction in boys with psychopathic tendencies? *Journal of Abnormal Child Psychology*, *29*, 499–511.

Brennan, P. A., Grekin, E. R., & Mednick, S. A. (1999). Maternal smoking during pregnancy and adult male criminal outcomes. *Archives of General Psychiatry*, *56*, 215–219.

Brennan, P. A., Grekin, E. R., & Mednick, S. A. (2003). Prenatal and perinatal influences on conduct disorder and serious delinquency. In B. B. Lahey, T. E. Moffitt, & A. Caspi (Eds.) *Causes of conduct disorder and juvenile delinquency*. New York: Guildford.

Buchanan, T. W., Bagley, S. L., Stansfield, R. B., & Preston, S. D. (2012). The empathic, physiological resonance of stress. *Society of Neuroscience*, *7*, 191–201.

Bugental, D. B., Martorell, G. A., & Barraza, V. (2003). The hormonal costs of subtle forms of infant maltreatment. *Hormones and Behaviour*, *43*, 237–244.

Byrd, A. L., Loeber, R., & Pardini, D. A. (2012). Understanding desisting and persisting forms of delinquency: The unique contributions of disruptive behaviour disorders and interpersonal callousness. *Journal of Child Psychology and Psychiatry*, *53*, 371–380.

Caspi, A. (2000). The child is father to the man: Personality continuities from childhood to adulthood. *Journal of Personality and Social Psychology*, *78*, 158–172.

Chabrol, H.,Van Leeuwen, N., Rodgers, R. F., & Gibbs, J. C. (2011). Relations between self-serving cognitive distortions, psychopathic traits, and antisocial behaviour in a non-clinical sample of adolescents. *Personality and Individual Differences*, *51*, 887–892.

Cicchetti, D., Rogosch, F. A., Toth, S. L., & Sturge-Apple, M. L. (2011). Normalizing the development of cortisol regulation in maltreated infants through preventive interventions. *Development and Psychopathology*, *23*, 789–800.

Dawes, M. A., Dorn, L. D., Moss, H. B., Yao, J. K., Kirisci, L., Ammerman, R. T., & Tarter, R. E. (1999). Hormonal and behavioural homeostasis in boys at risk for substance abuse. *Drug and Alcohol Dependency*, *55*, 165–176.

Dadds, M. R., Allen, J. L., Oliver, B. R., Faulkner, N., Legge, K., Moul, C., & Scott, S. (2012). Love, eye contact, and the developmental origins of empathy and v. psychopathy. *The British Journal of Psychiatry*, *200*, 191–196.

Dadds, M. R., El Masry, Y., Wimalaweera, S., & Guastella, A. J. (2007). Reduced eye-gaze explains 'fear blindness' in childhood psychopathic traits. *Journal of the American Academy of Child & Adolescent Psychiatry*, *47*, 455–463.

Dadds, M. R., Hawes, D. J., Frost, A. D. J., Vassallo, S., Bunn, P. B., Hunter, K., & Merz, S. (2009). Learning to 'talk the talk': The relationship of psychopathic traits to deficits in empathy across childhood. *Journal of Child Psychology and Psychiatry*, *50*, 599–606.

Dadds, M. R., Perry, Y., Hawes, D. J., Merz, S., Riddell, A. C., Haines, D. J., & Abeygunawardane, A. I. (2006). Attention to the eyes reverses fear-recognition deficits in child psychopathy. *British Journal of Psychiatry*, *189*, 280–281.

Dadds, M. R., & Salmon, K. (2003). Punishment insensitivity and parenting: Temperament and learning as interacting risks for antisocial behaviour. *Clinical Child and Family Psychology Review*, *6*, 69–86.

68 *Paul Frick and Elizabeth Shirtcliff*

Deater-Deckard, K., & Wang Z. (2012). Anger and irritability. In M. Zentner & R. L. Shiner (Eds.), *Handbook of temperament* (pp. 124–144). New York: Guildford.

Del Giudice, M., Ellis, B. J., & Shirtcliff, E. A. (2011). The Adaptive Calibration Model of stress responsivity. *Neuroscience and Biobehavioural Review, 35*, 1562–1592.

de Wied, M., van Boxtel, A., Matthys, W., & Meeus, W. (2012). Verbal, facial and autonomic responses to empathy-eliciting film clips by disruptive male adolescents with high versus low callous–unemotional traits. *Journal of Abnormal Child Psychology, 40*, 211–223.

Dodge, K. A., Lansford, J., Burks, V. S., Bates, J. E., Pettit, G. S., & Fontaine, R. (2003). Peer rejection and social information processing factors in the development of aggressive behaviour problems in children. *Child Development, 74*, 374–393.

Dodge, K. A, Lochman, J. E., Harnish, J. D., Bates, J. E., & Pettit, G. S. (1997). Reactive and proactive aggression in school children and psychiatrically impaired chronically assaultive youth. *Journal of Abnormal Psychology, 106*, 37–51.

Dodge, K. A., & Pettit, G. S. (2003). A biopsychological model of the development of chronic conduct problems in adolescence. *Developmental Psychology, 39*, 349–371.

Dodge, K. A., Pettit, G. S., McClaskey, C. L., & Brown, M. (1986). *Social competence in children. Monographs of the Society for Research in Child Development, 51*(Serial No. 213), 1–85.

Essex, M. J., Shirtcliff, E. A., Burk, L. R., Ruttle, P. L., Klein, M. H., & Slattery, M. J. (2011). Influence of early life stress on later hypothalamic–pituitary–adrenal axis functioning and its covariation with mental health symptoms: A study of the allostatic process from childhood into adolescence. *Development and Psychopathology, 23*, 1039–1058.

Fisher, P. A., Gunnar, M. R., Chamberlain, P., & Reid, J. B. (2000). Preventive intervention for maltreated preschool children: Impact on children's behaviour, neuroendocrine activity, and foster parent functioning. *Journal of the American Academy of Child and Adolescent Psychiatry, 39*, 1356–1364.

Fox, N. A., & Calkins, S. D. (2003). The development of self-control of emotion: Intrinsic and extrinsic influences. *Motivation and Emotion, 27*, 7–26.

Frick, P. J. (2012). Developmental pathways to conduct disorder: Implications for future directions in research, assessment, and treatment. *Journal of Clinical Child & Adolescent Psychology, 41*, 378–389.

Frick, P. J., Cornell, A. H., Barry, C. T., Bodin, S. D., & Dane, H. A. (2003). Callous-unemotional traits and conduct problems in the prediction of conduct problem severity, aggression, and self-report of delinquency. *Journal of Abnormal Child Psychology, 31*, 457–470.

Frick, P. J., Cornell, A. H., Bodin, S. D., Dane, H. A., Barry, C. T., & Loney, B. R. (2003). Callous–Unemotional traits and developmental pathways to severe aggressive and antisocial behaviour. *Developmental Psychology, 39*, 246–260.

Frick, P. J., Lilienfeld, S. O., Ellis, M., Loney, B., & Silverthorn, P. (1999). The association between anxiety and psychopathy dimensions in children. *Journal of Abnormal Child Psychology, 27*, 383–392.

Frick, P. J., & Morris, A. S. (2004). Temperament and developmental pathways to conduct problems. *Journal of Clinical Child and Adolescent Psychology, 33*, 54–68.

Frick, P. J., & Nigg, J. T. (2012). Current issues in the diagnosis of Attention Deficit Hyperactivity Disorder, Oppositional Defiant Disorder, and Conduct Disorder. *Annual Review of Clinical Psychology, 8*, 77–107.

Frick, P. J., & Viding, E. M. (2009). Antisocial behaviour from a developmental psychopathology perspective. *Development and Psychopathology, 21*, 1111–1131.

Frick, P. J., & White, S. F. (2008). The importance of callous–unemotional traits for the development of aggressive and antisocial behaviour. *Journal of Child Psychology and Psychiatry, 49*, 359–375.

Glenn, A. L., Raine, A., Venables, P. H., & Mednick, S. A. (2007). Early temperamental and psychophysiological precursors of adult psychopathic personality. *Journal of Abnormal Psychology, 116*, 508–518.

Hastings, P. D., Zahn-Waxler, C., & McShane, K. (2006). We are, by nature, moral creatures: Biological bases of concern for others. In M. Killen & J. Smetana (Eds.), *Handbook of moral development* (pp. 483–516). Mahwah, NJ: Lawrence Erlbaum Associates.

Hawes, D. J., & Dadds, M. R. (2005). The treatment of conduct problems in children with callous–unemotional traits. *Journal of Consulting and Clinical Psychology, 73*, 737–741.

Jones, A. P., Happe, F. G. E., Gilbert, F., Burnett, S., & Viding, E. (2010). Feeling, caring, knowing: Different types of empathy deficit in boys with psychopathic tendencies and autism spectrum disorder. *Journal of Child Psychology and Psychiatry, 51*, 1188–1197.

Jones, A. P., Laurens, K. R., Herba, C. M., Barker, G. J., & Viding, E. (2009). Amygdala hypoactivity to fearful faces in boys with conduct problems and callous–unemotional traits. *The American Journal of Psychiatry, 166*, 95–102.

Kagan, J. (2012). The biography of behavioural inhibition. In M. Zenter & R. L. Shiner (Eds.), *Handbook of temperament* (pp. 69–82). New York: Guilford.

Kahn, R. E., Frick, P. J., Youngstrom, E., Findling, R. L., & Youngstrom, J. K. (2012). The effects of including a callous–unemotional specifier for the diagnosis of conduct disorder. *Journal of Child Psychology and Psychiatry, 53*, 271–282.

Katz, L. F. (2007). Domestic violence and vagal reactivity to peer provocation. *Biological Psychology, 74*, 154–164.

Kimonis, E. R., Frick, P. J., Fazekas, H., & Loney, B. R. (2006). Psychopathy, aggression, and the emotional processing of emotional stimuli in non-referred girls and boys. *Behavioural Sciences and the Law, 24*, 21–37.

Kimonis, E. R., Frick, P. J., Muñoz, L. C., & Aucoin, K. J. (2008). Callous–unemotional traits and the emotional processing of distress cues in detained boys: Testing the moderating role of aggression, exposure to community violence, and histories of abuse. *Development and Psychopathology, 20*, 569–589.

Kimonis, E. R., Frick, P. J., Skeem, J., Marsee, M. A., Cruise, K., Muñoz, L. C., & Morris, A. S. (2008). Assessing callous–unemotional traits in adolescent offenders: Validation of the Inventory of Callous–Unemotional Traits. *Journal of the International Association of Psychiatry and Law, 31*, 241–252.

Kingston, L., & Priour, M. (1995). The development of patters of stable, transient, and school-age onset aggressive behaviour in young children. *Journal of the American Academy of Child and Adolescent Psychiatry, 34*, 348–358.

Kochanska, G. (1993). Toward a synthesis of parental socialization and child temperament in early development of conscience. *Child Development, 64*, 325–347.

Koob, G. F., & Le Moal, M. (2001). Drug addiction, dysregulation of reward, and allostasis. *Neuropsychopharmacology, 24*, 97–129.

Koob, G. F., & Le Moal, M. (2008). Addiction and the brain antireward system. *Annual Reviews in Psychology, 59,* 29–53.

Larson, J., & Lochman, J. E. (2003). *Helping schoolchildren cope with anger.* New York: Guilford.

Lemerise, E. A., & Maulden, J. (2010). Emotions and social information processing: Implications for understanding aggressive (and nonaggressive) children. In W. F. Arsenio & E. A. Lemerise (Eds.), *Emotions, aggression, and morality in children: Bridging development and psychopathology* (pp. 157–176). Washington, DC: American Psychological Association.

Lengua, L. J., West, S. G., & Sandler, I. N. (1998). Temperament as a predictor of symptomatology in children: Addressing contamination of measures. *Child Development, 69,* 164–181.

Lewis, M., & Ramsay, D. (2002). Cortisol response to embarrassment and shame. *Child Development, 73,* 1034–1045.

Loney, B. R., Frick, P. J., Clements, C. B., Ellis, M. L., & Kerlin, K. (2003). Callous-unemotional traits, impulsivity, and emotional processing in adolescents with antisocial behaviour problems. *Journal of Clinical Child and Adolescent Psychology, 32,* 66–80.

Loney, B. R., Frick, P. J., Ellis, M., & McCoy, M. G. (1998). Intelligence, psychopathy, and antisocial behaviour. *Journal of Psychopathology and Behavioural Assessment, 20,* 231–247.

Lotze, G. M., Ravindran, N., & Myers, B. J. (2010). Moral emotions, emotion self-regulation, callous–unemotional traits, and problem behaviour in children of incarcerated mothers. *Journal of Child and Family Studies, 19,* 702–713.

Lovallo, W. R. (2006). Cortisol secretion patterns in addiction and addiction risk. *International Journal Psychophysiology, 59,* 195–202.

Lovallo, W. R., Dickensheets, S. L., Myers, D. A., Thomas, T. L., & Nixon, S. J. (2000). Blunted stress cortisol response in abstinent alcoholic and polysubstance-abusing men. *Alcohol Clinical and Experimental Research, 24,* 651–658.

Lupien, S. J., Ouellet-Morin, I., Hupbach, A., Tu, M., Buss, C., & Walker, D. (2006). Beyond the stress concept: Allostatic load – A developmental biological and cognitive perspective. In D. Cicchetti & D. Cohen (Eds.), *Developmental psychopathology* (2nd ed., Vol. 2, pp. 578–628). Hoboken, NJ: John Wiley & Sons.

Marsh, A. A., Finger, E. C., Mitchell, D. G. V., Reid, M. E., Sims, C., Kosson, D. S., & Blair, R. J. R. (2008). Reduced amygdala response to fearful expressions in children and adolescents with callous-unemotional traits and disruptive behaviour disorders. *The American Journal of Psychiatry, 165,* 712–720.

Marsh, A. A., Finger, E. C., Schechter, J. C., Jurkowitz, I. T. N., Reid, M. E., & Blair, R. J. R. (2011). Adolescents with psychopathic traits report reductions in physiological responses to fear. *Journal of Child Psychology and Psychiatry, 52,* 838–841.

McMahon, R. J., & Forehand, R. L. (2003). *Helping the noncompliant child (2nd edition).* New York: Guilford.

McMahon, R. J., Witkiewitz, K., Kotler, J. S., & The Conduct Problems Prevention Research Group. (2010). Predictive validity of callous–unemotional traits measures in early adolescence with respect to multiple antisocial outcomes. *Journal of Abnormal Psychology, 119,* 752–763.

Miller, G. E., Chen, E., & Zhou, E. S. (2007). If it goes up, must it come down? Chronic stress and the hypothalamic-pituitary-adrenocortical axis in humans. *Psychological Bulletin, 133,* 25–45.

Moffitt, T. E. (2006). Life-course persistent versus adolescence-limited antisocial behaviour. In D. Cicchetti & D. J. Cohen (Eds.). *Developmental psychopathology, 2nd edition, vol. 3: Risk, disorder, and adaptation* (pp. 570–598). New York: Wiley.

Olds, D., Henderson, C. R., Cole, R., Eckenrode, J., Kiztman, H., Luckey, D., Pettitt, L., Sidora, K., Morris, P., & Powers, J. (1998). Long term effects of nurse home visitation on children's criminal and antisocial behaviour: 15-year follow-up of a randomized controlled trial. *JAMA: Journal of the American Medical Association, 280,* 1238–1244.

Pardini, D. A. (2006). The callousness pathway to severe violent delinquency. *Aggressive Behaviour, 32,* 1–9.

Pardini, D. A. (2011). Perceptions of social conflicts among incarcerated adolescents with callous–unemotional traits: 'You're going to pay. It's going to hurt, but I don't care.' *Journal of Child Psychology and Psychiatry, 52,* 248–255.

Pardini, D. A., & Byrd, A. L. (2012). Perceptions of aggressive conflicts and others' distress in children with callous–unemotional traits: 'I'll show you who's boss, even if you suffer and I get in trouble'. *Journal of Child Psychology and Psychiatry, 53,* 283–291.

Pardini, D. A., Lochman, J. E., & Frick, P. J. (2003). Callous–unemotional traits and social-cognitive processes in adjudicated youths. *Journal of the American Academy of Child and Adolescent Psychiatry, 42,* 364–371.

Pardini, D. A., Stepp, S., Hipwell, A., Stouthamer-Loeber, M., & Loeber, R. (2012). The clinical utility of the propose DSM-5 callous–unemotional subtype of conduct disorder in young girls. *Journal of the American Academy of Child and Adolescent Psychiatry, 51,* 62–73.

Pasalich, D. S., Dadds, M. R., Hawes, D. J., & Brennan, J. (2012). Do callous–unemotional traits moderate the relative importance of parental coercion versus warmth in child conduct problems? An observational study. *Journal of Child Psychology and Psychiatry, 52,* 1308–1315.

Patterson, G. R., Reid, J. R., & Dishion, T. J. (1992). *Antisocial boys.* Eugene, OR: Castalia.

Pilgrim, K., Marin, M. F., & Lupien, S. J. (2010). Attentional orienting toward social stress stimuli predicts increased cortisol responsivity to psychosocial stress irrespective of the early socioeconomic status. *Psychoneuroendocrinology, 35,* 588–595.

Preuss, D., & Wolf, O. T. (2009). Post-learning psychosocial stress enhances consolidation of neutral stimuli. *The Neurobiology of Learning and Memory, 92,* 318–326.

Raine, A. (2002). Biosocial studies of antisocial and violent behaviour in children and adults: A review. *Journal of Abnormal Child Psychology, 30,* 311–326.

Rothbart, M. K. (2012). Advances in temperament: History, concepts, and measures. In M. Zentner & R. L. Shiner (Eds.), *Handbook of temperament* (pp. 3–20). New York: Guildford.

Rothbart, M. K., & Bates, J. E. (1998). Temperament. In W. Damon (Ed.), *Handbook of child psychology: Vol. 3. Social, emotional, and personality development* (pp. 105–176). New York: Wiley.

Rowe, R., Maughan, B., Moran, P., Ford, T., Briskman, J., & Goodman, R. (2010). The role of callous unemotional traits in the diagnosis of conduct disorder. *Journal of Child Psychology and Psychiatry, 51,* 688–695.

Rubin, K. H., Bukowski, W., & Parker, J. G. (1998). Peer interactions, relationships, and groups. In W. Damon (Ed.), *Handbook of child psychology: Vol 3. Social, emotional, and personality development* (pp. 619–700). New York: Wiley.

Rubin, K. H., Burgess, K. B., Dwyer, K. M., & Hastings, P. D. (2003). Predicting preschoolers' externalizing behaviours from toddler temperament, conflict, and maternal negativity. *Developmental Psychology*, 39, 164–176.

Ruttle, P. L., Serbin, L. A., Stack, D. M., Schwartzman, A. E., & Shirtcliff, E. A. (2011). Adrenocortical attunement in mother-child dyads: Importance of situational and behavioural characteristics. *Biological Psychology*, 88, 104–111.

Ruttle, P. L., Shirtcliff, E. A., Serbin, L. A., Fisher, D. B., Stack, D. M., & Schwartzman, A. E. (2011). Disentangling psychobiological mechanisms underlying internalizing and externalizing behaviours in youth: Longitudinal and concurrent associations with cortisol. *Hormones and Behaviour*, 59, 123–132.

Salekin, R. T., Neumann, C. S., Leistico, A. R., & Zalot, A. A. (2004). Psychopathy in youth and intelligence: An investigation of Cleckley's hypothesis. *Journal of Clinical Child and Adolescent Psychology*, 33, 731–742.

Schwenck, C., Mergenthaler, J., Keller, K., Zech, J., Salehi, S., Taurines, R., & Freitag, C. M. (2012). Empathy in children with autism and conduct disorder: Group specific profiles and developmental aspects. *Journal of Child Psychology and Psychiatry*, 53, 651–659.

Sebastian, C. L., McCrory, E. J. P., Cecil, C. A. M., Lockwood, P. L., De Brito, S. A., Fontaine, N. M. G., & Viding, E. (2012). Neural responses to affective and cognitive theory of mind in children with conduct problems and varying levels of callous-unemotional traits. *Archives of General Psychiatry*, 69, 814–822.

Shaw, D. S., Gilliom, M., Ingoldsby, E. M., & Nagin, D. (2003). Trajectories leading to school-age conduct problems. *Developmental Psychology*, 39, 189–200.

Shaw, D. S., Owens, E., Vondra, J., & Keenan, K. (1996). Early risk factors and pathways in the development of early disruptive behaviour problems. *Development and Psychopathology*, 8, 679–699.

Shirtcliff, E. A., Granger, D. A., Booth, A., & Johnson, D. (2005). Low salivary cortisol levels and externalizing behaviour problems in youth. *Development and Psychopathology*, 17, 167–184.

Shirtcliff, E. A., Skinner, M., Obasi, E. M., & Haggerty, K. (under review). Positive parenting predicts calibration of cortisol functioning six years later in young adults.

Shirtcliff, E. A., Vitacco, M. J., Graf, A. R., Gostisha, A. J., Merz, J. L., & Zahn-Waxler, C. (2009). Neurobiology of empathy and callousness: implications for the development of antisocial behaviour. *Behavioural Science and the Law*, 27, 137–171.

Skinner, M. L., Shirtcliff, E. A., Haggerty, K. P., *et al.* (2011). Allostasis model facilitates understanding race differences in the diurnal cortisol rhythm. *Development and Psychopathology*, 23, 1167–1186.

Sorocco, K. H., Lovallo, W. R., Vincent, A. S., & Collins, F. L. (2006). Blunted hypothalamic-pituitary-adrenocortical axis responsivity to stress in persons with a family history of alcoholism. *International Journal of Psychophysiology*, 59, 210–217.

Stark, R., Wolf, O. T., Tabbert, K., Kagerer, S., Zimmermann, M., & Kirsch, P. (2006). Influence of the stress hormone cortisol on fear conditioning in humans: evidence for sex differences in the response of the prefrontal cortex. *Neuroimage*, 32, 1290–1298.

Stickle, T. R., Kirkpatrick, N. M., & Brush, L. N. (2009). Callous-unemotional traits and social information processing: Multiple risk factor models for understanding aggressive behaviour in antisocial youth. *Law and Human Behaviour*, 33, 515–529.

Theall, K. P., Drury, S. S., & Shirtcliff, E. A. (2012). Cumulative neighborhood risk of psychosocial stress and allostatic load in adolescents. *American Journal of Epidemiology*, 176 Suppl 7, S164–174.

Children at risk for serious conduct problems 73

Thomas, A., & Chess, S. (1977). *Temperament and development*. New York: New York University Press.

van Goozen, S. H., Fairchild, G., Snoek, H., & Harold, G. T. (2007). The evidence for a neurobiological model of childhood antisocial behaviour. *Psychological Bulletin, 133*, 149–182.

van Goozen, S. H., Matthys, W., Cohen-Kettenis, P. T., Buitelaar, J. K., & van Engeland, H. (2000). Hypothalamic-pituitary-adrenal axis and autonomic nervous system activity in disruptive children and matched controls. *Journal of the American Academy of Child and Adolescent Psychiatry, 39*, 1438–1445.

van Honk, J., Schutter, D. J., Hermans, E. J., & Putman, P. (2003). Low cortisol levels and the balance between punishment sensitivity and reward dependency. *Neuroreport, 14*, 1993–1996.

Viding, E., Frick, P. J., & Plomin, R. (2007). Aetiology of the relationship between callous-unemotional traits and conduct problems in childhood. *British Journal of Psychiatry, 49*, s33–s38.

Viding, E., Jones, A. P., Frick, P. J., Moffitt, T. E., & Plomin, R. (2008). Heritability of antisocial behaviour at nine-years: Do callous-unemotional traits matter? *Developmental Science, 11*, 17–22.

Waschbusch, D. A., Pelham, W. E., Jr., Jennings, J. R., Greiner, A. R., Tarter, R. E., & Moss, H. B. (2002). Reactive aggression in boys with disruptive behaviour disorders: behaviour, physiology, and affect. *Journal of Abnormal Child Psychology, 30*, 641–656.

Weems, C. F., & Carrion, V. G. (2007). The association between PTSD symptoms and salivary cortisol in youth: The role of time since the trauma. *Journal of Trauma and Stress, 20*, 903–907.

White, S. F., Marsh, A. A., Fowler, K. A., Schechter, J. C., Adalio, C., Pope, K., & Blair, R. J. R. (2012). Reduced amygdala response in youths with disruptive behaviour disorders and psychopathic traits: Decreased emotional response versus increased top-down attention to nonemotional features. *American Journal of Psychiatry, 169*, 750–758.

Willoughby, M. T., Waschbusch, D. A., Moore, G. A., & Propper, C. B. (2011). Using the ASEBA to screen for callous unemotional traits in early childhood: Factor structure, temporal, stability, and utility. *Journal of Psychopathology and Behavioural Assessment, 33*, 19–30.

Wootton, J. M., Frick, P. J., Shelton, K. K., & Silverthorn, P. (1997). Ineffective parenting and childhood conduct problems: The moderating role of callous-unemotional traits. *Journal of Consulting and Clinical Psychology, 65*, 301–308.

Yehuda, R. (1998). Psychoneuroendocrinology of post-traumatic stress disorder. *Psychiatric Clinics of North America, 21*, 359–379.

4 Biological approaches to externalising disorders and juvenile psychopathic traits

Moran D. Cohn, Arne Popma, Adrian Raine and Maaike Cima

Introduction

For as long as history records tell us, it has been normative to engage in minor forms of antisocial, delinquent and risk-taking behaviour during adolescence. Psychological models of adolescence have conceptualised such behaviour as important for exploration and transitioning to independence from parental supervision (Crone & Dahl, 2012). A wide array of social and psychological changes, such as a decrease in parental monitoring and an increase in susceptibility to peer group influences, mark the beginning of adolescence and may contribute to both social and antisocial forms of risk-taking and reward-seeking behaviour. Notably, these psychosocial changes are accompanied by a shift in levels of a variety of hormones which lead to profound physical changes, including substantial brain development (Blakemore, Burnett, & Dahl, 2010; Forbes & Dahl, 2010). In this respect, a large body of literature on the neural underpinnings of behavioural and psychosocial changes occurring during adolescence has formed over the past decades (Crone & Dahl, 2012). In concert, these studies have implicated the importance of several neural mechanisms in shaping development from childhood into adulthood. First, adolescence is marked by a substantial linear increase in the capacity to inhibit impulses, mediated by development of the prefrontal cortex (e.g. Rubia, Smith, Taylor, & Brammer, 2007; although see Crone & Dahl, 2012 for another point of view). Second, sensitivity to reward and loss, mediated by the ventral striatum and amygdala, shows a curvilinear pattern of increase in early adolescence followed by a decline from mid to late adolescence (Crone & Dahl, 2012). These findings may explain why even typically developing adolescents, when compared to children or adults, show more difficulties at inhibiting impulses associated with potential reward (social or material), even in the face of potential punishment (Steinberg, 2007). Adolescence is also marked by profound changes in sensitivity to particular social contexts, as evidenced by increased tendencies to engage in risk-taking behaviour in the context of (delinquent) peers (Gardner & Steinberg, 2005). Recent studies also suggest that empathy may be transiently reduced in adolescent boys, again potentially allowing for increased antisocial behaviour towards others (Van der Graaff et al., 2014). In sum, accumulating evidence supports a biopsychosocial model (Engel, 1977) in which biological predisposition interacts with both social and psychological factors explaining the normative increase in (antisocial) risk-taking and explorative behaviour in adolescence.

From a clinical perspective, this pattern of typical development and its associated neurobiological changes can be used as a background to understand atypical levels of antisocial behaviour in children and adolescents. Child and adolescent psychiatry classifies antisocial behaviour in minors as externalising psychiatric disorders (ED), encompassing both oppositional defiant disorder (ODD) and conduct disorder (CD), when they reach a level of severity and persistence that affects their overall functioning and/or inflicts serious harm on others. Children with ED are often very extraverted, under-controlled and act out their emotions. Often these children get involved in bullying, fighting and other types of violent behaviour. Similar to the differences between typical adolescents and both children or adults described above, children and adolescents with ED, when compared to age-matched controls, are characterised by deficits in cognitive functions such as inhibition, reward and loss processing as well as empathy. However, the deficits seen in ED cannot be reduced to 'exaggerated forms of typical adolescence', and the current review will instead employ the mentioned cognitive functions as a heuristic framework to describe the complicated brains that are currently thought to underlie ED.

While this review will focus on neuroimaging research in ED, we want to emphasise that these findings portray only part of the currently dominant biopsychosocial research approach to the development of ED. This approach is exemplified by gene-environment interaction studies showing that specific genes only put one at risk for antisocial development when social risk factors are also in place (e.g. MAOA maltreatment; Byrd & Manuck, 2014; notably, some biological 'risk factors' may actually be protective of adverse outcomes in positive social environments, cf. Belsky, Bakermans-Kranenburg, & Van Ijzendoorn, 2007), investigations of the effects of trauma on the developing brain that in turn may confer vulnerability to ED (e.g. McCrory, De Brito, & Viding, 2012), and longitudinal studies showing that parenting interventions may affect biological parameters of stress-regulation (Brotman et al., 2007; Cicchetti, Rogosch, Toth, & Sturge-Apple, 2011). These observations exemplify several important facts about behavioural neurobiology: (1) the relation between biology and behaviour is reciprocal (i.e. behaviour influences biological parameters and vice versa), (2) biological parameters are often not stable over time, especially during development from childhood to adulthood (e.g. Tottenham & Sheridan, 2009), and (3) complex behavioural constructs (like ED) cannot be explained by a single biological parameter but relate to a vast number of biological and environmental interacting factors (see Cicchetti & Posner, 2005 for a review on the interaction between neuroscience and psychology in general). Neurobiological research on ED has been criticised for not sufficiently taking into account these complexities (Loeber & Pardini, 2008) and, indeed, its validity and translational value may greatly increase when doing so, for example by taking up the challenge of

76 *Moran D. Cohn et al.*

investigating longitudinal changes in antisocial behaviour (e.g. Platje et al., 2013; Cohn et al., 2013). Notwithstanding these nuances, and as discussed in this chapter and other chapters in this book, studying biological parameters in relation to behaviour may help us understand developmental patterns of psychological functioning and psychiatric dysfunctioning. It may help to define new biologically plausible constructs of psychological functioning and more specific diagnostic subtyping. In turn, this may lead to more specific and effective prevention and treatment strategies (Beauchaine, Neuhaus, Brenner, & Gatzke-Kopp, 2008).

As such, this chapter will discuss neuroimaging findings in ED, using the cognitive framework described above. Notably, other chapters in this book discuss additional cognitive constructs that bear relevance to development of ED. For example, hyporeactivity (Raine, Reynolds, Venables, Mednick, & Farrington, 1998) and hyperreactivity (Cohn et al., 2013; Hodgins, 2007) of the fear neurocircuitry are also of importance in the development of ED but are discussed in two other chapters of this book (see Chapters 11 and 12). Here, we will first discuss the methodology of brain research on juveniles with ED, including its techniques and behavioural phenotyping approaches. Second, we will review the neuroimaging literature on ED with respect to three clinically relevant cognitive functions: (1) inhibition, (2) reward and loss processing, (3) and affective empathy. Finally, we will discuss potential practical implications of these findings.

Methods and behavioural constructs

The advent of high-resolution techniques such as magnetic resonance imaging (MRI) has substantially altered the field of neurobiological research in psychology and psychiatry at large. Previous biological studies on antisocial behaviour have often employed valid and pragmatic peripheral measures of brain function (e.g. neuropsychology [O'Brien, Frick, & Lyman, 1994]; hormone concentrations [Cima, Smeets, & Jelicic, 2008; Cima, Nicolson, De Lijster, & Popma, submitted; Popma et al., 2007] or heart rate [Ortiz & Raine, 2004]). Through these studies, insight has been gained into how arousal relates differentially to specific subtypes of antisocial behaviour. Moreover, studies into hormones such as testosterone have confirmed previous findings from animal studies (i.e. showing correlations between high adrenal hormones and aggression), but have also made clear, once more, that individual hormones interact with a vast amount of other factors (i.e. other hormones and environmental factors) in relation to antisocial behaviour (for example Popma et al., 2007; Platje et al., 2013). Both genetic and neuroimaging studies have allowed for investigating more 'central' biological parameters. A thorough review of genetic studies in ED is beyond the scope of this chapter but can be found in studies of Viding (Viding & Jones, 2008; Viding et al., 2012). Neuroimaging is an example of a recent, and still developing, technique that not only allows assessing both structure and function (fMRI) of the brain in a more direct manner, but its higher spatiotemporal resolution allows for a substantial increase in regional specificity (although see Logothetis, 2008 for its limitations). As such, the last decade has witnessed a tendency towards higher specificity in neurocognitive accounts of development of ED as well, moving from relatively simple models (e.g. 'hypofrontality' or 'fearlessness') to more sophisticated models incorporating multiple neural systems and – importantly – multiple behavioural dimensions of dysfunction (Blair, 2013).

In this respect, psychopathic traits (see also Chapters 4, 11 and 12) have been increasingly used in the study of the neural underpinnings of ED. While the criteria of ED capture oppositional and antisocial behaviour, the psychopathic traits construct refers to the characteristics of ED juveniles that bear resemblance to the personality traits seen in adult psychopaths. Although it has been argued that such characteristics cannot be seamlessly equated with its adult counterpart (Seagrave & Grisso, 2002), there is increasing evidence that in juveniles, high levels of psychopathic traits denote a subgroup of ED individuals showing the most severe and persistent antisocial behaviour (Frick, 2012) – similar to what has been reported in adults. Also in children and adolescents, the factor-analytic literature provides evidence for psychopathic traits to consist of three to four relatively independent factors or dimensions: (1) interpersonal, (2) affective (i.e. callous-unemotional traits), (3) impulsive and (4) antisocial traits (e.g. Neumann, Kosson, Forth, & Hare, 2006). Importantly, these factors are differentially associated with behavioural (Patrick, Hicks, Krueger, & Lang, 2005) and psychophysiological (Patrick, 1994) criterion variables. Recent studies suggests that these dimensions of psychopathic traits may also provide endophenotype-like entities, in that they represent atypical function of distinct neural systems (see also Chapter 4), also in ED juveniles. First evidence in this respect will be discussed below.

Inhibition

For a long time, deficient inhibition has been the mainstay of research on the neural underpinnings of antisocial and risky behaviour during adolescence. Similarly, lesion studies in adults have indicated that lesions to the prefrontal cortex – specifically the orbitofrontal cortex – result in disinhibited and antisocial behaviour in people not inclined to such behaviour before the lesion (Eslinger & Damasio, 1985). In addition, aberrant structure and function of several other prefrontal brain regions have since been implicated in the aetiology of antisocial behaviour. Yang and Raine (2009) have reported meta-analytic evidence for structural volumetric reductions in antisocial individuals not only in the orbitofrontal cortex, but also in the anterior cingulate cortex and dorsolateral prefrontal cortex (but not for the ventrolateral prefrontal cortex or medial prefrontal cortex). A plethora of cognitive functions involved in regulatory control, termed 'executive functions', have been attributed to these regions. These structural reductions are consistent with neuropsychological research, firmly suggesting the presence of deficits in executive functions relying on integrity of the orbitofrontal cortex in antisocial individuals (De Brito & Hodgins, 2009). However, there are indications for heterogeneity in this respect, and some have suggested that executive dysfunction is specific to the impulsive-antisocial dimensions of psychopathy (Ross, Benning, & Adams, 2007; Miller, Flory, Lynam, & Leukefeld, 2003; Whiteside & Lynam, 2001). In a recent study of juvenile delinquents, executive functioning (i.e. poor response inhibition) was indeed related to the antisocial dimension of psychopathy (Feilhauer, Cima, Korebrits, & Kunert, 2012). Moreover, at the same time the affective psychopathy dimension was related to better response inhibition, suggesting differential associations between psychopathy dimensions and response inhibition in children with ED (Feilhauer et al., 2012).

Although both functional paradigms and analytic strategies have often been biased towards detecting subcortical/ventral prefrontal dysfunction, functional MRI studies in juveniles with ED have been relatively consistent in not reporting functional reductions in dorsolateral regions of the prefrontal cortex. There have, however, been reports on ED juveniles displaying ventral prefrontal (orbitofrontal/ventromedial prefrontal [vmPFC] cortex) atypicalities, in terms of both function (Rubia et al., 2009; Finger et al., 2008; Finger et al., 2011), structure (Huebner et al., 2008; De Brito et al., 2009) and functional connectivity (Finger et al., 2012; Marsh et al., 2008; Marsh et al., 2011). Also in healthy children, cortical thickness of the orbitofrontal cortex has been associated with externalising behaviour tendencies (Ameis et al., 2014). However, the direction of these effects has not always been consistent, and their cognitive contexts (rewarded attention, punished reversal errors and reward, respectively) do not allow firm conclusions about inhibition. Similarly, anterior cingulate cortex abnormalities have also been commonly reported (Marsh et al., 2013; Lockwood et al., 2013; Sebastian et al., 2013; Sterzer, Stadler, Krebs, Kleinschmidt, & Poustka, 2005; Cohn et al., 2013) but, given their cognitive experimental context, these are likely to reflect its affective, rather than inhibitory functions (Bush, Luu, & Posner, 2000). Only two neuroimaging studies, from the same group, have specifically reported on inhibition-related deficits in ED. Rubia and colleagues (Rubia et al., 2008) used a tracking stop task to measure inhibition and reported that participants with pure CD, that is without co-morbid attention deficit/hyperactivity disorder (ADHD), show reduced activation in the posterior cingulate gyrus during inhibition failure, compared to controls. In the second study, on the other hand, Rubia and colleagues (Rubia et al., 2009) report that participants with pure CD show reduced activation in the superior temporal lobe and precuneus during interference inhibition in a Simon task. It is interesting that neither of these studies reports prefrontal deficits during inhibition in ED. One explanation may be that the recruitment strategy of these studies (aimed at participants with low levels of ADHD symptoms) has led to lower levels of impulsive-antisocial traits in their ED samples.

In summary, there are indications for ventral prefrontal atypicalities and for deficits in regulatory functions in antisocial juveniles. Studies in adults suggest that such deficits may be specifically associated with impulsive-antisocial psychopathic traits, but further research in this respect is needed. Similar to adolescent risk-taking in typical development (Crone & Dahl, 2012), however, antisocial behaviour in ED cannot be explained by inhibition deficits alone, and accumulating evidence suggests that reward and loss sensitivity should be taken into account to understanding its development more fully. A review of this literature is provided below.

Reward and loss sensitivity

There is considerable evidence for decision-making deficits in antisocial juveniles. For example, boys with ED show perseveration when engaged in a task that has a high chance of reward initially, but increasing rates of punishment later (Shapiro, Quay, Hogan, & Schwartz, 1988; Matthys, van Goozen, Snoek, & Van, 2004) and show poor passive avoidance learning in experiments with competing incentives (i.e. both reward and punishment; Newman, Widom, & Nathan, 1985). These are unlikely to be explained by deficient inhibition alone, as reward has been shown to moderate the association between decision-making deficits and antisocial behaviour (Newman & Kosson, 1986). As such, reward hypersensitivity (Scerbo et al., 1990) has been invoked as an additional explanation for some of the behaviours associated with antisocial or psychopathic traits. Gorenstein and Newman (1980) have posited that these results are the consequence of the psychopath's inability to modulate behaviour when engaged in a reward-oriented dominant response-set. In other words, reward hypersensitivity (Scerbo et al., 1990) may lead to an exclusive focus on the potential for rewarding outcomes, disregarding all other information – such as the potential for aversive consequences – as peripheral to the main goal. This approach is similar to the Response Modulation Hypothesis referred to later on and also discussed in Chapter 11.

Indeed, abnormalities in neural activation during incentive processing, i.e. atypical regional brain function during reward, loss or cues associated with these outcomes, have been reported in relation to psychopathic traits in healthy adults (Buckholtz et al., 2010; Carré, Hyde, Neumann, Viding, & Hariri, 2013) as well as in antisocial adults (Völlm et al., 2007) and juveniles with ED (Crowley et al., 2010; Gatzke-Kopp et al., 2009; Bjork, Chen, Smith, & Hommer, 2010; Finger et al., 2011; Rubia et al., 2009). However, the direction of these results has not been entirely consistent (for a review, see Byrd, Loeber, & Pardini, 2013), suggesting that multiple mechanisms may be at play. Moreover, there are indications for differential associations of reward and loss sensitivity with distinct dimensions of psychopathic traits (Ross et al., 2007; Wallace, Malterer, & Newman, 2009) and differences between subgroups of psychopathic individuals (Newman, MacCoon, Vaughn, & Sadeh, 2005). In this respect, we have recently shown that, in our sample of childhood arrestees, only those showing a developmental pattern characterised by persistent disruptive behaviour were characterised by reduced responsiveness of the ventral striatum during reward outcome and increased responsiveness of the amygdala during loss outcomes. In addition, callous–unemotional traits were associated with lower levels of amygdala responsiveness during reward outcome (Cohn et al., 2014). While previous studies in healthy adults have reported associations between ventral striatal reward processing deficits and impulsive-antisocial traits (Buckholtz et al., 2010; Carré et al., 2013), our findings converge with a study by O'Brien and Frick (1996), showing that reward dominance in ED juveniles is preferentially associated with callous-unemotional traits scores.

In summary, there are indications for multiple mechanisms underlying reward processing deficits in antisocial juveniles, associated with distinct phenotypes as captured by the dimensions of the psychopathy construct. As such, more precise phenotypical specification may advance our understanding of reward processing atypicalities in antisocial individuals, specifically relevant for clinical practice. For example, operant conditioning – the cornerstone of cognitive behavioural therapy (CBT) – relies heavily on the integrity of the reward neurocircuitry. Notably, there are indications for poor effectiveness of CBT in ED youths with high levels of callous-unemotional traits, which may be improved by adjunctive pharmacotherapy (Waschbusch, Carrey, Willoughby, King, & Andrade, 2007) – possibly due to its restoration of dopaminergic signalling. These considerations warrant further research on the effectiveness of pharmacological interventions on restoring reward sensitivity to typical levels. Finally, a recent study by White and colleagues (White et al., 2013), which used computational modelling to evaluate expected value and prediction error coding, yielded evidence for disrupted signalling of both in juveniles with ED – suggesting that some of the previous findings may actually result from a more basic alteration in the organisation of the dopaminergic system rather than from a simplistic reward hypersensitivity. However, replication of this finding is needed.

Affective empathy

While inhibitory deficits are thought to relate most strongly to the impulsive-antisocial dimensions of psychopathy, amygdala dysfunction during affective empathy has been convincingly argued to accompany its interpersonal-affective features (Blair, 2004; Blair, 2007; Blair, 2013). Specifically, Blair has suggested that such deficits may underlie the cruel behaviours and lack of regret and concern for others' suffering seen in adult psychopaths or juveniles high on psychopathic traits, and may therefore play an important role in the development of ED. While the sight of others' suffering elicits a form of sympathetic distress in healthy individuals, individuals high on psychopathic traits do not seem to have a functioning mechanism preventing them from harmful behaviour ('violence inhibition mechanism'; Blair, 2004). Indeed, there is increasing evidence for the notion that individuals with high levels of antisocial behaviour or psychopathic traits present with reduced amygdala function when viewing

Biological approaches to externalising disorders 81

pictures of sad faces (Marsh et al., 2008; Jones, Laurens, Herba, Barker, & Viding, 2009; Viding et al., 2012); although the opposite pattern has also been reported (Herpertz et al., 2008) – thought to index emotional contagion – and structural volumetric differences in the amygdala (Huebner et al., 2008; Yang, Raine, Narr, Colletti, & Toga, 2009; Sterzer, Stadler, Poustka, & Kleinschmidt, 2007; Fairchild et al., 2011). Converging evidence for psychopathy, and possibly ED, as disorders originating in atypical amygdalar neurodevelopment is provided by studies showing higher rates of cavum septum pellucidum – a perinatal neurodevelopmental problem indicative of limbic maldevelopment – in antisocial adults (Raine, Lee, Yang, & Colletti, 2010) and juveniles with ED (White et al., 2013). Moreover, low empathy is associated with low levels of arousal (Lorber, 2004; Van Hulle et al., 2013) that in turn might influence the ability to attach with other people (Choy, Farrington, & Raine, submitted; see Chapter 7 for the importance of attachment in relation to the development of conscience). Importantly, however, empathy is a multidimensional construct. First, there are clear distinctions between its affective (i.e. *sympathising* with others) and cognitive (i.e. *understanding* others) components – both in terms of factor-analytic studies (e.g. Dadds et al., 2008) and their association with psychopathology (e.g. Jones, Happe, Gilbert, Burnett, & Viding, 2010) – and associations between interpersonal-affective traits and empathy seem to be specific to the affective component (Jones et al., 2010). Second, there are variations in terms of complexity: simple contagion, for example, is thought to rely on the amygdala and insula (Blair, Morris, Frith, Perrett, & Dolan, 1999; Phillips et al., 1997) whereas moral judgement and mentalising about others' feelings also rely on integrity of the vmPFC, superior temporal sulcus (STS), and temporoparietal junction (Blair, 2007; Overgaauw, Güroglu, Rieffe, & Crone, 2013). Amygdala function in ED youths with psychopathic traits is not only reduced during emotional contagion (Marsh et al., 2008; Jones et al., 2009; Viding et al., 2012) and empathy for pain (Lockwood et al., 2013; Marsh et al., 2013; although see Decety, Michalska, Akitsuki, & Lahey, 2009), but also during more complex forms of empathic behaviour, i.e. moral judgement, amygdala function (and functional connectivity with orbitofrontal cortex; Marsh et al., 2011) have been associated with psychopathic traits (Glenn, Raine, & Schug, 2009).

However, studies on the neural correlates of callous-unemotional traits do not equivocally point to the amygdala: they are also relatively consistent in implicating dysfunction in the ACC and insula (Bjork, Chen, & Hommer, 2012; Lockwood et al., 2013; Marsh et al., 2013; Sebastian et al., 2012; Sebastian et al., 2013). Notably, both regions are linked more robustly to empathy for pain than is the amygdala (e.g. Engen & Singer, 2013; Bernhardt & Singer, 2012). Indeed, atypical regional brain function in both the ACC and insula in empathy for pain experiments have been reported in relation to callous-unemotional traits in children with conduct problems (Lockwood et al., 2013; Marsh et al., 2013). Moreover, lesions of the ACC have been noted to produce a 'lack of distress' – which may be argued to resemble some callous-unemotional traits (Corkin, Twitchell, & Sullivan, 1979), while its supposedly associated Stroop interference deficits – which are lacking in psychopathic individuals – are considered controversial (Cohen, Kaplan, Moser, Jenkins, & Wilkinson, 1999; Janer & Pardo, 1991). Furthermore, both the ACC and insula are essential parts of the neurocircuitry subserving fear conditioning (Sehlmeyer et al., 2009 – see Chapters 11 and 12). For a critical account on this literature see Blair, Peschardt, Budhani, Mitchell, and Pine (2006).

Atypical structure of other regions in the moral brain network has also been reported in relation to psychopathic traits: for instance, structural reductions have been observed in the superior temporal sulcus of psychopaths (de Oliveira-Souza et al., 2008; Müller et al., 2008). Moreover, this region has been shown to be most predictive of group-membership (psychopaths vs. healthy controls) in a multi-voxel pattern-analysis study (Sato et al., 2011). Similarly, cortical thickness reductions (another measure indicative of grey matter volume) in this region have been found in ED juveniles, and its thickness estimates were inversely associated with callous-unemotional traits (Wallace et al., 2014). Other studies have implicated deficient functioning and functional connectivity in the vmPFC (Finger et al., 2008) and the broader network subserving moral judgement (Pujol et al., 2012) in ED juveniles and adults, respectively, with high levels of psychopathic traits.

In summary, there is robust evidence for amygdala dysfunction during affective empathy in ED juveniles with high levels of psychopathic traits, and there are indications that these are specific to callous-unemotional/affective traits. Amygdala dysfunction is likely to extend to more complex forms of empathic behaviour, such as moral judgement, although there are indications for additional abnormalities in the extended empathy/moral brain network, such as the insula, ACC, STS and vmPFC. While these findings may reflect downstream consequences of a basic amygdala deficit, it seems premature at this point to conclude that there is no solid cognitive neuroscience account (Blair et al., 2006) of reduced '(para)limbic network' function in callous-unemotional traits and psychopathy (Kiehl, 2006). Moreover, it has to be noted that not all youths with ED present with reduced affective empathy (for review, see De Wied, Gispen-de Wied, & van Boxtel, 2010); such a deficit seems characteristic mostly of a subgroup of ED juveniles with additional high levels of callous-unemotional traits. Another subgroup, however, may be quite capable of feeling empathy, but present with situational decreases in such feelings due to factors such as hostile attribution bias or emotion dysregulation, which in turn lead to externalising behaviours. Again, these considerations underscore the relevance of taking into account heterogeneity among ED juveniles and the multidimensionality of the empathy construct.

In conclusion, there are strong indications for neural dysfunctions during inhibition, reward processing, affective empathy and fear processing (see Chapters 11 and 12) in juveniles with ED. Importantly, the list of cognitive functions and neural systems in which abnormalities have been reported in antisocial individuals is not complete. Most notably, an extensive line of research, mostly

Biological approaches to externalising disorders 83

performed by the group of Newman and colleagues (e.g. Newman, Curtin, Bertsch, & Baskin-Sommers, 2010; Baskin-Sommers, Curtin, & Newman, 2011), has investigated how attention moderates several of the deficits reported above. Its leading articulators suggest that a basic 'early bottleneck' dysfunction in attention allocation may underlie some if not most of these atypicalities. While decades of research by Newman and colleagues have resulted in substantial evidence for this position, others have convincingly argued against a 'general response modulation deficit' (e.g. Blair et al., 2006) as psychopaths are not lacking in inhibiting some forms of previously rewarded responses (e.g. extradimensional shifts, mediated by the dorsolateral prefrontal cortex). This issue remains unresolved and further research is warranted (see Chapter 11).

Overlap between neural dysfunctions related to internalising and externalising disorders

One of the most interesting findings from epidemiological studies on ED development during the past decades is the heterogeneity of outcomes associated with oppositional defiant disorder (Pardini & Fite, 2010; Loeber, Burke, & Pardini, 2009). To a lesser extent, the same holds true for conduct disorder (Kim-Cohen et al., 2003). While part of the juveniles showing antisocial behaviour will grow up to become antisocial adults (e.g. 30–40% of youths with conduct disorder; Robins, 1991; Robins & Price, 1991), a substantial proportion will not. While some of the latter individuals do not show significant psychiatric symptoms in adulthood, others will meet criteria for depression, anxiety disorder and schizophrenia (Kim-Cohen et al., 2003). Also in those who do show antisocial behaviour in adulthood, co-morbidity with internalising disorders is relatively common (Zoccolillo, 1992). While part of this association may be driven by psychosocial factors (e.g. low socio-economic status neighbourhoods, childhood maltreatment), neurobiological commonalities may also shed light on their covariance. Indeed, while there have been reports of divergent autonomic patterns relating to externalising versus internalising symptomatology (Dietrich et al., 2007), others have found that children with both externalising and internalising problems differ from externalising-only children with respect to their autonomic profile (Calkins, Graziano, & Keane, 2007). That is, children with a mixed profile of both externalising and internalising behaviour problems showed the greatest cardiac vagal regulation. In contrast, children with pure externalising profiles presented the least regulation, indicating that children with a combination of externalising and internalising symptoms revealing extreme physiological dysregulation. According to the assumption of Beauchaine (2001), an ideal level of vagal regulation relates to readiness to respond to environmental encounters. Extreme vagal withdrawal in response to these environmental encounters mirrors greater emotional lability, which is a likely characteristic of the children with a mixed behaviour problem profile (both externalising and internalising behaviours; Calkins et al., 2007). Neuroimaging research has suggested that emotional hyperreactivity is one of the cognitive atypicalities shared by disorders across the externalising-internalising spectrum, as it has been associated with some forms of ED (Cohn et al., 2013; Herpertz et al., 2008; Hodgins, 2007), as well as internalising (e.g. Goldin, Manber, Hakimi, Canli, & Gross, 2009) and personality disorders (Donegan et al., 2003). In addition, reward processing abnormalities have been argued to relate to most psychiatric disorders emerging during adolescence, including ED and internalising disorders (see Fairchild, 2011 for a review), and have been reported in a wide range of adult disorders (including depression; Stoy et al., 2012, obsessive-compulsive disorder; Figee et al., 2011, substance misuse; Hommer, Bjork, & Gilman, 2011, and schizophrenia; Juckel et al., 2006). Some of these biological commonalities may actually represent shared environmental risk factors. For example, atypicalities during reward processing and dopaminergic signalling have been related to childhood maltreatment (Dillon et al., 2009; Mehta et al., 2010) or preterm birth (Nosarti, 2013), and may provide the biological embedding of vulnerability to a wide range of psychiatric outcomes. However, it has to be noted that some biological markers may seem similar in externalising and internalising disorders cross-sectionally, but represent different developmental profiles (Ruttle et al., 2011). Biological correlates such as autonomic underarousal (Cornet, de Kogel, Nijman, Raine, & van der Laan, in press *a*), low resting heart rate (Lorber, 2004), and brain deficits and hormones influence the development of temperament which in turn can elicit a certain parenting style. The interaction of biological correlates with psychological (temperament development) and social (parenting style) factors predisposes an individual to the development of ED and may lead later on to criminal behaviour. As understanding their differential adult mental health outcomes may lead to the development of targeted preventive interventions, investigating shared biological risk factors could provide an interesting avenue for future research.

Practical implications

The basic neuroscientific nature of the literature reviewed above does not allow yet for firm recommendations with respect to clinical practice or implications for the legal system. Translational follow-up studies, examining neurobiological constructs in relation to clinical outcomes, are scarce, but provide preliminary evidence for the usefulness of neurobiological constructs in predicting treatment outcome (Cornet et al., in press *a*) and as markers of psychological improvement in treatment evaluation (Cornet, de Kogel, Nijman, Raine, van der Laan, in press *b*). Notwithstanding these limitations, several suggestions seem timely.

First, the literature provides abundant evidence for neurobiological heterogeneity within ED juveniles. These findings should motivate clinicians to differentiate between subtypes of antisocial juveniles, since they are likely to respond differently to treatment (e.g. Waschbusch et al., 2007; Hawes, Price, & Dadds, 2014). While further research is required to design optimised interventions for subgroups differing in neurobiological makeup, we speculate that differentiating between subgroups of ED juveniles may be essential with regard to (1) differential parenting approaches, e.g. adjusting the level of confrontation to a child's intrinsic reactivity (see Dadds & Rhodes, 2008 for an excellent discussion of this topic), and (2) differential effects of pharmacotherapy (see also Pardini & Frick, 2013; Hawes et al., 2014). In the latter respect, the literature on reward processing deficits in subgroups of ED juveniles suggests that dopaminergic pharmacotherapy may enhance sensitivity to behavioural therapy, and preliminary confirmation of this hypothesis has been provided (Waschbusch et al., 2007). Future studies in this respect are warranted.

The recent inclusion of psychopathic traits in the *Diagnostic and Statistical Manual of Mental Disorders*, version 5 (DSM-5), as a specifier to conduct disorder, termed 'limited prosocial emotions' (mostly focusing on callous–unemotional traits), will likely stimulate such subtyping practices both in research and clinical practice. Notably, though, we believe that neurobiological differences among ED juveniles are likely to be captured best by a multidimensional operationalisation of psychopathic traits, a notion that is clearly at odds with the simplistic notion of adequate versus 'limited prosocial emotions' embraced by DSM-5. As such, we applaud the inclusion of this specifier, but (1) emphasise that its clinical validity still requires rigorous validation (e.g. Colins & Vermeiren, 2013) and (2) suggest that it may need refining in future versions of the DSM to take into account the multidimensionality of the psychopathy construct and/or further subtyping based on within-trait heterogeneity with respect to callous–unemotional traits (e.g. Fanti, Demetriou, & Kimonis, 2013; Kimonis, Fanti, Isoma, & Donoghue, 2013). Finally, there are indications for the effects of early childhood experiences on neurobiological atypicalities, which in turn may confer vulnerability to internalising and externalising psychopathology, warranting not only primary prevention and early detection of family violence at the societal level, but also environmental enrichment programmes which have been shown to reduce antisocial outcomes in the general population (Raine, Mellingen, Liu, Venables, & Mednick, 2003) and may do so in at-risk samples.

Concluding remarks

The suggestions made above exemplify several of the potential uses of biological studies in ED juveniles. In a general sense, we have argued that such studies carry the promise of (1) more specific diagnostics, (2) targeted personalised interventions and development of new interventions, (3) enhanced risk assessment and (4) treatment evaluation (Popma & Raine, 2006). While most lay readers will applaud the clinical use of neurobiological measures, their use in forensic risk assessment and criminal law are not regarded without scepticism. Again, development in the field of neurobiological research on ED juveniles is paralleled by those in the field of neurobiological research on

86   *Moran D. Cohn et al.*

typical adolescence. In an excellent review, Steinberg (2009) ruminates on the validity of using the latter neuroscientific evidence to inform public policy, and finally decides:

> The brain science, in and of itself, does not carry the day, but when the results of behavioural science are added to the mix, I think it tips the balance toward viewing adolescent impulsivity, short-sightedness, and susceptibility to peer pressure as developmentally normative phenomena that teenagers cannot fully control.

Such considerations have led to appeals for (Steinberg, 2009) and actual establishment of separate legal systems for adolescents (as in the Dutch law system; e.g. Doreleijers & Fokkens, 2010). Similarly, it has been argued that 'neurocriminology' may change the judicial system in at least three areas: punishment, prediction and prevention (Glenn & Raine, 2013). Indeed, there have been initial examples of the use of neuroscience in the courtroom (e.g. Glenn & Raine, 2013; Appelbaum, 2009; Feigenson, 2006). While the question of whether evidence for neurobiological deficits would lower culpability in offenders is essentially philosophical in nature – with 'hard determinism' positions on free will suggesting it does and 'compatibilism' positions suggesting that it doesn't necessarily – neuroscientific findings do question the notion of a black and white picture of ED juveniles' freedom to control their actions, similar to the issue of adolescence. Indeed, there is empirical evidence that a mechanistic view of human nature is associated with lower tendencies towards retribution (Shariff et al., 2014), suggesting that exposure to debates about behavioural neuroscience, criminality and freedom may actually change the way we approach punishment. Future neurophilosophical research should be guiding in this respect, and clarify what levels of neuroscientific evidence should count as showing sufficient impairment of decision-making processes to diminish a defendant's culpability (Meynen, 2013). (Neuro)biological factors cannot be an excuse for responsibility, but they are associated with key constructs in criminological theories (Choy et al., submitted); for example, increased striatum volume is linked to reward-seeking, which in turn relates to crime (Glenn, Raine, Yaralian, & Yang, 2010) and may, in some instances, moderate the claim for responsibility. Therefore, prevention and intervention programmes should be delivered at a moment when brain functioning is still malleable to achieve optimal behavioural change.

Literature

Ameis, S.H., Ducharme, S., Albaugh, M.D., Hudziak, J.J., Botteron, K.N., Lepage, C., Zhao, L., Khundrakpam, B., Collins, D.L. & Lerch, J.P. (2014). Cortical thickness, cortico-amygdalar networks, and externalizing behaviours in healthy children. *Biological Psychiatry, 75,* 65–72.

Appelbaum, P. (2009). Law & psychiatry: Through a glass darkly: Functional neuroimaging evidence enters the courtroom. *Psychiatric Services, 60,* 21–23.

Baskin-Sommers, A.R., Curtin, J.J. & Newman, J.P. (2011). Specifying the attentional selection that moderates the fearlessness of psychopathic offenders. *Psychol Sci, 22,* 226–234.

Beauchaine, T.P. (2001). Vagal tone, development, and Gray's motivational theory: Toward an integrated model of autonomic nervous system functioning in psychopathology. *Development and Psychopathology, 13,* 183.

Beauchaine, T.P., Neuhaus, E., Brenner, S.L. & Gatzke-Kopp, L. (2008). Ten good reasons to consider biological processes in prevention and intervention research. *Development and Psychopathology, 20,* 745–774.

Belsky, J., Bakermans-Kranenburg, M.J. & Van IJzendoorn, M.H. (2007). For better and for worse differential susceptibility to environmental influences. *Current Directions in Psychological Science, 16,* 300–304.

Bernhardt, B.C. & Singer, T. (2012). The neural basis of empathy. *Annual Review of Neuroscience, 35,* 1–23.

Bjork, J.M., Chen, G. & Hommer, D.W. (2012). Psychopathic tendencies and mesolimbic recruitment by cues for instrumental and passively obtained rewards. *Biol Psychol, 89,* 408–415.

Bjork, J.M., Chen, G., Smith, A.R. & Hommer, D.W. (2010). Incentive-elicited mesolimbic activation and externalizing symptomatology in adolescents. *J. Child Psychol Psychiatry, 51,* 827–837.

Blair, R.J. (2004). The roles of orbital frontal cortex in the modulation of antisocial behaviour. *Brain Cogn, 55,* 198–208.

Blair, R.J. (2007). The amygdala and ventromedial prefrontal cortex in morality and psychopathy. *Trends Cogn Sci, 11,* 387–392.

Blair, R.J. (2013). The neurobiology of psychopathic traits in youths. *Nat Rev Neurosci, 14,* 786–799.

Blair, R.J., Peschardt, K.S., Budhani, S., Mitchell, D.G. & Pine, D.S. (2006). The development of psychopathy. *J Child Psychol Psychiatry, 47,* 262–276.

Blair, R.J., Morris, J.S., Frith, C.D., Perrett, D.I. & Dolan, R.J. (1999). Dissociable neural responses to facial expressions of sadness and anger. *Brain, 122,* 883–893.

Blakemore, S.-J., Burnett, S. & Dahl, R.E. (2010). The role of puberty in the developing adolescent brain. *Human Brain Mapping, 31,* 926–933.

Brotman, L.M., Gouley, K.K., Huang, K.Y., Kamboukos, D., Fratto, C. & Pine, D.S. (2007). Effects of a psychosocial family-based preventive intervention on cortisol response to a social challenge in preschoolers at high risk for antisocial behaviour. *Arch Gen Psychiatry, 64,* 1172–1179.

Buckholtz, J.W., Treadway, M.T., Cowan, R.L., Woodward, N.D., Benning, S.D., Li, R., Ansari, M.S., Baldwin, R.M., Schwartzman, A.N., Shelby, E.S., Smith, C.E., Cole, D., Kessler, R.M. & Zald, D.H. (2010). Mesolimbic dopamine reward system hypersensitivity in individuals with psychopathic traits. *Nat. Neurosci., 13,* 419–421.

Bush, G., Luu, P. & Posner, M.I. (2000). Cognitive and emotional influences in anteriour cingulate cortex. *Trends Cogn Sci, 4,* 215–222.

Byrd, A.L., Loeber, R. & Pardini, D.A. (2013). Antisocial behaviour, psychopathic features and abnormalities in reward and punishment processing in youth. *Clin Child Fam Psychol Rev., 17,* 125–156.

Byrd, A.L. & Manuck, S.B. (2014). MAOA, childhood maltreatment, and antisocial behaviour: Meta-analysis of a gene-environment interaction. *Biological Psychiatry, 75,* 9–17.

88 *Moran D. Cohn et al.*

Calkins, S.D., Graziano, P.A. & Keane, S.P. (2007). Cardiac vagal regulation differentiates among children at risk for behaviour problems. *Biological Psychology, 74,* 144–153.

Carré, J.M., Hyde, L.W., Neumann, C.S., Viding, E. & Hariri, A.R. (2013). The neural signatures of distinct psychopathic traits. *Soc Neurosci, 8,* 122–135.

Choy, O., Farrington, D. & Raine, A. (submitted). The need to incorporate autonomic arousal in developmental and life-course criminological research and theories.

Cicchetti, D. & Posner, M.I. (2005). Cognitive and affective neuroscience and developmental psychopathology. *Development and Psychopathology, 17,* 569–575.

Cicchetti, D., Rogosch, F.A., Toth, S.L. & Sturge-Apple, M.L. (2011). Normalizing the development of cortisol regulation in maltreated infants through preventive interventions. *Development and Psychopathology, 23,* 789–800.

Cima, M., Nicolson, N., De Lijster, J. & Popma. A. (submitted). Salivary cortisol patterns in psychopathic and non-psychopathic offenders.

Cima, M., Smeets, T. & Jelicic, M. (2008). Self-reported trauma, cortisol levels, and aggression in psychopathic and non-psychopathic prison inmates. *Biological Psychology, 78,* 75–86.

Cohen, R.A., Kaplan, R.F., Moser, D.J., Jenkins, M.A. & Wilkinson, H. (1999). Impairments of attention after cingulotomy. *Neurology, 53,* 819.

Cohn, M.D., Popma, A., van den Brink W., Pape, L.E., Kindt, M., Van Domburgh, L., Doreleijers, T.A. & Veltman, D.J. (2013). Fear conditioning, persistence of disruptive behaviour and psychopathic traits: An fMRI study. *Transl Psychiatry, 3,* e319.

Cohn, M.D., Veltman, D.J., Pape, L.E., van Lith, K., Vermeiren, R.R., van den Brink, W., Doreleijers, T.A. & Popma, A. (2014). Incentive processing in persistent disruptive behaviour and psychopathic traits: An fMRI study in adolescents. *Biological Psychiatry, 78,* 615–624.

Colins, O.F. & Vermeiren, R.R. (2013). The usefulness of DSM-IV and DSM-5 conduct disorder subtyping in detained adolescents. *The Journal of Nervous and Mental Disease, 201,* 736–743.

Corkin, S., Twitchell, T.E. & Sullivan, E.V. (1979). Safety and efficacy of cingulotomy for pain and psychiatric disorder. *Modern Concepts in Psychiatric Surgery,* 253–272.

Cornet, L.J., de Kogel, C.H., Nijman, H.L., Raine, A. & van der Laan, P.H. (in press *a*). Neurobiological factors as predictors of cognitive-behavioural therapy outcome in individuals with antisocial behaviour: A review of the literature. *International Journal of Offender Therapy and Comparative Criminology.*

Cornet, L.J., de Kogel, C.H., Nijman, H.L., Raine, A. & van der Laan, P.H. (in press *b*). Neurobiological changes after intervention in individuals with anti-social behaviour: A literature review. *Criminal Behaviour and Mental Health.*

Crone, E.A. & Dahl, R.E. (2012). Understanding adolescence as a period of social-affective engagement and goal flexibility. *Nat Rev Neurosci, 13,* 636–650.

Crowley, T.J., Dalwani, M.S., Mikulich-Gilbertson, S.K., Du, Y.P., Lejuez, C.W., Raymond, K.M. & Banich, M.T. (2010). Risky decisions and their consequences: Neural processing by boys with Antisocial Substance Disorder. *PLoS ONE, 5,* e12835.

Dadds, M.R. & Rhodes, T. (2008). Aggression in young children with concurrent callous–unemotional traits: Can the neurosciences inform progress and innovation in treatment approaches? *Philos.Trans.R Soc Lond B Biol Sci, 363,* 2567–2576.

Dadds, M.R., Hunter, K., Hawes, D.J., Frost, A.D., Vassallo, S., Bunn, P., Merz, S. & El Masry, Y. (2008). A measure of cognitive and affective empathy in children using parent ratings. *Child Psychiatry and Human Development, 39,* 111–122.

De Brito, S.A. & Hodgins, S. (2009). Executive functions of persistent violent offenders: A critical review of the literature. In S. Hodgins, E. Viding & A. Plodowski (Eds.), *The Neurobiological Basis of Violence: Science and Rehabilitation* (pp. 167–199). Oxford: Oxford University Press.

De Brito, S.A., Mechelli, A., Wilke, M., Laurens, K.R., Jones, A.P., Barker, G.J., Hodgins, S. & Viding, E. (2009). Size matters: Increased grey matter in boys with conduct problems and callous-unemotional traits. *Brain, 132*, 843–852.

Decety, J., Michalska, K.J., Akitsuki, Y. & Lahey, B.B. (2009). Atypical empathic responses in adolescents with aggressive conduct disorder: A functional MRI investigation. *Biol Psychol, 80*, 203–211.

de Oliveira-Souza, R., Hare, R.D., Bramati, I.E., Garrido, G.J., Azevedo, I.F., Tovar-Moll, F. & Moll, J. (2008). Psychopathy as a disorder of the moral brain: Fronto-temporo-limbic grey matter reductions demonstrated by voxel-based morphometry. *NeuroImage, 40*, 1202–1213.

De Wied, M., Gispen-de Wied, C. & van Boxtel, A. (2010). Empathy dysfunction in children and adolescents with disruptive behaviour disorders. *European Journal of Pharmacology, 626*, 97–103.

Dietrich, A., Riese, H., Sondeijker, F.E., Greaves-Lord, K., van ROON, A.R.I.E., Ormel, J., Neeleman, J. & Rosmalen, J.G. (2007). Externalizing and internalizing problems in relation to autonomic function: A population-based study in preadolescents. *Journal of the American Academy of Child & Adolescent Psychiatry, 46*, 378–386.

Dillon, D.G., Holmes, A.J., Birk, J.L., Brooks, N., Lyons-Ruth, K. & Pizzagalli, D.A. (2009). Childhood adversity is associated with left basal ganglia dysfunction during reward anticipation in adulthood. *Biol Psychiatry, 66*, 206–213.

Donegan, N.H., Sanislow, C.A., Blumberg, H.P., Fulbright, R.K., Lacadie, C., Skudlarski, P., Gore, J.C., Olson, I.R., McGlashan, T.H. & Wexler, B.E. (2003). Amygdala hyperreactivity in borderline personality disorder: Implications for emotional dysregulation. *Biological Psychiatry, 54*, 1284–1293.

Doreleijers, T.A.H. & Fokkens, J.W. (2010). *Minderjarigen en jongvolwassenen: pleidooi voor een evidence based Strafrecht*. The Hague: Sdu Uitgevers.

Engel, G.L. (1977). The need for a new medical model: A challenge for biomedicine. *Science, 196*, 129–136.

Engen, H.G. & Singer, T. (2013). Empathy circuits. *Current Opinion in Neurobiology, 23*, 275–282.

Eslinger, P.J. & Damasio, A.R. (1985). Severe disturbance of higher cognition after bilateral frontal lobe ablation patient EVR. *Neurology, 35*, 1731.

Fairchild, G. (2011). The developmental psychopathology of motivation in adolescence. *Dev.Cogn Neurosci, 1*, 414–429.

Fairchild, G., Passamonti, L., Hurford, G., Hagan, C.C., von dem Hagen, E.A., van Goozen, S.H., Goodyer, I.M. & Calder, A.J. (2011). Brain structure abnormalities in early-onset and adolescent-onset conduct disorder. *The American Journal of Psychiatry, 168*, 624–633.

Fanti, K.A., Demetriou, C.A. & Kimonis, E.R. (2013). Variants of callous-unemotional conduct problems in a community sample of adolescents. *J Youth Adolesc, 42*, 964–979.

Feigenson, N. (2006). Brain imaging and courtroom evidence: On the admissibility and persuasiveness of fMRI. *International Journal of Law in Context, 2*, 233–255.

Feilhauer, J., Cima, M., Korebrits, A. & Kunert, H. (2012). Differential associations between psychopathy dimensions, types of aggression, and response inhibition. *Aggressive behaviour, 38*, 77–88.

Figee, M., Vink, M., de, G.F., Vulink, N., Veltman, D.J., Westenberg, H. & Denys, D. (2011). Dysfunctional reward circuitry in obsessive-compulsive disorder. *Biol Psychiatry, 69,* 867–874.

Finger, E.C., Marsh, A., Blair, K.S., Majestic, C., Evangelou, I., Gupta, K., Schneider, M.R., Sims, C., Pope, K., Fowler, K., Sinclair, S., Tovar-Moll, F., Pine, D. & Blair, R.J. (2012). Impaired functional but preserved structural connectivity in limbic white matter tracts in youth with conduct disorder or oppositional defiant disorder plus psychopathic traits. *Psychiatry Res, 202,* 239–244.

Finger, E.C., Marsh, A.A., Blair, K.S., Reid, M.E., Sims, C., Ng, P., Pine, D.S. & Blair, R.J. (2011). Disrupted reinforcement signaling in the orbitofrontal cortex and caudate in youths with conduct disorder or oppositional defiant disorder and a high level of psychopathic traits. *The American Journal of Psychiatry, 168,* 152–162.

Finger, E.C., Marsh, A.A., Mitchell, D.G., Reid, M.E., Sims, C., Budhani, S., Kosson, D.S., Chen, G., Towbin, K.E., Leibenluft, E., Pine, D.S. & Blair, J.R. (2008). Abnormal ventromedial prefrontal cortex function in children with psychopathic traits during reversal learning. *Arch Gen Psychiatry, 65,* 586–594.

Forbes, E.E. & Dahl, R.E. (2010). Pubertal development and behaviour: Hormonal activation of social and motivational tendencies. *Brain and Cognition, 72,* 66–72.

Frick, P.J. (2012). Developmental pathways to conduct disorder: Implications for future directions in research, assessment, and treatment. *Journal of Clinical Child & Adolescent Psychology, 41,* 378–389.

Gardner, M. & Steinberg, L. (2005). Peer influence on risk taking, risk preference, and risky decision making in adolescence and adulthood: An experimental study. *Developmental Psychology, 41,* 625.

Gatzke-Kopp, L.M., Beauchaine, T.P., Shannon, K.E., Chipman, J., Fleming, A.P., Crowell, S.E., Liang, O., Johnson, L.C. & Aylward, E. (2009). Neurological correlates of reward responding in adolescents with and without externalizing behaviour disorders. *J Abnorm Psychol, 118,* 203–213.

Glenn, A.L., Raine, A. & Schug, R.A. (2009). The neural correlates of moral decision-making in psychopathy. *Mol. Psychiatry, 14,* 5–6.

Glenn, A.L., Raine, A., Yaralian, P.S. & Yang, Y. (2010). Increased volume of the striatum in psychopathic individuals. *Biol Psychiatry, 67,* 52–58.

Glenn, A.L. & Raine, A. (2013). Neurocriminology: Implications for the punishment, prediction and prevention of criminal behaviour. *Nature Reviews Neuroscience, 15,* 54–63.

Goldin, P.R., Manber, T., Hakimi, S., Canli, T. & Gross, J.J. (2009). Neural bases of social anxiety disorder: Emotional reactivity and cognitive regulation during social and physical threat. *Archives of General Psychiatry, 66,* 170–180.

Gorenstein, E.E. & Newman, J.P. (1980). Disinhibitory psychopathology: A new perspective and a model for research. *Psychol Rev, 87,* 301–315.

Hawes, D.J., Price, M.J. & Dadds, M.R. (2014). Callous–unemotional traits and the treatment of conduct problems in childhood and adolescence: A comprehensive review. *Clin Child Fam Psychol Rev, 17,* 248–267.

Herpertz, S.C., Huebner, T., Marx, I., Vloet, T.D., Fink, G.R., Stoecker, T., Shah, N.J., Konrad, K. & Herpertz-Dahlmann, B. (2008). Emotional processing in male adolescents with childhood-onset conduct disorder. *J Child Psychol Psychiatry, 49,* 781–791.

Hodgins, S. (2007). Persistent violent offending: What do we know? *Br J Psychiatry Suppl, 49,* s12–s14.

Hommer, D.W., Bjork, J.M. & Gilman, J.M. (2011). Imaging brain response to reward in addictive disorders. *Ann N Y Acad Sci, 1216*, 50–61.

Huebner, T., Vloet, T.D., Marx, I., Konrad, K., Fink, G.R., Herpertz, S.C. & Herpertz-Dahlmann, B. (2008). Morphometric brain abnormalities in boys with conduct disorder. *Journal of the American Academy of Child and Adolescent Psychiatry, 47*, 540–547.

Janer, K.W. & Pardo, J.V. (1991). Deficits in selective attention following bilateral anteriour cingulotomy. *Journal of Cognitive Neuroscience, 3*, 231–241.

Jones, A.P., Happe, F.G., Gilbert, F., Burnett, S. & Viding, E. (2010). Feeling, caring, knowing: Different types of empathy deficit in boys with psychopathic tendencies and autism spectrum disorder. *J Child Psychol Psychiatry, 51*, 1188–1197.

Jones, A.P., Laurens, K.R., Herba, C.M., Barker, G.J. & Viding, E. (2009). Amygdala hypoactivity to fearful faces in boys with conduct problems and callous–unemotional traits. *Am J. Psychiatry, 166*, 95–102.

Juckel, G., Schlagenhauf, F., Koslowski, M., Wustenberg, T., Villringer, A., Knutson, B., Wrase, J. & Heinz, A. (2006). Dysfunction of ventral striatal reward prediction in schizophrenia. *NeuroImage, 29*, 409–416.

Kiehl, K.A. (2006). A cognitive neuroscience perspective on psychopathy: Evidence for paralimbic system dysfunction. *Psychiatry Res, 142*, 107–128.

Kim-Cohen, J., Caspi, A., Moffitt, T.E., Harrington, H., Milne, B.J. & Poulton, R. (2003). Priour juvenile diagnoses in adults with mental disorder: Developmental follow-back of a prospective-longitudinal cohort. *Arch Gen Psychiatry, 60*, 709–717.

Kimonis, E.R., Fanti, K.A., Isoma, Z. & Donoghue, K. (2013). Maltreatment profiles among incarcerated boys with callous–unemotional traits. *Child Maltreat, 18*, 108–121.

Lockwood, P.L., Sebastian, C.L., McCrory, E.J., Hyde, Z.H., Gu, X., De Brito, S.A. & Viding, E. (2013). Association of callous traits with reduced neural response to others' pain in children with conduct problems. *Curr Biol, 23*, 901–905.

Loeber, R., Burke, J. & Pardini, D.A. (2009). Perspectives on oppositional defiant disorder, conduct disorder, and psychopathic features. *Journal of Child Psychology and Psychiatry, 50*, 133–142.

Loeber, R. & Pardini, D. (2008). Neurobiology and the development of violence: Common assumptions and controversies. *Philosophical Transactions of the Royal Society B: Biological Sciences, 363*, 2491–2503.

Logothetis, N.K. (2008). What we can do and what we cannot do with fMRI. *Nature, 453*, 869–878.

Lorber, M.F. (2004). Psychophysiology of aggression, psychopathy, and conduct problems: A meta-analysis. *Psychological Bulletin, 130*, 531.

Marsh, A.A., Finger, E.C., Fowler, K.A., Adalio, C.J., Jurkowitz, I.T., Schechter, J.C., Pine, D.S., Decety, J. & Blair, R.J. (2013). Empathic responsiveness in amygdala and anteriour cingulate cortex in youths with psychopathic traits. *J Child Psychol Psychiatry, 54*, 900–910.

Marsh, A.A., Finger, E.C., Fowler, K.A., Jurkowitz, I.T., Schechter, J.C., Yu, H.H., Pine, D.S. & Blair, R.J. (2011). Reduced amygdala-orbitofrontal connectivity during moral judgments in youths with disruptive behaviour disorders and psychopathic traits. *Psychiatry Res, 194*, 279–286.

Marsh, A.A., Finger, E.C., Mitchell, D.G., Reid, M.E., Sims, C., Kosson, D.S., Towbin, K.E., Leibenluft, E., Pine, D.S. & Blair, R.J. (2008). Reduced amygdala response to fearful expressions in children and adolescents with callous–unemotional traits and disruptive behaviour disorders. *The American Journal of Psychiatry, 165,* 712–720.

Matthys, W., van Goozen, S.H., Snoek, H. & Van, E.H. (2004). Response perseveration and sensitivity to reward and punishment in boys with oppositional defiant disorder. *Eur Child Adolesc Psychiatry, 13,* 362–364.

McCrory, E., De Brito, S.A. & Viding, E. (2012). The link between child abuse and psychopathology: A review of neurobiological and genetic research. *J R Soc Med, 105,* 151–156.

Mehta, M.A., Gore-Langton, E., Golembo, N., Colvert, E., Williams, S.C. & Sonuga-Barke, E. (2010). Hyporesponsive reward anticipation in the basal ganglia following severe institutional deprivation early in life. *J Cogn Neurosci, 22,* 2316–2325.

Meynen, G. (2013). A neurolaw perspective on psychiatric assessments of criminal responsibility: Decision-making, mental disorder, and the brain. *International Journal of Law and Psychiatry, 36,* 93–99.

Miller, J., Flory, K., Lynam, D. & Leukefeld, C. (2003). A test of the four-factor model of impulsivity-related traits. *Personality and Individual Differences, 34,* 1403–1418.

Müller, J.L., Gännsbauer, S., Sommer, M., Döhnel, K., Weber, T., Schmidt-Wilcke, T. & Hajak, G. (2008). Gray matter changes in right superior temporal gyrus in criminal psychopaths: Evidence from voxel-based morphometry. *Psychiatry Research: Neuroimaging, 163,* 213–222.

Neumann, C.S., Kosson, D.S., Forth, A.E. & Hare, R.D. (2006). Factor structure of the Hare Psychopathy Checklist: Youth Version (PCL: YV) in incarcerated adolescents. *Psychol Assess, 18,* 142–154.

Newman, J.P., Curtin, J.J., Bertsch, J.D. & Baskin-Sommers, A.R. (2010). Attention moderates the fearlessness of psychopathic offenders. *Biol Psychiatry, 67,* 66–70.

Newman, J.P. & Kosson, D.S. (1986). Passive avoidance learning in psychopathic and nonpsychopathic offenders. *J Abnorm Psychol, 95,* 252–256.

Newman, J.P., MacCoon, D.G., Vaughn, L.J. & Sadeh, N. (2005). Validating a distinction between primary and secondary psychopathy with measures of Gray's BIS and BAS constructs. *J Abnorm Psychol, 114,* 319–323.

Newman, J.P., Widom, C.S. & Nathan, S. (1985). Passive avoidance in syndromes of disinhibition: Psychopathy and extraversion. *Journal of Personality and Social Psychology, 48,* 1316.

Nosarti, C. (2013). Structural and functional brain correlates of behavioural outcomes during adolescence. *Early Human Development, 89,* 221–227.

O'Brien, B.S., Frick, P.J. & Lyman, R.D. (1994). Reward dominance among children with disruptive behaviour disorders. *J Psychopathology Behavioural Assessment, 16,* 131–145.

O'Brien, B.S. & Frick, P.J. (1996). Reward dominance: Associations with anxiety, conduct problems, and psychopathy in children. *Journal of Abnormal Child Psychology, 24,* 223–240.

Ortiz, J. & Raine, A. (2004). Heart rate level and antisocial behaviour in children and adolescents: A meta-analysis. *Journal of the American Academy of Child & Adolescent Psychiatry, 43,* 154–162.

Overgaauw, S., Güroglu, B., Rieffe, C. & Crone, E.A. (2013). Behaviour and neural correlates of empathy in adolescents. *Developmental Neuroscience, 36,* 210–219.

Pardini, D.A. & Fite, P.J. (2010). Symptoms of conduct disorder, oppositional defiant disorder, attention-deficit/hyperactivity disorder, and callous-unemotional traits as unique predictors of psychosocial maladjustment in boys: Advancing an evidence base for DSM-5. *J Am Acad Child Adolesc Psychiatry, 49,* 1134–1144.

Biological approaches to externalising disorders 93

Pardini, D.A. & Frick, P.J. (2013). Multiple developmental pathways to conduct disorder: Current conceptualizations and clinical implications. *Journal of the Canadian Academy of Child and Adolescent Psychiatry, 22,* 20.

Patrick, C.J. (1994). Emotion and psychopathy: Startling new insights. *Psychophysiology, 31,* 319–330.

Patrick, C.J., Hicks, B.M., Krueger, R.F. & Lang, A.R. (2005). Relations between psychopathy facets and externalizing in a criminal offender sample. *J Pers Disord, 19,* 339–356.

Phillips, M.L., Young, A.W., Seniour, C., Brammer, M., Andrew, C., Calder, A.J., Bullmore, E.T., Perrett, D.I., Rowland, D. & Williams, S.C.R. (1997). A specific neural substrate for perceiving facial expressions of disgust. *Nature, 389,* 495–498.

Platje, E., Jansen, L.M., Raine, A., Branje, S.J., Doreleijers, T.A., de Vries-Bouw, M., Popma, A., van Lier, P.A., Koot, H.M., Meeus, W.H. & Vermeiren, R.R. (2013). Longitudinal associations in adolescence between cortisol and persistent aggressive or rule-breaking behaviour. *Biol Psychol, 93,* 132–137.

Platje, E., Vermeiren, R.R., Raine, A., Doreleijers, T.A., Keijsers, L.G., Branje, S.J., Popma, A., van Lier, P.A., Koot, H.M., Meeus, W.H. & Jansen, L.M. (2013). A longitudinal biosocial study of cortisol and peer influence on the development of adolescent antisocial behaviour. *Psychoneuroendocrinology, 38,* 2770–2779.

Popma, A., Doreleijers, T.A., Jansen, L.M., van Goozen, S.H., Van, E.H. & Vermeiren, R. (2007). The diurnal cortisol cycle in delinquent male adolescents and normal controls. *Neuropsychopharmacology, 32,* 1622–1628.

Popma, A. & Raine, A. (2006). Will future forensic assessment be neurobiologic? *Child Adolesc Psychiatr Clin N Am, 15,* 429–444, ix.

Popma, A., Vermeiren, R., Geluk, C.A., Rinne, T., van den, B.W., Knol, D.L., Jansen, L.M., Van, E.H. & Doreleijers, T.A. (2007). Cortisol moderates the relationship between testosterone and aggression in delinquent male adolescents. *Biol Psychiatry, 61,* 405–411.

Pujol, J., Batalla, I., Contreras-Rodriguez, O., Harrison, B.J., Pera, V., Hernandez-Ribas, R., Real, E., Bosa, L., Soriano-Mas, C., Deus, J., Lopez-Sola, M., Pifarre, J., Menchon, J.M. & Cardoner, N. (2012). Breakdown in the brain network subserving moral judgment in criminal psychopathy. *Soc Cogn Affect Neurosci, 7,* 917–923.

Raine, A., Lee, L., Yang, Y. & Colletti, P. (2010). Neurodevelopmental marker for limbic maldevelopment in antisocial personality disorder and psychopathy. *Br J Psychiatry, 197,* 186–192.

Raine, A., Mellingen, K., Liu, J., Venables, P. & Mednick, S.A. (2003). Effects of environmental enrichment at ages 3–5 years on schizotypal personality and antisocial behaviour at ages 17 and 23 years. *The American Journal of Psychiatry, 160,* 1627–1635.

Raine, A., Reynolds, C., Venables, P.H., Mednick, S.A. & Farrington, D.P. (1998). Fearlessness, stimulation-seeking, and large body size at age 3 years as early predispositions to childhood aggression at age 11 years. *Archives of General Psychiatry, 55,* 745–751.

Robins, L.N. (1991). Conduct disorder. *Journal of Child Psychology and Psychiatry, 32,* 193–212.

Robins, L.N. & Price, R.K. (1991). Adult disorders predicted by childhood conduct problems: Results from the NIMH Epidemiologic Catchment Area project. *Psychiatry: Interpersonal and Biological Processes, 54,* 116–132.

Ross, S.R., Benning, S.D. & Adams, Z. (2007). Symptoms of executive dysfunction are endemic to secondary psychopathy: An examination in criminal offenders and noninstitutionalized young adults. *J Pers Disord, 21,* 384–399.

Ross, S.R., Moltó, J., Poy, R., Segarra, P., Pastor, M.C. & Montañés, S. (2007). Grays model and psychopathy: BIS but not BAS differentiates primary from secondary psychopathy in noninstitutionalized young adults. *Personality and Individual Differences, 43,* 1644–1655.

Rubia, K., Halari, R., Smith, A.B., Mohammad, M., Scott, S. & Brammer, M.J. (2009). Shared and disorder-specific prefrontal abnormalities in boys with pure attention-deficit/hyperactivity disorder compared to boys with pure CD during interference inhibition and attention allocation. *J Child Psychol Psychiatry, 50,* 669–678.

Rubia, K., Halari, R., Smith, A.B., Mohammed, M., Scott, S., Giampietro, V., Taylor, E. & Brammer, M.J. (2008). Dissociated functional brain abnormalities of inhibition in boys with pure conduct disorder and in boys with pure attention deficit hyperactivity disorder. *The American Journal of Psychiatry, 165,* 889–897.

Rubia, K., Smith, A.B., Halari, R., Matsukura, F., Mohammad, M., Taylor, E. & Brammer, M.J. (2009). Disorder-specific dissociation of orbitofrontal dysfunction in boys with pure conduct disorder during reward and ventrolateral prefrontal dysfunction in boys with pure ADHD during sustained attention. *The American Journal of Psychiatry, 166,* 83–94.

Rubia, K., Smith, A.B., Taylor, E. & Brammer, M. (2007). Linear age-correlated functional development of right inferiour fronto-striato-cerebellar networks during response inhibition and anteriour cingulate during error-related processes. *Human Brain Mapping, 28,* 1163–1177.

Ruttle, P.L., Shirtcliff, E.A., Serbin, L.A., Ben-Dat Fisher, D., Stack, D.M. & Schwartzman, A.E. (2011). Disentangling psychobiological mechanisms underlying internalizing and externalizing behaviours in youth: Longitudinal and concurrent associations with cortisol. *Hormones and Behaviour, 59,* 123–132.

Sato, J.R., de Oliveira-Souza, R., Thomaz, C.E., Basilio, R., Bramati, I.E., Amaro E Jr, Tovar-Moll, F., Hare, R.D. & Moll, J. (2011). Identification of psychopathic individuals using pattern classification of MRI images. *Soc Neurosci, 6,* 627–639.

Scerbo, A., Raine, A., O'Brien, M., Chan, C.J., Rhee, C. & Smiley, N. (1990). Reward dominance and passive avoidance learning in adolescent psychopaths. *J Abnorm Child Psychol, 18,* 451–463.

Seagrave, D. & Grisso, T. (2002). Adolescent development and the measurement of juvenile psychopathy. *Law Hum Behav, 26,* 219–239.

Sebastian, C.L., McCrory, E.J., Cecil, C.A., Lockwood, P.L., De Brito, S.A., Fontaine, N.M. & Viding, E. (2012). Neural responses to affective and cognitive theory of mind in children with conduct problems and varying levels of callous-unemotional traits. *Arch Gen Psychiatry, 69,* 814–822.

Sebastian, C.L., McCrory, E.J., Dadds, M.R., Cecil, C.A., Lockwood, P.L., Hyde, Z.H., De Brito, S.A. & Viding, E. (2013). Neural responses to fearful eyes in children with conduct problems and varying levels of callous-unemotional traits. *Psychol Med,* 1–11.

Sehlmeyer, C., Schoning, S., Zwitserlood, P., Pfleiderer, B., Kircher, T., Arolt, V. & Konrad, C. (2009). Human fear conditioning and extinction in neuroimaging: A systematic review. *PLoS ONE, 4,* e5865.

Shapiro, S.K., Quay, H.C., Hogan, A.E. & Schwartz, K.P. (1988). Response perseveration and delayed responding in undersocialized aggressive conduct disorder. *Journal of Abnormal Psychology, 97,* 371.

Biological approaches to externalising disorders 95

Shariff, A.F., Greene, J.D., Karremans, J.C., Luguri, J.B., Clark, C.J., Schooler, J.W., Baumeister, R.F. & Vohs, K.D. (2014). Free will and punishment: A mechanistic view of human nature reduces retribution. *Psychological Science*, 1–8.

Steinberg, L. (2007). Risk taking in adolescence new perspectives from brain and behavioural science. *Current Directions in Psychological Science, 16*, 55–59.

Steinberg, L. (2009). Should the science of adolescent brain development inform public policy? *American Psychologist, 64*, 739.

Sterzer, P., Stadler, C., Krebs, A., Kleinschmidt, A. & Poustka, F. (2005). Abnormal neural responses to emotional visual stimuli in adolescents with conduct disorder. *Biol Psychiatry, 57*, 7–15.

Sterzer, P., Stadler, C., Poustka, F. & Kleinschmidt, A. (2007). A structural neural deficit in adolescents with conduct disorder and its association with lack of empathy. *NeuroImage, 37*, 335–342.

Stoy, M., Schlagenhauf, F., Sterzer, P., Bermpohl, F., Hagele, C., Suchotzki, K., Schmack, K., Wrase, J., Ricken, R., Knutson, B., Adli, M., Bauer, M., Heinz, A. & Strohle, A. (2012). Hyporeactivity of ventral striatum towards incentive stimuli in unmedicated depressed patients normalizes after treatment with escitalopram. *J Psychopharmacol, 26*, 677–688.

Tottenham, N. & Sheridan, M.A. (2009). A review of adversity, the amygdala and the hippocampus: A consideration of developmental timing. *Frontiers in Human Neuroscience, 3*, 1–18.

Van der Graaff, J., Branje, S., De Wied, M., Hawk, S., Van Lier, P. & Meeus, W. (2014). Perspective taking and empathic concern in adolescence: Gender differences in developmental changes. *Developmental Psychology, 50*, 881.

Van Hulle, C., Zahn-Waxler, C., Robinson, J.L., Rhee, S.H., Hastings, P.D. & Knafo, A. (2013). Autonomic correlates of children's concern and disregard for others. *Social Neuroscience, 8*, 275–290.

Viding, E., Sebastian, C.L., Dadds, M.R., Lockwood, P.L., Cecil, C.A., De Brito, S.A. & McCrory, E.J. (2012). Amygdala response to preattentive masked fear in children with conduct problems: The role of callous-unemotional traits. *The American Journal of Psychiatry, 169*, 1109–1116.

Viding, E., Larsson, H., & Jones, A.P. (2008). Quantitative genetic studies of antisocial behaviour. *Philosophical Transactions of the Royal Society B: Biological Sciences, 363*, 2519–2527.

Völlm, B., Richardson, P., McKie, S., Elliott, R., Dolan, M. & Deakin, B. (2007). Neuronal correlates of reward and loss in Cluster B personality disorders: A functional magnetic resonance imaging study. *Psychiatry Res, 156*, 151–167.

Wallace, G.L., White, S.F., Robustelli, B., Sinclair, S., Hwang, S., Martin, A. & Blair, R.J. (2014). Cortical and subcortical abnormalities in youths with conduct disorder and elevated callous-unemotional traits. *Journal of the American Academy of Child & Adolescent Psychiatry, 53*, 456–465.

Wallace, J.F., Malterer, M.B. & Newman, J.P. (2009). Mapping Gray's BIS and BAS constructs onto factor 1 and factor 2 of Hare's Psychopathy Checklist – Revised. *Pers Individ Dif, 47*, 812–816.

Waschbusch, D.A., Carrey, N.J., Willoughby, M.T., King, S. & Andrade, B.F. (2007). Effects of methylphenidate and behaviour modification on the social and academic behaviour of children with disruptive behaviour disorders: The moderating role of callous/unemotional traits. *J Clin Child Adolesc Psychol, 36*, 629–644.

White, S.F., Brislin, S., Sinclair, S., Fowler, K.A., Pope, K. & Blair, R.J. (2013). The relationship between large cavum septum pellucidum and antisocial behaviour, callous–unemotional traits and psychopathy in adolescents. *J Child Psychol Psychiatry, 54*, 575–581.

White, S.F., Pope, K., Sinclair, S., Fowler, K.A., Brislin, S.J., Williams, W.C., Pine, D.S. & Blair, R.J. (2013). Disrupted expected value and prediction error signaling in youths with disruptive behaviour disorders during a passive avoidance task. *Am J Psychiatry, 170*, 315–323.

Whiteside, S.P. & Lynam, D.R. (2001). The five factor model and impulsivity: Using a structural model of personality to understand impulsivity. *Personality and Individual Differences, 30*, 669–689.

Yang, Y., Raine, A., Narr, K.L., Colletti, P. & Toga, A.W. (2009). Localization of deformations within the amygdala in individuals with psychopathy. *Arch Gen Psychiatry, 66*, 986–994.

Yang, Y. & Raine, A. (2009). Prefrontal structural and functional brain imaging findings in antisocial, violent, and psychopathic individuals: A meta-analysis. *Psychiatry Research: Neuroimaging, 174*, 81–88.

Zoccolillo, M. (1992). Co-occurrence of conduct disorder and its adult outcomes with depressive and anxiety disorders: A review. *Journal of the American Academy of Child & Adolescent Psychiatry, 31*, 547–556.

5 Juvenile offenders

Andries Korebrits

Introduction

Messages about different forms of juvenile crime reach the general public often through extensive media attention. Economic consequences of youth offending is estimated as at least £4 billion a year in England and Wales only (Report of the Independent Commission on Youth Crime and Antisocial Behaviour, 2010). Shootings at schools, robbery and violence committed by youths on the streets are mere examples of a very diverse pattern through which young people commit crimes, often also involving serious harm to other persons. These patterns of aggression possibly develop already from a very young age where they are called conduct disorder. Within the externalising spectrum disorders, conduct disorder constitutes a syndrome among children and youths with a prevalence between 5 and 10% of the population (Lahey, Miller, Gordon, & Riley, 1999; Korebrits & van den Boogaard, 2006). Several risk factors of developing from a violent child into an adult criminal have been distinguished (Farrington, 1991; Herrenkohl, et al., 2006). The appearance of early violence and delinquency comprises risk markers for later serious criminal behaviour and numerous other problems in social and mental health. Policy makers have to take into account that these troubled children and youth represent enormous costs to society – not only during this development but also later in life, as they are at risk of ending up in jail, losing their jobs, having social and mental health problems and so on (Cohen & Piquero, 2009). However, risk factors are only part of the picture. Although many children are being exposed to numerous of these so-called risk factors, two thirds of them never develop violent or persistent aggressive behaviour (Farrington, 1991). On the contrary, lots of these children do develop social and cognitive skills, adapt appropriately to their environment and show resilience and competence. Apparently, these children possess enough and strong protective factors that help them cope with the hard reality of their everyday life. Protective factors, like having an emotionally strong single parent, pursuing a professional career (doctor, artist) and motivational support through a teacher or coach, can build bridges toward a healthy future (Masten, 2001; Bartol & Bartol, 2009).

98   *Andries Korebrits*

In this chapter we will outline the impact of (early) risk but also protective factors on children and adolescents and their associations with the development of juvenile offending. To describe characteristics of (sub)groups, the theory of Moffitt (Moffitt, 1993) and the three-pathway model by Loeber (Loeber, Farrington, Stouthamer-Loeber, & White, 2008) will be highlighted. Moreover, neurobiological differences and differences in parenting styles contributing to a vulnerability of committing crimes will also be considered. Finally, this chapter ends with providing a short overview of existing and promising avenues for future treatment. Helping these troubled children and youths (including their families) at an early age with appropriate and sufficient therapies will be a challenge for the next decades.

Developmental characteristics of juvenile offenders

It is impossible to describe pathways to criminal behaviour in children and adolescents without taking into account the importance of developmental processes that take place during a person's life. Each child starts their own individual trajectory consisting of experiences and will be necessarily influenced by internal, at least partly genetical, characteristics such as intelligence and personality traits (Farrington, 1991). Thus each pathway will be different and heavily changed by life events such as changing school, moving from one town to another, disease and deaths in the family. So the life course of each individual will be a continuous process of change, depending on the adaptation to earlier experiences, and will be influenced by both risk and protective factors in different domains like family, school, peer groups and the community.

Chronological age will not define the beginning or ending of aberrant behaviour, as each child can and will interact with their environment in their own way. Looking at larger cohorts, Moffitt hypothesised that two types of offenders can be identified on the basis of the beginning of their offending: life-course-persistent (LCP) offenders and adolescence-limited (AL) offenders (Moffitt, 1993). The former begin criminal careers in childhood (before the age of 10); the latter begin their offending later around puberty. The LCP type, making up 5% of the population of juvenile offenders, present with four types of occurrences: early onset of offending, active offending during adolescence, escalation of offence seriousness and persistence in crime during adulthood. A much bigger group are the AL offenders, who have their crime peak at an adolescent age (Farrington, 1986) and do not have childhood histories of antisocial behaviour.

As Moffitt (1993) describes them, they 'are likely to engage in antisocial behaviour in situations where such responses seem profitable to them, but they are also able to abandon antisocial behaviour when pro-social styles are more rewarding' (p. 686). How these groups differ from each other besides age of onset remains unclear. In this regard, Moffitt refers to the interaction of neuropsychological deficits with adverse environmental conditions in early childhood for the aetiology of the LCP criminal development, but not for AL antisocial behaviour. According to her theory, the LCP anti-social behaviour relates to psychopathology, while the AL antisocial behaviour is described as a gap in biological and social maturity during adolescence. Although she emphasises the relationship between childhood onset conduct problems with the development of life-course persistent antisocial behaviour, 50 to 70% of children with early onset conduct problems outgrow their problem behaviour by the time they reach adolescence (Fergusson, Horwood, & Nagin, 2000; Odgers et al., 2007, 2008; Raine et al., 2005). A more recent prospective longitudinal study reported little evidence for differences between the groups (childhood-onset persistent, adolescent-onset and childhood-limited) regarding their exposure to childhood difficulties or intra-individual risk factors (Roisman, Monahan, Campbell, Steinberg, & Cauffman, 2010). All the groups were elevated on these measures as compared to a control-group, a finding in line with earlier research of Fergusson, Horwood, and Nagin (2000).

Although the taxonomy proposed by Moffitt (1993) of different behavioural trajectories related to antisocial and criminal development has been very useful in understanding the heterogeneity of antisocial behaviour, a more recent study showed that AL onset individuals resemble the childhood onset persistent individuals regarding childhood risk factors, personality traits, neuropsychological vulnerability and alterations in brain structure and function. Furthermore, not all childhood onset problems continue to develop into life-persistent criminal behaviour and not all AL problems seems to be limited to adolescence, often continuing into adulthood as well (Fairchild, van Goozen, Calder, & Goodyer, 2013). According to these authors, the quality of a child's early environment moderates the relationship between a biological vulnerability and the age of onset of antisocial behaviour. To examine the precise relationship between the effects of early environment adversity on externalised and internalised forms of psychopathology in relation to antisocial behaviour, conducting prospective longitudinal designs examining the presence of neural or structural abnormalities before the onset of antisocial behaviour enables researchers to establish the causal role of neurobiological variations in the aetiology and relationship between psychopathology and antisocial behaviour.

Another model regarding criminal development was introduced by Loeber, who described different trajectories from less serious problem behaviour to far more serious offences (Loeber et al., 2008). In this empirically based model three main but overlapping pathways are described: (1) the authority conflict pathway; (2) the covert; and (3) the overt pathway. Pre-delinquent offences take place in the authority conflict pathway, which is categorised by starting with stubborn behaviour and through defiance and disobedience leads to authority avoidance with truancy, running away and staying out late. More serious offences with a concealing nature and property damage modulated to fraud, auto theft and burglary. The overt pathway consists of violent offences developing from minor aggression through physical fighting to violent rape and homicide. In various samples this model has been validated and has shown that progression in offences takes place through these sorts of pathways, which can be of use in the juvenile justice system. Moreover, Loeber and Stouthamer-Loeber have modified Moffitt's onset-related pathway into five distinct subtypes (Loeber & Stouthamer-Loeber, 1998). To begin with, they discern two types of LCP offenders based on the starting point of serious aggression. The first, a preschool-onset subtype with a diagnosis of ADHD, where the ADHD symptoms play an important role in poor cognitive and academic functioning, ADHD symptoms potentiate oppositional behaviour and accelerated aggression, conduct problems and substance abuse, thus accounting for a severe disposition for serious, violent and chronic offending. A second, childhood-adolescent-onset subtype exists without clinical ADHD symptoms, where mainly oppositional behaviour persists and develops into serious aggression. The Moffitt limited-duration type (AL) is also split into two subtypes; the first comprises a childhood-beginning and childhood-limited subtype, while the other is similar to Moffitt's late adolescence subtype. The fifth and last subtype is a real late-onset subtype, with no early problems before late adolescence or adulthood, developing into serious aggression and antisocial behaviour.

The impact of very early offending is shown in several studies (Loeber & Farrington, 2012) and is characterised through a much larger percentage of serious, violent and chronic behaviour in a two to threefold manner compared to later starters. Child delinquents are more at risk at a later age to carry weapons, abuse drugs and join gangs, then adult offenders (Loeber & Farrington, 2012).

Risk factors

A substantial amount of evidence shows an association between these factors and aggression in later life, but one has to realise that having these risk factors does not necessarily mean some negative change in behaviour will happen. The mechanisms through which these factors influence behaviour are not fully understood and some precautions have to be taken when looking at these data. Risk factors on their own do not cause antisocial behaviour and their influence varies in time and with the developmental status of an individual.

The impact of risk factors is also cumulative, i.e. having several risk factors multiplies the chance of having more problems. Risk factors can be resolved on the basis of the domain in which they take place: the community, school, family, peers and individual risk factors. Below, extra-familial factors like peer group, inadequate schools and poverty will be described as well as familial-group risk factors, consisting of poor parental practices, parental psychopathology, family violence and large family size.

Extra-familial risk factors

Poverty, although differently defined in each country, presents as a strong predictor of limited child development. Poverty increases the risk of social and academic impairment in adolescence and later adult life. Poor people and their children are more likely to be exposed to violence, inappropriate living conditions, deficient medical care and unhealthy nutrition (Barbarin, 1993).

Social exclusion as an extra-familial risk factor has been shown to lead to acts of extreme violence both in Europe and the US, where young school shooters took the lives of fellow students and teachers. In retrospect almost all of them perceived themselves as rejected by their peers and the rest of society. The development of interactions with peers plays a central role in young people's social development. An early rejection by peers predicts very strongly later antisocial behaviour (Dodge, 2003). The reasons for peer rejection can be very different but violence and aggression seem to be an important mediating factor in developing, sustaining and increasing peer rejection. As an example, boys with ADHD are more impulsive and have less self-control while interacting with others. They will engage in loud and disrupting behaviour in the classroom, having trouble listening and an inability to restrain themselves early enough to comply with school and social rules. As a result their actions will negatively affect other youths, resulting in rejection by these youths and their peers (Coie, 2004). Peer rejection in girls, similar as in boys, relates to aggression, although girls express relationship aggression more subtly and often not through physical means (Prinstein & La Greca, 2004). When rejected by their peers, antisocial children seem to be drawn to groups of other deviant children, thus becoming members of these groups and developing even more antisocial and deviant behaviour (Bartol & Bartol, 2009).

The educational environment of children with antisocial tendencies developing into antisocial adolescents is also different from their non-violent peers. Already poor quality in day care outside the home results in lower development of language and cognitive skills. Exposure to long hours of care per week beginning in infancy, combined with less sensitive mother–child interactions, on top of modelling experiences in groups of children with more aggressive tendencies, may lead to a greater risk of persistent antisocial behaviour in later life (Vandell, 2004).

School failure and grade retention, as well as low intelligence in early school years, seem to be strong predictors of juvenile delinquency; retained children often fail to build normal social interactions with others and therefore feel rejected. Girls being expelled, suspended and held back in middle school years predicted offending by adolescent females (Wald & Losen, 2003). Thus grade retention, placement in special education and negative feedback from teachers makes the child feel socially rejected. Especially in ethnic minorities the impact on the development of antisocial behaviour seems to be more problematic. Research in African American children, for instance, showed that they are placed disproportionately in special education compared to other racial groups (Wang, Reynolds, & Walberg, 1986). School achievement, especially reading ability, plays an important role in preventing criminal behaviour, and youths with good competencies in this field show less aggressive behaviour, possibly through better social acceptance, enhanced motivation to learn at school and better chances of getting a job as a young adult (Petras et al., 2004).

102 *Andries Korebrits*

Individual risk factors

Next to these extra-familial risk factors, individual risk factors within the child or youth itself play a significant role in the expression of antisocial behaviour (Bartol & Bartol, 2009). Some of them appear as social risk factors such as the amount of aggressive behaviour demonstrated in early childhood, which is a very strong predictor of future criminal activities. Others are of a more cognitive nature like learning disorders, language problems and the overall cognitive abilities a child possesses. Within these individual risk factors expression of or control over anger and the ability to empathise with others are important in relation to development of antisocial behaviour (Tremblay & Le Marquand, 2001; Kiang, Moreno, & Robinson, 2004) and will be discussed thoroughly in other chapters of this book (for example, see Chapter 4). These paradigms overlap in a substantial way with more biologically oriented risk factors, which originate in physical and genetical substrates through which vulnerability and experience interact with each other to form the concept of the gene-environment interaction.

Family risk factors

Apart from the extra-familial and individual risk factors mentioned above, family risk factors play an important role in developing antisocial and criminal behaviour in youths. Especially parenting styles and practices have enormous influence on the prediction of aggressive behaviour (Chang, Schwartz, Dodge, & McBride-Chang, 2003; Baldry & Farrington, 2000). While rearing their children parents often use patterns of action and reaction to the situations in which they interact. These can be of an authoritarian nature, with parents who use a lot of rules and regulations through which they try to shape and control the child's behaviour. In this style of parenting there is little room for discussion and often punishment is used to enforce parents' will (Baumrind, 1991). In contrast to this type of parenting style Baumrind describes a more permissive style where parents serve as a resource for behaviour without monitoring and controlling. In between these two types of parenting styles, the authoritative style is a rational-oriented type of parenting, with communication-driven restrictions resulting in independence and individuality of the child. High controlling parental behaviour is associated with the development of antisocial behaviour, whereas an authoritative style, especially in girls, has protective aspects concerning aggressive behaviour development (Blitstein, Murray, Lytle, Birnbaum, & Perry, 2005; Hollister-Wagner, Foshee, & Jackson, 2001; Bartol & Bartol, 2009). Harsh punishment often in combination with an authoritarian parenting style is strongly correlated with a risk of violent behaviour in adolescence. However, it is not just a straightforward correlation, as it depends on the context in which it is given. For instance, this can be a cultural context but also the emotional control exhibited by the caregivers, while giving this punishment. Thus, parenting style and the message this sends out to the children influences the way children perceive the emotional charge of punishment and translate this into the child's own behaviour (Chang et al., 2003).

An important familial risk factor constitutes parents' own psychopathology, with or without the combination of substance abuse and criminality. Parents with antisocial personality disorders and especially mothers with depressive disorders pose a high risk of developing aggressive behaviour in their offspring. Often this is modulated through violence within the relationship between the parents and the child. Parents with psychopathology often have children exhibiting emotional disturbances, cognitive deficits and lacking social interaction skills.

Furthermore, when children witness violence between their parents this strongly affects these children, not only for physical violence but also for verbal abuse (Diamond & Muller, 2004; Mazulis, Hyde, & Clark, 2004; Murray, Janson, & Farrington, 2007). Children in these circumstances often become victims of violence and maltreatment themselves, with ratios of one in seven children in the entire population. Luckily not all of these children persist into criminal behaviour as an adult as both children and their families may show remarkable resilience and resourcefulness (Jaffee et al., 2005). Nevertheless, there is a strong association between maltreatment during childhood and later aggressive behaviour, especially when maltreatment continues for long durations in combination with an early start (Keiley, Howe, Bates, & Pettit, 2001). Abuse during a longer period in adolescence can also be very predictive of later antisocial activities (Thornberry, Ireland, & Smith, 2001). Maltreatment can be very diverse as it consists of different types of physical abuse, emotional neglect and most frequently, emotional abuse. Regarding sexual abuse, girls are four times more likely to experience this kind of maltreatment, with no gender differences in other kinds of abuse (Bartol & Bartol, 2005; 2009).

Considering other familial factors, parental monitoring has a strong association with aggressive behaviour, as has been shown in the Pittsburgh Youth Study. It increased the risk about 2.5-fold compared to better-supervised youths (Browning & Loeber, 1999). Another influencing factor can be sibling delinquency, especially when a sibling is in a close age range to the other child where the older child reinforces antisocial behaviour to the younger child (Coie & Miller-Johnson, 2001; Rowe & Gulley, 1992). In a study by Loeber and Stouthamer-Loeber (1986) it was shown that if siblings commit criminal activities, these activities tend to be similar to the ones that have been committed by older siblings like shoplifting and burglary. Not growing up in an environment with both biological parents present is a strong predictor of delinquent behaviour in later life, establishing the importance of looking at the influence of divorce, separation or desertion (Price & Kunz, 2003). Regarding these types of broken homes, Heck and Walsh (2000) presented findings that being deserted as a child related mostly to more serious crimes as an adult, as compared to children of divorced parents or those who had experienced a death in the direct family. When discussing these consequences of being

104　*Andries Korebrits*

brought up in a broken home situation, one must realise that there are many mechanisms through which this can occur. There is no logical and simple solution how this affects boys and girls differently, as distinct studies show different outcomes according to gender. A more robust finding considering the impact of development on criminal behaviour in children from divorced or separated parents is the age of the child. Divorce when children are very young shows a higher risk, as the child has fewer cognitive and social abilities to cope with the situation and fewer possibilities to engage with peers and talk about their problems.

Besides separation, the constellation of families seems to relate to antisocial behaviour. Children with antisocial behaviour come from larger families and boys originating from them tend to be in the middle of the birth order (MacCulloch, Gray, Philips, Taylor, & MacCulloch, 2004). Although this finding was repeated several times in earlier studies, an aetiological explanation was never given, neither why and how this depends on the social economic status of the family.

Protective factors

In contrast to the above-mentioned risk factors, more than half of the children who belong to so-called high-risk groups do not show violent behaviour as adults in spite of their high-risk backgrounds. In the last years many researchers have solely concentrated on studies on risk factors for antisocial activities but additionally a growing number of studies on protective factors have been conducted. Protective factors can be categorised into direct factors and buffering factors. Direct protective factors comprise, for instance, high or above-average intelligence, possibly resulting in better self-control or social information processing. The protective force of intelligence is not solely based on abstract abilities but more on social competency, flexibility and realistic planning (Werner, 1990). Especially, high-risk immigrants' language abilities show remarkable protective features (Schmitt-Rodermund & Silbereisen, 2008). Thus semantic and cognitive skills help to cope with adverse situations and probably go hand in hand with low feelings of helplessness and the confidence of being able to master problems in life (Herrenkohl et al., 2005). The buffering protective factors predict a low probability of violence in the presence of risk and often in interaction with them (Lösel & Farrington, 2012). Other individual protective factors are low impulsivity and a so-called easy temperament (Thomas & Chess, 1977), low levels of ADHD symptoms and enhanced anxiety and shyness.

Within the family protective factors, we see close relationships to at least one parent, intensive parental supervision, low physical punishment and parental disapproval of aggressive behaviour. In above-average socioeconomic status (SES) families there are many family activities and the parents model constructive coping. Moreover, they show positive parental attitudes toward the child's education (Loeber & Farrington, 2012). Good school achievement, a stronger bonding to school and forceful work motivation are parts of protective school factors, together with support and supervision by teachers, with clear classroom rules in schools with a positive climate (Hall et al., 2012; Pardini, Loeber, Farrington, & Stouthamer-Loeber, 2012). Of course peers also play an important protective role: having non-deviant good friends, being part of a peer group that disapproves of aggression, involvement in religious activities and interestingly being socially isolated can temporarily protect against antisocial behaviour (Farrington, Gallagher, Morley, St. Ledger, & West, 1988). On a biological level, having a higher heart rate level, a higher skin conductance arousal, the above-mentioned anxiousness and shyness, and possibly a high monoamine oxidase (MAO-A) activity results in buffering protective effects, although not all of these factors can be replicated (Kim-Cohen et al., 2006).

Findings in recent literature show that the concept of risk and protective factors as being opposite poles of a continuum is much too simple (Hall et al., 2012) as both can co-occur or have very different impacts depending on the sensitivity period when these factors occur (Bernat, Oakes, Pettingell, & Resnick., 2012; Henry, Tolan, Gorman-Smith, & Schoeny, 2012).

Treatment, principles and protocols

Although it is widely recognised that punishment and confinement does not work, it has been an integral part of international lawmaking and government policies in the last 10 decades (Cullen, 2007). Convictions in the 1960s and 70s have led to the belief that only incarceration alleviates crime and lowers recidivism. Against this stubborn point of view is a growing amount of evidence that treatment programmes available for large groups of juvenile delinquents can be effective. Before translating treatment into practice, key terms of what we refer to as best practice programmes must be distinguished and definitions should be generalised to guide research, development and programming (Howell, 2009).

'Evidence based'

This means that treatment decisions are not based on the preference and experience of the therapist, but grounded in sound scientific facts and data. Which treatment protocols are effective and which are less effective is preferably examined using randomised clinical trials (RCTs) in which participants are randomly assigned to get either the treatment of investigation or treatment as usual. Comparison between pre and post measures targeting behavioural change during treatment then indicate the most effective treatment protocol.

'Pilot programme'

This means a temporary research-based or theory-based project or programme that is eligible for funding from any source to determine whether evidence supports its continuation beyond the fixed evaluation period.

'Research based'

This means there is some research demonstrating effectiveness, but it does not yet meet the standard of evidence based, while *'theory-based'* programmes have had general support among treatment providers and experts. Based on experience or professional literature, these may have anecdotal or case study support and potential for becoming a research-based programme or practice (Howell, 2009, pp. 167–168). In trying to translate research evidence into successful practice for everyday use in juvenile delinquent settings, one can evaluate effects of a programme as it is implemented or draw on lists of model programmes with evidence of effectiveness, or use meta-analysis (Lipsey, 2005).

Regarding this, the so-called *'what works'* principles have been widely used, in contrast to 'nothing works' pessimistic views originating in the 1970s. In this concept one attempts a risk classification and directs more intensive programmes at high-risk offenders, with a focus on the specific factors associated with offending. Within these programs a structured learning style is used that requires active participation on the part of the offender and these have a high programme integrity. The level of intervention is matched to the risk based on the offending history. Cognitive behavioural interventions are used which help to improve problem solving and social interaction, but also address and challenge the attitudes, values and beliefs which support offending behaviour. They are based in the community to facilitate 'real-life' learning (Goldblatt & Lewis, 1998; Muncie, 2009). Effectiveness programmes differ as to their ability to inflict changes in serious and violent juvenile offenders. Treatment types used in institutionalised and non-institutionalised juvenile offenders with positive effects and consistent evidence try to influence interpersonal skills and use teaching family homes, cognitive behavioural programmes, group counselling, vocational training and mentoring. The same holds true for family counselling or therapy, integrated multimodal therapy (e.g. multisystemic therapy), remedial education or tutoring and life skills (Howell, 2009; Lipsey, 2005).

Considering their evidence-based effectiveness, a small group of interventions have been rigorously evaluated and demonstrated significant positive effects on reducing offending and related behaviour. Multisystemic therapy (MST) focuses on helping families deal more effectively with their children's behavioural problems and the risk factors contributing to delinquency including low levels of parental monitoring of activities, poor discipline practices, association with delinquent peers and poor school performances. MST also addresses barriers to family empowerment and effective functioning within the family ecology (Guerra, Kim, & Boxer, 2008; Henggeler et al., 1998; 2009).

Functional family therapy (FFT) was developed some decades ago and combines family system concepts, social learning theory, behavioural management and cognitive processes (Alexander & Parsons, 1973; Sexton & Alexander, 2000;

Waldron & Turner, 2008). FFT improves family problem-solving skills, enhances emotional bonds among members of the family and improves the ability of parents to provide structure and guidance to their children. Multidimensional Treatment Foster Care (MTFC) is used in a therapeutic living environment with foster parents and suits youths that do not live at home. Regarding the fact that custodial programmes are generally less effective than community-based programmes for any type of intervention, MTFC is especially noteworthy as an alternative to incarceration. Families from the community are recruited and trained to provide structure and behaviour management for these youths, and family therapy is provided for the youths' biological families (Chamberlain & Reid, 1997; Lipsey, 2006; Guerra et al., 2008).

Of course there are numerous other well-designed, promising interventions that would be worth mentioning here, especially treatment for specific offending groups. Violent gang-involved offenders, juvenile sexual delinquents, youths with mental health problems, substance abuse and trauma need to be considered, as well as juvenile offenders with special education needs and the female juvenile offender. They are and will be the object of further research in the near future, as we are developing our understanding of the causes and treatment of antisocial behaviour in youth. Our knowledge of risk and protective factors has increased enormously, but is still limited, for instance, about the dynamics of these factors, as is the knowledge about desistance from continued criminal activity. Why do some youth persist in antisocial criminal behaviour and others do not? More understanding of the developmental processes involved in the emergence and maintenance of criminal behaviour is necessary. How does this influence the appearance of antisocial behaviours at each stage of development? Which model helps best alter these thoughts and activities at the right time (sensitivity periods) to prevent escalation and lead to successful intervention?

Concluding remarks

Understanding developmental pathways to crime and indicating both risk as well as protective factors are relevant to prevent criminal careers. The balance between the amount of risk or protective factors and the impact of biological versus environmental influences varies across individuals. This is consistent with heterogeneity of diagnostic groups. Not all juveniles with externalising disorders or the presence of psychopathic traits are the same. By intervening at sensitive points during development, we may be able to change these risk factors for criminal outcome. Given the heterogeneity of diagnostic groups in relation to criminal careers, this raises intriguing questions regarding individual-focused treatment protocols. Considerations of treatment should integrate facets at all levels of risk, including biological, psychological and social. Examining more effective methods to prevent children and juveniles from developing into adult criminals is critical.

108   *Andries Korebrits*

Literature

Alexander, J.F., & Parsons, B.V. (1973). Short-term behavioural intervention with delinquent families: Impact on family process and recidivism. *Journal of Abnormal Psychology, 81*, 219–225.

Baldry, A.C., & Farrington, D.P. (2000). Bullies and delinquents, personal characteristics and parenting style. *Journal of Community & Applied Social Psychology, 1*, 17–31.

Bartol, C.R., & Bartol, A.M. (2005). *Criminal behaviour: A psychosocial approach* (7th ed.) Upper Saddle River, NJ: Prentice Hall.

Bartol, C.R., & Bartol, A.M. (2009). *Juvenile delinquency and antisocial behaviour: A developmental perspective 3rd ed.* Upper Saddle River, NJ: Prentice Hall.

Barbarin, O.A. (1993). Coping and resilience: Exploring the inner lives of African American children. *Journal of Black Psychology, 19*, 478–492.

Baumrind, D. (1991). Parenting styles and adolescent development. In J. Brooks, R. Lerner, & A.C. Petersen (Eds.), *The encyclopedia of adolescence*. New York: Garland.

Bernat, D.B., Oakes, J.M., Pettingell, S.L., & Resnick, M. (2012). Risk and direct protective factors for youth violence: Results from the National Longitudinal Study of Adolescent Health. *American Journal of Preventive Medicine, 43*, S57–S66.

Blitstein, J.L., Murray, D.M., Lytle, L.A., Birnbaum, A.S., & Perry, C.L. (2005). Predictors of violent behaviour in an early adolescent cohort: Similarities and differences across genders. *Health Education and Behaviour, 32*, 175–194.

Browning, K., & Loeber, R. (1999). *Highlights of findings from the Pittsburgh Youth Study*. OJJDP Fact Sheet. Washington DC: US Department of Justice, Office of Juvenile Justice and Delinquency Prevention.

Chamberlain, P., & Reid, J.B. (1997). Comparison of two community alternatives to incarceration for chronic juvenile offenders. *Journal of Consulting and Clinical Psychology, 6*, 624–633.

Chang, L., Schwartz, D., Dodge, K.A., & McBride-Chang, C. (2003). Harsh parenting in relation to child emotion regulation and aggression. *Journal of Family Psychology, 17*, 598–660.

Cohen, M., & Piquero, A. (2009). New evidence on the monetary value of saving a high risk youth. *J Quant Criminol, 25*(1), 25–49.

Coie, J.D. (2004). The impact of negative social experience on the development of antisocial behaviour. In J.B. Kuperschmidt & K.A. Dodge (Eds.), *Children's peer relations: From development to intervention*. Washington, DC: American Psychological Association.

Coie, J.D., & Miller-Johnson, S. (2001). Peer factors and interventions. In R. Loeber & D.P. Farrington (Eds.), *Child delinquents: Development, interventions and service needs*. Thousand Oaks, CA: Sage.

Cullen, E.T. (2007). Make rehabilitation corrections' guiding paradigms. *Criminology and Public Policy, 6*, 717–728.

Diamond, T., & Muller, R.T. (2004). The relationship between witnessing parental conflict during childhood and later psychological adjustment among university students. Disentangling confounding risk factors. *Canadian Journal of Behavioural Science, 36*, 295–309.

Dodge, K.A. (2003). Do social information-processing patterns mediate aggressive behaviour? In B.B. Lahey, T.E. Moffitt & A. Caspi (Eds.), *Causes of conduct disorder and juvenile delinquency*. New York: Guilford.

Fairchild, G., van Goozen, S.H.M., Calder, A.J., & Goodyer, I.M. (2013). Research review: Evaluating and reformulating the developmental taxonomic theory of antisocial behaviour. *Journal of Child Psychology and Psychiatry, 54*, 924–940.

Juvenile offenders 109

Farrington, D.P. (1986). Age and crime. In M. Tonry, N. Morris (Eds.), *Crime and justice: An annual review of research* (pp. 189–250). Chicago: University of Chicago Press.

Farrington, D.P., Gallagher, B., Morley, L., St. Ledger, R.J., & West, D.J. (1988). Are there any successful men from criminogenic backgrounds? *Psychiatry, 51*(2), 116–30.

Farrington, D.P. (1991). Antisocial personality from childhood to adulthood. *Psychologist, 4*, 389–394.

Fergusson, D.M., Horwood, L.J., & Nagin, D.S. (2000). Offending trajectories in a New Zealand birth cohort. *Criminology, 38*, 525–551.

Goldblatt, P., & Lewis, C. (1998). *Reducing offending, Home Office Research Study*, no. 187. London: HMSO.

Guerra, N.G., Kim, T.E., & Boxer, P. (2008). What works: Best practices with juvenile offenders. In R.D. Hoge, N.G. Guerra, & P. Boxer (Eds.), *Treating the juvenile offender*. New York: Guilford Press.

Hall, J.E., Simon, T.R., Mercy, J.A., Loeber, R., Farrington, D.P., & Lee, R.D. (2012). Centers for Disease Control and Prevention's expert panel on protective factors for youth violence perpetration: Background and overview. *American Journal of Preventive Medicine, 43*, 1–7.

Hall, J.E., Simon, T.R., Lee, R.D., & Mercy, J.A. (2012). Implications of direct protective factors for public health research and prevention strategies to reduce youth violence. *American Journal of Preventive Medicine, 43*, 76–83.

Heck, C., & Walsh, A. (2000). The effects of maltreatment and family structure on minor and serious delinquency. *International Journal of Offender Therapy and Comparative Criminology, 44*, 178–193.

Henggeler, S.W., Schoenwald, S.K., Borduin, C.M., Rowland, M.D., & Cunningham, P.B. (1998). *Multisystemic treatment of antisocial behaviour in children and adolescents*. New York: Guilford Press.

Henggeler, S.W., Letourneau, E.J., Chapman, J.E., Borduin, C.M., Schewe, P.A., & McCart, M.R. (2009). Mediators of change for multisystemic therapy with juvenile sexual offenders. *Journal of Consulting and Clinical Psychology, 77*(3), 451–462.

Henry, D.B., Tolan, P.H., Gorman-Smith, D., & Schoeny, M.E. (2012). Risk and direct protective factors for youth violence: Results from the Centers for Disease Control and Prevention's Multisite Violence Prevention Project. *American Journal of Preventive Medicine, 43*, 67–75.

Herrenkohl, T.I., Tajima, E.A., Whitney, S.D., & Huang, B. (2005). Protection against antisocial behaviour in children exposed to physically abusive discipline. *Journal of Adolescence Health, 36*(6): 457–465.

Herrenkohl, T.I., Maguin, E., Hill, K.G., Hawkins, J.D., Abbott, R.D., & Catalano, R.F. (2006). Developmental risk factors for youth violence. *Journal of Adolescent Health, 26*(3), 176–186.

Herrenkohl, T.I., Lee, J., & Hawkins. J.D. (2012). Risk versus direct protective factors and youth violence: Seattle Social Development Project. *American Journal of Preventive Medicine, 43*, 41–56.

Hollister-Wagner, G.H., Foshee, V.A., & Jackson, C. (2001). Adolescent aggression: Models of resilience. *Journal of Applied Social Psychology, 31*, 445–466.

Howell, J.C. (2009). *Preventing and reducing juvenile delinquency: A comprehensive framework* (2nd ed.). Thousand Oaks, CA: Sage.

Huizinga, D., Esbensen, F., & Weiher, A.W. (1996). The impact of arrest on subsequent delinquent behaviour. In R. Loeber, D. Huizinga, & T.P. Thornberry (Eds.), *Program of research on the causes and correlates of delinquency: Annual report*

1995–1996 (pp. 82–101). Washington, DC: Office of Juvenile Justice and Delinquency Prevention.

Jaffee, S.R., Caspi, A., Moffitt, T.E., Dodge, K.A., Rutter, M., Taylor, A., & Tully, L.A. (2005). Nature X nurture: Genetic vulnerabilities interact with physical maltreatment to promote conduct problems. *Development and Psychopathology, 17*, 67–84.

Keiley, K., Howe, T.R., Bates, J.E., & Pettit, G.S. (2001). The timing of child physical maltreatment: A cross-domain growth analysis of impact of adolescent externalizing and internalizing problems. *Development and Psychopathology, 13*, 891–912.

Kiang, L., Moreno, A.J., & Robinson, J.L. (2004). Maternal preconceptions about parenting predict child temperament, maternal sensitivity, and children's empathy. *Developmental Psychology, 40*, 1081–1092.

Kim-Cohen, J., Caspi, A., Taylor, A., Williams, B., Newcombe, R., Craig, I.W., & Moffitt, T.E. (2006). MAOA, maltreatment and gene-environment interaction predicting children's mental health: New evidence and a meta-analysis. *Molecular Psychiatry, 11*, 903–913.

Korebrits, A.M., & van den Boogaard, M. (2006). Disruptive behaviour disorders: A forensic psychiatric review. *Pedagogiek, 26*(3): 317–328.

Lahey, B.B., Miller, T.L., Gordon, R.A., & Riley, A.W. (1999). Developmental epidemiology of the disruptive disorders. In H.C. Quay & A.E. Hogan (Eds.), *Handbook of disruptive behaviour disorders* (pp. 23–48). New York: Kluwer Academic/Plenum.

Lipsey, M.W. (2005). The challenges of interpreting research for use by practitioners: Comments on the latest products from the Task Force on Community Preventive Services. *American Journal of Preventive Medicine, 28*, 1–3.

Lipsey, M.W. (2006). The effects of community based group treatment for delinquency. In K.A. Dodge, T.J. Dishion, & J.E. Lansford (Eds.), *Deviant peer influences in programs for youth: Problems and solutions* (pp. 162–184). New York: Guilford Press.

Loeber, R., Farrington, D.P., Stouthamer-Loeber, M., & White, H.R. (2008). *Violence and serious theft: Development and prediction from childhood to adulthood.* New York: Routledge.

Loeber, R., & Farrington, D.P. (2012). Advancing knowledge about direct protective factors that may reduce youth violence. *American Journal of Preventive Medicine, 43*, 24–27.

Loeber, R., & Stouthamer-Loeber, M. (1986). Family factors as correlates and predictors of juvenile conduct problems and delinquency. In M. Morris & M. Tonry (Eds.), *Crime and justice: An annual review of research* (Vol. 7). Chicago: University of Chicago Press.

Loeber, R., & Stouthamer-Loeber, M. (1998). Development of juvenile aggression and violence: Some common misconceptions and controversies. *American Psychologist, 53*, 242–259.

Lösel, F., & Farrington, D.P. (2012). Direct protective and buffering protective in the development of youth violence. *American Journal of Preventive Medicine, 43*, 8–23.

MacCulloch, S.I., Gray, N.S., Philips, H.K., Taylor, J., & MacCulloch, M.J. (2004) Birth order in sex-offending and aggressive-offending men. *Archives of Sexual Behaviour, 33*, 467–474.

Masten, A.S. (2001). Ordinary magic: Resilience processes in development. *American Psychologist, 56*, 227–238.

Mazulis, A.H., Hyde, J.S., & Clark, R. (2004). Father involvement moderates the effect of maternal depression during a child's infancy on child behaviour problems in kindergarten. *Journal of Family Psychology, 18*, 575–588.

Moffitt, T.E. (1993). Adolescence-limited and life-course-persistent antisocial behaviour: A developmental taxonomy. *Psychological Review, 100*, 674–701.

Muncie, J. (2009). *Youth and crime* (3rd ed.). Thousand Oaks, CA: Sage.

Murray, J., Janson, C.E., & Farrington, D.P. (2007). Crime in adult offspring of prisoners: A cross national comparison of two longitudinal samples. *Criminal Justice and Behaviour, 34*, 133–149.

Odgers, C.L., Caspi, A., Broadbent, J.M., Dickson, N., Hancox, R.J., Harrington, H., & Moffitt, T.E. (2007). Prediction of differential adult health burden by conduct problem subtypes in males. *Archives of General Psychiatry, 64*, 476–484.

Odgers, C.L., Moffitt, T.E., Broadbent, J.M., Dickson, N., Hancox, R.J., Harrington, H., & Caspi, A. (2008). Female and male antisocial trajectories: From childhood origins to adult outcomes. *Development and Psychopathology, 20*, 673–716.

Pardini, D.A., Loeber, R., Farrington, D.P., & Stouthamer-Loeber, M. (2012). Identifying direct protective factors for nonviolence. *American Journal of Preventive Medicine, 43*, 28–40.

Petras, H., Schaeffer, C.M., Ialongo, N., Hubbard, S., Muthen, B., Lambert, S., Poduska, J., & Kellam, S. (2004). When the course of aggression behaviour in childhood does not predict antisocial behaviour outcomes in adolescence and adulthood: An examination of potential explanatory variables. *Development and Psychopathology, 16*, 919–941.

Price, C., & Kunz, J. (2003). Rethinking the paradigm of juvenile delinquency as related to divorce. *Journal of Divorce and Remarriage, 39*, 109–133.

Prinstein, M.J., & La Greca, A.M. (2004). Childhood peer rejection and aggression predictors of adolescent girls' externalizing and health risk behaviours: A six-year longitudinal study. *Journal of Consulting and Clinical Psychology, 72*, 103–112.

Rowe, D.C., & Gulley, B. (1992). Sibling effects on substance abuse and delinquency. *Criminology, 35*, 217–233.

Raine, A., Moffitt, T.E., Caspi, A., Loeber, R., Stouthamer-Loeber, M., & Lynam, D. (2005). Neurocognitive impairments in boys on the life-course persistent antisocial path. *Journal of Abnormal Psychology, 114*, 38–49.

Roisman, G.I., Monahan, K.C., Campbell, S.B., Steinberg, L., & Cauffman, E. (2010). Is adolescence-onset antisocial behaviour developmentally normative? *Development and Psychopathology, 22*, 295–311.

Schmitt-Rodermund, E., & Silbereisen, R.K. (2008). Well-adapted adolescent ethnic German immigrants in spite of adversity: The protective effects of human, social and financial capital. *European Journal of Developmental Psychology, 5*, 186–209.

Scott, P.M. (2005). Evidenced based medicine? Show us the evidence. *JAAPA, 18*, 56–57.

Sexton, T.L., & Alexander, J.F. (2000). *Functional family therapy (Bulletin).* Washington, DC: Office of Juvenile Justice and Delinquency Prevention, Department of Justice.

Snyder, H.N. (1998). Serious, violent and chronic juvenile offenders: An assessment of the extent of and trends in officially recognized serious criminal behaviour in a delinquent population. In R. Loeber & D.P. Farrington (Eds.), *Serious and violent juvenile offenders: Risk factors and successful interventions* (pp. 428–444). Thousand Oaks, CA: Sage.

The Report of the Independent Commission on Youth Crime and Antisocial Behaviour (2010). *Time for a fresh start.* London: The Police Foundation.

Thomas, A., & Chess, S. (1977). *Temperament and development.* New York: Brunner/Mazel.

112 *Andries Korebrits*

Thornberry, T.P., Ireland, T.O., & Smith, C.A. (2001). The importance of timing: The varying impact of childhood and adolescent maltreatment on multiple problem outcomes. *Development and Psychopathology, 13*, 957–979.

Thornberry, T.P. (2005). Explaining multiple patterns of offending across the life course and across generations. *The Annals of the American Academy of Political and Social Science, 602*, 156–195.

Tremblay, R.E., & Le Marquand, D. (2001). Individual risk and protective factors. In R. Loeber & D.P. Farrington (Eds.), *Child delinquents: Development, intervention and service needs.* Thousand Oaks, CA: Sage.

Wald, J., & Losen, D. (2003). *Defining and directing a school-to-prison pipeline.* Cambridge, MA: Civil Rights Project at Harvard University.

Waldron, H.B., & Turner, C.W. (2008). Evidence-based psychosocial treatments for adolescent abuser: A review and meta-analysis. *Journal of Clinical Child and Adolescent Psychology* [Special Issue: Evidence Based Psychosocial Interventions for Clinical Child and Adolescent Disorders], *37*, 1–24.

Wang, M.C., Reynolds, M.C., & Walberg, H.J. (1986). Rethinking special education. *Educational Leadership, 44*, 26–31.

Werner, E.E. (1990). Antecedents and consequences of deviant behaviour. In K. Hurrelmann & F. Lösel (Eds.), *Health hazards in adolescence* (pp. 219–231). Berlin: W. de Gruyter.

Vandell, D.L. (2004). Early child care: The known and the unknown. *Merrill-Palmer Quarterly, 50*, 387–414.

6   Conscience

Moral cognitions, moral emotions and moral behaviour

Maaike Cima

Introduction

The overall aim of this chapter is to increase the understanding of conscience, including moral cognitions, moral emotions and moral behaviour. Morality is a key component of human social behaviour (Cimbora & McIntosh, 2003) that manifests itself in three important modalities: (1) cognitive morality, indicating how individuals think about rules of ethical conduct; (2) affective morality, which relates to how individuals feel about moral issues (Haidt, 2001; Koops, Brugman, & Ferguson, 2010; Prinz, 2006; Smetana, Killen, & Turiel, 2000); and (3) moral behaviour, referring to prosocial behaviour when in a certain situation (Brugman, 2010). In the literature there is an ongoing discussion whether cognitions or emotions guide moral behaviour. Some scholars state that the knowledge of right and wrong guides morally appropriate behaviour (Blasi, 1999; Colby & Kohlberg, 1987; Kohlberg, 1969; Nucci, 2002), whereas others argue that feelings of guilt, shame and empathy strongly guide a person's moral behaviour (Haidt, 2001; Prinz, 2006). This discussion raises questions about the meaning and understanding of conscience. For instance, is conscience mainly shaped by moral emotions; or is it predominantly composed of moral cognitions; or is conscience primarily related to moral behaviour?

According to Thompson and colleagues (Thompson, Meyer, & McGinley, 2006), conscience can be described as the cognitive, affective and relational processes that facilitate a person's action according to internalised standards, which are outlined by experience, personal interactions and community expectations (Thompson & Newton, 2010).

So far, studies regarding conscience have mainly focused on one of these aspects. Some studies concentrated on moral cognitions (Brugman & Aleva, 2004; Brugman et al., 2003; Nucci & Nucci, 1982) while others attended to moral emotions (Rozin et al., 1993; 1999). Moreover, studies examining moral cognitions often do not include several different angles of moral cognitions or descriptions are interchangeably used. For instance, some studies focus on moral developmental stages (Hare, 1996), while others report on moral reasoning (Brugman & Aleva, 2004; Brugman et al., 2003), and some describe moral judgements (Cima, Hauser, & Tonnaer, 2010). In fact, a person's judgements are often based on their reasoning patterns and indicate their moral developmental stage (see later on in this chapter) specifying their levels of moral development.

Research on moral emotions has focused mainly on using questionnaires tapping into empathy, guilt or shame. Additionally, studies using facial expressions recognition (Hastings, et al., 2008; Kosson et al., 2002), psychophysiological responses in reaction to emotional scenes (Brugman & Aleva, 2004; Brugman et al., 2003; Feilhauer, Cima, Benjamins, & Muris, 2013), and startle blink in reaction to emotional pictures (Flor, Birbaumer, Hermann, Ziegler, & Patrick, 2002; Levenston et al., 2000; Patrick et al., 1993) have been performed. To our knowledge, studies examining the individual's emotional state in relation to moral behaviour are sparse. There are some studies in which emotions were induced to investigate whether this had an effect on moral reasoning (Schnall et al., 2008; Valdesolo & DeSteno, 2006). Adjacent studies demonstrated relationship between empathy and antisocial behaviour (Miller & Eisenberg, 1988). However, such studies are mostly performed within healthy (student) subjects, or did not include the morally relevant emotions like the so-called self-conscious emotions of guilt and shame. Even disgust seems an important correlate of human moral sense, in the way that moral transgressions can evoke disgust, which in turn influences behavioural choices (Chapman, Kim, Susskind, & Anderson, 2009). But also fear and sadness are emotions relevant in relationship with moral behaviour (prosocial traits; Rothbart, Ahadi, & Hershey, 1994). Although studies on the relationship between lack of fear and antisocial psychopathic behaviour have been performed, studies on the interrelationship between moral emotions, moral cognitions and moral behaviour are sparse. One meta-analysis, examining the relationship between moral development and recidivism (Van Vugt et al., 2011), reported larger effect sizes for the relationship between moral cognition than for moral emotion with recidivism. However, moral cognition and moral emotion are often interconnected (Gibbs, 2010) in relation to moral behaviour (Van Vugt et al., 2011). Individuals lacking moral emotions do seem competent making moral judgements equal to healthy individuals (Pizarro, 2000; Cima et al., 2010), but often in these cases moral emotions are not guiding moral behaviour. Similarly, it has been demonstrated that both moral cognitions as well as moral emotions relate to prosocial as well as antisocial behaviour (Carlo, Mestre, Samper, Tur, & Armenta, 2010). According to the cognitive approach of morality, cognitions (such as mature stages of reasoning patterns) may buffer against the development of antisocial immoral behaviour (Gibbs, Arnold, Ahlborn, & Cheesman, 1994; Gibbs, 2003; Palmer, 2003), whereas the emotional approach suggests that empathic reaction and moral emotions (such as guilt and shame) seem important in the control of antisocial immoral behaviour (Blair, 1995; Feshbach, 1987; Kagan & Lamb, 1987). Although some theorists have attempted to integrate moral cognitions with moral actions (Bandura, 1991), or cognition and emotion (Gibbs, 2003; see Ma, 2013), research examining the integration of moral cognition and moral emotion in predicting moral behaviour is still warranted.

Studies regarding moral behaviour mainly focus on antisocial and/or aggressive behaviour (Blair, 1997). While antisocial and aggressive behaviour is morally inappropriate, moral behaviour also constitutes behaviour in which moral choices are not antisocial or aggressive, such as not helping an elderly person getting across the street. But also prosocial behaviour relates to moral behaviour as prosocial behaviour includes concerning for others or intentions to benefit others with empathy as an important underlying motivator (Eisenberg, Hofer, Sulik, & Liew, 2014; Gustavo, Crockett, Wolff, & Beal, 2012).

Since deficits in morality or conscience may be particularly present in youth with high levels of psychopathic traits (see Chapters 4, 6 and 11), specifically those high on the callousness dimension of psychopathy (Frick et al., 2003), the present chapter also reports the relationship between moral cognition, moral emotion and moral behaviour in psychopathic versus healthy control (youth) participants.

By unravelling the contribution of moral cognitions and moral emotions to moral behaviour, the current chapter will contribute to the knowledge of what conscience is and how to improve both diagnostic qualities of conscience and treatment regarding the development of conscience.

Development of conscience

Conscience develops far before the end of infancy (Stapert, 2010) and the fundamentals are established within the first three years of life (Laible & Thompson, 2000). A recent study reported that children as young as three months were able to distinguish social from non-social actions (Hamlin, Wynn, & Bloom, 2010). Also, prior research demonstrated that 12-month-olds associated positive actions with other positive actions and negative actions with other negative actions on a social interaction task (Kuhlmeier, Wynn, & Bloom, 2003; Premack & Premack, 1997), indicating the ability of young children to distinguish between antisocial and prosocial behaviour. In line with these findings, studies using 3-month-olds have repeatedly demonstrated that these infants were competent in evaluating social situations. For instance, their smiles were selectively social (Wolff, 1963), they were able to hold eye contact (Haith, Bergman, & Moore, 1977) and they were capable of distinguishing between different facial expressions (Barrera & Maurer, 1981; Bartrip, Morton, & De Schonen, 2001). These types of studies showed that young infants between the ages of 3 and 12 months were able to distinguish social from non-social acts, indicating some kind of moral knowledge present in very young infants. Accordingly, the domain theory of Turiel (2008) defined morality as based on the harmful consequences of one's act (Turiel, 2008, p. 904). Moral acts are those directly influencing another person (hitting results in pain), while conventional acts do not directly influence another person but are important in respect to social behaviour (wearing pyjamas to a restaurant). Research showed that young children are capable of distinguishing between moral versus conventional acts (Tisak & Turiel, 1988).

116   *Maaike Cima*

Moral emotions such as empathy, and the ability to distinguish right from wrongful actions, are already present in very young children (Turiel, 2008). However, there is no such thing as one coherent, complete theory regarding the development of conscience. Several theories exist, all with different views regarding the origins and components of conscience. Taken together, these theories might give a more complete and comprehensive view of what conscience actually includes.

Several approaches from history

Freud was one of the first to look at conscience from a psychological perspective. According to Freud, development of conscience is an unconscious process based on frustration. Some of his ideas are still incorporated in more contemporary theories. For instance, he described the development of conscience as an unconscious system that causes the child to feel guilty after having committed an act followed by parental punishment. In contemporary theories this concept is referred to as *passive avoidance learning*, where the child learns to avoid forbidden actions because of the negative consequences (punishment by the caregiver; e.g. Newman & Kosson, 1986). Some scholars state that this form of classic conditioning, in which the conditioned response elicits feelings of guilt and shame, is what we should call conscience (Raine, 2013). According to this view, moral emotions of guilt are seen as the core component of conscience.

Around 1930, behaviourists using behavioural experiments examined conscience. In short, they focused on the effect of negative authorisations on inappropriate behaviour. This theory concentrated on internalisation of values and norms in which conscience is mainly shaped by negative consequences. According to this view, conscience develops by conditioning of stimulus–response internalisation. The focus of such social learning lies mainly on moral behaviour.

In an attempt to incorporate the psycho–analytic view of Freud with the social learning views, Sears, Rau, and Alpert (1965) focused on both moral emotions as well as moral behaviour, although emotions and behaviour were modestly related. Around the same time, in 1960, the cognitive theory of Piaget (1932) became more prominent. He suggested that morality could be analysed by studying the development of moral judgement. In his view, the development of conscience can be divided into three important stages. These stages mature in correspondence with the cognitive developmental theory proposed by Piaget. See Table 6.1 for a description of these stages.

In 1969, Kohlberg extended Piaget's theory in which he revised the stage sequence proposed by Piaget and used moral dilemmas in a standard moral interview to examine moral reasoning and moral judgement (Kohlberg, 1969). Instead of Piaget's three moral stages, Kohlberg defined three levels, each consisting of two phases (see Table 6.1). Both Piaget and Kohlberg focused on moral cognition and stated that development of conscience relates to cognitive development focusing on the role of rational reasoning.

Table 6.1 Development of conscience according to Piaget (1932) versus Kohlberg (1981; 1984) versus Gibbs (2010)

Piaget levels	Kohlberg stages	Characteristics	Gibbs stadia	Characteristics
Stage 1 Moral realism				
Stage 2 Reciprocity	**Stage 1** Preconventional	Punishment orientation Instrumental orientation	**Stadia 1** Reasoning depends on concrete consequences of punishment versus reward	Immature
Stage 3 Democratic moral	**Stage 2** Conventional	Interpersonal orientation Authority orientation	**Stadia 2** Instrumental reasoning	
	Stage 3 Postconventional	Social contract orientation	**Stadia 3** Mutuality in relationships	Mature
		Universal-ethical orientation	**Stadia 4** Reasoning from norms and values of society	

According to the theory of Kohlberg (1981; 1984), higher moral developmental stages replace the lower moral developmental stages. Later on Gibbs attempted to integrate Kohlberg's and Hoffman's theories of morality into a four-stage model (i.e. sociomoral reflection maturity) where he emphasises the superficial and egocentric bias of the immature stages (1 and 2) versus the mutualistic, prosocial reasoning and understanding beyond the interpersonal sphere of the mature stages (3 and 4; Gibbs, 2010).

Moral development in Kohlberg's view, in which moral stages are followed according to the cognitive development and regardless of the context, is actually unlike what one would expect from an evolutionary view. From an evolutionary perspective, moral development should not so much depend on the moral stages regardless of the context, but should focus on flexible effective and efficient solutions depending on social problem situations. Depending on the context, a person might choose higher or lower stages of moral reasoning. In contrast to the notion of Kohlberg (1984) of consecutive moral stages, Krebs (2008) describes the possibility of several moral stages within one person, in which a person may switch between moral stages given a certain context. A person may have previously used higher moral stages but may prefer lower moral stages in specific social situations because in the

118   *Maaike Cima*

past this strategy has led to satisfying outcomes. In some settings there might be a conflict between prosocial wishes and antisocial needs (Verwaaijen & Bruggeman, 2010). In all of these abovementioned views, moral behaviour is a consequence of moral reasoning patterns. Instead of empathising cognitions as a core element of conscience, Hoffman (2000) approached conscience as prosocial feelings and behaviours, in which he especially emphasised the importance of empathy. In line with this, De Waal (1996) described empathy as the basics of moral behaviour. According to this author, similarities between humans and other animals exist as to the development of empathy and phylogenetic appearance of empathy (Hoffman, 2000; Preston & De Waal, 2002). De Waal builds on the evolutionary theory of Darwin, in that empathy is a phylogenetic continuous phenomenon. According to both Hoffman and De Waal, development of conscience relates to empathic distress in which, according to De Waal (1996), reciprocal altruism forms the core motive for development of conscience in humans.

Earlier, in the 1970s, Emde (1988) described social interactions in early development (within the first six months after birth) as the beginning of the socialisation process, which in his view is the core of moral development. The work of Emde was an important inspiration for Kochanska (2002), who performed a longitudinal study to the development of conscience. As Emde did, Kochanska concluded that early positive experiences in mutual interactions of child and a sensitive caregiver are essential for the successful development of conscience. Moreover, she emphasised important components related to conscience: socialisation and temperament (Kochanska, 2002).

Related components to conscience

Temperament

Several criminological studies have observed causal relationships between problematic development in infancy and antisocial behaviour in adolescence and adulthood (life course persistent offending; Farrington, 1995; Laan van der, Veenstra, Bogaerts, Verhulst, & Ormel, 2010; Loeber, & Hay, 2004; Moffitt, 1993). Current studies rely on different criminological theories (i.e. social control, lifestyle and social learning theories) and do not include children under the age of three years. However, research shows that the development of temperament, empathy and attachment takes place during the first two years of life (Greenberg, Speltz, & DeKlyen, 1993; Nigg, 2006; Thomas, & Chess, 1977). Temperament is often defined as individual differences in reactivity and self-regulation (Rothbart & Bates, 1998) with a biological basis of temperament influenced by inheritance, maturation and life experiences over time (Rothbart & Bates, 2008). The relationship between temperament and conscience relates to the capacity of inhibiting behaviour in association with moral emotions, especially guilt. Certain temperamental styles are related to the development of antisocial behaviour.

A review performed by Nigg (2006) showed that distinctive routes or pathways might lead to the development of specific antisocial behaviour. One pathway includes the Low Fear response, which is especially relevant in relation to the development of conscience (Nigg, 2006). One temperamental style is Effortful Control, designated as the ability to control behavioural impulses (Kochanska & Aksan, 2006). Reactive inhibition, or reactive control, relates to fearfulness and is a more stimulus-driven activation, relying on immediate incentive or affective reactions (Bijttebier & Roeyers, 2009; Kochanska & Aksan, 2006). These temperamental components in relationship with conscience mostly focus on Effortful Control, which starts to emerge early in the second year of life (Kochanska & Aksan, 2006). Effortful Control refers to the capacity to suppress dominant responses in favour of subdominant responses (Posner & Rothbart, 2000). It is built on the assumption that children experience anxious arousal when they commit immoral transgressions and this unpleasant feeling consequently leads to the suppression of repeating such behaviour in the future (Damasio, 1994). This passive avoidance learning, as mentioned earlier, relates especially to feelings of guilt and is an essential emotion in the development of conscience (Kochanska, 2002).

Similarly, a recent study in young children using the Affective Morality Index (AMI; Feilhauer et al., 2013) to distinguish between cognitive and affective morality showed that the combination of Callous-Unemotional traits (CU-traits) and externalising behaviour related to adequate cognitive morality but deficient affective morality. Children high on CU-traits and externalising behaviour knew how other persons should feel after committing an antisocial act (guilty), but failed to feel guilt themselves. Moreover, they reported feeling happy and excited after committing an antisocial act. This study supports the notion that children high on CU-traits have the knowledge of right and wrong (cognitive morality), but fail to experience the moral emotions typically associated with immoral behaviour (feeling guilt; affective morality). As with this study (Feilhauer et al., 2013), Kochanska (2002) found empirical support for the relationship between lack of guilt and externalising behaviour. More specifically, lack of guilt emerged as a precursor of later externalising and problematic behaviour. Development of adaptive guilt feelings relates to parental styles (Eisenberg, 2000; Meesters et al., submitted; Scarnier et al., 2009) and involves socialisation processes.

Socialisation

Through socialisation processes, the child learns certain standards and values, which are ingredients for developing conscience (Kohlberg, 1984). In the past, the socialisation process included obedience of children because of the negative consequences when disobeying (Thompson & Newton, 2010). Nowadays this concept has been expanded, including a parent-child discourse were parent and child tend to negotiate and discuss the child's misbehaviour by pointing out the negative effects of their behaviour on others. Research has demonstrated

120　*Maaike Cima*

that variations in such a moral discourse relate to alterations in the maturity of children's conscience (Laible & Thompson, 2000; Walker & Taylor, 1991).

This socialisation approach of conscience focuses on the reciprocal relationship between parent and child (Kochanska, 2002; Meesters et al., submitted). Accordingly, the child's willingness to obey parental values and standards depends on a responsive relationship. In that sense, there is a close relationship between socialisation and attachment. For instance, securely attached children are more likely to have experienced more responsive care. As a consequence, they are more compliant to internalise parental rules and demands (Londerville & Main, 1981; Kochanska & Thompson, 1997).

As a first step, for the socialisation process to take place, the child needs to bond with the primary caregiver (Ainsworth, Blehar, Waters, & Wall, 1978; Bowbly, 1982). Socialisation therefore relates to attachment styles in infancy that in turn interact with parental styles and temperament (Van Goozen, Snoek, Fairchild, & Harold, 2007).

Attachment

According to Bowbly (1982), attachment is defined as the relationship between infants and their primary caregiver(s). Through this relationship, depending on the responsiveness and sensitivity of infants and parent(s), infants learn to acquire trust and safety (Parker, Tuplin, & Brown, 1979). Several studies have demonstrated the relationship between insecure attachment during childhood and delinquency in adolescence (Greenberg et al., 1993; Hoeve et al., 2012). For instance, it has been shown that secure attachment profiles in young delinquents were extremely rare (Van Ijzendoorn et al., 1997). In line with this, several studies showed that disorganised and disoriented attachment were strong predictors of deviant and hostile behaviour (Lyons-Ruth, 1996; Speltz, Greenberg, & DeKlyen, 1990). In support of attachment theory, a study of Laible and Thompson (2000) showed that a parent–child discourse regarding sensitive topics was more frequent, more coherent and more emotionally open within securely attached children (Laible & Thompson, 2000). Recent research examined whether young infants of 9–12 months prefer a helper (good guy) over a hinderer (bad guy) in a puppet play (see also Hamlin et al. (2010) for explanation of this paradigm). The study showed that those infants who prefer the hinderer (bad guy) over a helper (good guy) were less securely attached to their primary caregiver and had a more difficult temperament (scored lower on Effortful Control; Cima, Hall, De Lijster, & Van Brakel, in preparation). Although this study was a pilot study, it showed that not all children have a preference for prosocial behaviour at a very young age. Of course, it remains unclear how this relates to future behavioural development. Longitudinal research into different developmental pathways is needed to establish whether a preference of antisocial behaviour at such a young age is a risk factor for developing antisocial behaviour.

Unlike some researchers who stress the importance of the socialisation process and attachment styles in the development of conscience, others are mainly interested in the genetic and biological processes relating to the development of conscience (e.g. Blair, 2003, 2006).

Neurobiological approach of conscience

In contrast to the socialisation processes, neurobiological views focus heavily on predisposition factors. For instance, according to Blair (2003), the amygdala and the ventromedial frontal cortex (VMFC) seem important in relation to empathy. This is based on findings in psychopathic individuals who show empathic defects, which, according to Blair, is due to the dysfunction of the amygdala and ventromedial prefrontal cortex (Blair, 2003). According to Iacoboni (2008), mirror neurons in these regions seem important for humans to learn from imitating others to understand other person's emotions (Iacoboni, 2008; Preston & De Waal, 2002). There is no certain spot in the brain where conscience can be located; there are probably certain networks or circuits of neurons that are interconnected and neural circuitries within the brain, involved by certain aspects of conscience. For example, when pain is experienced but also when observing pain in others, the anterior cingulate cortex, the anterior midcingulate cortex and the anterior insula are activated (Derbyshire, 2000; Price, 2000). Apparently, perceiving pain in others activates an unconscious somatic sensorimotor mirroring mechanism between the other and the self, including almost the whole neural pain matrix in the brain (Decety, Michalska, & Akitsuki, 2008). Individuals are incline to find others' pain and distress aversive and consequently learn to evade behaviour associated with distress. According to the Violent Inhibiton Theory of Blair (VIT, 2001; see also Chapter 10), psychopathic individuals are not prone in response to other persons' distress. Despite this failure to inhibit aggressive behaviour in response to others' distress, psychopathic individuals seem adequately able to recognize pain in others, which seemingly is not guiding their behaviour (Cima et al., in preparation). Brain areas involved in experiencing pain and perceiving pain in others overlap with circuits involved in emotional saliency, decision-making and moral reasoning (Decety et al., 2008; Decety & Cowell, 2014). Moreover, Raine and Yang (2006) argued that there is an overlap between specific brain areas associated with both antisocial behaviour and with moral reasoning. The neurobiological brain circuits related to conscience involve posterior superior temporal sulcus, amygdala, insula, ventromedial prefrontal cortex, dorsolateral prefrontal cortex and medial prefrontal cortex. These areas are particularly involved in moral cognition and empathic concern (Swaab, 2010; Decety & Cowell, 2014).

At a hormonal level, the neuropeptide oxytocin has gained interest as a buffer against social stress (Baumgartner et al., 2008), and is believed to play a key role in modulating social attachment and affiliated behaviour (Insel & Fernald, 2004; Winslow et al., 1993). According to Beech and Mitchell (2005), stressful

122   *Maaike Cima*

experiences may influence serotonergic neurotransmitters, consequently leading to alterations within the sensitivity of the oxytocin system. Since oxytocin is involved in social bonding, it seems important in relation to the socialisation process and therefore might be significant for the development of conscience. Moreover, increases in oxytocin levels relate to trust (Kosfeld, Heinrichs, Zak, Fischbacher, & Fehr, 2005), empathy (Hurlemann et al., 2010) and altruism (Barraza, McCullough, Ahmadi, & Zak, 2011). One would therefore expect that persons with low empathic ability would display lower levels of oxytocin. However, a recent study within male forensic patients varying in their levels of psychopathic traits showed that oxytocin levels were elevated in the forensic patient samples as compared to controls and correlated positively with psychopathy traits (Mitchell, Smid, Troelstra, Wever, Ziegler, & Beech, 2013). The authors explained these findings as a consequence of early childhood traumatic experiences within the forensic patient sample, which may have led to elevated oxytocin levels in adulthood. More specifically, increased oxytocin release consequently suppresses the release of the stress hormone cortisol. In a similar vein, Mitchell and colleagues (2013) argued that the combination of high oxytocin with low cortisol might extinguish the stress–and–fear reactions that normally relate to adequate social learning. Previous research already showed that early childhood traumatic experiences are associated with lower levels of cortisol in children, adolescents (Van Goozen, Matthys, Cohen-Kettenis, Buitelaar, & van Engeland, 2000) and adults (Cima, Smeets, & Jelicic, 2008; Cima, Nicolson, De Lijster, & Popma, submitted). Future research is needed to examine more precisely the relationship of hormones, neuropeptides and development of conscience.

As the above makes clear, there is no clear definition of what conscience actually includes. When talking about the development of conscience, often synonyms have been used in the literature, like conscience development (Kochanska & Aksan, 2006) and moral development (e.g. Blair, 2006; Kohlberg, 1984). Because of the overlap between these terms, the current chapter will use the term conscience development, which is described by Kochanska and Aksan (2006) as a personality system. However, Kochanska also describes conscience as stable over time and during distinct situations. As previously described in this chapter, moral stages may be more flexible over time and as discussed by others, may differ depending on the specific situation (Krebs, 2008; Verwaaijen & Bruggeman, 2010). However, in line with Kochanska and Aksan (2006), conscience is described here as consisting of three main mechanisms, including moral cognitions, moral emotions and moral behaviour (Kochanska & Aksan, 2006).

Conscience: moral cognition

According to the philosopher Kant (1781), conscience is a rational process that is based on what we think is right and wrong. In his view, the knowledge of what is right and wrong is a conscious, rational process based on justified principles. Conscience is therefore a cognitive reasoning process. Moral cognitions can be divided into measurements of moral stages, moral judgements of right and wrong, and moral reasoning: 'why is something morally permissible or not'. These aspects of moral cognitions are often recapitulated as moral competence. Several studies have now demonstrated that there is a discrepancy between moral competence (indicated by moral reasoning about what is morally right and wrong) and moral behaviour (Brugman, 2010). This is not in line with Plato's argument and the theory of Kohlberg (1981, p. 30): 'He who knows the good chooses the good' (Kohlberg, 1981). Or, as Gibbs put it, the knowledge of what is good becomes a motivator for corresponding actions (Gibbs, 2003). However, this seems not always to be the case.

Several studies showed mediators and moderators to be involved in the relationship between moral competence and behaviour (Boom & Brugman, 2005; Krebs, Denton, & Wark, 1997; Kuther & Higgins-D'Alessandro, 2000). In particular, self-serving cognitive distortions (Barriga, Gibbs, Potter, & Liau, 2001) and moral atmosphere (Boom & Brugman, 2005) seem important in this respect. Research demonstrating the importance of moral atmosphere showed that changes in the perception of school atmosphere (i.e. a more undisputed perception) reduced self-reported transgressive behaviour and related positively to prosocial behaviour (Brugman et al., 2003). Furthermore, moral reasoning in abstract hypothetical dilemmas (e.g. whether it is appropriate for you to hit the switch of a trolley approaching five workmen on the track, causing the trolley to go on another track where there is only one workman) seemed not always related to moral performance, as measured by reasoning in everyday practical moral dilemmas (e.g. you know your friend has stolen an MP3 player of another friend of yours; what would you do?). For instance, in a study by Krebs et al. (1997; 2002), it was demonstrated that participants may use higher-level reasoning in more hypothetical dilemmas as compared to everyday dilemmas. In line with this research, a recent study demonstrated that juvenile delinquents know the difference between right and wrong on hypothetical abstract dilemmas, but show lower moral reasoning levels in more practical everyday moral dilemmas (Cima, Korebrits, Stams, & Breumer, submitted). Moreover, in these more practical dilemmas they use cognitive distortions to ease their conscience. Indeed, cognitive distortions are an important mediator in the relationship between moral competence and moral behaviour (Barriga et al., 2001).

According to Gibbs (Gibbs, 1991), even persons with a lower stage of moral reasoning have the capacity of feeling guilty after committing an antisocial act. To ease one's conscience after committing an antisocial act, a person might employ cognitive distortions (Barriga et al., 2001). In other words, cognitive distortions enable a person to behave antisocially despite their knowledge of right and wrong. These cognitive distortions comprise internal beliefs such as blaming others for their actions (he provoked me), assuming the worst (if I did not hit him, he would have hit me) or minimising their behaviour (it is sometimes

124　*Maaike Cima*

healthy to have a fight; Gibbs et al., 1995). Correcting self-serving cognitive distortions might therefore lower the gap between knowing (right from wrong) and acting (behave antisocial). For instance, in a study by Larden, Melin, Holst, and Langstrom (2005) it was reported that delinquent adolescents aged 13 to 18 years exhibited less mature moral judgements and more cognitive distortions as compared to a non-clinical control sample. Interestingly, moral judgement and empathy were positively correlated and both constructs were negatively correlated with cognitive distortions, suggesting that cognitive distortions in particular are an important target for interventions (Helmond, Overbeek, Brugman, & Gibbs, 2014), although a single focus on cognitive distortions may not be sufficient to reduce delinquent behaviour given the multifaceted aetiology of delinquent behaviour (Van Stam et al., 2014).

Nevertheless, cognitive distortions seem to be an important mediator in the relationship between moral competence and moral behaviour. It seems that behaviour might be predicted by weighing the gains against the costs (Gibbs, 2003; helping a friend with a criminal act is important in case you need a favour from him later). However, in those individuals who anticipate feeling guilty after committing a criminal act, the emotion of guilt might be an inhibitor for helping a friend who plans to commit a crime (Baumeister, Vohs, DeWall, & Zhang, 2007). Indeed, according to emotion feedback theory (Baumeister et al., 2007), behaviour is little steered by currently felt emotions, but more by what one anticipates to feel when engaging in a certain behaviour. In other words, someone who anticipates feeling guilty after acting out badly will likely act less morally inappropriately as compared to individuals who anticipate feeling good after acting out badly (Feilhauer et al., 2013). So, anticipation of moral emotions may influence moral reasoning in guiding morally appropriate behaviour. However, in individuals lacking the capacity to anticipate moral emotions, morally appropriate behaviour may not occur despite their intact knowledge of right and wrong. Indeed, in a recent study (Cima et al., 2010), adult psychopaths demonstrated the same kind of nuanced decision-making strategies as do both non-psychopathic delinquents as well as healthy controls when presented with a wide range of moral dilemmas. These results revealed, for the first time, that psychopaths understand the difference between moral right and wrong, but such knowledge fails to guide their behaviour (Cima et al., 2010). In guiding morally appropriate behaviour, moral emotions may be more critical.

Conscience: moral emotion

According to the philosopher Hume (1751), conscience is an intuitive process, which is driven by emotions. In his view, emotions are crucial for moral judgement and are represented as a 'gut feeling' that something is good or bad. According to Hume's view, emotions make a person decide how to behave, and conscience in his view is therefore an emotional process.

Research in adults has indicated that some individuals seem to lack the human tendency to feel what others feel, i.e. sympathising, and to care about others, also called affective morality. The moral emotions that mostly relate to conscience include feelings of guilt, shame and empathy. Moreover, within the concept of empathy, there is a distinction between affective (feeling other people's pain) and cognitive empathy (understanding other people's pain; Jolliffe & Farrington, 2004; Preston & de Waal, 2002). Especially, psychopathic individuals do seem to understand what other people feel (Blair et al., 1996; Dolan & Fullam, 2004), but lack the ability to feel the emotion themselves (Ali, Amorim, & Chamorro-Premuzic, 2009; Cima et al., 2010; Hare, Hart, & Harpur, 1991). A recent study in young children showed that the combination of Callous-Unemotional traits (CU-traits; Frick et al., 2003) and externalising behaviour related not to adequate cognitive morality but to a failure in affective morality (Feilhauer et al., 2013). This study supports the notion that children high on CU-traits have the knowledge of right and wrong (cognitive morality), but fail to experience the moral emotions typically associated with immoral behaviour (feeling guilt; affective morality).

Some scientists have emphasised the importance of emotions in moral reasoning and moral judgement (Greene & Haidt, 2002). However, results that antisocial, psychopathic individuals, both adults (Cima et al., 2010) and juveniles (Cima et al., submitted), know the difference between right and wrong, but fail to behave morally appropriate, seem to support the view that moral emotions are not very important in moral reasoning, but specifically in guiding appropriate moral behaviour. Particularly, emotional empathy, the ability to feel emotional states of others, is important in relation to guiding morally appropriate behaviour. Emotional empathy is assumed to be present in infants as young as two years old (Verwaaijen & Bruggeman, 2010). The fact that this emotional empathy is also present in other species (de Waal, 1996) supports the notion that this is not so much learned behaviour but evolutionary behaviour anchored in the biology of the species to survive. In the brain, mirror neurons are involved in social emotions and situated within the insula (Wicker et al., 2003; Iacoboni, 2008). These neurons are specifically important in regard to emotional empathy, a potential protective factor for the development of antisocial behaviour (Verwaaijen & Bruggeman, 2010). Several studies support the importance of the role of moral emotions in relation to moral behaviour. Raine and Yang (2006) even argue that emotions are the driving force of moral actions. This is in line with research demonstrating that individuals lacking emotional capacity do have knowledge of right and wrong but regardless of this knowledge, behave morally inappropriately (Cima et al., 2010; Raine & Yang, 2006). This moral feeling, instead of knowing what is moral, is centred in the prefrontal cortex and amygdala and can be seen as the engine decoding the cognitive recognition that behaviour is immoral into behavioural inhibition (Raine & Yang, 2006).

126 Maaike Cima

Conscience: moral behaviour

According to the philosopher Rawls (1971), conscience is an intuitive process, which is unconscious and based on the grammar of actions. Criminal behaviour is without doubt morally inappropriate (Stams et al., 2006). Immoral behaviour seems not directly related to lack of moral competence (Cima et al., 2010; Nucci, 2001). However, there might be an indirect relationship in which processes guiding emotions are related to processes guiding moral competence (Lemerise & Arsenio, 2000). To behave morally adequately, individuals not only need to understand the point of view of others; they must also feel empathy (Hoffman, 2000).

Previous research showed that psychopathy is related to reduced empathic responding. In line with earlier findings (see Feilhauer et al., 2013; Cima et al., submitted), both aggressive and nonaggressive children appear to share a core moral value (it is not right for someone to do something bad; Arsenio & Lemerise, 2004). These findings support the notion as stated by Nucci (2001): 'Knowing the good is not always sufficient to motivate someone to do the good' (p. 196).

A possibility for an indirect relationship between moral competence and moral behaviour is the effects of diminished inhibitory control (Glenn & Raine, 2008; Hare, Hart, & Harpur, 1991), a deficit that may contribute to impulsive behaviour (Raine et al., 1998). This seems especially relevant in the context of anger provocation (Chase, O'Leary, & Heyman, 2001; Cima & Raine, 2009; Coie & Dodge, 1998; Kimbrell et al., 1999). Children who are easily provoked often demonstrate a hostile attribution bias and are consequently more likely to be aggressive and rejected (Coie & Dodge, 1998; Cima, Vancleef, Lobbestael, Meesters, & Korebrits, 2014; see also Chapter 8).

Research has demonstrated that antisocial and violent youth display clear aberrations in various aspects of morality. Most of these studies focused on cognitive morality, and although not all the results are univocal, they have generally shown that antisocial behaviour in children and adolescents is associated with deficits in cognitive morality judgements and higher levels of self-serving cognitive distortions (Barriga, Sullivan-Cosetti, & Gibbs, 2009; Nas, Brugman, & Koops, 2008; Stams et al., 2006). It is therefore important to extend diagnostic instruments with a measurement of cognitive distortions, empathy and moral behaviour in research on conscience.

How to measure conscience?

There is no unified instrument or task to measure conscience. Instead, several tools exist in which only one domain of conscience is measured. For instance, instruments like the Moral Judgment Interview (Colby & Kohlberg, 1987), SocioMoral Reflection Measure-Short Form Objective (SMR-SFO; Basinger, Brugman, & Gibbs, 2007) and Moral Judgment Sorting Task (Boom et al., 2001) measure moral cognition, in which moral reasoning is elicited to

Conscience   127

measure moral developmental stages. The Moral Sense Task (MST; Greene, Sommerville, Nystrom, Darley, & Cohen, 2001; Cima et al., 2010) includes several abstract dilemmas eliciting different arousal levels measuring moral judgements. The How I Think Questionnaire (HIT; Barriga et al., 2001; Nas et al., 2008) measures cognitive distortions as a measurement of cognitions within conscience. Meanwhile, measures like the Affective Moral Index (Cimbora & McIntosh, 2003; Feilhauer et al., 2013) and the Basic Empathy Scale (Jolliffe & Farrington, 2004) measure moral emotions, like the capacity to feel empathy or guilt. Interestingly, no instruments exist measuring moral behaviour. Below these instruments are described in more detail.

Cognition

To measure moral cognitions (both moral reasoning and moral judgement), it is common practice to use moral dilemmas to provoke a way of thinking. The Moral Judgment Interview (MJI; Colby & Kohlberg, 1987) involves a very extensive instruction manual in which various stages of moral development are inferred by the reasoning of a person in different moral problem situations. What the individual would do (action) given a certain moral situation is disregarded by this measurement. The focus entirely lies on the reasoning process, as to why that individual would act in a certain way. The MJI is therefore a measurement of moral cognition, since it taps into the capacity of an individual to generate abstract, hypothetical moral judgements based on their level of moral developmental stages as measured by their way of reasoning. The SRM-SFO (Sociomoral Reflection Measure – Short Form Objective; Basinger, Brugman, & Gibbs, 2007) is a third measure in a series of two previous SFM-SF instruments (Gibbs, Basinger, & Fuller, 1992). This measurement includes several moral problem situations, in which moral reasoning is provoked to evaluate a person's moral developmental stage.

To measure self-serving cognitive distortions, the How I Think Questionnaire has been proposed (Barriga et al., 2001; Nas et al., 2008). This questionnaire includes four different forms of cognitive distortions: (1) Self-centred, comprises items in which the needs and immediate rewards of a person's acquired status are so important that other people do not matter (egocentric bias); (2) Blaming others, involves items misattributing blame and guilt to external factors, like the environment or other persons; (3) Minimising/ mislabelling, including items describing how antisocial behaviour is not that bad; (4) Assuming the worst, comprises items with a hostile attribution bias (see Nas et al., 2008 for detailed information regarding the validity and reliability of this questionnaire).

As regards more hypothetical moral dilemmas, the MST has been developed assessing moral judgements (Greene et al., 2001; Greene, Nystrom, Engell, Darley, & Cohen 2004). In this test, sets of hypothetical dilemmas are used, varying in the degree of eliciting emotional arousal (see Box 6.1; Cima et al., 2010).

Box 6.1 Example of an impersonal and personal dilemma

Impersonal example

While on vacation on a remote island, you are fishing from a seaside dock. You observe a group of tourists board a small boat and set sail for a nearby island. Soon after their departure you hear over the radio that there is a violent storm brewing, a storm that is sure to intercept them. The only way that you can ensure their safety is to warn them by borrowing a nearby speedboat. The speedboat belongs to a miserly tycoon who has hired a fiercely loyal guard to make sure that no one uses his boat without permission. To get to the speedboat you will have to lie to the guard. Would you lie to the guard to borrow the speedboat and warn the tourists about the storm?

Personal example

You are a young student on a field trip with the rest of your class and your teacher. Your teacher is a mean person who makes everyone around him miserable, including you. It occurs to you that if you were to push your teacher off a very high bridge he would fall to his death and everyone would think it was an accident. Is it morally permissible for you to push your teacher off of the bridge to get him out of your life?

Emotion

The Affective Morality Index (AMI; Cimbora & McIntosh, 2003) and the Basic Empathy Scale (BES; Jolliffe & Farrington, 2004) involve questionnaires measuring moral emotions. The AMI includes short vignettes in which the main character has committed an antisocial act. Questions are focused on moral reasoning about moral emotions in items such as: 'How do you think the main character would feel after committing such an act?'. To adapt this instrument for direct moral emotions, and at the same time enabling the study to differentiate between moral emotions in others versus self, we adjusted this instrument with questions like: 'How would you feel after committing such an antisocial act?' and: 'Would you do it again?' (Feilhauer et al., 2013). This instrument is therefore suitable for measuring moral emotions in response to hypothetical events. The BES (Jolliffe & Farrington, 2004) consists of questions like: 'I do not care much about my friends' feelings', 'I do not get upset when other people cry' and 'I understand how people feel, most of the time even before they tell me how they feel'. Scores on this questionnaire can distinguish between affective and cognitive empathy. The higher the scores on this questionnaire, the more empathic the respondent.

Conscience 129

Can we treat our conscience?

Several psychological training programmes exist, such as Equip (Gibbs et al., 1995) and Aggression Replacement Training (ART; Glick & Goldstein, 1987), in which moral developmental stages are measured and evaluated. Equip is a multi-component treatment programme for juvenile delinquents (Gibbs et al., 1995). In this programme moral reasoning and cognitive distortions are evaluated and corrected. Although it has been shown that cognitive distortions are decreased in juvenile delinquents after administration of this programme (Nas, Brugman, & Koops, 2005) and sociomoral development (moral reasoning) is increased with a small to moderate effect size (Stams et al., 2006), whether reduction of these self-serving cognitive distortions and improved moral reasoning leads to less antisocial behaviour is unclear (Brugman, Bink, Nas, & van den Bos, 2007). Indeed, a recent study showed improvement on cognitive distortions after a cognitive intervention treatment programme for juvenile offenders, but did not report on the effects on behaviour (McGlynn, Hahn, & Hagan, 2013). Similarly, there seems to be an overall effect of Equip on sociomoral development (social skills, moral judgement and cognitive distortions) but the impact of Equip on recidivism did not reach significance, at least not in male or mixed gender samples (Stams et al., 2006). As mentioned earlier, it has been suggested that a treatment focus on cognitive distortions might not be sufficient to adequately change behaviour, especially externalising behaviour (Helmond, Overbeek, Brugman, & Gibbs, 2014; Van Langen, Stams, Van Vugt, Wissink, & Asscher, 2014). A more integrated approach targeting both moral emotions and moral cognitions might be necessary to change behaviour.

In the ART programme (Glick & Goldstein, 1987), participants are challenged to take another perspective on a moral situation, to transfer participants into one-half or more of the successive moral stages. However, as argued before, persons may find themselves in different moral stages using distinct moral reasoning patterns depending on the situation. Following this line of reasoning, it might not be very effective to transfer individuals into one-half or more of the successive moral stages, since moral reasoning levels may be very dependent on the given situations. Differences in reasoning patterns may be due to evaluating personal gains (Krebs, 2008), but may also be due to the lack of care not only for others, but also for themselves. Because of this carelessness about themselves, they do not care about the long-term consequences of their behaviour, but instead focus on immediate reward (Laub & Sampson, 2003). The question therefore remains whether stimulating a person into higher moral developmental stages leads successfully to changes in behaviour (Kohlberg, 1984; Boom et al., 2010 (in Brugman, 2010; see also Chapter 8). Although some studies showed a relationship between moral cognitions and delinquency, or even recidivism (e.g. Leeman, Gibbs, & Fuller, 1993), until now, the effects of improving behaviour by intervening on cognitions are still small (Blasi, 1980; Stams et al., 2006; Van Vught et al., 2011).

Moreover, to recognise and internalise consequences of one's behaviour, one needs to first restore self-esteem and self-worth (Brugman, 2010).

130   *Maaike Cima*

Although empirical evidence is lacking, many delinquent youth who have a lack of care for others also have a lack of care for themselves (Laub & Sampson, 2003; Brugman, 2010). In the literature there is some debate regarding the level of self-esteem in relation to externalising delinquent behaviour. Some authors argue that high levels of self-esteem relate to aggression and crime (e.g. Baumeister, Smart, & Boden, 1996), while others argued that low self-esteem may put a person at risk for externalising problem behaviour such as delinquency (Fergusson & Horwood, 2002; Sprott & Doob, 2000). More recently, a study within three different samples of subjects (11–14-year-old participants with diverse nationality; cohort of births between April and May 1972 from New Zealand; and undergraduate students) showed a relationship between low self-esteem and aggression independent of narcissism (Donnellan, Trzesniewski, Robins, Moffitt, & Caspi, 2005). It seems that in some cases aggression is a way to protect the low self-esteem that is left to decrease the negative feelings about oneself. In other cases, low self-esteem may infer a lack of emotion or carelessness regarding the world – others as well as oneself. In even other cases, aggression, especially shame-based aggression, seems illustrative of a vulnerable form of high self-esteem (Baumeister et al., 1996). Treatment should therefore focus on restoring an unbalance in self-esteem to improve behavioural evaluation, and consequently moral reasoning patterns.

Concluding remarks

There is no single overarching theory regarding conscience. Several theories explain certain aspects of conscience, like moral cognitions (Kant, 1902), moral reasoning (Gibbs, 2003), moral emotions (Hume, 1972; Greene & Haidt, 2002) and moral behaviour (Rawls, 1971; Nucci, 2001). We argue in accordance with Kochanska (2002) that conscience actually comprises all these components of cognition, emotions and behaviour. We therefore suggest that diagnostic tools measuring conscience should consist of a test-battery tapping into all these different components. Furthermore, since research has demonstrated that antisocial, psychopathic individuals do not seem to lack knowledge of right and wrong (one aspect of conscience) but do seem to be impaired in moral emotions and/or moral developmental stages, this supports the view that a lack of conscience can be within the one to three components of conscience. A deficit in one of these three components may indicate lack of conscience.

Regarding the development of conscience, several theories exist. Summarising these theories, one might conclude that certain basic elements of conscience are innate, e.g. the mechanism to empathise, mirror neurons and the capacity to distinguish right from wrong. However, these basic elements are nurtured by adequate parenting styles in combination with temperament, socialisation and attachment. Therefore, children who have a lack of conscience may suffer from an interaction of difficult temperament or neurobiological set-up with a non-optimal environment (Parker et al., 1979) in which ineffective socialisation plays an important role. Moreover, a child with a difficult temperament is more likely to elicit harsh, inconsistent and negative socialisation (Patterson, Reid, & Dishion, 1992; Paulussen Hoogeboom, Stams, Hermanns, & Peetsma, 2007). This consequently may lead to antisocial behaviour (Eisenberg & Valiente, 2002), which indirectly interacts with the development of certain relevant brain areas. Research regarding the innate aspects of conscience is sparse. One study by Schonfeld, Mattson, and Riley (2005) demonstrates that those children with prenatal exposure to alcohol use were less morally matured. Especially, moral judgements including connecting with others were related to prenatal alcohol exposure. Although prenatal influences regarding moral development are sparse, these kinds of studies stress the importance of the relationship between brain development and moral maturation.

Future studies should therefore extend previous research in which it will be examined whether we indeed are all born with a conscience. But from what we know so far, it seems that we are all born with the basic elements to develop an adequate conscience. During development these basic elements need to be adequately nurtured at key points to properly develop an adequate conscience. More mature developmental stages seem not to be a guarantee for adequate moral behaviour. An individual with a mature moral developmental stage may in a certain situations still behave morally inappropriately (Krebs, 2008). Focusing treatment on shifting moral developmental stages may therefore not be sufficient. However, the question remains whether we want to teach children morally appropriate motives in guiding their behaviour (Kant, 1902), or whether we want them to behave morally appropriately regardless of the underlying moral reasons (Rawls, 1971). Indeed, already in 1980, Blasi concluded that the knowledge of right and wrong does not relate to behaviour. In evaluating one's own behaviour, individuals strive for consistency between cognition and behaviour. When a person does not behave according to his own moral understanding, this may consequently lead to the use of cognitive distortions to repair the cognitive dissonance. Therefore the discrepancy between cognition and behaviour may be due to several factors: (1) The use of cognitive distortions enables a person to behave morally inappropriately despite their knowledge of right and wrong; (2) a lack of self-esteem may make them insensitive to the negative consequences for themselves, or their behaviour; (3) deficits in emotional processes might guide morally appropriate behaviour despite their moral knowledge. Treatment should therefore focus on self-esteem, moral emotions and cognitive distortions. Tracing the appearance of factors most importantly influencing moral conduct is still a challenge for current scientific research.

Literature

Ainsworth, M.D.S., Blehar, M.C., Waters, E., & Wall, S. (1978). *Patterns of attachment: A psychological study of the Strange Situation*. Hillsdale, New York: Erlbau.

Ali, F., Amorim, I.S., & Chamorro-Premuzic, T. (2009). Empathy deficits and trait emotional intelligence in psychopathy and Machiavellianism. *Personality and Individual Differences, 47*, 758–762.

132 Maaike Cima

Alvik, A., Tongersen, A.M., Allen, O.O., & Lindeman, R. (2011). Binge alcohol exposure once a week in early pregnancy predicts temperament and sleeping problems in the infant. *Early Human Development, 87*, 827–833.

Arsenio, W.F., & Lemerise, E.A. (2004). Aggression and moral development: Integrating social information processing and moral domain models. *Child Development, 75*, 987–1002.

Bandura, A. (1991). A social cognitive theory of moral thought and action. In: W.M. Kurtines & J.L. Gewirtz (Eds,). *Handbook of moral behavior and development* (pp. 45–103). Hillsdale, NJ: Lawrence Erlbaum Associates.

Barriga, A.Q., Morrison, E.M., Liau, A.K., & Gibbs, J.C. (2001). Moral cognition: Explaining the gender difference in antisocial behaviour. *Merrill-Palmer Quarterly, 47*, 532–562.

Basinger, K.S., Brugman, D., & Gibbs, J.C. (2007). *Sociomoral reflection measure: Short form objective* (SRM-SFO). Unpublished instrument, Urbana University, OH.

Baumeister, R.F., Smart, L., & Boden, J.M. (1996). Relation of threatened egotism to violence and aggression: The dark side of high self-esteem. *Psychological Review, 103*, 5–33.

Baumeister, R.F., Vohs, K.D., DeWall, C.N., & Zhang, L. (2007). How emotion shapes behavior: Feedback, anticipation, and reflection, rather then direct causation. *Personality and Social Psychology Review, 11*, 167–203.

Baumgartner, T., Heinrichs, M., Vonlanthen, A., Fischbacher, U., & Fehr, E. (2008). Oxytocin shapes the neural circuitry of trust and trust adaptation in humans. *Neuron, 58*, 639–650.

Barraza, J.A., McCullough, M.E., Ahmadi, S., & Zak, P.J. (2011). Oxytocin infusion increases charitable donations regardless of monetary resources. *Hormones and Behavior, 60*, 148–151.

Barrera, M.E., & Maurer, D. (1981). The perception of facial expressions by the three-month-old. *Child Development, 52*(1), 203–206.

Barriga, A.Q., Gibbs, J.C., Potter, G., & Liau, A.K. (2001). *The How I Think Questionnaire Manual.* Champaign, IL: Research Press.

Barriga, A.Q., Sullivan-Cosetti, M., & Gibbs, J.C. (2009). Moral cognitive correlates of empathy in juvenile delinquents. *Criminal Behaviour and Mental Health, 19*, 253–264.

Bartrip, J., Morton, J., & De Schonen, S. (2001). Responses to mother's face in 3 week to 5-month-old infants. *British Journal of Developmental Psychology, 19*(2), 219–232.

Beech, A.R., & Mitchell, I.J. (2005). A neurobiological perspective on attachment problems in sexual offenders and the role of selective serotonin re-uptake inhibitors in treatment of such problems. *Clinical Psychology Review, 25*, 153–182.

Bijttebier, P., & Roeyers, H. (2009). Temperament and vulnerability to psychopathology: Introduction to the special section. *Journal of Abnormal Child Psychology, 37*(3), 305–308.

Blair, R.J.R. (1995). A cognitive developmental approach to morality: Investigating the psychopath. *Cognition, 57*, 1–29.

Blair, R.J.R. (1997). Moral reasoning and the child with psychopathic tendencies. *Personality and Individual Differences, 22*, 731–739.

Blair, R.J.R. (2001). Neurocognitive models of aggression, the antisocial personality disorders, and psychopathy. *Journal of Neurology, Neurosurgery, and Psychiatry, 71*, 727–731.

Blair, R.J.R. (2003). Neurobiological basis of psychopathy. *The British Journal of Psychiatry, 182*, 5–7.

Blair, R.J.R. (2006). The emergence of psychopathy: Implications for the neuropsychological approach to developmental disorders. *Cognition, 101*, 414–442.

Blair, R.J.R., Sellars, C., Strickland, I., Clark, F., Williams, A. O., & Smith, M. (1996). Theory of mind in the psychopath. *Journal of Forensic Psychiatry, 7*, 15–25.

Blasi, A. (1980). Bridging moral cognition and moral action: A critical review of the literature. *Psychological Bulletin, 88*, 1–45.

Blasi, A. (1999). Emotions and moral motivation. *Journal of the Theory of Social Behavior, 29*, 1–19.

Boom, J., & Brugman, D. (2005). In W. van Haaften et al. (Eds.), *Moral sensibilities and education III: The adolescent* (pp. 87–112). Bemmel: Concorde.

Boom, J., Brugman, D., & van der Heijden, P.G.M. (2001). Hierarchical structure of moral stages assessed by a sorting task. *Child Development, 72*, 535–548.

Bowbly, J. (1982). *Attachment and loss: Vol. 1.* New York: Basic Books.

Brugman, D. (2010). Moral reasoning competence and the moral judgment-action discrepancy in young adolescents. In W. Koops, D. Brugman, & T.J. Ferguson (Eds.), *The development and structure of conscience* (pp. 119–133). London: Psychology Press.

Brugman, D., & Aleva, A.E. (2004). Developmental delay or regression in moral reasoning by juvenile delinquents. *Journal of Moral Education, 33*, 319–336.

Brugman, D., Podolskij, A.I., Heymans, P.G., Boom, J., Karabanova, O., & Idobaeva, O. (2003). The development and structure of conscience. *International Journal of Behavioral Development, 27*, 289–300.

Brugman, D., Bink, M.D., Nas, C.N., & Bos, J.K. van den (2007). Kunnen delinquent jongeren elkaar helpen in hun sociale ontwikkeling? Effecten peer-hulpprogramma EQUIP op denkfouten en recidive. *Tijdschrift voor Criminologie, 49*, 153–119.

Brugman, D., & Weisfelt, M.E.W. (2000). Moral competence and professional reasoning by Dutch auditors. *Research on Accounting Ethics, 7*, 105–142.

Carlo, G., Mestre, M.V., Samper, P., Tur, A., & Armenta, B.E. (2010). Feelings or cognitions? Moral cognitions and emotions as longitudinal predictors of prosocial and aggressive behaviour. *Personality and Individual Differences, 48*, 872–877.

Chapman, H.A., Kim, D.A., Susskind, M., & Anderson, A.K. (2009). In bad taste: Evidence for the oral origins of moral disgust. *Science, 323*, 222–226.

Chase, K. A., O'Leary, K. D., & Heyman, R. E. (2001). Categorizing partner-violent men within the reactive-proactive typology model. *Journal of Consulting and Clinical Psychology, 69*, 567–572.

Cima, M., & Raine, A. (2009). Distinct characteristics of psychopathy relate to different subtypes of aggression. *Personality and Individual Differences, 47*, 835–840.

Cima, M., Hall, R., De Lijster, J., & Van Brakel, H. (in preparation). The relationship between attachment, temperament and preference of antisocial behavior in nine month old children.

Cima, M., Hauser, M., & Tonnaer, F. (2010). Psychopaths know right from wrong, they just don't care. *Social Cognitive and Affective Neuroscience, 6*, 1–9.

Cima, M., Korebrits, A., Stams, G.J., & Bleumer, P. (submitted). Moral development, cognition, emotion and behavior in male youth with varying levels of psychopathic traits.

Cima, M., Nicolson, N., De Lijster, J., & Popma, A. (submitted). Salivary cortisol patterns in psychopathic and non-psychopathic offenders.

Cima, M., Smeets, T., & Jelicic, M. (2008). Self-reported trauma, cortisol levels, and aggression in psychopathic and non-psychopathic prison inmates. *Biological Psychology, 78*, 75–86.

Cima, M., Vancleef, L., Lobbestael, J., Meesters, C., & Korebrits, A. (2014). Don't you dare look at me, or else: Negative and aggressive interpretation bias, callous unemotional traits and type of aggression. *Journal of Child and Adolescent Behavior, 2*, http://dx.doi.org/10.4172/jcalb.1000128.

Cimbora, D.M., & McIntosh, D.N. (2003). Understanding the link between moral emotions and behaviour. In A.V. Clark, (Ed.), *Psychology of moods* (pp. 1–27). New York: Nova Science Publishers.

Coie, J.K., & Dodge, K.A. (1998). Aggression and antisocial behavior. In W. Damon & N. Eisenberg (Eds.), *Handbook of child psychology*, 5th edition. Volume 3. New York: John Wiley & Sons.

Colby, A., & Kohlberg, L. (1987). *The measurement of moral judgment: Theoretical foundation and research validation.* Vol. 1. Cambridge: Cambridge University Press.

Damasio, A.R. (1994). *Descartes' error: Emotion, reason and the human brain.* New York: Putnam.

Decety, J., & Cowell, J.M. (2014). Friends or foes: Is empathy necessary for moral behaviour? *Perspectives on Psychological Science, 9,* 525–537.

Decety, J., Michalska, K.J., & Akitsuki, Y. (2008). Who caused the pain? An fMRI investigation of empathy and intentionality in children. *Neuropsychologia, 46,* 2607–2614.

Derbyshire, S.W.G. (2000). Exploring the pain 'neuromatrix'. *Current Review of Pain, 4,* 467–477.

De Waal, F. (1996). *Good natured: The origins of right and wrong in humans and other animals.* London: Harvard University Press.

Dolan, M., & Fullam, R. (2004). Theory of mind and mentalizing ability in antisocial personality disorders with and without psychopathy. *Psychological Medicine, 34,* 1093–1102.

Donnellan, M.B., Trzesniewski, K.H., Robins, R.W., Moffitt, T.E., & Caspi, A. (2005). Low self-esteem is related to aggression, antisocial behaviour, and delinquency. *Psychological Science, 16,* 328–335.

Eisenberg, N. (2000). Emotion, regulation, and moral development. *Annual Review of Psychology, 51,* 665–697.

Eisenberg, N., Hofer, C., Sulik, M., & Liew, J. (2014). The development of prosocial moral reasoning and a prosocial orientation in young adulthood: Concurrent and longitudinal correlates. *Developmental Psychology, 50,* 58–70.

Eisenberg, N., & Valiente, C. (2002). Parenting and children's prosocial and moral development. In M.H. Bornstein (Ed.), *Handbook of parenting* (pp. 111–142). London: Lawrence Erlbaum Associates.

Emde, R.N. (1988). Development terminable and interminable: I. Innate and motivational factors from infancy. *International Journal of Psycho-Analysis, 69,* 23–42.

Farrington, D.P. (1995). The development of offending and antisocial behaviour from childhood: Key findings from the Cambridge study on delinquent development. *Journal of Child Psychology and Psychiatry, 36,* 929–964.

Feilhauer, J., Cima, M., Benjamins, C.A., & Muris, P. (2013). Knowing right from wrong, but just not always feeling it: Relations among callous–unemotional traits, psychopathological symptoms, and cognitive and affective morality judgments in 8- to 12-year-old boys. *Child Psychiatry and Human Development, 44,* 709–716.

Fergusson, D.M., & Horwood, L.J. (2002). Male and female offending trajectories. *Development and Psychopathology, 14,* 159–177.

Feshbach, N.D. (1987). Parental empathy and child adjustment/maladjustment. In N. Eisenberg & J. Strayer (Eds.), *Empathy and its developemt.* New York: Cambridge University Press.

Conscience 135

Flor, H., Birbaumer, N., Hermann, C., Ziegler, S., & Patrick, C.J. (2002). Aversive Pavlovian conditioning in psychopaths: Peripheral and central correlates. *Psychophysiology, 39,* 505–518.

Frick, P.J., Cornell, A.H., Bodin, S.D., Dane, H.E., Barry, C.T., & Loney, B.R. (2003). Callous-unemotional traits and developmental pathways to severe conduct problems. *Developmental Psychology, 39,* 246–260.

Gibbs, J.C. (1991). Sociomoral development delay and cognitive distortion: Implications for the treatment of antisocial youth. In W. Kurtines & J. Gewirtz (Eds.), *Handbook of moral behaviour and development* (pp. 95–110). Hillsdale, NJ: Lawrence Erlbaum Associates.

Gibbs, J.C. (2003). *Moral development and reality: Beyond the theories of Kohlberg and Hoffman.* Thousand Oaks, CA: Sage Publications.

Gibbs, J.C. (2010). *Moral development and reality: Beyond the theories of Kohlberg and Hoffman* (2nd ed.). Boston, MA: Pearson, Allyn & Bacon.

Gibbs, J.C., Arnold, K.D., Ahlborn, H.H., & Cheesman, F.L. (1994). Facilitation of sociomoral reasoning in delinquents. *Journal of Consulting and Clinical Psychology, 52,* 37–45.

Gibbs, J.C, Basinger, K.S., & Fuller, R. (1992). *Moral maturity: Measuring the development of sociomoral reflection.* Hillsdale: Erlbaum.

Gibbs, J.C., Potter, G.B., & Goldstein, A.P. (1995). *The EQUIP program: Teaching youth to think and act responsibly through a peer-helping approach.* Champaign, IL: Research Press.

Glenn A.L., & Raine, A. (2008). The neurobiology of psychopathy. *Psychiatric Clinics of North America, 31,* 463–475.

Glick, B., & Goldstein, A. P. (1987). Aggression replacement training. *Journal of Counseling and Development, 65*(7), 356–362.

Greenberg, M.T., Speltz, M.L., & DeKlyen, M. (1993). The role of attachment in the early development of disruptive behavior problems. *Development and Psychopathology, 5,* 191–213.

Greene, J.D., & Haidt, J. (2002). How (and where) does moral judgment work? *Trends in Cognitive Science, 6,* 517–523.

Greene, J.D., Nystrom, L.E., Engell, A.D., Darley, J.M., & Cohen, J.D. (2004). The neural bases of cognitive conflict and control in moral judgment. *Neuron, 44,* 389–400.

Greene, J.D., Sommerville, R.B., Nystrom, L.E., Darley, J.M., & Cohen, J.D. (2001). An fMRI investigation of emotional engagement in moral judgment. *Science, 293,* 2105–2108.

Gustavo, C., Crockett, L.J., Wolff, J.M., & Beal, S.J. (2012). The role of emotional reactivity, self-regulation, and puberty in adolescents' prosocial behaviors. *Social Development, 21*(4), 667–685.

Haidt, J. (2001). The emotional dog and its rational tail: A social intuitionist approach to moral judgment. *Psychological Review, 108,* 814–834.

Haith, M., Bergman, T., & Moore, M. (1977). Eye contact and face scanning in early infancy. *Science, 198,* 853–855.

Hamlin, J.K., Wynn, K., & Bloom, P. (2010). Three-month-olds show a negativity bias in their social evaluations. *Developmental Science, 1,* 1–7.

Hare, R.D. (1996). Psychopathy and antisocial personality disorder: A case of diagnostic confusion. *Psychiatric Times, 13,* 39–40.

Hare, R.D., Hart, S.D., & Harpur, T.J. (1991). Psychopathy and the DSM-IV criteria for antisocial personality disorder. *Journal of Abnormal Psychology, 100,* 391–398.

Hastings, M.E., Tangney, J.P., & Stuewig, J. (2008). Psychopathy and identification of facial expressions of emotion. *Personality and Individual Differences, 44,* 1474–1483.

136   *Maaike Cima*

Helmond, P., Overbeek, G., Brugman, D., & Gibbs, J.C. (2014). A meta-analysis on cognitive distortions and externalizing problem behavior: Associations, moderators, and treatment effectiveness. *Criminal Justice and Behavior, 37*, 695–708.

Hoeve, M., Stams, G.J.J.M., Van der Put, C.E, Dubas, J.S., Van der Laan, P.H., & Gerris, R. M. (2012). A meta-analysis of attachment and juvenile delinquency. *Journal of Abnormal Child Psychology, 40*, 771–785.

Hoffman, M.L. (2000). *Empathy and moral development: Implications for caring and justice.* Cambridge: Cambridge University Press.

Hume, D. (1751). *An enquiry concerning the principles of morals.* London: A. Millar.

Hurlemann, R., Patin, A., Onur, O.A., Cohen, M.X., Baumgartner, T., Metzler, S., & Kendrick, K.M. (2010). Oxytocin enhances amygdala-dependent, socially reinforced learning and emotional empathy in humans. *Journal of Neuroscience, 30*, 4999–5007.

Iacoboni, M. (2008). *Mirroring people: The new science of how we connect with others.* New York: Farrar, Straus, and Giroux.

Insel, T.R., & Fernald, R.D. (2004). How the brain processes social information: Searching for the social brain. *Annual Review of Neuroscience, 27*, 697–722.

Jolliffe D., & Farrington D.P. (2004). Empathy and offending: A systematic review and meta- analysis. *Aggression and Violent Behavior, 9*, 441–476.

Kagan, J., & Lamb, S. (1987). *The emergence of morality in young children.* Chicago: University of Chicago Press.

Kant, I. (1781). *Kritik der reinen vernunft [Critique of pure reason].* Hamburg: Felix Meiner Verlag.

Kimbrell, T.A., George, M.S., Parekh, P.I., Ketter, T.A., Podell, D.M., & Danielson, A.L. (1999). Regional brain activity during transient self-induced anxiety and anger in healthy adults. *Biological Psychiatry, 46*, 454–465.

Kochanska, G. (2002). Mutually responsive orientation between mothers and their young children: A context for the early development of conscience. *Current Directions in Psychological Science, 11*, 191–195.

Kochanska, G., & Aksan, N. (2004). Conscience in childhood: Past, present, and future. *Merrill-Palmer Quarterly, 50*, 299–310.

Kochanska, G., Forman, D.R., Aksan, N., & Dunbar, S. (2005). Pathways to conscience: Early mother-child mutually responsive orientation and children's moral emotion, conduct, and cognition. *Journal of Child Psychology and Psychiatry, 46*, 19–34.

Kochanska, G., & Aksan, N. (2006). Children's conscience and self-regulation. *Journal of Personality, 74*, 1587–1618.

Kochanska, G., & Thompson, R. A. (1997). The emergence and development of conscience in toddlerhood and early childhood. In J.E. Gursec & L. Kuczynski (Eds.), *Parenting and children's internalization of values: A handbook of contemporary theory* (pp. 53–77). New York: Wiley.

Kohlberg, L. (1969). Stage and sequence: The cognitive developmental approach to socialization. In D.A. Goslin (Ed.), *Handbook of socialization theory and research* (pp. 347–480). Chicago: Rand McNally.

Kohlberg, L. (1981). *Essays on moral development: Vol 1. The philosophy of moral development.* New York: Harper & Row.

Kohlberg, L. (1984). *The psychology of moral development: Essays on moral development (Vol. 2).* San Francisco: Harper & Row.

Koops, W., Brugman, D., & Ferguson, T.J. (2010). The development of conscience: Concepts and theoretical and empirical approaches. An introduction. In W. Koops,

D. Brugman, T.J. Ferguson, & A.F. Sanders (Eds.), *The development and structure of conscience* (pp. 1–22). Hove: Psychology Press.

Kosfeld, M., Heinrichs, M., Zak, P.J., Fischbacher, U., & Fehr, E. (2005). Oxytocin increases trust in humans. *Nature, 435,* 673–676.

Kosson, D.S., Suchy, Y., Mayer, A.R., & Libby, J. (2002). Facial affect recognition in criminal psychopaths. *Emotion, 2*(4), 398–411.

Krebs, D.L. (2008). Morality: An evolutionary account. *Perspectives of Psychological Science, 3,* 149–172.

Krebs, D.L., Denton, K., & Wark, G. (1997). The forms and functions of real-life moral decision-making. *Journal of Moral Education, 26,* 131–143.

Krebs, D.L., Denton, K., Wark, G., Couch, R., Racine, T., & Krebs, D.L. (2002). Interpersonal moral conflicts between couples: Effects of type of dilemma, role, and partner's judgments on level of moral reasoning and probability of resolution. *Journal of Adult Development, 9,* 307–316.

Kuhlmeier, V., Wynn, K., & Bloom, P. (2003). Attribution of dispositional states by 12-month-olds. *Psychological Science, 14,* 402–408.

Kuther, T.L., & Higgins-D'Alessandro, A. (2000). Bridging the gap between moral reasoning and adolescent engagement in risky behavior. *Journal of Adolescence, 23,* 409–422.

Laan, A.M. van der, Veenstra, R., Bogaerts, S., Verhulst, F.C., & Ormel, J. (2010). Serious, minor, and non-delinquents in early adolescence: The impact of cumulative risk and promotive factors. The TRAILS study. *Journal of Abnormal Child Psychology, 38*(3), 339–351.

Laible, D.J., & Thompson, R.A. (2000). Mother-child discourse, attachment security, shared positive affect, and early conscience development. *Child Development, 71,* 1424–1440.

Larden, M., Melin, L., Holst, U., & Langstrom, N. (2005). Moral judgement, cognitive distortions and empathy in incarcerated delinquent and community control adolescents. *Psychology Crime & Law* 10.1080/10683160500036855

Laub, J.H., & Sampson, R.J. (2003). *Shared beginnings, divergent lives: Delinquent boys to age 70.* Cambridge, MA: Harvard University Press.

Leeman, L.W., Gibbs, J.C., & Fuller, D. (1993). Evaluation of a multi-component group treatment program for juvenile delinquents. *Aggressive Behavior, 19,* 281–292.

Lemerise, E.A., & Arsenio, W.F. (2000). An integrated model of emotion processes and cognition in social information processing. *Child Development, 71,* 107–118.

Levenston, G.K., Patrick, C.J., Bradley, M.M., & Lang, P.J. (2000). The psychopath as observer: Emotion and attention in picture processing. *Journal of Abnormal Psychology, 109,* 373–389.

Loeber, R., & Hay, D.F. (2004). Key issues in the development of aggression and violence from childhood to early adulthood. *Annual Review of Psychology, 48,* 371–410.

Londerville, S., & Main, M. (1981). Security of attachment, compliance, and maternal training methods in the second year of life. *Developmental Psychology, 17,* 289–299.

Lyons-Ruth, K. (1996). Attachment relationships among children with aggressive behaviour problems: The role of disorganized early attachment patterns. *Journal of Consulting and Clinical Psychology, 64,* 64–73.

Ma, H.K. (2013). The moral development of the child: An integrated model. *Frontiers in Public Health, 1,* 1–17.

McGlynn, A.H., Hahn, P., & Hagan, M.P. (2013). The effect of a cognitive treatment program for male and female juvenile offenders. *International Journal of Offender Therapy and Comparative Criminology, 57,* 1107–1119.

138   *Maaike Cima*

Meesters, C., Cima, M., Muris, P., Roelofs, J., & Colenbrander, C. (submitted). Relationships between child- and parent-reported attachment style and symptoms of anxiety disorders and depression in non-clinical children.

Miller, P.A., & Eisenberg, N. (1988). The relation of empathy to aggressive and externalizing/antisocial behavior. *Psychological Bulletin, 103*, 324–344.

Mitchell, I.J., Smid, W., Troelstra, J., Wever, E., Ziegler, T.E., & Beech, A.R. (2013). Psychopathic characteristics are related to high basal urinary oxytocin levels in male forensic patient. *The Journal of Forensic Psychiatry & Psychology, 24*, 309–318.

Moffit, T.E. (1993). Adolescence-limited and life-course-persistent antisocial behavior: A developmental taxonomy. *Psychological Review, 4*, 674–701.

Nas, C.N., Brugman, D., & Koops, W. (2005). Effects of the EQUIP programme on the moral judgement, cognitive distortions, and social skills of juvenile delinquents. *Psychology, Crime, & Law, 11*, 421–434.

Nas, C.N., Brugman, D., & Koops, W. (2008). Measuring self-serving cognitive distortions with the 'How I Think' questionnaire. *European Journal of Psychological Assessment, 24*, 181–189.

Newman, J., & Kosson, D., (1986). Passive avoidance learning in psychopathic and nonpsychopathic offenders. *Journal of Abnormal Psychology, 95*(3), 252–256.

Nigg, J.T. (2006). Temperament and developmental psychopathology. *Journal of Child Psychology and Psychiatry, 47*(3/4), 395–422.

Nucci, L.P. (2001). *Education in the moral domain.* Cambridge: Cambridge University Press.

Nucci, L.P. (2002). Because it is the right thing to do. *Human Development, 45*, 125–129.

Nucci, L.P., & Nucci, M.S. (1982). Children's responses to moral and social conventional transgressions in free-play settings. *Child Development, 53*, 1337–1342.

Palmer, E.J. (2003). An overview of the relationship between moral reasoning and offending. *Australian Psychologist, 38*, 165–174.

Parker, G., Tuplin, H., & Brown, L.B. (1979). A parental bonding instrument. *British Journal of Medical Psychology, 52*, 1–10.

Patrick, C.J., Bradley, M.M., & Lang, P.J. (1993). Emotion in the criminal psychopath: Startle reflex modification. *Journal of Abnormal Psychology, 102*, 82–92.

Patterson, G.R., Reid, J.B., & Dishion, T.J. (1992). *A social learning approach: Vol. 4: Antisocial boys.* Eugene, OR: Castalia Press.

Paulussen Hoogeboom, M.C., Stams, G.J.J.M., Hermanns, J.M.A., & Peetsma, T.T.D. (2007). Child negative emotionality and parenting from infancy to preschool: A meta-analytic review. *Developmental Psychology, 43*, 438–453.

Piaget, J. (1932). *The moral judgment of the child.* New York: Harcourt, Brace & World.

Pizarro, D. (2000). Nothing more than feelings? The role of emotions in moral judgment. *Journal for the Theory of Social Behaviour, 30*, 355–375.

Posner, M.I., & Rothbart, M.K. (2000). Developing mechanisms of self-regulation. *Development and Psychopathology, 12*, 427–441.

Premack, D., & Premack, A.J. (1997). Infants attribute value +/- to the goal-directed actions of self-propelled objects. *Journal of Cognitive Neuroscience, 9*, 848–856.

Preston, S.D., & de Waal, F.B.M. (2002). Empathy: Its ultimate and proximate bases. *Behavioral and Brain Sciences, 25*, 1–20.

Price, D.D. (2000). Psychological and neural mechanisms of the affective dimension of pain. *Science, 288*, 1769–1772.

Prinz, J. (2006). The emotional basis of moral judgments. *Philosophical Explorations, 9*, 29–43.

Raine, A. (2013). The anatomy of violence: The biological roots of crime. New York: Pantheon Books.

Raine, A., Meloy, J.R., Bihrle, S., Stoddard, J., LaCasse, L., & Buchsbaum, M.S. (1998). Reduced prefrontal and increased subcortical brain functioning assessed using positron emission tomography in predatory and affective murderers. *Behavioral Science and the Law, 16*, 319–332.

Raine, R., & Yang, Y. (2006). Neural foundations to moral reasoning and antisocial behavior. *Social Cognitive and Affective Neuroscience, 1*, 203–213.

Rawls, J. (1971). *A theory of justice.* Cambridge, MA: Harvard University Press.

Rothbart, M.K., Ahadi, S.A., & Hershey, K.L. (1994). Temperament and social behavior in childhood. *Merrill-Palmer Quarterly, 40*, 21–39.

Rothbart, M.K., & Bates, J.E. (1998). Temperament. In W. Damon (Series Ed.) & N. Eisenberg (Vol. Ed.), *Handbook of child psychology: Vol. 3. Social, emotional, and personality development (5th ed.)* (pp. 105–176). New York: Wiley.

Rothbart, M.K., & Posner, M.I. (2006). Temperament, attention, and developmental psychopathology. In D. Cicchetti (Ed.), *Handbook of developmental psychopathology.* Hoboken, NJ: Wiley.

Rozin, P., Loewry, L., Imada, S., & Haidt, J. (1999). The CAD triad hypothesis: A mapping between three moral emotions (contempt, anger, disgust) and three moral codes (community, autonomy, divinity). *Journal of Personality Social Psychology, 76*, 574–586.

Rozin, P., Haidt, J., & McCauley, C.R. (1993) Disgust: The body and soul of emotion. In T. Dalgleish and M. Power (Eds.,), *Handbook of cognition and emotions*, (pp. 575–659). London: Wiley Guilford Press.

Sagi, A., & Hoffman, M.L. (1976). Empathic distress in the newborn. *Developmental Psychology, 32*, 720–729.

Scarnier, M., Schmader, T., & Lickel, B. (2009). Parental shame and guilt: Emotional reactions to a child's wrong- doing. *Personal Relationships, 16*, 205–220.

Schnall, S., Haidt, J., Clore, G.L., & Jordan, A.H. (2008). Disgust as embodied moral judgment. *Personality and Social Psychology Bulletin, 34*, 1096–1109.

Schonfeld, A.M., Mattson, S.N., & Riley, E.P. (2005). Moral maturity and delinquency after prenatal alcohol exposure. *Journal of Studies of Alcohol and Drugs, 66*, 545–554.

Sears, R.R., Rau, L., & Alpert, R. (1965). *Identification and child rearing.* Stanford, CA: Stanford University Press.

Smetana, J.G., Killen, M., & Turiel, E. (2000). Moral reasoning. In W. Craig (Ed.), *Childhood social development: The essential readings* (pp. 273–304). Oxford: Blackwell Publisherd Ltd.

Speltz, M.L., Greenberg, M.T., & DeKlyen, M. (1990). Attachment in preschoolers with disruptive behavior: A comparison of clinic-referred and nonproblem children. *Development and Psychopathology, 2*, 31–46.

Sprott, J.B., & Doob, A.N. (2000). Bad, sad, and rejected: The lives of aggressive children. *Canadian Journal of Criminology, 42*, 123–133.

Stams, G.J.J.M., Brugman, D., Dekovic, M, Van Rosmalen, L., Van der Laan, P.H., & Gibbs, J.C. (2006). The moral judgment of juvenile delinquents: A meta-analysis. *Journal of Abnormal Child Psychology, 34*, 697–713.

Stapert, W. (2010). Conscience development: A review of theory and research. *Tijdschrift voor Psychiatrie, 52*, 433–443.

Swaab, D. (2010). *Wij zijn ons brein: Van baarmoeder tot Alzheimer.* Amsterdam/Antwerpen: Contact.

Thomas, A., & Chess, S. (1977). *Temperament and development.* New York: New York University Press.

140 Maaike Cima

Thompson, R.A., & Newton, E.K. (2010). Emotion in early conscience. In W.F. Arsenio & E.A. Lemerise (Eds.), *Emotions, aggression, and morality in children: Bridging development and psychopathology* (pp. 13–31). Washington DC: American Psychological Association.

Thompson, R.A., Meyer, S., & McGinley, M. (2006). Understanding values in relationship: The development of conscience. In M. Killen & J. Smetana (Eds.), *Handbook of moral development* (pp. 267–297). Mahwah, NJ: Lawrence Erlbaum Associates.

Tisak, M.S., & Turiel, E. (1988). Variation in seriousness of transgressions and children's moral and conventional concepts. *Developmental Psychology, 24*, 352–357.

Turiel, E. (2008). The development of morality. In W. Damon & R.M. Lerner (Eds.), *Child and adolescent development* (pp. 473–514). Toronto: John Wiley & Sons.

Valdesolo, P., & DeSteno, D. (2006). Manipulations of emotional context shape moral judgment. *Psychological Science, 17*, 476–477.

Van Goozen, S.H., Snoek, H., Fairchild, G., & Harold, G.T. (2007). The evidence for a neurobiological model of childhood antisocial behavior. *Psychological Bulletin, 1333*(1), 149–182.

Van Goozen, S.H., Matthys, W., Cohen-Kettenis, P.T., Buitelaar, J.K., & van Engeland, H. (2000). Hypothalamic-pituitary-adrenal axis and autonomic nervous system activity in disruptive children and matched controls. *Journal of the American Academy of Child and Adolescent Psychiatry, 39*, 1438–1445.

Van Ijzendoorn, M.H., Feldbrugge, J.T.T.M., Derks, F.C.H., De Ruiter, C., Verhages, M.F.M., Philipe, M.W.G., Van der Staak, C.P.F., & Riksen Walraven, J.M.A. (1997). Attachment representations of personality disordered criminal offenders. *American Journal of Orthopsychiatry, 67*(3), 449–459.

Van Langen, M.A.M., Stams, G.J.J.M., Van Vugt, E.S., Wissink, I.B., & Asscher, J.J. (2014). Explaining female offending and prosocial behaviour: The role of empathy and cognitive distortions. *Laws, 3*, 706–720.

Van Stam, M.A., Van der Schuur, W.A., Tserkezis, S., Van Vugt, E.S., Asscher, J.J., Gibbs, J.C., & Stams, G.J.J.M. (2014). The effectiveness of Equip on sociomoral development and recidivism reduction: A meta-analytic study. *Children and Youth Services Review, 38*, 260–275.

Van Vugt, E.S., Gibbs, J.C., Stams, G.J.J.M., Bijleveld, C., Van der Laan, P.H., & Hendriks, J. (2011). Moral development and recidivism: A meta-analysis. *International Journal of Offender Therapy and Comparative Criminology, 55*, 1234–1250.

Verwaaijen, A.A.G., & Bruggeman, F.M.J. (2010). De teddybeer voeldoet niet meer: Persisterend delictgedrag bij adolescenten. In T. Dorelijers, J. ten Voorde, & M. Moerings (Red.,), *Strafrecht en forensische psychiatrie voor 16- tot 23-jarigen* (pp. 141–157). Den Haag: Boom Uitgevers.

Walker, L.J., & Taylor, J.H. (1991). Family interactions and the development of moral reasoning. *Child Development, 62*, 264–283.

Wicker, B., Keysers, C., Plailly, J., Royet, J.P., Gallese, V., & Rizzolatti, G. (2003). Both of us disgusted in my insula: The common neural basis of seeing and feeling disgust. *Neuron, 40*, 655–664.

Winslow, J.T., Shapiro, L.E., Carter, C.S., & Insel, T.R. (1993). Oxytocin and complex social behaviors: Species comparisons. *Psychopharmology Bulletin, 29*, 409–414.

Wolff, P. (1963). Observations on the early development of smiling. In B.M. Foss (Ed.), *Determinants of infant behavior* (pp. 113–138). London: Methuen.

Part III

Psychopathology and crime

7 Deception

Faking good or bad

*Kim Van Oorsouw, Marco Jelicic
and Maaike Cima*

Introduction

In the *Diagnostic and Statistical Manual of Mental Disorders V* (DSM-5; APA, 2013), malingering is defined as: 'The intentional production of false or grossly exaggerated physical or psychological symptoms motivated by external incentives' (p. 726). This psychiatric classification system does not provide specific criteria for malingering as it does not recognise malingering as a psychiatric disorder. The DSM-5 rather sees it as a 'condition that may be the focus of clinical attention' (pp. 726–727).

Deception, faking of good and bad, is a relevant issue to mental health experts, especially those who are involved in forensic assessments. Defendants may fabricate mental health problems to diminish their criminal responsibility or competency to stand trial (Tysse, 2005). In both civil as well as criminal forensic examinations, the examinee may engage in a considerable degree of response distortion (Rogers, Sewell, & Goldstein, 1994). Malingering may seriously compromise the integrity of these evaluations when undetected. In such cases, false claims regarding the mental state of a suspect or claimant may have societal consequences such as acquittal in court, diminished responsibility convictions, lenient sentences or financial compensation (Conroy & Kwartner, 2006; Iverson, 2006). Over the last few years, the awareness of the importance of including response distortion tests in forensic mental health assessments has been increasing. In this chapter, several types of malingering, risk groups as well as tools to detect malingering of psychiatric and neurocognitive symptoms will be described.

Types of deception

Two different types of deception in forensic assessments can be distinguished, namely faking bad and faking good. Faking bad, better known as malingering, refers to a deliberate exaggeration, fabrication or misattribution of symptoms to obtain a desired external goal (e.g. Berry, Bear, Rinaldo, & Wetter, 2002; Boon, Gozna, & Hall, 2008; Van Oorsouw & Merckelbach, 2010). Such a goal could be financial compensation for psychological or physical injuries, obtaining prescription medicines or reducing criminal responsibility. Faking good

144   *Kim Van Oorsouw et al.*

refers to the exaggeration of positive features resulting in a systematic denial of complaints that normal people experience in their daily life, also to reach an external goal such as, for example, termination of mandatory psychiatric treatment (Cima, Van Bergen, & Kremer, 2008).

Faking bad is a strategy that is seen in both the civil and criminal arena. Psychiatrists and neurologists often see personal injury claimants with memory or other cognitive problems. In some cases their complaints are indeed caused by the injury, but many people involved in personal injury litigation are fabricating or exaggerating their symptoms (Cassidy et al., 2000). In fact, in up to 60% of these cases, cognitive problems are exaggerated (Mittenberg, Patton, Canyock, & Condit, 2002; Schmand et al., 1998). Therefore, neuropsychologists should be aware of the possibility that some examinees may be feigning their complaints for external reasons such as financial gain. The prevalence of the two different types of deceptive behaviours depends on the goal the person involved wants to achieve. A suspect of a serious offence who is awaiting his trial may feign insanity (fake bad) to escape a lengthy incarceration. When feigning is not detected, this suspect may be admitted to a forensic psychiatric hospital for mandatory treatment. Continuing to report symptoms may now obstruct the beneficial effects of therapy. Subsequently, the patient's goals may change because exhibiting signs of mental illness may extend his stay in the hospital. The patient's new goal may be to minimise pathology (fake good) to leave the clinic as soon as possible.

Faking good differs from defensiveness in the sense that it is not just the denial of psychiatric symptoms (e.g. 'I sometimes hear voices in my head'), but also the denial of common symptoms (e.g. intrusive thoughts, checking whether you have locked the door), and it does not depend on social context as social desirability does (Cima et al., 2008). Faking good is often observed in patients who wish to have their treatment terminated, or those who are reevaluated for their risk of recidivism because they are seeking probation.

This chapter will focus on malingering and deception in the forensic and criminal legal context. More specifically, malingering in psychopaths, in sex offenders and malingered crime-related amnesia will be discussed. Also, several tests and procedures to assess the veracity of feigned psychiatric and neurocognitive symptoms in forensic settings will be described.

Malingering and psychopathy

A childhood diagnosis of oppositional defiant disorder (ODD) and conduct disorder (CD) often precedes a later diagnosis of antisocial personality disorder (APD) or psychopathy. Children with ODD and CD have a tendency to deceive. They often lie to obtain goods or favors or to avoid obligations (APA, 2013, p. 99). Early lying and deception in these disorders is often a developmental marker of more severe violent behaviours that are yet to come (Waldman, Singh, & Lahey, 2006; see Chapter 4 of this book). CD children with callous unemotional (CU) traits are especially at risk of developing psychopathy.

Psychopathy is a personality construct that is characterised by superficial charm, inflated self-worth, impulsiveness, irresponsibility and callousness in conjunction with antisocial behaviour (Hare, 1991; Vitacco, Neumann, & Jackson, 2005). It is believed that people who have psychopathic personality features are more likely to engage in a variety of conning and deceptive behaviours such as pathological lying, conning and manipulation than those without these features (Cleckley, 1941; Edens, Buffington, & Tomicic, 2000; Hare & Neumann, 2009; Porter & Woodworth, 2007; see Chapter 11 for a more detailed description of this disorder). Because psychopaths are very skilled in deceiving others, many clinicians think that psychopaths are very prone to and capable of fabricating symptoms of mental disorders in mental health settings. This is related to the idea that the majority of psychopaths also meet the criteria for APD (Decuyper, De Fruyt, & Buschman, 2008). According to DSM-5 (APA, 2013), individuals with APD display an elevated tendency to malinger. Thus, one would expect a relationship between psychopathy and malingering. However, only a few empirical studies that addressed the question of whether psychopathic personality traits predict an increased ability to malinger yielded a direct relation between psychopathy and malingering.

In fact, the findings in this research area are rather mixed. Gacono, Meloy, Sheppard, and Roske (1995) demonstrated that incarcerated offenders who feigned insanity did indeed score higher on a measure of psychopathy. Poythress, Edens, and Watkins (2001), on the other hand, failed to find a relationship between psychopathy scores and malingering on a variety of instruments (see also Kucharski, Duncan, Egan, & Falkenbach, 2006). However, they did find that high scores on the Psychopathic Personality Inventory (PPI) were related to a more extensive history of engaging in various types of deception than those with low PPI scores. Edens et al. (2000) also showed that high levels of psychopathy were related to a willingness to feign mental illness as well as to the belief that they would be able to go undetected while doing so. Yet psychopathy levels were not related to an objective ability to successfully feign mental illness. These findings seem to suggest that psychopathic traits are associated with attitudes that encourage the engagement in malingering in adversarial forensic settings. These attitudes seem to be related to the grandiose and self-serving features of psychopathy, as measured by the Machiavellian Egocentricity subscale of the PPI (Edens et al., 2000). In line with this, Cima and Van Oorsouw (2013) investigated whether the relationship between psychopathy and claims of crime-related amnesia was typical for only a subtype of psychopaths. Since previous research demonstrated that claims of (genuine) amnesia are more likely to occur in impulsive and reactive acts of violence, it was expected that psychopaths scoring high on the PPI impulsive antisocial factor (PPI-2) would be more likely to claim amnesia than those scoring high on the PPI Fearless Dominance factor (PPI-1). Indeed, it turned out that only PPI-2 scores were predictive of claims of amnesia. It also appeared that the PPI-2 subtype of psychopathy had a higher tendency to malinger (i.e. fake bad) than the other subtype (see Cima & Van Oorsouw, 2013).

146   *Kim Van Oorsouw et al.*

In addition, Cima, Pantus, and Dams (2007) demonstrated that context may play a role in the relationship between psychopathy and malingering. They found that, prior to conviction (i.e. when there was something to gain), malingering and psychopathy were related, whereas after conviction (i.e. when in prison or a forensic mental health institution) these constructs were unrelated. According to Cima et al. (2007), differentiating between the types of deception could be important when investigating the psychopathy-malingering link. Most studies that have investigated this link looked at the tendency of psychopaths to exaggerate psychiatric symptoms (i.e. faking bad). However, considering the context of a forensic setting, they may also gain from the denial of psychopathology (i.e. faking good). This issue was investigated by Cima et al. (2008) using the supernormality scale – revised (SS-R). This scale consists of 50 items measuring the tendency to deny common symptoms, also called dissimulation. It was expected that higher psychopathy scores would be related to higher rates of faking good. In contrast to their expectations, psychopathy was not related to faking good.

To sum up, psychopathy and malingering (faking bad) seem to be related to some extent, and this is particularly the case for the impulsive antisocial facet of psychopathy. Thus, screening for impulsive antisocial traits and malingering might be informative in assessing the veracity of symptoms reported by psychopathic offenders. Such screening should be considered in the light of the purpose of the assessment and the nature of the charges.

Malingering in sex offenders

Paraphilias are sexual deviations with behaviours or sexual urges focusing on unusual objects, activities or situations (DSM-5; APA, 2013). These deviations may result in deviant and illegal sexual activities such as exhibitionism and pedophilia, which could result in long prison sentences. An important feature of pedophilia and sexually abusive behaviour is lying, minimisation and defensiveness in addition to cognitive distortions. This may be expressed in the use of deceptive acts to lure a victim, in rationalisations for the illegal act (e.g. incest as a form of education), but also in denial or minimisation of the effects of the act on the victim (Ward, Gannon, & Keown, 2006). Denial and lying about previous sexual offences interfere with the acceptance of responsibility and increase the risk of future offending. Sex offending often starts at a young age where the offenders lie about and minimise the act (Barbaree, Marshall, & Hudson, 1993; Curwen, 2003). According to Baker, Tabacoff, Tornusciolo, and Eisenstadt (2003), children's prevarications may be related to family factors. These authors showed that lying, family deception and family myths are more common in families of sexually abused children than in families without a history of child abuse. The presence of lying and deception in such families increased the likelihood that these children would engage in sexual offending themselves.

An important factor in the assessment of malingering in sex offenders is whether the sex offenders acknowledge their sexually deviant behaviour (admitters) or whether they deny this (non-admitters). For example, many pedo-philes may have cognitive distortions such as maladaptive beliefs and attitudes and problematic thinking styles (Friestad, 2012; Gannon et al., 2007; Ward, 2000). As a consequence they excuse and rationalise their behaviour or blame the sexual acts on the victim (e.g. the victim desires the sex, consents to the sex). These offenders do not see sexual contact between adults and children as a crime because of their distorted beliefs, and will approach children without hesitation using positive affect and explicit planning (approach goal offenders). Not all sex offenders hold distorted views about the appropriateness of sexual contact with children, despite their sexual preference for children. Such offenders often try to avoid contact with children because they realise it is wrong (avoidant goal offender). However, when they do commit a sex offence, this is often a result of poor self-regulation or inadequate coping (Bickley & Beech, 2003). Depending on the offence pathway, either resulting from distorted cognitive beliefs or poor self-regulation in high-risk situations, different types of interventions should be selected. Also, these offenders may differ in their motivations to deny or minimise their responsibility when they commit a sex offence. Approach goal offenders, for example, may show reduced awareness of the impact of their abuse on the victim as compared to avoidant goal offenders.

Especially for the non-admitting sex offenders, it is important to use vali-dated instruments that provide insight in their response style. In doing this, one of course needs to distinguish between non-admitters who are guilty (those who falsely deny their offence) and those who are innocent (falsely accused). Also of importance is to accurately identify persons who have deviant sexual interest but who have not committed a crime (e.g. for risk assessments) and those who have been found guilty of committing a sex offence. Finally, the setting has to be considered in the assessment of malingering in sex offenders because motivations to deceive may be different at pretrial, after conviction, in treatment or in research settings (see Lanyon & Thomas, 2008). A related issue was shown in a study of blame attribution of Cima et al. (2007) in which forensic patients attributed their behaviour to mental illness but demonstrated higher guilt-feeling scores as compared to prison inmates. Interestingly, sex-ual offenders who were prisoners showed the lowest guilt-feeling attribution, while sexual offenders who were forensic patients had the highest guilt-feeling attribution scores. Since earlier research reported a tendency of sex offenders to present themselves in a desirable way (Cima et al., 2003), the authors suggests that the forensic sexual offenders may demonstrate a social desirable response tendency in an attempt to gain sympathy and/or earlier parole (Cima et al., 2007). Methods to assess response style and tendency to malinger may be useful and will be discussed later in this chapter.

Simulated amnesia

In the legal domain, simulated amnesia is probably the most common form of amnesia (Cima, Merckelbach, Nijman, Knauer, & Hollnack, 2002; Schacter,

148   *Kim Van Oorsouw et al.*

1986). About 25–40% of the offenders of violent crimes claim amnesia (Cima, Nijman, Merckelbach, Kremer, & Hollnack, 2004; Kopelman, 1995). Pretending to have no memory of an offence is often an elegant way to use the right to remain silent or to get a mitigated punishment. According to Tysse (2005), genuine amnesia could lead to an incompetency-to-stand-trial verdict because when someone has no memory of his crime, one cannot assist in one's own defence. He states that:

> someone who is unable to recall the facts, events and circumstances surrounding his alleged criminal act . . . his inability to testify to facts which may establish an effective alibi, or to offer evidence in excuse, justification or extenuation would seem to bring the amnesic clearly within the very purpose of the competency rule.
>
> (p. 336)

A well-known example of a case of feigned amnesia is the case of Rudolf Hess. This prominent Nazi leader simulated amnesia for his Third Reich period at the start of the Nuremberg trials. Hess successfully fooled several mental health experts into believing his amnesia was genuine. However, when he discovered that because of his feigned amnesia, he could not respond to allegations, Hess suddenly announced during his trial that he had been feigning his memory loss (Gilbert, 1971).

Similar to a feigned mental disorder, crime-related amnesia may be used as a strategy by defendants and convicts who think they may get personal gain from it. Especially those who are not yet convicted (pretrial) appear to use this strategy. In an exploratory study, it was found that amnesia claims were more frequent in people awaiting trial for a serious crime than in those convicted of such an offence (Van Oorsouw & Cima, 2007). In offenders sent to a forensic mental hospital, continuous feigning may obstruct therapy where remembering the crime plays an important role. Not recalling the crime prevents the development of offence pathways and the learning of relapse prevention strategies (Marshall, Serran, Marshall, & Fernandez, 2005).

Research has demonstrated that feigning amnesia may actually undermine genuine memories of a crime. That is, college students who were asked to feign amnesia for a mock crime recalled up to 20% fewer correct crime details when asked to respond honestly one week later as compared to cooperative participants who reported about the crime honestly from the beginning (Van Oorsouw & Merckelbach, 2004, 2006). Apparently, not recalling crime details as part of an amnesia strategy makes the crime memories more difficult to access at a later time.

A type of crime-related amnesia that is frequently claimed is memory loss due to an alcoholic blackout. Alcohol is reported to be implicated in about 50% of all violent crimes (Haggard-Grann, Hallqvist, Langstrom, & Moller, 2006). Sigurdsson and Gudjonsson (1994) found that 64% of the prisoners they interviewed were said to have been intoxicated at the time of their crime.

Several studies have indicated that alcohol intoxication seriously undermines memory of crime-related information (Van Oorsouw & Merckelbach, 2012). Even at moderate levels of intoxication (average blood alcohol concentrations (BACs) of 0.06%), participants recall 20% fewer correct crime details as compared to sober controls. At higher levels of intoxication (average BACs of 0.16%) recall was reduced by more than 30% compared to sober controls. However, this does not mean that we should blindly accept a claim of alcohol blackout in an intoxicated offender. A study that investigated the relation between BAC and blackout claims in driving under the influence (DUI) suspects demonstrated that 85% of the drivers who claimed an alcohol blackout had caused a serious car accident. In those who did not claim an alcohol blackout, 35% were involved in an accident. This suggests that claiming a blackout may serve a strategic purpose (Van Oorsouw, Merckelbach, Nijman, Ravelli, & Mekking-Pompen, 2004).

When an offender claims alcohol amnesia it is important to gather information about intoxication levels (BACs). Examining the characteristics of the amnesia may also provide clues about the veracity of crime-related amnesia (Jelicic & Merckelbach, 2007). In people with genuine memory loss, amnesic periods are usually gradual and blurred in onset and termination. Such people are usually able to recall fragments of events that occurred during their amnesic period. An amnesic episode of sudden onset and termination without 'islands of memory' would be suggestive of feigned amnesia. In contrast with feigners, people with bona fide memory loss often think that hints and cues might help to retrieve their lost memories. Sometimes, people feigning memory loss report amnesia not compatible with the neuropsychological literature (e.g. amnesia for basic personal facts such as one's own name or one's mother tongue). Note that absence of atypical amnesia characteristics does not always imply that the claimed crime-related amnesia is genuine. There is reason to believe that offenders with knowledge of real amnesia may feign memory loss in a convincing way.

Detecting deception and malingering

When confronted with an offender suspected of denial of symptoms (e.g. sex offenders), exaggeration of symptoms (e.g. in accountability assessment) or feigning of amnesia, several tools are available to the mental health expert to detect deception. First of all, self-report tests with embedded validity indicators such as the Minnesota Multiphasic Personality Inventory (MMPI-2; Butcher, Dahlstrom, Graham, Tellegen, & Kaemmer, 1989) can be used. This 567-item self-report inventory assesses personality traits and psychological symptoms, but also includes validity scales that assess underreporting of symptoms (L, K, S scales), over-reporting of, for example, depressive symptoms (Fb scale), rare symptoms reported in the general population (F scale) or psychiatric patients (Fp scale). The frequency scale (F) combined with the infrequency-psychopathology scale (Fp) can be used to evaluate the probability that the patient or defendant is malingering. Endorsement of a substantial number of items on the F scale (e.g. 'There is something wrong with my mind') would be suggestive of the exaggeration of psychological distress. In addition, the exaggeration of more subtle symptoms (e.g. 'No one seems to understand me') can be identified with the dissimulation scale (DS). Overall defensiveness and denial on certain MMPI scales can also be informative. Non-admitting sex offenders are often more defensive on the L and K scales compared to controls (Sewell & Salekin, 1997). Thus, the MMPI-2 profile can give an impression of a patient's tendency to distort his responses to exaggerate or deny psychopathology. However, interpreting the MMPI-2 requires extensive training.

The Structured Inventory of Malingered Symptomatology (SIMS; Smith & Burger, 1997) and the Structured Interview of Reported Symptoms (SIRS; Rogers, 1992) are other instruments that can be used to detect malingering. These instruments were developed to assess over-reporting of psychiatric and neurocognitive symptoms. The SIMS is a self-report questionnaire consisting of 75 items that screen for fabricated symptoms in the domains of low intelligence, affective disorder, neurological impairment, psychosis and amnesia. The items ask about bizarre and non-existing symptoms that are not reported by patients who genuinely suffer from these disorders. People exaggerating or fabricating their symptoms will more often respond with 'yes' to questions such as: 'Sometimes I lose all feeling in my hands so that it is as if I am wearing a glove'. When the total score on symptoms endorsed exceeds the cut-off, the person is suspected of malingering. Note that the SIMS should only be used as a screen for malingering. Especially in schizophrenic patients, a high SIMS score may not always be indicative of feigning (Peters, Jelicic, Moritz, Hauschildt, & Jelinek, 2013). Only when an abnormal SIMS score is backed by other test results and collateral information evidencing malingering can a person be labeled a malingerer (see Merckelbach, Peters, Jelicic, Brands, & Smeets, 2006). The SIRS works according to a similar principle as the SIMS, but with an interview format. Using 172 items which can be subdivided into eight scales tapping into rare, subtle, unusual and extreme symptoms, lack of symptoms and inconsistency between reported and observed symptoms (e.g. 'Is the government trying to keep track of your actions? Is it using military aircraft to do this?' and 'Do you become nervous and fidgety whenever you use the bathroom?'), this instrument also screens for malingered symptoms (Rogers, 2008). The SIRS also provides additional information about self-defensiveness, self-appraisal of honesty and inconsistent responding. The scores on the subscales can classify the examinee as feigning, not feigning or indeterminate.

Assessing deception in sex offenders is not a straightforward issue. The Multiphasic Sex Inventory (MSI-II; Nichols & Molinder, 1996) is a self-report instrument that assesses normal and sexually deviant interests. It includes six validity scales to identify persons who are defensive or who want to manipulate their findings. Yet little research has been conducted on the reliability and validity of these scales, thereby questioning their usefulness. Another under-researched method is the use of penile plethysmography (PPG) which measures penile erection in response to certain sexual stimuli. One could argue that PPG does not rely on conscious processes and the question of deception would therefore be irrelevant. It simply assesses the sexual deviant interest regardless of overt denial. However, there is considerable variability in PPG assessments which appears to be related to differences in testing procedures (Howes, 1995, 2003; Marshall & Fernandez, 2000). The more realistic the material, the more effective it is in eliciting a response. As one can imagine, using deviant assessment material (e.g. child pornography) for research purposes raises ethical discussions (see Seto, 2001). In some countries showing realistic assessment to offenders is therefore not allowed. Also, different types of sex offenders show different patterns of sexual arousal on PPG depending on their sexual preference. For example, rapists are difficult to identify using PPG because they often prefer erotic stimuli depicting consensual sex and not forced sexual acts (Looman, 2000). In addition, familial and non-familial pedophiles show different patterns of arousal to adult and child material (Blanchard et al., 2006). And what to conclude from non-responders? Non-responding could be related to anxiety about the criminal proceedings, but it could also be a consequence of deliberate obstruction of the test procedure. When instructed malingerers were asked about deceptive strategies used to suppress responding, many of them answered: 'avoiding looking at the stimulus' and 'generating alternative thoughts' (Lanyon & Thomas, 2008). Faking became more difficult when forced to look at the stimulus using a semantic tracking task. Despite attempts to increase the usefulness of PPG procedures, the conclusion remains that this technique cannot be regarded as an accurate measure to classify sex offenders. The method is not standardised, lacks reliability and is insufficient for individual classification in legal settings. In addition sex offenders are able to deceive on the PPG, and it is difficult to detect or prevent faking on this technique (Marshall & Fernandez, 2000, 2001).

Another measure to assess deception in sex offenders is the polygraph test. Despite criticism from the scientific community and the courts, this test has been shown to be useful in monitoring sex offenders postconviction. English and co-workers (2000 as cited in Lanyon & Thomas, 2008) demonstrated the effectiveness of this method by testing 180 sex offenders before and after postconviction polygraph testing. After the polygraph test, there was an increase of 80–200% in admitting sex crimes compared to before the test was administered. Admitting may benefit treatment and reduce recidivism. Thus, as long as the offenders believe that the polygraph can accurately detect deception, many of them will admit their offences. This 'bogus-pipeline' use of the polygraph has demonstrated its utility in several studies and may therefore be useful in the rehabilitation of sex offenders (see Gannon, Keown, & Polaschek, 2007).

To assess a person's tendency to simulate amnesia, the SIMS can be administered in combination with other tools designed to detect feigned memory problems. Examples of these instruments are the Test of Memory Malingering (TOMM; Tombaugh, 1996), the Amsterdam Short Term Memory test (ASTM; Schmand & Lindeboom, 2005), and the Word Memory Test (WMT; Green, Lees-Haley, & Allen, 2002). These tests require passive recognition of previously learned pictures or words. Because people with genuine memory disorders perform nearly perfectly on these tests, suboptimal performance on them may indicate that memory problems are being exaggerated. Note that a nontrivial percentage of bona fide psychiatric patients appear to score below the cut-off on the WMT (Gorissen, Sanz, & Schmand, 2005). Hence, an abnormal score on the TOMM, ASTM or WMT, just like a high SIMS score, does not necessarily mean that someone is malingering his memory problems. A person should not be labeled a malingerer unless an abnormal TOMM, ASTM or WMT score is backed by other test results and collateral information highly suggestive of malingering.

One limitation of the SIMS and other standard malinger instruments is that, in many criminal cases, the problem is not so much a global amnesia claim as an amnesia claim that specifically focuses on the crime. In such cases, the Symptom Validity Test (SVT; Denney, 1996) might be useful. SVT consists of a forced choice procedure in which offenders who claim amnesia are asked a series of questions about details of the crime and/or the crime scene. For each question, the offender must choose between two equally plausible answers – one of which is correct and the other of which is incorrect. Bona fide amnesia for a crime should result in random performance on the SVT. That is, true memory loss will result in approximately half of the answers being correctly answered. Below chance performance, in which the incorrect answer is chosen significantly more often than the correct one, indicates deliberate avoidance of correct answers, and, hence, preserved memory for the offence. SVT is based on binomial statistics, which has the clear advantage of quantifying memory performance. Thus, one can determine the exact probability that someone with genuine amnesia answers only seven of 25 true-false questions correctly (according to binomial statistics, this probability is less than 5%). Thus, below chance performance on an SVT procedure provides strong evidence for feigned memory loss for criminal acts.

Concluding remarks

In forensic assessments, it is necessary to take the possibility of faking good and bad into account. Several tests and tools are available to find out whether the examinee is exaggerating or denying their symptoms. Deception detection is often a complex issue. For example, the stage of the trial may affect an examinee's motivation to distort their responses (pre- or post-trial). By keeping these complexities in mind and by using a combination of assessment tools, the mental health expert may gain a good idea of the authenticity of the examinee's symptoms (or lack thereof).

Literature

American Psychiatric Association (2013). *Diagnostic and statistical manual of mental disorders* (5th ed.). Washington, DC: American Psychiatric Association.

Baker, A., Tabacoff, R., Tornusciolo, G., & Eisenstadt, M. (2003). Family secrecy: A comparative study of juvenile sex offenders and youth with conduct disorders. *Family Process, 42,* 105–116.

Barbaree, H.E., Marshall, W.L., & Hudson, S.M. (1993). *The juvenile sex offender.* New York: Guilford Press.

Berry, D.T.R., Bear, R.A., Rinaldo, J.C., & Wetter, M.W. (2002). Assessment of malingering. In J.N. Butcher (Ed.), *Clinical personality assessment: Practical approaches* (2nd ed., pp. 269–302). New York: Oxford University Press.

Bickley, J.A., & Beech, A.R. (2003). Implications for treatment of sexual offenders of the Ward and Hudson model of relapse. *Sexual Abuse: A Journal of Research and Treatment, 15,* 121–134.

Blanchard, R., Kuban, M.E., Blak, T., Cantor, J.M, Klasssen, P., & Dickey, R. (2006). Phallometric comparison of pedophilic interest in nonadmitting sexual offenders against stepdaughters, biological daughters, other biologically related girls, and unrelated girls. *Sexual Abuse: A Journal of Research and Treatment, 18,* 1–14.

Boon, J., Gozna, L., & Hall, S. (2008). Detecting 'faking bad' on the Gudjonsson Suggestibility Scales. *Personality and Individual Differences, 44,* 263–272.

Butcher, J.N., Dahlstrom, W.G., & Graham, J.R. (1989). *Manual for the restandardized Minnesota Multiphasic Personality Inventory: MMPI-2.* Minneapolis: University of Minnesota Press.

Cassidy, J.D., Carroll, L.J., Cote, P., Lemstra, M., Berglund, A., & Nygren, A. (2000). Effect of eliminating compensation for pain and suffering on the outcome of insurance claims for whiplash injury. *New England Journal of Medicine, 342,* 1179–1186.

Cima, M., Hollnack, S., Kremer, K., Knauer, E., Schellbach-Matties, R., Klein, B., & Merckelbach, H. (2003). Strukturierter Fragebogen Simulierter Symptome Die deutsche Version des Structured Inventory of Malingered Symptomatology. *SIMS, Nervenarzt, 11,* 977–986.

Cima, M., Merckelbach, H., Butt, C., Kremer, K., Knauer, E., & Schellbach-Matties, R. (2007). It was not me: Attribution of blame for criminal acts in psychiatric offenders. *Forensic Science International, 168,* 143–147.

Cima, M., Merckelbach, H., Nijman, H., Knauer, E., & Hollnack, S. (2002). I can't remember your honour: Offenders who claim amnesia. *German Journal of Psychiatry, 5,* 24–34.

Cima, M., Nijman, H., Merckelbach, H., Kremer, K., & Hollnack, S. (2004). Claims of crime-related amnesia in forensic patients. *International Journal of Law and Psychiatry, 27,* 215–221.

Cima, M., Pantus, M., & Dams, L. (2007). Simulation und Dissimulation in Abhängigkeit vom Strafrechtlichen Kontext und der persönlichkeit. *Praxis der Rechtspsychologie, 17,* 47–62 [Simulation and dissimulation depending on juridical context and personality traits].

Cima, M., Van Bergen, S., & Kremer, K. (2008). Development of the Supernormality Scale Revised and its relationship with psychopathy. *Journal of Forensic Science, 53,* 975–981.

154 *Kim Van Oorsouw et al.*

Cima, M., & Van Oorsouw, K. (2013). The relationship between psychopathy and crime-related amnesia. *International Journal of Law & Psychiatry, 36*, 23–29.

Cleckley, H.M. (1941). *The mask of sanity: An attempt to reinterpret the so-called psychopathic personality.* Saint Louis: MO. Mosby Company.

Conroy, M.A., & Kwartner, P.P. (2006). Malingering. *Applied Psychology in Criminal Justice, 2*, 29–51.

Curwen, T. (2003). The importance of offense characteristics, victimization history, hostility, and social desirability in assessing empathy of male adolescent sex offenders. *Sexual Abuse: A Journal of Research and Treatment, 15*, 347–364.

Decuyper, M., De Fruyt, F., & Buschman, J. (2008). A five-factor model perspective on psychopathy and comorbid Axis-II disorders in a forensic-psychiatric sample. *International Journal of Law and Psychiatry, 31*(5), 394–406.

Denney, R.L. (1996). Symptom validity testing of remote memory in a criminal forensic setting. *Archives of Clinical Neuropsychology, 11*, 589–603.

Edens, J.F., Buffington, J.K., & Tomicic, T.L. (2000). An investigation of the relationship between psychopathic traits and malingering on the psychopathic personality inventory. *Assessment, 7*, 281–296.

Friestad, C. (2012). Making sense, making good or making meaning? Cognitive distortions as targets of change in offender treatment. *International Journal of Offender Therapy and Comparative Criminology, 56*, 465–482.

Gacono, C.B., Meloy, J.R., Sheppard, K., Speth, E., & Roske, A. (1995). A clinical investigation of malingering and psychopathy in hospitalized NGRI patients. *Bulletin of the American Academy of Psychiatry and the Law, 23*, 387–397.

Gannon, T.A., Keown, K., & Polaschek, D.L. (2007). Increasing honest responding on cognitive distortions in child molesters: The bogus pipeline revisited. *Sexual Abuse, 19*, 5–22.

Gannon, T.A., Ward, T., & Collie, R. (2007). Cognitive distortions in child molesters: Theoretical and research developments over the past two decades. *Aggression and violent Behaviour, 12*, 402–416.

Gilbert, G.M. (1971). *Nürnberger Tagebuch: Gespräche der Angeklagten mit dem Gerichtspsychologen [Nurnberger Diary: Interviews of the accused with legal psychologists].* Frankfurt am Main: Fisher.

Gorissen, M., Sanz, J.C., & Schmand, B. (2005). Effort and cognition in schizophrenia patients. *Schizophrenia Research, 78*, 199–208.

Green, P., Lees-Haley, P.R., & Allen, L.M. (2002). The Word Memory Test and the validity of neuropsychological test scores. *Brain Injury, 15*, 1045–1060.

Haggard-Grann, U., Hallqvist, J., Langstrom, N., & Moller, J. (2006). The role of alcohol and drugs in triggering criminal violence: A case cross-over study. *Addiction, 101*, 100–108.

Hare, R.D. (1991). *The Hare Psychopathy Checklist-Revised manual.* Toronto, Canada: Multi-Health Systems.

Hare, R.D., & Neumann, C.S. (2009). Psychopathy: Assessment and forensic implications. *The Canadian Journal of Psychiatry, 54*, 791–802.

Howes, R.J. (1995). A survey of plethysmographic assessment in North America. *Sexual Abuse: A Journal of Research and Treatment, 7*, 9–24.

Iverson, G.L. (2006). Ethical issues associated with the assessment of exaggeration, poor effort, and malingering. *Applied Neuropsychology, 13*, 77–90.

Jelicic, M., & Merckelbach, H., (2007). Evaluating the authenticity of crime-related amnesia. In S.A. Christianson (Ed.), *Offenders' memory of violent crimes* (p. 215–234). Chichester: Wiley.

Kopelman, M.D. (1995). The assessment of psychogenic amnesia. In A.D. Baddeley, B.A. Wilson & F.N. Watts (Eds.), *Handbook of memory disorders* (pp. 427–448). New York: Wiley.

Kucharski, L.T., Duncan, S., Egan, S.S., & Falkenbach, D.M. (2006). Psychopathy and malingering of psychiatric disorder in criminal defendants. *Behavioural Sciences and the Law, 24,* 633–644.

Lanyon, R.I., & Thomas, M.L. (2008). Detecting deception in sex offender assessment. In R. Rogers, (Ed.), *Clinical Assessment of Malingering and Deception.* New York: Guilford.

Looman, J. (2000). Sexual arousal in rapists as measured by two stimulus sets. *Sexual Abuse: A Journal of Research and Treatment, 12,* 235–248.

Marshall, W.L., Serran, G., Marshall, L.E., & Fernandez, Y.M. (2005). Recovering memories of the offense in 'amnesic' sexual offenders. *Sexual Abuse: A Journal of Research and Treatment, 17,* 31–38.

Marshall, W.L., & Fernandez, Y.M. (2000). Phallometric testing with sexual offenders: Limits to its value. *Clinical Psychology Review, 20,* 807–822.

Marshall, W.L., & Fernandez, Y.M. (2001). Phallometry in forensic practice. *Journal of Forensic Psychology Practice, 1,* 77–87.

Merckelbach, H., Peters, M., Jelicic, M., Brands, I., & Smeets, T. (2006). Detecting malingering of Ganser-like symptoms with tests: A case study. *Psychiatry and Clinical Neurosciences, 60,* 636–638.

Mittenberg, W., Patton, C., Canyock, E.M., & Condit, D.C. (2002). Base rate of malingering and symptom exaggeration. *Journal of Clinical and Experimental Neuropsychology, 24,* 1094–1102.

Nichols, H.R., & Molinder, I. (1996). *Multiphasic sex inventory II handbook.* Tacoma, WA: Nichols & Molinder Assessments.

Peters, M.J.V., Jelicic, M., Moritz, S., Hauschildt, M., & Jelinek, L. (2013). Assessing the boundaries of over-reporting using the Structured Inventory of Malingered Symptomatology in a clinical schizophrenia sample: Its relationship with symptomatology and neurocognitive dysfunctions. *Journal of Experimental Psychopathology, 4,* 64–77.

Porter, S., & Woodworth, M. (2007). 'I'm sorry I did it . . . but he started it': A comparison of the official and self-reported homicide descriptions of psychopaths and non-psychopaths. *Law and Human Behaviour, 31,* 91–107.

Poythress, N.G., Edens, J.F., & Watkins, M.M. (2001). The relationship between psychopathic personality features and malingering symptoms of major mental illness. *Law and Human Behaviour, 25,* 567–582.

Rogers, R., Sewell, K., & Goldstein, A. (1994). Explanatory models of malingering: A prototypical analysis. *Law and Human Behaviour, 18,* 543–552.

Rogers, R. (1992). *Structured interview of reported symptoms.* Odessa, FL: Psychological Assessment Resources.

Rogers, R. (2008). An introduction to response styles. In R. Rogers (Ed.), *Clinical assessment of malingering and deception* (3rd ed., pp. 3–13). New York: Guilford.

Schacter, D.L. (1986). Feeling-of-knowing ratings distinguish between genuine and simulated forgetting. *Journal of Experimental Psychology: Learning, Memory, and Cognition, 9,* 39–54.

Schmand, B., & Lindeboom, J. (2005). *The Amsterdam Short Term Memory Test.* Leiden: PITS.

Schmand, B., Lindeboom, J., Schagen, S., Heijt, R., Koene, T., & Hamburger, H.L. (1998). Cognitive complaints in patients after whiplash injury: The impact of malingering. *Journal of Neurology, Neurosurgery, Psychiatry, 64,* 339–343.

Seto, M.C. (2001). The value of phallometry in the assessment of male sex offenders. *Journal of Forensic Psychology Practice, 1,* 65–75.

Sewell, K.W., & Salekin, R.T. (1997). Understanding and detecting dissimulation in sex offenders. In R. Rogers (Ed.), *Clinical assessment of malingering and deception* (2nd ed., pp. 328–350). New York: Guilford Press.

Sigurdsson, J.F., & Gudjonsson, G.H. (1994). Alcohol and drug intoxication during police interrogation and the reasons why suspects' confess to the police. *Addition, 89,* 985–997.

Smith, G.P., & Burger, G.K. (1997). Detection of malingering: Validation of the structured inventory of malingered symptomatology (SIMS). *Journal of American Academic Psychiatry and the Law, 25,* 183–189.

Tombaugh, T.N. (1996). *Test of memory malingering.* Los Angeles: Western Psychological Services.

Tysse, J.E. (2005). The right to an imperfect trial: Amnesia, malingering and competency to stand trial. *William Mitchell Law Review, 32,* 353–387.

Van Oorsouw, K., Merckelbach, H., Ravelli, D., Nijman, H., & Mekking-Pompen, I. (2004). Alcohol blackouts for criminally relevant behaviour. *Journal of the American Academy of Psychiatry and the Law, 32,* 364–370.

Van Oorsouw, K., & Cima, M. (2007). Expectations and claims of amnesia in psychiatric inmates. In S.A. Christianson (Ed.), *Offenders' memories of violent crimes* (pp. 191–213). Chichester: Wiley.

Van Oorsouw, K., & Merckelbach, H. (2004). Feigning amnesia undermines memory for a mock-crime. *Applied Cognitive Psychology, 18,* 505–518.

Van Oorsouw, K., & Merckelbach, H. (2006). Simulating amnesia and memories of a mock crime. *Psychology, Crime & Law, 12,* 261–271.

Van Oorsouw, K., & Merckelbach, H. (2010). Detecting malingered memory problems in the civil and criminal arena. *Legal and Criminological Psychology, 15,* 97–115.

Van Oorsouw, K., & Merckelbach, H. (2012). Effects of alcohol on crime-related memories: A field study. *Applied Cognitive Psychology, 26,* 82–90.

Vitacco, M.J., Neumann, C.S., & Jackson, R.L. (2005). Testing a four-factor model of psychopathy and its association with ethnicity, gender, intelligence, and violence. *Journal of Consulting and Clinical Psychology, 73,* 466–476.

Waldman, I.D., Singh, A.L., & Lahey, B.B. (2006). Dispositional dimensions and the causal structure of child and adolescent conduct problems. In R.R. Krueger & J.L. Tackett (Eds.), *Personality and psychopathology* (pp. 112–152). New York: Guilford Press.

Ward, T. (2000). Sexual offenders' cognitive distortions as implicit theories. *Aggression and Violent Behaviour, 5,* 491–507.

Ward, T., Gannon, T., & Keown, K. (2006). Beliefs, values and action: The judgment model of cognitive distortions in sexual offenders. *Aggression and Violent Behaviour, 1,* 232–340.

8 Aggression

*Franca Tonnaer, Maaike Cima
and Arnoud Arntz*

Introduction

Human aggression, violence and deviant behaviour are not only a great cost for society – up to $40.2 billion yearly only for England and Wales and 3.3% of the gross domestic product in America (Waters et al., 2004) – but have also great consequences for general health as they are among the world's foremost causes of death (Krug, Dahlberg, Mercy, Zwi, & Lozano, 2002). Moreover, violence is often stated as a preventable public health problem (Gilligan, 1997). A search for literature on human aggression shows that different terms, such as aggression and violence, are frequently used interchangeably (Perry, 2001), although they actually differ in meaning. Therefore, the current chapter starts by defining the different concepts. Furthermore, the current chapter will further outline several subtypes of aggression and explain the concept of impulsivity in the context of aggression and forensic risk assessment. Thereby, several developmental theories of aggression will be presented. More specifically, theories emphasising biological, psychological and social origins of aggression will be reported. The chapter will finally describe some interventions for aggressive problem behaviour.

Concept

Violence is defined by the World Health Organization as the 'intentional use of physical force or power, threatened or actual, against a person, or against a group or community, that either results in or has a high likelihood of resulting in injury, death, psychological harm, maldevelopment or deprivation' (Krug et al., 2002, p. 4).

Aggression can be defined as 'hostile, injurious or destructive behaviour' (Siever, 2008, p. 429). While violence and aggression are both defined as behaviour, violence explicitly includes the use of physical force or power towards someone or a group. Aggression is a broader concept also comprising verbal aggression, non-directed behavioural acts out of frustration and threat. Thus, violence includes aggression, but not all aggression results in violence. Another important qualification for behaviour to be perceived as aggressive or violent is the violation of normative believes and shared rules of society

158 *Franca Tonnaer et al.*

(Tedeschi, Gaes, & Rivera, 1977). Behaviour that is prohibited, criminal and in violation of normative believes and social rules is defined as *deviant behaviour* (Perry, 2001).

Aggression can be described referring to its style or response modulation including verbal aggression, physical aggression and sexual aggression; its immediacy with direct versus indirect aggression; its instigation as unprovoked versus retaliate aggression; the duration of consequences as transient or long-term; its type of harm as physical versus psychological; its visibility as overt and covert aggression; its response quality as action versus failure to act aggressive; and the target of the aggression, self-directed or other directed (Siever, 2008; Krahé, 2001).

Subtypes of aggression

Within the concept of aggression, different subtypes exist. The most frequently stated subtypes are those defined by its goal direction, reactive vs. proactive (Babcock, Sharp, Tharp, Hepner, & Stanford, 2014). Reactive aggression indicates spontaneous and emotion-driven responses to perceived threats (Cima & Raine, 2009), and proactive aggression refers to forethought and planned, goal-directed aggression (Raine et al., 2006). Reactive aggression is also called hostile, impulsive, injurious, destructive, instinct or angry aggression (Anderson & Bushman, 2002), in which there is a lack of regulating anger (Cima & Siep, in press), while proactive aggression is often called instrumental aggression as it is used to obtain some goal other than harming the victim per se (Berkowitz, 1993). In this type of aggression anger is often overregulated, in the sense that aggression is controllably focused to accomplish certain goals, in the presence of lacking empathy. This distinction between reactive and proactive aggression is not only present in psychology, but also in law settings where it refers to 'one single act' (e.g. murder) which can either be reactive (e.g. manslaughter) or proactive (e.g. first degree murder, Cima & Raine, 2009, p. 383).

Although reactive and proactive aggression refer to underlying motives of behaviour (driven by defence or driven by deliberate purpose) in which certain individuals tend to display primarily reactive or primarily proactive aggression, in practice they often overlap (an aggressive act can have aspects of both types) and tend to co-occur in individuals (Hubbard, Morrow, Romano, Meghan, & McAuliffe, 2010). Distinguishing subtypes of aggression is nevertheless useful (Cima & Raine, 2009), since they indicate certain episodes of aggression instead of fixed traits (Hubbard et al., 2010), which might be useful in directing treatment choice (Barker et al., 2010). A process that plays an important role in reactive aggression is impulsivity.

Aggression and impulsivity

The self-control theory of crime or the general theory of crime relates aggression to impulsivity and thereby focuses on reactive, impulsive aggression.

More specifically, it states that crime is a result of a lack of self-control, by an impulsive personality and in criminal opportunities (Gottfredson & Hirschi, 1990). Moreover, research shows that a lack of self-control (impulsivity) indeed is a core factor in predicting crime (Pratt & Cullen, 2000; Vazsonyi & Belliston, 2007). Furthermore, research has demonstrated a relation between impulsivity and aggression or violent crime (Lane & Cherek, 2000; Scarpa & Raine, 2000; Swann & Hollander, 2002). There is, however, little consensus regarding the definition of impulsivity. For example, Evenden (1999) introduced 28 terms to describe impulsivity. The International Society for Research on Impulsivity (ISRI) defines impulsivity as: 'behaviour without adequate thought, the tendency to act with less forethought than do most individuals of equal ability and knowledge, or a predisposition towards rapid, unplanned reactions to internal or external stimuli without regard to the negative consequences of these reactions'. Recently an impulsivity model was presented, including three distinctive impulsivity dimensions capturing various impulsive behaviours ranging from sensation seeking to impulsive decision making and response (dis)inhibition (Tonnaer, Cima, & Arntz, 2015b). In fact, research on this three-dimensional impulsivity model showed that the impulsivity dimension '(inadequate) Response Inhibition' was the essential predictor for reactive aggressive behaviour (Tonnaer, Cima, & Arntz, 2015c), again showing that a lack of impulse control is associated with aggressive actions (Gottfredson & Hirschi, 1990).

Clinical practice also shows a clear link between impulse control problems and aggressive behaviour (Swann & Hollander, 2002). For example, the *Diagnostic and Statistical Manual of Mental Disorders* (DSM-5, APA, 2013) includes a category of impulsive control disorders such as pyromania and pathological gambling, but also incorporates the intermitted explosive disorder ([IED], APA, 2013). The IED is characterised by frequent episodes of extreme anger or physical outburst leading to destructiveness or violence. Importantly, the reactive impulsive aggression in the intermitted explosive disorder is defined as a disproportionate reaction to provocation.

Impulsive reactive aggression is driven by lack of anger regulation. Several studies have shown neurocognitive correlates of underlying anger (e.g. Denson, Perderson, Ronquillo, & Nandy, 2009; Fabiansson, Denson, Moulds, Grisham, & Schira, 2012; Lindquist et al., 2012). Until recently, neurocognitive studies regarding impulsivity and reactive aggression reported an imbalance between prefrontal cortical control and excessive bottom-up signals of negative affect by limbic regions (Raine et al., 1998). In a study of Dambacher et al. (2014) examining neural mechanisms underlying lack of self-control, an overlap of neural correlates for failed motor response inhibition and reactive aggression in healthy subjects was located at the anterior insula, indicating that this brain area is involved in both motor impulsivity and reactive aggression. A recent functional imaging study regarding resting-state within aggressive violent offenders focusing on reactive aggression showed that an anger provocation significantly increased amygdala connectivity with

160   *Franca Tonnaer et al.*

(para)limbic regions in a violent offender group and decreased connectivity in a non-violent control group (Siep, Tonnaer, van de Ven, Arnzt, & Cima, 2015). Prior to the provocation, connectivity within the violent offender group was stronger, while after provocation, results showed a significant decrease in amygdala–medial prefrontal functional connectivity in the violent group but an increase in the control group. These results point to a dominance of emotion processes in reactive aggression, in which the emotional processes seem to have the potential to grow out of control (especially when provoked), as indicated by the lack a of medial prefrontal cortex regulation (Siep et al., 2015). These types of studies, in which violent subjects are provoked into an anger state to elicit aggressive behaviour while examining neurocognitive correlates, are important to understand the biological underlying mechanisms of reactive aggression.

Theories regarding the development of aggression: short historical overview

Instinct

In 1920 Freud described the dual instinct theory in his book named *Beyond the Pleasure Principle* (Freud, 1955). In his view, behaviour is driven by instincts. Based on biological processes ('drives'), energy builds up and has to be released. Aggression was viewed by Freud as a primary reactive drive (Thompson, Arora, & Sharp, 2002). Acting out aggressively is a way to release, but as it is often forbidden people usually develop other ways to deal with it – these ways are called 'defence mechanisms'. An individual acts aggressively to obtain intrapsychic stability. However, the theory has been criticised because it lacks operational definitions, and empirical evidence largely builds on case studies without stringent operationalisation. Nevertheless, the Freudian approach was a source of inspiration for the frustration–aggression hypothesis (Krahé, 2001).

The *frustration-aggression hypothesis* as proposed by Dollard, Doob, Miller, Mowrer, and Sears (1939) describes aggression as a result of frustration. In the view of Dollard and colleagues frustration – as an emotional experience – is created when an external trigger interferes with goal-directed behaviour. Frustration subsequently activates the desire to act aggressively, leading to reactive aggressive behaviour against the source of frustration (Vitaro & Brendgen, 2005). Research has indeed demonstrated a relationship between frustration and aggression, with frustration leading to more reactive aggressive behaviour (Berkowitz & LePage, 1967). However, this theory is quite stringent, stating that 'aggression always presupposes the existence of frustration' and 'contrawise, that the existence of frustration always leads to some form of aggression' (Dollard et al., 1939, p. 1). Not surprisingly, in 1994, the founders of the frustration–aggression hypothesis – driven by Miller – nuanced the original statement in two ways: first, they state that frustration can initiate aggression, but doesn't automatically result in aggressive behaviour. For instance, aggressive behaviour can be inhibited by the notion of punishment. Second, they modified the statement that frustration always causes aggression, now claiming that frustration can cause a number of different reactions in which aggression is one, but not the only (Miller, Sears, Mowrer, Doob, & Dollard, 1941). Even so, either version of the frustration–aggression hypotheses did not receive consistent empirical support (Baron, 1977). Lorenz (1974) was the first to offer an *aetiological model of aggression*. His model – sometimes described as a hydraulic model of emotional or instinctive pressures – described how a constant input of aggressive energy within an individual leads to aggressive behaviour based on the intensity of the trigger and the quantity of aggression. Although Lorenz believed that aggression was innate, originating from the failure of a certain instinct but not necessary reactive, current literature classifies his theory as a theory of reactive aggression (Dodge, 2006). However, Lorenz's theory has been criticised because of the lack of operational definitions. Lorenz did not define aggressive energy, and neither did he present a way of measuring the amount of energy presented in an individual, making it impossible to test his theory.

In 1989 Berkowitz reformulated the frustration–aggression hypotheses to the *cognitive neoassociation theory (CNT)*, a new aggression theory based on the relation between frustration and aggression. Although Berkowitz proposed his theory explaining merely hostile aggression, it is also relevant to other types of aggression. Berkowitz states that all aversive events – frustration, but also provocations, pain, loud noises, uncomfortable temperature – empower negative affect, which is a powerful instigator of anger and aggression (Berkowitz, 1989, 1990, 1993). In his view, negative affect automatically triggers diverse thoughts, memories, expressive motor reactions and physiological responses associated with both fight and flight reactions. The fight reactions do have an aggressive nature, where the flight reactions have a nature of fear. In memory, concepts with related connotations or concepts triggered together automatically form an associative network and become more strongly associated. Aversive primes triggered during fight reactions, as well as the actual responses, become associated with an event, linking aggressive thoughts, emotions and behavioural tendencies to each other in memory (Collins & Loftus, 1975). For example, in memory a link between angry feelings and approach motivation – more specifically, the motivation to approach the source of anger – is formed, leading to stronger memory associations for approach in case of aversive events. The CNT incorporates higher-order cognitive processes such as appraisal (e.g. considering the consequences of an aggressive act) and causal attributions (e.g. exploring the cause of negative affect) but refers to aggressive behaviour as an automatic, uncontrolled reaction to an aversive event (Anderson, Bushman, 2002). So, the CNT not only includes the frustration–aggression hypothesis (Dollard et al., 1939), but broadens it to aversive experiences in general, and provides a broadly applicable cognitive concept on the cause of reactive aggression. It thus gives an explanatory framework for aggressive preference in specific individuals (Berkowitz, 1989).

162 *Franca Tonnaer et al.*

Social theories

The social learning theory (Bandura, 1983; Mischel, 1973) states that individuals learn aggressive behaviour in the same way as they learn other complex forms of social behaviour, either by direct experience or by observing others. The learning theory offers useful concepts explaining aggression by describing the beliefs and expectations driving social behaviour (Anderson & Bushman, 2002). For instance, Bandura did not believe that individuals have an aggressive nature, but that both reactive and proactive aggression is learned by instrumental conditioning in which behaviour is influenced by its consequences and reinforcement, and modelled by the observation of aggressive models (Bandura & Ribes-Inesta, 1976).

A related social theory attributing behaviour to the social habitat is the *differential association theory*, developed by Sutherland (1939). Sutherland believed that criminal 'definitions' or associations are learned by interaction with other deviant individuals, causing an overexposure to rationale, motives etc. favouring crime-related 'definitions' above pro social ones. His theory is most useful in explaining deviance, and both reactive and proactive aggression in adolescent and youth groups due to peer influence and exposure to criminal behaviour. However, there are many comments on the theory, with the lack of defining the core concept 'definitions' and the mechanisms involved in learning criminal behaviour as the main critique along with the lack of empirical support (Akers & Lee, 1996; Pfohl, 1994). Moreover, the theory lacks an explanation on the origin of criminal behaviour (Warr & Stafford, 1991).

Another theory focusing on the labelling of information as the former described excitation transfer theory is the *labelling theory*. This theory shifts the focus from the individual to its social environment, stating that deviance is not intrinsic but socially determined behaviour. Becker (1963) described this by stating that:

> Social groups create deviance by making the rules whose infraction constitutes deviance, and by applying those rules to particular people and labelling them as outsiders. From this point of view, deviance is not a quality of the act the person commits, but rather a consequence of the application by others of rules and sanctions to an 'offender'. The deviant is one to whom that label has successfully been applied; deviant behaviour is behaviour that people so label.
>
> (Becker, 1963, p. 9)

Thus, individuals are labelled by groups and behaviour is judged in accordance with the stereotypes of this group. In other words, aggressive behaviour, either reactive or proactive, is defined by the norms of the group, and not by some forces inside the individual. The most prominent critique of the labelling theory is given by Sagarin (1975), stating that an individual is more than only a label. Furthermore, this labelling theory ignores the process of becoming deviant.

Still another theory explaining aggression as a social learning process is the *social interaction theory (of coercive action)* introduced by Tedeschi and Felson in 1994 which focuses on proactive, instrumental aggression. They describe proactive aggression as aggression used to protect someone's positive self-identity as toughness by means of threat, punishment or bodily force. The type of response is a decision-making process based on past learning experiences, weighing the costs of aggressive behaviour (Anderson & Bushman, 2002).

Lastly, according to the *script theory* (Tomkins, 1954), reactive as well as proactive aggression can be learned by the acquisition of scripts. The theory proposes that behaviour is based on scripts, representing specific behavioural patterns. Scripts are sets of repeatedly associated concepts in memory, used to guide our behaviour (Anderson & Bushman, 2002; Schank & Abelson, 1997). The more specific sets are associated, the stronger the connection between the concepts, possibly forming a unitary concept. Even few repetitions might change individual expectations and behavioural intentions (Marsh, Hicks, & Bink, 1998). Huesmann (1988) states that when youngsters are presented with aggressive scripts, e.g. in video games of the mass media, they learn aggressive scripts, ultimately believing that aggressive behaviour is a normal response.

Biological theories

On a neurobiological level, a prominent theory concerning the aetiological and biological origin of aggression is the *frontal lobe dysfunction theory* (e.g. Hawkins & Trobst, 2000; Séguin, 2013; Swann & Hollander, 2002), which proposes a relation between dysfunctional abnormalities in the frontal brain regions related to reactive aggression and increased aggressive antisocial behaviour (Blair, 2004; Brower & Price, 2001). More specifically, the frontal lobe dysfunction theory refers to deficits in frontal lobe functioning that lead to inhibition problems and therefore to increased aggression (Barratt, 1994; Blair, 2004; Raine, Lencz, Bihrle, Lacasse, & Colletti, 2000). Indeed, a series of brain imaging studies have supported the notion of reduced cortical inhibition in violent offenders (Raine, Buchsbaum, & Lacasse, 1997; Raine et al., 2000). In particular, research has focused on the role of the medial prefrontal cortex (mPFC) and reactive aggression, which is strongly associated with impulse control and self-regulation (Bobadilla, Wampler, & Taylor, 2012). The frontal lobe dysfunction theory is supported by brain imaging studies showing abnormalities in the frontal lobe in persons displaying reactive aggression (Brower & Price, 2001). However, not all persons with prefrontal lesions show aggressive behaviour (Raine et al., 2000). Often these studies do not distinguish between different forms of frontal lobe dysfunctions like encoding of emotional material (e.g. happy vs. angry; Guastella, Kenyon, Alvares, Carson, & Hickie, 2010) or emotion recognition (e.g. stressors; Raine et al., 2000). Up to now, no study has reliably demonstrated a characteristic pattern of frontal network dysfunction predictive of violent crime in offenders (Brower & Price, 2001). However, literature reviews of functional and structural neuroimaging

164   *Franca Tonnaer et al.*

studies show distinct functional pathways for anger experience and anger perception (Lindquist, Wager, Kober, Bliss-Moreau, & Barrett, 2012) and support the frontal lobe dysfunction theory, implying that a combination of decreased medial prefrontal activity (the orbitofrontal, the anterior medial, medial frontal and superior frontal cortex) along with increased subcortical activity (the medial-temporal lobe, including the amygdala, hippocampus and basal ganglia) is related to antisocial behaviour and reactive aggression (see also below: '*aggression and impulsivity*'; Bufkin & Luttrell, 2005; Fabian, 2010).

Research on *autonomic reactivity and psychophysiology* suggests a link between under arousal – e.g. low resting heart rate and skin conductance – and aggressive behaviour (Glenn, Raine, Venables, & Mednick, 2007; King, 2012). This is in accordance with the earlier mentioned excitation transfer theory (Zillmann, 1983), giving a central role for arousal and the cognitive judgement of the experienced arousal leading to aggressive behaviour. It is believed that individual variability in arousal levels influence their behaviour to maintain an optimal arousal level (Kohn, Cowles, & Lafreniere, 1987).

Also, a *hormonal influence* on aggressive behaviour is suggested (King, 2012). Most research focuses on testosterone and cortisol. Testosterone is one of the steroid male hormones from the androgen group. Research on sex differences in aggressive behaviour during adolescence suggests a strong role for testosterone (Archer, 2009; Terburg, Morgan, & van Honk, 2009; Terburg, Peper, Morgan, & van Honk, 2009). Higher levels of testosterone have been associated with higher dominance behaviour, aggression in response to provocation, and sexual and violent offending (Englander, 2003; Mehta & Beer, 2009). More specifically, research suggests a link between testosterone and the control of aggressive responding, with administering testosterone resulting in more aggressive responses (Archer, 2009; Kouri, Lukas, Pope, & Olivia, 1995; Mehta & Beer, 2009). Testosterone is positively associated with the tendency of a person to respond aggressively, due to reduced activation of the neural circuitry of impulse control and self-regulation located in the medial orbitofrontal cortex (Mehta & Beer, 2009). A recent study focusing on reactive aggression showed a mediating effect for testosterone, with reduced testosterone levels mediating positive intervention programme effects in social provocations (Carré, Iselin, Welker, Hariri, & Dodge, 2014). In contrast, *low* cortisol levels have been linked to general aggressive behaviour, especially in males (Cima, Smeets, & Jelicic, 2008; Cima, Nicolson, de Lijster, & Popma, 2015; Feilhauer, Cima, Korebrits, & Nicolson, 2013; King, 2012; Poustka et al., 2010). Cortisol hormone levels reflect the stress reactivity in the hypothalamic–pituitary–adrenal (HPA) axis of the individual (Poustka et al., 2010). Apparently, low stress responses are associated with aggressive behaviour, which is apparently at odds with theories stating that high arousal fuels aggression. Moreover, research reveals an intertwined relationship between aggressive behaviour and reactive as well as proactive and both testosterone and cortisol levels (Terburg et al., 2009). For instance, Popma and colleagues (2007) found that cortisol moderates the relationship between testosterone and aggression in male delinquent adolescents. They found that only individuals with low cortisol levels showed a relation between testosterone and aggression (Popma et al., 2007). Another example is given by Pavlov, Chistiakov, and Chekhonin (2012), who found that an imbalance in the testosterone and cortisol ratios in the sense of increased testosterone levels and reduced cortisol levels enhances the tendency towards reactive aggressive behaviour, due to a reduced activation of the neural circuitry of impulse control. These findings led to a testosterone-cortisol hypothesis of reactive aggression (van Honk, Harmon-Jones, Morgan, & Schutter, 2010) in which the combination of high levels of testosterone and low levels of cortisol predisposes one to aggression by means of threat perception, biases towards punishment or reward, and an increase or decrease in neuronal control over subcortical structures (Montaya, Terburg, Bos, & van Honk, 2012). Moreover, testosterone mediates aggression by increasing the vasopressin gene expression at the amygdala, which is hypothesised to facilitate aggressive approach behaviour (Schulkin, 2003).

Turning to the *neurotransmitters*, recently, serotonin (5-hydroxytryptamine; 5-HT; Bevilacque et al., 2010; Montoya et al., 2012; van Honk et al., 2010) but also dopamine and serotonin have been related to especially reactive aggression (King, 2012). Dopamine has a function in the neural reward system, and high dopamine levels reduce the threshold to respond to a perceived threat, increasing the readiness for reactive aggressive response (Pavlov et al., 2012). However, serotonin facilitates prefrontal inhibition, and as a result, increased serotonin activity inhibits aggression. Lowered serotonin activity can enhance aggressive responses (Summers et al., 2005), especially in those individuals prone to reactive aggression due to a high testosterone-cortisol ratio (Montoya et al., 2011; van Honk et al., 2010). Serotonin seems especially relevant in relation to self-control. In a study of Seo, Patrick, and Kennealy (2008) it was demonstrated that low serotonin might be a vulnerability factor for impulsive aggression, in which high levels of dopamine contribute additionally to this serotonergic insufficiency. Returning to biological factors, twin and adoptive studies (Miles & Carey, 1997) have indicated that heritable factors influence a person's tendency to behave aggressively. These types of studies for instance showed genetic components as shared genes better explained (up to 50%) aggressive behaviour than family and other environmental factors could (Crowe, 1975; Miles & Carey, 1997). For instance, adult criminal adoptees whose biological as well as adoptive parents were criminal had the highest likelihood of becoming criminal themselves, followed by criminal adoptees whose biological parents, but not adoptive parents had criminal records (Cloninger, Sigvardsson, Bohman, & von Knorring, 1982). Further, the influence of genetic and family environment varied with age, with genetic factors become increasingly important with age (Miles & Carey, 1997). These results differ from reviews of adoption studies and the intergeneration transmission of violent behaviour (Mednick, Brennan, & Kandel, 1988), but they are broadly consistent with more recent studies on a genetic component in antisocial behaviour. These studies show relationships between delinquency,

166   Franca Tonnaer et al.

criminality, and antisocial personality in the sense that adopted children whose biological parents were diagnosed with antisocial personality disorder tend to have higher rates of antisocial behaviour themselves (Kline, 2004; Taylor, Loney, Bobadilla, Iacono, & McGue, 2003). On the other hand, the failure to detect specific genes that explain the heritability suggested by these studies, despite the enormous amounts of money and effort put into human genome research, has created a crisis in the field. As yet, it is unclear what explains the heritability findings from twin and adoption studies.

Integrative theories

In contrast to the learning theories on the origins of aggression, the *excitation transfer theory* (Zillmann, 1983), originating from Schachter and Singer's (1962) two-factor theory of emotion, is a biological oriented theory stating that emotion is a function of both cognitive factors and physiological arousal. According to this theory, reactive aggression is the experiencing of physiological arousal including the transfer of arousal from environmental emotional cues (Schachter & Singers, 1962). Likewise, Zillmann (1983) argued that a combination of physiological arousal and cognitive judgement shapes the emotional experience of anger. The level of arousal determines the intensity of the emotional response while the labelling of arousal is essentially determining the kind of emotion. Interestingly, mislabelling by transferring arousal from a neutral or even irrelevant source to the arousal elicited by an aversive stimulation can cause a longer and stronger experience of anger (Anderson & Bushman, 2002). This may extend over long periods of time if the heightened arousal is labelled consciously to anger, making an individual ready to aggress even when the source of anger is gone.

A related theory searching for aetiologically determined reactive aggression and the central role of self-control is the *self-control theory of crime*, often referred to as *the general theory of crime*. The theory developed by Gottfredson and Hirschi (1990) proposes crime to be a result of a lack of self-control, an impulsive personality and criminal opportunities. Most crime has an impulsive, opportunistic nature, showing a lack of control. In the quest for the origin of crime, Gottfredson and Hirschi (1990) pointed to the strong relationship between criminal behaviour and age, with self-control improving with age due to several components such as hormonal development and socialisation (Hirschi & Gottfredson, 1983). Empirical evidence has suggested that a lack of self-control (impulsivity) indeed is a core factor in predicting crime (Baumeister & Vohs, 2007; Pratt & Cullen, 2000; Vazsonyi & Belliston, 2007). The prefrontal cortex enables self-control in humans. As mentioned above, aggressive behaviour is also associated with deficits in the basal-orbital prefrontal cortex (Damasio, Grabowski, Frank, Galaburda, & Damasio, 1994). This brain area involves a dopaminergic neuronal circuit, which underlies reactivity, arousal modulation and attention modulation. In children prenatally exposed to cocaine, this pathway seems disrupted related to a general aggressive behavioural tendency later in life (Mayes, 1999; Bendersky, Bennett, & Lewis, 2006). Other prenatal factors related to the development of aggression and antisocial behaviour include prenatal depression (Hay, Pawlby, Waters, Perra, & Sharp, 2010), alcohol (Streissguth, Barr, Bookstein, Sampson, & Olson, 1999), smoking (Huijbregts, Seguin, Zoccolillo, Boivin, & Tremblay, 2008) and stress (Zohsel et al., 2013). Such biological-environmental factors influence the brain make-up of the child, and constitute one group of factors that result in individual child differences regarding the degree in which they are vulnerable to their environment. For instance, maltreatment in children has been related to aggressive antisocial behaviour in some, but not all cases (see Box 8.1 for an example of a gen X environment interaction example).

As to the different aetiological theories regarding aggression, the *differential susceptibility theory* may best explain why some individuals develop reactive and/ or proactive aggressive response tendencies while others do not. According to this theory, individuals with a biological predisposition are sensitive to both negative as well as positive environmental influences. For instance, similarly to the study of Caspi et al. (2002; see Box 8.1), in a study of Bakermans-Kranenburg and Ijzendoorn (2006) the effect of genes (dopamine receptor D4 7-repeat polymorphism; DRD4-7R) in combination with the sensitivity of the mother was examined in relation to externalising behaviour including aggression. The authors reported that children with the DRD4-7R allele in combination with an insensitive mother demonstrated more externalised behaviour compared to children with the same allele but sensitive mothers. Children with the DRD4-7R allele and sensitive mothers showed the least externalised disorders, while the sensitivity of the mother had no effect on children without this DRD4-7R allele.

Many hypotheses about what genetic and other biological factors determine children's vulnerability have been proposed, but after promising results the initial enthusiasm has been dampened due to the failure to replicate early findings (Duncan & Keller, 2011; Duncan, Pollastri, & Smoller, 2014). At the moment, despite the attractiveness of the theory, it is not clear what biological factors exactly influence the child's vulnerability to environmental influences.

Box 8.1   Interaction of vulnerability and environmental influences

Maltreated children with low MAO-A levels were more likely to develop antisocial behaviour later on in life, compared to children who were also maltreated but had high MAO-A levels. These results suggest that traumatised stressful experiences may be a risk factor in some but not all cases of victims, and that the person's sensitivity to negative environmental factors seems moderated by their genetic makeup (Caspi et al., 2002).

(continued)

168   *Franca Tonnaer et al.*

> *(continued)*
>
> This also accords with a more recent study by Obradovic, Bush, Stamperdahl, Adler, and Boyce (2010) in which 5-year-old children with elevated levels of cortisol reactivity were identified by their teachers as less prosocial when they were raised under adverse conditions. When these children were raised under better circumstances, they displayed the most prosocial behaviour even in comparison with children with low cortisol reactivity. These findings indicate that more vulnerable individuals are more sensitive to environmental influences, both associated with negative as well as positive surroundings.

In 2002, Anderson and Bushman integrated some of the above-mentioned theories (as the cognitive neoassociation theory, the social learning theory, the script theory, the social interaction theory and the excitation transfer theory) on aggression into one social cognitive model named the *General Aggression Model* (GAM, Anderson & Bushman, 2002), as a framework for understanding reactive as well as proactive aggression and violence. According to the GAM, aggression can be learned either by instrumental conditioning (Bandura & Ribes-Inesta, 1976), by learning to label information (Becker, 1963), by attributing behaviour to asocial habitat (Sutherland, 1939), by social interaction (Tedeschi & Felson, 1994) or by frequent confrontation with aggressive scripts (Huesmann, 1988).

The model distinguished three different learning structures. First, *perceptual schemata* are used to identify everyday psychical objects; second, *person schemata* consist of beliefs of individuals and stereotypes; third, *behavioural scripts* contain behavioural guides. Furthermore, the GAM recognises four different stages in explaining aggressive behaviour (see Figure 8.1, re-used from Krahé (2013)), namely (1) *input variables* coming from (a) the individual ('person') and (b) input from the environment ('situation'); (2) cognitive, affective and arousal information *processing* routes; (3) several complex *decision processes and (re)appraisal* from relative automatic processes as immediate appraisal to more controlled cognitive processes as reappraisal (Anderson & Bushman, 2002) determining response expression, leading to (4) either thoughtful, proactive or impulsive reactive action *outcomes*. It is important to note that the focus of the model is on aggression, and all elements described in the GAM are denoted towards aggressive behaviour, but the opposite perspective like anti-aggressive beliefs and attitudes is equally important (Anderson & Carnagey, 2004). The idea is that because the GAM integrated various theories that each focus on a different aspect of aggression, it is more inclusive and capable of explaining aggressive acts based on multiple motives. Likewise, its integrated view on aggression demands comprehensive interventions targeting the multiple influential factors and developmental trajectories responsible for aggressive behaviour (Anderson & Bushman, 2002).

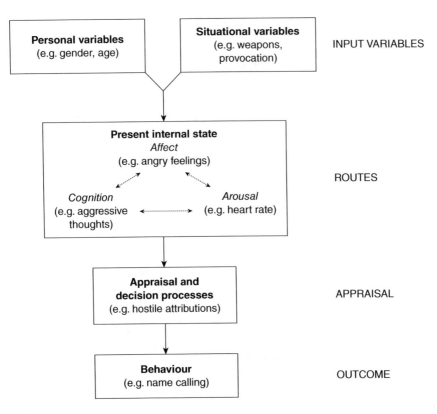

Figure 8.1 The General Aggression Model

Interventions

Most interventions focus on reactive aggression (Buchmann, Hohmann, Brandeis, Banaschewski, & Poustka, 2014), while prevention primarily focuses on proactive aggression (Henggeler, Cunningham, Pickrel, Schoenwald, & Brondino, 1996). However, interventions based on cognitive behavioural approaches and aimed to alter cognitions like Aggression Replacement Training (ART; Goldstein, 1996) and Stress Inoculation Treatment (SIT; Novaco, 1975) are promising in reducing reactive as well as proactive aggressive behaviour (de Ruiter & Hildebrand, 1999). ART is a programme originally targeting juvenile delinquents in penitentiary institutions by improving their anger management by anger-control training, social skills training and moral reasoning training (Goldstein, 1996; National Center, 2007). ART is a multimodal treatment empowering the adolescent using aspects of the learning theory as observations. Another multimodal treatment combining cognitive and affective coping strategies is the SIT for anger management in stressful events (Novaco, 1975). The SIT empowers individuals by training them in coping techniques

170   *Franca Tonnaer et al.*

such as cognitive restructuring, relaxation training, interpersonal communication skills training and training in using social support systems (Meichenbaum, 1996). A recent meta-analysis showed that such cognitive behavioural treatment techniques are effective in decreasing aggression (Smeets et al., 2014), and reactive as well as proactive (Down, Willner, Watts, & Griffiths, 2011). Smeets and colleagues (2014) also examined possible moderators in predicting treatment response. Although no significant predictors were identified, better standardisation of predictors and outcome measures across studies is required to be able to reliably recognise responders and non-responders to aggression reduction treatment.

Interventions not only focusing on the individual but also on their interactions with others like multisystemic therapy (MST; Borduin, 1999; Henggeler, Schoenwald, Borduin, Rowland, & Cunningham, 1998) seem to present encouraging results. MST is home-based family therapy based on Bronfenbrenner's (1979) theory of social ecology combined with interventions on empirical known risk factors (such as criminal environment, low intelligence, school dropout etc.) for antisocial behaviour in youth (Henggeler, Cunningham, Pickrel, Schoenwald, & Brondino, 1996; Lahey, Moffitt, & Caspi, 2003; see also Chapter 5). MST focuses on the family, school, community and peers as a system and not solely on the adolescent with antisocial behavioural problems. Therefore, the parents are coached in interventions as showing more warmth and learning how to more effectively discipline their children (Curtis, Ronan, & Borduin, 2004; Henggeler et al., 1996). Results of a meta-analysis on the effectiveness of MST did show that MST is indeed effective, with families that received MST versus alternatives functioning up to 70% better (Curtis et al., 2004). Even more promising, earlier research demonstrated long-term reductions in criminal activity and general aggression after MST (Henggeler et al., 1996, p. 1). Additionally, results also showed that MST is most effective in targeting family relations more than in individual adjustment or peer relations (Curtis et al., 2004).

Interventions tapping into a neurological level involve pharmacotherapy interventions. Various pharmacotherapies are available aiming to reduce (mostly reactive) aggressive behaviour (Swann & Hollander, 2002). Historically, most acute care settings used a combination of antipsychotic medication and benzodiazepines. However, the results show only a modestly effect for antipsychotic medication in reducing reactive aggressive behaviour and other non-cognitive behavioural symptoms (Antonius et al., 2013; Schneider, Pollock, & Lyness, 1990) and mostly in patients with acute psychotic symptoms (Swanson et al., 2008). However, atypical antipsychotics tend to show positive effects in anger management (Buckley, 1999). For example, a study showed a reduction in interpersonal sensitivity, impulsivity and anger in borderline personality-disordered individuals using olanzapine (Schulz, Camlin, Berry, & Jesberger, 1999). Benzodiazepines are prescribed to reduce symptoms of hyperactivity and attention, insomnia and panic related to anxiety problems (Swann & Hollander, 2002). Research shows that benzodiazepines are not advised for long-term use, but only in case of acute reactive aggressive outburst in which they seem effective (Citrome & Volavka, 1997). However, over the last few years, more has become known about the mechanisms underlying aggression (and impulsivity) and possible positive effects of different pharmacotherapies such as mood stabilisers, monoamine-oxidase inhibitors (MAOIs), antidepressants, anticonvulsants and beta-blockers (Swann & Hollander, 2002). A mood stabiliser commonly used is valproate (e.g. available as divalproex sodium), originally developed for the treatment of mania and epilepsy, but now applied in a variety of psychiatric disorders such as panic disorders, borderline personality disorder and drug withdrawal, and successful in the reduction of reactive aggression and impulsivity (Huband, Ferriter, Nathan, & Jones, 2010) by, for example, the reduction in patients' irritability in personality-disordered individuals (Hollander et al., 2001; Kavoussi & Coccaro, 1998).

Another commonly used mood stabiliser in individuals with depression symptoms is lithium, which aims to increase the serotonin function leading to less reactive aggression (Sheard, Marini, Bridges, & Wagner, 1976). MAOIs, mostly prescribed in cases of depression symptoms, seem to be successful in anger management, reducing anger and hostility in borderline personality-disordered individuals (Soloff et al., 1993). In addition, antidepressants and more specific selective serotonin reuptake inhibitors (SSRIs) seem to be effective in reducing reactive aggressive behaviour by increasing serotonin levels (Conacher, 1997; Phan, Lee, & Coccaro, 2011). Anticonvulsants are mostly prescribed in cases of epilepsy and seizures, but seem to show a reduction of aggressive behaviour (Young & Hillbrand, 1994). However, little research has been done on the anti-aggressive effects of anticonvulsants such as carbarnazepine on reactive aggression and persistent aggression (Huband, Ferriter, Nathan, & Jones, 2010; Young & Hillbrand, 1994), but the number of reports is growing (Eatmon & Daniel, 2014; Stanford, Anderson, Lake, & Baldridge, 2009). Beta-blockers have been introduced, targeting situational anxiety (Conacher, 1997). However, caution towards the use of beta-blockers in reactive aggressive individuals is needed because studies only show positive results on agitation and aggression in demented geriatric facilities (Shankle, Nielson, & Cotman, 1995) and in reactive aggressive patients with brain damage (Kavoussi & Coccaro, 1998). Moreover, in several studies, beta-blockers were prescribed in addition to other (e.g. antipsychotic) medication (Conacher, 1997; Silver, Yudofsky, Kogan, & Katz, 1986).

Improving anger behavioural control to decrease aggression may also be fruitful, using treatment focusing on up-regulating prefrontal cortex functions supporting enhanced ability to reappraise negative emotions. In this regard, research has shown that reappraisal is the most affective anger regulation strategy (Denson, Moulds, & Grisham, 2012; Fabiansson et al., 2012) and may lead to less negative interpretational biases, consequently altering the behavioural response to perceived threat in reactive impulsive aggression (Siep et al., 2015). Supportive recent studies demonstrated neurobiological changes after

172   *Franca Tonnaer et al.*

behavioural interventions (see for review Cornet, De Kogel, Nijman, Raine, & de Laan, 2014; Karlsson, 2011; Vaske, Galyean, & Cullen, 2011). Moreover, some studies documented the predictive value of neurobiological factors in behavioural treatment success (see for review Cornet, De Kogel, Nijman, Raine, & de Laan, 2013). These types of studies give important insight into the variability of the treatment response.

An upcoming development in examining interventions and treatment of aggression and hostility are studies focusing on nutrition, especially omega 3 fatty acids (Hibbeln, Ferguson, & Blasbalg, 2006). In a well-designed placebo-controlled study, a reduction of 26% of incidents was reported within 231 young adult offenders (Gesch et al., 2002). In a recent study this relationship between nutrition supplements and aggressive incidents was repeated in adult male prisoners in the Netherlands, demonstrating again a reduction of 34% in the experimental group compared to a 14% increase in the control group. Although there was a relationship between supplements and reported inci-dents (observed behaviour), there was no association between supplements and other measures of aggression (Zaalberg, Nijman, Bulten, Stroosma, & van der Staak, 2010). Research regarding aggression reduction and nutrition is still very premature, but so far seems a promising avenue for future research, in which underlying mechanisms may be further examined.

Concluding remarks

As earlier theories explain aggression as an instinctive, innate system, more recent theories describe it as a learning process in which some individuals may have a biological predisposition, making them more vulnerable to react aggressively in certain circumstances. Environmental influences regarding the development of aggression are based on social learning and labelling models. Although several types of aggression have been identified (i.e. reactive versus proactive; direct versus indirect; verbal versus physical; hostile versus instru-mental), little attention so far has been given to the influence of these different subtypes of aggression in their possible moderating role in treatment response. There is, however, some evidence that these subtypes of aggression benefit from distinct treatment components. Reactive aggressors seem to have more profit from psychosocial interventions based on anger control (Barker et al., 2010; Vitaro, Brendgen, & Barker, 2006), while children and adolescents with severe problems of conduct disorder and proactive aggression in general are often more unwilling to engage in and are unaffected by treatment, resulting in less clinical improvement (Barker et al., 2010; Haas et al., 2011; Masi et al., 2011). Interventions for proactive aggression should instead focus on teach-ing the individual alternative strategies in achieving instrumental goals, such as negotiation and compromising (Hubbard et al., 2010). Additionally, inter-ventions including an emotional component targeting callous unemotional traits often related to this subtype of aggression (Frick & White, 2008; see also Chapter 3) seem important.

Cognitive Behavioural Therapy focusing on cognitions (cognitive distortions) and emotion (anger reappraisal), but also pharmacology and nutrition treatment, all seem promising opportunities in reducing reactive as well as proactive aggression. However, more research on predictors and possible moderators of treatment response in decreasing aggression is needed. Deficits in emotion regulation (see also Introduction) – either a lack of regulating anger (reactive aggression) or controlled focused anger emotions in the presence of lacking empathy (instrumental goal-directed aggression) – seem essential in understanding treatment aimed at helping individuals to control their aggressive behaviour more effectively.

Literature

Akers, R., & Lee, G. (1996). A longitudinal test of social learning theory: Adolescent smoking. *Journal of Drug Issues, 26,* 317–343.

American Psychiatric Association. (2013). *Diagnostic and statistical manual of mental disorders (5th ed.).* Arlington, VA: American Psychiatric Publishing.

Anderson, C. A., & Bushman, B. J. (2002). Human aggression. *The Annual Review of Psychology, 53,* 27–51.

Anderson, C. A., & Carnagey, N. L. (2004). Violent evil and the General Aggression Model. In A. Miller (Ed.), *The social psychology of good and evil* (pp. 168–192). New York: Guilford Publications.

Antonius, D., Sinclair, S. J., Shiva, A., Messinger, J. W., Maile, J., Siefert, C. J., Belfi, B., Malaspina, D., & Blais, M. A. (2013). Assessing the heterogeneity of aggressive behaviour traits: Exploratory and confirmatory analyses of the reactive and instrumental aggression Personality Assessment Inventory (PAI) scales. *Violence and Victims, 28,* 587–601.

Archer, J. (2009). Does sexual selection explain human sex differences in aggression? *Behavioural and Brain Sciences, 32,* 249–311.

Babcock, J. C., Sharp, C., Tharp, A., Hepner, W., & Stanford, M. A. (2014). Similarities and differences in impulsive/premeditated and reactive/proactive bimodal classifications of aggression. *Aggression and Violent Behaviour, 19,* 251–262.

Bakermans-Kranenburg, M. J., & Ijzendoorn, M. H. (2006). Gene-environment interaction of the dopamine D4 receptor (DRD4) and observed maternal insensitivity predicting externalizing behaviour in pre-schoolers. *Developmental Psychobiology, 48,* 406–409.

Bandura, A. (1983). Psychological mechanism of aggression. In R. G. Geen & E. I. Donnerstein (Eds.), *Aggression: Theoretical and empirical reviews* (pp. 1–40). New York: Academic Press.

Bandura, A., & Ribes-Inesta, E. (1976). *Analysis of delinquency and aggression.* Mahwah, NJ: Lawrence Erlbaum Associates.

Barker, E. D., Vitaro, F., Lacourse, E., Fontaine, N. M. G., Carbonneau, R., & Tremblay, R.E. (2010). Testing the developmental distinctiveness of male proactive and reactive aggression with a nested longitudinal experimental intervention. *Aggressive Behaviour, 36,* 127–140.

Baron, R. (1977). *Human aggression.* New York: Plenum.

Barratt, E. S. (1994). Impulsiveness and aggression. In J. S. Monahan & H. J. Steadman (Eds.), *Violence and mental disorder: Developments in risk assessment* (pp. 61–79). Chicago: University of Chicago Press.

174   *Franca Tonnaer et al.*

Baumeister, R. F., Smart, L., & Boden, J. M. (1996). Relation of threatened egotism to violence and aggression: The dark side of high self-esteem. *Psychological Review, 103,* 5–33.

Baumeister, R. F., & Vohs, K. D. (2007). Self-regulation, ego-depletion, and motivation. *Social and Personality Psychology Compass, 1,* 115–128.

Becker, H. S. (1963). *Outsider: Studies in the sociology of deviance.* New York: The Free Press.

Bendersky, M., Bennett, D., & Lewis, M. (2006). Aggression at age 5 as a function of prenatal exposure to cocaine, gender, and environmental risk. *Journal of Pedriatric Psychology, 31,* 71–84.

Berkowitz, L. (1989). Frustration-aggression hypothesis: Examination and reformulation. *Psychological Bulletin, 106,* 59–73.

Berkowitz, L. (1990). On the formation and regulation of anger and aggression: A cognitive neoassociationistic analysis. *American Psychologist, 45,* 494–503.

Berkowitz, L. (1993). Pain and aggression: Some findings and implications. *Motivation and Emotion, 17,* 277–293.

Berkowitz, L., & LePage, A. (1967). Weapons as aggression-eliciting stimuli. *Journal of Personality and Social Psychology, 7,* 202–207.

Bevilacque, L., Doly, S., Kaprio, J., Yuan, Q., Tikkanen, R., & Paunio, T (2010). A population specific HTR2B stop codon predisposes to severe impulsivity. *Nature, 468,* 1061–1066.

Blair, R. J. R. (2004). The roles of the orbital frontal cortex in the modulation of antisocial behaviour. *Brain and Cognition, 55,* 198–208.

Bobadilla, L., Wampler, M., & Taylor, J. (2012). Proactive and reactive aggression are associated with different physiological and personality profiles. *Journal of Social and Clinical Psychology, 31,* 458–487.

Borduin, C. M. (1999). Multisystemic treatment of criminality and violence in adolescents. *Journal of the American Academy of Child & Adolescent Psychiatry, 38,* 242–249.

Buchmann, A., Hohmann, S., Brandeis, D., Banaschewski, T., & Poustka, L. (2014). Aggression in children and adolescents. In K. A. Miczek & A. Meyer-Lindenberg (Eds.), *Neuroscience of aggression.* New York: Springer.

Buckley, P. F. (1999). The role of typical and atypical antipsychotic medications in the management of agitation and aggression. *Journal of Clinical Psychiatry, 60,* 52–60.

Bufkin, J. L., & Luttrell, V. (2005). Neuroimaging studies of aggressive and violent behaviour. Current findings and implications for criminology and criminal justice. *Trauma, Violence, & Abuse, 6,* 176–191.

Carré, J. M., Iselin, A-M. R., Welker, K. M., Hariri, A. R., & Dodge, K A. (2014). Testosterone reactivity to provocation mediates the effect of early intervention on aggressive behaviour. *Psychological Science, 25,* 1140–1146.

Carré, J. M., & McCormick, C. M. (2008). In your face: Facial metrics predict aggressive behaviour in the laboratory and in varsity and professional hockey players. *Proceedings of the Royal Society, 275,* 2651–2656.

Caspi, A., McClay, J., Moffitt, T. E., Mill, J., Martin, J., Craig, I. W., Taylor, A., & Poulton, R. (2002). Role of genotype in the cycle of violence in maltreated children. *Science, 297,* 851–854.

Cima, M., & Raine, A. (2009). Distinct characteristics of psychopathy relate to different subtypes of aggression. *Personality and Individual Differences, 47,* 835–840.

Cima, M., Nicolson, N., de Lijster, J., & Popma, A. (2015). Salivary cortisol reactivity patterns in psychopathic and non-psychopathic offenders. Manuscript submitted for publication.

Cima, M., Smeets, T., & Jelicic, M. (2008). The relationship between trauma self reports, levels of cortisol, and aggression in psychopathic and non-psychopathic prison inmates. *Biological Psychology, 78,* 75–86.

Cima, M., Tonnaer, F., & Lobbestael, J. (2007). Moral emotions in predatory and impulsive offenders using implicit measures. *Netherlands Journal of Psychology, 4,* 144–155.

Citrome, L., & Volavka, J. (1997). Psychopharmacology of violence. Part I: assessment and acute treatment. *Psychiatric Annals, 27,* 691–695.

Cloninger, C. R., Sigvardsson, S., Bohman, M., & von Knorring, A. L. (1982). Predisposition to petty criminality in Swedish adoptees, II: Cross-fostering analysis of gene-environment interaction. *Archives of General Psychiatry, 39,* 1242–1249.

Collins, A. M., & Loftus, E. F. (1975). A spreading activation of semantic processing. *Psychological Review, 82,* 407–428.

Conacher, G. N. (1997). Pharmacological approaches to impulsive and aggressive behaviour. In C. D. Webster & M. A. Jackson (Eds.), *Impulsivity: theory, assessment, and treatment* (pp. 394–408). New York: Guilford Press.

Cornet, L., De Kogel, C., Nijman, H., Raine, A., & van der Laan, P. (2013). Neurobiological factors as predictors of cognitive-behavioural therapy outcome in individuals with antisocial behaviour: A review of the literature. *International Journal of Offender Therapy and Comparative Criminology, 9,* 1–18.

Cornet, L., De Kogel, C., Nijman, H., Raine, A., & van der Laan, P. (2015). Neurobiological changes after intervention in individuals with anti-social behaviour: A literature review. *Criminal Behaviour and Mental Health, 25,* 10–27.

Crick, N. R., & Dodge, K. A. (1994). A review and reformulation of social information processing mechanisms in children's adjustment. *Psychological Bulletin, 115,* 74–101.

Crowe, R. R. (1975). An adoptive study of psychopathology: Preliminary results from arrest records and psychiatric hospital records. In R. R. Fieve, D. Rosenthal, & H. Brill (Eds.), *Genetic research in psychiatry* (pp. 95–103). Baltimore: Johns Hopkins University Press.

Curtis, N. M., Ronan, K. R., & Borduin, C. M. (2004). Multisystemic treatment: A meta-analysis of outcome studies. *Journal of Family Psychology, 18,* 411–419.

Damasio, H., Grabowski, T., Frank, R., Galaburda, A. M., & Damasio, A. R. (1994). The return of Phineas Gage: Clues about the brain from the skull of a famous patient. *Science, 264,* 1102–1105.

Dambacher, F., Sack, A. T., Lobbestael, J., Arnts, A., Brugman, S., & Schuhman, T. (2014). Out of control: Evidence for anterior insula involvement in motor impulsivity and reactive aggression. *Social Cognitive and Affective Neuroscience, 17,* 1–9.

Denson, T. F., Moulds, M. L., & Grisham, J. R. (2012). The effects of rumination, reappraisal, and distraction on anger experience. *Behaviour Therapy, 43,* 355–364.

Denson, T. F., Pederson, W. C., Ronquillo, J., & Nandy, A. S. (2009). The angry brain: Neural correlates of anger, angry rumination, and aggressive personality. *Journal of Cognitive Neuroscience, 21,* 734–744.

de Ruiter, C., & Hildebrand, M. (1999). *Behandelingsstrategieën bij Forensich-psychiatrische patiënten. [Treatment strategies with forensic psychiatric patients].* Bohn Stafleu van Loghum: Houten.

Dodge, K. A. (2006). Translational science in action: Hostile attributional style and the development of aggressive behaviour problems. *Development and Psychopathology, 18,* 791–814.

176   *Franca Tonnaer et al.*

Dodge, K. A., & Coie, J. D. (1987). Social information processing factors in reactive and proactive aggression in children's peer groups. *Journal of Personality and Social Psychology, 53,* 1146–1158.

Dollard, J., Doob, L. W., Miller, N. E., Mowrer, O. H., & Sears, R. R. (1939). *Frustration and aggression.* New Haven: Yale University Press.

Down, R., Willner, P., Watts, L., & Griffiths, J. (2011). Anger management groups for adolescents: A mixed-methods study of efficacy and treatment preferences. *Clinical Child Psychology & Psychiatry, 16,* 33–52.

Duncan, L. E., & Keller, M. C. (2011). A critical review of the first 10 years of candidate gene-by-environment interaction research in psychiatry. *American Journal of Psychiatry, 168,* 1041–1049.

Duncan, L. E., Pollastri, A. R., & Smoller, J. W. (2014). Mind the gap: Why many geneticists and psychological scientists have discrepant views about gene–environment interaction (GXE) research. *American Psychologist, 69,* 249–268.

Eatmon, C. V., & Daniel, J. S. (2014). Should you use an anticonvulsant to treat impulsivity and aggression? *Current Psychiatry, 13,* 49–51.

Englander, E. K. (2003). *Understanding violence (2nd ed.).* Mahwah: Lawrence Erlbaum Associates.

Evenden, J. L. (1999). Varieties of impulsivity. *Psychopharmacology, 146,* 348–361.

Fabian, J. M. (2010). Neuropsychological and neurological correlates in violent and homicidal offenders: A legal and neuroscience perspective. *Aggression and Violent Behaviour, 15,* 209–223.

Fabiansson, E. C., Denson, T. F., Moulds, M. L., Grisham, J. R., & Schira, M. M. (2012). Don't look back in anger: Neural correlates of reappraisal, analytical rumination, and angry rumination during recall of an anger-inducing autobiographical memory. *NeurImage, 59,* 2974–2981.

Feilhauer, J., Cima, M., Korebrits, A., & Nicolson, N. (2013). Salivary cortisol and psychopathy dimensions in detained antisocial adolescents. *Psychoneuroendocrinology, 38,* 1586–1595.

Frick, P. J., & White, S. F. (2008). Research review: The importance of callous unemotional traits for developmental models of aggressive and antisocial behaviour. *Journal of Child Psychology and Psychiatry, 49,* 359–375.

Freud, S. (1955). *Beyond the pleasure principle.* (J. Strachey, Trans.). London: Hogarth Press (Original work published in 1920).

Gesch, C. B., Hammond, S. M., Hampson, S. E., Eves, A., & Crowder, M. J. (2002). Influence of supplementary vitamins, minerals and essential fatty acids on the antisocial behaviour of young adult prisoners. Randomised, placebo-controlled trial. *British Journal of Psychiatry, 181,* 22–28.

Gilligan, J. (1997). *Violence: Reflections on a national epidemic.* New York: Vintage Books.

Glenn, A. L., Raine, A., Venables, P., & Mednick, S.A. (2007). Early temperamental and psychophysiological precursors of adult psychopathic personality. *Journal of Abnormal Psychology, 116,* 508–518.

Goldstein, A. P. (1996). Aggression replacement training: Teaching prosocial behaviours to antisocial youth. In R. Ross, D. H. Antonowicz, & K. Dhuluval (Eds.), *Effective delinquency prevention and offender rehabilitation.* Ottawa: AIR Training and Publications.

Gottfredson, M. R., & Hirschi, T. (1990). *General theory of crime.* Stanford: Stanford University Press.

Guastella, A. J., Kenyon, A. R., Alvares, G. A., Carson, D. S., & Hickie, I. B. (2010). Intranasal arginine vasopressin enhances the encoding of happy and angry faces in humans. *Biological Psychiatry, 67,* 1220–1222.

Haas, S. M., Waschbusch, D. A., Pelham, W. E. Jr, King, S., Andrade, B. F., & Carrey, N. J. (2011). Treatment response in CP/ADHD children with callous/unemotional traits. *Journal of Abnormal Child Psychology, 39,* 541–552.

Hawkins, K. A., & Trobst, K. K. (2000). Frontal lobe dysfunction and aggression: Conceptual issues and research findings. *Aggression and Violent Behaviour, 5,* 147–157.

Hay, D. F., Pawlby, S., Waters, C. S., Perra, O. & Sharp, D. (2010). Mothers' antenatal depression and their children's antisocial outcomes. *Child Development, 81,* 149–165.

Huesmann, L. R. (1988). An information processing model for the development of aggression. *Aggressive Behavior, 14,* 13–24.

Henggeler, S. W., Cunningham, P. B., Pickrel, S. G., Schoenwald, S. K., & Brondino, M. J. (1996). Multisystemic therapy: An effective violence prevention approach for serious juvenile offenders. *Journal of Adolescence, 19,* 47–61.

Henggeler, S. W., Schoenwald, S. K., Borduin, C. M., Rowland, M. D., & Cunningham, P. B. (1998). *Multisystemic treatment of antisocial behaviour in children and adolescents.* New York: Guilford.

Hibbeln, J. R., Ferguson, T. A., & Blasbalg, T. L. (2006). Omega-3 fatty acid deficiencies in neurodevelopment, aggression and autonomic dysregulation: Opportunities for intervention. *International Review of Psychiatry, 18,* 107–118.

Hirschi, T., & Gottfredson, M. R. (1983). Age and the explanation of crime. *American Journal of Sociology, 89,* 552–584.

Hollander, E., Allen, A., Lopez, R. P., Bienstock, C. A., Grossman, R., Siever, L. J., Merkatz, L., & Stein, D. J. A. (2001). Preliminary double-blind, placebo-controlled trial of divalproex sodium in borderline personality disorder. *Journal of Clinical Psychiatry, 62,* 199–203.

Huband, N., Ferriter, M., Nathan, R., & Jones, H. (2010). Antiepileptics for aggression and associated impulsivity. *Cochrane Database of Systematic Reviews, Issue 2,* Art. No.: CD003499.

Hubbard, J. A., Morrow, M. T., Romano, L. J., & McAuliffe, M. D. (2010). The role of anger in children's reactive versus proactive aggression: review of findings, issues of measurement, and implications for intervention. In W. F. Arsenio & E. A. Lemerise (Eds.), *Emotions, aggression, and morality in children: Bridging development and psychopathology.* Washington DC: American Psychological Association.

Huijbregts, S., Seguin J., Zoccolillo, M., Boivin, M., & Tremblay, R. E. (2008). Maternal prenatal smoking, parental antisocial behaviour, and early childhood physical aggression. *Development and Psychopathology, 20,* 437–453.

Karlsson, H. (2011). How psychotherapy changes the brain: Understanding the mechanisms. *Psychiatric Times, 28,* 1–5.

Kavoussi, R. J., & Coccaro, E. F. (1998). Divalproex sodium for impulsive aggressive behaviour in patients with personality disorder. *Journal of Clinical Psychiatry, 59,* 676–680.

King, B. (2012). Psychological theories of violence. *Journal of Human Behaviour in the Social Environment, 22,* 553–571.

Kline, K. (2004). *Conduct disorder, antisocial personality disorder, and psychopathy.* Unpublished presentation, Florida State University at Panama.

Kohn, P. M., Cowles, M. P., & Lafreniere, K. (1987). Relationships between psychometric and experimental measures of arousability. *Personality and Individual Differences, 8,* 225–231.

178 *Franca Tonnaer et al.*

Kouri, E. M., Lukas, S. E., Pope, H. G., & Olivia, P. S. (1995). Increased aggressive responding in male volunteers following the administration of gradually increasing doses of testosterone cypionate. *Drug and Alcohol Dependence, 40,* 73–79.

Krahé, B. (2001). *The social psychology of aggression.* Philadelphia: Psychology Press.

Krahé, B. (2013). *The social psychology of aggression* (2nd ed.). New York: Psychology Press.

Krug, E. G., Dahlberg, L. L., Mercy, J. A., Zwi, A. B., & Lozano, R. (2002). *World report on violence and health.* Geneva: World Health Organization.

Lahey, B., Moffitt, T. E., & Caspi, A. (2003). *The causes of conduct disorder and serious juvenile delinquency.* New York: Guilford Press.

Lane, S. D., & Cherek, D. R. (2000). Analysis of risk taking in adults with a history of high risk behaviour. *Drug and Alcohol Dependence, 60,* 179–187.

Lindquist, K. A., Wager, T. D., Kober, H., Bliss-Moreau, E., & Barrett, L. F. (2012). The brain basis of emotion: A meta-analytic review. *Behavioural and Brain Sciences, 35,* 121–202.

Lorenz, K. (1974). *On aggression.* New York: Harcourt Brace Jovanovich.

Marsh, R. L., Hicks, J. L., & Bink, M. L. (1998). Activation of completed, uncompleted and partial completed intentions. *Journal of Experimental Psychology: Learning, Memory and Cognition, 24,* 350–361.

Masi, G., Manfredi, A., Milone, A., Muatori, P., Polidori, L., Ruglioni, L., & Muratori, F. (2011). Predictors of nonresponse to psychosocial treatment in children and adolescents with disruptive behaviour disorders. *Journal Child Adolescent Psychopharmacology, 21,* 51–55.

Mayes, L.C. (1999). Developing brain and in utero cocaine exposure: Effects on neural ontogeny. *Development and Psychopathology, 4,* 685–714.

Mednick, S. A., Brennan, P., & Kandel, E. (1988). Predisposition to violence. *Aggressive Behaviour, 14,* 25–33.

Mehta, P. H., & Beer, J. (2009). Neural Mechanisms of the testosterone–aggression relation: The role of orbitofrontal cortex. *Journal of Cognitive Neuroscience, 22,* 2357–2368.

Meichenbaum, D. (1996). Stress inoculation training for coping with stressors. *The Clinical Psychologist, 49,* 4–7.

Mellow, A. M., Solano-Lopez, C., & Davis, S. (1993). Sodium valproate in the treatment of behavioural disturbance in dementia. *Journal of Geriatric Psychiatry and Neurology, 6,* 205–209.

Miles, D. R., & Carey, G. (1997). Genetic and environmental architecture of human aggression. *Journal of Personality and Social Psychology, 72,* 207–217.

Miller, N. E., Sears, R. R., Mowrer, O. H., Doob, L. W., & Dollard, J. (1941). The frustration–aggression hypothesis. *Psychological Review, 48,* 337–342.

Mischel, W. (1973). Toward a cognitive social learning reconceptualization of personality. *Psychological Review, 80,* 252–283.

Montoya, E. R., terburg, D., Bos, P.A., & van Honk, J. (2011). Testosterone, cortisol, and serotonin as key regulators of social aggression: A review and theoretical perspective. *Motivation and Emotion, 36,* 65–73.

National Center. (2007). *Aggression Replacement Training® (ART®): Factsheet.* Waltham: The National Center for Mental Health Promotion and Youth Violence Prevention.

Novaco, R. W. (1975). *Anger control: The development and evaluation of an experimental treatment.* Lexington: Heath.

Nyth, A. L., & Gottfries, C. G. (1990). The clinical efficacy of citalopram in treatment of emotional disturbances in dementia disorders. A Nordic multicentre study. *British Journal of Psychiatry, 157,* 894–901.

Obradovic, J., Bush, N. R., Stamperdahl, J., Adler, N. E., & Boyce, W. T. (2010). Biological sensitivity to context: The interactive effects of stress reactivity and family adversity on socioemotional behaviour and school readiness. *Child Development, 81,* 270–289.

Pavlov, K. A., Chistiakov, D. A., & Chekhonin, V. P. (2012). Genetic determinants of aggression and impulsivity in humans. *Journal of Applied Genetics, 53,* 61–82.

Perry, B. D. (2001). The neurodevelopmental impact of violence in childhood. In D. Schetky & E. P. Benedek (Eds.), *Textbook of child and adolescent forensic psychiatry* (pp. 221–238). Washington: American Psychiatric Press.

Pfohl, S. (1994). *Images of deviance and social control: A sociological history,* 2nd ed. New York: McGraw-Hill.

Phan, K. L., Lee, R., & Coccaro, E. F. (2011). Personality predictors of anti-aggressive response to fluoxetine: Inverse association with neuroticism and harm avoidance. *International Clinical Psychopharmacology, 26,* 278–283.

Pokhrel, P., Sussman, S., Sun, P., Kniazer, V., & Masagutov, R. (2010). Social self-control, sensation seeking, and substance use in samples of US and Russian adolescents. *American Journal of Health Behaviour, 34,* 374–384.

Popma, A., Vermeiren, R., Geluk, C. A. M. L., Rinne, T., van den Brink, W., Knol, D. L., Jansen, L. M. C., van Engeland, H., & Doreleijers, T. A. H. (2007). Cortisol moderates the relationship between testosterone and aggression in delinquent male adolescents. *Biological Psychiatry, 61,* 405–411.

Poustka, L., Maras, A., Hohm, E., Fellinger, J., Holtmann, M., Banaschewski, T., Lewicka, S., Schmidt, M. H., Esser, G., & Laucht, M. (2010). Negative association between plasma cortisol levels and aggression in a high-risk community sample of adolescents. *Journal of Neural Transmission, 117,* 621–627.

Pratt, T. C., & Cullen, F. T. (2000). The empirical status of Gottfredsons and Hirschi's General Theory of Crime: A meta analysis. *Criminology, 38,* 931–964.

Raine, A., Buchsbaum, M. S., & La Casse, L. (1997). Brain abnormalities in murderers indicated by positron emission tomography. *Biological Psychiatry, 42,* 495–508.

Raine, A., Dodge, K., Loeber, R., Gatzke-Kopp, L., Lynam, D., Reynolds, C., Stouthamer-Loeber, M., & Liu, J. (2006). The reactive-proactive aggression questionnaire: Differential correlates of reactive and proactive aggression in adolescent boys. *Aggressive Behaviour, 32,* 159–171.

Raine, A., Lencz, T., Bihrle, S., Lacasse, L., & Colletti, P. (2000). Reduced prefrontal gray matter volume and reduced autonomic activity in antisocial personality disorder. *Archives of General Psychiatry, 57,* 119–127.

Raine, A., Meloy, J. R., Bihrle, S., Stoddard, J., Lacasse, L., & Buchsbaum, M. S. (1998). Reduced prefrontal and increased subcortical brain functioning assessed using positron emission tomography in predatory and affective murderers. *Behavioural Sciences and the Law, 16,* 319–332.

Sagarin, E. (1975). *Deviants and deviance.* New York: Praeger.

Scarpa, A., & Raine, A. (2000). Violence associated with anger and impulsivity. In J. C. Borod (Eds.), *The neuropsychology of emotion: Series in affective science* (pp. 320–339). New York: Oxford University Press.

Schachter, S., & Singer, J. (1962). Cognitive, social, and physiological determinants of emotional state. *Psychological Review, 69,* 379–399.

180 *Franca Tonnaer et al.*

Schank, R. C., & Abelson, R. P. (1977). *Scripts, plans, goals and understanding: An inquiry into human knowledge structures.* Hillsdale: Erlbaum.

Schneider, L. S., Pollock, V. E., & Lyness, S. A. A. (1990). Metaanalysis of controlled trials of neuroleptic treatment in dementia. *Journal of the American Geriatrics Society, 38,* 553–563.

Schulkin, J. (2003). *Rethinking homeostasis: Allostatic regulation in physiology and pathophysiology.* Cambridge, MA: MIT Press.

Schulz, S. C., Camlin, K. L, Berry, S. A., & Jesberger, J. A. (1999). Olanzapine safety and efficacy in patients with borderline personality disorder and comorbid dysthymia. *Biological Psychiatry, 46,* 1429–1435.

Séguin, J. R. (2013). The frontal lobe and aggression. *European Journal of Developmental Psychology, 6,* 100–119.

Seo, D., Patrick, C. J., & Kennealy, P. J. (2008). Role of serotonin and dopamine system interactions in the neurobiology of impulsive aggression and its comorbidity with other clinical disorders. *Aggression and Violent Behaviour, 13,* 383–395.

Shankle, W. R., Nielson, K. A., & Cotman, C. W. (1995). Low-dose propranolol reduces aggression and agitation resembling that associated with orbitofrontal dysfunction in elderly demented patients. *Alzheimer Disease & Associated Disorders, 9,* 233–237.

Sheard, M. H., Marini, J. L., Bridges, C. I., & Wagner, E. (1976). The effect of lithium on impulsive aggressive behaviour in man. *American Journal of Psychiatry, 133,* 1409–1413.

Siep, N., Tonnaer, F., van de Ven, V., Arntz, A., & Cima, M. (2015). *Out of control: Anger provocation increases limbic and decreases medial prefrontal cortex connectivity with the left amygdala in reactive aggressive violent offenders.* Manuscript submitted for publication.

Siever, L. J. (2008). Neurobiology of aggression and violence. *American Journal of Psychiatry, 165,* 429–442.

Silver, J. M., Yudofsky, S. C., Kogan, M., & Katz, B. L. (1986). Elevation of thiouridazine plasma levels by propanolol. *American Journal of Psychiatry, 143,* 1290–1292.

Smeets., K. C., Leeijen, A. A. M., van der Molen, M. J., Scheepers, F. E., Buitelaar, J. K., & Rommelse, N. N. J. (2015). Treatment moderators of cognitive behaviour therapy to reduce aggressive behaviour: A meta-analysis. *European Child and Adolescent Psychiatry, 24,* 255–264.

Soloff, P. H., Cornelius, J., George, A., Nathan, S., Perel, J. M., & Ulrich, R. F. (1993). Efficacy of phenelzine and haloperidol in borderline personality disorder. *Archives of General Psychiatry, 50,* 377–385.

Stanford, M. S., Anderson, N. E., Lake, S. L., & Baldridge, R. M. (2009). Pharmacologic treatment of impulsive aggression with antiepileptic drugs. *Current Treatment Options in Neurology, 11,* 383–390.

Streissguth, A. P., Barr, H. M., Bookstein, F. L., Sampson, P. D., & Olson, H. C. (1999). The long-term neurocognitive consequences of prenatal alcohol: A 14-year study. *Psychological Science, 10,* 186–190.

Summers, C. H., Korzan, W. J., Lukkes, J. L., Watt, M. J., Forster, G. L., Øverli, Ø., Höglund, E., Larson, E. T., Ronan, P. J., Matter, J. M., Summers, T. R., Renner, K. J., & Greenberg, N. (2005). Does serotonin influence aggression? Comparing regional activity before and during social interaction. *Physiological and Biochemical Zoology, 78,* 679–694.

Sutherland, E. H. (1939). *Principles of criminology,* 3rd ed. Philadelphia: J.B. Lippincott.

Swann, A. C., & Hollander, E. (2002). *Impulsivity and aggression: Diagnostic challenges for the clinician: A monograph for continuing medical education credit*. Chicago: ACCESS Medical Group.

Swanson, J. W., Swartz, M. S., Van Dorn, R. A., Volavka, J., Monahan, J., Stroup, T. S., & Lieberman, J. A. (2008). Comparison of antipsychotic medication effects on reducing violence in people with schizophrenia. *British Journal of Psychiatry, 193,* 37–43.

Taylor, J., Loney, B. R., Bobadilla, L., Iacono, W. G., & McGue, M. (2003). Genetic and environmental influence on psychopathy: Findings from an adolescent male twin cohort. *Journal of Abnormal Child Psychology, 31,* 633–645.

Tedeschi, J. T., Gaes, G. G., & Rivera, A. N. (1977). Aggression and the use of coercive power. *Journal of Social Issues, 33,* 101–125.

Tedeschi, J. T., & Felson, R. B. (1994.) *Violence, aggression, & coercive actions*. Washington: APA.

Terburg, D., Morgan, B., & van Honk, J. (2009). The testosterone–cortisol ratio: A hormonal marker for proneness to social aggression. *International Journal of Law and Psychiatry, 32,* 216–223.

Terburg, D., Peper, J. S., Morgan, B., & van Honk, J. (2009). Sex differences in human aggression: The interaction between early developmental and later activational testosterone. *Behavioural and Brain Sciences, 32,* 280–290.

Thompson, D. A., Arora, T., & Sharp., S. (2002). *Bullying – Effective strategies for long term improvement*. London: Routledge/Falmer.

Tomkins, S. S. (1954). *Script theory: Differential magnification of affects*. Fourteenth International Congress of Psychology. Montreal, Canada.

Tonnaer, F., & Chakhssi, F. (2007). *Incident profiling on patients characteristics*. 5th EU Violence in Clinical Psychiatry, Amsterdam.

Tonnaer, F., Cima, M., & Arntz, A. (2015a). *Explosive matters: Aggression induction: what works?* Manuscript in preparation.

Tonnaer, F., Cima, M., & Arntz, A. (2015b). *A three-dimensional model of impulsivity*. Manuscript submitted for publication.

Tonnaer, F., Cima, M., & Arntz, A. (2015c). *Are executive (dys)functioning and impulsivity both vulnerability factors for aggression?* Manuscript submitted for publication.

Van Honk, J., Harmon-Jones, E., Morgan, B. A., & Schutter, D. L. G. (2010). Socially explosive minds: The triple imbalance hypothesis of reactive aggression. *Journal of Personality, 78,* 67–94.

Vaske, J., Galyean, K., & Cullen, F. T. (2011). Toward a biosocial theory of offender rehabilitation: Why does cognitive-behavioural therapy work? *Journal of Criminal Justice, 39,* 90–102.

Vazsonyi, A. T., & Belliston, L. M. (2007). The family> low self-control > deviance: A cross-cultural and cross-national test of self-control theory. *Criminal Justice and Behaviour, 34,* 505–530.

Vitaro, F., & Brendgen, M. (2005). Proactive and reactive aggression: A developmental perspective. In R. E. Tremblay, W. M. Hartup, & J. Archer (Eds.), *The developmental origins of aggression* (pp. 178–201). New York: Guilford Press.

Vitaro, F., Brendgen, M., & Barker, E. D. (2006). Subtypes of aggressive behaviours: A developmental perspective. *International Journal of Behavioural Development, 30,* 12–19.

Warr, M., & Stafford, M. (1991). The influence of delinquent peers: What they think or what they do? *Criminology, 29,* 851–866.

182 *Franca Tonnaer et al.*

Waters, H., Hyder, A., Rajkotia, Y., Basu, S., Rehwinkel, J. A., & Butchart, A. (2004). *The economic dimensions of interpersonal violence*. Geneva: World Health Organization.

Young, J. L., & Hillbrand, M. (1994). Carbamazepine lowers: Aggression: A review. *Bulletin of the American Academy of Psychiatry and the Law, 22,* 53–61.

Zaalberg, A., Nijman, H., Bulten, E., Stroosma, L., & van der Staak, C. (2010). Effects of nutritional supplements on aggression, rule-breaking, and psychopathology among young adult prisoners. *Aggressive Behaviour, 36,* 117–126.

Zillmann, D. (1983). Arousal and aggression. In R. G. Geen & E. I. Donnerstein (Eds.), *Aggression: Theoretical and empirical reviews* (pp. 75–102). New York: Academic Press.

Zohsel, K., Buchmann, A. F., Blomeyer, D., Hohm, E., Schmidt, M. H., Esser, G., Brandeis, D., Banaschewski, T., & Lauch, M. (2013). Mothers' prenatal stress and their children's antisocial outcomes – a moderating role for the Dopamine D4 Receptor (DRD4) gene. *Journal of Child Psychology and Psychiatry, 55,* 69–76.

9 Personality disorders and crime

Jill Lobbestael and René Cane

Introduction

The available literature concerning the relationship between personality disorders (PDs) and criminal behaviour is, in general terms, limited and in many cases contradictory (Berman, Fallon, & Coccaro, 1998). The incongruous nature of the evidence arises from studies indicating, for example, that there is no relationship between PDs and aggression (Gardner, Leibenluft, O'Leary, & Cowdry, 1991), studies demonstrating that all serious offenders present high rates of PDs and studies showing that each PD may be related to particular types of offending (Davison & Janca, 2012; Roberts & Coid, 2010). Despite the controversy, the presence of a PD is already considered by many a risk factor for violent re-offending and has been included in some risk assessment tools (Davison & Janca, 2012). Therefore, this chapter focuses on the available research on the relationship between PDs and crime.

This chapter starts by explaining the general concept of PDs, including a description of all 10 PDs according to the DSM-IV-TR criteria. The relationship between antisocial PD and psychopathy will be shortly addressed, as will the categorical versus dimensional operationalisation of PDs. In this chapter we will also summarise findings on the relationship between PDs and crime. The first line of evidence for this relationship is the high prevalence rates of PDs in violent samples. We will also address some controversies on this matter, gender distributions and the effect of high comorbidity levels among PDs. Additionally, the motivations for crime among different PD patient groups will be outlined, as will the challenge of reliably assessing PDs in these samples, and how the different PDs are related to offence. The second line of evidence on the relationship between PDs and crime shows that patients with certain PDs, i.e. antisocial, borderline and narcissistic PDs, have been shown to display high levels of aggression. Finally, the methodological limitations of studies assessing the relationship between PDs and crime are addressed. This chapter is restricted to studies using adult samples because formal PD diagnoses can only be made after age 18. The relationship between crime and psychopathy will not be included because psychopathy is not a formal DSM diagnosis. It is beyond the scope of this chapter to discuss the aetiological models of PDs (interested readers are referred to e.g. Widiger, 2012).

The 10 personality disorders

PDs refer to a pattern of rigid and self-defeating traits. They are characterised by three Ps; pathological because the traits deviate from normality and from the expectation of one's culture, persistent because of their long-lasting nature and traceability to adolescence or early adulthood, and pervasive because they express themselves in a broad range of personal and social situations. A PD can manifest itself in cognitive, affective, interpersonal and/or impulse control areas, and leads to significant impairment. In contrast to the clinical disorders on axis I of the DSM, PDs are so deeply entrenched into personality that they feel like an intrinsic part of the person who suffers from it, which is why it is termed ego–syntonic. As a consequence, many PD patients lack insight into the pathological nature of their personality. PD diagnoses are based on a polythetical classification, meaning that a diagnosis can be made with only a proportion of the items that define the disorder. Consequently, the clinical image of two people that suffer from the same PD can be quite diverse, with e.g. 256 possible ways of meeting borderline PD criteria (Johansen, Karterud, Pedersen, Gude, & Falkum, 2004). The DSM-IV-TR classifies PDs on axis II. There are 10 different PDs, which are part of one of three clusters.

Box 9.1 Cluster A personality disorder (see DSM-5)

Cluster A, or the odd and eccentric cluster, includes three personality disorders (PDs) – paranoid, schizoid and schizotypal – that share social awkwardness and withdrawal. Paranoid PD refers to distrust and suspiciousness of others, and a malevolent interpretation of others' motives. At least four out of seven criteria need to be present:

1   suspects, without sufficient basis, that others are exploiting, harming or deceiving him or her
2   preoccupied with unjustified doubts about the loyalty or trustworthiness of friends or associates
3   reluctant to confide in others because of unwarranted fear that the information will be used maliciously against him or her
4   reads hidden meanings or threatening meanings into benign remarks or events
5   persistently bears grudges, i.e. is unforgiving of insults, injuries or slights
6   perceives attacks on his or her character or reputation that are not apparent to others and is quick to react angrily or to counterattack
7   has recurrent suspicions, without justification, regarding fidelity of spouse or sexual partner.

Schizoid PD patients show detachment from social relationships and only display a restricted range of emotional expressions, as indicated by four (or more) of the following:

1 neither desires nor enjoys close relationships, including being part of a family
2 almost always chooses solitary activities
3 has little, if any, interest in having sexual experiences with another person
4 takes pleasure in few, if any, activities
5 lacks close friends or confidants other than first-degree relatives
6 appears indifferent to the praise or criticism of others
7 shows emotional coldness, detachment or flattened affectivity.

The final Cluster A PD, schizotypal PD, presents itself through extreme social and interpersonal deficits. These patients show discomfort with and reduced capacity for close relationships. There are *cognitive* or perceptual distortions, and behaviour is eccentric. At least five out of the following criteria need to be present:

1 ideas of references (excluding delusions of reference)
2 odd beliefs or thinking that influences behaviour and is inconsistent with subcultural norms (e.g. superstitiousness, belief in clairvoyance, telepathy or 'sixth sense'; in children and adolescents, bizarre fantasies or preoccupations)
3 unusual perceptual experiences, including bodily illusions
4 odd thinking and speech (e.g. vague, circumstantial, metaphorical, over-elaborate or stereotyped)
5 suspiciousness or paranoid ideation
6 inappropriate or constricted affect
7 behaviour or appearance that is odd, eccentric or peculiar
8 lack of close friends or confidants other than first-degree relatives
9 excessive social anxiety that does not diminish with familiarity and tends to be associated with paranoid fears rather than negative judgements about self.

Relationship between antisocial PD and psychopathy

In 1941, Cleckley published *The Mask of Sanity* establishing the actual definition of psychopathy (Blair, Mitchell, & Blair, 2005). The main aspects of psychopathy were described like this:

186 *Jill Lobbestael and René Cane*

interpersonally, psychopaths are grandiose, arrogant, callous, superficial, and manipulative; affectively, they are short-tempered, unable to form strong emotional bonds with others, and lacking in empathy, guilt or remorse; and behaviourally, they are irresponsible, impulsive, and prone to violate social and legal norms and expectations.

(Hart & Hare, 1997)

This conceptualisation of psychopathy thus focuses on the interpersonal characteristic of the patient and not on criminal history. In this sense, it is possible to distinguish between psychopaths who end up in prison or mental institutions and psychopaths that are 'not criminals', for example white collar psychopaths. Based on Cleckley's ideas, Hare constructed his Psychopathy Checklist which is currently the most used assessment tool to diagnosed psychopathy (Hare, 1991).

Therefore historically, the symptomatological description of psychopathy has fundamentally referred to an affective and interpersonal dimension (Coid & Ullrich, 2010). It is here that we find the main difference between psychopathy and antisocial PD; while the diagnosis of psychopathy is based on personality traits, the diagnosis of antisocial PD emphasises the behavioural dimension of the disorder, like frequently breaking the law, uninterested in their own or others' safety, inability to conform to social norms and irresponsibility. Therefore, the main difference between these two constructs might be found in the fact that while criminal behaviour is a component of antisocial PD, it could be considered only as a correlate of psychopathy (Skeem & Cooke, 2010). In fact, some have argued that psychopathy is conceptually more related to narcissistic and histrionic PDs than to antisocial PD (Blackburn, 2007). These definitional differences may explain why the prevalence of antisocial PD in forensic populations is almost three times higher than the prevalence of psychopathy. Furthermore, it may also explain why the relationship between both disorders is asymmetric; that is, the majority of offenders who meet criteria for antisocial PD are not psychopaths, but the majority of psychopaths also meet criteria for antisocial PD (Decuyper, De Fruyt, & Buschman, 2008). In any case, it is probably the association between this two disorders and criminal behaviour that has played a major role in consolidating the idea among mental health professionals that individuals with PDs are prone to aggressive and criminal behaviour (Berman et al., 1998; Hart & Hare, 1996).

Box 9.2 Cluster B personality disorder (see DSM-5)

The dramatic, emotional and erratic Cluster B is characterised by impulse control and emotional regulation problems. Antisocial, borderline, histrionic and narcissistic personality disorders (PDs) are part of Cluster B.

The antisocial PD consists of two parts. First, there has to be an adult pattern of disregard for and violation of the rights of others occurring since age 15. For this A-criterion of antisocial PD, at least three of the following need to be present:

1 failure to conform to social norms with respect to lawful behaviours as indicated by repeatedly performing acts that are grounds for arrest
2 deceitfulness, as indicated by repeated lying, use of aliases or conning others for personal profit or pleasure
3 impulsivity or failure to plan ahead
4 irritability and aggressiveness, as indicated by repeated physical fights or assaults
5 reckless disregard for safety of self or others
6 consistent irresponsibility, as indicated by repeated failure to sustain consistent work behaviour or honour financial obligations
7 lack of remorse, as indicated by being indifferent to or rationalising having hurt, mistreated or stolen from another.

The second prerequisite for the antisocial PD diagnosis is that a conduct disorder had to be present with onset before age 15. This way, antisocial PD is the only axis II disorder for which non-adult criteria are formulated in the DSM. Conduct disorder criteria include at least three indices of aggression to people or animals, property destruction, deceitfulness, theft or rule violations.

The second disorder of Cluster B is borderline PD, where the central term is instability. This instability appears in interpersonal relationships, self-image, affects and/or marked impulsivity. Specifically, at least five of the following criteria need to be present:

1 frantic efforts to avoid real or imagined abandonment
2 a pattern of unstable and intense interpersonal relationships characterised by alternating between extremes of idealisation and devaluation
3 identity disturbance: markedly and persistently unstable self-image or sense of self
4 impulsivity in at least two areas that are potentially self-damaging (e.g. spending, sex, substance abuse, reckless driving, binge eating)
5 recurrent suicidal behaviour, gestures or threats, or self-mutilating behaviour
6 affective instability due to a marked reactivity of mood (e.g. intense episodic dysphoria, irritability or anxiety usually lasting a few hours and only rarely more than a few days)
7 chronic feelings of emptiness

(continued)

(continued)

8   inappropriate, intense anger or difficulty controlling anger (e.g. frequent displays of temper, constant anger, recurrent physical fights)

9   transient, stress-related paranoid ideation or severe dissociative symptoms.

Excessive emotionality and attention seeking are hallmark criteria of the histrionic PD. At least five criteria need to be present:

1   uncomfortable in situations in which he or she is not the centre of attention

2   interaction with others is often characterised by inappropriate sexually seductive or provocative behaviour

3   displays rapidly shifting and shallow expression of emotions

4   consistently uses physical appearance to draw attention to self

5   a style of speech that is excessively impressionistic and lacking in detail

6   shows self-dramatisation, theatricality and exaggerated expression of emotion

7   suggestible, i.e. easily influenced by others or circumstances

8   considers relationships to be more intimate than they actually are.

The final Cluster B disorder is narcissistic PD, referring to grandiosity (in fantasy or behaviour), need for admiration and lack of empathy. Five or more criteria need to be present:

1   a grandiose sense of self-importance (e.g. exaggerates achievements and talents, expects to be recognised as superior without commensurate achievements)

2   preoccupied with fantasies of unlimited success, power, brilliance, beauty or ideal love

3   believes that he or she is 'special' and unique and can only be understood by, or should associate with, other special or high-status people (or institutions)

4   requires excessive admiration

5   a sense of entitlement, i.e. unreasonable expectations of especially favourable treatment or automatic compliance with his or her expectations

6   interpersonally exploitative, i.e. takes advantage of others to achieve his or her own ends

7   lacks empathy: is unwilling to recognise or identify with the feelings and needs of others

8   often envious of others or believes that others are envious of him or her

9   shows arrogant, haughty behaviours or attitudes.

Personality disorders and crime 189

Box 9.3 Cluster C personality disorder (see DSM-5)

Finally, Cluster C is the anxious and fearful cluster, including avoidant, dependent and obsessive-compulsive personality disorders (PDs). Avoidant PD patients display social inhibition, feelings of inadequacy and hypersensitivity to negative evaluation. This is expressed in at least four of the following criteria:

1 avoids occupational activities that involve significant interpersonal contact, because of fears of criticism, disapproval or rejection
2 unwilling to get involved with people unless certain of being liked
3 shows restraint within intimate relationships because of the fear of being shamed or ridiculed
4 preoccupied with being criticised or rejected in social situations
5 inhibited in new interpersonal situations because of feelings of inadequacy
6 views self as socially inept, personally unappealing or inferior to others
7 unusually reluctant to take personal risks or to engage in any new activities because they may prove embarrassing.

The second Cluster C PD is dependent PD, which is primarily characterised by an extreme need for other people, to a point where the person is unable to make any decisions or take an independent stand on their own. There is a fear of separation, clinging and submissive behaviour. People with dependent PD have a marked lack of decisiveness, self-confidence and are self-denigrating. At least five of the following criteria need to be present:

1 a hard time in making everyday decisions without getting reassurance and advice from others
2 cannot show disagreement with others for fear of being rejected
3 difficulty in doing things on their own
4 will do almost anything to get support of others
5 when alone, overcome by a feeling of discomfort or helplessness
6 when one caring or supporting relationship ends they are compelled to seek another
7 preoccupation with and unrealistic fear of being left alone to care for themselves.

The obsessive–compulsive PD is part of Cluster C, with an extreme preoccupation with orderliness, perfectionism and mental and interpersonal control,

(continued)

(continued)

at the expense of flexibility, openness and efficiency. Four or more of the following criteria need to be present:

1. preoccupied with details, rules, lists, order, organisation or schedules to the extent that the major point of the activity is lost
2. shows perfectionism that interferes with task completion (e.g. unable to complete a project because his or her own overly strict standards are not met)
3. excessively devoted to work and productivity to the exclusion of leisure activities and friendships (not accounted for by obvious economic necessity)
4. overconscientious, scrupulous and inflexible about matters of morality, ethics or values (not accounted for by cultural or religious identification)
5. unable to discard worn-out or worthless objects even when they have no sentimental value
6. reluctant to delegate tasks or to work with others unless they submit to exactly his or her way of doing things
7. adopts a miserly spending style towards both self and others; money is viewed as something to be hoarded for future catastrophes
8. shows rigidity and stubbornness.

Categorical or dimensional operationalisation of PDs

There is an ongoing debate on whether PDs should be best seen as categorical concepts, as conceptualised in the DSM-IV, or whether a dimensional view would better justify PD pathologies. Taxometric studies investigate this question in a data-driven manner. Based on large samples, the distributions of the datasets are compared to their fits on dimensional versus categorical structures. For most PDs, including borderline, paranoid and cluster C PDs, greater evidence was found for a latent dimensional structure (e.g. Arntz et al., 2009). In contrast, schizotypal PD fitted better with a taxonic, categorical structure (e.g. Haslam, 2003). Findings on antisocial PD were mixed (e.g. Ayers, 2000; Edens, Marcus, Lilienfeld, & Poythress, 2006). While the DSM-5 workgroup initially suggested major changes to the PD section, including the removal of half of the axis II disorders and the introduction of a prototypic matching procedure (Skodol et al., 2011; Widiger, 2011), it was recently decided that all 10 PDs would be preserved categorically because of the major criticism raised by scholars in the PD field and the premature state of empirical research on several PDs. A new trait-specific methodology will be included, though, in a separate area of the DSM-5. Future research is necessary to decide how to accurately diagnose PDs in clinical practice. In this chapter, both studies using categorical and dimensional views on PDs are included.

Prevalence of PDs in criminal samples

Although findings are mixed, in general PD rates have been shown to be high among prisoner samples. A review based on more than 20 000 prisoners concluded that 65% of men and 47% of women suffered from a PD (Fazel & Danesh, 2002). There is also initial evidence that PD rates are even higher among violent recidivists (Putkonen, Komulainen, Virkkunen, Eronen, & Lönnqvist, 2003). Compared to a community sample, the odds ratio of having a PD in incarcerated samples was estimated at 8.6 (Butler, Andrews, Allnutt, Sakashita, & Smith, 2006). Longitudinal studies confirmed that having PD symptoms or diagnoses strongly increased the risk for violence among community samples. Johnson and colleagues, for example, followed more than 700 adolescents into adulthood and found that those with a PD diagnosis had an elevated base rate for violence of 14.4% (Johnson et al., 2000). Another study following 500 persons over 20 years showed that PD symptoms in early adulthood partly mediated the effect between earlier childhood risk factors and perpetrating partner violence in adulthood (Ehrensaft, Cohen, & Johnson, 2006).

Turning to prevalence rates of specific PDs in prisoner samples, it seems that in fact most PDs have been observed to some degree. Conclusions are hampered, though, by the substantial heterogeneity between the prevalence rates across studies which is likely due to different assessment methods (questionnaires versus interviews) and subsamples (e.g. forensic psychiatric patients, sexual offenders, maximum–security offenders). Nonetheless, antisocial PD appears the predominant PD type among prisoners, with around 50% diagnosed males and 20% females, and a 10 times higher chance of diagnosing among prisoners compared to the general population (Fazel & Danesh, 2002; Ullrich et al., 2008). It has to be noted, though, that antisocial PD is almost always accompanied by substance abuse, which might independently steer or strengthen the relationship between antisocial PD and violence (Fountoulakis, Leucht, & Kaprinis, 2008). This positive relationship between antisocial PD and criminal behaviour constitutes a problem by itself. The diagnostic criteria for antisocial PD not only include personality traits such as irritability, impulsiveness and lack of remorse, but mainly focus on behavioural aspects such as failure to conform to social norms, deception in different forms and the legal consequences of such behaviours (APA, 2000). In other words, repeated criminal behaviour is a criterion for antisocial PD and therefore it is easy to imagine why it has been argued that any possible relationship between antisocial PD and criminal behaviour might be tautological (Berman et al., 1998).

As with antisocial PD, borderline PD also includes anger and related problems in the diagnostic criteria and therefore it is not surprising to find considerable evidence indicating higher rates of borderline PD in prison populations compared to community samples (Sansone & Sansone, 2009). Prevalence rates of borderline PD in prison samples vary between 10 and 70% (e.g. Black et al., 2007; Coid, 2003) with a review suggesting borderline PD dominates in female incarcerated samples (25%, Fazel & Danesh, 2002). Similarly, Burke (2005) observed that the prevalence of borderline PD in a forensic sample among men was 5.3% and among women 11.5%. Interestingly, there is evidence showing that rates of borderline PD among men in forensic populations are similar to rates in the general population whereas female rates in the forensic population are much higher (Sansone & Sansone, 2009). Around 90% of offenders showed at least one and 78% at least two borderline PD criteria, most frequently impulsivity (Black et al., 2007). There is some preliminary evidence that specifically the borderline PD traits of affect instability, unstable relationships (Raine, 1993) and identity diffusion (Leichsenring, Kunst, & Hoyer, 2003) would predispose to violence. In contrast, the majority of studies showed that relationships between borderline PD and violence disappeared after controlling for other comorbidity rates like antisocial PD, conduct disorder, history of childhood maltreatment, length of therapy stay and substance abuse (see Allen & Links, 2012, for a review). This was, for example, the case in two longitudinal community-based studies (Berman et al., 1998; Johnson et al., 2000). One likely explanation is that violence is not due to a borderline PD trait-based tendency, but the presence of comorbid conditions known to elevate risk for violence (Allen & Links, 2012).

Between 7 and 48% of prisoner samples were estimated to adhere to the narcissistic PD criteria (Coid, 2003; Harsch, Bergk, Steinert, Keller, & Jockusch, 2006; Leue, Borchard, & Hoyer, 2004; Ullrich et al., 2008). Histrionic PD appeared to be the least prevalent cluster B disorder among prisoners, with estimates between 0 and 21% (Coid, 2003; Harsch et al., 2006; Leue et al., 2004; Ullrich et al., 2008). A diagnosis of any cluster B PD significantly predicted if there was self-reported violence of incarcerated females within the institution (Warren et al., 2002). The overall prevalence of any cluster B disorder varied between 30 and 60% (Butler et al., 2006; Leue et al., 2004), with an odds ratio of 14.1 in prison samples compared to community samples (Butler et al., 2006).

Second in line are cluster C PDs, assumed to be present in 20 to 40% of prisoners, with an odds ratio of 7.3 compared to the community sample (Butler et al., 2006; Harsch et al., 2006; Leue et al., 2004). Among non-patients, dependent PD was the only cluster C PD to relate to interview-assessed aggression (Berman et al., 1998). Bornstein (2012) concluded from a literature search that dependent PD patients are especially triggered to aggress when important relationships are threatened, resulting in an increased risk for domestic violence and child abuse. Estimates of avoidant PD in criminal samples vary between 5 and 24%, and those of obsessive-compulsive PD between 0 and 11%.

Of cluster A PDs, paranoid PD diagnoses are quite frequent, with figures ranging between 7 and 46% (Coid, 2003; Harsch et al., 2006; Rotter, Way, Steinbacher, Sawyer, & Smith, 2002; Ullrich et al., 2008). Assessing the full range of PDs in a non-clinical sample, paranoid traits were found to uniquely predict interview-measured aggression, even when controlled for antisocial and borderline PD traits (Berman et al., 1998). This suggests that the tendency to be suspicious and unforgiving of perceived slights likely puts paranoid PD patients at risk for aggression. Estimates of schizotypal and schizoid PD traits are lower (between 0 and 23%, Coid, 2003; Harsch et al., 2006; Rotter et al., 2002; Ullrich et al., 2008). Schizoid PD was the only PD that has been observed to correlate negatively with aggression, likely because limited social interactions provide limited opportunities to engage in aggression. Overall, cluster A PDs are the least likely to be found in prisoners (13 to 27%, Butler et al., 2006; Harsch et al., 2006). Compared to community samples, the odds ratio of having a cluster A PD in a forensic population is 14.1 (Butler et al., 2006).

Comorbidity

Some findings suggest that different constellations of axis II comorbidity may be associated with particular forms of violence. In this regard, for example, Hernandez-Avila et al. (2000) observed that antisocial PD patients with a comorbid diagnosis of schizoid and borderline PD were significantly more involved in violent crimes. In this same line of research, Keeney, Festinger, Marlowe, Kirby, and Platt (1997) found that a diagnosis of antisocial PD with paranoid and narcissistic PD comorbidity was associated with higher numbers of crimes against persons, even controlling for alcohol and drug abuse. More research is necessary to learn how specific PD comorbidities relate to violence.

Relationship between specific PDs and offence types

Quite a large body of research aimed to link the different PDs to specific offence types. Several studies have shown significant associations between antisocial PD and a diversity of crimes such as firearm offences, robbery, theft, burglary, violent offences, fraud and drug offences (Coid, 1998; Hodgins, Mednick, Brennan, Schulsinger, & Engberg, 1996; Rasmussen & Levander, 1996; Roberts & Coid, 2010). Since repeated criminal behaviour is a criterion for antisocial PD, these broad associations between criminal behaviour and antisocial PD may merely confirm criminal versatility (Roberts & Coid, 2010).

One study found borderline PD to predict self-reported partner-aggression in women, even when controlled for other PD types (Weinstein, Oltmanns, & Gleason, 2012). However, in the study by Roberts and Coid (2010) based on the national survey of mental disorders in prisoners in England and Wales, the authors observed that borderline PD was not associated with any of the different offending behaviours in their list. Their explanation for this was based on one of the major difficulties when studying possible relationships between a particular PD and criminal behaviour, namely comorbidity. Specifically, they assumed it was probably the comorbidity between borderline PD and other PDs that caused the association between borderline PD and criminality types to disappear when controlling for other PDs. There is in fact substantial evidence indicating high associations between borderline PD and other cluster

194 *Jill Lobbestael and René Cane*

B disorders (Becker, Grilo, Edell, & McGlashan, 2000; Stuart et al., 1998), particularly with antisocial PD.

In that same study, it was observed that narcissistic PD was significantly associated with offences such as fraud and forgery (Roberts & Coid, 2010), possibly as a means to display dominance. Narcissistic PD subjects in the forensic sample of Coid (2002) appeared to be more involved in violent acts towards other inmates and staff. According to the author, this association reflects core features of narcissistic PD such as lack of empathy, pervasive grandiosity, hyper-sensitivity to others' evaluations and an inflated self-image. In relation to histrionic PD, Roberts and Coid (2010) and Warren and South (2009) both failed to observed any association between this disorder and specific criminal offences.

One of the few studies addressing offence types in cluster A and C PDs was conducted by Roberts and Coid (2010). The authors observed that in relation to cluster A PDs, paranoid PD was significantly associated with robbery and blackmail but negatively associated with driving offences. In addition, schizotypal PD was significantly associated with arson but negatively associated with robbery and blackmail. Finally, schizoid PD appeared associated with kidnap, burglary and theft. In a study conducted by Warren et al. (2002) on 261 incarcerated female felons, a diagnosis of any cluster A PDs significantly predicted current convictions of any violent crimes including and excluding homicide, and conviction for prostitution. Regarding cluster C, it was observed that avoidant, dependent and obsessive-compulsive PDs were significantly associated with offences such as criminal damage, violent offences (with or without firearm) and firearm offences respectively. Furthermore, significant negative associations were observed between avoidant PD and firearm offences, and between dependent PD and criminal damage. Finally, any cluster C PD among incarcerated females predicted not being incarcerated for drug crime and being incarcerated for regulatory crimes (Warren et al., 2002). Taken together, most PDs (except histrionic PD) have been linked to one or some types of offence, while antisocial PD is related to a broad spectrum of offences.

Assessment methods of PDs in forensic samples

The prevalence rates of PDs and relations with offence types outlined above are all based on self-reported or interview-based assessment of PDs. There are several reasons, though, to doubt the validity of patient-provided information in forensic samples, like high levels of deceitfulness, the tendency to malinger symptoms to excuse themselves from blame or withholding negative information that might have negative legal consequences (Allard & Grann, 2000; Cima, 2003; Haywood, Grossman, & Hardy, 1993). Some studies examined the convergence between self-reported and informant-based (e.g. treatment providers) PD assessment in forensic samples. Overall, informants observed more PD pathology in these patients than the patients did themselves (Allard & Grann, 2000; Keulen-de-Vos et al., 2011; Whyte, Fox, & Coxell, 2006).

One study concluded that the PD diagnoses changed by the supplementary data given by informants in 20% of the cases (Allard & Grann, 2000). These findings are in line with a study on cognitive schema assessment showing that therapists reported more maladaptive schemas when compared to the forensic patients themselves (Lobbestael, Arntz, Löbbes, & Cima, 2009). Findings on agreement between patient and observer reports for cluster B disorders are particularly inconsistent, with one study showing a higher agreement which was hypothesised to stem from these disorders more often being the focus of treatment (Allard & Grann, 2000), and another study finding the opposite pattern of informants reporting more borderline, narcissistic and (trend effect) antisocial PD than the patients themselves (Keulen-de-Vos et al., 2011). Importantly, the observed discrepancy in patient-observer-assessed PD pathology could also result from treatment providers overestimating the pathology levels in their patients. Knowing which assessment type is closer to the 'clinical truth' is difficult. Nonetheless, because of the generally lower estimations of psychopathology in forensic patients, there are reasons to assume that the PD prevalence rates mentioned above are likely an underestimation of the true PD rates.

Motivation for crimes in PDs

Knowledge of the motivation for crime is valuable for therapeutically lowering violent recidivism. Coid (2002) interviewed prisoners about their motives to commit offences, and linked these to their PD diagnoses. He concluded that crimes of paranoid PD patients mostly stemmed from their sensitive and vengeful traits. Schizoid PD patients were mostly motivated to commit crime as an acting out of homicidal fantasies. Distorted affective functioning resulting in taking pleasure in crimes proved to motivate schizotypal PD patients for crime. Borderline PD patients reported often acting violently as a way to relieve tension or dysphoria. Desire to express their toughness and low stress tolerance led histrionic PD patients to engage in offences. Furthermore, the crimes committed by narcissistic PD offenders were motivated by their intolerance of rules, receiving a standard treatment in prison that conflicted with their high expectations and seeing violence as the sole solution to interpersonal difficulties. Finally, avoidant PD patients' motivation for crime was based on anxiety and an intolerance of being associated with other prisoners. The antisocial PD diagnosis was too broadly associated with specific types of crime and motivations for it to permit conclusions. More research like this on the motivations for crime in specific PDs is necessary to better understand the dynamics leading to crime.

Relationship between PDs and aggression

In this section, we will turn to the relationship between PDs and aggression, as a proxy of crime. Three specific PDs are selected that have a strong empirical

196 *Jill Lobbestael and René Cane*

line of evidence regarding aggression, namely antisocial, narcissistic and borderline PD. In the reported studies, aggression is measured either through self-report or through behavioural paradigms. Some of these studies differentiate between reactive and proactive types of aggression. Reactive aggression refers to uncontrolled or impulsive outbursts of anger that serve as a defensive reaction to goal blocking, provocation or frustration. Proactive aggression, on the other hand, is a relatively non-emotional and often premeditated or planned display of aggression, to further one's goals of power, money or external gains (Dodge & Coie, 1987). Factor analyses have consistently found evidence for this bimodal distinction of outperforming, viewing aggression as a unitary concept (Ross & Babcock, 2009). Although opposite in nature and motives, these two types of aggression are often correlated. Hence, individuals can engage in both types of aggression, leading to the view that reactive and proactive aggression are separate dimensions rather than distinct categories (Cima & Raine, 2009; Poulin & Boivin, 2000).

Antisocial PD and aggression

Antisocial PD has been consistently linked with increased levels of aggression in imprisoned samples across gender and ethnicity (e.g. Dunsieth et al., 2004; Warren et al., 2002). A survey among a British household population concluded that the presence of antisocial PD diagnoses increased the risk of having caused victims injuries by 24% (Coid et al., 2006). In these epidemiological studies, antisocial PD was highly comorbid with substance abuse, making it unclear to which degree antisocial PD independently predicted aggression. We are aware of only one study linking antisocial PD to more aggressive responses on a behaviour task using the Point Subtraction Aggression Paradigm, a competitive reaction time task where aggression is operationalised as the points the subject subtracts from a virtual opponent. This effect stood strong even after controlling for cocaine abuse, craving and withdrawal symptoms (Moeller et al., 1997). Given the small sample, however, these findings can only be considered preliminary.

Antisocial PD traits have been shown to relate to both reactive and proactive types of general aggression (Lobbestael, Cima, & Arntz, 2013; Walters, 2007) and physical aggression (Ostrov & Houston, 2008). When looking at relational aggression, the antisocial PD diagnosis was only related to proactive aggression (Ostrov & Houston, 2008). Finally, male batterers with an antisocial PD diagnosis were found to be motived to reactive aggression in reaction to violence displayed by their female partner, which these men likely interpreted as provocative. Male batterers also engaged in proactive aggression, which was motivated by a need to control their female partner after they displayed dominant behaviour (Ross & Babcock, 2009).

Taken together, although a strong epidemiological link was evidenced between antisocial PD and violence, hardly anything is known from behavioural studies. The tautological relationship with aggression might have caused

Personality disorders and crime 197

this lack of studies. Antisocial PD patients proved to be motivated to aggression both for reactive and proactive reasons.

Narcissistic PD and aggression

For several decades, there was a fierce battle between researchers assuming that high levels versus low levels of self-esteem predisposed to aggression. Inconsistent findings in both research lines, however, led many scholars to conclude that neither ends of this simple self-esteem spectrum were relevant in predicting aggression (for an overview see Bushman & Thomaes, 2011). That is when the inflated self-view, central to narcissistic PD, became the focus of aggression studies. A theoretical link between narcissism and aggression was already put forward in the 1970s, with the psychodynamic conceptualisation of narcissistic rage (Kernberg, 1975; Kohut, 1971).

All existing studies on the relation between narcissistic PD and aggression used non-clinical samples. Here, narcissism is typically assessed with the Narcissistic Personality Inventory (NPI, Raskin & Hall, 1979), a self-report instrument. The NPI primarily assesses the typical type of narcissism, i.e. self-assured extraverts that are preoccupied with receiving attention and admiration from others, who are also referred to as having overt narcissism (Wink, 1991). These overt narcissistic aspects are also mostly considered in the DSM-IV criteria. Overt narcissists are generally described as interpersonally disruptive, bossy, aggressive and even cruel (Wink, 1991). Overt narcissism has been linked to reactive aggression through the concept of threatened egotism. Aggression is thereby designated as being a defensive response when the highly favourable self-view is challenged by less favourable external appraisals (Baumeister & Boden, 1998; Baumeister, Smart, & Boden, 1996). This view was supported by several studies linking overt narcissism to aggression specifically after provocation or social rejection. Bushman & Baumeister (1998), for example, observed that participants high in narcissism that were given negative feedback on an essay they wrote administered more noise blasts (i.e. physical aggression) to their opponents in a competitive reaction time task. In another study, an ego-threat was induced by bogus negative feedback on an IQ test. Here, narcissism positively correlated to the level of negative feedback they provided about an experimenter while aware of possibly harmful consequences of such feedback (i.e. verbal aggression, Stucke & Sporer, 2002). Finally, narcissism was found to positively correlate to physical aggression to a person they were previously rejected by (i.e. not selected to be part of his/her group, Twenge & Campbell, 2003). These studies evidencing the ego-threat hypothesis in narcissism is in line with those demonstrating a link between self-reported narcissism traits and reactive aggression. In their review, Bettencourt, Talley, Benjamin, and Valentine (2006) came to a similar conclusion of participants high in narcissism only displaying more aggression than their lower-scoring counterparts under conditions of provocation.

There are other studies available, though, that failed to replicate narcissistic rage following ego-threat (e.g. study 1 of Bushman & Baumeister, 1998), or found narcissism scores to predispose to aggression (i.e. amount of electric shocks given to opponent in a learning task), even in the absence of ego-threat (Martinez, Zeichner, Reidy, & Miller, 2008; Reidy, Foster, & Zeichner, 2010; Reidy, Zeichner, Foster, & Martinez, 2008). Narcissism traits were even shown to (also) correlate with self-reported proactive aggression (Fossati, Borroni, Eisenberg, & Maffei, 2010; Seah & Ang, 2008; Washburn, McMahon, King, Reinecke, & Silver, 2004), suggesting that narcissists might also use aggression in an instrumental way.

Overt narcissism is opposed by covert narcissism. While covert narcissists share a cognitive-affective preoccupation with the self with overt narcissism manifested through conceit and arrogance, a tendency to give in to one's own needs and disregard for others (Wink, 1991), feelings of grandeur are largely unconscious in covert narcissists. Instead, they openly display themselves as timid and insecure and lacking self-confidence and initiative while being hypersensitive, anxious and depressed. Although covert narcissists avoid much social contact, when they do become close to others they may reveal their grandiose fantasies, which often comes as a surprise to the friends and partners who had thought of them as shy, humble persons (Kernberg, 1986; Wink, 1991). Covert narcissists are also described as defensive, hostile and insisting upon having their own way (Wink, 1991). The only experimental study that assessed the relationship between covert narcissism and the aggression types found a unique relationship to reactive aggression (Fossati et al., 2010).

Borderline PD and aggression

Clinical lore holds that borderline PD creates a higher risk of aggression (Allen & Links, 2012). There is some evidence showing that borderline PD patients report higher levels of aggression when compared to non-patient controls (Dougherty, Bjork, Huckabee, Moeller, & Swann, 1999) and non-cluster B patients (McCloskey et al., 2009). In a study where participants rated their behaviour after each social interaction during 20 days on an electronic diary, borderline PD patients indeed reported more quarrelsome behaviour than non-patient controls (Russel, Moskowitz, Zuroff, Sookman, & Paris, 2007). Using a similar experienced-sample methodology, borderline PD patients reported their rage to often result from perceived rejection (Berenson, Downey, Rafaeli, Coifman, & Leventhal Paquin, 2011). Such a rejection-rage link in borderline PD was further supported by faster pronunciation of rage-words after priming with rejection-related words (Berenson et al., 2011).

Although theories have explained the risk of aggression in borderline PD in terms of their high impulsivity levels (Látalová & Praško, 2010), findings on whether aggression displayed by borderline PD patients is predominantly reactive or proactive in nature are contradictory. Ostrov and Houston (2008) found borderline PD to relate to both reactive and proactive types of relational aggression, but another study concluded male batterers to respond with violence in reaction to their female partners' display of distress, suggesting a reactive function only of aggression in this subsample (Ross & Babcock, 2009).

Behavioural aggression studies in borderline PD solely relied on the Point Subtraction Aggression Paradigm (Cherek, 1981; Golomb, Cortez-Perez, Jaworski, Mednick, & Dimsdale, 2007), where participants compete in an online computer game against a virtual opponent who provokes the participant by subtracting points. When the participant subtracts money from the opponent as a counterattack, this is considered an aggressive act. Using the PSAP, borderline PD patients were found to respond with three times more aggressive responses compared to non-patients (Dougherty et al., 1999; McCloskey et al., 2009; New et al., 2009). Aggression levels did not differ, however, from those of non–cluster B patients (McCloskey et al., 2009).

Taken together, the handful of studies addressing the relationship between aggression and borderline PD did confirm this link using both experienced sampling and behavioural methods. More research is required, however, to determine how specific aggression is for borderline PD patients, and whether their displayed aggression is mostly reactive or proactive in nature.

Methodological limitations

As mentioned by Berman et al. (1998), one of the major criticisms commonly addressed to the studies investigating possible associations between PDs and criminal behaviour is that most of these studies have been conducted in forensic samples or psychiatric inpatients. This type of sampling may be confounded with other variables and therefore not truly reveal the association between PD and criminal behaviour. A second limitation emerges from the assessment tools used in most of these studies. Many include self-reports or clinician-rated assessment tools. Despite the psychometric properties of such assessment instruments, each of them presents particular limitations which are possible to find in the related literature. Finally, most of these studies lack control for comorbidity. This raises the question of whether PD pathology sufficiently predicts specific criminal behaviour or whether this relationship is driven by more complex constellations of overall psychopathology. Further research is needed to answer this question.

Concluding remarks

PDs are enduring patterns of pathological traits that are traceable to early adulthood and express themselves across several aspects in life. Ten different PDs are defined that are grouped in either cluster A (paranoid, schizoid, schizotypal), cluster B (antisocial, borderline, histrionic, narcissistic) or cluster C (avoidant, dependent, obsessive-compulsive). The diagnosis of psychopathy has a strong overlap with the behavioural antisocial PD criteria, but requires additional personality traits. Studies on the prevalence of PDs in forensic samples are not always directly comparable because of differences in study populations and assessment methods. Nonetheless, while the prevalence of PDs in the general populations is estimated at around 3%, as many as one third to one half of the prisoner samples are estimated to suffer from one or more PDs. Although PDs across all clusters have been associated with crime, antisocial, borderline and narcissistic PDs are most commonly observed in forensic samples. It is difficult to draw firm conclusions on the unique contribution of these PDs to crime, though, because of the partly tautological relation between crime and some PD criteria, and the high comorbidity rates of these PDs with other disorders, including substance abuse. Some studies suggest basing PD assessment on patient-reports but these likely underestimate true PD pathology in forensic samples. More research is needed on the motivations of different PD groups to aggress. Antisocial PD appears to relate to a diversity of crimes, and other PDs have been associated with specific types of offences. Some research lines took a broader stand and studied how antisocial, borderline and narcissistic PDs relate to aggression. There are surprisingly few studies on how antisocial PD is associated with aggression, but the ones that did evidence such a link mainly did so through self-report. Narcissistic PD traits have been vastly related to aggressive behaviour mainly using laboratory aggression paradigms. Borderline PD patients were also found to both report higher aggression levels, and react more aggressive in laboratory settings. Aggression in antisocial PD patients can stem both from reactive and proactive motivations. Proactive, instrumental motivations sometimes steer narcissistic PD patients' aggression, but research primarily supports this patient group to respond with aggression in response to provocation (reactive aggression). Findings on the reactive versus proactive motivation for aggression in borderline PD patients are mixed. Overcoming methodological drawbacks like using confined samples, failing to account for comorbidities and sole reliance on self-report are challenges for future studies on the relationship between PDs and crime.

Literature

Allard, K., & Grann, M. (2000). Personality disorders and patient-informant concordance on DIP-Q self-report in a forensic psychiatric inpatient setting. *Nordic Journal of Psychiatry, 54*(3), 195–200.

Allen, A., & Links, P. S. (2012). Aggression in borderline personality disorder: Evidence for increased risk and clinical predictors. *Current Psychiatry Reports, 14,* 62–69.

American Psychiatric Association. (2000). *Diagnostic and statistical manual of mental disorders (Revised 4th ed.).* Washington, DC: American Psychiatric Association.

Arntz, A., Bernstein, D. P., Gielen, D., van Nieuwenhuyzen, M., Penders, K., Haslam, N., & Ruscio, J. (2009). Taxometric evidence for the dimensional structure of Cluster-C, Paranoid, and Borderline Personality Disorders. *Journal of Personality Disorders, 23*(6), 606–628.

Ayers, W. A. (2000). Taxometric analysis of borderline and antisocial personality disorders in a drug and alcohol dependent population. *Dissertation Abstracts International: Section B: The Sciences and Engineering, 61*(3-B), 1684.

Baumeister, R. F., & Boden, J. M. (1998). Aggression and the self: High self-esteem, low self-control, and ego threat. In R. G. Geen & E. Donnerstein (Eds.), *Human aggression: Theories, research, and implications for social policy*. San Diego, CA: Academic Press.

Baumeister, R. F., Smart, L., & Boden, J. M. (1996). Relation of threatened egotism to violence and aggression: The dark side of high self-esteem. *Psychological Review, 103*, 5–33.

Becker, M. E., Grilo, C. M., Edell, W. S., & McGlashan, T. H. (2000). Comorbidity of borderline personality disorder with other personality disorders in hospitalized adolescents and adults. *American Journal of Psychiatry, 157*(12), 2011–2016.

Berenson, K. R., Downey, G., Rafaeli, E., Coifman, K. G., & Leventhal Paquin, N. (2011). The rejection-rage contingency in borderline personality disorder. *Journal of Abnormal Psychology*. doi: 10.1037/a0023335

Berman, M. E., Fallon, A. E., & Coccaro, E. F. (1998). The relationship between personality psychopathology and aggressive behaviour in research volunteers. *Journal of Abnormal Psychology, 107*(4), 651–658.

Bettencourt, B. A., Talley, A., Benjamin, A. J., & Valentine, J. (2006). Personality and aggressive behaviour under provoking and neutral conditions: A meta-analytic review. *Psychological Bulletin, 132*(5), 751–777.

Black, D. W., Gunter, T., Allen, J., Blum, N., Arndt, S., Wenman, G., & Sieleni, B. (2007). Borderline personality disorder in male and female offenders newly committed to prison. *Comprehensive Psychiatry, 48*, 400–405.

Blackburn, R. (2007). Personality disorder and antisocial deviance: Comments on the debate on the structure of the Psychopathy Checklist – Revised. *Journal of Personality Disorders, 21*(2), 142–159.

Blair, J., Mitchell, D. R., & Blair, K. (2005). *The psychopath: Emotion and the brain*. Malden, MA: Blackwell.

Bornstein, R. F. (2012). Illuminating a neglected clinical issue: Societal costs of interpersonal dependency and dependent personality disorder. *Journal of Clinical Psychology, 68*(7), 766–781.

Burke, J. M. (2005). Male borderline personality disorder with comorbid disorders as contrasted to females with comorbid disorders in a correctional setting. *Diss Abstr Int, 65*, 4885B.

Bushman, B. J., & Baumeister, R. F. (1998). Threatened egotism, narcissism, self-esteem, and direct and displaced aggression: Does self-love or self-hate lead to violence? *Journal of Personality and Social Psychology, 75*, 219–229.

Bushman, B. J., & Thomaes, S. (2011). When the narcissistic ego deflates, narcissistic aggression inflates. In W. K. Campbell, J. D. Miller & N. J. Hoboken (Eds.), *The handbook of narcissism and narcissistic personality disorder: Theoretical approaches, empirical findings, and treatments*. New York: John Wiley & Sons.

Butler, T., Andrews, G., Allnutt, S., Sakashita, C., & Smith, N. E. (2006). Mental disorders in australian prisoners: A comparison with a community sample. *Australian and New Zealand Journal of Psychiatry, 40*, 272–276.

Cherek, D. R. (1981). Effects of smoking different doses of nicotine on human aggressive behaviour. *Psychopharmacology, 75*, 339–349.

Cima, M. (2003). *Faking good, bad and ugly: Malingering in forensic psychiatry inpatients*. Maastricht, the Netherlands: Maastricht University.

Cima, M., & Raine, A. (2009). Distinct characteristics of psychopathy relate to different subtypes of aggression. *Personality and Individual Differences, 47*, 835–840.

202 Jill Lobbestael and René Cane

Cleckley, H. M. (1941). *The mask of sanity: An attempt to reinterpret the so-called psychopathic personality*. St. Louis, MO: The C. V. Mosby Company.

Coid, J. W., & Ullrich, S. (2010). Antisocial personality disorder is on a continuum with psychopathy. *Comprehensive Psychiatry, 51*(4), 426–433.

Coid, J. W., Yang, M., Roberts, A., Ullrich, S., Moran, P., Bebbington, P., & Singleton, N. (2006). Violence and psychiatric morbidity in the national household population of Britain: Public health implications. *The British Journal of Psychiatry, 189*(1), 12–19.

Coid, J. W. (1998). Axis II disorders and motivation for serious criminal behaviour. In A. E. Skodol (Ed.), *Psychopathology and violent crime*. Washington, DC: American Psychiatric Press.

Coid, J. W. (2002). Personality disorders in prisoners and their motivation for dangerous and disruptive behaviour. *Criminal Behaviour and Mental Health, 12*, 209–226.

Coid, J. W. (2003). The co-morbidity of personality disorder and lifetime clinical syndromes in dangerous offenders. *The Journal of Forensic Psychiatry & Psychology, 14*(2), 341–366.

Davison, S., & Janca, A. (2012). Personality disorder and criminal behaviour: What is the nature of the relationship? *Current Opinion in Psychiatry, 25*, 39–45.

Decuyper, M., De Fruyt, F., & Buschman, J. (2008). A five-factor model perspective on psychopathy and comorbid Axis-II disorders in a forensic-psychiatric sample. *International Journal of Law and Psychiatry, 31*(5), 394–406.

Dodge, K. A., & Coie, J. D. (1987). Social-information-processing factors in reactive and proactive aggression in children's peer groups. *Journal of Personality and Social Psychology, 53*(6), 1146–1158.

Dougherty, D. M., Bjork, J. M., Huckabee, H. C., Moeller, F. G., & Swann, A. C. (1999). Laboratory measures of aggression and impulsivity in women with borderline personality disorder. *Psychiatry Research, 85*(3), 315–326.

Dunsieth, N. W., Nelson, E. B., Brusman-Lovins, L. A., Holcomb, J. L., Beckman, D., Welge, J. A., & McElroy, S. L. (2004). Psychiatric and legal features of 113 men convicted of sexual offenses. *Journal of Clinical Psychiatry, 65*(3), 293–300.

Edens, J. F., Marcus, D. K., Lilienfeld, S. O., & Poythress, N. G. (2006). Psychopathic, not psychopath: Taxometric evidence for the dimensional structure of psychopathy. *Journal of Abnormal Psychology, 115*, 131–144.

Ehrensaft, M. K., Cohen, P., & Johnson, J. G. (2006). Development of personality disorder symptoms and the risk for partner violence. *Journal of Abnormal Psychology, 115*, 474–483.

Fazel, S., & Danesh, J. (2002). Serious mental disorder in 23 000 prisoners: A systematic review of 62 surveys. *The Lancet, 359*, 545–550.

Fossati, A., Borroni, S., Eisenberg, N., & Maffei, C. (2010). Relations of proactive and reactive dimensions of aggression to overt and covert narcissism in nonclinical adolescents. *Aggressive Behaviour, 36*, 21–27.

Fountoulakis, K. N., Leucht, S., & Kaprinis, G. S. (2008). Personality disorders and violence. *Current Opinion in Psychiatry, 21*, 84–92.

Gardner, D. L., Leibenluft, E., O'Leary, K. M., & Cowdry, R. W. (1991). Self-ratings of anger and hostility in borderline personality disorder. *Journal of Nervous and Mental Disease, 179*, 157–161.

Golomb, B., Cortez-Perez, M., Jaworski, B., Mednick, S., & Dimsdale, J. (2007). Point subtraction aggression paradigm: Validity of a brief schedule of use. *Violence Vict., 22*, 95–103.

Personality disorders and crime 203

Hare, R. D. (1991). *The Hare Psychopathy Checklist revised.* Toronto, Ontario: Multi-Health Systems.

Harsch, S., Bergk, J. E., Steinert, T., Keller, F., & Jockusch, U. (2006). Prevalence of mental disorders among sexual offenders in forensic psychiatry and prison. *International Journal of Law and Psychiatry, 29,* 443–449.

Hart, S. D., & Hare, R. D. (1996). Psychopathy and risk assessment. *Current Opinion in Psychiatry, 9*(6), 380–383.

Hart, S. D., & Hare, R. D. (1997). Psychopathy: Assessment and association with criminal conduct. In M. Stoff, J. Breiling & J. D. Maser (Eds.), *Handbook of antisocial behaviour* (pp. 22–35). New York: Wiley.

Haslam, N. (2003). The dimensional view of personality disorders: A review of the taxometric evidence. *Clinical Psychology Review, 23,* 75–93.

Haywood, T. W., Grossman, L. S., & Hardy, D. W. (1993). Denial and social desirability in clinical examinations of alleged sex offenders. *Journal of Nervous and Mental Disease, 181*(3), 183–188.

Hernandez-Avila, C. A., Burleson, J. A., Poling, J., Tennen, H., Rounsaville, B. J., & Kranzler, H. R. (2000). Personality and substance use disorders as predictors of criminality. *Comprehensive Psychiatry, 41,* 276–283.

Hodgins, S., Mednick, S. A., Brennan, P. A., Schulsinger, F., & Engberg, M. (1996). Mental disorder and crime: Evidence from a Danish birth cohort. *Archives of General Psychiatry, 54,* 489–496.

Johansen, M., Karterud, S., Pedersen, G., Gude, T., & Falkum, E. (2004). An investigation of the prototype validity of the borderline DSM-IV construct. *Acta Psychiatrica Scandinavica, 109*(4), 289–298.

Johnson, J. G., Cohen, P., Smailes, E., Kasen, S., Oldham, J. M., Skodol, A. E., & Brook, J. S. (2000). Adolescent personality disorders associated with violence and criminal behaviour during adolescence and early adulthood. *American Journal of Psychiatry, 157,* 1406–1412.

Keeney, M. M., Festinger, D. S., Marlowe, D. B., Kirby, K. C., & Platt, J. J. (1997). Personality disorders and criminal activity among cocaine abusers. *Problems of drug dependence 1997: Proceedings of the 59th annual scientific meeting of the college on problems of drug dependence (Research Monograph No. 178).* National Institute on Drug Abuse.

Kernberg, O. F. (1975). *Borderline conditions and pathological narcissism.* New York: Jason Aronson, Inc.

Kernberg, O. F. (1986). *Severe personality disorders: Psychotherapeutic strategies.* New Haven, CT: Yale University Press.

Keulen-de-Vos, M., Bernstein, D. P., Clark, L. A., Arntz, A., Lucker, T. P. C., & Spa de, E. (2011). Patient versus informants reports of personality disorders in forensic patients. *The Journal of Forensic Psychiatry & Psychology, 22*(1), 52–71.

Kohut, H. (1971). *The analysis of the self.* New York: International Universities Press.

Látalová, K., & Praško, J. (2010). Aggression in borderline personality disorder. *Psychiatric Quarterly, 81,* 239–251.

Leichsenring, F., Kunst, H., & Hoyer, J. (2003). Borderline personality organization in violent offenders: Correlations of identity diffusion and primitive defense mechanisms with antisocial features, neuroticism, and interpersonal problems. *Bulletin of the Menninger Clinic, 67,* 314–327.

Leue, A., Borchard, B., & Hoyer, J. (2004). Mental disorders in a forensic sample of sexual offenders. *European Psychiatry, 19,* 123–130.

204 *Jill Lobbestael and René Cane*

Lobbestael, J., Arntz, A., Löbbes, A., & Cima, M. (2009). A comparative study of patients and therapists' reports of schema modes. *Journal of Behaviour Therapy and Experimental Psychiatry, 40*(4), 571–579.

Lobbestael, J., Cima, M., & Arntz, A. (2013). The relationship between adult reactive and proactive aggression, hostile interpretation bias, and antisocial personality disorder. *Journal of Personality Disorders, 27*(1), 53–66.

Martinez, M. A., Zeichner, A., Reidy, D. E., & Miller, J. D. (2008). Narcissism and displaced aggression: Effects of positive, negative and delayed feedback. *Personality and Individual Differences, 44*(1), 140–149.

McCloskey, M. S., New, A., Siever, L. J., Goodman, M., Koenigsberg, H. W., Flory, J. D., & Coccaro, E. F. (2009). Evaluation of behavioural impulsivity and aggression tasks as endophenotypes for borderline personality disorder. *Journal of Psychiatric Research, 43*, 1036–1048.

Moeller, F. G., Dougherty, D. M., Rustin, T., Swann, A. C., Allen, T. J., Shah, N., & Cherek, D. R. (1997). Antisocial personality disorder and aggression in recently abstinent cocaine dependent subjects. *Drug and Alcohol Dependence, 44*, 175–182.

New, A. S., Hazlett, E. A., Newmark, R. E., Zhang, J., Triebwasser, J., Meyerson, D., & Buchsbaum, M. S. (2009). Laboratory induced aggression: A positron emission tomography study of aggressive individuals with borderline personality disorder. *Biological Psychiatry, 66*, 1107–1114.

Ostrov, J. M., & Houston, R. J. (2008). The utility of forms and functions of aggression in emerging adulthood: Association with personality disorder symptomatology. *Journal of Youth and Adolescence, 37*, 1147–1158.

Poulin, F., & Boivin, M. (2000). Reactive and proactive aggression: Evidence of a two-factor model. *Psychological Assessment, 12*(2), 115–122.

Putkonen, H., Komulainen, E. J., Virkkunen, M., Eronen, M., & Lönnqvist, J. (2003). Risk of repeat offending among violent female offenders with psychotic and personality disorders. *The American Journal of Psychiatry, 160*(5), 947–951.

Raine, A. (1993). Features of borderline personality and violence. *Journal of Clinical Psychology, 49*, 277–281.

Raskin, R. N., & Hall, C. S. (1979). A narcissistic personality inventory. *Psychological Reports, 45*(2), 590.

Rasmussen, K., & Levander, S. (1996). Crime and violence among psychiatric patients in a maximum security psychiatric hospital. *Criminal Justice and Behaviour, 23*(3), 455–471.

Reidy, D. E., Foster, J. D., & Zeichner, A. (2010). Narcissism and unprovoked aggression. *Aggressive Behaviour, 35*, 1–9.

Reidy, D. E., Zeichner, A., Foster, J. D., & Martinez, M. A. (2008). Effects of narcissistic entitlement and exploitativeness on human physical aggression. *Personality and Individual Differences, 44*, 865–875.

Roberts, A. D. L., & Coid, J. W. (2010). Personality disorder and offending behaviour: Findings from the national survey of male prisoners in England and Wales. *The Journal of Forensic Psychiatry & Psychology, 21*(2), 221–237.

Ross, J. M., & Babcock, J. C. (2009). Proactive and reactive violence among intimate partner violent men diagnosed with antisocial and borderline personality disorder. *Journal of Family Violence, 24*, 607–617.

Rotter, M., Way, B., Steinbacher, M., Sawyer, D., & Smith, H. (2002). Personality disorders in prison: Aren't they all antisocial? *Psychiatric Quarterly, 73*, 337–349.

Russel, J. J., Moskowitz, D. S., Zuroff, D. C., Sookman, D., & Paris, J. (2007). Stability and variability of affective experience and interpersonal behaviour in borderline personality disorder. *Journal of Abnormal Psychology, 116*(3), 578–588.

Sansone, R. A., & Sansone, L. A. (2009). Borderline personality and criminality. *Psychiatry Research, 6*(10), 16–20.

Seah, S. L., & Ang, R. P. (2008). Differential correlates of reactive and proactive aggression in Asian adolescents: relations to narcissism, anxiety, schizotypical traits, and peer relations. *Aggressive Behaviour, 34*, 553–562.

Skeem, J. L., & Cooke, D. J. (2010). Is criminal behaviour a central component of psychopathy? Conceptual directions for resolving the debate. *Psychological Assessment, 22*(2), 433–445.

Skodol, A. E., Bender, D. S., Morey, L. C., Alarcon, R. D., Siever, L. J., Clark, L. A., & Oldham, J. M. (2011). Proposed changes in personality and personality disorder assessment and diagnosis for DSM-5 Part I: Description and rationale. *Personality Disorders: Theory, Research, and Treatment, 2*(1), 4–22.

Stuart, S., Pfohl, B., Battaglia, M., Bellodi, L., Grove, W., & Cadoret, R. (1998). The co-occurrence of DSM-III-R personality disorders. *Journal of Personality Disorders, 12*, 302–315.

Stucke, T. S., & Sporer, S. L. (2002). When a grandiose self-image is threatened: Narcissism and self-concept clarity as predictors of negative emotions and aggression following ego-threat. *Journal of Personality, 70*(4), 509–532.

Twenge, J. M., & Campbell, W. K. (2003). "Isn't it fun to get the respect that we're going to deserve?" Narcissism, social rejection, and aggression. *Personality and Social Psychology Bulletin, 29*, 261–272.

Ullrich, S., Deasy, D., Smith, J., Johnson, B., Clarke, M., Broughton, N., & Coid, J. (2008). Detecting personality disorder in the prison population of England and Wales: Comparing case identification using the SCID-II screen and SCID-II clinical interview. *The Journal of Forensic Psychiatry & Psychology, 19*(3), 301–322.

Walters, G. D. (2007). Measuring proactive and reactive criminal thinking with PICTS, correlations with outcome expectancies and hostile attribution biases. *Journal of Interpersonal Violence, 22*(4), 371–385.

Warren, J. I., Burnette, M. L., South, S. C., Chauhan, P., Bale, R., & Friend, R. (2002). Personality disorders and violence among female prison inmates. *The Journal of the American Academy of Psychiatry and the Law, 30*, 502–509.

Warren, J. I., & South, S. C. (2009). A symptom level examination of the relationship between Cluster B personality disorders and patterns of criminality and violence in women. *International Journal of Law and Psychiatry, 32*, 10–17.

Washburn, J. J., McMahon, S. D., King, C. A., Reinecke, M. A., & Silver, C. (2004). Narcissistic features in young adolescents: Relations to aggression and internalizing symptoms. *Journal of Youth and Adolescence, 33*(3), 247–260.

Weinstein, Y., Oltmanns, T. F., & Gleason, M. E. J. (2012). Borderline but not antisocial personality disorder symptoms are related to self-reported partner aggression in late middle-age. *Journal of Abnormal Psychology, 121*(3), 692–698.

Whyte, S., Fox, S., & Coxell, A. (2006). Reporting of personality disorder symptoms in a forensic inpatient sample: effects of mode of assessment and response style. *The Journal of Forensic Psychiatry & Psychology, 17*(3), 431–441.

Widiger, T. A. (2011). A shaky future for personality disorders. *Personality Disorders: Theory, Research, and Treatment, 2*, 54–67.

Widiger, T. A. (Ed). (2012). *The Oxford handbook of personality disorders*. New York: Oxford University Press.

Wink, P. (1991). Two faces of narcissism. *Journal of Personality and Social Psychology, 61*(4), 590–597.

10 Contemporary approaches to psychopathy

Inti A. Brazil and Maaike Cima

Introduction

Within the forensic field, the construct of psychopathy is without doubt an important clinical concept. Although this construct is relatively old, originating from the work of Cleckley (1941), today there is still debate regarding the conceptual boundaries of psychopathy as an expression of criminal deviant behaviour. Despite the conceptual discussion, there is a certain amount of consensus on the notion that the core characteristics of psychopathy include callousness, irresponsibility, antisocial tendencies and a lack of empathy and guilt. These characteristics can be divided into different clusters or domains, like interpersonal, affective and behavioural clusters (Hare, Hart, & Harpur, 1991; Patrick, Fowles, & Krueger, 2009). However, there is still no consensus regarding the exact content of these clusters. Although in the past 20 years, researchers and clinicians have relied heavily on the classification of psychopathy as a personality disorder, it is still not fully recognised as such in the current (5th) edition of the *Diagnostic and Statistical Manual of Mental Disorders* (DSM). Recently, there has been much debate about current ideations of various personality disorders, which have become even more prominent due to the development of the 5th edition of the DSM. The divergence in conceptualisations has become increasingly visible for relatively opaque personality disorders such as psychopathy. In this chapter, we will first provide a description of currently dominant conceptualisations of psychopathy as a construct reflecting personality traits. In addition, we also review other major accounts that emphasise the role of aberrant cognitive and neurobiological functioning in this disorder. Finally, we will present a selection of recent insights obtained using various approaches originating from the fields of neuroscience and social cognition.

Psychopathy and personality

The existence of personality structures that resemble the condition nowadays referred to as clinical psychopathy can be found in writings that date back several centuries (Arrigo & Shipley, 2001). For instance, in the early 1800s Prichard (1835) described a condition characterised by disturbed affective functioning. Also, these individuals seemed less capable to attend to social norms and rules. They were considered to lack the willpower to control themselves and to follow social norms and were therefore considered 'morally insane'. Now, almost two centuries later, the idea that emotional disturbances and lack of morality play key roles in psychopathy is still prominently present (Blair, 2007), although the exact operationalisation of the clinical construct is still a matter of debate.

Still, in the past 20 years researchers and clinicians have relied heavily on the definition of psychopathy as a personality disorder that is typified by disturbed affect and interpersonal style combined with antisocial behavioural tendencies (Hare, Hart, & Harpur, 1991). This has been fuelled by the development of the Psychopathy Checklist (Hare, 1980) and its successor the Psychopathy Checklist – Revised (PCL-R) (Hare, 2003), which have solidified this conceptualisation of psychopathy in the field of forensic mental health and also in the legal system. However, there are also other instruments for measuring psychopathy that are based on different conceptualisations. Therefore, we will provide a short description of the PCL-R and its main properties, as well as a brief overview of two other influential (predominantly personality-based) models of psychopathy.

Psychopathy according to the PCL-R

The PCL-R consists of 20 items that are scored based on information from clinical history files combined with a semi-structured interview. Each item represents a certain behavioural tendency that is scored as either completely absent (0), moderately present (1) or prominently present (2). This yields a dimensional total score ranging between 0 and 40, but the total score has also been used to indicate the presence of psychopathy when a predefined cut-off score is exceeded. A cut-off score of 30 is usually maintained in North America, meaning that individuals scoring equal to or higher than 30 can be considered psychopathic. European countries often maintain a cut-off score ≥26 (Cooke & Michie, 1999; but see Bolt, Hare, & Neumann, 2007) in clinical and legal practice and this cut-off score has been extended to research on psychopathy (e.g. Brazil et al., 2013; Cima, Tonnaer, & Hauser, 2010; Hildebrand, De Ruiter, & Nijman, 2004; Rasmussen, Storsæter, & Levander, 1999).

Factor analyses have shown that the PCL-R measures two correlated factors. Factor 1 consists of items that capture behaviours related to interpersonal and affective functioning (e.g. glibness, lack of empathy, manipulativeness) and Factor 2 describes aspects related to a deviant lifestyle and antisocial behaviour (e.g. parasitic lifestyle, juvenile delinquency; Hare & Neumann, 2006; Harpur, Hare, & Hakstian, 1989). Interestingly, while Hare and colleagues argue that both factors are key components of psychopathy, others have argued that antisociality is of secondary importance to psychopathy (Cooke, Michie, & Hart, 2006).

Cooke and colleagues (2006) believe that the antisocial behaviour seen in psychopathy is a consequence of psychopathy rather than a central feature.

208   *Inti A. Brazil and Maaike Cima*

Using sophisticated analytic approaches, they have argued that the PCL-R captures three factors that are representative of the core features of psychopathy (Cooke et al., 2006). These factors are 'arrogant and deceitful interpersonal style', 'deficient affective experience' and 'impulsive and irresponsible behavioural style' (Cooke & Michie, 2001). Nine PCL-R items (e.g. criminal versatility, poor behavioural control, early behavioural problems) did not load on any of the three factors and were regarded as indexes for antisocial tendencies rather than psychopathy. Therefore, it was argued that antisociality was not a core feature of psychopathy, but rather a consequence of the core features captured by the three-factor model.

Hare and his co-workers have criticised the empirical validity of the psychometric choices that led to the discovery of the three-factor model (e.g. Bolt et al., 2007), and have worked on further refinement of the original two-factor model. The resulting body of work has shown that each factor can be subdivided in two facets, which lead to the emergence of the four-factor model of psychopathy (Hare, 2003). More specifically, Factor 1 can be subdivided into a facet that captures interpersonal traits and a second facet that measures distortions in affective functioning. Factor 2 can be decomposed into a facet capturing lifestyle and impulsivity and a facet representing antisocial behavioural tendencies. Nowadays, Factor 1 is often labelled 'interpersonal/affective' and Factor 2 'impulsive/antisocial' to denote both the two superordinate factors and the presence of the four facets.

Other conceptualisations and measures of psychopathy

Despite the fact that Hare's definition of psychopathy has been very influential in the modern view on psychopathy, others have argued that this conceptualisation places too much focus on maladaptive aspects of psychopathy (Patrick & Bernat, 2009). In his seminal work, Cleckley (1982) described what seem to be different expressions of a similar core deficit in individuals with psychopathy. He described callous and unemotional individuals with a tendency to be disinhibited and engaging in antisocial and destructive behaviours, but also that some of these individuals appeared to be well skilled in understanding social conventions and using them to their advantage. Based on these observations Cleckley formulated 16 criteria for diagnosing psychopathy, which were later grouped into three categories: (1) criteria related to positive psychological functioning and adequate social adjustment in general, (2) a set of items related to disinhibited and antisocial tendencies, sexual promiscuity, reduced learning from experience and lack of foresight, and (3) criteria reflecting disturbed affective and interpersonal functioning (Patrick, 2006).

Some researchers have argued that the conceptualisation used by Hare only captures the maladaptive aspects of psychopathy and cannot account for the indicators of positive adjustment (Patrick & Bernat, 2009). Also, it has been proposed that psychopathy should be measured dimensionally rather than categorically and that psychopathic tendencies can also be measured among the general population rather than only in offender samples (Lilienfeld & Andrews, 1996; Neumann, Schmitt, Carter, Embley, & Hare, 2012; Patrick & Bernat, 2009). These ideas have led to the development of alternative frameworks that seek to explain psychopathy from a broader perspective and not only as a clinical condition present in offender samples. Next, we will briefly discuss two prominent frameworks based on such conceptualisations of psychopathy.

Based on Cleckley's items, Lilienfeld and Andrews (1996) proposed that psychopathy can be described in terms of individual variations on eight common personality traits such as anxiety, fear and impulsivity, and individuals are considered increasingly psychopathic as the these traits become more prominent. To measure the traits they used student samples to develop the Psychopathy Personality Inventory (PPI), a self-report questionnaire that indexes scores on eight general personality traits. Psychometric research has shown that the traits cluster into two independent higher-order factors initially termed fearless dominance (PPI-I) and antisocial impulsivity (PPI-II) (Benning, Patrick, Hicks, Blonigen, & Krueger, 2003). The PPI-I is believed to reflect social-affective functioning and the PPI-II captures behaviours related to externalising proneness. Thus, to a certain extent these higher-order factors show parallels with Factors 1 and 2 of the PCL-R, respectively. One key difference with the PCL-R is that this approach to psychopathy is not bounded by the presence of specific criminal tendencies, making it suitable to assess psychopathy-related tendencies in non-criminal samples (Sellbom, Ben-Porath, Lilienfeld, Patrick, & Graham, 2005). However, it has been pointed out that extreme scores on psychopathic traits in samples of healthy individuals who generally do not pose a threat to society (i.e. non-clinical psychopathy) cannot be equated with the severe pathological expression of psychopathy seen in offenders scoring high on the PCL-R (i.e. clinical psychopathy (Koenigs, Baskin-Sommers, Zeier, & Newman, 2011). In addition, it has been shown that the PPI has poor psychometric properties in offender populations and that the two-factor structure found in healthy community samples is not viable in offender samples (Neumann, Malterer, & Newman, 2008), also supporting the claim that this self-report measure might not be suitable for assessing clinical psychopathy (see also Miller & Lynam, 2012, for confirmations of caution, especially for the PPI-I fearless dominance factor and its poor relationship with the PCL-R).

It should be mentioned that despite the concerns regarding the usefulness of self-report measures to assess psychopathy, Neumann and colleagues have succeeded in developing an instrument known as the Self-Report Psychopathy Scale (SRP) that seems capable of measuring psychopathic tendencies reliably in offender and healthy samples and in both males and females (Paulhus, Neumann, & Hare, in press).

More recently, Patrick and colleagues (2009) have developed the Triarchic model of psychopathy. The core of this model is that psychopathy can be conceptualised dimensionally based on three components that resemble those proposed by Cleckley. This framework tries to account for the different manifestations of psychopathy in terms of individual variations on these three core dimensions and their interactions. The components are disinhibition, meanness and boldness, and the tenet is that each can be indexed individually by measuring unique behavioural and neurobiological markers reflective of an underlying genetic predisposition (called endophenotypes). Disinhibition is held to reflect a general inclination towards problems with impulse control and negative affectivity and is related to pathological behaviours such as addiction, reactive aggression and criminality. Meanness captures maladaptive phenotypic expressions related to reduced affective responsivity such as lack of empathy, sensation seeking and a tendency to be confrontational and to seek personal gratification at the expense of others. The predominance of these two facets in an individual is assumed to be influenced by the presence of a difficult temperament (e.g. high irritability, proneness to experience excessive frustration and anger). Boldness describes phenotypic markers indicative of characteristics such as low-stress reactivity and neuroticism, calmness, social efficacy and social dominance. Importantly, both meanness and boldness are believed to be phenotypic expressions of an underlying biological predisposition towards experiencing low fear, but the expression of this predisposition as either meanness or boldness may depend (in part) on the interactions with environmental factors such as parenting style. According to the Triarchic conceptualisation of psychopathy, the combination of meanness and disinhibition can result in the characteristics often seen in offenders with psychopathy, while the combination of boldness and disinhibition can be observed in individuals with reduced fear reactivity but positive psychological functioning and adequate social adjustment.

In addition, this model postulates that antisocial individuals without psychopathy are characterised by high disinhibition and relatively low meanness and boldness. This highlights that although psychopathy and general antisociality show overlap at the behavioural level, they should not be equated. This notion has been subject to considerable debate in psychiatry, partly because the 5th edition of the DSM does not include psychopathy as a separate disorder but as part of antisocial personality disorder (ASPD). The importance of distinguishing psychopathy from generic antisocial tendency is also bolstered by studies showing that while 50 to 80% of offenders can be diagnosed with ASPD, only 20% of these individuals score above the threshold on the PCL-R (Hare, 1998). Also, more recent approaches employing electrophysiology have shown that psychopathy and generic antisocial tendency differ at the neurocognitive level despite resulting in similar behaviour.

Neurocognitive models of psychopathy

In contrast to the personality-based frameworks described in the previous section, other scientists have defined psychopathy from a cognitive and/or neurobiological point of view. The technological advances of the last three decades have been pivotal in increasing our understanding of the basic cognitive and

Contemporary approaches to psychopathy 211

neurobiological mechanisms driving animal and human behaviour. Findings from studies on cognition in the general population have also facilitated research aimed at understanding abnormal cognition in various personality disorders, including psychopathy. In this section we will discuss some very influential cotemporary models of psychopathy that seek to explain psychopathy as a disorder characterised by cognitive and/or neurobiological dysfunctions rather than one predominantly based on personality factors. It is important to note that our use of the term 'cognitive' refers to both affective and non-affective processes that take place in the brain. First, we will discuss the low-fear hypothesis (Lykken, 1995), followed by the response modulation hypothesis (Patterson & Newman, 1993) and the integrated emotion systems model (Blair, 2005). These three theories have been very influential in understanding various aspects of cognition and neurobiology in psychopathy. We will end this section with a brief overview of other, less dominant frameworks that have also been gaining empirical support.

The low-fear accounts of psychopathy

David Lykken (1995) argued that a deficiency in processing and responding to anxiety- and fear-evoking events lies at the core of psychopathy. This idea led to the development of fear-centred accounts of psychopathy, which have received a considerable amount of empirical support throughout the years, and offer an explanation for various psychophysiological and cognitive impairments seen in psychopathy. The psychophysiological abnormalities include impaired autonomic conditioning (Hare & Quinn, 1971), impaired acquisition of conditioned fear responses (Hare, 1965a), reductions in galvanic skin response in anticipation of threat (Hare, 1965b) and impaired fear-potentiated startle (Patrick, 1994). Also, healthy individuals are held to experience fear in the light of impending aversive outcomes and associate this fear with the actions that induced it, resulting in avoidance of these actions. This form of associative learning is known as fear-conditioning (Maren & Quirk, 2004). As individuals with psychopathy show reduced fear responsivity, they should demonstrate impairments in associating fear with the actions inducing it. This would ultimately result in weaker associations and thus the endurance of undesirable behaviours. Indeed, a study conducted by Birbaumer and colleagues (2005) found impaired fear-conditioning in offenders with psychopathy, while another study from the same lab found evidence for a more general impairment in aversive affective conditioning (Flor, Birbaumer, Hermann, Ziegler, & Patrick, 2002).

Fear is also believed to play a key role in the acquisition of social behaviour through a process known as social fear learning, a process that occurs according to the same associative learning principles as classical fear-conditioning (Olsson & Phelps, 2007). Impairments in social fear learning are believed to hamper the socialisation process, leading to disturbed empathic processing and moral development (Blair, 2006). From the perspective of the low-fear accounts it

212   *Inti A. Brazil and Maaike Cima*

can be predicted that reduced fear reactivity should have a detrimental effect on social fear learning and the moralisation process. While this explanation for the antisocial behaviour seen in psychopathy is very appealing, it leans heavily on the assumption that fear is a unitary system, an assumption that has been challenged by neuroscientific evidence (Blair, Mitchell, & Blair, 2005). In addition, Blair et al. (2005) argued that the low-fear hypotheses also suffers from other weaknesses such as underspecificity and disconcordance with the literature on moral development. One might argue, however, that the model proposed by Blair in which he attributes poor socialisation and moral development to low responsiveness of the amygdala and subsequent functional connectivity with the ventromedial prefrontal cortex (VMPFC) is not so different from the low-fear hypothesis. Moreover, complex constructs such as socialisation and moral development are probably not located in one specific brain area (see also Chapter 6). Indeed Kiehl and colleagues have provided evidence from large samples for dysfunction in more widely distributed, functionally connected regions, which likely work together for proper moral socialisation (Anderson & Kiehl, 2012).

Problems with relating complex behavioural constructs to psychopathic traits have led to other explanatory frameworks that are more consistent with neuroscientific theories in general and empirical findings in specifically psychopathy research. However, the position that disturbances in processing affective information are the main determinants of psychopathy has repeatedly been challenged by an alternative account of psychopathy known as the response modulation hypothesis (Baskin-Sommers, Curtin, Li, & Newman, 2011; Patterson & Newman, 1993). This framework will be discussed in the following section.

The response modulation hypothesis

The response modulation (RM) hypothesis is one of the oldest frameworks among contemporary neurocognitive accounts of psychopathy, finding its roots in cognitive research performed in the 1980s by Newman and his co-workers. Originally, RM was not developed as an account of psychopathy, per se. Rather, it pointed out common features underlying many forms of disinhibited behaviour in general. Its application to psychopathy was inspired by the apparent 'fearlessness' in animals with septal lesions, along with the very typical response perseveration also seen in incarcerated psychopaths (Patterson & Newman, 1993). This theory has been subjected to revisions and refinements throughout the years (Baskin-Sommers et al., 2011; Gorenstein & Newman, 1980; MacCoon, Wallace, & Newman, 2004; Patterson & Newman, 1993), but the core of the RM hypothesis remains that psychopathy is characterised by an inability to automatically regulate goal-directed behaviour because of a deficiency in modulating attention to accommodate meaningful information that is of secondary importance to ongoing behaviour (Hiatt & Newman, 2006). Thus, RM has been further specified into an alternative framework with 'attention switching' as being the more fundamental deficit in relation

Contemporary approaches to psychopathy   213

to psychopathy. That is, psychopathic individuals are believed to be unable to shift their focus of attention away from information that is of primary importance for their current goals (e.g. win money) and therefore neglect information that is unattended or that provides secondary/peripheral information (e.g. cues signalling that they will lose money, others' negative emotional reactions). By defining psychopathy as a disorder of attention rather than one of affect, this account differs fundamentally from other emotion-based theories of psychopathy.

Throughout the years, Newman and his colleagues have collected an extensive amount of data and have gathered a lot of evidence supporting their position that various impairments seen in psychopathy are driven by a problem with (re)allocation of attention. For instance, they have shown that the reduced fear reactivity typically associated with psychopathy is moderated by limited attentional capacity rather than amygdala-mediated impairments in affective processing (Newman, Curtin, Bertsch, & Baskin-Sommers, 2010). The RM hypothesis has also been held to account for various other types of behavioural impairments seen in psychopathy, such as passive avoidance learning (Newman & Kosson, 1986), response perseveration (Newman, Patterson, & Kosson, 1987) and incorporation of secondary contextual information in speech (Hiatt & Newman, 2006).

Most of the evidence in favour of the RM hypothesis has been acquired using behavioural paradigms, thus precluding direct assessment of the underlying neurocognitive mechanisms. However, in their more recent work, Newman and colleagues have been employing neuroscientific methodologies to further specify the possible neurocognitive correlates of their theory (Baskin-Sommers et al., 2011; Newman et al., 2010). This has led to the development of the latest refinement of the RM model, which postulates that the abnormal selective attention seen in psychopathy is due to an early attention bottleneck (Baskin-Sommers et al., 2011). More specifically, it is argued that a bottleneck in early selective attention results in an overfocus on relevant information because information that is secondary of nature is filtered out in a very early stage of processing. As a consequence, psychopathic individuals are less aware of the presence of contextual information relevant for guiding goal-directed behaviour, resulting in the endurance of less appropriate/sub-optimal behaviour. Still, the RM hypothesis has been criticised for not being compatible with modern neurobiological accounts of attention and for not providing a specification for the neurocognitive mechanisms driving the shift of attention (Blair & Mitchell, 2009). Next, we will turn to a model that was developed based on neurobiology that claims to offer a better account of psychopathy than the low-fear accounts and the RM hypothesis.

The integrated emotion systems model

The integrated emotion systems (IES) model is currently the leading neurobiological theory of psychopathy, as it has a strong neuroscientific basis and can account for a large amount of behavioural and neuroscientific findings. Before discussing how the IES model links brain systems to psychopathic behaviour, a general description of the main brain regions and overlapping networks incorporated in the model will be provided.

One of the central tenets of the IES model is that a large portion of the behavioural disturbances seen in psychopathy is primarily driven by deficient functioning of the amygdala and specific prefrontal brain areas, in which especially the interaction between the amygdala and orbitofrontal cortex (OFC) has received a great deal of attention (Blair, 2005). The orbitofrontal cortex is located in the front of the brain above the upper extremities of the eye sockets (see Figure 10.1A) and is believed to play a central role in functions such as reward processing, decision-making, associative learning (Wallis, 2007) and social cognition (Beer, John, Scabini, & Knight, 2006; Rushworth, Behrens, Rudebeck, & Walton, 2007). It is strongly connected to the amygdala, an almond-shaped structure located in the deeper region of the medial temporal lobe well known for its importance for affective functioning (see Figure 10.1B). Some OFC and amygdala functions appear to overlap as they share reciprocal connections with each other and work

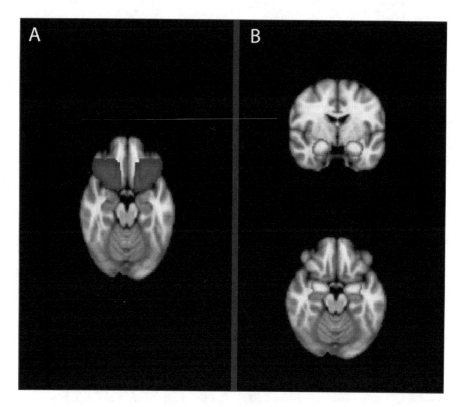

Figure 10.1 Location of the orbitofrontal cortex and amygdala

Contemporary approaches to psychopathy 215

together in processing emotional information and incorporating expected reinforcement information into higher-order decision-making. But additionally, the amygdala is involved in autonomic processes such as threat detection (Davis & Whalen, 2001), the modulation of fear- and anxiety-potentiated startle (Robinson, Overstreet, Allen, Pine, & Grillon, 2012), and the modulation of general stimulus saliency (Cunningham & Brosch, 2012).

One question that arises is how a relatively small structure like the amygdala can be implicated in so many different autonomic and cognitive functions. Part of the answer lies in a growing body of empirical evidence pointing out that the amygdala is a modular structure rather than a unitary one. The amygdala consists of 13 anatomically interconnected nuclei (Sah, Faber, De Armentia, & Power, 2003), which have been parcellated into three subregions based on their connectivity patterns (Bzdok, Laird, Zilles, Fox, & Eickhoff, 2013). Others refer to two primary subdivisions of the amygdala known as the central nuclei (CeN) and the basolateral nuclei (BLA) based on differences in evolutionary development (Moul, Killcross, & Dadds, 2012).

The latter subdivision played a key role in the development the IES model and three interacting neural networks centred on the amygdala have been incorporated in this model: (1) a forebrain system that is believed to provide sensory input to the amygdala through reciprocal connections, (2) a network anchored in the CeN that projects downwards to various structures located in the brain stem and (3) a system with reciprocal connections between the BLA and various frontocortical regions that is held to modulate goal-directed behaviour (Blair et al., 2005). These systems, as well as their mutual interactions, are proposed to drive various cognitive deficiencies characteristic of psychopathy. More specifically, the IES model postulates that psychopathic behaviour is driven by impairments in representing affective information, thus leading to disturbances in specific associative learning processes in the amygdala that are modulated by OFC (Blair, 2005). The premise is that psychopathic individuals are less capable of linking negative outcomes (e.g. loss of money) and the corresponding negative affective states (feeling sad about losing money) to the event that led to the negative outcome. One prediction that follows is that individuals with psychopathy should show impairments when they have to adapt their behaviour to move away from undesirable outcomes. Indeed, psychopathic offenders have been found to show impairments in avoiding stimuli that lead to punishment (Newman & Kosson, 1986) and also in adapting their behaviour when previously rewarded stimuli start leading to punishment (Budhani & Blair, 2004; Mitchell, Colledge, Leonard, & Blair, 2002; Newman et al., 1987).

Other neurocognitive models of psychopathy

A lot of research has been conducted within each of the major frameworks described previously, but there are also other models of psychopathy. One of these models is the differential amygdala activation model (DAAM), which has been put forth as a model that can unify the IES model and the RM hypothesis. The DAAM is a new model that still needs direct empirical support, but the assumption is that it is of incremental value in explaining psychopathy because this model might also account for data that cannot be fully explained by the IES model or the RM hypothesis individually (Moul et al., 2012). The DAAM was developed based on the structural and functional differences between the CeN and the BLA. In essence, the DAAM predicts that the affective and attentional deficits seen in psychopathy are caused by an imbalance in the activation of the CeN and the BLA. The CeN is proposed to show normal or even superior functioning in psychopathy, while the BLA is held to be underactivated. One of the predictions is that the impaired automatic shift of attention in psychopathy formalised in the RM hypothesis is (at least in part) due to hyporeactivity of the BLA, as this structure has been implicated in reflexive allocation of attention. Another assumption is that the impairments in associative learning found in psychopathy (cf. IES model) are driven by a preference to encode the 'general motivational valence' of reward and punishment rather than the magnitude of the outcomes (Moul et al., 2012). Thus, psychopathic individuals are believed to have a learning bias and therefore tend to encode the hedonic aspects of an outcome (e.g. winning money feels good vs. losing money feels bad) rather than the magnitude of the outcome (e.g. how much money was won or lost). The first empirical evidence of this learning bias has been provided by a recent study by Moul and Dadds (2013) in children high in psychopathic traits, but more research is needed to substantiate the claims made by the model in both children and adult populations marked by psychopathy.

While the theories with a strong neuroscientific basis are centred around relationships with and within the amygdala, another theory known as the paralimbic dysfunction model (Kiehl, 2006) has focused on a wider range of interconnected brain regions that seem to be abnormal in psychopathy. This model is based on a large body of extant findings from neuropsychology, volumetric reductions, lesion studies, event-related potentials (ERPs), structural and functional imaging studies in psychopathy, implicating a wide range of regions that are interconnected and are part of a widely distributed neuroanatomical network called the paralimbic cortex (Anderson & Kiehl, 2012). Until recently, this theory has been less prominent in the literature. There is, however, a growing consensus regarding structural abnormalities in limbic/paralimbic brain regions in psychopathy (Ermer, Cope, Nyalakanti, Calhoun, & Kiehl, 2012; Ermer, Cope, Nyalakanti, Calhoun, & Kiehl, 2013). Conflicting findings regarding brain morphology in psychopathy may be due to using different subgroups of psychopathic individuals. For instance, in some studies structural magnetic resonance imaging (sMRI) was used to investigate the morphology of the amygdala in samples with psychopathy. One study found volumetric reductions in some subregions of the amygdala, while other areas were enlarged (Boccardi et al., 2011). In sharp contrast, Yang et al. (2009) reported reductions in the same areas that were found to be

Contemporary approaches to psychopathy 217

enlarged in the study by Boccardi et al. (2011). Similarly, the latter study also found reduced volumes in the anterior cingulate cortex, while another study found no differences (Glenn, Yang, Raine, & Colletti, 2010). The study of Boccardi et al. (2011) used psychopathic individuals who also met criteria for substance abuse, which stresses the importance of accounting for relevant co-occurring disorders in psychopathy. Indeed, Ermer and colleagues found reductions in amygdala volumes when controlling for substance, brain size and age (Ermer et al., 2013). Considering a wider range of brain regions offering a more complete understanding of the neural underpinnings of psychopathy is appealing.

Current developments in psychopathy research

Although among researchers and clinicians there have been arguments over the years regarding cause and operationalisation of psychopathy (for a recent example see Lilienfeld et al., 2012; Lynam & Miller, 2012), there is overall agreement among experts regarding some of the essential characteristics of psychopathy. Discussions regarding the operationalisation of the construct have fuelled a large amount of research by scientists with competing clarifications. This research, along with the employment of novel scientific approaches, has yielded important insights and is currently broadening the scope of the research on psychopathy. The following sections will provide an outline of these novel developments through brief discussions of some topics that are currently emerging in the literature on psychopathy.

Disentangling psychopathy from antisocial personality disorders

There has been a long-standing discussion about the relationship between ASPD and psychopathy (for a historical decomposition see Arrigo & Shipley, 2001). The intertwinement of these disorders became especially evident when the diagnostic criteria for psychopathy were merged with those for ASPD in the 4th and psychopathy is still absent as a separate disorder in the 5th edition of the DSM. The DSM has repeatedly been criticised for its focus on maladaptive antisocial behaviour, thus neglecting the personality factors that are differentially at play in psychopathy relative to ASPD (Hare et al., 1991). This early critique was predominantly formulated at the level of personality structures and findings from behavioural studies, but neuroscientific insights are suggesting that it might be possible to separate psychopathy from ASPD based on patterns of neurocognitive processing.

One of the approaches has been to use electrophysiology to visualise and probe for possible differences in neurocognitive processing in psychopathy. This can be achieved by assessing event-related potentials (ERPs), for example, which are electrophysiological markers that reflect information processing in the brain. There are several types of ERPs, each related to one or more aspects of cognitive processing. Recent studies have used ERPs to compare neurocognitive functioning between offenders with PCL-defined psychopathy vs. offenders without psychopathy (henceforth referred to as non-psychopathic offenders). For instance, Baskin-Sommers and colleagues (2011) have found that psychopathic offenders show an exaggerated ERP response in an early time window and they propose that this is reflective of abnormal early attention processing. This was interpreted as additional support for the early attention bottleneck postulated by the RM hypothesis. Verona et al. (2012) found that another ERP component, the P300, was modulated by negative emotional content in healthy control participants and non-psychopathic offenders, but not in the psychopathic subjects. The non-psychopathic offenders showed an overreaction to the negative affective content, while the psychopathic group showed underreactivity. Another study found that both psychopathy and antisociality were related to reduced recruitment of cognitive resources relative to a healthy control group, but that psychopathic individuals were still able to process the information appropriately despite the reduced overall ERP activity (Brazil et al., 2012). More specifically, the task required participants to distinguish between one frequent and two low frequent stimuli. Both psychopathic and non-psychopathic offenders showed reduced overall activity relative to healthy controls, but similar to the healthy controls the psychopathic group still showed different types of activity for each stimulus. In contrast, the non-psychopathic group failed to differentiate between the low frequent stimuli. Thus, the group with psychopathy used fewer cognitive resources to carry out the same computations as the healthy controls, while the non-psychopathic offenders were not able to process all the information appropriately. One of the interpretations was that psychopathy might be related to more efficient (superior) processing of certain types of information, while antisociality is linked to a general processing impairment. Moreover, some earlier research also showed that psychopathy can be differentiated from antisociality without psychopathy using psychophysiological methods (Kiehl, Hare, McDonald, & Brink, 1999; Patrick, Bradley, & Lang, 1993; Williamson, Harpur, & Hare, 1991). Together, these studies provide direct psychophysiological evidence in favour of a clinical distinction between psychopathy and generic antisocial tendency.

Social cognition

Social cognition refers to an area of research focused on understanding the cognitive basis of social behaviour and this area has become increasingly visible in the empirical literature. A study by Ermer and Kiehl (2010) showed specific impairments in different aspects of social cognition, which could not be explained by antisocial tendency, but were specific to psychopathy. Studies on social cognition are also emerging in the literature on psychopathy and several aspects are being tackled. For instance, in a recent study Brazil and colleagues (2011) investigated the observation of others' actions in psychopathy using ERPs. The task employed required participants to sit across from another individual (the experimenter) and observe the experimenter performing a

Contemporary approaches to psychopathy 219

speeded response task. Electrophysiological recordings were made during the entire task and participants were instructed to keep track of the amount of errors committed by the experimenter. The results showed that psychopathy is related to intact processing of the outcome of own actions (in terms of correct vs. incorrect) but impaired processing of the outcomes of others' actions. It was concluded that the latter impairment might play an important role in abnormal associative learning processes throughout the psychopathic individual's life, thus possibly also facilitating the acquisition of antisocial behaviour.

Other studies have focused on moral reasoning in psychopathy. Neuro-scientific findings indicate that similar brain areas are involved in emotional processing and moral decision-making (Greene, 2003; Moll et al., 2002), thus supporting the dominant perspective that emotional processes are related to morality (Prinz, 2006; Young & Koenigs, 2007). Given this relationship between emotions and morality, it can be predicted that a lack of emotions should lead to a lack of moral knowledge. However, research has shown that adult psychopathic offenders (generally believed to lack moral emotions) seem to know the difference between right and wrong (Cima, Tonnaer, & Hauser, 2010), which suggests that moral reasoning regarding good and bad does not necessarily depend on moral emotions (see Chapter 6 for more details on moral reasoning and psychopathic characteristics). Similarly, a recent study showed that juvenile psychopathic offenders do seem to know the difference between right and wrong (Cima, Korebrits, Stams, & Bleumer, submitted) despite their lower stages of moral reasoning, thus corroborating previous findings in adult psychopathy (Cima et al., 2010). Indeed, juvenile delinquents with psycho-pathic tendencies have been found to show poor moral judgement relative to delinquents without psychopathy and non-delinquent juveniles (for an exten-sive review see Stams et al., 2006). This is in line with studies showing that juvenile delinquents with psychopathic tendencies trail behind in their moral development and consequently do not make the transition to higher stages of moral reasoning (Blasi, 1980; Campagna & Harter, 1975; Fodor, 1973; Nelson, Smith, & Dodd, 1990; Smetana, 1990).

Finally, there are relatively few studies on economic social decision-making in psychopathy. Research on social decision-making tries to address the direct and indirect influences of the social context on the decisions we make by using paradigms originally derived from research in economics (for a review see Sanfey & Rilling, 2011). Such paradigms include the Ultimatum Game and its many derivatives, the Dictator game and the Public Goods game, to name a few. The essence of these games is that people have to make decisions about dividing money or other assets with other individuals, and several measures can be calculated to index concepts like fairness and intentionality (Radke, Güroğlu, & de Bruijn, 2012), egalitarianism (Fehr, Rützler, & Sutter, 2011) and also social emotions such as guilt aversion (Chang, Smith, Dufwenberg, & Sanfey, 2011) and regret (Giourgetta et al., 2012). These topics are also of interest for psychopathy because they can help us understand the role of social context in explaining facets of psychopathic behaviour. For example,

Koenigs et al. (2010) investigated economic decision-making in psychopathy and found that psychopathic participants with low trait anxiety (referred to as primary psychopaths in their study) accepted less unfair financial offers in a Ultimatum Game and also offered less money to the other person in a Dictator game. In contrast, Radke and colleagues (2013) did not find any differences between offenders with psychopathy and a healthy control sample, but they did find that a third group consisting of non-psychopathic offenders failed to adjust behaviour according to the contextual demands.

Taken together, studying social cognition from various perspectives is proving to be very useful in understanding the impact of social context on decision-making and behaviour in psychopathy. The first results show the added value of research in this area and highlight the importance of pursuing this line of research in the future.

Concluding remarks

The goal of this chapter has been to provide an overview of current perspectives on psychopathy and also to highlight some of the novel developments in the field. The first section revolves around contemporary conceptualisations of psychopathy as a personality construct. The operationalisation of psychopathy followed by Hare in the development of the PCL-R has been very influential in establishing the currently dominant conception of psychopathy. Although the PCL-R was initially developed as a dimensional measure of psychopathy, it is often used to dichotomise this dimension for the classification of behaviour into psychopathic or non-psychopathic. This feature has made the PCL-R of great value in both clinical and legal settings. However, other conceptualisations exist in which psychopathy is defined as the presence of extreme variations in common personality traits (Lilienfeld & Andrews, 1996) or as a combination of personality facets with a strong genetic background (Patrick et al., 2009) among the general population.

Others have described psychopathy in terms of abnormal neurocognition. The IES model and the RM hypothesis have generated competing neurocognitive explanations for the core dysfunctions in psychopathy. On one hand, the IES model builds on previous models positing that the core feature of psychopathy lies in abnormal affective processing and impairments in specific amygdala–centred associative learning processes. In contrast, the RM hypothesis postulates that psychopathy is not primarily typified by affective dysfunctions but by abnormalities in early selective attention processes. Arguably, these two theories have been the most prominent in the literature on psychopathy research in the last decade. But while both models can accommodate a large amount of data, there are also empirical results that do not fit neatly in either of these frameworks (Boccardi et al., 2011; Brazil et al., 2013; Moul & Dadds, 2013; von Borries et al., 2010). This has contributed to the development of other neurocognitive accounts of psychopathy. Although the IES model is much in agreement with the paralimbic dysfunction hypothesis in that amygdala and OFC are dysfunctional in psychopathy, the paralimbic dysfunction hypothesis postulates impairments in a wider range of brain regions (e.g. ACC, PCC, insula, temporal pole and so on), which are highly interconnected with the primary limbic structures. Recently, a great deal of extant literature adds credence to the paralimbic dysfunction hypothesis demonstrating dysfunction extending beyond the amygdala and OFC (see Anderson & Kiehl, 2012).

Besides the empirical work generated by these models, there is also an increasing amount of studies targeting other questions relevant for our understanding of psychopathy. These include, but are not limited to, the differentiation of psychopathy and generic antisociality from a neurocognitive point of view and the assessment of various aspects of social cognition. The results are promising and highlight the importance of embracing novel ideas and empirical approaches to increase our understanding of psychopathy, and further studies in these areas will be of great value for research on psychopathy.

Literature

Anderson, N. E., & Kiehl, K. A. (2012). The psychopath magnetized: Insights from brain imaging. *Trends in Cognitive Sciences, 16*(1), 52–60.

Arrigo, B. A., & Shipley, S. (2001). The confusion over psychopathy (I): Historical considerations. *International Journal of Offender Therapy and Comparative Criminology, 45*(3), 325–344.

Baskin-Sommers, A., Curtin, J. J., Li, W., & Newman, J. P. (2011). Psychopathy-related differences in selective attention are captured by an early event-related potential. *Personality Disorders: Theory, Research, and Treatment, 3*(4), 370–378.

Beer, J. S., John, O. P., Scabini, D., & Knight, R. T. (2006). Orbitofrontal cortex and social behaviour: Integrating self-monitoring and emotion-cognition interactions. *Journal of Cognitive Neuroscience, 18*(6), 871–879.

Benning, S. D., Patrick, C. J., Hicks, B. M., Blonigen, D. M., & Krueger, R. F. (2003). Factor structure of the psychopathic personality inventory: Validity and implications for clinical assessment. *Psychol Assess, 15*(3), 340–350.

Birbaumer, N., Veit, R., Lotze, M., Erb, M., Hermann, C., Grodd, W., & Flor, H. (2005). Deficient fear conditioning in psychopathy: A functional magnetic resonance imaging study. *Archives of General Psychiatry, 62*(7), 799–805.

Blair, R. J. R. (2005). Applying a cognitive neuroscience perspective to the disorder of psychopathy. *Development & Psychopathology, 17*(3), 865–891.

Blair, R. J. R. (2006). Dissociable systems for empathy. In *Novartis Foundation Symposium* (Vol. 278, p. 134). Chichester, New York: John Wiley.

Blair, R. J. R. (2007). The amygdala and ventromedial prefrontal cortex in morality and psychopathy. *Trends in Cognitive Sciences, 11*(9), 387–392.

Blair, R. J. R., & Mitchell, D. G. V. (2009). Psychopathy, attention and emotion. *Psychological Medicine, 39*(04), 543–555.

Blair, R. J. R., Mitchell, D. R., & Blair, K. (2005). *The psychopath: Emotion and the brain*. Oxford: Wiley-Blackwell.

Blasi, A. (1980). Bridging moral cognition and moral action: A critical review of the literature. *Psychological Bulletin, 88*(1), 1–45.

Boccardi, M., Frisoni, G. B., Hare, R. D., Cavedo, E., Najt, P., Pievani, M., & Repo-Tiihonen, E. (2011). Cortex and amygdala morphology in psychopathy. *Psychiatry Research: Neuroimaging, 193*(2), 85–92.

Bolt, D. M., Hare, R. D., & Neumann, C. S. (2007). Score metric equivalence of the Psychopathy Checklist – Revised (PCL-R) across criminal offenders in North America and the United Kingdom. *Assessment, 14*(1), 44–56.

Brazil, I. A., Maes, J. H. R., Scheper, I., Bulten, B. H., Kessels, R. P., Verkes, R. J., & De Bruijn, E. R. A. (2013). Reversal deficits in psychopathy in explicit but not implicit learning conditions. *Journal of Psychiatry and Neuroscience*, Epub ahead of print.

Brazil, I. A., Mars, R. B., Bulten, B. H., Buitelaar, J. K., Verkes, R. J., & De Bruijn, E. R. (2011). A neurophysiological dissociation between monitoring one's own and others' actions in psychopathy. *Biological Psychiatry, 69*(7), 693–699.

Brazil, I. A., Verkes, R. J., Brouns, B. H. J., Buitelaar, J. K., Bulten, B. H., & de Bruijn, E. R. A. (2012). Differentiating psychopathy from general antisociality using the P3 as a psychophysiological correlate of attentional allocation. *PloS One, 7*(11), e50339.

Budhani, S., & Blair, R. J. R. (2004). Response reversal and children with psycho-pathic tendencies: Success is a function of salience of contingency change. *Journal of Child Psychology and Psychiatry, 46*(9), 972–981.

Bzdok, D., Laird, A. R., Zilles, K., Fox, P. T., & Eickhoff, S. B. (2013). An investigation of the structural, connectional, and functional subspecialization in the human amygdala. *Human Brain Mapping, 34*(12), 3247–3266.

Campagna, A. F., & Harter, S. (1975). Moral judgment in sociopathic and normal children. *Journal of Personality and Social Psychology, 31*(2), 199–205.

Chang, L. J., Smith, A., Dufwenberg, M., & Sanfey, A. G. (2011). Triangulating the neural, psychological, and economic bases of guilt aversion. *Neuron, 70*(3), 560–572.

Cima, M., Korebrits, A., Stams, G. J., & Bleumer, P. (submitted). Moral development, cognition, emotion and behaviour in male youth with varying levels of psycho-pathic traits.

Cima, M., Tonnaer, F., & Hauser, M. D. (2010). Psychopaths know right from wrong but don't care. *Social Cognitive and Affective Neuroscience, 5*(1), 59–67.

Cleckley, H. (1941). *The mask of sanity: An attempt to reinterpret the so-called psychopathic personality.* Oxford: Mosby.

Cleckley, H. M. (1982). *The mask of sanity.* St. Louis, MO: Mosby.

Cooke, D. J., & Michie, C. (1999). Psychopathy across cultures: North America and Scotland compared. *Journal of Abnormal Psychology, 108*(1), 58–68.

Cooke, D. J., & Michie, C. (2001). Refining the construct of psychopathy: Towards a hierarchical model. *Psychological Assessment, 13*(2), 171.

Cooke, D. J., Michie, C., & Hart, S. D. (2006). Facets of clinical psychopathy. In C. J. Patrick (Ed.), *Handbook of psychopathy* (pp. 91–106). New York: The Guilford Press.

Cunningham, W. A., & Brosch, T. (2012). Motivational salience amygdala tuning from traits, needs, values, and goals. *Current Directions in Psychological Science, 21*(1), 54–59.

Davis, M., & Whalen, P. J. (2001). The amygdala: Vigilance and emotion. *Molecular Psychiatry, 6*(1), 13–34.

Ermer, E., Cope, L. M., Nyalakanti, P. K., Calhoun, V. D., & Kiehl, K. A. (2012). Aberrant paralimbic gray matter in criminal psychopathy. *Journal of Abnormal Psychology, 121*(3), 649.

Ermer, E., Cope, L. M., Nyalakanti, P. K., Calhoun, V. D., & Kiehl, K. A. (2013). Aberrant paralimbic gray matter in incarcerated male adolescents with psychopathic traits. *Journal of the American Academy of Child & Adolescent Psychiatry*, *52*(1), 94–103.

Ermer, E., & Kiehl, K. A. (2010). Psychopaths are impaired in social exchange and precautionary reasoning. *Psychological Science*, *21*(10), 1399–1405.

Fehr, E., Rützler, D., & Sutter, M. (2011). The development of egalitarianism, altruism, spite and parochialism in childhood and adolescence. *European Economic Review*, *64*, 369–383.

Flor, H., Birbaumer, N., Hermann, C., Ziegler, S., & Patrick, C. J. (2002). Aversive Pavlovian conditioning in psychopaths: Peripheral and central correlates. *Psychophysiology*, *39*(4), 505–518.

Fodor, E. M. (1973). Moral development and parent behaviour antecedents in adolescent psychopaths. *The Journal of Genetic Psychology*, *122*(1), 37–43.

Giourgetta, C., Grecucci, A., Bonini, N., Coricelli, G., Demarchi, G., Braun, C., & Sanfey, A. G. (2012). Waves of regret: A meg study of emotion and decision-making. *Neuropsychologia*, *51*, 38–51.

Glenn, A. L., Yang, Y., Raine, A., & Colletti, P. (2010). No volumetric differences in the anterior cingulate of psychopathic individuals. *Psychiatry Research: Neuroimaging*, *183*(2), 140–143.

Gorenstein, E. E., & Newman, J. P. (1980). Disinhibitory psychopathology: A new perspective and a model for research. *Psychological Review*, *87*(3), 301–315.

Greene, J. (2003). From neural 'is' to moral 'ought': What are the moral implications of neuroscientific moral psychology? *Nature Reviews Neuroscience*, *4*(10), 846–850.

Hare, R. D. (1965a). Acquisition and generalization of a conditioned-fear response in psychopathic and nonpsychopathic criminals. *The Journal of Psychology*, *59*(2), 367–370.

Hare, R. D. (1965b). Temporal gradient of fear arousal in psychopaths. *Journal of Abnormal Psychology*, *70*(6), 442–445.

Hare, R. D. (1980). A research scale for the assessment of psychopathy in criminal populations. *Personality and Individual Differences*, *1*(2), 111–119.

Hare, R. D. (1998). Psychopathy, affect and behaviour. In *Psychopathy: Theory, research and implications for society* (pp. 105–137). Dordrecht: Kluwer.

Hare, R. D. (2003). *Manual for the revised psychopathy checklist* (2nd ed.). Toronto, ON: Multi-Health Systems.

Hare, R. D., Hart, S. D., & Harpur, T. J. (1991). Psychopathy and the DSM-IV criteria for antisocial personality disorder. *Journal of Abnormal Psychology*, *100*(3), 391–398.

Hare, R. D., & Neumann, C. S. (2006). The PCL-R assessment of psychopathy. In C. J. Patrick (Eds.), *Handbook of psychopathy* (pp. 58–88). New York: The Guilford Press.

Hare, R. D., & Quinn, M. J. (1971). Psychopathy and autonomic conditioning. *Journal of Abnormal Psychology*, *77*(3), 223.

Harpur, T. J., Hare, R. D., & Hakstian, A. R. (1989). Two-factor conceptualization of psychopathy: Construct validity and assessment implications. *Psychological Assessment: A Journal of Consulting and Clinical Psychology*, *1*(1), 6–17.

Hiatt, K. D., & Newman, J. P. (2006). Understanding psychopathy: The cognitive side. In C. J. Patrick (Ed.), *Handbook of psychopathy* (pp. 334–352). New York: Guilford Press.

Hildebrand, M., De Ruiter, C., & Nijman, H. (2004). PCL-R psychopathy predicts disruptive behaviour among male offenders in a Dutch forensic psychiatric hospital. *Journal of Interpersonal Violence*, *19*(1), 13–29.

Kiehl, K. A. (2006). A cognitive neuroscience perspective on psychopathy: Evidence for paralimbic system dysfunction. *Psychiatry Res, 142*(2–3), 107–128.

Kiehl, K. A., Hare, R. D., McDonald, J. J., & Brink, J. (1999). Semantic and affective processing in psychopaths: An event-related potential (ERP) study. *Psychophysiology, 36*(6), 765–774.

Koenigs, M., Baskin-Sommers, A., Zeier, J., & Newman, J. P. (2011). Investigating the neural correlates of psychopathy: A critical review. *Molecular Psychiatry, 16*(8), 792–799.

Koenigs, M., Kruepke, M., & Newman, J. P. (2010). Economic decision-making in psychopathy: A comparison with ventromedial prefrontal lesion patients. *Neuropsychologia, 48*(7), 2198–2204.

Lilienfeld, S. O., & Andrews, B. P. (1996). Development and preliminary validation of a self-report measure of psychopathic personality traits in noncriminal populations. *Journal of Personality Assessment, 66*(3), 488–524.

Lilienfeld, S. O., Patrick, C. J., Benning, S. D., Berg, J., Sellbom, M., & Edens, J. F. (2012). The role of fearless dominance in psychopathy: Confusions, controversies, and clarifications. *Personality Disorders: Theory, Research, and Treatment, 3*(3), 327–340.

Lykken, D. T. (1995). *The antisocial personalities.* Hillsdale, NJ: Lawrence Erlbaum Associates.

Lynam, D. R., & Miller, J. D. (2012). Fearless dominance and psychopathy: A response to Lilienfeld et al.

MacCoon, D. G., Wallace, J. F., & Newman, J. P. (2004). Self-regulation: Context-appropriate balanced attention. *Handbook of self-regulation: Research, theory, and applications* (pp. 422–444). New York, Guilford Press.

Maren, S., & Quirk, G. J. (2004). Neuronal signalling of fear memory. *Nature Reviews Neuroscience, 5*(11), 844–852.

Miller, J. D., & Lynam, D. R. (2012) An examination of the Psychopathic Personality Inventory's nomological network: A meta-analytic review. *Personality Disorders: Theory, Research, and Treatment, 3*, 305–326.

Mitchell, D. G. V., Colledge, E., Leonard, A., & Blair, R. J. R. (2002). Risky decisions and response reversal: Is there evidence of orbitofrontal cortex dysfunction in psychopathic individuals? *Neuropsychologia, 40*(12), 2013–2022.

Moll, J., de Oliveira-Souza, R., Eslinger, P. J., Bramati, I. E., Mourão-Miranda, J., Andreiuolo, P. A., & Pessoa, L. (2002). The neural correlates of moral sensitivity: A functional magnetic resonance imaging investigation of basic and moral emotions. *The Journal of Neuroscience, 22*(7), 2730–2736.

Moul, C., & Dadds, M. R. (2013). Learning-style bias and the development of psychopathy. *Journal of Personality Disorders, 27*(1), 85–98.

Moul, C., Killcross, S., & Dadds, M. R. (2012). A model of differential amygdala activation in psychopathy. *Psychological Review, 119*(4), 789–806.

Nelson, J. R., Smith, D., J, & Dodd, J. (1990). The moral reasoning of juvenile delinquents: A meta-analysis. *Journal of Abnormal Child Psychology, 18*(3), 231–239.

Neumann, C. S., Malterer, M. B., & Newman, J. P. (2008). Factor structure of the Psychopathic Personality Inventory (PPI): Findings from a large incarcerated sample. *Psychological Assessment, 20*(2), 169–174.

Neumann, C. S., Schmitt, D. S., Carter, R., Embley, I., & Hare, R. D. (2012). Psychopathic traits in females and males across the globe. *Behavioural Sciences & the Law, 30*(5), 557–574.

Newman, J. P., Curtin, J. J., Bertsch, J. D., & Baskin-Sommers, A. R. (2010). Attention moderates the fearlessness of psychopathic offenders. *Biological Psychiatry*, *67*(1), 66–70.

Newman, J. P., & Kosson, D. S. (1986). Passive avoidance learning in psychopathic and nonpsychopathic offenders. *Journal of Abnormal Psychology*, *95*(3), 252–256.

Newman, J. P., Patterson, C. M., & Kosson, D. S. (1987). Response perseveration in psychopaths. *Journal of Abnormal Psychology*, *96*(2), 145–148.

Olsson, A., & Phelps, E. A. (2007). Social learning of fear. *Nature neuroscience*, *10*(9), 1095–1102.

Patrick, C. J. (1994). Emotion and psychopathy: Startling new insights. *Psychophysiology*, *31*(4), 319–330.

Patrick, C. J. (2006). Back to the future: Cleckley as a guide to the next generation of psychopathy research. In C. J. Patrick (Ed.). New York: Guilford Press.

Patrick, C. J., & Bernat, E. M. (2009). Neurobiology of psychopathy: A two process theory. In G. G. Bernston & J. T. Cacioppo (Eds.), *Handbook of neuroscience for the behavioural sciences* (pp. 1110–1131). New York: John Wiley & Sons.

Patrick, C. J., Bradley, M. M., & Lang, P. J. (1993). Emotion in the criminal psychopath: Startle reflex modulation. *Journal of Abnormal Psychology*, *102*(1), 82.

Patrick, C. J., Fowles, D. C., & Krueger, R. F. (2009). Triarchic conceptualization of psychopathy: Developmental origins of disinhibition, boldness, and meanness. *Development and psychopathology*, *21*(3), 913–938.

Patterson, C. M., & Newman, J. P. (1993). Reflectivity and learning from aversive events: Toward a psychological mechanism for the syndromes of disinhibition. *Psychological Review*, *100*(4), 716–736.

Paulhus, D. L., Neumann, C. S., & Hare, R. D. (in press). *Manual for the Hare Self-Report Psychopathy scale*. Toronto, ON: Multi-Health Systems.

Prichard, J. C. (1835). *A treatise on insanity and other disorders affecting the mind* (Vol. 1835). London: Sherwood, Gilbert and Piper.

Prinz, J. (2006). The emotional basis of moral judgments. *Philosophical Explorations*, *9*(1), 29–43.

Radke, S., Brazil, I. A., Scheper, I., Bulten, B. H., & De Bruijn, E. R. (2013). Unfair offers, unfair offenders? Fairness considerations in incarcerated individuals with and without psychopathy. *Frontiers in Human Neuroscience*, *7*, 406.

Radke, S., Güroğlu, B., & de Bruijn, E. R. (2012). There's something about a fair split: Intentionality moderates context-based fairness considerations in social decision-making. *PloS One*, *7*(2), e31491.

Rasmussen, K., Storsæter, O., & Levander, S. (1999). Personality disorders, psychopathy, and crime in a Norwegian prison population. *International Journal of Law and Psychiatry*, *22*(1), 91–97.

Robinson, O. J., Overstreet, C., Allen, P. S., Pine, D. S., & Grillon, C. (2012). Acute tryptophan depletion increases translational indices of anxiety but not fear: Serotonergic modulation of the bed nucleus of the stria terminalis. *Neuropsychopharmacology*, *37*, 1963–1971.

Rushworth, M. F., Behrens, T. E., Rudebeck, P. H., & Walton, M. E. (2007). Contrasting roles for cingulate and orbitofrontal cortex in decisions and social behaviour. *Trends in Cognitive Sciences*, *11*(4), 168–176.

Sah, P., Faber, E. S. L., De Armentia, M. L., & Power, J. (2003). The amygdaloid complex: Anatomy and physiology. *Physiological Reviews*, *83*(3), 803–834.

Sanfey, A. G., & Rilling, J. K. (2011). Neural bases of social decision making. *Neuroscience of Decision Making*, 223.

226 *Inti A. Brazil and Maaike Cima*

Sellbom, M., Ben-Porath, Y. S., Lilienfeld, S. O., Patrick, C. J., & Graham, J. R. (2005). Assessing psychopathic personality traits with the MMPI–2. *Journal of Personality Assessment, 85*(3), 334–343.

Smetana, J. G. (1990). Morality and conduct disorders. In M. Lewis & S. M. Miller (Eds.), *Handbook of developmental psychopathology* (pp. 157–179). New York: Plenum Press.

Stams, G. J., Brugman, D., Deković, M., van Rosmalen, L., van der Laan, P., & Gibbs, J. C. (2006). The moral judgment of juvenile delinquents: A meta-analysis. *Journal of Abnormal Child Psychology, 34*(5), 692–708.

Verona, E., Sprague, J., & Sadeh, N. (2012). Inhibitory control and negative emotional processing in psychopathy and antisocial personality disorder. *Journal of Abnormal Psychology, 121*(2), 498–510.

Von Borries, A. K. L., Brazil, I. A., & Bulten, B. H. (submitted). The psychopathic personality inventory: Factor structure and validity in (non)-criminal populations.

Von Borries, A. K. L., Brazil, I. A., Bulten, B. H., Buitelaar, J. K., Verkes, R. J., & de Bruijn, E. R. A. (2010). Neural correlates of error-related learning deficits in individuals with psychopathy. *Psychological Medicine, 40*(9), 1443–1451.

Wallis, J. D. (2007). Orbitofrontal cortex and its contribution to decision-making. *Annual Review of Neurosciemce, 30*, 31–56.

Williamson, S., Harpur, T. J., & Hare, R. D. (1991). Abnormal processing of affective words by psychopaths. *Psychophysiology, 28*(3), 260–273.

Yang, Y., Raine, A., Narr, K. L., Colletti, P., & Toga, A. W. (2009). Localization of deformations within the amygdala in individuals with psychopathy. *Archives of General Psychiatry, 66*(9), 986–994. doi:10.1001/archgenpsychiatry.2009.110

Young, L., & Koenigs, M. (2007). Investigating emotion in moral cognition: A review of evidence from functional neuroimaging and neuropsychology. *British Medical Bulletin, 84*, 69–79.

11 Violent offenders

Neurobiology and crime

Alexandria K. Johnson and Andrea L. Glenn

Introduction

Much of the current research on the neurobiology of crime has examined samples of individuals who meet criteria for disorders that commonly result in criminal behaviour, such as antisocial personality disorder (APD) and psychopathy. Although these disorders are not directly indicative of criminal behaviour, they are highly correlated. To better understand the complex relationship between neurobiological risk factors and crime, it is helpful to first review the theories that help us understand how anomalies in certain brain regions and hormone levels can lead to deficits that may predispose someone to APD, psychopathy and criminal activity. Some of the key brain regions implicated in this type of behaviour include the prefrontal cortex, the amygdala and the hippocampus. The prefrontal cortex, and in particular the orbitofrontal region, plays a large role in decision-making and inhibition, whereas the amygdala and hippocampus are involved in emotional processing. In this chapter we attempt to clarify how neurobiological research has begun to elucidate how deficits in particular brain regions might put someone at risk for criminal behaviour, in hopes to better understand its aetiology. In addition to considering specific brain regions, we discuss how hormones such as testosterone and cortisol have been implicated in criminal behaviour. This information could lead to advances in the treatment and management of individuals whose actions lead to their involvement in the criminal justice system.

Disorders associated with crime

Research has shown that certain clinical diagnoses increase the likelihood of criminal behaviour. It is important to note that a categorical label of either APD or psychopathy does not necessarily equate to criminal activity, as in the case of 'successful' psychopaths, a term used to refer to people who exhibit many of the criteria used to identify psychopathy, yet do not have a criminal record. However, a disproportionate number of people who meet criteria for psychopathy can be found in correctional settings (Hare, 1991) and psychopathy is a risk factor for violence (Leistico, Salekin, DeCoster, & Rogers, 2008; Spidel et al., 2007; Swogger, Walsh, & Kosson, 2007) as well as increased likelihood

228 *Alexandria K. Johnson and Andrea L. Glenn*

to reoffend (Leistico, Salekin, DeCoster, & Rogers, 2008; Neumann & Hare, 2008; Quinsey, Rice, & Harris, 1995). Relatedly, APD is overrepresented in the criminal justice system with rates of APD in prison around 47% for men and 21% for women (Fazel & Danesh, 2002) in comparison to estimated rates of 3% and 1%, respectively, in the general population (Gibbon et al., 2010). Because APD and psychopathy significantly increase the risk for criminal behaviour, a great deal of research on neurobiology and crime has focused on these diagnoses.

Neurobiological models of criminal behaviour

Several models have been proposed to explain how the brain differences observed in individuals with APD or psychopathy may increase the likelihood of criminal behaviour.

The low-fear hypothesis

The low-fear hypothesis suggests that the deviant behaviours often associated with psychopathic traits are a result of a deficit in fear (Fowles, 1980; Lykken, 1995). In healthy individuals who process fear in the typical manner, a form of associative learning, known as fear conditioning, occurs (Maren & Quirk, 2004). Through fear conditioning, actions that result in fearful situations become associated with fear and are thus avoided. Among those who do not process fear in the typical manner, this associative link may be weaker. Supporting the idea that those with psychopathic tendencies do not exhibit associative learning when conditioned through aversive stimuli, studies have shown that while people with psychopathy respond similarly to a control group when presented with unconditioned stimuli (i.e. painful pressure, unpleasant odour), they do not demonstrate a similar response to conditioned stimuli (Birbaumer et al., 2005; Flor, Birbaumer, Hermann, Ziegler, & Patrick, 2002). This indicates that although people with psychopathic traits find pain or bad smells displeasing in the same way the control subjects do, exposure to the aversive stimuli does not become associated with the stimulus with which it has been paired. A failure to form such a link would make it difficult to learn from negative consequences or change behaviour as a result of negative consequences. In terms of unlawful behaviour, if a link is not made between the behaviour and the punishment that results from the behaviour, punishment is not likely to serve as a deterrent to acting in the same way in the future, regardless of the person finding punishment unpleasant.

Because those who lack the ability to be conditioned to have a fear of punishment do not effectively link bad behaviour to negative consequences, a lack of fear may inhibit socialisation. Long before a person ever enters the judicial system, parental attempts at discouraging bad behaviour, whether through time-outs, spankings or reduced privileges, are unlikely to work if the behaviour-punishment link does not properly form. The amygdala, which will be an important brain region of discussion throughout this chapter, has been suggested to be tied to this lack of fear and the process of fear conditioning (Patrick, 1994).

The response modulation hypothesis

The response modulation hypothesis suggests that those high in psychopathic traits are poor at processing any type of information (including but not limited to fear and punishment cues) that is peripheral to their primary goal, and that this lack of attention explains the demonstrated reduction in startle response (Newman, Curtin, Bertsch, & Baskin-Sommers, 2010). This theory offers an alternative interpretation of the previously mentioned fear-potentiated startle finding, suggesting that those with psychopathic traits become so focused on the goal or reward at hand that they may fail to integrate or consider additional information. This theory differs from the low-fear hypothesis in that it focuses on cognitive rather than emotional deficits associated with psychopathy and antisocial behaviour. Research supporting this theory has shown that when performing certain Stroop-type tasks, which require the individual to block out distracting and irrelevant information, participants who score high on psychopathic traits outperform controls, indicating that they more effectively ignore interfering information in favour of an attentional bias that focuses more closely on goal-relevant information (Hiatt, Schmitt, & Newman, 2004). This theory calls attention to the role of higher-order brain processes in regulating emotion (Newman et al., 2010).

The integrated emotion systems (IES) model

The IES model (Blair, 2005) attempts to integrate a wide variety of previous findings, including those in the low-fear literature, into a comprehensive model that more directly links specific brain regions to well-established deficits observed among individuals with psychopathy. The specific brain regions that are key to the IES model will be mentioned briefly here, but will be covered in greater detail later in this chapter.

The IES model indicates that individuals with psychopathy demonstrate a reduced ability to form associations between a stimulus and its subsequent reinforcement, a task that relies on specific regions of the amygdala. This reduced ability to form associations results in a lowered ability to respond to cues of distress in others or to be socialised, resulting in a lack of empathy (Blair, 2005). Although this model views psychopathy as primarily a result of deficits in processes stemming from the amygdala, the model also postulates that different types of aggression are differentially associated with particular brain regions. Reactive aggression is a hostile or angry reaction to perceived danger, threat or frustration that is typically impulsive or driven by emotions. Instrumental aggression, on the other hand, is driven primarily by a desire for a particular goal and any violence or injury that occurs is secondary to the attainment of

230　*Alexandria K. Johnson and Andrea L. Glenn*

the particular goal (e.g. Woodworth & Porter, 2002). According to the IES model, reactive aggression is the result of dysfunction in the orbital and ventrolateral frontal cortex whereas instrumental aggression is the result of dysfunction in the amygdala, which produces difficulties in socialisation (Blair, 2005). In sum, a poorly socialised person who does not relate to the distress felt by others and who may also become easily frustrated and have a hard time inhibiting physical impulses may be at an increased likelihood of getting into fights with others and would also be less likely to refrain from criminal activity over feelings of guilt for potential victims.

The differential amygdala activation model (DAMM)

The DAMM (Moul, Killcross, & Dadds, 2012) is a model that was proposed as a way of unifying existing emotional (i.e. low-fear hypothesis, IES) and cognitive (i.e. response modulation hypothesis) models of the origin of psychopathic characteristics. This theory is based in part on research showing that although participants with psychopathic traits often have difficulty recognising fearful faces, their ability to do so is improved if they are explicitly instructed to focus on the eyes of a face (Dadds, El Masry, Wimalaweera, & Guastella, 2008). It has been previously demonstrated that those high in psychopathic traits have a decreased ability to recognise and accurately identify fearful facial expressions (e.g. Blair et al., 2004). This deficit is thought to be related to the inability to recognise distress cues in others, which is important in socialisation. However, if the inability to recognise fear improves with instruction on where to look, this suggests that some attention problems, as proposed in the response modulation hypothesis, may be at least partially responsible for this deficit. This finding indicates that those with psychopathic traits do not entirely lack the ability to recognise fear because correcting where attention is focused ameliorates the fear recognition deficit. In addition, the finding that facial recognition can be improved through instruction offers the possibility to improve emotional processing.

One of the central tenets of the DAMM is that the amygdala does not function as a singular unit. Examining the two major regions of the amygdala, the basolateral amygdala (BLA) and the central amygdala (CeA), separately is said to explain the mixed results that have been obtained by previous researchers who have studied the amygdala as a singular entity. The division within the amygdala will be expanded on later in the chapter, but for now it is important to note that the DAMM proposes that psychopathic characteristics are the result of an underactive BLA and a normally functioning, or possibly overactive, CeA (Moul et al., 2012). To fully understand the DAMM, it is necessary to clearly understand these two subregions.

The paralimbic system dysfunction model

This model draws upon existing research that is available using a variety of different methodology to determine that a wide range of brain areas are likely responsible for psychopathic traits. Based upon a review of the available findings from a wide array of sources, it is surmised that the abnormalities observed in psychopathy must extend beyond commonly implicated brain regions such as the prefrontal cortex or the amygdala. The brain structures implicated in this model are part of the paralimbic system (Kiehl, 2006). This model is based upon cytoarchitetonics, a field of study that uses neuronal similarities to identify regions of the brain that are closely related to one another (Anderson & Kiehl, 2012). The IES and the paralimbic models are in agreement with one another that dysfunctions in the amygdala and the orbitofrontal cortex (OFC) lead to psychopathic traits. The paralimbic system dysfunction model includes other related regions in addition to the OFC and the amygdala.

The limbic system

Amygdala

As previously stated, the most current neurocognitive models used to conceptualise psychopathy and its related behaviours like crime (i.e. the IES, the DAMM and the paralimbic system dysfunction model) emphasise the importance of the amygdala (Blair, 2005; Moul et al., 2012; Anderson & Kiehl, 2012). The amygdala is an almond-shaped region located deep in the brain, within the medial temporal lobe. The amygdala is highly connected to the orbitofrontal cortex (OFC), located in the front of the brain in the area just behind the eye sockets. The OFC and the amygdala share information and work together to process emotional information and then incorporate that information into higher-order decision-making. Overall, the amygdala is an important area for causing a person to be alert to important information, process emotions and adjust behaviour via reinforcement. The amygdala has been shown to be important for vigilance, avoidance, evaluating emotionally significant stimuli (Davis & Whalen, 2001) and fear-related responses (Sah, Faber, De Armentia, & Power, 2003). The amygdala is a complex structure made up of approximately 13 connected nuclei (Sah et al., 2003) that can then be grouped into two main regions, the BLA and CeA (Moul et al., 2012).

The BLA is cited as the region of the amygdala that reflexively causes gaze to shift to the eyes of a face (Gamer & Büchel, 2009). Therefore, according to the DAMM an underactive BLA would result in a failure to automatically attend to the eyes, but once the gaze is deliberately fixed on the eye region of a face, fear can be recognised normally (Moul et al., 2012). Discovering the cause of a lack of fear recognition and a means to correct the problem is critical in that an inability to recognise fear in others is thought to be closely associated with difficulty in becoming properly socialised. This could be due to an inability to connect precipitating events to their adverse consequences or to a lack of ability to emotionally grasp the negative effects that cruel actions have on their recipient (Blair et al., 2004). A poor understanding of the cause and effect relationship between actions and consequences and a lack of empathy for one's victims are outcomes that make someone less likely to be persuaded away from a criminal lifestyle.

Information is passed from the BLA region of the amygdala to the CeA region of the amygdala, where it is encoded and processed. Research showing that the previously observed emotional deficits are accounted for once attention is focused on the appropriate stimulus (the eyes of the face), and thus the BLA defect has been circumvented, indicates that the CeA in those with psychopathic traits is functioning normally (Moul et al., 2012). This is why the DAMM hypothesises that BLA is underactive, but the CeA is likely functioning normally among those with psychopathic traits.

Blair's IES model also recognises that the BLA and CeA can be considered separate but related fear systems (Blair, 2004). The CeA controls aversive conditioning, whereas the BLA controls instrumental learning, or the ability to change a response based on punishment (Killcross, Robbins, & Everitt, 1997). In other words, the separable fear system that the IES model proposes is one in which the CeA plays a role in the ability to form a conditioned stimulus-unconditioned response association and the BLA is responsible for encoding the emotional valence associated to a conditioned stimulus. Between the two systems, those with psychopathic traits have a deficit in forming associations between a stimulus and punishment. This ultimately leads to difficulty with emotional learning and socialisation (Blair, 2005).

In sum, previous research has offered substantial support indicating that psychopathic characteristics are in some way associated with abnormalities within the amygdala. The most recent neurocognitive models of psychopathy are beginning to look at specific subregions of the amygdala to further delineate the relationship between abnormalities in the emotional and cognitive processing of psychopaths and amygdala differences.

Hippocampus

The hippocampus is responsible for consolidating information and memories from experienced events and storing them in long-term memory. Although previous research has shown that the volume of the hippocampus does not significantly differ between controls and participants with either APD or psychopathy (Barkataki, Kumari, Das, Taylor, & Sharma, 2006; Laakso et al., 2001; Raine et al., 2004), one study has shown a negative correlation between the volume of the posterior hippocampus and the severity of psychopathy among an offender sample (Laakso et al., 2001). Furthermore, Boccardi and colleagues (2010) found no significant differences in overall volume of the hippocampi between a sample of offenders and a control sample. However, when looking at the surface of particular areas of the hippocampi, the offender group did show a significant pattern of differences from the control group. This finding suggests that while overall volume of the hippocampi may not differ among offenders, it is possible that intricacies of the hippocampal structure may differ from that of healthy controls.

Additionally, although Raine and colleagues (2004) did not find overall volume differences, they did find that the right and left hippocampi were structurally asymmetrical, with the right anterior hippocampus being greater than the left anterior hippocampus among those classified as psychopaths with criminal records. This hippocampal abnormality was not present among those classified as psychopaths without a criminal record or among healthy control participants. In addition to structural differences, aggressive children with conduct disorders demonstrated lower activation in both the amygdala and the hippocampus compared to control subjects (Sterzer, Stadler, Krebs, Kleinschmidt, & Poustka, 2005). In sum, these studies indicate that the overall volume of the hippocampus is not likely associated with criminal behaviour, but certain structural abnormalities may be.

The prefrontal cortex

The PFC is important for decision-making, planning, moderating behaviour and the ability to concentrate, think abstractly, solve problems and behave in a socially appropriate manner. The PFC is also responsible for executive functioning, which includes the ability to determine good and bad, understand consequences, work towards goals, predict outcomes and suppress urges. Structurally, the PFC of subjects diagnosed with APD has been shown to have 11.0% less grey matter compared to a group of healthy controls (Raine et al., 2000). Similarly, so-called unsuccessful psychopaths showed a 22.3% reduction in grey matter compared to healthy controls, whereas successful psychopaths did not differ significantly from controls in terms of grey matter (Yang et al., 2005). In this case, a score ≥ 23 on the Psychopathy Checklist – Revised (PCL-R; Hare, 1991) was required to be in either psychopathy group. Successful psychopaths were those who had never been convicted of a crime, as opposed to unsuccessful psychopaths who had. A meta-analysis of brain imaging studies conducted among individuals with APD offered further support that such individuals show deficits in both the functioning and structure of the PFC, and this is a finding that has been replicated across many studies (Yang & Raine, 2009). In fact, there is some support that structural differences in the grey matter volume of males and females with APD may partially explain the gender difference in prevalence rates of APD (Raine, Yang, Narr, & Toga, 2009). In this study, the gender difference in antisocial behaviour between men and women was reduced by 77.3% when the difference in grey matter in the PFC was controlled.

Considered as a whole, these studies suggest that antisocial and criminal behaviour may be partially ascribed to reduced grey matter in the PFC. Reduced grey matter in the PFC may result in a reduced ability to inhibit behaviour, weigh outcomes and generally make well-thought-out decisions. Having less ability than others to perform this type of mental processing could result in more impulsive and less informed decision-making, and possibly more criminal behaviour.

It is worth reiterating that although the PFC is often treated as a singular structure, studies have indicated that it can be further divided into more specific areas such as the orbitofrontal cortex (OFC), the dorsolateral prefrontal cortex, the ventrolateral prefrontal cortex and the medial prefrontal cortex (Öngür, Ferry, & Price, 2003; Petrides & Pandya, 1999, 2001). Areas in the orbital network are responsible for receiving and integrating sensory information, whereas areas in the medial network output information to the hypothalamus and brainstem, influencing autonomic processes (Öngür & Price, 2000). Investigating these subregions adds specificity to our knowledge of PFC abnormalities (Yang & Raine, 2009).

The orbitofrontal cortex

The orbitofrontal cortex (OFC), a specific region of the PFC, is closely linked to the amygdala and is important for processes such as reward processing, decision-making and associative learning (Wallis, 2007). The amygdala and the OFC work in close connection with one another to integrate emotionally valenced information into the higher-order decision-making process. Previous research has found that among psychopaths with a criminal record, the connection between the amygdala and the OFC is significantly weaker compared to controls (Craig et al., 2009). In this study, it was found that the degree of impairment was correlated with the degree of antisocial behaviour (Craig et al., 2009). Similar findings have been observed in youth with conduct disorder, who displayed weaker connections between the amygdala and the PFC while viewing images of people in pain (Decety, Michalska, Akitsuki, & Lahey, 2009). A weak connection between the amygdala and the OFC could mean that emotional information is not being integrated into the decision-making process in the same way as it is for others. This could potentially result in behaviour that does not account for the impact that the behaviour will have on others. Many crimes have victims, and a lack of consideration for the emotions of the victims involved is likely to make it easier for a person to commit criminal acts against others without feelings of guilt to cause them to reconsider their actions.

Furthermore, as mentioned within the IES model, it has been hypothesised that people with abnormalities in the OFC and ventrolateral cortex might be more likely to engage in reactive aggression. The orbitofrontal cortex is responsible for integrating sensory information into the decision-making process and is involved in learning and decision-making about emotional and reward-driven behaviour (Kringelbach, 2005). The ventrolateral cortex is believed to be an area responsible for inhibiting and overriding movement and reorienting attention to information that is outside of the primary focus of attention (Levy & Wagner, 2011). As such, it is possible that individuals with deficits within these regions may become easily frustrated as a result of not having their desires met and also have a reduced ability to inhibit or control their subsequent behaviours (Blair, 2005). Additional research into how specific regions within the PFC as well as other brain regions relate to specific types of aggression may lead to a more precise understanding of the mechanisms driving various criminal behaviours.

Other brain regions

The temporal cortex

When structural brain scans of youth with early onset conduct disorder (CD) were compared to scans of matched control participants, the youth with CD had significantly less temporal lobe grey matter volume (Kruesi, Casanova, Mannheim, & Johnson-Bilder, 2004). Incarcerated inmates with psychopathy have also shown a similar reduction in temporal lobe volume (Dolan, Deakin, Roberts, & Anderson, 2002). Furthermore, a study of dementia found that when the disease was localised to the right temporal lobe, loss of empathy was an associated symptom (Perry et al., 2001). Taken together, these studies indicate that reduced volume in the temporal cortex may lead to a lessened ability to empathise, and thus to antisocial behaviour.

The corpus callosum

The corpus callosum is the largest white matter bundle in the brain and is responsible for connecting the two hemispheres of the brain. It has been suggested that anger and aggression can be explained in part by a dominant left frontal hemisphere that contributes to a bias favouring approach motivation, or being driven to seek rewards rather than driven by a fear of punishment (Sutton & Davidson, 1997). A review of recent literature indicates that abnormalities in the corpus callosum may play a role in approach-related motivation (Schutter & Harmon-Jones, 2013). It is possible that tapping into a bias towards approach motivation, rather than using punitive measures, may offer a more effective avenue for treatment. In a study looking at the effects of an intensive programme designed to treat adolescent offenders, it was found that this particular reward-based treatment was found to be effective at reducing recidivism after a four-year follow-up period. Moreover, the youth enrolled in this treatment were those who had proven to be unmanageable and disruptive in typical correctional facilities (Caldwell, McCormick, Umstead, & Van Rybroek, 2007). Individuals with psychopathy have been observed to have greater white matter volume and length within the corpus callosum, reduction in the thickness of the corpus callosum and increased interconnectivity between the two brain hemispheres (Raine et al., 2003). These callosal differences are believed to reflect differences in the brain's developmental process. Increased volume was found to be associated with deficits in interpersonal and affective functioning (Raine et al., 2003). Overall, these studies indicate that differences in the connection between the brain hemispheres may result in hypersensitivity to reward among those who engage in antisocial behaviour.

Other neurobiological correlates of crime

Altered levels of hormones and neurotransmitters have also been linked to criminal behaviour. The hormones cortisol and testosterone have commonly been associated with antisocial behaviour. Cortisol is a part of the body's stress response system and serves to mobilise the body's resources and to provide energy in times of stress (Kudielka and Kirschbaum, 2005). Evidence suggests that cortisol levels are reduced in antisocial children, adolescents and adults. In children, low cortisol levels have been associated with externalising behaviour and low anxiety (van Goozen et al., 1998) as well as symptoms of CD (Oosterlaan et al. 2005). In adolescents, low cortisol has been associated with CD (Pajer et al., 2001) and callous-unemotional traits (Loney, Butler, Lima, Counts, & Eckel, 2006). Low cortisol levels have also been observed in violent adults (Virkkunen, 1985) and offenders with psychopathic traits (Holi et al., 2006). Lower levels of cortisol may indicate that individuals are less responsive to stressors and may be less fearful of negative consequences such as potential punishment.

Testosterone has also been associated with aggressive behaviour. Males have several times the amount of testosterone as females. Because there are large sex differences in antisocial behaviour, it has been hypothesised that testosterone may contribute to aggressive behaviour. Elevated testosterone levels have indeed been linked to antisocial behaviour and violent crime in adults (Banks & Dabbs, 1996), but studies of aggressive children and adolescents have yielded mixed results (Loney et al., 2006; Maras et al., 2003). It has been argued that testosterone may not be linked to aggression per se, but to social dominance (Archer, 2006), whether within healthy or antisocial groups, which may account for some of the mixed results.

More recently, it has been hypothesised that the ratio between cortisol and testosterone may be important (van Honk & Schutter, 2006). Cortisol is thought to promote withdrawal behaviour, whereas testosterone promotes approach-related behaviour. Thus, an imbalance in the relative levels of these, with more testosterone relative to cortisol, may result in excessive approach-related behaviour (e.g. aggression) and reduced withdrawal (e.g. fearlessness, lack of inhibition). Some evidence has been found to support this hypothesis in adults with psychopathic traits (Glenn et al., 2011).

Biosocial hypotheses

Researchers studying how biology and environment may interact to influence individual differences have examined how a host of environmental factors may influence the trajectory of crime. For example, previous research on violent offenders that takes into account the effects of severe physical child abuse found brain differences that indicate that dysfunction in the right temporal cortex combined with serious child abuse may put someone at greater likelihood of violently offending as an adult. However, good right hemisphere functioning may be a protective factor among those who were seriously abused as children but do not go on to violently offend later in life (Raine et al., 2001).

Dual hazards

The dual hazard hypothesis surmises that biological risk factors, when combined with social risk factors, put someone at an overall risk factor that is greater than the sum of its parts. For example, in a study of aggression in children, it was found that being a victim of community violence was associated with increased proactive aggression, but only among those children who had a low resting heart rate. Witnessing community violence was found to be positively related to reactive aggression, but only among children whose heart rate was highly variable (Scarpa, Tanaka, & Haden, 2008). Indeed, in a Swedish sample 40% of adoptees who had biological parents who were criminals *and* received poor parenting from their adoptive parents became criminal offenders, compared to 12.1% who had only genetic risk factors, 6.7% with only environmental factors and 2.9% among those who had neither risk factor (Cloninger, Sigvardsson, Bohman, & von Knorring, 1982).

Social push

An alternative perspective for considering how social and biological factors interact is the social push hypothesis, suggesting that biological risk factors may be more important when there are fewer social factors that would predispose to crime (Raine, 2002). That is, for individuals who are raised with few environmental factors that would predispose them to crime, biological factors play a larger role in determining future criminal behaviour. However, among individuals who are raised in an environment where there are relatively more social risk factors, these environmental influences play a greater role in influencing future antisocial behaviour.

Concluding remarks

Many different models for explaining disorders closely linked to crime have been proposed. More recent models have begun to focus more specifically on structural and functional abnormalities in the brain. These brain abnormalities are being integrated into theories regarding how brain regions might help explain cognitive, emotional and behavioural deficits that have long been observed. In addition to homing in on specific brain regions, these models attempt to connect emotional-based deficit accounts of psychopathy with attentional-based deficit explanations of psychopathy. These more recent models are promising in terms of expanding on clarifying earlier models of psychopathy, although more research is required.

A variety of brain areas are likely related to criminal behaviour, with the amygdala and OFC as two heavily researched regions. It is important, however,

238 *Alexandria K. Johnson and Andrea L. Glenn*

to continue to expand research to other likely candidate regions, as complex behaviours such as criminal activity likely stem from the interplay of integrated networks within the brain. It is important also to consider how factors within the social environment influence biological risk factors that may predispose someone to crime. A better understanding of the aetiology of criminal behaviour will hopefully lead to improved interventions and reduced recidivism in the future.

Literature

Anderson, N. E., & Kiehl, K. A. (2012). The psychopath magnetized: insights from brain imaging. *Trends in Cognitive Sciences, 16*(1), 52–60.

Archer, J. (2006). Testosterone and human aggression: an evaluation of the challenge hypothesis. *Neuroscience and Biobehavioural Reviews, 30*, 319–345.

Banks, T., & Dabbs, J. M. (1996). Salivary testosterone and cortisol in a delinquent and violent urban subculture. *Journal of Social Psychology, 136*, 49–56.

Barkataki, I., Kumari, V., Das, M., Taylor, P., & Sharma, T. (2006). Volumetric structural brain abnormalities in men with schizophrenia or antisocial personality disorder. *Behavioural Brain Research, 169*(2), 239–247.

Birbaumer, N., Veit, R., Lotze, M., Erb, M., Hermann, C., Grodd, W., & Flor, H. (2005). Deficient fear conditioning in psychopathy: a functional magnetic resonance imaging study. *Archives of General Psychiatry, 62*(7), 799–805.

Blair, R. J. R. (2004). The roles of orbital frontal cortex in the modulation of antisocial behaviour. *Brain and Cognition, 55*(1), 198–208.

Blair, R. J. R. (2005). Applying a cognitive neuroscience perspective to the disorder of psychopathy. *Development and Psychopathology, 17*(03), 865–891.

Blair, R. J. R., Mitchell, D. G. V., Peschardt, K. S., Colledge, E., Leonard, R. A., Shine, J. H., & Perrett, D. I. (2004). Reduced sensitivity to others' fearful expressions in psychopathic individuals. *Personality and Individual Differences, 37*(6), 1111–1122.

Boccardi, M., Ganzola, R., Rossi, R., Sabattoli, F., Laakso, M. P., Repo-Tiihonen, E., & Tiihonen, J. (2010). Abnormal hippocampal shape in offenders with psychopathy. *Human Brain Mapping, 31*(3), 438–447.

Caldwell, M. F., McCormick, D. J., Umstead, D., & Van Rybroek, G. J. (2007). Evidence of treatment progress and therapeutic outcomes among adolescents with psychopathic features. *Criminal Justice and Behaviour, 34*(5), 573–587.

Cloninger, R., Sigvardsson, S., Bohman, M., & von Knorring, A. (1982). Predisposition to petty criminality in Swedish adoptees. *Archives of General Psychiatry, 39*, 1242–1247.

Craig, M. C., Catani, M., Deeley, Q., Latham, R., Daly, E., Kanaan, R., & Murphy, D. G. (2009). Altered connections on the road to psychopathy. *Molecular Psychiatry, 14*(10), 946–953.

Dadds, M. R., El Masry, Y., Wimalaweera, S., & Guastella, A. J. (2008). Reduced eye gaze explains 'fear blindness' in childhood psychopathic traits. *Journal of the American Academy of Child & Adolescent Psychiatry, 47*(4), 455–463.

Davis, M., & Whalen, P. J. (2001). The amygdala: vigilance and emotion. *Molecular Psychiatry, 6*(1), 13–34.

Decety, J., Michalska, K. J., Akitsuki, Y., & Lahey, B. B. (2009). Atypical empathic responses in adolescents with aggressive conduct disorder: a functional MRI investigation. *Biological Psychology, 80*(2), 203–211.

Dolan, M. C., Deakin, J. F. W., Roberts, N., & Anderson, I. M. (2002). Quantitative frontal and temporal structural MRI studies in personality-disordered offenders and control subjects. *Psychiatry Research: Neuroimaging, 116*(3), 133–149.

Fazel, S., & Danesh, J. (2002). Serious mental disorder in 23000 prisoners: a systematic review of 62 surveys. *Lancet, 359*(9306), 545–550.

Flor, H., Birbaumer, N., Hermann, C., Ziegler, S., & Patrick, C. J. (2002). Aversive Pavlovian conditioning in psychopaths: peripheral and central correlates. *Psychophysiology, 39*(4), 505–518.

Fowles, D. C. (1980). The three arousal model: implications of Gray's two-factor learning theory for heart rate, electrodermal activity, and psychopathy. *Psychophysiology, 17*(2), 87–104.

Gamer, M., & Büchel, C. (2009). Amygdala activation predicts gaze toward fearful eyes. *The Journal of Neuroscience, 29*(28), 9123–9126.

Gibbon, S., Duggan, C., Stoffers, J., Huband, N., Vollm, B. A., Ferriter, M., & Lieb, K. (2010). Psychological interventions for antisocial personality disorder. *Cochrane Database of Systematic Reviews, 16*(6), 1–118.

Glenn, A. L., Raine, A., Schug, R. A., Gao, Y., & Granger, D. A. (2011). Increased testosterone-to-cortisol ratio in psychopathy. *Journal of Abnormal Psychology, 120*, 389–399.

Hare, R. D. (1991). *The Hare Psychopathy Checklist – revised*. Toronto, Ontario: Multi-Health Systems.

Hiatt, K. D., Schmitt, W. A., & Newman, J. P. (2004). Stroop tasks reveal abnormal selective attention among psychopathic offenders. *Neuropsychology, 18*(1), 50.

Holi, M., Auvinen-Lintunen, L., Lindberg, N., Tani, P., & Virkkunen, M. (2006). Inverse correlation between severity of psychopathic traits and serum cortisol levels in young adult violent male offenders. *Psychopathology, 39*, 102–104.

Kiehl, K. A. (2006). A cognitive neuroscience perspective on psychopathy: evidence for paralimbic system dysfunction. *Psychiatry Research, 142*(2), 107–128.

Killcross, S., Robbins, T. W., & Everitt, B. J. (1997). Different types of fear-conditioned behaviour mediated by separate nuclei within amygdala. *Nature, 388*(6640), 377–380.

Kringelbach, M. L. (2005). The human orbitofrontal cortex: linking reward to hedonic experience. *Nature Reviews Neuroscience, 6*(9), 691–702.

Kruesi, M. J., Casanova, M. F., Mannheim, G., & Johnson-Bilder, A. (2004). Reduced temporal lobe volume in early onset conduct disorder. *Psychiatry Research: Neuroimaging, 132*(1), 1–11.

Kudielka, B. M., & Kirschbaum, C. (2005). Sex differences in HPA axis responses to stress: a review. *Biological Psychiatry, 69*, 113–132.

Laakso, M. P., Vaurio, O., Koivisto, E., Savolainen, L., Eronen, M., Aronen, H. J., & Tiihonen, J. (2001). Psychopathy and the posterior hippocampus. *Behavioural Brain Research, 118*(2), 187–193.

Leistico, A. R., Salekin, R. T., DeCoster, J., & Rogers, R. (2008). A large-scale meta-analysis relating the Hare measures of psychopathy to antisocial conduct. *Law And Human Behaviour, 32*, 28–45.

Levy, B. J., & Wagner, A. D. (2011). Cognitive control and right ventrolateral prefrontal cortex: reflexive reorienting, motor inhibition, and action updating. *Annals of the New York Academy of Sciences, 1224*(1), 40–62.

Loney B. R., Butler, M. A., Lima, E. N., Counts, C. A., & Eckel, L. A. (2006). The relation between salivary cortisol, callous-unemotional traits, and conduct problems

240 *Alexandria K. Johnson and Andrea L. Glenn*

in an adolescent non-referred sample. *The Journal of Child Psychology and Psychiatry*, *47*, 30–36.

Lykken, D. T. (1995). *The antisocial personalities*. Hillsdale, NJ: Lawrence Erlbaum.

Maras, A., Laucht, M., Gerdes, D., Wilhelm, C., Lewicka, S., Haack, D., Malisova, L., & Schmidt, M. H. (2003). Association of testosterone and dihydrotestosterone with externalizing behaviour in adolescent boys and girls. *Psychoneuroendocrinology*, *28*(7), 932–940.

Maren, S., & Quirk, G. J. (2004). Neuronal signalling of fear memory. *Nature Reviews Neuroscience*, *5*(11), 844–852.

Moul, C., Killcross, S., & Dadds, M. R. (2012). A model of differential amygdala activation in psychopathy. *Psychological Review*, *119*(4), 789.

Neumann, C., & Hare, R. (2008). Psychopathic traits in a large community sample: links to violence, alcohol use, and intelligence. *Journal Of Consulting And Clinical Psychology*, *76*, 893–899.

Newman, J. P., Curtin, J. J., Bertsch, J. D., & Baskin-Sommers, A. R. (2010). Attention moderates the fearlessness of psychopathic offenders. *Biological Psychiatry*, *67*, 66–70.

Öngür, D., Ferry, A. T., & Price, J. L. (2003). Architectonic subdivision of the human orbital and medial prefrontal cortex. *Journal of Comparative Neurology*, *460*(3), 425–449.

Öngür, D., & Price, J. L. (2000). The organization of networks within the orbital and medial prefrontal cortex of rats, monkeys and humans. *Cerebral Cortex*, *10*(3), 206–219.

Oosterlaan, J., Geurts, H. M., Dirk, K., & Sergeant, J. A. (2005). Low basal salivary cortisol is associated with teacher-reported symptoms of conduct disorder. *Psychiatry Research*, *134*, 1–10.

Pajer, K., Gardner, W., Rubin, R. T., Perel, J., & Neal, S. (2001). Decreased cortisol levels in adolescent girls with conduct disorder. *Archives of General Psychiatry*, *58*, 297–302.

Patrick, C. J. (1994). Emotion and psychopathy: startling new insights. *Psychophysiology*, *31*(4), 319–330.

Perry, R. J., Rosen, H. R., Kramer, J. H., Beer, J. S., Levenson, R. L., & Miller, B. L. (2001). Hemispheric dominance for emotions, empathy and social behaviour: evidence from right and left handers with frontotemporal dementia. *Neurocase*, *7*(2), 145–160.

Petrides, M., & Pandya, D. N. (1999). Dorsolateral prefrontal cortex: comparative cytoarchitectonic analysis in the human and the macaque brain and corticocortical connection patterns. *European Journal of Neuroscience*, *11*(3), 1011–1036.

Petrides, M., & Pandya, D. N. (2001). Comparative cytoarchitectonic analysis of the human and the macaque ventrolateral prefrontal cortex and corticocortical connection patterns in the monkey. *European Journal of Neuroscience*, *16*(2), 291–310.

Quinsey, V. L., Rice, M. E., & Harris, G. T. (1995). Actuarial prediction of sexual recidivism. *Journal of Interpersonal Violence*, *10*, 85–105.

Raine, A. (2002). Biosocial studies of antisocial and violent behaviour in children and adults: a review. *Journal of Abnormal Child Psychology*, *30*(4), 311–326.

Raine, A., Ishikawa, S. S., Arce, E., Lencz, T., Knuth, K. H., Bihrle, S., & Colletti, P. (2004). Hippocampal structural asymmetry in unsuccessful psychopaths. *Biological Psychiatry*, *55*(2), 185–191.

Raine, A., Lencz, T., Bihrle, S., LaCasse, L., & Colletti, P. (2000). Reduced prefrontal gray matter volume and reduced autonomic activity in antisocial personality disorder. *Archives of General Psychiatry*, *57*(2), 119–127.

Raine, A., Lencz, T., Taylor, K., Hellige, J. B., Bihrle, S., Lacasse, L., & Colletti, P. (2003). Corpus callosum abnormalities in psychopathic antisocial individuals. *Archives of General Psychiatry, 60*(11), 1134–1142.

Raine, A., Park, S., Lencz, T., Bihrle, S., LaCasse, L., Widom, C. S., & Singh, M. (2001). Reduced right hemisphere activation in severely abused violent offenders during a working memory task: an fMRI study. *Aggressive Behaviour, 27*(2), 111–129.

Raine, A., Yang, Y., Narr, K. L., & Toga, A. W. (2009). Sex differences in orbitofrontal gray as a partial explanation for sex differences in antisocial personality. *Molecular psychiatry, 16*(2), 227–236.

Sah, P., Faber, E. S. L., De Armentia, M. L., & Power, J. (2003). The amygdaloid complex: anatomy and physiology. *Physiological Reviews, 83*(3), 803–834.

Scarpa, A., Tanaka, A., & Haden, S. C. (2008). Biosocial bases of reactive and proactive aggression: the roles of community violence exposure and heart rate. *Journal of Community Psychology, 36,* 969–988.

Schutter, D. J., & Harmon-Jones, E. (2013). The corpus callosum: a commissural road to anger and aggression. *Neuroscience & Biobehavioural Reviews, 37*(10), 2481–2488.

Spidel, A., Vincent, G., Huss, M. T., Winters, J., Thomas, L., & Dutton, D. (2007). The psychopathic batterer: subtyping perpetrators of domestic violence. In H. Hervé & J. C. Yuille (Eds.), *The psychopath: Theory, research, and practice* (pp. 327–342). Mahwah, NJ: Lawrence Erlbaum.

Sterzer, P., Stadler, C., Krebs, A., Kleinschmidt, A., & Poustka, F. (2005). Abnormal neural responses to emotional visual stimuli in adolescents with conduct disorder. *Biological psychiatry, 57*(1), 7–15.

Sutton, S. K., & Davidson, R. J. (1997). Prefrontal brain asymmetry: a biological substrate of the behavioural approach and inhibition systems. *Psychological Science, 8*(3), 204–210.

Swogger, M., Walsh, Z., & Kosson, D. (2007). Domestic violence and psychopathic traits: distinguishing the antisocial batterer from other antisocial offenders. *Aggressive Behaviour, 33,* 253–260.

van Goozen, S. H. M., Matthys, W., Cohen-Kettenis, P. T., Thijssen, J. H. H., & van Engeland, H. (1998). Adrenal androgens and aggression in conduct disorder prepubertal boys and normal controls. *Biological Psychiatry, 43,* 156–158.

van Honk, J., & Schutter, D. J. L. G. (2006). Unmasking feigned sanity: a neurobiological model of emotion processing in primary psychopathy. *Cognitive Neuropsychiatry, 11*(3), 285–306.

Virkkunen, M. (1985). Urinary free cortisol secretion in habitually violent offenders. *Acta Psychiatrica Scandinavica, 72,* 40–44.

Wallis, J. D. (2007). Orbitofrontal cortex and its contribution to decision-making. *Annual Review of Neuroscience, 30,* 31–56.

Woodworth, M., & Porter, S. (2002). In cold blood: characteristics of criminal homicides as a function of psychopathy. *Journal of Abnormal Psychology, 111*(3), 436.

Yang, Y., & Raine, A. (2009). Prefrontal structural and functional brain imaging findings in antisocial, violent, and psychopathic individuals: a meta-analysis. *Psychiatry Research: Neuroimaging, 174*(2), 81–88.

Yang, Y., Raine, A., Lencz, T., Bihrle, S., LaCasse, L., & Colletti, P. (2005). Volume reduction in prefrontal gray matter in unsuccessful criminal psychopaths. *Biological Psychiatry, 57*(10), 1103–1108.

12 Safe community reintegration of sex-offenders through Circles of Support and Accountability

Mechtild Höing and Bas Vogelvang

Introduction

It all started in 1994. A sex-offender named Charlie, 41-years-old, was about to return to Hamilton, Ontario, his Canadian home town. Charlie had served a seven-year prison sentence for sexual abuse of a young boy. Before his release, the prison psychologist contacted local reverend Harry Nigh to discuss possibilities of organising social support for Charlie. Harry suggested creating a 'circle of support' for Charlie in Hamilton and recruited members from his Mennonite congregation and community to be part of a small circle 'so that Charlie would have somebody in the community when he landed, like a surrogate family. We informally called our group "Charlie's Angels"' (Höing et al., 2011, p. 6). The group of volunteers supported Charlie with his reintegration, but also held him accountable for his actions and opinions. Charlie was supported by this group for 12 years. He then died, without having re-offended.

Several months after the Circle in Hamilton took off, a second Circle started in Toronto for a released sex-offender named Wray. Around that time, police and probation services became interested in this new approach. They became increasingly involved in assisting the Circles initiative. The Canadian Correctional Services Chaplaincy incorporated Circles of Support and Accountability (COSA) into their Community Chaplaincy projects and started to provide basic materials like project guidelines and training manuals through a website. Today, there are COSA sites in all Canadian provinces.

Almost 20 years after the first Canadian Circle, the COSA initiative has spread to the United States, the United Kingdom, the Netherlands and Belgium. More European countries, such as Spain, Bulgaria, Latvia and Ireland, have introduced Circles. In short, a faith-based, grassroots initiative came a long way. It has inspired hundreds of citizens to become involved, it has prevented many new victims, it has supported many offenders in building a crime-free life, it has inspired societal discussion about reintegration following serious crime and – as we will discuss in the last section of this chapter – it has also challenged the traditional forensic psychology treatment paradigm in many ways.

Safe community reintegration of sex offenders 243

The Circle model

COSA is aimed at preventing recidivism by addressing some of the key risk factors for re-offending: social isolation and emotional loneliness. A Circle provides a medium- to high-risk sex-offender with a group of three to six trained volunteers, preferably from the local community, who meet with the sex-offender ('core member' in a Circle) weekly. Volunteers support the core member by modelling pro-social behaviour, offering moral support and assisting with practical needs. They hold the core member accountable by challenging pro-offending attitudes, beliefs and behaviour. The volunteers are assisted by an outer Circle of professionals. Volunteers report their concerns to the professionals who – when necessary – can take appropriate measures to prevent the core member from re-offending. Volunteers do so not directly, but report to a Circle coordinator whose task is to share information between inner and outer Circles and support and supervise the Circle process.

The inner Circle

The inner Circle should reflect the diversity in society and constitute both male and female members from different ages and backgrounds. Although a Circle should offer core members the opportunity to learn from different perspectives, all Circle volunteers should share some key qualities. Competent Circle volunteers are able to express empathy and their belief in restorative justice. They have good communication skills, and are good problem-solvers and team-workers. They have a balanced lifestyle and can handle the emotions of self and others. They can set and maintain clear boundaries, and act in a respectful and constructive manner. They also should be able to accept supervision and support from the Circle coordinator. Circle volunteers are compensated for all costs they incur in their function. Some basic safety rules are set up to prevent any unnecessary risk.

The outer Circle

The outer Circle is formed of the professionals who are involved in the core member's process of re-entering society. Usually the following organisations and professionals are involved: sex-offender treatment provider, probation organisation (probation officer) and local police officer, preferably with special assignment to the neighbourhood where the core member lives and responsibility for public protection and sex-offender registration. Members of the outer Circle have their own professional responsibility and involvement with the core member and operate within the rules and regulations of their organisation and profession. It is good practice that the inner and outer Circle get to know each other and are able to exchange views and expectations and set clear boundaries between their distinct roles.

244　*Mechtild Höing and Bas Vogelvang*

The role of the outer Circle is primarily to support the core member in their functioning within the Circle (as part of their own professional involvement with the core member) and to give advice to volunteers (through the Circle coordinator) on specific topics. They monitor the Circle process through monthly updates from the Circle coordinator. In case of immediate risk, the professionals are informed directly through the Circle coordinator to be able to take whatever steps are necessary to prevent relapse, for example informing justice authorities.

The Circle coordinator

Each Circle is supported and supervised by a Circle coordinator, who is a professional with specific expertise in coaching and supervision as well as expertise in sex-offender management. In the Netherlands, Circle coordinators are professionals from the probation organisation, but in other countries other organisations may be able to deliver the necessary expertise.

The role of the Circle coordinator is crucial in the whole Circle process and his or her major concern is the development of a positive group dynamic. They are involved in the recruiting, selection, training and supervision of volunteers and deals with all practical issues that need to be solved before a Circle can get started. After attending the first three preparatory meetings (without core member) and the first Circle meeting with the core member, they step back and are informed about the ongoing Circle through Circle minutes from the volunteers and contact minutes. The Circle coordinator contacts the volunteer(s) whenever the minutes give them reason to.

Whenever necessary, the Circle coordinator may suggest interventions to the volunteers and/or attend Circle meetings, or intervene to support group development. Volunteers are also individually supported and supervised by the Circle coordinator.

On a quarterly basis, the Circle coordinator assists the volunteers in the evaluation of the core member's dynamic risks and strengths with the Dynamic Risk Review (Bates & Wager, 2012), a standardised evaluation instrument. Apart from that, the regional project offers a 24/7 back-up by telephone to the inner Circle – in case of any emergency that might occur.

Exchange of information

The exchange of information within the inner Circle, between inner and outer Circle and between members of the outer Circle, is – apart from the personal engagement of the volunteers – one of the strengths of the Circles model, based on the key motto 'no more secrets'. From the very first Circle meeting on, the core member is invited to talk freely about what will help avoid re-offending and the risk factors they experience in daily life. Volunteers and core members sign a Circle agreement in which rules about honesty, openness, privacy policies and exchange of information with each other and with other institutions are set.

Safe community reintegration of sex offenders 245

For adequate functioning of Circles, it is fundamental that no information from both the inner and outer Circle is shared with the outside world. Within Circles there are no secrets, but for the outside world, what is discussed in Circles is secret. However, to ensure public safety and to reassure citizens and former victims, it is possible that Circles can decide to inform others about the existence of a Circle around a core member, without giving any details.

Support

Each Circle project is embedded in a local network of organisations who are involved in sex-offender rehabilitation and risk management. Since the reintegration of sex-offenders into society is often also an issue of public safety and managing public opinion, it is also important to establish good relationships with the local administration and local newspapers.

On a national level, the success and financial sustainability of Circles is dependent on government policies, justice authorities' decisions, non-governmental sources of income such as charitable trusts and, not least, public opinion. It is helpful to establish and maintain supportive relationships with influential persons within national boards and for instance the justice department, with journalists from national media and to keep them well informed.

Sex-offenders

Subtypes

Sex-offender typologies have been made along different lines, e.g. victim preference (child molester vs. rapist), motivation for the offence (sexual or non-sexual), degree and function of aggression used, psychological needs, age of victims (pre-pubescent, adolescent or peers) and modus operandi, e.g. hands-on, hands-off (Robertiello & Terry; 2007). Ward and Hudson (1998) have categorised sex-offenders by their pathways to sexual offending in the 'self regulation model of sexual offending'. This model describes both the individual's goals with respect to motives of offending behaviour (approach versus avoidance goals), and the manner in which the individual attempts to achieve these goals (passive versus active regulation), resulting in four pathways that lead to sexual offending. The model has been proven valid and enables differentiation between offender types. Rapists and child molesters with male victims are more represented in the approach pathways, while others show more variability in their offence pathway (Yates & Kingston, 2006). Bogaerts, Vanheule, and Desmet (2006) categorised a subgroup of sex-offenders – child molesters – by adult attachment style (secure versus insecure), and concluded that child molesters with an insecure adult attachment style suffer from more personality disorders than child molesters with a secure attachment style, with a very strong connection between schizoid personality disorder and insecure adult attachment style. The daily life symptoms of both schizoid personality disorder and insecure adult attachment style are similar in many respects and are typical risk factors for sexual offending: intimacy deficits, loneliness and impaired interpersonal functioning (Hanson & Morton-Bourgon, 2005). See Chapter 6 for the importance of attachment styles in relation to the development of conscience.

Recidivism

Recidivism rates have been shown to be different for sex-offender subtypes and continuously rise with longer periods of follow-up (see Table 12.1). Recidivism studies show that sexual recidivism is generally low in the first five years of follow-up (10–15%, Hanson & Bussiere, 1998; Hanson & Morton-Bourgon, 2004), but recidivism rates climb up to 23% after a follow-up period of 25 years (Dahle, Janka, Gallasch-Nemitz, & Lehmann, 2009; Nieuwbeerta, Blokland, & Bijleveld, 2003) and are even higher among sex-offenders with psychiatric disorders (De Ruiter & de Vogel, 2004). It may be concluded that some sex-offenders face a considerable risk of re-offending during long periods of their life, and need long-term support and monitoring.

Table 12.1 Recidivism studies

Study	Follow-up (years)	Population	N	Recidivism %
Schönberger, De Kogel, & Bregman, 2012	3	Sex offenders who have been in court-ordered psychiatric care (TBS)	253	5.2
Hanson & Bussiere, 1998	4–5	All sex offenders	23393	13.4
		Rapists	1839	18.9
		Child molesters	9603	12.7
Hanson & Morton-Bourgon, 2004	5–6	All sex offenders	20440	13.7
Dahle et al., 2009	8	All sex offenders	2446	23
De Ruiter & de Vogel, 2004	12	Sex offenders who have been in court-ordered psychiatric care (TBS)	121	39
		Rapists	94	33
		Child molesters	27	59
Nieuwbeerta et al., 2003	25	All sex offenders	488	29
		Rapists	242	24
		Child molesters	143	28

Safe community reintegration of sex offenders 247

These are typically sex-offenders that might benefit from a Circle. In COSA projects, structured risk assessment is used to identify the level of risk of potential core members.

Risk assessment

In the past decades, much effort has been put into the development of valid tools to assess sex-offenders' risk of re-offending. Many official decisions (e.g. decisions about conditional release, level of treatment intensity, duration of supervision) are based on such risk assessments. Risk assessment procedures are categorised into assessment of static, dynamic and acute-dynamic risk factors (Ward & Beech, 2004). Static factors are biographical and historical data like number of previous sex offences (more means higher risk) and type of victim (extra-familial victim and male victim means higher risk). Dynamic risk factors are personality characteristics of the core member that can be worked on, but only change slowly, like personality disorders or cognitive distortions. Acute-dynamic risk factors are characteristics of the offender or of their environment that can change quickly, like low self-regulation through consumption of alcohol or drugs, and access to possible victims (Ward & Beech, 2004). Based on five meta-studies, Mann, Hanson, and Thornton (2010) identified the following risk factors: sexual preoccupation, deviant sexual arousal, offence-supportive cognitions, emotional identification with children, lack of intimate relations with adults, an impulsive lifestyle, lack of self-regulation, lack of problem-solving skills, low adherence to rules and regulations, hostility (especially towards women), negative social influences, callousness and abuse of power and dysfunctional coping styles (e.g. using sex as coping). According to Mann et al. (2010), the potential risk of recidivism may be calculated from the existence of these risk factors, but they do not necessarily explain actual recidivism or inform the development of preventive interventions. The meaning and potential impact these risk factors have on the daily life of the offender must be taken into account. They must be seen as personal 'dispositions' that that can or cannot become apparent in ways of acting and thinking, in the self-presentation and in the interaction of the sex-offender with others and with their environment. This implies close monitoring of the sex-offender in their own environment, and interventions that are tailored to their specific situation and needs.

Selection of core members in COSA

The criteria and procedures for the selection of core members are described in several project manuals, e.g. Caspers and Vogelvang (2012). Circles are intended for medium to high-risk sex-offenders who have served their sentence and want to re-integrate into society. While gender or type of sexual offence is no criterion for selection, some offender characteristics speak against participating in a Circle. Potential core members who seek to join a Circle only to increase their chances of a positive judgement by the court and otherwise show

248 *Mechtild Höing and Bas Vogelvang*

no motivation to adopt a non-criminal life style are not eligible, since it will be difficult for them to cooperate with volunteers on common targets. Neither are sex-offenders who have a low risk of re-offending eligible, since Circles are an intensive and costly measure, and means should be allocated to where the risk of re-offending is highest and where other options are not available or not thought suitable. Also, volunteers must be able to do their work safely, therefore core members with significantly aggressive or antisocial behaviour problems are not eligible. Specific psychiatric problems (e.g. ADHD, autism) must be addressed by very careful selection and sometimes additional training of volunteers. Psychiatric problems which obstruct the cooperation in a Circle (like psychosis, severe addiction to drugs or alcohol) must be taken care of first.

Potential core members must show a substantial need for social support, for example because they are isolating themselves, or there is simply no-one left in their own social network, or because the re-settlement after detention has evoked harsh community reactions. Core members must be willing to share information about their offence and their specific risk and risk factors with the volunteers, and must agree to the exchange of risk-related information between inner and outer Circle. They agree on two main principles: 'no more victims' and 'no secrets'.

As a result of risk factors for re-offending and the selection criteria of COSA, the 'typical' core member in a COSA Circle is a middle-aged repeat offender, a medium to high-risk child abuser with little or no other social support, who is socially isolated, lacks intimate adult relationships and shows marked deficits in social skills and skills to cope with daily problems (Wilson, Picheca, & Prinzo, 2007a; Bates, Macrae, Williams, & Webb, 2012).

The COSA intervention model

COSA has been developed as a practice-based intervention, initially based on Christian values of inclusion and redemption. In recent years, the model has been acknowledged by experts as one of the most promising approaches to safe sex-offender reintegration (e.g. De Kogel & Nagtegaal, 2008). A scientific underpinning of the workings of COSA has resulted in a COSA intervention model (Saunders & Wilson, 2003; Wilson, Bates, & Völlm, 2010; Höing, Bogaerts, & Vogelvang, 2013). This intervention model (Fig. 12.1) illustrates how COSA aims to prevent recidivism by supporting the core members' process of becoming a full desister. Desistance is a concept that refers to a situation where the offender not only stops offending, but also participates in society as a responsible member and consolidates their new social role by developing a positive narrative identity (Maruna, 2001). These main targets of desistance are achieved by working towards intermediate targets: the improvement of the sex-offender's human and social capital.

Human, social and psychological capital targets

Human capital targets are aiming at reducing some of the core dynamic risk factors: self-regulation skills, problem-solving and coping skills, social skills

Safe community reintegration of sex offenders 249

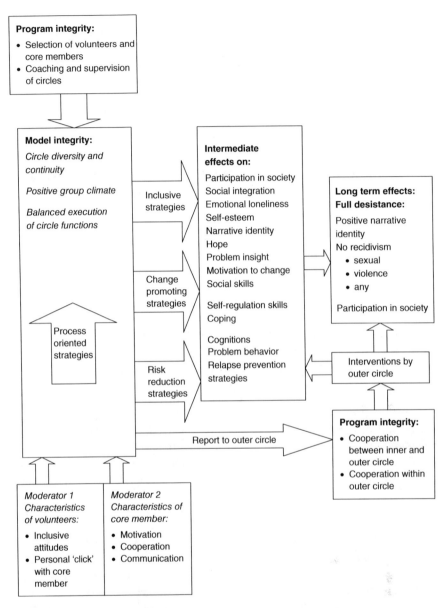

Figure 12.1 The Circles of Support and Accountability intervention model

and lack of problem awareness. COSA also aims to reduce intimacy deficits and develop adequate and appropriate intimate relationships, and on changing offence-supportive cognitions and cognitive distortions. These are addressed in COSA in a non-professional way, especially cognitive distortions like blaming the victim and minimising the offence.

250   *Mechtild Höing and Bas Vogelvang*

The improvement of the core member's social capital is probably the most prominent target of Circles, as COSA provides a surrogate social network and supports the core member in developing a stronger or new personal pro-social network.

Increased hope for a better future, increased self-esteem and a sustained motivation to change are intermediate targets that support the process of change. In the positive psychology literature these characteristics are referred to as 'psychological capital' (Luthans, Avolio, Avey, & Norman, 2007).

Effective strategies and Circle characteristics

Effective Circles are characterised by a balanced execution of four strategies: inclusive strategies, change-promoting strategies, risk reduction strategies and process-oriented strategies (Höing et al., 2013).

The inclusive function of a Circle is accomplished by several activities and strategies. The most frequent inclusive Circle activity is the regular meeting and group discussion – a COSA Circle is mainly a 'talking circle'. Being part of a social community (again) for the core member means something to live up to and fosters the need to adopt norms and attitudes of this group of members of the public, who offer their time, personal commitment and presence. Inclusion is also expressed by providing moral and practical support within the core member's own context. Engaging in social activities together serves their social needs, provided they are conducted with respect for the privacy and the interests of the core member. Social activities give a boost to the growth of their 'normal' identity and self-esteem and help them improve their social skills. Change-promoting activities are mainly targeted at improving the social and problem-solving skills of the core member by giving practical advice and tips and tricks to solve daily problems and by encouraging new behaviour, like taking up hobbies, health activities or volunteer work and positive appraisal of new behaviour. More directive strategies are also used, e.g. confronting the core member with the consequences of their actions, requesting specific behaviour like doing homework, confronting the core member with an observed lack of effort and holding them accountable for their own process of change.

Risk-reducing strategies undertaken by the Circle include discussing the relapse prevention plan, monitoring the core member's behaviour, confronting the core member with risk-related information and reporting risk concerns to the professionals. Monitoring is typically targeted at problem-solving behaviour and risk-related behaviour. Process-oriented strategies indirectly contribute to Circle effectiveness by supporting the development of a positive group dynamic and a balanced execution of the three former mentioned Circle functions. The continuous reflection and evaluation processes that Circle volunteers and Circle coordinators (but less so the core member) are engaged in leads to interventions that change the balance in the regular Circle functions, like putting more stress on the core member's own responsibility, or loosening the monitoring 'grip' and offering more social activities.

A positive group dynamic and an atmosphere of mutual trust and openness are crucial for the balanced execution of effective Circle functions (Höing et al., 2013). This is achieved by a combination of careful assessment and of volunteers and core members, and a successful transition through the different stages of group development. The Circle coordinator supervises this process and intervenes if necessary. Nevertheless, some Circles adopt dysfunctional activities or develop a negative group dynamic, sometimes causing the premature closure of a Circle or replacement of volunteers.

Circles research

Since COSA is a relatively new and small-scale approach, research into its effectiveness is still scarce. Nevertheless, results so far are promising. In a Canadian study, Wilson et al. (2007b) reported a significant reduction of recidivism rates of 60 sex-offenders who had been in a Circle compared to 60 matched controls who had not (medium follow-up: 55 months for COSA group and 53 months for controls). While 16.7% of controls sexually re-offended, only 5% of the COSA group did – a reduction of 70%. Also, general re-offence rates were lower (28.3% in the COSA group vs. 43.3% in the control group). In 2009, Wilson, Cortoni, and McWhinnie conducted a national replication study, including 44 sex-offenders in Circle projects throughout the country, matched pairwise with 44 controls. Time at risk was 35 months for the COSA group vs. 38 months for the controls. Groups were comparable on all matching criteria except Static 99 scores, with the controls having a higher level of risk. The COSA group showed 83% less sexual re-offending and 71% less general re-offending than controls. In a sub-sample of 19 COSA members and 18 controls, with equal Static 99 scores and time at risk (36 months), none of the COSA group re-offended sexually, while five controls did. General re-offence rates of the COSA members were reduced by 83% (Wilson et al., 2009). Violent recidivism was reduced by 73% and general recidivism by 71%.

In the United States, Duwe (2013) conducted a randomised controlled trial with 62 sex-offenders (31 in test group, 31 in control group). After three years, 65% of the control group offenders had been rearrested for a new offence compared with 39% of the COSA participants. Research into recidivism rates of 60 core members in the UK (Bates et al., 2012) showed that after a mean follow-up period of 36 months, only one core member had recidivated (1.6%) and two (3.6%) had been taken back into custody due to violation of parole rules. In a matched control study, Bates, Williams, Wilson, and Wilson (2013) compared 71 core members to 71 matched controls (follow-up 55 months). While 4.2% of the core members sexually re-offended (non-contact offences), 16.9% of the controls did, mostly with contact offences (14.1% of controls).

Concluding remarks

Circles of Support and Accountability are both a pragmatic and ethical approach to the problem of sex-offenders re-entering society. Circles combine

252 *Mechtild Höing and Bas Vogelvang*

an inclusive strategy with respect for the victims' and society's needs for safety with respect for the basic human needs of the sex-offender and their need for rehabilitation.

In the past 20 years, the Circles approach has challenged the forensic psychology treatment paradigm in several ways. In the first place, Circles seem to stretch the definition of what can be called 'treatment'. Circles were never designed or intended to be a form of forensic treatment, but their effects are quite similar to forensic psychology treatment effects. On the other hand, categorising Circles effects as 'natural change' also misses the point, because Circles do intend to influence the core member in many ways and in a strategic fashion. Their effects can therefore not be categorised under 'spontaneous' recovery. In our view, the crucial point here is that, in Circles, volunteers, the core member and forensic treatment specialists decide to *depend upon each other* within a formal context to reach a set of common goals. In this way, Circles blur the border between professional 'treatment' and non-professional, selfless citizen 'investment'.

The second way in which Circles challenge the traditional forensic treatment paradigm is the ethical foundation of the model. For volunteers, joining Circles is a moral obligation (with many facets, ranging from preventing new victims to leaving no-one behind, not even sex-offenders). The question of 'scientific proof' or the 'evidence-based quality' of Circles is not the primary motivation for volunteers to join. They might even find this aspect hardly interesting or even irrelevant (and probably also the core member). Circle volunteers thus replace the value of mutual research-informed acting – a Hippocratic oath for forensic psychologists – with adopted moral values that inspire their selfless investment. For some forensic psychologists, this may be hard to swallow, but others will welcome it. In Circles, empiricists and believers join forces.

On the other hand, it is important to emphasise that the Circles model supports the mainstream forensic treatment paradigm in many ways as well. The risk principle in the 'what works' paradigm states that the intensity of an intervention must parallel the risk of re-offending, and the needs principle states that interventions (only) need to target problem areas that will maintain or increase the sex-offender's risk level. The selection criteria and volunteer actions in Circles mirror these principles, for instance by the focus volunteers place on cognitive and emotional self-regulation and social inclusion. This is also the case for the responsivity principle, emphasising both interventions that match the motivation and personal values and interests of the offender, and a flexible, tailored approach.

Finally, Circles promote desistance from crime. The desistance paradigm is still less well known in forensic psychology. As discussed earlier in this chapter, life-changing events and unselfish volunteer care can provide elements for a new script or 'narrative identity' of the sex-offender that will pull them towards a crime-free life; desistance. Sexual preferences and feelings of guilt and remorse cannot be erased by Circles, but a life worth living can be achieved by focusing on new values, such as friends, work and (not always) family, and their meaning in everyday life. Circles thus challenge forensic psychology to think

Safe community reintegration of sex offenders   253

further than managing risks and changing individual behaviour patterns. They invite the field of forensic psychology to extend this narrowly defined role and consider joining forces with inspired citizens to create lives worth living as the best remedy against creating new victims.

Literature

Bates, A., Macrae, R., Williams, D., & Webb, C. (2012). Ever-increasing circles: A descriptive study of Hampshire and Thames Valley Circles of Support and Accountability 2002–09. *Journal of Sexual Aggression, 18*(3), 355–373.

Bates, A., Williams, D., Wilson, C., & Wilson, R. (2013). Circles South East: The first 10 years 2002–2012. *International Journal of Offender Therapy and Comparative Criminology, online first: April 24, 2013.* DOI: 10.1177/0306624X13485362

Bates, A., & Wager, N. (2012) Assessing dynamic risk in the community: The DRR and Circles of Support and Accountability. *Forensic Update, (108)*, British Psychological Society.

Bogaerts, S., Vanheule, S., & Desmet, M. (2006). Personality disorders and romantic adult attachment: A comparison of secure and insecure attached child molesters. *International Journal of Offender Therapy and Comparative Criminology, 50*(2), 139–147.

Caspers, J., & Vogelvang, B. (2012). *Circles-NL. Basidocument implementatie. [Circles-NL. Implementation protocol]*. Hertogenbosch: Avans University of Applied Sciences, Expertisecentrum Veiligheid/Circles-NL.

Dahle, K., Janka, C., Gallasch-Nemitz, F., & Lehmann, R. (2009). Tatcharakteristika, Rückfallrisiko und Rückfallprognose bei Sexualstraftätern vom Jugend-bis ins Seniourenalter. [Offence characteristics, risk of reoffending and relapse propensity in sex offenders from youth to old age.] *Forensische Psychiatrie, Psychologie, Kriminologie, 3*(3), 210–220.

De Kogel, C. H., & Nagtegaal, M. H. (2008). *Toezichtprogramma's voor delinquenten en forensisch psychiatrische patiënten [Supervision programs for delinquents and forensic mental health clients]*. Den Haag: WODC.

De Ruiter, C., & de Vogel, V. (2004). Recidive bij behandelde zedendelinquenten. [Recidivism rates in treated sex offenders]. *Tijdschrift voor Seksuologie, 28*(3), 92–102.

Duwe, G. (2013). Can Circles of Support and Accountability (COSA) work in the United States? Preliminary results from a randomized experiment in Minnesota. *Sexual Abuse: A Journal of Research and Treatment, 25*(2), 143–165.

Hanson, R. K., & Bussiere, M. T. (1998). Predicting relapse: A meta-analysis of sexual offender recidivism studies. *Journal of Consulting and Clinical Psychology, 66*(2), 348.

Hanson, R. K., & Morton-Bourgon, K. (2004). *Predictors of sexual recidivism: An updated meta-analysis.* Ottawa, ON: Public Safety and Emergency Preparedness Canada.

Hanson, R. K., & Morton-Bourgon, K. E. (2005). The characteristics of persistent sexual offenders: A meta-analysis of recidivism studies. *Journal of Consulting and Clinical Psychology, 73*(6), 1154.

Höing, M. et al. (2011). *European Handbook. COSA, Circles of Support and Accountability.* Hertogenbosch: Circles Europe: Together for Safety; c/o Avans University of Applied Sciences, Centre for Public Safety and Criminal Justice.

Höing, M., Bogaerts, S., & Vogelvang (2013). Circles of support and accountability: How and why they work for sex offenders. *Journal of Forensic Psychology Practice, 13*(4), 267–295.

254 *Mechtild Höing and Bas Vogelvang*

Luthans, F., Avolio, B. J., Avey, J. B., & Norman, S. M. (2007). Positive psychological capital: Measurement and relationship with performance and satisfaction. *Personnel Psychology, 60*(3), 541–572.

Mann, R. E., Hanson, R. K., & Thornton, D. (2010). Assessing risk for sexual recidivism: Some proposals on the nature of psychologically meaningful risk factors. *Sexual Abuse: A Journal of Research and Treatment, 22*(2), 191–217.

Maruna, S. (2001). *Making good*. Washington, DC: American Psychological Association Books.

Nieuwbeerta, P., Blokland, A., & Bijleveld, C. (2003). Lange termijn recidive van daders van seksuele delicten. [Long-term recidivism of sex offenders]. *Tijdschrift voor Criminologie, 45*, 369–377

Robertiello, G., & Terry, K. J. (2007). Can we profile sex offenders? A review of sex offender typologies. *Aggression and Violent Behaviour, 12*(5), 508–518.

Saunders, R., & Wilson, C. (2003) 'The Three Key Principles' in *Circles of Support and Accountability in the Thames Valley – Interim Report*. London: Quaker Communications.

Schönberger, H. C. M., De Kogel, C. H., & Bregman, I. M. (2012). Kenmerken en recidivecijfers van ex-terbeschikkinggestelden met een zedendelict. [Characteristics and recidivism rates of sex offenders who have been in court ordered forensic psychiatric mental health care.] *Memorandum 2012-1*. The Hague: WODC.

Ward, T., & Beech, A. R. (2004). The etiology of risk: A preliminary model. *Sexual Abuse: A Journal of Research and Treatment, 16*(4), 271–284.

Ward, T., & Hudson, S. M. (1998). A model of the relapse process in sexual offenders. *Journal of Interpersonal Violence, 13*(6), 700–725.

Wilson, C., Bates, A., & Völlm, B. (2010). Circles of support and accountability: An innovative approach to manage high-risk sex offenders in the community. *Open Criminology Journal, 3*, 48–57.

Wilson, R. J., Cortoni, F., & McWhinnie, A. (2009). Circles of Support and Accountability: A Canadian national replication of outcome findings. *Sexual Abuse: A Journal of Research and Treatment, 21*, 412–430.

Wilson, R. J., Picheca, J. E., & Prinzo, M. (2007a). Evaluating the effectiveness of professionally-facilitated volunteerism in the community-based management of high-risk sexual offenders: Part One – Effects on participants and stakeholders. *The Howard Journal of Criminal Justice, 46*(3), 289–302.

Wilson, R. J., Picheca, J. E., & Prinzo, M. (2007b). Evaluating the effectiveness of professionally – facilitated volunteerism in the community-based management of high-risk sex offenders: Part Two – A comparison of recidivism rates. *The Howard Journal of Criminal Justice, 46*(4), 327–337.

Yates, P. M., & Kingston, D. A. (2006). The self-regulation model of sexual offending: The relationship between offence pathways and static and dynamic sexual offence risk. *Sexual Abuse: A Journal of Research and Treatment, 18*(3), 259–270.

13 Psychotic disorders and violence

What do we know so far?

Maarten Peters, Henk Nijman and Joost à Campo

Introduction

Paranoia going wrong

13 March 2011 started as a quite normal day for J., a 24-year-old man who was living with his parents in a rural area in the South of the Netherlands. J. was diagnosed with schizophrenia of the paranoid type. He received antipsychotic medication for this condition. However, he did not take it on a regular basis. Besides that, he was diagnosed with substance and alcohol abuse.

In the afternoon, he was chilling in his room, listening to music. At that time he lit up a cigarette. All of a sudden his mother entered the room. She argued that he was not allowed to smoke inside. The situation escalated and J. started hitting his mother on her chest and in her face. She fell to the floor. J. ran to the kitchen where he took a big kitchen knife. He returned to his room where his mother was lying unconscious. He started cutting her throat, after which she bled to death. J. got out of the house. A day later, the local police authorities arrested him. At that time, he looked confused. In his statements he claimed:

> There was somebody in my room, but not my mother. I felt threatened, as if an alien had taken over my mother. He was trying to control me. I had to do something otherwise I lost control. So I acted. It had to be stopped.

The case presented above describes the prototypical circumstances under which a person with a psychotic disorder may become severely violent. Nevertheless, it should be noted that the majority of patients suffering from a psychotic disorder would not engage in severe physical violence. This case triggers several questions: what about the link between psychotic disorders, more specifically schizophrenia, and violence? Are there specific symptoms that increase the risk of violent outbursts? Furthermore, what contrasts patients residing in a forensic psychiatric clinic or prison with patients in a regular mental health setting? In this chapter we want to answer these specific questions using the current state of scientific knowledge. But first we would like to start with defining the core features of psychotic disorders.

256 *Maarten Peters et al.*

Schizophrenia-spectrum and other psychotic disorders

There is no doubt that psychoses are among the most serious forms of psychopathology. A clear conceptual definition is the following: 'Loss of ego-boundaries or a gross impairment in reality testing' (*Diagnostic and Statistical Manual of Mental Disorders*, fourth edition text revision; DSM-IV-TR, American Psychiatric Association, 2000, p. 297). The core features of these diagnostic categories are: delusions, hallucinations, disorganised thinking (speech), grossly disorganised or abnormal motor behaviour (including catatonia) and negative symptoms (DSM-5, American Psychiatric Association, 2013).

Delusions

These can be defined as fixed false beliefs that are held with conviction and are not open to change in the light of disconfirming evidence. Central to delusions are disorders in the content of thinking. People are, for example, convinced that they are being followed or watched. On a content level, various themes can be central in delusions, like grandiosity, persecutory, referential, somatic or nihilistic and erotomanic (American Psychiatric Association, 2013). Bizarre delusions are defined as those fixed false beliefs that are clearly implausible that cannot be understood by peers from the same culture and do not derive from ordinary life experiences (DSM-5, American Psychiatric Association, 2013, p. 87). An example of this would be the belief that aliens have taken control over humans, as was the case in our example of J.

Hallucinations

These can be described as sensory experiences one can have within all senses, without the presence of a clear external stimulus and which are not under voluntary control. The most known example of hallucinations is hearing voices, referred to as auditory hallucinations. In cases in which the voices patients hear are telling the patient what to do or how to act, the term 'command hallucinations' is used.

Disorganised thinking

This is also defined as formal thought disorder. This feature can best be inferred from the speech of the patient. Most of the time there is no logical structure in the way of thinking, in that patients often switch from one topic to the other (i.e. derailment). This must be to a level that it clearly interferes with effective communication.

Grossly disorganised or abnormal motor behaviour (including catatonia)

As described in the DSM-5, this:

> may manifest itself in a variety of ways, ranging from childlike 'silliness' to unpredictable agitation. Problems may be noted in any form of goal

directed behaviour, leading to difficulties in performing activities of daily living. *Catatonic behaviour* is a marked decrease in reactivity to the environment. This ranges from resistance to instructions (*negativism*); to maintaining a rigid, inappropriate or bizarre posture; to a complete lack of verbal and motor responses (*mutism* and *stupor*).

(DSM-5, American Psychiatric Association, 2013, p. 88)

Apart from that, catatonic behaviour can also be seen as excessive movement without a clear goal and cause. It should be stated that catatonia is not schizophrenia-spectrum specific, but can also be found in other disorders like bipolar disorder or depression.

Negative symptoms

These can be defined as general a loss or lack of specific experiences and interests. This stands in contrast to positive symptoms that mostly add on specific experiences. Two negative symptoms that are frequently prominent within schizophrenia are diminished emotional expression and avolition. Avolition is expressed in a clearly diminished amount of self-initiated purposeful behaviour.

As described above, symptoms of schizophrenia-spectrum and other psychotic disorders may involve disorders of thought, perception and behaviour. One of the most frequently diagnosed and severest forms of psychosis is schizophrenia. After studying a large number of epidemiological studies performed since 1960, Eaton and colleagues (1995) arrived at a point prevalence of between 0.6 and 8.3 cases of schizophrenia per 1000 in the general population. According to Tandon, Keshavan, and Nasrallah (2008), the annual incidence of schizophrenia averages 15 per 100,000, the point prevalence averages approximately 4.5 per population of 1000, and the risk of developing the illness over one's lifetime averages 0.7%. These rates also accord with the prevalence rates of schizophrenia published in the DSM-5, ranging from 0.3%–0.7%. It should be noted that prevalence rates also vary by ethnic groups, across countries and by geographic origin for immigrants.

One of the tragedies of this disorder is that it often affects young people in the bloom of their life. Expectations about life are not fulfilled and goals have to be adjusted. Timely recognition of a developing psychosis is essential to limit the suffering and damage for the patient and his or her family. It is, however, no exception that people are psychotic for months or even years in some cases, before it is recognised. Problematic behaviour is then considered as mere obstinacy, unsociability or laziness and/or blamed on drug abuse. Our natural tendency to place behaviour of patients within the boundaries of reason feeds the reluctance to diagnose individuals as psychotic or schizophrenic. Particularly in the case of serious disruptive violent behaviour, it is very important to detect disorders in thought and perception. Schizophrenia is relatively often also undetected for a long time, as patients may be very reluctant to share or express their delusional ideas because of

258   *Maarten Peters et al.*

paranoia and fears, and psychotic patients generally lack insight at first in their symptoms and ideas may be caused by a psychiatric illness. As mentioned earlier, patients have fixed beliefs that their (delusional) thoughts and sensory experiences are correct and therefore will not readily seek psychiatric help by themselves (à Campo, 2004).

Diagnostic classification and aetiology

Classification

According to the newest version of the DSM (DSM-5, American Psychiatric Association, 2013) the following categories of psychotic disorders can be diagnosed: schizotypal (personality) disorder, brief psychotic disorder, schizophreniform disorder, schizophrenia, schizoaffective disorder, substance/medication-induced psychotic disorder, psychotic disorder due to another medical condition, catatonia, other specified schizophrenia-spectrum and other psychotic disorder, and unspecified schizophrenia-spectrum and other psychotic disorder. Elaborating on all of these disorders is beyond the scope of this chapter. The interested reader is referred to the DSM-5. What all these diagnoses have in common is that they all encompass one or more of the core features described above.

Diagnosing schizophrenia-spectrum and other psychotic disorders should be done by trained clinicians. Apart from that, the general guidelines of the DSM-5 are that:

> Clinicians should first consider conditions that do not reach full criteria for a psychotic disorder or are limited to one domain of psychopathology. Then they should consider time-limited conditions. Finally, the diagnosis of a schizophrenia-spectrum disorder requires the exclusion of another condition that may give rise to psychosis.
>
> (DSM-5, American Psychiatric Association, 2013, pp. 88–89)

To screen for possible prodromal stages, diagnose and/or determine the severity of the disorders in the schizophrenia-spectrum and other psychotic disorders, several (semi-)structured interview, rating scales and self-report questionnaires are available. Examples of screeners for prodromal stages and psychotic complaints are the Psychotic Symptom Rating Scale (PSYRATS; Haddock, McCarron, Tarrier, & Faragher, 1999; severity and different dimensions of hallucinations and delusions), the Community Assessment of Psychic Experiences (CAPE; Stefanis et al., 2002; self-report questionnaire measuring psychotic experiences within the general population) and the Comprehensive Assessment of At Risk Mental State (CAARMS; Yung et al. 2005; vulnerability to develop psychosis). Examples of structured and semi-structured interviews to diagnose schizophrenia-spectrum and psychotic disorders are the

Comprehensive Assessment of Symptoms and History (CASH; Andreasen, Flaum, & Arndt, 1992; investigating schizophrenia and affective disorders), the Schedules for Clinical Assessment in Neuropsychiatry 2.1 (SCAN 2.1; World Health Organization, 1999), the Structured Interview for DSM-IV Axis I Disorders (SCID-I; First et al., 1996) or the Composite International Diagnostic Interview (CIDI; World Health Organization, 1999). To determine the severity and course of symptomatology, the Positive and Negative Syndrome Scale (PANSS; Kay, Fiszbein, & Opler, 1987) or the Brief Psychiatric Rating Scale (BPRS; Overall & Gorham, 1962) can be used.

Currently, the new DSM-5 includes a scale in which the severity of the primary symptoms of schizophrenia-spectrum disorders and psychosis, as well as depression, mania and cognitive deficits, can be assessed on a more dimensional scale. This can be found in section III, 'Assessment measures' (see clinician-rated dimensions of psychosis symptom severity, p. 743–744 of the DSM-5).

Phases

The course of a psychotic disorder, and more specifically schizophrenia, is characterised by a specific sequence of phases. The first phase can be described as a premorbid phase in which subtle and non-specific subclinical cognitive, social and motor deficits are in the foreground (Schenkel & Silverstein, 2004). Persons within this phase start to socially withdraw in a subtle way. This is then followed by the prodromal phase characterised by subclinical positive symptoms and declining functions (Schultze-Lutter, 2009). In the acute or active phase, the first psychotic episode defines the formal onset of schizophrenia, mostly known by active positive symptoms such as auditory hallucinations, deficits in formal thinking, etc. These psychotic episodes can be cyclic: 'with partial and variable degrees and duration of inter-episode remission with accrual of disability with each episode of illness' (Tandon, Nasrallah, & Keshavan, 2009, p. 7). The last phase is the chronic or more stable phase. In this phase, often the acute mostly positive symptoms are not in the foreground, but instead negative symptoms and cognitive deficits are.

The diagnostic process is a listing of factors that contribute to the probability of the diagnosis. As described above, modern clinicians also have scales, questionnaires and additional medical technical tools at their disposal to help them gain insight into what is wrong with the patient. This, however, bears the risk of seeming evidence. Especially in people with more serious psychopathology, such as psychosis, the literal communicativeness about aberrations of thought, experience or perception is temporarily or permanently limited. The craft of listening to and looking at the patient threatens to become obsolete (Van der Ploeg, 2001).

Aetiology

How do people develop a schizophrenia-spectrum disorder? As with most psychiatric disorders, the exact aetiology is still to be unravelled and is a topic of scientific discussion. There is, however, consensus that there is a clear genetic vulnerability within schizophrenia-spectrum and other psychotic disorders (e.g. Vorstman & Kahn, 2011). A specific biological marker for this disorder, however, has not been found yet (Tandon et al., 2008). One of the strongest models in this sense is the dopamine hypothesis, which now is in its third version (Howes & Kapur, 2009), stating that the neurotransmitter dopamine and dopaminergic mechanisms are central to the development of schizophrenia-spectrum and psychosis in general in which multiple socio-cultural factors interact to result in dopamine dysregulation, leading up to psychosis-proneness in general. Indeed, there are several environmental factors known to increase the risk for developing psychotic symptoms in genetically vulnerable people. These environmental factors can include both biological and psychosocial risk factors during the perinatal period, early and late childhood, adolescence and early adulthood, like infections, etc. Furthermore, growing up in an urban environment (big cities) may be one of the risk factors in the development of psychosis in vulnerable people. A meta-analysis by Krabbendam and Van Os (2005) found a prevalence rate that was twice as high in the city compared to rural areas. Whether this relationship is causal (urbanicity leading to psychosis) or selective (the city attracting people with a genetic vulnerability) remains a topic of scientific debate. Other examples of risk factors are male gender, life events, a critical family environment (high expressed emotions), a history of migration and substance abuse (mainly cannabis use). How then can these environmental factors influence the risk of developing a psychotic disorder? It is hypothesised that sensitisation plays an important role in this cascade. If you are exposed to a negative event, you can become more vulnerable to react to similar events in the future. This can be because people will react more strongly to the same event or will react more strongly to minor events. For example, it has been found that people with a psychotic vulnerability react strongly to life events, but also to minor daily stressors, so-called daily hassles (e.g. Myin-Germeys & Van Os, 2007). Genetic factors and gene-environment interactions together should explain more than 80% of the liability for developing schizophrenia (Tandon et al., 2008).

Recent studies have also highlighted the importance of psychological mechanisms in explaining the formation and maintenance of specific symptomatology. In 2009, Beck and colleagues (2009) attempted to integrate these findings in an integrated cognitive model to explain the development and maintenance of the variety of symptoms that characterise schizophrenia. According to this model, vulnerable individuals appraise daily stressors in a negative way and perceive situations as more threatening than other people. The stress can lead to a dysregulation of the hypothalamic-pituitary-adrenal (HPA) axis in vulnerable persons, who react more strongly to stress (i.e. sensitisation). This dysregulation of the HPA axis then potentially affects the dopaminergic brain circuitry. These endocrine and biochemical brain abnormalities then interact with the already limited cognitive resources, leading to further exhaustion of cognitive capacities. Of special importance in the development and maintenance of full-blown psychosis are maladaptive beliefs about oneself, the others and the future. Examples of these beliefs could be: 'I'm vulnerable' or 'People are against me'. In general, vulnerable individuals seem to have more negative beliefs about themselves and others. These dysfunctional beliefs in turn lead to certain behaviours, such as social withdrawal, and increase the level of suspiciousness and anxiety. When these beliefs that they call schemas become stronger, new situations are more easily interpreted in a schema-congruent manner. The dysfunctional beliefs distort information processing, leading to a biased way of thinking: common biases include attending only to certain types of information (attention bias), seeking only information that confirms one's beliefs (confirmation bias) and interpreting information as being related to or directed against oneself (self-referential bias). According to this model, when the beliefs become hypersalient, the individual's ability to test reality reduces.

Cognitive deficits related to psychosis

One of the most important psychological domains in scientific research nowadays is to study how cognitive deficits relate to the development and maintenance of schizophrenia-spectrum symptomatology. Table 13.1 gives a brief overview of the deficits in the most prominent cognitive domains. An elaboration on each of these domains is beyond the scope of this chapter, but we will highlight how some of these deficits can be involved in increasing the risk of the development of psychotic symptoms.

Related to neurocognitive deficits, the consistent finding is that overall, there is a large decrease in all these six domains of neurocognitive functioning in patients suffering from schizophrenia (see, for example, Heinrichs & Zakzanis, 1998; Reichenberg & Harvey, 2007). In schizophrenia-spectrum

Table 13.1 Overview of the most important cognitive domains and deficits related to schizophrenia: spectrum

Domain	Deficits
Neurocognition	Processing speed Memory and learning Attention Working memory Executive functions (e.g. cognitive flexibility) Language comprehension
Metacognition	Illness insight Meta-memory (e.g. confidence) Reasoning bias (e.g. jumping to conclusions (JTC) bias) Source monitoring
Social cognition	Theory of mind Emotion perception Attribution style

262 *Maarten Peters et al.*

disorders, a general neurocognitive decline is seen, with a general decrease of 1 to 1.5 SD on intelligence indices (e.g. Krabbendam & Aleman, 2011). However, within these domains a substantial heterogeneity is found. Furthermore, most of these neurocognitive deficits are not schizophrenia-spectrum specific (i.e. are also found in other mental disorders). For this reason, researchers have tried to identify the schizophrenia-specific deficits.

In the search for disorder-specific deficits, several memory biases (e.g. Peters et al., 2007; Peters, Hauschildt, Moritz, S., & Jelinek, 2013) and meta-memory deficits (how schizophrenia-spectrum patients self-reflect on their own memory processes; Dunlosky & Metcalfe, 2009) have been investigated. It seems that patients suffering from schizophrenia are less confident in their true (i.e. correct) memory traces while at the same time they seem overconfident in incorrect memory traces in comparison to healthy and psychiatric controls (e.g. Moritz, Woodward, & Ruff, 2003). Furthermore, from a liberal acceptance point of view, schizophrenic patients are very liberal in accepting incomplete information as sufficient when judging this information (Moritz, Woodward, Jelinek, & Klinge, 2008).

The ability to infer mental states is known in the literature as 'mentalising' or 'theory of mind' (Bozikas et al., 2011). Theory of mind (ToM) is essential for social and behavioural adaptation, including the ability to empathise and feel guilt (Baron-Cohen, 1995). We use these mentalising abilities to explain and predict another person's behaviour. Studies in schizophrenia have confirmed that patients with schizophrenia have deficits in ToM (e.g. Pickup & Frith, 2001).

Another factor that is known to be a core characteristic of schizophrenia is the so-called jumping to conclusions (JTC) bias. This is the tendency to make extremely hasty decisions based on little evidence (Moritz & Woodward, 2005). Moritz and Woodward (2005) and Ziegler, Rief, Werner, Mehl, and Lincoln (2008) contend that this reasoning bias explains both the development and maintenance of a number of non-elaborated delusional beliefs, as it is likely to lead to a premature rejection of alternative explanations.

Cognitive flexibility falls within the range of executive functioning, which is the ability to alter a behavioural response in the face of changing contingencies (set-shifting; Bonilha et al., 2008). Impairments in cognitive flexibility in schizophrenia patients have been demonstrated (Bonilha et al., 2008).

Psychosis and violence

The annual prevalence of schizophrenia in the Netherlands is estimated at 0.5% of the Dutch population. The number of new cases (incidence) per year is 10 to 20 per 100,000 persons. Because of their potential violent behaviour, a number of psychotic patients come into contact with the criminal justice system, either the regular prison system or the forensic psychiatric care system.

Annual prevalence rates of schizophrenia-spectrum and/or related psychotic disorders among prisoners have shown that in, for example, England and Wales

Psychotic disorders and violence   263

these rates are approximately 10 times higher than in the household population (Coid & Ullrich, 2011). In a systematic review including 33,588 prisoners, about 5.5% suffered from psychotic symptoms (Fazel & Seewald, 2012). This may lead to the conclusion that schizophrenia patients more frequently end up in jail due to violent and aggressive outbursts compared to non-schizophrenia patients and thus they might be more prone to become violent or at least show aggressive behaviour. Related to the clinical context, obviously, patients with psychotic disorders are also admitted, either voluntarily or involuntarily, to the civil psychiatric care system, and a smaller percentage of these patients also has a history of aggressive and/or behaviour towards others (e.g. Raja & Azzoni, 2005; Steinert, 2002).

The study of the relationship between psychosis and violence has a long history. In one of those prototypical studies, Monahan and Appelbaum (2000) followed discharged patients from the MacArthur Risk Assessment Study for 10 years to explore whether these individuals would act violently in the future. It appeared that 9% of the patients with schizophrenia and 17.2% of the ones with other psychotic disorders were violent at some point in the first 20 weeks after they were discharged. The percentages of the discharged patients suffering from other mental disorders that became violent were as follows: 15% of those suffering from bipolar disorder, 19% of the depressed patients, 29% of the patients suffering from substance misuse disorders and 25% of the patients suffering from a personality disorder (Monahan & Appelbaum, 2000).

Recently, a number of systematic reviews and meta-analyses on the relationship between psychosis and violence have appeared (e.g. Bo, Abu-Akel, Kongerslev, Haahr, & Simonsen, 2011; Douglas, Guy, & Hart, 2009; Fazel, Gulati, Linsell, Geddes, & Grann, 2009a; Hodgins, 2008; Large & Nielssen, 2011; Witt, van Dorn, & Fazel, 2013). In conclusion, these studies have found a positive relation between psychosis and violence. However, this relationship is more complex than generally assumed. In the remainder of this chapter, we will give a brief overview of the consensus up to now regarding the different risk factors for violent and aggressive behaviour in schizophrenia-spectrum and related psychotic disorders. First, we will start with addressing the kinds of violent and aggressive behaviour schizophrenia-spectrum patients are engaged in.

Types of violent behaviour

With respect to violence, several studies provide consistent support for the fact that schizophrenia-spectrum patients who offend tend to victimise persons that are close to them (e.g. Nestor & Haycock, 1997; Nijman, Cima, & Merckelbach, 2003). Regarding the type of violence, there seems to be an association between schizophrenia and homicide (Fazel et al., 2009a). To get further insight into the nature of the crimes of psychotic patients, Nijman and colleagues (2003) investigated the psychiatric and criminal background of 111 forensic psychotic patients and compared them with 197 non-psychotic offenders residing in two forensic clinics in the Netherlands and Germany.

In comparing these two groups, these authors found that the psychotic offenders were more often first-time offenders who were convicted for severe physical assaults targeted at intimates such as first-degree relatives. Sexual assaults were rare among this group of psychotic offenders. In this study it was further reported that of the 111 offences these patients were convicted for, 33 were related to crimes with fatal consequences for someone close or least known to the psychotic offenders before the crime was committed. In this subsample of psychotic patients who committed lethal crimes, some specific characteristics were found: fewer previous arrest records, late onset of criminal activity and fewer addiction problems. This would show a more fine-grained differentiation in psychotic subsamples to investigate the link between psychosis and violence in the future.

Risk factors contributing to violence in psychosis

As described above, recent review articles and meta-analyses have reported a positive though limited association between mainly schizophrenia and violence (e.g. Douglas et al., 2009; Witt et al., 2013). For clinical and forensic practice it is of interest to know what the possible risk and future protective factors could be and the possible mechanisms mediating this relationship. In the following section, we will provide a brief overview of the most important risk factors for violence in schizophrenia-spectrum and related psychotic disorders.

Positive psychotic symptoms

Several studies conclude that mainly positive symptoms related to psychotic disorders are clearly associated with violence (e.g. Walsh, Buchanan, & Fahy, 2002; Bo et al., 2011). This is based on the hypothesis that specific symptoms (i.e. positive symptoms such as hallucinations and delusions and negative symptoms such as avolition and affective flattening) may precipitate violent acts (Hodgins, 2008). For example, McNiel, Eisner, and Binder (2000) found a positive association between command hallucinations and violence incidents (see also Junginger, 1995). A recent study by Reynolds and Scragg (2010) investigated which factors of command hallucinations are essential for patients to comply with; for example, harm-others hallucinations. They found that beliefs, such as a commanding voice that was more powerful than the self and of a higher social rank than the self, were associated with compliance.

Concerning delusions, a link has been found between persecutory delusions (Swanson et al., 2006) and violence offences in psychotic patients. Furthermore, threat/control-override (TCO; Bjørkly, 2002) symptoms are also related to violence offences in this patient group. When experiencing these TCO symptoms, the patient feels gravely threatened by someone intending to cause them harm and over which they have no self-control (Link & Stueve, 1994). The combination of TCO symptoms and substance abuse further increases the likelihood of violent behaviour (Swanson et al., 2006). Recently, Witt and colleagues (2013) found in their systematic review and meta-regression of 110 studies relating psychosis to violence that lack of illness insight was strongly associated to violence, as with higher PANSS scores (moderate association). They did not find a significant association between violence and negative symptomatology factor indices.

Substance abuse

Overall, there is a large body of scientific evidence linking substance abuse to violence (e.g. Fazel, Långström, Hjern, Grann, & Lichtenstein, 2009b) and to increased risk of violent behaviour in psychotic patients (e.g. Elbogen & Johnson, 2009). For example, Arseneault, Moffitt, Caspi, Taylor, and Silva (2000) examined a birth cohort of young adults and concluded that individuals that fulfilled the criteria for marijuana, alcohol dependence and schizophrenia-spectrum disorders were respectively 3.8 times, 1.9 times and 2.5 times more likely to act violently than the control group.

Overall, it can be concluded that substance abuse can strongly intensify the relationship between violence and schizophrenia-spectrum, as many patients suffering from schizophrenia also suffer from (comorbid) dependency disorders. So for risk assessment indications, it is important to consider substance abuse as an additional risk factor for becoming violent within schizophrenia-spectrum and related disorders.

First episode of psychosis

Large and Nielssen (2011) conducted a systematic review and meta-analysis, exploring the incidence of violence in patients suffering from a first-episode psychosis. These authors concluded that a substantial portion of patients suffering from a first psychosis commit a violent act or aggressive incident before being treated for their symptoms. In their meta-analysis, the following factors were associated with violence committed by patients presenting with first psychotic episode: young age, prior offending, substance use and a lack of education. They concluded that 'more serious violence was associated with measure of the length of time patients have experienced symptoms without receiving treatment' (Large & Nielssen, 2012, p. 215).

Demographic and premorbid factors

In a recent systematic review and meta-regression study by Witt et al. (2013), these authors investigated a wide range of demographic and premorbid factors that could be related to violence in psychotic disorders within 110 studies. These authors found a number of demographic factors that were related to violence risk: the patient being violently victimised (strong association), recent homelessness, history of homelessness, being male (moderate association), non-white ethnicity and being from a lower socio-economic status

266 *Maarten Peters et al.*

(weak association). When exploring premorbid factors, they found moderate associations with childhood physical or sexual abuse, parental history of criminal involvement and parental history of alcohol misuse.

Antisocial background/psychopathy

In a recent review article on risk factors for violence among psychotic patients, Bo et al. (2011) reviewed the literature on the role of comorbid personality pathology in increasing the violence risk in psychotic patients. Despite the controversy surrounding this topic (i.e. can one assess a personality diagnosis within this schizophrenia-spectrum group in a reliable and valid way?), most of the research on the associations between personality dimensions, violence and schizophrenia-spectrum has focused on psychopathy and antisocial personality disorder (APD).

In their review article, Bo and colleagues conclude:

> Overall, these findings underscore the relevance of including personality features when assessing risk for future violence among patients with schizophrenia. That is not to say that the symptomatology of patients with schizophrenia does not predict or influence the tendency to engage in delinquent behaviour, but rather that among a specific group of patients with schizophrenia (i.e. psychopathic traits or severe personality pathology), evidence suggests that personality features or traits have a higher predictive value in risk assessment evaluations than do symptoms or states related to schizophrenia.
>
> (Bo et al., 2011, p. 717)

Neuropsychological indicators

As described above, patients with a psychotic disorder show marked deficits in various neuropsychological functions (e.g. Krabbendam & Aleman, 2011; Pijnenborg & Krabbendam, 2012). However, when investigating the possible relationship between neuropsychological indicators and violence, Witt and colleagues (2013) did not find any significant association between violence and the Wechsler Adult Intelligent Scale (WAIS) total and subscale scores, the National Adult Reading Test (NART) or error rates (perseverative errors) on the Wisconsin Card Sorting Test. Until now, no firm associations have been found, although the research in this specific field is scarce.

Forensic treatment factors

The main treatment modality for forensic patients suffering from a psychotic disorder is the administration of antipsychotic medication. In the vast majority of psychotic patients, consistent use of antipsychotic medication reduces the (positive) symptoms of their illness, which can also substantially lower the risk of becoming violent. It should be noted, though, that in a general sense the evidence for the anti-aggressive effects of various psychotropic agents, among which are antipsychotics, antidepressants, anticonvulsants and β-adrenergic-blocking drugs, is still limited (for a systematic review on the effects of pharmacotherapy in treating aggressive behaviour see Goedhard et al., 2006). Of the antipsychotic drugs, the newer, so-called atypical antipsychotic agents appear to have somewhat better effects in reducing aggression than typical antipsychotics, but again, there is still a paucity of empirical research on this topic.

Considering the potential anti-aggressive effects of (atypical) antipsychotic agents, it sounds logical and has been backed up by scientific research that treatment non-adherence (either to psychopharmacological or psychological treatment) is moderately to strongly associated with an increased violence risk (e.g. Witt et al., 2013). In treatment adherence, having some insight into one's own illness is an important issue, as psychotic patients who completely lack insight into the fact that their symptoms are the result of a psychiatric disorder on average will also judge the need for (pharmacological) treatment as low. Because of this, the main components in the treatment of psychotic forensic patients, apart from the use of antipsychotic medication, are often intensive psycho-education about their psychiatric disorder, as well as improvement of skills and gaining more insight into warning signals that signal a worsening of their psychiatric condition (Nijman, van Marle, & Kavelaars, 2006; Fluttert, 2011). In a general sense, however, research investigating projects for behavioural change during forensic psychiatric treatment in reducing violence risks is still limited (e.g. Nijman, de Kruyk, & van Nieuwenhuizen, 2004).

Besides antipsychotic medication, psychosocial therapies are often provided as adjuncts to antipsychotic medication to help alleviate symptoms and improve treatment adherence, like psycho-education, cognitive behaviour therapy, cognitive remediation, social skills training and assertive community therapy both in the clinical field (e.g. Tandon et al., 2010) and potentially also in the forensic field. As stated previously, the research on this topic in the forensic field is still rather limited.

Psychotic patients in clinical or forensic care: is there any difference?

A psychotic individual may end up in general mental health care or forensic mental health care. In the latter case, if an individual has been found not criminally responsible or incompetent to stand trial, they are referred to forensic treatment services (Seto, Harris, & Rice, 2004). Many (involuntarily) admitted psychotic patients in general mental health care institutions are also admitted as a result of violent or disruptive behaviour. The focus of the treatment that is offered, however, is generally very different in forensic psychiatric settings when compared to general psychiatric hospitals. An important difference between general mental health care and forensic mental health care is that forensic services strongly focus on the reduction of aggressive and criminal

268   *Maarten Peters et al.*

behaviour whereas general psychiatric services mainly focus on reducing psychotic symptoms (Hodgins, 2009).

On closed psychiatric admissions wards of general mental health institutions, the vast majority of the patients that are treated suffer from psychotic disorders such as schizophrenia leading to disruptive, dangerous behaviour. They are often a threat to themselves or others and this is why they are involuntarily admitted. Adequate treatment of the psychotic condition almost always leads to a diminishing of the disruptive conduct. Acts of violence in those cases can merely be seen as the outcome of their fear and anxiety related to delusions and hallucinations rather than criminal intent. Lack of insight into their disorder and the absence of help-seeking opens the way to criminalisation and/or victimisation.

To illustrate how complex things can turn out in cases of psychotic disorders in relation to disruptive violent behaviour, we present three case-reports. The first concerning Mr A. has been published previously in more detail (see à Campo, Nijman, Merckelbach, & Yeates-Frederikx, 2001).

Case-report A

Mr A. is a 35-year-old man who had initially been diagnosed as suffering from borderline personality disorder with antisocial characteristics. He had a long history of aggressive behaviour and drug abuse. Because of his acts of violence to what seemed to be random passengers on the street, he had been locked up in jail for three years. When Mr A. entered the consulting room after admission to a general psychiatric hospital, the large tattoos on his neck were striking to the psychiatrist. One side of his neck displayed '666' in black ink, while the other side showed a tattoo of a pentagram. When asked about this, Mr A. at first was reluctant to talk about the meaning of his tattoos, but he finally explained that the tattoos were recently engraved in his neck 'to serve Satan'. Further examination of his thoughts and perceptions made it clear that the patient had suffered from paranoid delusions since adolescence.

Once Mr A. was diagnosed with paranoid schizophrenia, his treatment was also changed. Mr A. was now administered antipsychotic medication. As a result of this, his delusions disappeared and his overall psychiatric condition improved markedly. Mr A. became a more cooperative man, and was in full control of his aggressive impulses. After a few months, his thoughts and perceptions also became relatively normal and he started to gain insight into his illness. Furthermore, he became aware of the social impact of his tattoos, namely that people avoided him. In retrospect, Mr A. says the following about his disease:

> When I was ill, I thought I lived with Satan and therefore I needed to have his signs in my neck. Living with Satan forced me to do violence to innocent people. Now that I have come to my senses, I want those tattoos to be removed. I am ashamed and I hope I will never get so confused again.

Psychotic disorders and violence   269

At his request, the tattoos were removed by plastic surgery (see à Campo et al., 2001).

Case-report B

In the late 1990s a young man, Mr B., 20-years-old, was involuntarily admitted to a closed psychiatric ward. He was a student in physics who lived with his parents and had few social contacts. He stopped going to college and gradually withdrew himself from social life. The room in his parents' house became his world and there was a growing sympathy with an extreme right-wing political ideology. At night he listened to heavy metal songs with forbidden fascistic lyrics. His mother was concerned but couldn't correct her son's behaviour. When she heard him talking and screaming in his room while there were no other people, she consulted the general practitioner. However, her son didn't want to talk to a doctor. Later on, the general practitioner asked a psychiatrist to visit the young man. The psychiatrist couldn't do anything as long as there was no specific demand for care by Mr B. himself.

Some weeks later the young man threw his furniture out of the window and set the furniture on fire in the street. His mother alerted the police and fire brigade. Nevertheless, the police hesitated to arrest Mr B. He stated that he wanted to draw attention to his vision of the world being totally rotten. The solution was to burn everything down. The police consulted a psychiatrist who concluded that Mr B. suffered from paranoid delusions. An involuntary admission followed.

At the psychiatric admission ward, the patient told the psychiatrist that he had no problems at all. He had the idea that a new world war could clean up this whole mess. So he had the plan that he himself could create World War Three by spreading some posters all over town with aggressive provocative statements. Nobody could be trusted and he didn't accept any help such as antipsychotic medication.

In the weeks and months that followed, the patient behaved superficially correctly but didn't mingle with other patients. One day a drawing was found in his room with a plan to escape from the ward by eliminating therapists and setting a fire. Because of the serious threat, the psychiatrist ordered a second opinion to explore the possibility of starting antipsychotic medication to reduce the danger. When the patient heard that even in second opinion the conclusion was that it was best to start antipsychotic medication, he eventually accepted treatment. After some weeks the paranoid delusions diminished. In three months the patient could go home with an intensive treatment plan by an Assertive Community Treatment (ACT) team. After 13 years, unfortunately, the patient stopped his medication because he was stable and wanted to try to live his life without any drug. This resulted in an attack with a Molotov cocktail directed to the local police department in response to imperative hallucinations. This led to seclusion in a closed forensic psychiatric admission ward where the antipsychotic medication was restarted.

Case-report C

A 35-year-old woman had been treated for schizophrenia of the disorganised type for several years. It was almost impossible for her to manage her daily life because she couldn`t plan the steps that had to be taken to reach a certain goal. Even under slight stress she could become paranoid and hostile. In the past she sometimes took some drugs, mainly cannabis or amphetamines, to feel more comfortable.

A multidisciplinary ACT team offered the treatment she needed. A psychiatrist took care of the overall treatment planning, consisting of supportive psychotherapy, psycho-education and pharmacotherapy. She weekly had an appointment with her case-manager who also visited her at her home when necessary.

One day the patient came to the office of her case-manager who had to give her the usual three-weekly dose of antipsychotic medication by injection. The routine medication administration resulted in an almost lethal incident. While the case-manager was preparing the injection, the patient took a knife out of her bag and stabbed the case-manager in his back. The case-manager managed to press the alarm button on his mobile telephone and soon help from co-workers arrived. They called an ambulance to rush their wounded colleague to the nearest hospital and brought the aggressive woman to a seclusion room. After two days of observation and wound treatment, the case-manager could leave the hospital with no lasting physical damage.

In the seclusion room the patient told the consulted psychiatrist that she didn't want to die of the poison they wanted to inject in her. For her, the stabbing of her case-manager was an act of self-defence. The patient was not arrested but could stay at the closed ward where she had been secluded after the aggressive incident.

In court, the judgement was that the patient couldn't be held responsible for her assault, because she acted in a state of paranoid psychosis. The patient had to be treated in a closed ward of a psychiatric hospital, the hospital where she was already in therapy.

From these case vignettes, it can be concluded that there is a fine line between clinical and forensic practice for schizophrenia-spectrum disorders. Can we find sociodemographical or psychiatric risk factors that determine which patient will end up in a forensic or clinical setting? This was the central question of a case file study that was carried out by two of the authors in collaboration with a graduate student (à Campo, Timmermans, & Peters, unpublished manuscript). In this case file study, patients with psychotic symptoms that were involuntarily admitted within forensic mental health care ($n = 10$) and patients with psychotic symptomatology that were involuntarily admitted to general mental health care ($n = 20$) were investigated. All patients were admitted within the Mondriaan institute, either in the forensic department in Heerlen, or in a general psychiatry ward in the department in Heerlen or in Maastricht in the Netherlands. Demographics, clinical variables, psychiatric and criminal history and violent incidents were taken into account. The results indicated that the groups resembled each other with regard to demographical variables and psychiatric history. However, forensic patients ($n = 10$) had significantly more diagnoses, were more likely to have comorbid substance problems and were more likely to be convicted in the past, in contrast to civil psychotic patients ($n = 20$). No associations between violence and psychosis-specific symptoms were found.

Concluding remarks

From the literature it becomes clear that the risk of becoming violent is increased in patients with psychotic disorders, with different risk factors unrelated to psychotic symptomatology also contributing to this increase. Nevertheless, only a minority of psychotic patients will engage in severe physical assaults towards others.

In case a severe physical assault is performed by a psychotic patient, the victims are relatively often first intimates (e.g. parents) or people well known (e.g. a neighbour) to the patient.

In the treatment of violent psychotic patients, regardless of whether they are admitted to a forensic psychiatric institution or a general mental health institute, the administration of antipsychotic medication is the main component, supplemented by psychosocial treatments. Research on the efficacy and risk management of psychosocial interventions for psychotic patients in the forensic context is rather limited and warrants further attention.

Pharmacological treatment with antipsychotics is often hampered by low treatment adherence, which is often the result of a lack of illness insight. This makes intensive psycho-education about the psychiatric disorder and the consequences of treatment non-adherence another essential focus (apart from pharmacotherapy) of treatment of (violent) psychotic patients.

Literature

American Psychiatric Association (2000). *Diagnostic and statistical manual of mental disorders, fourth edition text revision* (DSM-IV-TR). Arlington, VA: American Psychiatric Association.

American Psychiatric Association (2013). *Diagnostic and statistical manual of mental disorders, fifth edition* (DSM-5). Arlington, VA: American Psychiatric Association.

Andreasen, N. C., Flaum, M., & Arndt, S. (1992). The Comprehensive Assessment of Symptoms and History (CASH): An instrument for assessing diagnosis and psychopathology. *Archives of General Psychiatry, 49,* 615–623.

Arseneault, L., Moffitt, T. E., Caspi, A., Taylor, P. J., & Silva, P. A. (2000). Mental disorders and violence in a total birth cohort: results from the Dunedin study. *Archives of General Psychiatry, 57,* 979–986.

Baron-Cohen, S. (1995). *Mindblindness: An essay on autism and theory of mind.* Cambridge, MA: MIT Press.

Beck, A. T., Rector, N. A., Stolar, N., & Grant, P. (2009). An integrative cognitive model of schizophrenia. In A. T. Beck, N. A. Rector, N. Stolar, & P. Grant (Eds.), *Schizophrenia: Cognitive theory, research, and therapy.* New York: Guilford Press.

272 Maarten Peters et al.

Bjørkly, S. (2002). Psychotic symptoms and violence toward others – A literature review of some preliminary findings: Part 1: Delusions. *Aggression and Violent Behaviour, 7,* 617–631.

Bo, S., Abu-Akel, A., Kongerslev, M., Haahr, U. H., & Simonsen, E. (2011). Risk factors for violence among patients with schizophrenia. *Clinical Psychology Review, 31,* 711–726.

Bonilha, L., Molnar, C., Horner, M. D., et al. (2008). Neurocognitive deficits and prefrontal cortical atrophy in patients with schizophrenia. *Schizophrenia Research, 101,* 142–151.

Bozikas, V. P., Giannakou, M., Kosmidis, M. H., et al. (2011). Insights into theory of mind in schizophrenia: The impact of cognitive impairment. *Schizophrenia Research, 130,* 130–136.

Campo, à, J. M. L. G., Nijman, H. L. I., Merckelbach, H. L. G. J., & Yeates-Frederikx, M. H. M. (2001). Changes in appearance and psychosis. *Psychiatry. Interpersonal and Biological Processes, 64,* 165–167.

Campo, à, J. M. L. G. (2004). *Changes in appearance and psychosis.* Maastricht, the Netherlands: Maastricht University Press.

Coid, J., & Ullrich, S. (2011). Prisoners with psychosis in England and Wales: Diversion to psychiatric inpatient services? *International Journal of Law and Psychiatry, 34,* 99–108.

Douglas, K. S., Guy, L. S., & Hart, S. D. (2009). Psychosis as a risk factor for violence to others: A meta-analysis. *Psychological Bulletin, 135,* 679–706.

Dunlosky, J., & Metcalfe, J. (2009). *Metacognition.* Thousand Oaks, CA: Sage Publications.

Eaton, W. W., Tien, A. Y., & Poeschla, B. D. (1995). Epidemiology of schizophrenia. In J. A. den Boer, H. G. M. Westenberg, & H. M. van Praag (Eds.), *Advances in the neurobiology of schizophrenia* (pp. 27–57). New York: John Wiley & Sons.

Elbogen, E. B., & Johnson, S. C. (2009). The intricate link between violence and mental disorder: Results from the national epidemiologic survey on alcohol and related conditions. *Archives of General Psychiatry, 66,* 152–161.

Fazel, S., & Seewald, K. (2012). Severe mental illness in 33,588 prisoners worldwide: Systematic review and meta-regression analysis. *British Journal of Psychiatry, 200,* 364–373.

Fazel, S., Gulati, G., Linsell, L., Geddes, J. R., & Grann, M. (2009a). Schizophrenia and violence: Systematic review and meta-analysis. *Plos Medicine, 6,* 1–14.

Fazel, S., Långström, N., Hjern, A., Grann, M., & Lichtenstein, P. (2009b). Schizophrenia, substance abuse, and violent crime. *JAMA, the Journal of the American Medical Association, 301*(19), 2016–2023.

First, M. B., Spitzer, R. L., Gibbon, M. et al. (1996). *Structured Clinical Interview for DSM IV Axis I Disorders (SCID-I).* Washington DC: American Psychiatric Press.

Fluttert, F. (2011). Management of inpatient aggression in forensic mental health nursing: The application of the Early Recognition Method (Ph.D. thesis). Utrecht: Utrecht University.

Goedhard, L. E., Stolker, J. J., Heerdink, E. R., Nijman, H. L. I., Olivier, B., & Egberts, T. C. G. (2006). Pharmacotherapy for the treatment of aggressive behaviour in general adult psychiatry: A systematic review. *Journal of Clinical Psychiatry, 67,* 1013–1024.

Haddock, G., McCarron, J., Tarrier, N., & Faragher, E. B. (1999). Scales to measure dimensions of hallucinations and delusions: The psychotic symptom rating scales (PSYRATS). *Psychological Medicine, 29,* 879–889.

Heinrichs, R. W., & Zakzanis, K. K. (1998). Neurocognitive deficit in schizophrenia: A quantitative review of the evidence. *Neuropsychology, 12*, 426–445.

Hodgins, S. (2008). Violent behaviour among people with schizophrenia: A framework for investigation of causes, and effective treatment, and prevention. *Philosophical Transactions of the Royal Society, 363*, 2505–2518.

Hodgins, S. (2009). Editorial: The interface between general and forensic psychiatric services. *European Psychiatry, 24*, 354–355.

Howes, O. D., & Kapur, S. (2009). The dopamine hypothesis of schizophrenia: Version III – The final common pathway. *Schizophrenia Bulletin, 35*, 549–562.

Junginger, J. (1995). Command hallucinations and the prediction of dangerousness. *Psychiatric Services, 46*, 911–914.

Kay, S. R., Fiszbein, A., & Opler, L. A. (1987). The positive and negative syndrome scale (PANSS) for schizophrenia. *Schizophrenia Bulletin, 13*, 261–276.

Krabbendam, L., & Aleman, A. (2011). Cognitieve stoornissen [Cognitive deficits]. In W. Cahn, L. Krabbendam, I. Myin-Germeys, R. Bruggeman & L. De Haan (Eds). Handboek schizofrenie [Handbook of schizophrenia] (pp. 265–280). Utrecht: de Tijdstroom.

Krabbendam, L., & Os, J. van (2005). Schizophrenia and urbanicity: A major environmental influence: conditional on genetic risk. *Schizophrenia Bulletin, 31*, 795–799.

Large, M. M., & Nielssen, O. (2011). Violence in first-episode psychosis: A systematic review and meta-analysis. *Schizophrenia Research, 125*, 209–220.

Link, B., & Stueve, A. (1994). Psychotic symptoms and the violent/illegal behaviour of mental patients compared to the community. In J. Monahan & H. Steadman (Eds.), *Violence and mental disorder: Development in risk assessment* (pp. 137–158). Chicago, IL: University of Chicago Press.

McNiel, D. E., Eisner, J. P., & Binder, R. L. (2000). The relationship between command hallucinations and violence. *Psychiatric Services, 51*, 1288–1292.

Monahan, J., & Appelbaum, P. (2000). Reducing violence risk: Diagnostically based clues from the MacArthur violence risk assessment study. In S. Hodgins (Eds.), *Effective prevention of crime and violence among the mentally ill* (pp. 19–34). Alphen aan den Rijn, the Netherlands: Kluwer Academic Publishers.

Moritz, S., Woodward, T. S., Jelinek, L., & Klinge, R. (2008). Memory and metamemory in schizophrenia: A liberal acceptance account of psychosis. *Psychological Medicine, 38*, 825–832.

Moritz, S., Woodward, T. S., & Ruff, C. C. (2003). Source monitoring and memory confidence in schizophrenia. *Psychological Medicine, 33*, 131–139.

Moritz, S., & Woodward, T. S. (2005). Jumping to conclusions in delusional and non-delusional schizophrenic patients. *British Journal of Clinical Psychology, 44*, 193–207.

Myin-Germeys, I., & Os, J. van. (2007). Stress reactivity in psychosis: Evidence for an affective pathway to psychosis. *Clinical Psychology Review, 27*, 409–424.

Nestor, P. G., & Haycok, J. (1997). Not guilty by reason of insanity of murder: Clinical and neuropsychological characteristics. *Journal of the American Academy of Psyciatry and the Law, 25*, 161–171.

Nijman, H., Cima, M., & Merckelbach, H. (2003). Nature and antecedents of psychotic patients' crimes. *Journal of Forensic Psychiatry and Psychology, 14*, 542–553.

Nijman, H., de Kruyk, C., & van Nieuwenhuizen, C. (2004). Behavioural changes during forensic psychiatric (TBS) treatment in the Netherlands. *International Journal of Law and Psychiatry, 27*, 79–85.

274   Maarten Peters et al.

Nijman, H. L. I., van Marle, H., & Kavelaars, M. (2006). Psychotische patiënten in de TBS: Achtergronden, delictgedrag en behandeling. *Pedagogiek, 26,* 291–300.

Overall, J. E., & Gorham, D. R. (1962). The Brief Psychiatric Rating Scale. *Psychological Reports, 10,* 799–812.

Peters, M. J. V., Hauschildt, M., Moritz, S., & Jelinek, L. (2013). Impact of emotional valence on memory and meta-memory in schizophrenia using video sequences. *Journal of Behaviour Therapy and Experimental Psychiatry, 44,* 77–83.

Peters, M. J. V., Cima, M., Smeets, T., de Vos, M., Jelicic, M., & Merckelbach, H. (2007). Did I say that or did you? Executive dysfunctions in schizophrenic patients affect memory efficiency, but not source attributions. *Cognitive Neuropsychiatry, 12,* 391–411.

Pickup, G., & Frith, C. (2001). Theory of mind impairments in schizophrenia: Symptomatology, severity, and specificity. *Psychological Medicine, 31,* 207–220.

Pijnenborg, G. H. M., & Krabbendam, L. (2012). Neuropsychologische diagnostiek bij mensen met een psychothsche kwetsbaarheid (pp. 143–165). In M. van der Gaag, T. Staring, & L. Vamaggia (Eds.), *Handboek psychose.* Assen: Koninklijke Van Gorcum.

Raja, M., & Azzoni, A. (2005). Hostility and violence of acute psychiatric inpatients. *Clinical Practice and Epidemiology in Mental Health, 1,* 11–19.

Reichenberg, A., & Harvey, P.D. (2007). Neuropsychological impairents in schizophrenia: Integration of performance-based and brain imaging findings. *Psychological Bulletin, 133,* 833–858.

Reynolds, N., & Scragg, P. (2010). Compliance with command hallucinations: The role of power in relation to the voice, and social rank in relation to the voice and others. *Journal of Forensic Psychiatry and Psychology, 21,* 121–138.

Schenkel, L. S., & Silverstein, S. M. (2004). Dimensions of premorbid functioning in schizophrenia: A review of neuromotor, cognitive, social, and behavioural domains. *Genetic, Social, and General Psychol. Monogr., 130,* 241–270.

Schultze-Lutter, F., (2009). Subjective symptoms of schizophrenia in research and the clinic: the basic symptom concept. *Schizophrenia Bulletin, 35,* 5–8.

Seto, M. C., Harris, G. T., & Rice, M. E. (2004). The criminogenic, clinical, and social problems of forensic and civil psychiatric patients. *Law and Human Behaviour, 28,* 577–586.

Stefanis, N. C., Hanssen, M., Smirnis, N. K., et al. (2002). Evidence that three dimensions of psychosis have a distribution in the general population. *Psychological Medicine, 32,* 347–358.

Steinert, T. (2002). Prediction of inpatient violence. *Acta Psychiatrica Scandinavia, 106,* 133–141.

Swanson, J. W., Swartz, M. S., Van Dorn, R. A., et al. (2006). A national study of violent behaviour in persons with schizophrenia. *Archives of General Psychiatry, 63,* 490–499.

Tandon, R., Keshavan, M. S., & Nasrallah, H. A. (2008). Schizophrenia, 'just the facts': What we know in 2008. 2. Epidemiology and etiology. *Schizophrenia Research, 102,* 1–18.

Tandon, R., Nasrallah, H. A., & Keshavan, M. S. (2009). Schizophrenia, 'just the facts': 4. Clinical features and conceptualization. *Schizophrenia Research, 110,* 1–23.

Tandon, R., Nasrallah, H. A., & Keshavan, M. S. (2010). Schizophrenia, 'just the facts': 5. Treatment and prevention: Past, present, and future. *Schizophrenia Research, 122,* 1–23.

Vorstman, J., & Kahn, R. (2011). Genetica. In W. Cahn, L. Krabbendam, I. Myin-Germeys, R. Bruggeman, & L. De Haan (Eds), *Handboek schizofrenie [Handbook of schizophrenia]* (pp. 215–228). Utrecht: de Tijdstroom.

Walsh, E., Buchanan, A., & Fahy, T. (2002). Violence and schizophrenia: Examining the evidence. *British Journal of Psychiatry, 180,* 490–495.

Witt, K., van Dorn, R., & Fazel, S. (2013). Risk factors for violence in psychosis: Systematic review and meta-regression analysis of 110 studies. *Plos One, 8,* 1–15.

World Health Organization (1992). *Schedules for clinical assessment in neuropsychiatry.* Geneva: World Health Organization.

World Health Organization (1999). *SCAN 2:1. Schedules for clinical assessment in neuropsychiatry.* Geneva: World Health Organization.

Yung, A. R., Yuen, H. P., McGorry, P. D., et al. (2005). Mapping the onset of psychosis: The comprehensive assessment of at-risk mental states. *Australian and New Zealand Journal of Psychiatry, 39,* 964–971.

Ziegler, M., Rief, W., Werner, S. M., Mehl, S., & Lincoln, T. M. (2008). Hasty decision-making in a variety of tasks: Does it contribute to the development of delusions? *Psychology and Psychotherapy: Theory, Research and Practice, 81,* 237–245.

14 Aggressive behaviour in offenders with intellectual disabilities

Theories and treatment

Marije Keulen-De Vos and Karin Frijters

Introduction

Intellectual disability[1] (ID) is a generalised disorder that involves impairments of mental abilities that impact intellectual functioning and adaptive behaviour, such as reasoning, learning and problem-solving skills. There is no specific age requirement, but the onset of symptoms is typically in early childhood. According to the DSM-5, ID equals an IQ score of 70 of below (APA, 2013). Approximately 1 to 2% of the general population has an intellectual disability, whereas prevalence rates among forensic psychiatric patients typically vary between 3 and 50% (e.g. Deb, Thomas, & Bright, 2001a; Holland, 2004). Many people with IDs show high-challenging or aggressive behaviour. Definitions of aggressive behaviour vary, but the most common forms are physical aggression, sexual aggression, self-injurious behaviour, temper tantrums, screaming and shouting (Deb et al., 2001b; Myrbakk & von Tetzchner, 2008). Although the true extent of aggressive behaviour in ID populations is unclear, some studies report prevalence rates ranging from 11 to 60%, which would suggest that the prevalence rates are up to three to five times higher than in non-disabled individuals (Hogue et al., 2006; Janssen, Schuengel, & Stolk, 2002; McClintock, Hall, & Oliver, 2003; Rojahn, Zaja, Turygin, Moore, & van Dingen, 2012; Sturmey, 2002; Taylor, Novaco, Gillmer, Robertson, & Thorne, 2005). Higher rates of aggressive behaviour are found in institutionalised and secure settings. This is not surprising because aggressive behaviour is often the reason why they are institutionalised or admitted to a forensic psychiatric hospital in the first place (Benson & Brooks, 2008; Bhaumik et al., 2009; Embregts, Didden, Schreuder, Huitink, & van Nieuwenhuijzen, 2009). Studies demonstrate that offenders with IDs are more likely to be convicted for sexual offences, arson, theft and burglary, and criminal damage compared to non-ID offenders (Asscher, van der Put, & Stams, 2012; van den Bogaard, Embregts, Hendriks, & Heestermans, 2013; Embregts et al., 2010; Simpson & Hogg, 2001). ID offenders are also responsible for a substantial amount of aggressive incidents within forensic settings. This behaviour can interfere with participating in social activities and can lead to social rejection; it can also impair new learning skills, cause physical injury to self and others and can incur great costs (Novaco & Taylor, 2008; Travis & Sturmey, 2013). In general, crime and violence have an enormous impact on society in terms of damage to persons and property, the effect on the quality of life of victims and their families, as well as the costs of prosecuting offenders and detaining them for prolonged periods of time.

A clear understanding of an offender's aggressive and violent behaviour is a prerequisite for determining suitable treatment interventions to reduce such behaviour. In this chapter, we describe possible determinants for aggressive and criminal behaviour in individuals with intellectual disabilities, and subsequently review available treatment options.

Theories on aggressive and criminal behaviour

Why do some people become criminals? Over the last decades, there is an increased interest in pathways to criminal behaviour and forensic treatment, as is evidenced, for example, by a growing literature on pathways to criminal behaviour and treatments for sex offenders and substance-abused offenders (e.g. Jones, 2004; Marshall & Serran, 2001; Murphy & Ting, 2010; Ward & Beech, 2006; Ward et al., 2004). The interest in offending and intellectual disabilities (ID), though, has a long history (Lindsay, Sturmey, & Taylor, 2004). In the late 19th century, scholars like Lewis Terman (1877–1956) assumed that ID was a key factor in unlawful behaviour. In fact, intellectual disabilities were considered to be part of a general deficit that also included immorality, promiscuous sexual behaviour, criminality and substance misuse. According to Terman (1911), 'all feeble-minded [ID] individuals are potential criminals'. This view was nuanced at the end of the 20th century because research had failed to establish a causal relationship between low intelligence and crime. Furthermore, other variables, such as socio-economic status, were believed to influence the trajectory of criminal behaviour (e.g. Hirschi & Hindelang, 1977; Simons, 1978). Echoing this perspective, during the 20th and 21st century, several theories and determinants for criminal behaviour in offenders with intellectual disabilities have been suggested.

In recent years, the relationship between *biological factors* and violent behaviour has been increasingly recognised. For example, a large body of research implicates that abnormalities in brain structures (i.e. amygdala, frontal lobe, prefrontal cortex), biochemicals or neurotransmitter imbalance (i.e. opiate receptor dysregulation, dopaminergic or serotonergic imbalance) play a key role in mediating aggressive and violent behaviour (e.g. Blair, Mitchell, & Blair, 2005; Darrow, Follette, Maragakis, & Dystra, 2011; Dolan, Anderson, & Deakin, 2001; Raine & Yang, 2006). Some research findings suggest that impairments in genetic and brain functions may also enhance the propensity for violence in the subgroup of intellectually disabled offenders (Pillman et al., 1999; Schuurs-Hoeijmakers et al., 2013; Woodcock, Oliver, & Humpreys, 2009). For example, behavioural phenotypes such as Prader-Willi syndrome (i.e. a chromosomal disorder in which seven genes are deleted of unexpressed) and Fragile X syndrome are associated with intellectual disabilities.

278   *Marije Keulen-De Vos and Karin Frijters*

They also often coincide with self-injurious behaviour, temper outbursts and negative emotional behaviour (Chevalère, Postal, Jauregui, Copet, Laurier, & Thuilleaux, 2013; Woodcock, Humphreys, & Oliver, 2009; Yang et al., 2013). Also, twin and adoption studies suggest that inheritance plays a role; there is often a similarity between ID offenders and their parents (Lindsay, Sturmey, & Taylor, 2004; Farrington, 1995). For example, parents of ID offenders have often been convicted for a criminal offence, or are diagnosed with psycho-pathology (Hayes, 2012). Although it is likely that inheritance plays a role, it is unclear what exactly is inherited (i.e. IQ, oppositionality, propensity to depression etc.). Some studies cast doubt on the heritability of ID; for example, studies of institutionalised individuals found that more than half of them had parents without an intellectual disability (e.g. Beirne-Smith, Patton, & Kim, 2006). Also, not all intellectually disabled offenders have genetic or brain abnormalities, but there is an increased likelihood.

Psychological factors are also important agents in the development of aggressive behaviour in intellectually disabled individuals.

Cognitions

On a cognitive level, several factors have been identified. First, aggressive ID offenders are often flawed in the processing of social information (Van Nieuwenhuizen et al., 2006). An adequate encoding and interpretation of other people's intentions generates a (behaviour) response; subsequently, a failure to interpret other people's intent can lead to problem-solving deficits and ultimately to an inadequate (behavioural) response. Research has suggested that, in ID offenders, information in social situations is encoded as 'hostile' or 'provocative' which consequently generates an aggressive response (Basquill, Nezu, Nezu, & Klein, 2004; Jahoda, Pert, & Trower, 2006a; Larkin, Jahoda, & MacMahon, 2013; Lindsay, 2007; Pert, Jahoda, & Squire, 1999). Secondly, the erroneous appraisal of interpersonal information may be related to an ID offender's normative beliefs about aggression (Tyrer et al., 2006). During childhood, offenders with ID have often been exposed to violence or have been a witness to parental violence. This may contribute to the development of normative beliefs that violence is a normal part of everyday life. A possible third cognitive factor that mediates violent behaviour in individuals with intellectual disabilities is a limited repertoire of coping strategies. For example, they typically lack skills with regard to communication, problem solving and interpersonal conflicts (Embregts et al., 2010; McClintock, Hall, & Oliver, 2003; McClure, Halpern, Wolper, & Donahue, 2003; Novaco & Taylor, 2008; Sturmey, 2002). A fourth and related factor is ignorance of knowledge or skills. For example, studies on sex offenders with intellectual disabilities typically report that these offenders have limited knowledge about sexual acts and sexual relationships (Lindsay, 2002; Rice, Harris, Lang, & Chaplin, 2008). It is argued that this sexual naivety rather than sexual deviance lies at the heart of sexual offending in

Aggressive behaviour in offenders with intellectual disabilities   279

individual with IDs (Day, 1994; Michie, Lindsay, Martin, & Grieve, 2006). This hypothesis is often referred to as the 'counterfeit deviance hypothesis' (Hingsburger, Griffiths, & Quinsey, 1991; Griffiths, Hingsburger, Hoath, & Ioannou, 2013). Moreover, intellectually disabled individuals often have a lack of understanding of how their own actions affect others (Hoitzing van Lankveld, Kok, & Curfs, 2010; Tyrer et al., 2006). Whether this is related to a lack of knowledge or a lack of empathy, or theory of mind, remains unclear. Little research has been conducted on this subject. Also, a lack of empathy or theory of mind may not be specific for *sex* offenders with ID. For example, a recent study by Ralfs and Beail (2012) has shown that there is no differ- ence between empathy in sex offenders with IDs and ID offenders who were committed for other types of crimes. Furthermore, the studies on empathy and theory of mind in ID offenders that have been conducted report mixed results. For example, Proctor and Beail (2007) reported that ID offenders have better, rather than poorer, empathy and theory of mind than offenders with normal intelligence, whereas Nader-Grosbois, Houssa, and Mazzone (2013) report that, in a sample of children with externalising behaviour disor- ders and IDs, developmental age does predict the ability to understand other people's mental states. A fifth cognitive factor is moral reasoning or how someone thinks about moral issues. According to Kohlberg (1969), there are six hierarchical stages of moral development. In stage one, individuals abide by the rules to avoid punishment. In other words, an action is perceived as immoral if one is punished for it.

At stage two, morality remains at a superficial level; actions are judged based on how they serve individual needs. For example, an action is perceived as moral if the act is in someone's own interest. In stage three, moral development is focused on living up to social expectations. In the fourth stage, people start to consider society when making judgements; laws and conventions are obeyed because of their importance in society. In the fifth and sixth stage, moral devel- opment progresses from being driven by social contracts with individuals or communities to being driven by universal principles. Many scholars have criti- cised Kohlberg stage theory on moral development. For example, it has been suggested that no one would ever achieve the final two stages of moral devel- opment, or that cultural variations are not accounted for (e.g. Gibbs, Basinger, Grime, & Snarey, 2007). Nevertheless, it is has shaped our thinking about moral reasoning. If moral cognitions are related to moral behaviour, individuals with intellectual or cognitive impairments are predisposed to deficits in moral judgement and, therefore, at risk for violent and criminal behaviour. There is limited research on moral development in ID offenders. The albeit limited evidence suggests that ID offenders are functioning at a lower stage of moral judgement compared to non-ID offenders (Goodwin, Gudjohnsson, Morris, Perkins, & Young, 2012; Langdon, Murphy, Clare, & Palmer, 2010; Lindsay et al., 2004). For example, a study by Van Vugt and colleagues (2011) found that moral reasoning of sex offenders with intellectual disabilities, as meas- ured with the Sociomoral Reflection Measure – Short Form (SRM-SF; Gibbs,

Emotions

On an emotional level, emotion regulation is believed to be a salient factor in the development of aggressive behaviour in individuals with intellectual disabilities. Although individuals with IDs can reliably identify their own emotions (McClure et al., 2003), their ability to recognise emotions in *others* may be hampered (Rojahn, Rabold, & Schneider, 1995; Zoja & Rojahn, 2008). For example, some studies show that individuals with IDs have difficulties in interpreting emotional stimuli in interpersonal situations (Matheson, Jahoda, & MacLean, 2005; Woodcock & Rose, 2007), although others contradict these findings (Jahoda, Pert, & Trower, 2006b). In the literature, there does seem to be consensus on the theory that individuals with IDs have deficits in regulating their emotions (e.g. McClure et al., 2003; Sappok et al., 2013; Taylor, Novaco, Gillmer, & Robertson, 2004). ID offenders often have a limited response repertoire when they are emotionally aroused; aggressive behaviour may be a default response in situations that are perceived as hostile or anger provoking (Taylor, Novaco, Guinian, & Street, 2004). The inability to adequate regulate emotions is evident as early as in early childhood. Children with an ID are ill equipped in dealing with emotional experiences, possibly due to their parent's inability to express and regulate emotions (Berkovits & Baker, 2013; Green & Baker, 2011; Haynes, Gillmore, Shochet, Campbell, & Roberts, 2013). The regulation of emotions not only directs behaviours but it is also anchored in social interaction and influences self-esteem and social competence (Ciarrochi & Scott, 2006; Sappok et al., 2013). The emotional dysregulation is in concordance with research findings that individuals with IDs have low self-esteem and come across as socially incompetent (Ali, Hassiotis, Strydom, & King, 2012; Janssen, Schuengel, & Stolk, 2002; Johnson, 2012; Paterson, McKenzie, & Lindsay, 2012; Rey, Extremera, Durán, & Ortiz-Tallo, 2012). Second, it has also been theorised that attachment is of importance in the development of violent behaviour in ID offenders. Attachment refers to the emotional bond between an infant and parent or caregiver. This bond is of critical importance because it affects social and emotional development; it promotes the ability to regulate arousal levels and cope with disturbing emotions (Cassidy, 1994). After birth, an infant has an inborn biological need to maintain close contact with the primary caregivers, although he/she is not born with the capacity to actually do so. It's the caregiver's response to distress signals and other social experiences, and the child's responsiveness to these responses, that shape an emotional bond (Ainsworth, Blehar, Waters, & Wall, 1978; Bartholomew, 1990; Bowlby, 1944, 1973).

Aggressive behaviour in offenders with intellectual disabilities 281

For example, soothing behaviour leads to a secure attachment, whereas separation and emotional deprivation will result in insecure attachment. Studies show that attachment organisations in childhood influence the attachment representations in adulthood (Mitchell & Beech, 2011; Weinfield, Sroufe, & Egeland, 2000; Weinfield, Whaley, & Egeland, 2004). Secure attachment serves as a buffer to deal with distress and adverse experiences in life, whereas insecure attachment causes the individual to become vulnerable and ill equipped to deal with negative life events (Lindberg, Fugett, & Lounder, 2013; Rutgers et al., 2007). Research suggests a link between insecure attachment and aggressive or high-challenging behaviour (Craissati, 2009; Dozier et al., 1999; Finzie et al., 2001; Michell & Beech, 2011; Weinfield, Sroufe, Egeland, & Carlson, 2008). Whether someone forms secure attachment relationships early in life determines whether someone develops effective coping strategies to deal with stressful situations. For example, traumatic life events result in insecure attachment relationships which, in turn, lead to an inability to deal with stress (Janssen et al., 2002). There is limited research on attachment issues in offenders in general and on ID offenders specifically. Studies in non-offenders samples do suggest that children and adults with intellectual disabilities are at risk of experiencing non-secure attachment relationships (Atkinson et al., 1999; Clegg & Sheard, 2002; Penketh, 2011; Schuengel, de Schipper, Sterkenburg, & Kef, 2013). For example, individuals with intellectual disabilities often grow up in pathogenic environments. Low parental educational levels, psychopathology of the primary caregiver, parental referral to mental health care and family dysfunction prevail. Also, ID offenders have often been a witness to parental violence, or been subjected to abuse. In fact, ID offenders have suffered more physical and sexual abuse compared to offenders without an intellectual disability (Embregts et al., 2010; Novaco & Taylor, 2008; Strickler, 2001). The combination of stress and insecure attachment may put individuals with intellectual disabilities at risk for developing behavioural problems (Janssen et al., 2002).

Behaviour

Although behaviour is often influenced by emotions and cognitions, we feel it is warranted to discuss behaviour factors that explain or contribute to aggression in ID offenders separately. On a behavioural level, behavioural disinhibition may be a contributing factor to challenging behaviour in ID offenders because the inability to control behaviour impulses is connected to impulsive behaviour (Friedman & Miyake, 2004; Reynolds, Ortengren, Richards, & de Wit, 2006; White et al., 1994). Although this may apply to all types of offenders, it is believed that behavioural disinhibition is pronounced in patients with lower IQ levels (Ogilvie et al., 2011; Parry & Lindsay, 2003). For example, a study by Gleaser & Deane (1999) showed that sex offenders with intellectual disabilities had poor anger management and impulse control compared to sex offenders with normal IQ levels. The high prevalence of substance abuse in individuals with IDs may influence behavioural disinhibition. For example, ID offenders regularly have a history of alcohol or cannabis abuse, although other substances also occur (McGillivray & Moore, 2001; Plant, McDermott, Chester, & Alexander, 2011). The use of substances often precedes or coincides with impulsive and aggressive behaviour (Lammers et al., 2014; Lindsay et al., 2013b; Ruiz et al., 2012). Another cognitive factor that may be of explanatory value in ID offenders is self-regulation or arousal. Ward and Hudson (1998) have proposed a pathways model for sexual offences which is based on self-regulation. According to this model, four basic pathways can be distinguished. The first is the approach/explicit pathways that refer to a strong desire to sexually offend and the use of explicit plans to do so. In the approach/automatic pathway, an individual's default behavioural pattern is to sexually offend. The third and fourth pathway refers to avoidant self-regulation patterns. In the third pathway, the individual tries to avoid sexually offensive behaviour but fails to use effective strategies. The fourth pathway refers to a passive stance to avoid sexual offending (Ward et al., 2004; Ward & Hudson, 1998). Keeling and Rose (2005) have proposed that the approach/automatic or avoidant/passive pathway are the most likely pathways for sex offenders with intellectual disabilities due to sexual naivety and a lack of coping strategies. Limited research has shown ambiguous results regarding the pathways model in ID offenders. Some studies have shown that these offenders offend via active pathways (Keeling, Rose, & Beech, 2006; Lindsay, Steptoe, & Beech, 2008), whereas another study has shown that both the approach and avoidant approach are common in ID sex offenders (Langdon, Maxted, Murphy, & OTSEC-ID GROUP, 2007). Based on these results, no direct inferences can be made regarding the validity of the pathways model in ID offenders.

Overall

People with intellectual disabilities who show aggressive behaviour are often diagnosed with a co-morbid psychiatric disorder or personality disorder; prevalence rates typically vary between 20 and 64% (Dias, Ware, Kinner, & Lennox, 2013; Dosen, 1993; Glaser & Florio, 2004). ID often co-occurs with mental disorders like depression (<11%), autistic spectrum disorders (5–30%), schizophrenia (< 9%), substance use disorders, attention deficit hyperactivity disorder (ADHD; < 15%) and cluster B personality disorders (i.e. antisocial, borderline PD; 31–57%) (van den Bogaard et al., 2013; Chapman & Wu, 2012; Copper, Smiley, Morrison, Williamson, & Allan, 2007; Deb et al., 2001a; Hogue et al., 2006; Lindsay et al., 2006; Lindsay et al., 2013a; Matson & Shoemaker, 2009; O'Brien et al., 2010; Owen, 2012; Reid, Lindsay, Law, & Sturmey, 2004; Smith, & O'Brien, 2004; Tenneij, Didden, Stolker, & Koof, 2009). These psychiatric disorders may moderate the impact of ID on offending (Andrews & Bonta, 2006). For example, it is likely that intellectual disability in combination with an antisocial personality pattern would increase the propensity to violence. Alternatively, certain mental disorders may manifest differently in

ID offenders compared to non-ID offenders. Individuals with intellectual disabilities, who are, to a certain extent, unable to communicate their experiences and problems, may manifest behaviour problems. For example, 'depression' may be expressed by irritability and agitation instead of an overt depressive mood (Deb, Matthews, Holt, & Bouras, 2001; Tyrer et al., 2006). However, psychiatric and personality disorders cannot explain aggressive behaviour in individuals with ID by itself since similar disorders are diagnosed in non-ID populations (Lindsay et al., 2013a).

Environmental or social factors

These are also important factors in aggressive behaviour in people with intellectual disabilities. According to social-learning theory, we learn by observation (Bandura, 1973). In other words, the environment in which we live serves as a model for behaviour. The childhood of ID offenders is often characterised by family pathology and dysfunction, parental separation and abuse. Moreover, they have often been a witness to parental violence and intoxicated states of caregivers (Lindsay et al., 2004; Männynsalo, Putkonen, Lindberg, & Kotilainen, 2009; Novaco & Taylor, 2008). This exposure serves as a blueprint for a child's cognitions and behaviour. Domestic violence or social disadvantage in combination with psychological impairments may aggravate aggressive tendencies (Watts & McNulty, 2013). Individuals with IDs are also vulnerable because they often lack economic independency. Families who live in poverty or hold a low socio-economic position are often less able to access welfare institutions and specialised educational programmes (Duncan & Brooks-Gunn, 2000; Hatton & Emerson, 2009; Strickler, 2001). Children with intellectual disabilities are often in need of specialised education, and early treatment because of occurring psychopathology (i.e. conduct disorders). Thus, a lack of financial means can result in disadvantageous development through adolescence into adulthood.

In general, aggressive behaviour is likely to have social consequences, either positive or negative. For example, Matson and Kozlowski (2012) point out three maintaining contingencies of aggressive behaviour in ID offenders: attention, escape and tangibles. Because of their cognitive impairments, individuals with intellectual disabilities are often unable to ask for attention in a verbal manner. Therefore, aggression is often exhibited to gain attention or ask for help. Although this behaviour typically elicits negative attention, the attention reinforces the behaviour all the same (Didden, 2007; Matson & Kozlowski, 2012). Alternatively, aggressive behaviour may be engaged in an attempt to (temporarily) avoid or escape undesirable social demands, situations or people. In other instances, aggression is used to obtain tangible objects or permission to engage in certain activities (Embregts et al., 2009; Matson & Kozlowski, 2012). Aggressive behaviour may lead to the possession of these objects or permission to engage in activities, which, in turn, reinforces the behaviour. Thus aggressive behaviour in ID offenders is typically maintained by social functions

284   *Marije Keulen-De Vos and Karin Frijters*

rather than by non-social functions (i.e. physical discomfort) (Embregts et al., 2009; Matson & Mayville, 2001; Rojahn et al., 2012). A third environmental factor is social support. Social support has a positive influence on someone health and well-being. It enhances the feeling of belonging, sense of security and experience of affection. In that sense, social support can serve as a buffer against stressful situations or live events, whereas the (perceived) lack of supportive social network is a risk factor for violence (Douglas & Skeem, 2005; McCarthy, Tarrier, & Gregg, 2002; Ozbay et al., 2007; Rihmer, Belsö, & Kiss, 2002). Many individuals with intellectual disabilities have impoverished personal relationships. They do not only have relatively few social relationships, they also have relatively little social contact at all (Hauser, Olson, & Drogin, 2014; McVilly, Stancliffe, Parmenter, & Burton-Smith, 2006). Moreover, people with IDs have very few relationships with people who do not have IDs themselves (Robertson et al., 2001).

Treatment

Treatment in ID offenders is focused on accepting and compensating impairments, and stimulating or increasing competencies. It typically consists of therapeutic approaches or interventions that are also used in non-ID offenders, while certain interventions have been specifically adapted for ID offenders. On a *biological level*, pharmacological management is the treatment of choice. There are two groups of medication that are commonly used: (1) psychotropic medication that acts on the central nervous system to reduce aggression and stabilise mood changes, and (2) hormonal or anti-libidinal medication (i.e. medroxy-progesterone acetate) to decrease the level of testosterone so as to decrease sexual arousal in sex offenders. The first group of medications usually includes antipsychotic (i.e. risperidone, haloperidol) and antidepressant drugs (i.e. sertraline, fluoxetine) (Benson & Brooks, 2008; Bhaumik et al., 2009; Lambrick & Glaser, 2004; Lindsay, 2002; McGillivray & McCabe, 2004; Oliver-Africano, Murphy, & Tyrer, 2009). The use of medications has increased dramatically over the past few decades, although the empirical evidence is best described as minimal. For example, a randomised clinical trial by Tyrer and colleagues (2008) showed that 86 patients who were randomly assigned to risperidone, haloperidol or a placebo responded equally on measures of aggression. Some studies state that there is some evidence that psychotropic medications are effective in managing behavioural problems in adults with IDs (Deb, Sohanpal, Soni, Lenôtre, & Unwin, 2007; Deb et al., 2008), whereas other studies go a step further by stating that there is no evidence whatsoever that these medications are effective.

For example, a systematic review by Brylewski and Duggan (2007) concluded that there is, in fact, no evidence whether antipsychotic medication helps or harms aggressive individuals with IDs. Matson and Neal (2009) state in their review that 'the adoption of psychotropic drugs to treat challenging behaviour [in individuals with IDs] is at present a risky notion' (p. 582), because the

Aggressive behaviour in offenders with intellectual disabilities   285

evidence for its use is largely based on anecdotal evidence, (non-controlled) case studies or studies that are methodologically constraint (e.g. Simon, Blubaugh, & Pippidis, 1996; Samuel, Attard, & Kyriakopoulos, 2013). Randomised clinical trials are often considered the Holy Grail in conducting research; however, these methods may not always be feasible from a logistical or ethical point of view. Overall, the empirical evidence shows that the use of pharmacological as a routine or standalone treatment is debatable. Its use, however, might facilitate psychologically based treatment.

There is a multitude of available *psychologically based* treatments for aggressive individuals with an intellectual disability. On a *cognitive and behavioural level*, treatments vary from cognitive behavioural treatment (CBT; Beck et al., 1990) to anger management approaches, skills training and educational treatment. The central characteristic of cognitive treatment is the focus on cognitive restructuring; the modification of a patient's ways of thinking to change behaviour. The premise of behavioural treatment is to improve competencies and skills while decreasing undesirable behaviour. Anger management programmes for ID offenders are often based on the aggression model by Novaco (1977) which stated that aggression consists of a physical, cognitive and behavioural component. Therefore, these CBT-derived treatments usually employ reduction of biological arousal, cognitive restructuring or reappraisal and behavioural skills training (Jones, 2007; Lindsay, 2007; Rose, West, & Clifford, 2000). Skills training, sometimes referred to as positive programming, is used in both sex and non-sex offenders with an intellectual disability. Common components of skills trainings are social skills, problem-solving skills, assertiveness training, communication skills, education about anger and other emotions, and education about sex (e.g. Craig et al., 2006; Whitaker, 2001). Anger management programmes are delivered either in a group or individual format. There is evidence that CBT and anger management programmes, or components of the treatment, are effective in individuals with intellectual disabilities (Barron, Hassiotis, & Banes, 2002; Burns et al., 2003; Lindsay, Allan, MacLeod, Smart, & Smith, 2003; Lindsay & Smith, 1998; Nicoll, Beail, & Saxon, 2013; Rose et al., 2000; Rose, Jenkins, O'Conner, Jones, & Felce, 2002; Taylor et al., 2004). However, little research has been conducted in offenders with IDs. In a study by Taylor and colleagues (2005), a CBT-derived anger management programme was effective in reducing anger in 40 offenders with IDs and a long history of aggressive and violent behaviour. The treatment consisted of 18 sessions that were administered in an individual format. Patients reported lower levels of aggression after completion of the treatment (Taylor et al., 2005). Social skills training have often been advocated as a suitable treatment for offending behaviour in individuals with IDs. However, the effectiveness of these trainings is hardly explored in offender samples. For example, the study by Travis and Sturmey (2013) is one of the few that has been conducted. Offenders who participated in a behavioural skills training showed a decline in aggressive responses and an increase in social desirable behaviour (Travis & Sturmey, 2013). However, only three offenders with an ID participated in this study. Therefore, no conclusions can be drawn from it. A two-year Dutch, CBT-derived programme for aggressive ID offenders ('Grip on Aggression' [GoA]; Didden, Niehoff, Valenkamp, & Rutten, 2013) has recently been formally approved by the Dutch Ministry of Safety and Justice's accreditation commission. The programme consists of seven modules. The first three are educational and consist of interventions such as education about aggression, enhancing motivation for treatment and recognising arousal. In modules 4–7, the individual is encouraged to apply new insights and skills (Didden et al., 2013). Research has shown that GoA is effective in reducing aggressive behaviour and increasing insight in ID offenders (Drieschner, Niehoff, Didden, Rutten, & Valenkamp, 2012).

Few treatments tap into the *emotional origins* of aggression in individuals with an ID. Sometimes non-verbal or arts therapies, such as such as drama, art, music, dance and movement therapies, and psychomotor therapy, are used to treat the emotional component or origins of aggression (Reiss, Quayle, Brett, & Meux, 1998; Smeijsters & Cleven, 2006). Non-verbal therapies may be effective in evoking and reprocessing patients' emotions because these therapies are particularly suitable for patients who have difficulty in accessing and expressing their emotions verbally – difficulties that are prevalent in ID offenders. Individuals with IDs typically have difficulty in this area. In general, there is increasing evidence that emotions are important in certain forms of cognitive processing or that cognitions are processed unconsciously (e.g. David, Miclea, & Opre, 2003; David & Szentagotai, 2006; Greenwald, 1992). Therefore, non-verbal therapies may facilitate cognitive treatment. There are very few studies about non-verbal therapies in intellectually disordered offenders (e.g. Pim Hoek, personal communication, 27 February 2014; Hooper, Wigram, Carson, & Lindsay, 2011; Royal College of Psychiatrists, 2003; Soltani, Roslan, Abdullah, Jan, 2011), therefore little can be concluded from them with regard to its effectiveness.

Another type of treatment that tapes into emotional or mental states is Mentalisation-Based Treatment (MBT). MBT is a form of psychodynamic psychotherapy that focuses on mental states such as needs, feelings and beliefs that influence behaviour (Bateman & Fonagy, 2006). The foundation of MBT is mentalisation, which can be defined as the ability to perceive and interpret your own behaviour and that of others as meaningful and intentional, based on a person's own mental states. In other words, it is the ability to recognise your own and others' mental states. The overall goals of MBT are better behaviour control, increased affect regulation, more intimate relationships and the ability to pursue life goals (Bateman & Fonagy, 2006; Fonagy, 1991). MBT has originally been developed for borderline (non-forensic) PD patients, but it is also sometimes applied in individuals with intellectual disabilities because they also have difficulty with mentalisation or empathising with others and social situations (Neijmeijer, Moerdijk, Veneberg, & Muuse, 2009). However, no scientific research on the effectiveness of MBT in ID populations has been conducted yet.

Aggressive behaviour in offenders with intellectual disabilities 287

A third treatment approach that may be effective in ID offenders is Schema Therapy ([ST]; Young, Klosko, & Weishaar, 2003). The pillars of ST are early maladaptive schemas, dysfunctional coping styles and schema modes or fluctuating emotional states that temporarily dominate a person's thinking, feeling and behaviour. See Keulen-de Vos, Bernstein and Arntz (2013) for a detailed description of these concepts and therapeutic techniques in forensic patients. These concepts are believed to originate from adverse childhood experiences and early temperament. ST is strongly influenced by the attachment theories of Ainsworth et al. (1978) and Bowlby (1973). ST's basic therapeutic style is known as limited reparenting, which means that the therapist provides warmth, empathy, recognition and validation of emotions, or empathic confrontation and limit setting. Individuals with an ID have often lacked the experience of these interpersonal features. Although ST is adapted for forensic patients (Bernstein, Arntz, & de Vos, 2007; Keulen-de Vos et al., 2013), it has not been applied to intellectually disabled offenders yet. A group of Dutch scholars and clinicians are now in the process of adapting forensic ST to offenders with intellectual disabilities (Keulen-de Vos, personal communication, 13 May 2013).

On a *social level*, individuals with an ID who are prone to aggressive behaviour are often removed from situations that provoke this behaviour. This strategy can be considered a reactive strategy, because it is focused on managing challenging behaviour when it occurs instead on reducing this behaviour (Whitaker, 2001). Nevertheless, removing a patient from particular situations can be effective because it may prevent other people getting hurt. Another intervention that taps into the social origins of aggressive behaviour in individuals with an intellectual disability is contingency management or operant conditioning (Catania, 2013; Lloyd & Kennedy, 2014). The primary aim of contingency management is that the patient learns to link certain situations or behaviours to their favourable or unfavourable consequences (Catania & Harnad, 1988; Vollmer & Hackenberg, 2001). In other words, aggressive behaviour is punished whereas appropriate behaviour is reinforced. The use of contingency management may be salient for offenders where staff have considerable control over the institutional environment, enabling them to deliver reinforcements selectively. Research has shown that skilful use of contingency management results in reductions in violent or aggressive behaviour in ID offenders (Carr, Severtson, & Lepper, 2009; Chowdury & Benson, 2011; Kurtz, Boelter, Jarmolowicz, Chin, & Hagopian, 2011; Lloyd & Kennedy, 2014). A critical note, however, is that it is unlikely that an operant approach will continue to yield reductions of aggression when these patients leave a forensic setting, and the ability to contingently manage their behaviour is lost. Also, as previously mentioned, negative attention may still reinforce the undesired behaviour. A third social intervention that is used in individuals with an ID is 'curricular revisions'. This technique is employed to change the perceived social undesirableness of social demands (Dunlap, Kern-Dunlap, Clarke, & Robbins, 1991). If patients' tasks or demands are adjusted or redefined,

288   *Marije Keulen-De Vos and Karin Frijters*

social demands are no longer perceived as undesirable or aversive and aggressive behaviour is likely to extinct. Research has shown that this intervention is effective in individuals with an ID (e.g. Lloyd & Kennedy, 2014; Shogren, Faggella-Luby, Bae, & Wehmeyer, 2004).

Therapy usually consists of different components, thus interventions tap into both biological and/or psychological functioning, as well as into environmental factors or the social context. In addition to the aforementioned biologically, psychologically and socially based treatments, different *therapeutic models* are commonly used. Forensic treatment for intellectually disabled offenders who display aggressive behaviour is often based on one of the following models: the risk-need-responsivity (RNR) model (Andrews & Bonta, 2006), the 'good lives' model (GLM) (Ward, Mann, & Gannon, 2007); the old me/new me model (Haaven, 2000, 2006), and/or the 'social competency model' (SCM; Slot & Spanjaard, 1999; Bartels, 2001). The RNR model consists of three principles: risk, need and responsivity. The risk principle states that patients who are at high risk should receive a higher intensity of health services than patients who are at low risk. The need principle assumes that treatment should be targeted at needs that are related to criminal behaviour, so-called criminogenic needs. The responsivity principle states that the treatment must be responsive to the patient's characteristics and personal circumstances (Andrews & Bonta, 2006; Andrews et al., 1990). Numerous studies have been carried out to examine the usefulness of the RNR model in various types of offenders, including offenders with an intellectual disability (e.g. Frize, Kenny, & Lennings, 2008; Hocken, Winder, & Grayson, 2013; Lindsay et al., 2013b). According to this model, to determine the adequate level of mental health service, an offender's criminogenic needs ought to be assessed. However, treatment should also focus on general needs and strengths, such as physical health, quality of life, social and cultural factors, personal abilities and interests, because they add to a patient's risk for violence (Bonta & Andrews, 2007; Serin, Lloyd, Helmus, Derkzen, & Luong, 2013). A model that focuses on these needs and strengths is the GLM (Ward et al., 2006). The GLM focuses on promoting an offender's well-being and abilities. A patient is taught to focus on his primary needs, and how he can lead a 'good life' with regard to living, working, social relationships and leisure activities. The GLM is a general rehabilitation theory, developed to suit all types of offenders (including ID offenders), but in practice it is mainly used in sexual (ID) offenders (Aust, 2010; Hoitzing et al., 2010; Whitehead, Ward, & Collie, 2007). Working with individuals with an intellectual disability calls for the use of simplified and, if possible, visualised concepts. A theoretical model that taps into these requirements is the 'old me/new me' model by Haaven (2000, 2006). In this strengths-based model, the 'old me' refers to those features that lead up to and culminate in the commission of violent behaviour. The 'new me' refers to the new characteristics and new behaviours to live a life without violent and criminal behaviour. By formulating the 'new me', a patient is urged to take control over his own life and to make appropriate choices accordingly. In essence, this model focuses on rehabilitation. A pictorial model is used to visually present these concepts to an individual with an ID; for example, smileys, arrows and stop-signs are used to indicate the direction of outcome (Haaven, 2006; Lambrick & Glaser, 2004). We recommend the literature by Haaven (2006) for a detailed description of the old me/new me model. The SCM (Slot & Spanjaard, 1999; Bartels, 2001), a model that is commonly used in the Netherlands, states that there needs to be a balance between an individual's tasks and skills for an individual to be competent to deal with the challenges of everyday life. In individuals with an ID, the tasks that need to be carried out are substantially hampered by the individual's intellectual impairment, lack of protective factors and environmental stressors. According to this model, aggressive behaviour can be prevented or reduced if the individual's skills and protective factors are enhanced or if tasks are alleviated (Slot & Spanjaard, 1999; Bartels, 2001).

Case example

Background – John is a 20-year-old intellectually disabled man with an index offence of arson, which he committed while under the influence of alcohol. He has been admitted to a forensic psychiatric hospital for ID offenders. John grew up in an unsafe environment in which he was emotionally neglected. For example, he experienced many unpleasant and unsafe situations with his father. His father drank a lot which caused him to be violent and unpredictable. His mother did not dare to go against him. Consequently, John became very anxious. He tried to control his fear by exercising extreme control (powerlessness versus power). John suppresses his problems; he is unable to talk about it. Because of the insecure environment during his childhood and the humiliations by his father, John has become very suspicious and vigilant. He suffers from a sense of inferiority and low self-esteem. Letting go of control, showing emotions and making mistakes are associated with danger and being punished. John wants to be normal and tries everything to fit in. As a result, he is strongly influenced by his environment; he hangs out with the wrong kind of friends, and starts drinking a lot of alcohol. He can defend himself well, but he is constantly trying to fit in. He tries to impress others, and because of his mistrust, he's easily aggrieved. Typically, when he drinks, he loses control and his behaviour becomes inappropriate and impulsive. Because of his intellectual disability, he is unable to understand situations and grasp the consequences of his actions. In short, John is a vulnerable, gullible young man with a low sense of self who is easily wounded. He is very afraid of losing control; however, under the influence of alcohol that's exactly what happens. Prior to the arson, he drank a lot and did not get enough attention from a girl (who, instead, spent much attention on someone else). He became jealous, walked away and set a fire out of anger.

Treatment – On a biological level, pharmacological management was used to manage his ADHD symptoms. Because of this, John is more at ease and better able to let things sink in. In terms of psychological treatment, John

290   *Marije Keulen-De Vos and Karin Frijters*

was offered a CBT group for arsonists, addiction treatment and individual Eye Movement Desensitisation and Reprocessing (EMDR; Shapiro, 2001) and Psychomotor Therapy (PMT). The CBT group programme focused on the crime scenario analyses, gaining insight in risk factors and enhancing coping skills. The crime analyses were conducted with the BAREPTI format that focuses on what happened in the events leading up to the crime, during and after the crime with regard to behaviour (B), attitudes (A), relations, (R), emotions (E), physical state (P), thoughts (T) and interests (I). Subsequently, high-risk events, feelings and thoughts are identified, and a relapse prevention plan is set up. Additionally, John learned new, alternative coping skills (instead of arson) with regard to communication, emotions (i.e. anger) and assertiveness. In general, CBT focused on John's mistrust and controlling thoughts, for example through the use of the Socratic dialogue. Addiction treatment consisted of psycho-education and skills training that targeted craving for alcohol and the ability to say no to alcohol. The EMDR treatment focused on the traumatic events with his father, for example a situation where his drunken father threatened his mother, sister and himself. In PMT, John practised alternative strategies to feel safe and to have control. He learned to deal with loss of control and discovered that it's not a bad thing to lose control. John learned that he can feel safe and secure, unlike in the past. PMT also focused on building self-confidence (i.e. getting stronger) and learning to relax. This treatment was used as an experiential treatment. On a social level, John was offered a safe environment on the unit where staff members are reliable, predictable and congruent. In addition, he had daily meetings with the staff to prevent problems adding up and to learn how to disclose. Talking about problems and other desirable behaviour was systematically reinforced, whereas negative behaviour (i.e. sulking, being crabby) was ignored and aggression led to a time-out (i.e. principles of operant conditioning).

Treatment effects – John has learned to express his anger in a more socially accepted way. He knows that keeping problems to himself and the use of alcohol are important risk factors for him. As a result, he thinks and acts differently now. He has processed the traumatic life events with his father and is not afraid of him anymore. Furthermore, the relationship between father and son has been restored. John's self-image is positive; also his feelings of inferiority, mistrust and fear have diminished. He is more resilient, less gullible and less prickly. In short, the treatment has been successful. John has been transferred to an assisted-living community project. He has his own home, but also has a community support system. His prospects are much improved.

Concluding remarks

In intellectually disabled offenders, no single determinant for aggressive or high-challenging behaviour can be identified, nor do we know for certain whether the aforementioned factors are indeed of importance. Perhaps it is the *interplay* between multiple factors, such as biological, psychological and environmental features, that plays a key role in the development or maintenance of violent behaviour in these individuals. However, it may also be that we just don't know why these individuals are prone to violence. When reviewing the aforementioned aetiological factors in aggressive behaviour in ID offenders, one can conclude that the aetiology of this behaviour is not markedly different in non-ID offenders. Is there a difference in violence between individuals with IDs and non-disabled individuals? Maybe we are all, more or less, the same when it comes to violent behaviour; perhaps it is solely the low level of cognitive abilities that sets the non-disabled apart from the disabled. Although the body of literature on challenging or aggressive behaviour in individuals with an ID has increased over the years, there is still a gap between what we know and what we need to know. Given the high prevalence of aggression in individuals with an ID, the aetiology, assessment of needs and treatment of these offenders are areas in need of far greater attention. For example, there is a large body of research on treatment of individuals with IDs who have a history of aggressive behaviour. Although there may be similarities between these individuals and *offenders*, there is very little research to draw conclusions on this matter. Also, more research is needed to examine the effectiveness of treatment approaches; that is, the way that we deal with our patients. Perhaps we don't have to develop brand new treatments or adapt existing treatments in terms of *techniques*. Perhaps we should adjust our programmes in the way that we *approach* these individuals. For example, individuals with an intellectual disability are more likely to benefit from treatment if the content is presented visually, in short chunks and over a much longer period of time (Clare & Mosher, 2005). However, at this point, it is premature to make definite recommendations with regard to which treatment (approach) is most effective for ID offenders. Also, the fact that a treatment is effective does not necessarily mean that we understand the cause(s) of the behaviour. In general, treatment should always be based on a conceptual, theoretical framework. In other words, the cause(s) of a behaviour should underpin treatment and have a link to the techniques applied. If we better understand the reason for aggression in individuals with an ID, we will have a better notion of what might work for these individuals, under which circumstances, when and where. As a result, the (cost) effectiveness of forensic treatment for these offenders may be improved.

Note

1 A variety of terms are used in the literature to cover the group of patients that have IQs lower than 70 (i.e. 'intellectual disability', 'developmental disability', 'mental retardation'). In this chapter, we use the term intellectual disability (ID) because this term is used by the DSM-5.

Literature

Ainsworth, M. D. S., Blehar, M. C., Waters, E., & Wall, S. (1978). *Patterns of attachment: A psychological study of the strange situation*. Hillsdale, NJ: Lawrence Erlbaum.

Ali, A., Hassiotis, A., Strydom, A., King, M. (2012). Self stigma in people with intellectual disabilities and courtesy stigma in family carers: A systematic review.

292   *Marije Keulen-De Vos and Karin Frijters*

Research in Developmental Disabilities, 33, 2122–2140. http://dx.doi.org/10.1016/j.ridd.2012.06.013

American Psychiatric Association (2013). *Desk reference to the diagnostic criteria from DSM-5.* Washington, DC: APA.

Andrews, D. A., & Bonta, J.L. (2006). *The psychology of criminal conduct,* 4th edition. Cincinnati, OH: Anderson.

Andrews, D. A., Zinger, I., Hoge, R. D., Bonta, J., Gendreau, P., & Cullen, F. T. (1990). Does correctional treatment work? A clinically relevant and psychologically informed meta-analysis. *Criminology, 28*(3), 369–404. doi: 10.1111/j.1745-9125.1990.tb01330.x

Asscher, J. J., van der Put, C. E., & Stams, G. J. J. M. (2012). Differences between juvenile offenders with and without intellectual disability in offense type and risk factors. *Research in Developmental Disabilities, 33*, 1905–1913. doi: 10.1016/j.ridd.2012.05.022

Atkinson, L., Chisholm, V. C., Scott, B., Goldberg, S., Vaughn, B. E., Blackwell, J., et al. (1999). Atypical attachment in infancy and early childhood among children at developmental risk. III. Maternal sensitivity, child functional level, and attachment in Down syndrome. *Monographs of the Society for Research in Child Development, 64* (3), 45–66.

Aust, S. (2010). Is the Good Lives Model of offender treatment relevant to sex offenders with a learning disability? *Journal of Learning Disabilities and Offending Behavior, 1*(3), 33–39. doi: 10.5042/jldob.2010.0627

Bandura, A. (1973). *Aggression: A social learning analysis.* Englewood Cliffs: Prentice Hall.

Barron, P., Hassiotis, A., & Banes, J. (2002). Offenders with intellectual disability: The size of the problem and therapeutic outcomes. *Journal of Intellectual Disability Research, 46*(6), 454–463. doi: 10.1046/j.1365-2788.2002.00432.x

Bartels, A. A. J. (2001). Het sociaal-competentiemodel en de kinder en jeugdpsychotherapie: Ontstaan, betekenis, stand-van-zaken, toekomst. [The social-competency model in child psychotherapy: Origins, meaning, status and future]. *Kinder- en Jeugdpsychotherapie, 28*(2), 5–22.

Bartholomew, K. (1990). Avoidance of intimacy: An attachment perspective. *Journal of Social and Personality Relationships, 7*(2), 147–178. doi: 10.1177/0265407590072001

Basquill, M. F., Nezu, C. M., Nezu, A. M., & Klein, T. L. (2004). Aggression-related hostility bias and social problem-solving deficits in adult males with mental retardation. *American Journal of Mental Retardation, 109*(3), 255–263. doi: 10.1352/0895-8017

Bateman, A., & Fonagy, P. (2006). *Mentalization-Based Treatment for borderline personality disorder: A practical guide.* New York: Oxford University Press.

Beck, A. T., & Freeman, A. M. (1990). *Cognitive therapy for personality disorders.* New York: The Guilford Press.

Beirne-Smith, M., Patton, J. R., & Kim, S. H. (2006). *Mental retardation: An introduction to intellectual disabilities,* 7th edition. Upper Saddle River: Pearson Merrill Prentice Hall.

Benson, B. A., & Brooks, W. T. (2008). Aggressive challenging behavior and intellectual disability. *Current Opinion in Psychiatry, 21*(5), 454–458. doi: 10.1097/YCO.0b013e328306a090

Berkovits, L. D., & Baker, B. L. (2013). Emotion dysregulation and social competence: Stability, change and predictive power. *Journal of Intellectual Disability Research,* doi: 10.1111/jir.12088 [Epub ahead of print]

Bernstein, D. P., Arntz, A., & de Vos, M. E. (2007). Schema-Focused Therapy in forensic settings: Theoretical model and recommendations for best clinical practice. *International Journal of Forensic Mental Health, 6*(2), 169–183.

Bhaumik, S., Watson, J. M., Devapriam, J., Raju, L. B., Tin, N. N., Kiani, R., Talbott, L., Parker, R., Moore, L., Majumdar, S. K., Ganghadaran, S. K., Dixon, K., Das Gupta, A., Barrett, M., & Tyrer, F. (2009). Aggressive challenging behavior in adults with intellectual disability following community resettlement. *Journal of Intellectual Disability Research, 53*(3), 298–302. doi: 10.1111/j.1365-2788.2008.01111.x

Blair, J. R. J, Mitchell, D., & Blair, K. (2005). *The psychopath: Emotion and the brain.* Oxford: Blackwell Publishing Ltd.

Bogaard, K. J. H. M. van den, Embregts, P. J. C. M., Hendriks, A. H. C., & Heestermans, M. (2013). Comparison of intellectual disabled offenders with a combined history of sexual offenses and other offenses versus intellectual disabled offenders without a history of sexual offenses on dynamic client and environmental factors. *Research in Developmental Disabilities, 34*, 3226–2324. doi: 10.1016/j.ridd.2013.06.027

Bonta, J., & Andrews, D. A. (2007). *Risk-need-responsivity model for offender assessment and rehabilitation* (User Report 2006–7). Ottawa, Ontario: Public Safety Canada.

Bowlby, J. (1944). Forty-four juvenile thieves: Their characters and home-life. *International Journal of Psycho-Analysis, 25*, 19–52.

Bowlby, J. (1973). Attachment and loss: Volume 2. Separation, anxiety and anger. In J. Cassidy & P. R. Shaver (Ed.). (2008). *Handbook of attachment: Theory, research, and clinical applications.* New York: Guilford Press.

Brylewski, J., & Duggan, L. (2007). Antipsychotic medication for challenging behavior in people with intellectual disability: A systematic review of randomized controlled trials. *Cochrane Database Systematic Review, 3*, CD000377.

Burns, M., Bird, D., Leach, C., & Higgins, K. (2003). Anger management training: The effects of a structured program on the self-reported anger experience of forensic inpatients with learning disability. *Journal of Psychiatric and Mental Health Nursing, 10*(5), 569–577. doi: 10.1046/j.1365-2850.2003.00653.x

Carr, J. E., Severtson, J. M., & Lepper, T. L. (2009). Noncontingent reinforcement is an empirically supported treatment for problem behavior exhibited by individuals with developmental disabilities. *Research in Developmental Disabilities, 30*(1), 44–57. doi:10.1016/j.ridd.2008.03.002

Cassidy, J. (1994). Emotion regulation: Influences of attachment relationships. *Monographs of the Society for Research in Child Development, 59*(2–3), 228–249. doi: 10.1111/j.1540-5834.1994.tb01287.x

Catania, A. C. (2013). *Learning,* 5th edition. New York: Sloan Publishing.

Catania, A. C., & Harnad, S. (Eds.). (1988). *The selection of behavior: The operant behaviorism of B.F. Skinner: Comments and consequences.* Cambridge: Cambridge University Press.

Chapman, S. L. C., & Wu, L. T. (2012). Substance abuse among individuals with intellectual disabilities. *Research in Developmental Disabilities, 33*(4), 1147–1156. doi:10.1016/j.ridd.2012.02.009

Chevalère, J., Postal, V., Jauregui, J., Copet, P., Laurier, V., & Thuilleaux, D. (2013). Assessment of executive functions in Prader-Willi Syndrome and relationship with intellectual level. *Journal of Applied Research in Intellectual Disabilities, 26*, 309–318. doi: 10.1111/jar.12044

Chowdury, M., & Benson, B. A. (2011). Use of differential reinforcement to reduce behavior problems in adults with intellectual disabilities: A methodological review. *Research in Developmental Disabilities, 32*(2), 383–394. doi: 10.1016/j.ridd.2010.11.015

294 *Marije Keulen-De Vos and Karin Frijters*

Ciarrochi, J., & Scott, C. (2006). The link between emotional competence and well-being: A longitudinal study. *British Journal of Guidance & Counselling, 34*(2), 231–243. doi: 10.1080/03069880600583287

Clare, I., & Mosher, S. (2005). Working with people with aggressive behavior. In T. Riding, C. Swann, & B. Swan (Eds.), *The handbook of forensic learning disabilities* (pp. 73–95). Oxford: Radcliffe Medical Press, Ltd.

Clegg, J. A., & Sheard, C. (2002). Challenging behavior and insecure attachment. *Journal of Intellectual Disability Research, 46*(6), 503–506. doi: 10.1046/j.1365-2788.2002.00420.x

Copper, A., Smiley, E., Morrison, J., Williamson, A., & Allan, L. (2007). Mental ill-health in adults with intellectual disabilities: Prevalence and associated factors. *The British Journal of Psychiatry, 190*, 27–35. doi: 10.1192/bjp.bp.106.022483

Craig, L. A., Stringer, I., & Moss, T. (2006). Treating sexual offenders with learning disabilities in the community: A critical review. *International Journal of Offender Therapy and Comparative Criminology, 50*(4), 369–390. doi: 10.1177/0306624X05283529

Craissati, J. (2009). Attachment problems and sex offending. In A. R. Beech, L. A. Craig, & K. D. Browne (Eds.), *Handbook of assessment and treatment of sexual offenders* (pp. 13–38). Chichester, UK: Wiley.

Darrow, S. M., Follette, W. C., Maragakis, A., & Dykstra, T. (2011). Reviewing risk for individuals with developmental disabilities. *Clinical Psychological Review, 31*, 472–477. doi:10.1016/j.cpr.2010.11.008

David, D., Miclea, M., & Opre, A. (2003). The information processing approach to the human mind: Basic and beyond. *Journal of Clinical Psychology, 60*(4), 353–369. doi: 10.1002/jclp.10250

David, D., & Szentagotai, A. (2006). Cognitions in cognitive-behavioral psychotherapies: Toward an integrative model. *Clinical Psychology Review, 26*(3), 284–298. doi: 10.1016/j.cpr.2005.09.003

Day, K. (1994). Male mentally handicapped sex offenders. *British Journal of Psychiatry, 165*, 630–639. doi:10.1192/bjp.165.5.630

Deb, S., Chaplin, R., Sohanpal, S., Unwin, G., Soni, R., & Lenôtre, L. (2008). The effectiveness of mood stabilizers and antiepileptic medication for the management of behavior problems in adults with intellectual disability: A systematic review. *Journal of Intellectual Disability Research, 52*(2), 107–113. doi: 10.1111/j.1365-2788.2007.00965.x

Deb, S., Matthews, T., Holt, G., & Bouras, N. (2001). *Practical guidelines for the assessment and diagnoses of mental health problems in adults with intellectual disability.* Brighton: Pavilion.

Deb, S., Thomas, M., & Bright, C. (2001a). Mental disorders in adults with intellectual disability: Part I: Prevalence of functional psychiatric illness among a community-based population aged 16 and 64 years. *Journal of Intellectual Disability Research, 45*(6), 495–505. doi: 10.1046/j.1365-2788.2001.00374.

Deb, S., Thomas, M., & Bright, C. (2001b). Mental disorders in adults with intellectual disability: Part II: The rate of behavior disorders among a community-based population aged 16 and 64 years. *Journal of Intellectual Disability Research, 45*(6), 506–514. doi: 10.1046/j.1365-2788.2001.00373.x

Deb, S., Sohanpal, S. K., Soni, R., Lenôtre, L., & Unwin, G. (2007). The effectiveness of antipsychotic medication in the management of behavioral problems in adults with intellectual disabilities. *Journal of Intellectual Disability Research, 51*, 766–777. doi: 10.1111/j.1365-2788.2007.00950.x

Dias, S., Ware, R. S., Kinner, S. A., & Lennox, N. G. (2013). Co-occurring mental disorder and intellectual disability in a large sample of Australian prisoners. *The Australian and New Zealand Journal of Psychiatry, 47*(10), 938–944. doi: 10.1177/0004867413492220.

Didden, R. (2007). Functional analysis methodology in developmental disabilities. In: P. Sturmey (Ed.), *Functional analysis in clinical treatment* (pp. 65–86). Burlington: Academic Press.

Didden, R., Niehoff, H., Valenkamp, M., & Rutten, E. (2013). *Theoriehandleiding Grip of Agressie (GoA): Behandelprogramma voor mensen met een lichte verstandelijke beperking en ernstig agressief (delict)gedrag*. [Theoretical manual Grip on Aggression: A treatment program for individuals with mild intellectual disabilities and aggressive (criminal) behavior. Zwolle & Woerden, the Netherlands: Trajectum & Van Montfoort.

Dolan, M., Anderson, I. M., & Deakin, J. F. W. (2001). Relationship between 5-HT function and impulsivity and aggression in male offenders with personality disorders. *British Journal of Psychiatry, 178*, 352–359. doi: 10.1192/bjp.178.4.352

Dosen, A. (1993). Mental health and mental illness in persons with mental retardation: What are we talking about? In R. J. Fletcher & A. Dosen (Eds.), *Mental health aspects of mental retardation: Progress in assessment and treatment*, (pp. 23–39). New York: Lexington Books.

Douglas, K. S., & Skeem, J. L. (2005). Violence risk assessment: Getting specific about being dynamic. *Psychology, Public Policy, and Law, 11*(3), 347–383. doi: 10.1037/1076-8971.11.3.347

Dozier, M., Stovall, K. C., & Albus, K. (1999). Attachment and psychopathology in adulthood. In: J. Cassidy & P. R. Shaver (Eds.), *Handbook of attachment theory and research* (pp. 497–519). New York: Guilford Press.

Drieschner, K., Niehoff, H., Didden, R., Rutten, E., & Valenkamp, M. (2012). *Beoordelings- en evaluatiehandleiding Grip op Agressie (GoA): Behandelprogramma voor mensen met een lichte verstandelijke beperking en ernstig agressief (delict)gedrag*. [Evaluation manual Grip on Aggression: A treatment program for individuals with mild intellectual disabilities and aggressive (criminal) behavior. Zwolle & Woerden, the Netherlands: Trajectum & Van Montfoort.

Duncan, G. J., & Brooks-Gunn, J. (2000). Family poverty, welfare reform, and child development. *Child Development, 71*(1), 188–196. doi: 10.1111/1467-8624.00133

Dunlap, G., Kern-Dunlap, L., Clarke, S., & Robbins, F.R. (1991). Functional assessment curricular revision, and severe behavior problems. *Journal of Applied Behavior Analysis, 24*(2), 387–397. doi: 10.1901/jaba.1991.24-387

Embregts, P., van den Bogaard, K., Hendriks, L., Heestermans, M., Schuitemaker, M., & van Wouwe, H. (2010). Sexual risk assessment for people with intellectual disabilities. *Research in Developmental Disabilities, 31*, 760–767. doi:10.1016/j.ridd.2010.01.018

Embregts, P., Didden, R., Schreuder, N., Huitink, C., & van Nieuwenhuijzen, M. (2009). Aggressive behavior in individuals with moderate to borderline intellectual disabilities who live in residential facility: An evaluation of functional variables. *Research in Developmental Disabilities, 30*, 682–688. doi:10.1016/j.ridd.2008.04.007

Farrington, D. P. (1995). The development of offending and antisocial behavior from childhood: Key findings from the Cambridge study in delinquent development.

296 *Marije Keulen-De Vos and Karin Frijters*

Journal of Child Psychology and Psychiatry, 36(6), 929–964. doi: 10.1111/j.1469-7610.1995.tb01342.x

Finzi, R., Ram, A., Har-Even, D., Shnitt, D., & Weizman, A. (2001). Attachment styles and aggression in physically abused and neglected children. *Journal of Youth and Adolescence, 30*, 769–786.

Fonagy, P. (1991). Thinking About thinking: Some clinical and theoretical considerations in the treatment of a borderline patient. *International Journal of Psychoanalyses, 72*(4), 639–656.

Friedman, N. P., & Miyake, A. (2004). The relations among inhibition and interference control functions: A latent variable analysis. *Journal of Experimental Psychology: General, 133*(1), 101–135. doi: 10.1037/0096-3445.133.1.101

Frize, M., Kenny, D., & Lennings, C. (2008). The relationship between intellectual disability, indigenous status and risk of reoffending in juvenile offenders on community orders. *Journal of Intellectual Disability Research, 52*(6), 510–519. doi: 10.1111/j.1365-2788.2008.01058.x.

Gibbs, J. C., Basinger, K. S., & Fuller, D. (1992). *Moral maturity: Measuring the development of sociomoral reflection.* Hillsdale, NJ: Erlbaum.

Gibbs, J. C., Basinger, K. S., Grime, R. L., & Snarey, J. R. (2007). Moral judgment development across cultures: Revising Kohlbergs's universality claims. *Developmental Review, 27*, 443–500. doi:10.1016/j.dr.2007.04.001

Glaser, W., & Florio, D. (2004). Beyond specialist programmes: A study of the needs of offenders with intellectual disabilities requiring psychiatric attention. *Journal of Intellectual Disability Research, 48*(6), 591–602. doi: 10.1111/j.1365-2788.2004.00628.x

Gleaser W., & Deane K. (1999). Normalisation in an abnormal world: A study of prisoners with intellectual disability. *International Journal of Offender Therapy and Comparative Criminology, 43*(3), 388–356. doi: 10.1177/0306624X99433007

Goodwin, E. J., Gudjohnsson, G. H., Morris, R., Perkins, D., & Young, S. (2012). The relationship between sociomoral reasoning and intelligence in mentally disordered offenders. *Personality and Individual Differences, 53*, 974–979. doi: 10.1016/j.paid.2012.07.01

Green, S., & Baker, B. (2011). Parents' emotion expression as a predictor of child's social competence: Children with or without intellectual disability. *Journal of Intellectual Disability Research, 55*(3), 324–338. doi: 10.1111/j.1365-2788.2010.01363.x

Greenwald, A. G. (1992). Unconscious cognition reclaimed. *American Psychologist, 47*(6), 766–779. doi: 10.1037/0003-066X.47.6.766

Griffiths, D., Hingsburger, D., Hoath, J., & Ioannou, S. (2013). 'Counterfeit deviance' revisited. *Journal of Applied Research in Intellectual Disabilities, 26*(5), 471–480. doi: 10.1111/jar.12034.

Haaven, J. L. (2006). The evolution of the old me/new me model. In G. D. Blasingame, (Ed.), *Practical treatment strategies for person with intellectual disabilities: Working with forensic clients with severe and sexual behavior problems.* Brandon: Safer Society Press.

Haaven, J. L., & Coleman, E. M. (2000). Treatment of the developmentally disabled sex offender. In D. R. Laws, S. M. Hudson, & T. Ward (Eds.), *Remaking relapse prevention with sex offenders: A sourcebook* (pp. 167–186). Thousand Oaks, CA: Sage.

Hatton, C., & Emerson, E. (2009). Poverty and the mental health of families with a child with intellectual disabilities. *Psychiatry, 8*(11), 433–437.

Hauser, M. J., Olson, E., & Drogin, E. Y. (2014). Psychiatric disorders in people with intellectual disability (intellectual developmental disorder): Forensic aspects. *Current Opinion in Psychiatry*. doi: 10.1097/YCO.0000000000000036. [Epub ahead of print].

Hayes, S. C. (2012). People with intellectual and developmental disabilities in the criminal justice system. In J.K. Luiselli (Ed.), *The handbook of high-risk challenging behaviors in people with intellectual and developmental disabilities* (pp. 211–228). Baltimore: Paul H. Brookes Publishing Co.

Haynes, A., Gillmore, L., Shochet, I., Campbell, M., & Roberts, C. (2013). Factor analyses of the self-report version of the strengths and difficulties questionnaire in a sample of children with intellectual disabilities. *Research in Developmental Disabilities, 34*, 847–854. doi: 10.1016/j.ridd.2012.11.008

Hingsburger, D., Griffiths, D., & Quinsey, V. (1991). Detecting counterfeit deviance: Differentiating sexual deviance from sexual inappropriateness. *Habilitative Mental Healthcare Newsletter, 10*(9), 51–54.

Hirschi, T., & Hindelang, M. J. (1977). Intelligence and delinquency: A revisionist view. *American Sociological Review, 42*, 571–587.

Hocken, K., Winder, B., & Grayson, A. (2013). Putting responsivity into risk assessment: The use of the Structured Assessment of Risk and Need (SARN) with sexual offenders who have an intellectual disability. *Journal of Intellectual Disabilities and Offending Behavior, 4*(3/4), 77–89. doi: 10.1108/JIDOB-05-2013-0009

Hogue, T., Steptoe, L., Taylor, J. L., Lindsay, W. R., Mooney, P., Pinkney, L., Johnston, S., Smith, A. H. W., & O'Brien, G. (2006). A comparison of offenders with intellectual disability across three levels of security. *Criminal Behavior and Mental Health, 16*, 13–28. doi: 10.1002/cbm.52

Hoitzing, B., van Lankveld, J., Kok, G., & Curfs, L. (2010). Behandelprogramma's voor plegers van seksueel grensoverschrijdend gedrag met een licht verstandelijke beperking in Nederland. [Treatment programs for Dutch sex offenders with mild intellectual disabilities]. *Tijdschrif voor Seksuologie, 34*, 19–32.

Holland, A. J. (2004). Criminal behavior and developmental disability: An epidemiological perspective. In: W. R. Lindsay, J. L. Taylor, & P. Sturmey (Eds.), *Offenders with developmental disabilities,* (pp. 23–34). Chichester, UK: Wiley & Sons.

Hooper, J., Wigram, T., Carson, D., & Lindsay, B. (2011). The practical implication of comparing how adults with and with intellectual disability respond to music. *British Journal of Learning Disabilities, 39*, 22–28. doi: 10.1111/j.1468-3156. 2010.00611.x

Jahoda, A., Pert, C., & Trower, P. (2006a). Frequent aggression and attribution of hostile intent in people with mild to moderate intellectual disabilities: An empirical investigation. *American Journal on Mental Retardation, 111*(2), 90–99. doi: 10.1352/ 0895-8017(2006)111[90:FAAAOH]2.0.CO;2

Jahoda, A., Pert, C., & Trower, P. (2006b). Socioemotional understanding and frequent aggression in people with mild to moderate intellectual disabilities. *American Journal on Mental Retardation, 111*(2), 77–89. doi: 10.1352/0895-8017(2006)111[77:SUAF AI]2.0.CO;2

Janssen, C. G. C., Schuengel, C., & Stolk, J. (2002). Understanding challenging behavior in people with severe and profound intellectual disability: A stress-attachment model. *Journal of Intellectual Disability Research, 46*(6), 445–453. doi: 10.1046/j.1365-2788.2002.00430.x

Johnson, P. (2012). The prevalence of low self-esteem in an intellectually disabled forensic population. *Journal of Intellectual Disability Research, 56*(3), 317–325. doi: 10.1111/j.1365-2788.2011.01447.x

Jones, L. (2004). Offence paralleling behavior (OPB) as a framework for assessment and intervention with offenders. In A. Needs & G. Towels (Eds.). *Applying psychology to forensic practice* (pp. 34–63). Malden, MA: Blackwell.

Jones, J. (2007). Persons with intellectual disabilities in the criminal justice system: Review of issues. *International Journal of Offender Therapy and Comparative Criminology, 51*(6), 723–733. doi: 10.1177/0306624X07299343

Keeling, J. A., & Rose, J. L. (2005). Relapse prevention with intellectually disabled sex offenders. *Sexual Abuse: A Journal of Research & Treatment, 17*(4), 407–423. doi: 10.1177/107906320501700405

Keeling, J. A., Rose, J. L., & Beech, A. R. (2006). A comparison of the application of the self-regulation model of the relapse process for mainstream and special needs offenders. *Sexual Abuse: A Journal of Research & Treatment, 18*(4), 373–382. doi: 10.1007/s11194-006-9030-3

Keulen-de Vos, M. E., Bernstein, D. P., & Arntz, A. (2013). Schema therapy for offenders with aggressive personality disorders. In R. C. Tafrate & D. Mitchell (Eds.), *Forensic CBT: A Practitioner's Guide* (pp. 66–83). Chichester, UK: Wiley Blackwell.

Kohlberg, L. (1969). Stage and sequence: The cognitive developmental approach to socialization. In D. A. Goslin (Ed.), *Handbook of socialization theory and research* (pp. 380–437). Chicago: Rand McNally.

Kurtz, P. F., Boelter, E. W., Jarmolowicz, D. P., Chin, M. D., & Hagopian, L. P. (2011). An analysis of functional communication training as an empirically supported treatment for problem behavior displayed by individuals with intellectual disability. *Research in Developmental Disabilities, 32*(6), 2935–2942. doi: 10.1016/j.ridd.2011.05.009

Lambrick, F., & Glaser, W. (2004). Sex offenders with an intellectual disability. *Sexual Abuse: A Journal of Research and Treatment, 16*(4), 381–392. doi: 10.1177/107906320401600409

Lammers, S. M. M., Soe-Agnie, S. E., de Haan, H. A., Bakkum, G. A. M., & Nijman, H. J. M. (2014). Middelengebruik en criminaliteit: een overzicht. [Substance use and crime: a review]. *Tijdschrift voor Psychiatrie, 56*(1), 32–39.

Langdon, P. E., Clare, I. C. H., & Murphy, G. H. (2010). Developing an understanding of the literature relating to moral development of people with intellectual disabilities. *Developmental Review, 30*, 273–293. doi:10.1016/j.dr.2010.01.001

Langdon, P. E., Murphy, G. H., Clare, I. C. H., & Palmer, E. J. (2010). The psychometric properties of the Socio-Moral Reflection Measure – Short Form and the Moral Theme Inventory for men with and without intellectual disabilities. *Research in Developmental Disabilities, 31*, 1204–1215. doi:10.1016/j.ridd.2010.07.025

Langdon, P. E., Maxted, H., Murphy, G. H., & SOTSEC-ID GROUP (2007). An exploratory evaluation of the Ward and Hudson offending pathways model with sex offenders who have intellectual disability. *Journal of Intellectual & Developmental Disabilities, 32*(2), 94–105. doi: 10.1080/13668250701364686

Larkin, P., Jahoda, A., & MacMahon, K. (2013). The social information processing model as a framework for explaining frequent aggression in adults with mild to moderate intellectual disabilities: A systematic review of the evidence. *Journal of Applied Research in Intellectual Disabilities, 26*, 447–465. doi: 10.1111/jar.12031

Lindberg, M. A., Fugett, A., & Lounder, L. (2013). The attachment and clinical issues questionnaire: A new methodology for science and practice in criminology and forensics. *International Journal of Offender Therapy and Comparative Criminology, 20*(10), 1–20. doi: 10.1177/0306624X13492397

Lindsay, W. R. (2002). Research and literature on sex offenders with intellectual and developmental disabilities. *Journal of Intellectual Disability Research, 46*(1), 74–85. doi: 10.1046/j.1365-2788.2002.00006.x

Lindsay, W. R. (2007). Offenders with mild intellectual and developmental disabilities: Epidemiology, assessment and treatment. In R. Didden & X. Moonen (Eds.), *Met het oog op behandeling: Effectieve behandeling van gedragsstoornissen bij mensen met een lichte verstandelijke beperking* (pp. 41–53). Utrecht/Den Dolder: Landelijk Kenniscentrum LVG/Expertisecentrum De Borg.

Lindsay, W. R., Allan, R., MacLeod, F., Smart, N., & Smith A. H. (2003). Long-term treatment and management of violent tendencies of men with learning disabilities convicted of assault. *Mental Retardation, 41*, 47–56. doi: 10.1352/0047-6765 (2003)041<0047:LTTAMO>2.0.CO;2

Lindsay, W. R., Carson, D., Holland, A. J., Taylor, J. L., O'Brien, G., & Wheeler, J. (2013a). The impact of known criminogenic factors on offenders with intellectual disability: Previous findings and new results on ADHD. *Journal of Applied Research in Intellectual Disabilities, 26*, 71–80. doi:10.1111/jar.12011

Lindsay, W. R., Holland, A. J, Carson, D., Taylor, J. L., O'Brien, G., Steptoe, L., & Wheeler, J. (2013b). Responsivity to criminogenic need in forensic intellectual disability services. *Journal of Intellectual Disability Research, 57*(2), 172–181. doi:10.1111/j.1365-2788.2012.01600.x

Lindsay, W. R., Hogue, T., Taylor, J. L., Mooney, P., Steptoe, L., Johnston, S., O'Brien, G., & Smith, A. H. W. (2006). Two studies on the prevalence and validity of personality disorders in three forensic intellectual disability samples. *The Journal of Forensic Psychiatry and Psychology, 17*(3), 485–506. doi: 10.1080/14789940600821719

Lindsay, W. R., & Smith, A. H. W. (1998). Responses to treatment for sex offenders with intellectual disability: A comparison of men with 1- and 2-year probation sentences. *Journal of Intellectual Disability Research, 42*(5), 346–353. doi: 10.1046/j.1365-2788.1998.00147.x

Lindsay, W. R., Steptoe, L., & Beech, A. T. (2008). The Ward and Hudson pathways model of the sexual offence process applied to offenders with intellectual disability. *Sexual Abuse: A Journal of Research and Treatment, 20*(4), 379–392. doi: 10.1177/1079063208323369

Lindsay, W. R., Sturmey, P., & Taylor, J. L. (2004). Natural history and theories of offending in people with developmental disabilities. In W. R. Lindsay, P. Sturmey, & J.L. Taylor (Eds.). *Offenders with developmental disabilities* (pp. 3–22). Chichester: John Wiley & Sons Ltd.

Lloyd, B. P., & Kennedy, C. H. (2014). Assessment and treatment of challenging behavior for individuals with intellectual disability: A research review. *Journal of Applied Research in Intellectual Disabilities*. doi: 10.1111/jar.12089. [Epub ahead of print].

Männynsalo, L., Putkonen, H., Lindberg, N., & Kotilainen, I. (2009). Forensic psychiatric perspective on criminality associated with intellectual disability: A nationwide register-based study. *Journal of Intellectual Disability Research, 53*(3), 279–288. doi: 10.1111/j.1365-2788.2008.01125.x

300 *Marije Keulen-De Vos and Karin Frijters*

Marshall, W. L., & Serran, G. A. (2001). Improving the effectiveness of sexual offender treatment. *Trauma, Violence & Abuse, 1*(3), 203–222. doi: 10.1177/152483800000 1003001

Matheson, E., Jahoda, A., & MacLean W. E. (2005). Emotional understanding in aggressive and nonaggressive individuals with mild or moderate mental retardation. *American Journal on Mental Retardation, 110*(1), 57–67. doi: 10.1352/0895-8017 (2005)110<57:EUIAAN>2.0.CO;2

Matson, J. L., & Kozlowski, A. M. (2012). Environmental determinants of aggressive behaviour. In J. L. Luiselli (Ed.), *The handbook of high-risk challenging behaviors in people with intellectual and developmental disabilities* (pp. 63–81). Baltimore: Paul H. Brookes Publishing Co.

Matson, J. L., & Mayville, E. A. (2001). The relationship of functional variables and psychopathology to aggressive behavior in persons with severe and profound mental retardation. *Journal of Psychopathology and Behavioral Assessment, 23*(1), 3–9. doi: 10. 1023/A:1011083221991

Matson, J. L., & Neal, D. (2009). Psychotropic medication use for challenging behaviors in persons with intellectual disabilities: An overview. *Research in Developmental Disabilities, 30*, 572–586. doi:10.1016/j.ridd.2008.08.007

Matson, J. L., & Shoemaker, M. (2009). Intellectual disability and its relationship to autism spectrum disorders. *Research in Developmental Disabilities, 30*(6), 1107–1114. doi: 10.1016/j.ridd.2009.06.003

McCarthy, E., Tarrier, N., & Gregg, L. (2002). The nature and timing of seasonal affective symptoms and the influence of self-esteem and social support: A longitudinal prospective study. *Psychological Medicine, 32*(8), 1425–1434. doi: 10.1017/ S0033291702006621

McClintock, K., Hall, S., & Oliver, C. (2003). Risk markers associated with challenging behaviors in people with intellectual disabilities: A meta-analytic study. *Journal of Intellectual Disability Research, 47*(6), 405–416. doi: 10.1046/j.1365-2788. 2003.00517.x

McClure, K. S., Halpern, J., Wolper, P. A., & Donahue, J. J. (2003). Emotion regulation and intellectual disabilities. *Journal on Developmental Disabilities, 15*(2), 38–44.

McGillivray, J. A., & Moore, M. R. (2001). Substance use by offenders with mild intellectual disability. *Journal of Intellectual and Developmental Disability, 26*(4), 297–310. doi:10.1080/13668250120087317

McVilly, K. R., Stancliffe, R. J., Parmenter, T. R., Burton-Smith, R. M. (2006). 'I get by with a little help from my friends': Adults with intellectual disability discuss loneliness. *Journal of Applied Research in Intellectual Disabilities, 19*(2), 191–203. doi: 10.1111/j.1468-3148.2005.00261.x

Michie, A. M., Lindsay, W. R., Martin, V., & Grieve, A. (2006). A test of counterfeit deviance: a comparison of sexual knowledge in groups of sex offenders with intellectual disability and controls. *Sexual Abuse: A Journal of Research and Treatment, 18*(3), 271–278. doi: 10.1177/107906320601800305

Mitchell, I. J., & Beech, A. R. (2011). Towards a neurobiological model of offending. *Clinical Psychology Review, 31*, 872–882. doi:10.1016/j.cpr.2011.04.001

Murphy, C. M., & Ting, L. (2010). The effects of treatment for substance use problems on intimate partner violence: A review of empirical data. *Aggression and Violent Behavior, 15*, 325–333. doi:10.1016/j.avb.2010.01.006

Myrbakk, E., & von Tetzchner, S. (2008). Psychiatric disorders and behavior problems in people with intellectual disability. *Research in Developmental Disabilities, 29*, 316–332. doi:10.1016/j.ridd.2007.06.002

Aggressive behaviour in offenders with intellectual disabilities 301

Nader-Grosbois, N., Houssa, M., & Mazzone, S. (2013). How could Theory of Mind contribute to the differentiation of social adjustment profiles of children with externalizing behavior disorders and children with intellectual disabilities? *Research in Developmental Disabilities, 34*, 2642–2660. doi: 10.1016/j.ridd.2013.05.010

Neijmeijer, L., Moerdijk, L., Veneberg, G., & Muuse, C. (2009). Licht verstandelijk gehandicapten in de GGZ: Een verkennend onderzoek. Utrecht: Trimbos-instituut.

Nicoll, M., Beail, N., & Saxon, D. (2013). Cognitive Behaviral Treatment for anger in adults with intellectual disabilities: A systematic review and meta-analysis. *Journal of Applied Research in Intellectual Disabilities, 26*, 47–62. doi: 10.1111/jar.12013

Nieuwenhuijzen, M. van, de Castro, B. O., van der Valk, I., Wijnroks, L., Vermeer, A., & Matthys, W. (2006). Do social information-processing models explain aggressive behavior by children with mild intellectual disabilities in residential care? *Journal of Intellectual Disability Research, 50*(11), 801–812. doi: 10.1111/j.1365-2788.2005.00773.x

Novaco, R. W. (1977). A stress inoculation approach to anger management in the training of law enforcement officers. *American Journal of Community Psychology, 5*(3), 327–346. doi: 10.1007/BF00884700

Novaco, R. W., & Taylor, J. L. (2008). Anger and assaultiveness of male forensic patients with developmental disabilities: Links to volatile parents. *Aggressive Behavior, 34*, 380–393. doi: 10.1002/ab.20254

O'Brien, G., Taylor, J. L., Lindsay, W. R., Holland, A. J., Carson, D., Steptoe, L., Middleton, C., Price, K., & Wheeler, J. R. (2010). A multicentre study of adults with learning disabilities referred to services for antisocial or offending behaviour: demographic, individual, offending and service characteristics. *Journal of Learning Disabilities and Offending Behavior, 1*, 5–15. doi:10.5042/jldob.2010.0415

Ogilvie, J., Stewart, A., Chan, R. C. K., & Shum, D. H. K. (2011). Neuropsychological measures of executive function and antisocial behavior: A meta-analysis. *Criminology, 49*(4), 1063–107. doi: 10.1111/j.1745-9125.2011.00252.x

Oliver-Africano, P., Murphy, D., & Tyrer, P. (2009). Aggressive behavior in adults with intellectual disability: defining the role of drug treatment. *CNS Drugs, 23*(11), 903–913. doi: 10.2165/11310930-000000000-00000.

Owen, M. J. (2012). Intellectual disability and major psychiatric diagnoses: A continuum of neurodevelopmental causality. *The British Journal of Psychiatry, 200*, 268–269. doi: 10.1192/bjp.bp.111.105551

Ozbay, F., Johnson, D. C., Dimoulas, E., Morgan, C. A., Charney, D., & Southwick, S. (2007). Social support and resilience to stress: From neurobiology to clinical practice. *Psychiatry, 4*(5), 35–40.

Parry, C. J., & Lindsay, W. R. (2003). Impulsiveness as a factor in sexual offending by people with mild intellectual disability. *Journal of Intellectual Disability Research, 47*(6), 483–487. doi: 10.1046/j.1365-2788.2003.00509.x

Paterson, L., McKenzie, K., & Lindsay, B. (2012). Stigma, social comparison and self-esteem in adults with an intellectual disability. *Journal of Applied Research in Intellectual Disabilities, 25*, 166–176. doi: 10.1111/j.1468-3148.2011.00651.x

Penketh, V. J. (2011). *Attachment in adults with intellectual disabilities: The examination of the psychometric properties of the Manchester Attachment Scale – Third Party Observational Measure (MAST).* [Dissertation manuscript]. University of Manchester.

Pert, C., Jahoda, A., & Squire, J. (1999). Attribution of intent and role-taking: Cognitive factors as mediators of aggression with people who have mental retardation. *American Journal on Mental Retardation, 104*(5), 399–409. doi: 10.1352/0895-8017(1999)104<0399:AOIARC>2.0.CO;2

302 *Marije Keulen-De Vos and Karin Frijters*

Pillman, F., Rohde, A., Ullrich, S., Draba, S., Sannemüller, U., & Marneros, A. (1999). Violence, criminal behavior and the EEG: Significance of left hemispheric focal abnormalities. *The Journal of Neuropsychiatry and Clinical Neurosciences, 11*(4), 454–457.

Plant, A., McDermott, E., Chester, V., & Alexander, R. T. (2011). Substance misuse among offenders in a forensic intellectual disability service. *Journal of Learning Disabilities and Offending Behaviour, 2*(3), 127–135. doi: 10.1108/20420921111186589

Proctor, T., & Beail, N. (2007). Empathy and theory of mind in offenders with intellectual disability. *Journal of Intellectual and Developmental Disability, 32*(2), 82–93. doi:10.1080/13668250701373331

Raine, A. and Yang, Y. (2006). The neuroanatomical bases of psychopathy: A review of brain imaging findings. In C. J. Patrick (Ed.), *Handbook of psychopathy* (pp. 278–295). New York: The Guildford Press.

Ralfs, S., & Beail, N. (2012). Assessing components of empathy in sex offenders with intellectual disabilities. *Journal of Applied Research in Intellectual Disabilities, 25,* 50–59. doi: 10.1111/j.1468-3148.2011.00648.x

Reiss, D., Quayle, M., Brett, T., & Meux, C. (1998). Dramatherapy for mentally disordered offenders: Changes in levels of anger. *Criminal Behaviour and Mental Health, 8*(2), 139–153. doi: 10.1002/cbm.232

Reid, A. H., Lindsay, W. R., Law, L., & Sturmey, P. (2004). The relationship of offending behavior and personality disorder in people with developmental disabilities. In W. R. Lindsay, J. L. Taylor, & P. Sturmey (Ed.), *Offenders with developmental disabilities,* (pp. 289–303). Chichester, UK: Wiley & Sons.

Rey, L., Extremera, N., Duran, A., & Ortiz-Tallo, M. (2012). Subjective quality of life of people with intellectual disabilities: The role of emotional competence on their subjective wellbeing. *Journal of Applied Research in Intellectual Disabilities, 26*(2), 146–156. doi:10.1111/jar.12015

Reynolds, B., Ortengren, A., Richards, J., & de Wit, H. (2006). Dimensions of impulsive behavior: Personality and behavioral measures. *Personality and Individual Differences, 40,* 305–315. doi: 10.1016/j.paid.2005.03.024

Rice, M. E., Harris, G. T., Lang, C., & Chaplin, T. C. (2008). Sexual preferences and recidivism of sex offenders with mental retardation. *Sexual Abuse: A Journal of Research and Treatment, 20*(4), 409–425. doi: 10.1177/1079063208324662

Rihmer, Z., Belsö, N., & Kiss, K. (2002). Strategies for suicide prevention. *Current Opinion in Psychiatry, 15*(1), 83–87.

Robertson, J., Emerson, E., Gregory, N., Hatton, C., Kessissoglou, S., Hallam, A., & Linehan, C. (2001). Social networks of people with mental retardation in residential settings. *Mental Retardation, 39,* 201–214. doi: 10.1352/0047-6765(2001)039<0201:SNOPWM>2.0.CO;2

Rojahn, J., Rabold, D. E, & Schneider, F. (1995). Emotion specificity in mental retardation. *American Journal of Mental Retardation, 99,* 477–486.

Rojahn, J., Zaja, R. H., Turygin, N., Moore, L., & van Ingen, D. J. (2012). Functions of maladaptive behavior in intellectual and developmental disabilities: behavior categories and topographies. *Research in Developmental Disabilities, 33,* 2020–2027. http://dx.doi.org/10.1016/j.ridd.2012.05.025

Rose, J., Jenkins, R., O'Conner, C., Jones, C., & Felce, D. (2002). A group treatment for men with learning disabilities who sexually offend or abuse. *Journal of Applied Research in Learning Disabilities, 15,* 138–150.

Rose, J., West, C., & Clifford, D. (2000). Group interventions for anger in people with intellectual disabilities. *Research in Developmental Disabilities, 21*(3), 171–181. doi: 10.1016/S0891-4222(00)00032-9

Royal College of Psychiatrists (2003). *Psychotherapy and learning disability.* London: Council Report CR116.

Ruiz, M. A., Douglas, K. S., Edens, J. F., Nikolova, N. L., & Lilienfeld, S. O. (2012). Co-occurring mental health and substance use problems in offenders: implications for risk assessment. *Psychological Assessment, 24*(1), 77–87. doi: 10.1037/a0024623

Rutgers, A. H., van IJzendoorn, M. H., Bakermans-Kranenburg, M. J., Swinkels, S. H. N., van Daalen, E., Dietz, C., Naber, F. B. A., Buitelaar, J. K., & van Engeland, H. (2007). Autism, attachment and parenting: A comparison of children with autism spectrum disorder, mental retardation, language disorder, and non-clinical children. *Journal of Abnormal Child Psychology, 35,* 859–870. doi: 10.1007/s10802-007-9139-y

Samuel, R., Attard, A., & Kyriakopoulos, M. (2013). Mental state deterioration after switching from brand-name to generic olanzapine in an adolescent with bipolar affective disorder, autism and intellectual disability: A case study. *BMC Psychiatry, 13,* 244–246. doi: 10.1186/1471-244X-13-244

Sappok, T., Budczies, J., Bölte, S. Dziobek, I., Dosen, A., & Diefenbacher, A. (2013). Emotional development in adults with autism and intellectual disabilities: A retrospective, clinical analysis. *PLoS ONE, 8*(9), e74036. doi:10.1371/journal.pone.0074036

Schuengel, C., de Schipper, J. C., Sterkenburg, P. S., & Kef, S. (2013). Attachment, intellectual disabilities and mental health: Research, assessment and intervention. *Journal of Applied Research in Intellectual Disabilities, 26,* 34–46. doi: 10.1111/jar.12010

Schuurs-Hoeijmakers, J. H. M., Vulto-van Stifhout, A. T., Vissers, L. E. L. M. et al. (2013). Identification of pathogenic gene variants in small families with intellectual disabled siblings by exome sequencing. *Journal of Medical Genetics, 10,* 1–10. doi: 10.1136/jmedgenet-2013-101644

Serin, R. C., Lloyd, C. D., Helmus, L., Derkzen, D. M., & Luong, D. (2013). Does intra-individual change predict offender recidivism? Searching for the Holy Grail in assessing offender change. *Aggression and Violent Behavior, 18*(1), 32–53. doi: 10.1016/j.avb.2012.09.002

Shapiro F. (2001). *EMDR: Eye movement desensitization of reprocessing: Basic principles, protocols and procedures* (2nd ed.). New York: Guilford Press.

Shogren, K. A., Faggella-Luby, M. N., Bae, S. J., & Wehmeyer, M. L. (2004). The effect of choice-making as an intervention for problem behavior: A meta-analysis. *Journal of Positive Behavior Interventions, 6*(4), 228–237. doi: 10.1177/10983007040060040401

Simon, E. W., Blubaugh, K. M., & Pippidis, M. (1996). Substituting traditional antipsychotics with risperidone for individuals with mental retardation. *Mental Retardation, 34,* 359–366.

Simons, R. L. (1978). The meaning of the IQ delinquency relationship. *American Sociological Review, 43,* 268–270.

Simpson, M. K., & Hogg, J. (2001). Patterns of offending among people with intellectual disability: A systematic review. Part I: Methodology and prevalence data. *Journal of Intellectual Disability Research, 45*(5), 384–396. doi: 10.1046/j.1365-2788.2001.00345.x

304 *Marije Keulen-De Vos and Karin Frijters*

Slot, N. W., & Spanjaard, H. J. M. (1999). *Competentievergroting in de residentiele jeug-dzorg: Hulpverlening voor kinderen en jongeren in tehuizen.* [Enhancing competency in residential youth care: The care for children in orphanages]. Utrecht: De Tijdstroom.

Smeijsters, H., & Cleven, G. (2006). The treatment of aggression using arts therapies in forensic psychiatry: Results of a qualitative inquiry. *The Arts in Psychotherapy, 33*, 37–58. doi: 10.1016/j.aip.2005.07.001

Smith, A. H. W., & O'Brien, G. (2004). Offenders with dual diagnoses. In W. R. Lindsay, J. L. Taylor, & P. Sturmey (Eds.), *Offenders with developmental disabilities* (pp. 242–263). Chichester, UK: Wiley & Sons.

Soltani, A., Roslan, S., Abdullah, M. C., Jan, C. C. (2011). Facilitating flow experience in people with intellectual disability using a music intervention program. *International Journal of Psychological Studies, 3*(2), 54–63. doi: 10.5539/ijps.v3n2p54

Strickler, H. L. (2001). Interaction between family violence and mental retardation. *Mental Retardation, 39*(6), 461–471. doi: 10.1352/0047-6765(2001)039<0461:IBFVAM>2.0.CO;2

Sturmey, P. (2002). Treatment interventions for people with aggressive behavior and intellectual disability. In G. Holt & N. Bouras (Ed.), *Autism and related disorders: The basis handbook for mental health, primary care and other professional* (pp. 42–56). World Psychiatric Association/Royal College of Psychiatrists, London: Gaskel.

Taylor. J. L., Novaco, R., Gillmer, B. T., Robertson, A., & Thorne, I. (2005). Individual cognitive-behavioral anger treatment for people with mild-borderline intellectual disabilities and histories of aggression: A controlled trial. *British Journal in Clinical Psychology, 44*(3), 367–382. doi: 10.1348/014466505X29990

Taylor, J. L., Novaco, R. W., Gillmer. B. T., & Roberton, A. (2004). Treatment of anger and aggression. In W. R. Lindsay, J. L. Taylor, & P. Sturmey (Eds.), *Offenders with developmental disabilities,* (pp. 201–219). Chichester, UK: Wiley.

Taylor. J. L., Novaco, R., Guinian, C., & Street, N. (2004). Development of an imaginal provocation test to evaluate treatment for anger problems in people with intellectual disabilities. *Clinical Psychology and Psychotherapy, 11*(4), 233–246. doi: 10.1002/cpp.411

Tenneij, N. H., Didden, R., Stolker, J. J., & Koot, H. M. (2009). Markers for aggression in inpatient treatment facilities for adults with mild to moderate intellectual disability. *Research in Developmental Disabilities, 30*, 1248–1257. doi:10.1016/j.ridd.2009.04.006

Terman, L. (1911). *The measurement of intelligence.* Boston, MA: Houghton Mifflin.

Travis, R.W., & Sturmey, P. (2013). Using behavioral skills training to treat aggression in adults with mild intellectual disability in a forensic setting. *Journal of Applied Research in Intellectual Disabilities, 26*, 481–488. doi: 10.1111/jar.12033

Tyrer, F., McGrother, C. W., Thorp, C. F., Donaldson, S., Bhaumik, S., Watson, J. W., & Hollin, C. (2006). Physical aggression towards others in adults with learning disabilities: Prevalence and associated factors. *Journal of Intellectual Disability Research, 50*(4), 295–304. doi: 10.1111/j.1365-2788.2005.00774.x

Tyrer, P., Oliver-Africano, P. C., Ahmed, Z., Bouras, N., Cooray, S., Deb, S. et al. (2008). Risperidone, haloperidol, and placebo in the treatment of aggressive challenging behavior in patients with intellectual disability: A randomized controlled trial. *Lancet, 371*, 57–63.

Vollmer, T. R., & Hackenberg, T. D. (2001). Reinforcement contingencies and social reinforcement: Some reciprocal relations between basis and applied research. *Journal of Applied Behavior Analysis, 34*(2), 241–253.

Vugt, E. van, Asscher, J., Stams, G. J., Hendriks, J., Bijleveld, C., & Van der Laan, P. (2011). Moral judgment of young sex offenders with and without intellectual disabilities. *Research in Developmental Disabilities, 32*, 2841–2846. doi:10.1016/j.ridd.2011.05.022

Ward, T., & Beech, A. (2006). An integrated theory of sexual offending. *Aggression and Violent Behavior, 11*, 44–63. doi:10.1016/j.avb.2005.05.002

Ward, T., Bickley, J., Webster, S. D., Fisher, D., Beech, A., & Eldridge, H. (2004). *The self-regulation model of the offence and relapse process: A manual: Vol. 1. Assessment.* Victoria, Canada: Pacific Psychological Assessment Corporation.

Ward, T., Mann, R. E. & Gannon, T. A. (2007). The good lives model of offender rehabilitation: Clinical implications. *Aggression and Violent Behavior: A Review Journal, 12*, 87–107. doi: 10.1016/j.avb.2006.03.004

Ward, T., & Hudson, S. M. (1998). A model of the relapse process in sexual offenders. *Journal of Interpersonal Violence, 13*, 700–725. doi: 10.1177/088626098013006003

Watts, S. J., & McNulty, T. L. (2013). Childhood abuse and criminal behaviour: Testing a general strain theory model. *Journal of Interpersonal Violence, 28*(15), 3023–3040. doi: 10.1177/0886260513488696

Weinfield, N. S., Sroufe, L. A., & Egeland, B. (2000). Attachment from infancy to early adulthood in a high-risk sample: Continuity, discontinuity, and their correlates. *Child Development, 71*, 695–702. doi: 10.1111/1467-8624.00178

Weinfield, N. S., Sroufe, A., Egeland, B., & Carlson, E. (2008). Individual differences in infant–caregiver attachment: Conceptual and empirical aspects of security. In J. Cassidy & P. R. Shaver (Eds.), *Handbook of attachment: Theory, research, and clinical applications* (pp. 78–101) (second edition). New York: Guilford.

Weinfield, N. S., Whaley, G. J. L., & Egeland, B. (2004). Continuity, discontinuity, and coherence in attachment from infancy to late adolescence: Sequelae of organization and disorganization. *Attachment & Human Development, 6*, 73–97. doi: 10.1080/14616730310001659566

Whitaker, S. (2001). Anger control for people with learning disabilities: A critical review. *Behavioral and Cognitive Psychotherapy, 29*(3), 277–293. doi: 10.1017/S1352465801003022

White, J. L., Moffitt, T. E., Caspi, A., Bartusch, D. K., Needles, D. J., Stouthamer-Loeber, M. (1994). Measuring impulsivity and examining its relationship to delinquency. *Journal of Abnormal Psychology, 103*(2), 192–205. doi: 10.1037/0021-843X.103.2.192

Whitehead, P. R., Ward, T., & Collie, R. M. (2007). Time for a change: Applying the Good Lives Model of Rehabilitation to a high-risk violent offender. *International Journal of Offender Therapy and Comparative Criminology, 51*, 578–598.

Woodcock, K. A., Humphreys, G. W., & Oliver, C. (2009). Dorsal and ventral stream mediated visual processing in genetic subtypes of Prader-Willi syndrome. *Neuropsychologia, 47*, 2367–2373. doi: 10.1016/j.neuropsychologia.2008.09.019

Woodcock, K. A., Oliver, C., & Humpreys, G. W. (2009). A specific pathway can be identified between genetic characteristics and behavior profiles in Prader-Willi syndrome via cognitive, environmental and physiological mechanisms. *Journal of Intellectual Disability Research, 53*(6), 493–500. doi: 10.1111/j.1365-2788.2009.01167.x

Woodcock, K. A., & Rose, J. (2007). The relationship between facial expressions and self-reported anger in people with intellectual disabilities. *Journal of Applied Research in Intellectual Disability, 20*, 279–284. doi: 10.1111/j.1468-3148.2006.00326.x

Yang, L., Zhan, G. D., Ding, J. J., Wang, H. J., Ma, D., Huang, G. Y., Zhou, W. H. (2013). Psychiatric illness and intellectual disability in the Prader-Willi syndrome with different molecular defects – A meta analysis. *PLoS One, 8*(8), e72640. doi: 10.1371/journal.pone.0072640

Young, J. E., Klosko, J., & Weishaar, M. (2003). *Schema therapy: A practitioner's guide.* New York: Guilford Press.

Zoja, R. H., & Rojahn, J. (2008). Facial emotion recognition in intellectual disabilities. *Current Opinion in Psychiatry, 21*, 441–444. doi: 10.1097/YCO.0b013e328 305e5fd

15 Autism and (violent) offending

An overview of current knowledge, risk factors and treatment

Lysandra Podesta and Anna M.T. Bosman

Introduction

In Newtown, Connecticut, December 2012, a 20-year-old adolescent with a form of autism first killed his mother and, subsequently, drove to his former primary school and took the lives of 26 people. Many of them were primary school children. After this killing spree he committed suicide (Barron, 2012).

Reports of extreme, sensational cases like this example of the second-deadliest school shooting in the US have caused some to link Autism Spectrum Disorder (ASD; Mr Lanza, the shooter, was diagnosed with Asperger syndrome; Berger & Santora, 2013) to being able to act out highly aggressive (deadly) actions. Advocates and experts on ASD fear that media messages will send out the wrong signal by reinforcing the belief that people with ASD are dangerous, thereby creating a new stereotype image of ASD stating that it is a disorder which causes some individuals to act in extremely violent ways (Shah & Ujifusa, 2013). Another expressed fear is that of false stereotypes and stigmatisation (Howlin, 2004) leading to less adequate guidance for people with ASD. If individuals with mental health problems are, in fact, viewed as dangerous, they might be isolated from society, which prevents substantive contact with other people and threatens recovery and learning experiences to, one day, be able to function (again) in society.

Although it is often highlighted by the media that an offender has an ASD diagnosis, the connections between autism and these acts are not so straightforward. The goal of this chapter is to illustrate what exactly is known about the relationship between ASD, aggression and criminal acts and what the causes of this apparent link could be. First, we need to understand what ASD is.

ASD is a common developmental disorder which impacts all aspects of one's development and often affects daily life functioning, social interaction and well-being severely. Estimated prevalence rates are around 1/90 in Western countries (Baird et al., 2006; Dyck, 2009). A remarkable 92% of parents of children with ASD report problems with mood and behaviour, such as tantrums, aggression and self-injury (Mayes & Calhoun, 2011). In comparison to children with intellectual disability, children with autism tend to have more emotional and behavioural problems (Einfeld, Tonge, Gray, & Taffe, 2007) that persist into adulthood, albeit the problems most likely have by then become less severe (Gray et al., 2012). Regardless of this improvement, as people become older ASD renders most people reliant on lifelong support (Ganz, 2007).

According to the DSM-5 (American Psychiatric Association, 2013), the latest version of the DSM series, ASD comprises multiple symptoms organised in two main categories: social communication deficits and restricted behaviour or interests. Formerly known discrete disorders which were described within the pervasive developmental disorders (Autistic Disorder or classic autism, Asperger syndrome, Pervasive Developmental Disorder – Not Otherwise Specified, and Childhood Disintegrative Disorder) are incorporated into what is now known as Autism Spectrum Disorder and are used interchangeably in this chapter with 'autism'.

The similarities between individuals with ASD are the behavioural criteria on which the disorder is based. Yet extreme interindividual differences exist regarding level of functioning in childhood and adulthood. Noteworthy differences exist between lower-functioning individuals (with IQ scores below roughly 70, mostly with Autistic Disorder) and higher-functioning individuals (who have, by definition, average to high intellectual ability and are often diagnosed with Asperger syndrome). The associated social problems can range from being nonverbal to having relatively small difficulties with managing and understanding social interaction (Kasari, Locke, Gulsrud, & Rotheram-Fuller, 2011).

The precise cause of autism is still unknown. Genetic causes can be found for approximately 10–20% of (mostly low-functioning) ASD cases, including the X-linked genetic syndrome called Fragile X, which is associated with intellectual disability and autism (Abrahams & Geschwind, 2008). The aetiology of ASD behaviours will likely be diverse and complex, illustrating that ASD is highly heterogeneous.

Regarding adaptive behaviour, which entails being able to function in one's environment, a wide variety of skills can be observed (Oswald & DiSalvo, 2003). Nevertheless, particularly in people with average or high intellectual ability, adaptive behaviour tends to lag behind the skills that are expected based on their intellectual functioning (Bölte & Poustka, 2002; Kanne et al., 2011). Even high-functioning adults often experience severe difficulty with functioning in society, for instance in work settings (Baldwin, Costley, & Warren, 2014). The result is a combination of good intellectual ability with problematic social development and trouble applying learned abilities in daily life.

Apart from low versus high-functioning ASD, a gender distinction between people with ASD is apparent. ASD expresses itself differently in women than it does in men. Women with ASD display less repetitive behaviour, have more internalising problems (such as depression and anxiety; Kreiser & White, 2014) and are more sensitive than their male counterparts (Lai et al., 2011). This less obvious clinical expression of ASD is assumed to be one of the reasons the proportion of males to females seems to be overestimated, as women are regularly missed or misdiagnosed (Kreiser & White, 2014).

The clinical picture of autism is often complex and great interindividual variance exists. Shocking behavioural extremes, as illustrated at the beginning, will only be present in a small minority. Nevertheless, it is important to understand what exactly is known about the relationship between ASD and offending and aggression, as the results of extreme behavioural or emotional reactions might cause disastrous situations.

The large variability in how ASD presents itself has led to various theories with respect to underlying (brain) mechanisms and influential factors in the environment and development of people with ASD. This has complicated the field's attempt to untangle the web of relevant factors when explaining the causes of ASD symptoms and associated problems. Nevertheless, certain behavioural and cognitive patterns are generally present and these might be used as explanatory causes for aggression and delinquency. In this chapter, before moving on to the discussion of factors connected to criminality in ASD, an overview is presented of the current knowledge about offending and aggression in individuals with ASD. After the risk factors for delinquency and aggression associated with and inherent to ASD are discussed, the connections and differences between autistic and psychopathic behaviour are highlighted. Finally, options for treatment and their known efficacy are reviewed.

Aggression and delinquency in ASD

Whereas many studies have focused on children and adolescents who engage in aggressive or delinquent behaviour, adult studies on this subject are relatively scarce. In this part of the chapter, the contemporary knowledge about this topic is discussed.

Children and adolescents

Problem behaviour

As noted above, challenging behaviour, defined as socially unacceptable behaviour, including aggression, tantrums, destructive acts and self-injury, in young people with low and higher-functioning ASD is common (up to 94.3% shows at least one challenging behaviour) and tends to be chronic (Matson, Mahan, Hess, Fodstad, & Neal, 2010). Especially parents with low socioeconomic status (SES) are often unable to cope with the present problem behaviour of their child and may not be able to afford expensive or long therapies. Low SES is, because of this, associated with problem behaviour (including irritability, low frustration tolerance, tantrums, aggression and self-injury) of children who are 6–16-years-old (Mayes & Calhoun, 2011).

A large-scale study by Kanne and Mazurek (2011), including 1380 children and adolescents varying greatly in IQ, revealed prevalence rates of 68% for aggression towards a caregiver and 49% towards other people. Surprisingly, aggression was *unrelated* to intellectual ability (unlike in the general population),

310 *Lysandra Podesta and Anna M. T. Bosman*

ASD symptom severity and gender. Even though in the general population boys act aggressively more often than girls (NICHD Early Child Care Research, 2004), this gender difference was not found in ASD. However, Kaartinen et al. (2014), who assessed inhibition of children's reactive aggression using a computerised task, found that girls with ASD reacted less aggressively than girls without ASD, whereas boys reacted with more severe aggression as a response to mild aggressive acts. All children were considered to be high functioning, with total IQ scores above 70. Thus high-functioning girls seem more able to inhibit aggressive impulses. Additional aspects that might increase the chance of demonstrating aggression were age (younger participants showed more aggression), repetitive behaviour (linked to aggression) and heightened communication and social problems (Kanne & Mazurek, 2011). High rates of externalising problems are also suggested in other studies. Hartley and colleagues (2008) showed that 22% of children aged between 1 and 5 scored as clinically significant on the Aggression subscale of the Child Behavior Checklist (Achenbach & Rescorla, 2000). Externalising behaviour was found to be related to the level of functioning of the child; poorer quality of expressive language, nonverbal cognitive functioning and adaptive skills. This is in line with other studies which found a correlation between lower adaptive skills and aggression (Vieillevoya & Nader-Grosbois, 2008). This might be related to the fact that these children do not tend to act in disruptive ways for reaching social goals (such as gaining attention), but, for instance, to escape demands and avoid certain sensory stimuli (Reese, Richman, Belmont, & Morse, 2005). If they are unable to express their wish to escape or continue with soothing repetitive behaviours or self-injury in a non-violent manner, the situation might elicit aggression.

Offenders

For some, challenging behaviour leads to contact with the police and the criminal justice system. Only few prevalence studies of youngsters with ASD in the criminal justice system have been conducted (Vermeiren et al., 2006), suggesting an overrepresentation of young people with ASD. Of the juvenile offenders between 15 and 22 years, 15% met the criteria of ASD and 3% of Asperger syndrome (Siponmaa & Kristiansson, 2001). A crime prevalence study of the general ASD population with approximately 50% low-functioning young people indicated that 5% in the South Carolina Autism and Developmental Disabilities Monitoring Program (SC ADDM) had at one point been charged with one or more offences in the Department of Juvenile Justice or South Carolina Law Enforcement Division (Cheely et al., 2012).

Other studies report a significantly higher crime rate. The prevalence of ASD in family court cases in Japan, involving 14–19 year olds, was 18.2% in a unique criminal case court (Kumagami & Matsuura, 2009). In three other courts, 3.2% of 335 examined cases turned out to have ASD. Almost all of the offenders with ASD were high-functioning individuals and male. With respect to types of offending, it appears that offences directed at people (like assaults) were more common in youth with ASD, whereas property offences (e.g. arson and trespassing) were less common (Cheely et al., 2012). A possible explanation is that, as a result of impairments in executive functioning, individuals with ASD will lash out in a violent manner when provoked (or when they believe they are, due to negatively interpreting the social situation), rather than contemplating the crime. Compared with a comparison group, youth with ASD were more often charged with the offence of disturbing schools, which might be linked to being a victim of bullying (Cheely et al., 2012).

In sum, youth with ASD appear to be somewhat over-represented when it comes to offending and certain types of offending seem more common. Comorbid intellectual disability is less likely in charged youth. This group possibly has a diminished chance to engage in criminal acts, because they receive more supervision or are institutionalised, or because they are less likely to be prosecuted in general.

Note that, when youth with ASD *are* convicted and sentenced to prison, they seem to have severe difficulty with adjusting to this setting (with unfamiliar routines, non-preferred rituals and gaining an understanding of all social hierarchies), which ultimately may lead to solitary confinement (Paterson, 2008). It is therefore highly important that necessary support is given to these individuals.

Adults

In the general population approximately 1% of individuals commit crimes (see King & Murphy, 2014). Offenders (with and without intellectual disability) tend to be similar when it comes to societal standing. Unemployment is common and many are unmarried and poorly educated (MacEachron, 1979). Even in high-functioning ASD, it appears that many are unemployed (50% of those with Asperger syndrome; Jennes-Coussens, 2006), which is a known risk factor for offending. In adults with serious mental illness, violent acts are reported more often than in the general population (2.9%; Van Dorn, Volavka, & Johnson, 2012). Studies on offending adults with ASD focus on either crime rates within the ASD population or on ASD prevalence within the justice system. An important caveat is needed here: Most studies suffer from substantial methodological issues, which makes it impossible to draw final conclusions with a fair amount of certainty (Mouridsen, 2012).

Criminality and aggression in ASD

An early review of the literature on the combination of ASD with violent behaviour (i.e. acts that could lead to being charged, like murder or arson and that caused significant physical injury to other people) indicated that just three out of 132 individuals with Asperger syndrome displayed violent behaviour, indicating the rarity of these acts (Ghaziuddin, Tsai, & Ghaziuddin, 1991). A more recent, Swedish longitudinal study included 422 hospitalised people

312   *Lysandra Podesta and Anna M. T. Bosman*

with ASD (Långström, Grann, Ruchkin, Sjöstedt, & Fazel, 2009). Only 31 individuals (7%) were convicted for violent offences of a nonsexual nature and two were convicted for sexual offences. However, in this study, the prevalence of being convicted for offences related to violence was different for people with Asperger syndrome (20%) than for people with Autistic Disorder (3%), suggesting high-functioning individuals are convicted for violent crimes more often. With regards to all forms of offending in high-functioning individuals, official and self-report data suggest a surprisingly low rate of criminal activities (when compared to people without ASD; Woodbury-Smith, Clare, Holland, & Kearns, 2006). Other studies seem to agree with a lack of increased susceptibility to criminal offences in general within the ASD population (Mouridsen, Rich, Isager, & Nedergaard, 2008). Of studies that used a general population comparison group, like Mouridsen et al. (2008), the prevalence of crime in ASD seemed to be equal (for Asperger syndrome) or lower than in the comparison groups. So, if anything, the total crime rate in ASD is equal to the general population, albeit a difference is often found between individuals with Asperger syndrome and those with Autistic Disorder.

ASD in forensic settings

Scragg and Shah (1994) found that 1.5% of (male) individuals with ASD (hospitalised in a forensic hospital in the UK) met strict criteria of Asperger syndrome. Another study by Hare et al. (1999) included 1305 patients in a special forensic hospital in the UK of which only 21 (1.6%) were diagnosed with Asperger syndrome. In a Swedish study, 1.3% of the male individuals with Autistic Disorder were arsonists and 0.3% committed other crimes, compared to 7.1% arsonists and 1% offenders regarding other crimes of male individuals with Asperger syndrome (Enayati et al., 2008). Regarding women with Autistic Disorder, arson was found in 0% of the cases, whereas 2.5% of the women with Asperger syndrome were found to be arsonists. Women with ASD might be over-represented in the population of female offenders (presumably due to the more complex clinical presentation of women who have been diagnosed with ASD): Over 10% have been found to (probably) have ASD (Crocombe, Mills, & Wing, 2006).

A recent review of the literature suggests poor evidence for an overrepresentation of ASD in the criminal justice system (King & Murphy, 2014) and another review study shows that only 11 of the 147 studies supported the link between ASD and violent crimes (Bjørkly, 2009). Compared with matched groups with schizophrenia and personality disorders, the individuals with Asperger syndrome showed an even lower rate of violent offences (Murphy, 2003).

Types of offending

Illicit drug taking was reported less often in high-functioning individuals with ASD, but offences related to 'criminal damage' and violent behaviour were reported more often than in a general population community sample (Woodbury-Smith, Clare, Holland, & Kearns, 2006). Violent acts were the most common offending behaviour (81%), followed by threatening conduct (75%) and destructive behaviour (50%) in 16 English adults with Asperger syndrome (Allen et al., 2008). Although some studies suggest a link between certain crimes and ASD, like the often mentioned arson (e.g. Mouridsen et al., 2008), other studies contradict this presumed connection (see King & Murphy, 2014). However, those individuals who do commit arson might mainly do so because of an intense interest in fire (Woodbury-Smith et al., 2010).

Although patterns in types of criminal acts are not greatly supported by research, patterns in prominent types of offending could differ between groups of individuals within the ASD population. People with ASD who are violent offenders tend to have severe mental health issues and function better intellectually when compared to sexual offenders with ASD (Søndenaa et al., 2014). When sexual offences occur, it is mostly due to a lack of social understanding (e.g. when displaying sexual acts in public settings, like masturbation; see Sevlever, Roth, & Gillis, 2013 for an overview).

In conclusion, certain crimes appear less common in ASD (as individuals with ASD tend to be law abiding and willing to follow rules; Howlin, 2004), whereas violent crimes might happen more often than in the general population, at least in high-functioning autism. These acts seem mostly a reaction to provocation, instead of premeditated crimes, warranting a focus on predisposing factors in the environment and characteristics of people with ASD which might cause someone with ASD to act in criminal ways.

Comorbidity

It is plausible that individuals with ASD who commit (violent) crimes have certain characteristics and triggers for violence that are different from the general population. ASD brings about a myriad of associated difficulties including comorbidity, which involves additional psychiatric diagnoses or meeting the criteria of these disorders. Estimates of the prevalence of comorbidity reach 70% (Simonoff et al., 2008) to 80.9% (in children with PDD-NOS; de Bruin, Ferdinand, Meester, de Nijs, & Verheij, 2006). Whereas ASD is generally seen as the prototypical disorder for social difficulties, many other psychiatric classifications are also associated with interpersonal problems (e.g. OCD, ADHD, schizophrenia and personality disorders; APA, 2013) or aggression, which makes the clinical presentation even more complicated. The presence of comorbidity is known to be related to more severe and persistent (social) problems and negative outcomes, including criminal behaviour (Connor et al., 2003; de Bruin et al., 2006).

ADHD and ODD

Note that the DSM-IV did not allow a diagnosis that combines ASD with, for instance, Attention Deficit Hyperactivity Disorder (ADHD), albeit this

314   *Lysandra Podesta and Anna M. T. Bosman*

combination has nonetheless oftentimes been given. Whether comorbidity with ADHD in children with ASD resembles ADHD or really is additional ADHD cannot be decided upon as long as the aetiology of both disorders is not clear (Gadow et al., 2008). The majority of children with ASD have ADHD symptoms (APA, 2013) and, according to Gadow et al. (2008), the screening rate of individuals between 6 and 12 years of age who were referred reached over 50%, meaning that half of these individuals met the criteria for at least one subtype of ADHD: A developmental disorder associated with problematic behaviour. Montes and Halterman (2007) found that children with ASD who also had AD(H)D were at greater odds to engage in bullying than children without this comorbidity, also when age, gender and household income were controlled for. In this population, girls did not have a decreased chance of showing this behaviour.

The combination of ASD and ADHD comprises social problems combined with behavioural disinhibition, which is believed to make aggressive acts more likely (Guttmann-Steinmetz, Gadow, & DeVincent, 2009). This combination is often associated with oppositional defiant disorder (ODD) and aggression (Gadow, DeVincent, & Drabick, 2008; Singh et al., 2006), which is more pronounced for children with combined and hyperactive-impulsive subtypes of ADHD compared to inattention. But note, some characteristics of ODD appeared to be frequently present (e.g. 'angry and resentful' and 'loses temper'), whereas others were less prevalent, namely those of a more social nature (e.g. 'argues with adults' and 'tries to get even'), which might provide clues regarding causes of aggressive acts.

Anxiety, mood disorders, loneliness and trauma

There are cases that suggest a possible link between trauma and criminality in ASD. Murrie, Warren, Kristiansson, and Dietz (2002) report about a person with low average intelligence who set houses on fire, because small details reminded him of the houses of peers who had harassed him when he was young. People with ASD might be vulnerable to developing Posttraumatic Stress Disorder, an anxiety disorder associated with aggression (Kivisto, Moore, Elkins, & Rhatigan, 2009). In Mehtar and Mukkades (2011), 26% had a trauma history and 17% had a PTSD diagnosis, which is more than the lifetime PTSD prevalence of 6% to 8% in the general population (Kessler, Petukhove, Sampson, Zaslavsky, & Wittchen, 2012). Mandell, Walrath, Manteuffel, Sgro, and Pinto-Martin (2005) emphasise that a history of abuse should be considered when confronted with problematic behaviours in ASD; 18.5% had been physically abused and 16.6% had experienced sexual abuse and these were associated with behaviours such as self-injury, acting out, and suicidal and abusive behaviour.

In an article of Murrie and colleagues (2002), a young man with average intelligence was described as a person who peeped at girls in a locker room through a hole he made himself. He had, as personality testing elucidated, a tendency to escape in fantasies when severely stressed. This could have had something to do with his criminal acts. This man had spent his youth mostly isolated from his peers and was severely anxious and depressed. He missed his only friend from home when he went to college and he did not fit into relationships developing around him. Important people in the life of an adolescent or (young) adult are the family. Unfortunately, families with a family member with ASD often function poorly. Parents report more parental stress, equally so when the child has high-functioning ASD (Rao & Beidel, 2009). Poor family functioning is, in turn, a known risk factor for delinquency (Stouthamer-Loeber, Loeber, Wei, Farrington, & Wikstrorm, 2002). Particularly people with ASD are at risk of having a modest social network, which entails not having many people for practical or emotional support. The risk of becoming isolated from social life is enhanced in ASD and may increase the risk of delinquency. Two individuals described in Palermo (2004) also had comorbid mood disorders. There probably is, for some individuals with ASD, a link between mood disorders or trauma, poor emotional regulation and crimes. Anxiety and mood disorders are among the most common and debilitating problems associated with ASD (White, Oswald, Ollendick, & Scahill, 2009). Emotion regulation problems paired with severe anxiety, depression and/or irritability (and a traumatic past) might lead to aggressive acts (McLaughlin, Hatzenbuehler, Mennin, & Nolen-Hoeksema, 2011). The combination of ASD with bipolar disorder is associated with aggression and delinquency (Weissman & Bates, 2010). Emotion regulation problems in ASD are assumed to be practically universal (Mazefsky et al., 2013) and cognitive reappraisal is used less often, which is associated with increased negative emotion experience. This, in turn, is associated with problem behaviour, including aggression and tantrums (Samson, Hardan, Lee, Phillips, & Gross, 2015). In ASD, extreme emotional reactions seem to go along with fewer options for expressing these (e.g. through verbalisation or facial expression; Losh & Capps, 2006).

This has an impact on quality of life, as illustrated by a study which included 12 men with Asperger syndrome, who all reported lower quality of life when compared to matched controls (Jennes-Coussens, 2006) and a qualitative study which showed that most individuals with ASD who committed crimes did so because of an accumulation of stress, (e.g. due to relationship and work problems), which led to poor mental health (Allen et al., 2008).

Substance use, psychosis and personality disorders

A longitudinal study of 422 people with ASD (of whom 105 had Asperger syndrome and the rest had Autistic Disorder) revealed that comorbid psychopathology was associated with violent convictions; those who were offenders had more comorbidity (Långstrøm, Grann, Ruchkin, Siøstedt, & Fazel, 2009). Comorbid psychotic disorder, personality disorders and substance use disorders were linked to violent offending. Schizophrenia was the most common (25%) among offenders with Asperger syndrome (Allen et al., 2008).

316 *Lysandra Podesta and Anna M.T. Bosman*

Långstrøm et al. (2009) concluded that offending in ASD is related to the same (comorbid) risk factors as in the general population. King and Murphy (2014), however, point out that studies showing that comorbid disorders are associated with crime in ASD are carried out in mental health settings, in which people are more likely to have comorbid diagnoses.

In conclusion, a connection between offending and ASD is inconclusive and concomitant psychopathological factors could be the main driving force behind criminal behaviour, instead of ASD itself (Palermo, 2004). The findings suggest that many individuals with ASD commit crimes because of severely impaired mental health. Yet some people with ASD seem to commit crimes when no comorbidity is present (15% in a review by Newman & Ghaziuddin, 2008). Certain factors inherent to ASD (such as emotion regulation problems and sensory sensitivity, as discussed below) are sometimes thought to be risk factors for (violent) criminal acts.

Internal factors in ASD related to offending

Intensity of emotions and hyperreactivity

ASD is assumed to be associated with hyperarousal (heightened reactivity or elevated basal levels of the nervous system). The limbic system is involved in emotion regulation, but there are indications that this regulation is altered in ASD, which is not only associated with internalising problems, but also with aggression (McLaughlin, Hatzenbuehler, Mennin, & Nolen-Hoeksema, 2011). Magnée, de Gelder, van Engeland, and Kemner (2007) examined facial electromyographic responses to emotional information. They found that this high-functioning sample had strong automatic, emotional reactions to facial expressions (presented together with voices) of happiness and fear. However, ambiguous or neutral faces are often interpreted as negative (Eack, Mazefsky, & Minshew, 2014). Additionally, direct gaze is associated with intense emotional reactions in ASD (Dalton et al., 2005). This might be related to, as rat models of autism show, hyperreactive and hyperconnected amygdalae and medial prefrontal cortices, which are associated with a 'fight or flight' reaction (Makram, Rinaldi, & Makram, 2007). What this entails is that face-to-face social interaction (which is viewed as normal in society) could be seen as threatening or overwhelming for a person with ASD. In turn, this will influence social behaviour and will probably cause social withdrawal (related to internalising problem behaviour or avoiding sensory stimuli) or lead to 'fight' reactions; in other words, aggression. For example, when looking other people in the eyes is avoided, possibly because of sensitivity to emotional information, which is prevalent in the eye region, important social information could be missed. Less experience with social interaction and picking up social information to a lesser degree will make it more difficult to cope with and learn from social interactions. In turn, a lack of social insight might be related to crimes.

Sensory processing differences

Regarding sensory processing, several types of extreme sensory processing are reported. Patterns of sensory processing differences can differ greatly between individuals, but 94.4% reported extreme sensory processing of at least one type. Some might experience disabling sensory sensitivity, because it renders an everyday life environment unbearable, whereas others often drown out sensory information and may become largely unresponsive (Crane, Goddard, & Pring, 2009). Even within one individual, hypersensitivity to, for instance, sound can be accompanied by hyposensitivity to touch. That person might become aggressive when confronted with certain intolerable sounds, whereas he or she could often bump into objects in daily life because of hyposensitivity. Not only do differences between senses often exist, but sensitivity can even vary regarding one sense within an individual (switching from hyper- to hyposensitivity and back, as expressed by, for instance, low cortical evoked response reliability in reaction to sensory stimuli; Dinstein et al., 2012). The precise mechanisms behind these differences are still unknown.

Whatever the case, when hypersensitivity of some of the senses is present, overloading these senses can cause a hyperarousal state associated with panic or aggression. Some crimes have been reported to be committed due to feelings of an extreme sense of urgency to escape overwhelming sensory sensations. In Bjørkly (2009), sensory hypersensitivity was the second largest (21%) cause of violent crimes. Having difficulty expressing needs or noticing increasing emotional tension (due to a lack of awareness of one's emotions) might make timely interfering with the increasing hyperarousal difficult, leading to extreme behavioural reactions.

Alternatively, a shutting out of sensory input due to sensory overload will lead to a (social) withdrawal: A self-created state of isolation (Liss, Mailloux, & Erchull, 2008). This can be related to a lack of felt connection to other people; to be socially engaged, fight, flight and shutdown responses need to be absent (Porges, 2003). This dissociation from others or one's own emotions is also seen in, for instance, PTSD. While both options (hyper- and hypoarousal) are possible, it seems that mostly sensory hypersensitivity is typical in offending individuals with ASD (Bjørkly, 2009).

Cognitive difficulties

Multiple cognitive differences appear to be associated with ASD. Executive functioning, which is a cluster of abilities involving processes such as inhibition, planning and task switching, is assumed to be impaired in ASD (O'Hearn, Asato, Ordaz, & Luna, 2008). These functions are presumed needed for everyday activities and affect complex behaviour (e.g. social interaction). Deficits in executive functioning have been proposed as an underlying factor of behavioural symptoms of ASD (Pennington & Ozonoff, 1996). Average executive functioning is associated with 'optimal' developmental outcomes, albeit some

318   *Lysandra Podesta and Anna M. T. Bosman*

differences compared to typically developing individuals remain also in individuals who no longer meet the criteria of ASD (e.g. working memory and attention shifting; Troyb et al., 2014).

Another theory states that due to lack of central coherence, people with ASD might not be able to (immediately) see the whole. A recent version of this theory (for an overview, see Happé & Frith, 2005), however, focuses on a bias towards and superiority in local (detail-oriented) processing. Individuals with ASD appear to be able to process information globally, when required to do so. Local forms of information processing may cause trouble with understanding general meaning and being able to experience the whole in people with ASD. Traditional theories of ASD include Theory of Mind (mentalising) impairment, which refers to the cognitive ability to explain and predict behaviour in other people. These skills are necessary to know that other people have knowledge, intentions and desires that are different from one's own and to recognise these in oneself and others (for a review, see Baron-Cohen, 2001). However, not every child with ASD fails false-belief tasks used to measure Theory of Mind. According to Happé (1995), 15% to 60% pass the false-belief test. Children with proper language abilities tend to have a relatively intact Theory of Mind (Baron-Cohen, Leslie, & Frith, 1985; Tager-Flusberg & Joseph, 2005). When Theory of Mind develops later, as it usually does in ASD, (communicating with) other people may seem highly confusing and this can be related to aggressive behaviour (e.g. Werner, Cassidy, & Juliano, 2006).

These cognitive deviations in people with ASD can serve as a *protective* factor for certain crimes and for some people, as they limit long term planning and organisation of premeditated crimes. On the other hand, however, they might also affect understanding social situations and regulating and processing emotions adversely. A weak central coherence is thought to be associated with preoccupations and can lead to criminal behaviour due to a disconnection with the social environment (Haskins & Silva, 2006). Furthermore, when attention shifting is difficult, interests can become obsessional, which in turn increase the chance of certain crimes (e.g. arson). It also makes it difficult to handle situations and emotions in a manner that can be considered flexible or adaptable (see White et al., 2014).

Distinction between ASD and psychopathy

Regarding empathy in ASD, cognitive empathy seems to be diminished (being able to understand other people, Theory of Mind and recognising facial emotions; Harms, Martin, & Wallace, 2010). However, affective empathy (emotional resonance, e.g. feeling distress when other people are in distress; Decety, 2011) is intact (Dziobek et al., 2008). In fact, affective empathy in ASD might yield a susceptibility to empathic overarousal, according to the empathy–imbalance hypothesis (see Smith, 2009). Senland and Higgins-D'Alessandro (2013) found that adolescents with high-functioning

Autism and (violent) offending 319

ASD had higher empathic personal distress and similar empathic concern, but lower moral reasoning than typically developing adolescents. The adolescents reported struggles using empathic feelings to support their actions when encountering spontaneous socio-moral situations, leading to lower scores on 'moral reasoning'. These findings support the view that individuals with ASD are overwhelmed by affective empathy (and experience difficulty using this information to back up actions). This entails an empathy-deficit opposite to the pattern of antisocial personality disorder and psychopathy (Blair, 2005).

Although callous-unemotional traits (characteristic for psychopathy) are associated with a lack of affective empathy, this is usually not the case in ASD. In Murphy (2007), all people with Asperger syndrome in a high-security psychiatric care setting scored below the British and North-American cut-off point for psychopathy. A small minority of individuals with ASD, however, develop severely antisocial behaviour, which is associated with callous-unemotional traits. This appears to be unrelated to ASD traits and may reflect an unfortunate 'double hit' (Rogers, Viding, Blair, Frith, & Happé, 2006). Note, however, that characteristics such as 'reacts unsympathetically when another child is upset' measure the callous-unemotional trait, but this behaviour could be elicited by other things than not *wanting* or not caring to help. It is necessary to focus on underlying factors of similar behaviour to understand the differences. In Soderstrom, Rastam, and Gillberg (2002), antisocial temperament (high novelty seeking, low harm avoidance and low reward dependence) was not found at all in adults with Asperger syndrome; other personality types, especially those involving high harm avoidance, e.g. fear of uncertainty and worry, seemed typical of this sample.

Usually, people with ASD, unlike psychopaths, wish to escape overwhelming sensory stimulation or overwhelming emotions (associated with *reactive* violence), which is a different drive than the instrumental, manipulative or social force that drives the crimes of psychopaths that can lead to *proactive* violence (for a complete overview, see Bjørkly, 2009). There are additional striking differences between criminal people with ASD and people with psychopathy; psychopaths have a reduced response to sensory stimuli, whereas people with ASD tend to be (sensory, and, as described earlier, emotionally) hyperreactive. Furthermore, instead of manipulative interactions, people with ASD tend to lack these and when asked about the crime, psychopaths often deny, but individuals with ASD usually confess quickly.

This quick confession might be due to overwhelming emotions. Allen et al. (2008) found that most individuals in court felt highly anxious, despite the fact that some will come across as arrogant or uninterested (Archer & Hurley, 2013). Many people with ASD suppress expression of emotions. In this group, a common self-control coping mechanism which comprises limiting facial expressions and controlling emotions makes an individual *seem* unemotional, whereas blood-pressure and sympathetic activation is, in fact, elevated (Dan-Glauser & Gross, 2011; Samson, Huber, & Gross, 2012). Another explanation is that they do not know how they feel (i.e. alexithymia is common in ASD and is associated with suppression; Bird & Cook, 2013; Buck, 2003). In ASD, emotions (including empathic concern) might be drowned out because these are experienced as overwhelming. In some, this numbing might also be related to crime. When obsession or habit is combined with lack of feeling, this can elicit delinquency (e.g. sexual offences in higher-functioning individuals; Allan et al., 2008).

One important characteristic influencing criminality and confessing is general harm avoidance. Law-abiding behaviour is likely to be more present in ASD than in the general population (Howlin, 2004). People with ASD are unlikely to wilfully break rules or laws. They are also more inclined to avoid conflict and confrontation than controls. This may lead to overly compliant behaviour when it comes to suggestions or requests, even when this has negative consequences as a suspect (North, Russel, & Gudjonsson, 2008).

In sum, committing crimes appears to be triggered by other factors than wanting to cause deliberate harm or gain certain benefits, as would be the case in psychopathy. In fact, due to their will to please, people with ASD may even be lured into criminal acts when these are not triggered by unmanageable emotions or impulses, maybe especially so when they experience great loneliness or a wish to be accepted. A media example illustrates this line of reasoning. Snodgrass, an individual with ASD with no history of buying or selling drugs, was persuaded by an undercover officer to sell a small amount of marijuana. He thought that the officer was a fellow student and his friend, which led to a traumatic arrest and loss of his only friend (Autism Speaks, 2014; Erdely, 2014). Interestingly, while this kind of behaviour is usually explained by social naivety (Murrie, Warren, Kristiansson, & Dietz, 2002), this boy (who had ASD, among other psychiatric disorders) reported he was worried about his troubled friend and believed him when he said he needed drugs to cope with personal problems. This shows that at least part of the ASD population is not only socially motivated, but also wishes to help others and wants to be accepted even when this goes against generally law-abiding behaviour. Highly socially motivated individuals with ASD might be at risk for being lured into delinquency.

External factors in ASD related to offending

Some external factors will be common in people with ASD, like being unemployed and having a small social network (discussed earlier). These are, in turn, connected to criminality. Sometimes, the influence of risk factors on criminality is aggravated when combined with ASD symptoms.

An important external factor is victimisation. Children with autism are usually victims rather than bullies (Zablotsky, Bradshaw, Anderson, & Law, 2013). ASD characteristics like intense emotional or behavioural reactions and uncommon interests make someone a vulnerable target (Gray, 2004). Apart from the commonly mentioned negative effects of being victimised, such as internalising and externalising symptoms and sometimes even suicide, several outcomes have been related to being bullied regarding children with ASD specifically.

Examples are emotional trauma and being scared for one's safety (Zablotsky et al., 2013), aggression, agitation, hyperactivity, self-injury, but also exacerbation of ASD symptoms, like deterioration in social skills (Mehtar & Mukaddes, 2011). The link between mental health problems and being bullied is bidirectional, meaning that children who are bullied will be at risk for new mental health problems and these problems will further elevate the risk of being bullied (Fekkes et al., 2006). Long-lasting or severe experiences could affect development (for instance, via PTSD) and may elicit criminal acts (e.g. the case previously noted in which a man burned down houses because details of these reminded him of houses of people who had harassed him).

Additional support for the assumed relationship between victimisation and offending in high-functioning people with ASD is provided by Kawakami et al. (2012). In this group, physical abuse and neglect are important predictors for criminal acts and a late diagnosis is correlated with criminal behaviour. Moreover, late diagnoses are also more common in high-functioning ASD, due to less obvious clinical expressions or better coping mechanisms. All these factors increase the risk of developing criminal behaviour. Perhaps these individuals never received adequate help when they were young, causing the combination of risk factors for criminality, like comorbid (mood) disorders and disappointments regarding societal functioning, to become more complicated over the years.

Treatment

General treatment for people with ASD

Multiple treatment options are available for young people with ASD used to either manage accompanying problems or target ASD symptoms. However, the vast majority of these options lack a solid empirical basis (Goin-Kochel et al. 2007; Schechtman, 2007). A study by Goin-Kochel et al. (2007) has shown that parents report that, on average, eight therapies had been tried for their child. This number illustrated the daunting task parents face when trying to help their child cope with problems and act in acceptable ways. The authors found a trend in the types of therapies that were currently implemented. Behavioural or educational therapies were used most often for young individuals. Examples are Applied Behavior Analysis (ABA, which is empirically validated; Foxx, 2008), Speech Therapy and Sensory Integration. Social Stories, in which social situations are explained, and social skills training were more often used in adolescence and in individuals diagnosed with Asperger syndrome. Psychotropic medication was most used in adolescence, possibly because, during the transition of middle childhood to adolescence, problems are considered to become too severe for behavioural treatment alone to alleviate them.

The most commonly administered psychotropic medications are antidepressants, psychostimulants and antipsychotics (Martin, Scahill, Klin, & Volkmar, 1999). Green et al. (2006) reported that 52% of parents currently used at least

322   Lysandra Podesta and Anna M.T. Bosman

one type of medication for their child. A study including 353 youths from 3 to 21 years of age with ASD revealed that 46.7% of these young participants had used at least one type of medication in the past year (Witwer & Lecavalier, 2005). The type of medication was related to the (1) age of the individuals (older participants used medication more often), (2) adaptive skills and being socially competent (lower skills were linked to more medication use) and (3) problematic behaviour (when more problem behaviour was displayed, medication had a higher chance of being the treatment of choice). Having more adaptive skills was associated with more psychostimulant use.

Treatment of aggression and challenging behaviour in youth

Neither therapy nor medication can cure ASD. Nevertheless, comorbid (disturbing) problems are often targeted for treatment. Multiple pharmacological treatments that are supposed to reduce problem behaviour are abundant. Methylphenidate has been found to improve symptoms of hyperactivity and impulsivity in children with ASD, but the repetitive/stereotyped behaviour and ODD remain unaffected (Posey et al., 2007). Important downsides include: aggravating stereotypes, behavioural problems and side effects like weight loss (Malone, Gratz, Delaney, & Hyman, 2005). Furthermore, serotonin reuptake inhibitors, generally used to treat depression and anxiety (Kapczinski et al., 2003), are associated with improvements in certain challenging behaviours in ASD (Taylor et al., 2012) through helping people with ASD feel better emotionally, albeit the efficacy for reaching this goal appears limited (Malone et al., 2005). Antipsychotic medication has often been used to treat problems such as aggression, panic and hyperactivity (Kirino, 2014) and issues like emotional instability and repetitive behaviour in ASD (Malone et al., 2005). The Research Units on Pediatric Psychopharmacology Autism Network (RUPP, 2002) found that irritable behaviour and hyperactivity decreased through treatment with risperidone. This medicine has been approved (in the US; Food and Drug Administration) for particularly treating aggression and irritability (including tantrums, aggression and self-injury) in minors with ASD, and is now, in addition to aripiprazole, the antipsychotic drug of choice. However, debilitating side effects include weight gain and metabolic changes (Beherec et al., 2011; Dinnissen, Dietrich, van den Hoofdakker, & Hoekstra, 2015).

Several behavioural treatments are available to treat aggression and oppositional behaviour. Functional communication training is associated with positive results by helping individuals express their needs (for an overview, see Matson & Jang, 2014). For example, a training that helps clients to say 'I don't understand' could provide the child with the needed assistance, making aggressive behaviour unnecessary. Additionally, intensive behavioural interventions have been used successfully to treat problem behaviour in children and adolescents (Howlin, Magiati, & Charman, 2009) and the empirically confirmed effectiveness of ABA is also found regarding treatment of aggression (Brosnan & Healy, 2011). Yet a combination of behavioural

Autism and (violent) offending   323

treatment and medication could hold the greatest promise for reducing aggressive behaviour. For example, Frazier et al. (2010) showed that antipsychotic medication could decrease the number of required intensive behavioural intervention sessions in children. Importantly, behavioural treatments that have been confirmed to be effective in controlled laboratory settings might, in reality, not be performed with the same intensity and thoroughness in community-based, mental health clinics (Brookman-Frazee, Taylor, & Garland, 2010) and community services possibly have insufficient specialised knowledge on ASD (Brookman-Frazee et al., 2009).

To complicate things even further, additional troublesome areas of functioning could precipitate or aggravate aggression. Treating these might indirectly help alleviate aggression (e.g. sleep difficulties; Goldman et al., 2011; Malow et al., 2009). Importantly, trauma might be missed, as aggression and self-injury fluctuates and parents can fail to see that behavioural differences result from trauma and the child may have problems expressing these experiences in decodable ways (e.g. sexual abuse; Edelson, 2010). An individually tailored treatment plan that encompasses careful assessment of additional comorbid problems and which is also accommodated to the individual's level of functioning could be extremely important for successfully treating the problem behaviour of an individual with ASD.

Treatment of aggression and challenging behaviour in adults

A disproportional emphasis has been laid on studying aggression and problem behaviour in children or adolescents with ASD. Including adult participants is particularly important, considering that adult aggression could have more far-reaching consequences. After all, an adult can create more harm (see a review of related literature, in which only five of the 42 reviewed articles included adult participants; Matson & Cervantes, 2014) and may get in more serious trouble by breaking the law. With regards to sexual abuse and offending, treatment has often focused on prevention, possibly because not much is known about specific treatments for these behaviours (Sevlever, Roth, & Gillis, 2013). However, some forms of therapy have been shown to be successful for harmful behaviour in adults with ASD.

When it appears that problem behaviour has clear environmental antecedents, it may be useful to choose applied behaviour analysis for helping the individual change his or her aggressive reactions (as is the case in children and adolescents). If the cause of delinquent behaviour is a lack of emotion recognition, this can be accommodated for by training (Golan & Baron-Cohen, 2006). But pharmacological treatment is probably best when challenging behaviour is either extreme or antecedents cannot be identified (see Matson, Sipes, Fodstad, & Fitzgerald, 2011).

In short, all kinds of treatment will have certain drawbacks. Pharmacological treatment often has side effects and psychological and behavioural treatments are labour intensive (Matson, Mahan, & LoVullo, 2009). Comorbid psychiatric

324   *Lysandra Podesta and Anna M. T. Bosman*

diagnoses are often present in individuals with ASD and it is recommended to treat these because they may generate delinquent or aggressive acts. Prevention also seems important, because 94.4% of people with criminal activity were recidivists (Kawakami et al., 2012) and, despite traditional intervention or without intervention, challenging behaviours tend to be chronic (Murphy et al., 2005).

Concluding remarks

Although there is an awareness that individuals with ASD often need lifelong assistance to develop and use their potential (Howlin, 2005), effective and appropriate services are scarce (Gerhardt & Lainer, 2011). The discussed literature suggests that problems associated with or inherent to ASD might form risk factors and risk factors might exacerbate ASD symptoms, which, in turn, will be new risk factors for criminality. Note that most people with 'only' ASD do not commit crimes; criminal behaviour is not inherent to the disorder. Nevertheless, certain internal and external (risk) factors may aggravate problematic behaviour and offending.

Using medication or redirecting challenging behaviour alone will not remove causes such as trauma, hyperactivity or prolonged social isolation. It is doubtful whether individuals with ASD currently get the help they need for factors underlying criminal behaviour. A focus on these factors is justified and treating these problems in people with ASD may be more complicated or last longer.

Literature

Abrahams, B. S., & Geschwind, D. H. (2008). Advances in autism genetics: On the threshold of a new neurobiology. *Nature Reviews: Genetics, 9*(5), 341–355. doi: 10.1038/nrg2346

Achenbach, T. M., & Rescorla, L. A. (2000). *Manual for the ASEBA preschool forms and profiles.* Burlington, VT: University of Vermont Department of Psychiatry.

Allen, D., Evans, C., Hider, A., Hawkins, S., Peckitt, H., & Morgan, H. (2008). Offending behaviour in adults with Asperger's syndrome. *Journal of Autism and Developmental Disorder, 38,* 748–758.

American Psychiatric Association (2013). *Diagnostic and statistical manual of mental disorders* (Fifth ed.). Arlington, VA: American Psychiatric Publishing.

Archer, N., & Hurley, E. A. (2013). A justice system failing the autistic community. *Journal of Intellectual Disabilities and Offending Behaviour, 4,* 7.

Autism Speaks (2014). *Rolling Stone looks at story of high-schooler with autism arrested for selling drugs.* Retrieved from: https://www.autismspeaks.org/news/news-item/rolling-stone-looks-story-high-schooler-autism-arrested-selling-drugs

Baird, G., Simonoff, E., Pickles, A., Chandler, S., Loucas, T., Meldrum, D., & Charman, T. (2006). Prevalence of disorders of the autism spectrum in a population cohort of children in South Thames: The Special Needs and Autism Project (SNAP). *Lancet, 368,* 210–215. doi: 10.1016/S0140-6736(06)69041-7

Baldwin, S., Costley, D., & Warren, A. (2014). Employment activities and experiences of adults with high-functioning autism and Asperger's disorder. *Journal of Autism and Developmental Disorder, 44*(10), 2440–2449.

Baron-Cohen, S. (2001). Theory of mind and autism: A review. *Special Issue of the International Review of Mental Retardation, 23*, 1–35.

Baron-Cohen, S., Leslie, A. M., & Frith, U. (1985). Does the autistic child have a 'theory of mind'? *Cognition, 21*, 37–46.

Barron, J. (2012). Nation reels after gunman massacres 20 children at school in Connecticut. *The New York Times*. Retrieved from: http://www.nytimes.com/2012/12/15/nyregion/shooting-reported-at-connecticut-elementary-school.html

Beherec, L., Lambrey, S., Quilici, G., Rosier, A., Falissard, B., & Guillin, O. (2011). Retrospective review of Clozapine in the treatment of patients with Autism Spectrum Disorder and severe disruptive behaviors. *Journal of Clinical Psychopharmacology, 31*(3), 341–344.

Berger, J., & Santora, M. (2013). Chilling look at Newtown killer, but no 'why'. *The New York Times*. Retrieved from: http://www.nytimes.com/2013/11/26/nyregion/sandy-hook-shooting-investigation-ends-with-motive-still-unknown.html

Bird, G., & Cook, R. (2013). Mixed emotions: The contribution of alexithymia to the emotional symptoms of autism. *Translational Psychiatry, 3*, e285. doi: 10.1038/tp.2013.61

Bjørkly, S. (2009). Risk and dynamics of violence in Asperger's syndrome: A systematic review of the literature. *Aggression and Violent Behavior, 14*, 306–312. doi: 10.1016/j.avb.2009.04.003

Blair, R. J. R. (2005). Responding to the emotions of others: Dissociating forms of empathy through the study of typical and psychiatric populations. *Consciousness and Cognition, 14*, 698–718.

Bölte, S., & Poustka, F. (2002). The relation between general cognitive level and adaptive behavior domains in individuals with autism with and without co-morbid mental retardation. *Child Psychiatric and Human Development, 33*, 165–172.

Brookman-Frazee, L. I., Baker-Ericzén, M., Stahmer, A., Mandell, D., Haine, R. A., & Hough, R. L. (2009). Involvement in youths with autism spectrum disorders or intellectual disabilities in multiple public service systems. *Mental Health Research in Intellectual Disabilities, 2*, 201–219.

Brookman-Frazee, L. I., Taylor, R., & Garland, A. F. (2010). Characterizing community-based mental health services for children with autism spectrum disorders and disruptive behavior problems. *Journal of Autism and Developmental Disorders, 40*(10), 1188–1201. doi: 10.1007/s10803-010-0976-0

Brosnan, J., & Healy, O. (2011). A review of behavioral interventions for the treatment of aggression in individuals with developmental disabilities. *Research in Developmental Disabilities, 32*(2), 437–446.

Buck, R. (2003). Emotional expression, suppression, and control: Nonverbal communication in cultural context. *Journal of Intercultural Communication Research, 32*, 47–65.

Cheely, C. A., Carpenter, L. A., Letourneau, E. J., Nicholas, J. S., Charles, J., & King, L. B. (2012). The prevalence of youth with Autism Spectrum Disorders in the criminal justice system. Journal of Autism and Developmental Disorders, *42*, 1856–1862. doi: 10.1007/s10803-011-1427-2

Connor, D. E., Edwards, G., Fletcher, K. E., Baird, J., Barkley, R. A., & Steingard, R. J. (2003). Correlates of comorbid psychopathology in children with ADHD. *Journal of the American Academy of Child and Adolescent Psychiatry, 42*, 193–200. doi: 10.1097/00004583-200302000-00013.

326 *Lysandra Podesta and Anna M. T. Bosman*

Crane, L., Goddard, L., & Pring, L. (2009). Sensory processing in adults with autism spectrum disorders. *Autism, 13*, 215–228. doi: 10.1177/1362361309103794

Crocombe, J., Mills, R., & Wing, L. (2006). *Autism spectrum disorders in the high security hospitals of the United Kingdom. A summary of two studies.* London: National Autistic Society.

Dalton, K. M., Nacewicz, B. M., Johnstone, T., Schaefer, H. S., Gernsbacker, M. A., Goldsmith, H. H., & Davidson, R. J. (2005). Gaze fixation and the neural circuitry of face processing in autism. *Nature Neuroscience, 8*, 519–526. doi: 10.1038/nn1421

Dan-Glauser, E. S., & Gross, J. J. (2011). The temporal dynamics of two response-focused forms of emotion regulation: Experiential, expressive, and autonomic consequences. *Society for Psychophysiological Research, 48*, 1309–1322. doi: 10.1111/j.1469-8986.2011.01191.x

De Bruin, E. I., Ferdinand, R. F., Meester, S., de Nijs, P. F. A., & Verheij, F. (2007). High rates of psychiatric co-morbidity in PDD-NOS. *Journal of Autism and Developmental Disorder, 37*(5), 877–886. doi: 10.1007/s10803-006-0215-x

Decety, J. (2011). Dissecting the neural mechanisms mediating empathy. *Emotion Review, 3*, 92–109.

Dinnissen, M., Dietrich, A., Van den Hoofdakker, B. J., & Hoekstra, P. J. (2015). Clinical and pharmacokinetic evaluation of risperidone for the management of autism spectrum disorder. *Expert Opinion of Drug Metabolism & Toxicology, 11*(1), 111.

Dinstein, I., Heeger, D. J., Lorenzi, L., Minshew, N. J., Malach, R., & Behrmann, M. (2012). Unreliable evoked responses in autism. *Neuron, 75*(6), 981–991. doi: 10.1016/j.neuron.2012.07.026

Dyck, P. C. (2009). Prevalence of parent-reported diagnosis of autism spectrum disorder among children in the US. *Pediatrics, 124*, 1395–1403.

Dziobek, I., Rogers, K., Fleck, S., Bahnemann, M., Heekeren, H. R., Wolf, O. T., & Convit, A. (2008). Dissociation of cognitive and emotional empathy in adults with Asperger syndrome using the Multifaceted Empathy Test (MET). *Journal of Autism and Developmental Disorders, 38*(3), 464–473.

Eack, S. M., Mazefsky, C. A., & Minshew, N. J. (2014). Misinterpretation of facial expressions of emotion in verbal adults with autism spectrum disorder. *Autism, 19*(3), 308–315. doi: 10.1177/1362361314520755

Edelson, G. (2010). Sexual abuse of children with autism: Factors that increase risk and interfere with recognition of abuse. *Disability Studies Quarterly, 31*(2), 189–200. doi: 10.1007/s11195-013-9286-8

Einfeld, S. L., Tonge, B. J., Gray, K. M., & Taffe, J. (2007). Evolution of symptoms and syndromes of psychopathology in young people with mental retardation. *International Review of Research in Mental Retardation – Developmental Epidemiology of Mental Retardation and Developmental Disabilities, 33*, 247–265.

Enayati, J., Grann, M., Lubbe, S., & Fazel, S. (2008). Psychiatric morbidity in arsonists referred for forensic psychiatric assessment in Sweden. *Journal of Forensic Psychiatry and Psychology, 19*, 139–147.

Erdely, S. R. (2014). The entrapment of Jesse Snodgrass. *Rolling Stone.* Retrieved from: http://www.rollingstone.com/culture/news/the-entrapment-of-jesse-snodgrass-20140226

Fekkes, M., Pijpers, F. I., Fredriks, A. M., Vogels, T., & Verloove-Vanhorick, S. P. (2006). Do bullied children get ill, or do ill children get bullied? A prospective cohort study on the relationship between bullying and health-related symptoms. *Pediatrics, 117*, 1568–1574.

Foxx, R. M. (2008). Applied behavior analysis treatment of autism: The state of art. *Child and Adolescent Psychiatric Clinics of North America, 28*, 821–834.

Frazier, T. W., Youngstrom, E. A., Havcook, T., Sinoff, A., Dimitriou, F., Knapp, J., & Sinclair, L. (2010). Effectiveness of medication combined with intensive behavioral intervention for reducing aggression in youth with autism spectrum disorder. *Journal of Child and Clinical Psychopharmacology, 20*, 167–177. doi: 10.1089/cap.2009.0048

Gadow, K. D., DeVincent, C. J., & Drabick, D. A. G. (2008). Oppositional defiant disorder as a clinical phenotype in children with autism spectrum disorder. *Journal of Autism and Developmental Disorders, 38*, 1302–1310. doi:10.1007/s10803-007-0516-8

Ganz, M. L. (2007). The lifetime distribution of the incremental societal costs of autism. *Archives of Pediatrics & Adolescent Medicine, 161*(4), 343–349. doi:10.1001/archpedi.161.4.343

Gerhardt, P. F., & Lainer, I. (2011). Addressing the needs of adolescents and adults with autism: A crisis on the horizon. *Journal of Contemporary Psychotherapy, 41*(1), 37–45. doi: 10.1007/s10879-010-9160-2

Ghaziuddin, M., Tsai, L., & Ghaziuddin, N. (1991). Brief report: Violence in Asperger syndrome, a critique. *Journal of Autism and Developmental Disorders, 21*, 329–354. doi: 10.1007/BF02207331

Goin-Kochel, R., Myers, B., MacKintosh, V. (2007). Parental reports on the use of treatments and therapies for children with autism spectrum disorders. *Research in Autism Spectrum Disorders, 1*, 195–209.

Golan, O., & Baron-Cohen, S. (2006). Systemizing empathy: Teaching adults with Asperger syndrome or high-functioning autism to recognize complex emotions using interactive multimedia. *Developmental Psychopathology, 18*, 591–617.

Goldman, S. E., McGrew, S., Johnson, K. P., Richdale, A. L., Clemons, T., & Malow, B. A. (2011). Sleep is associated with problem behaviors in children and adults with Autism Spectrum Disorders. *Research in Autism Spectrum Disorders, 5*(3), 1223–1229.

Gray, C. (2004). Gray's guide to bullying: The original series of articles, parts I–III. *Jenison Autism Journal, 16*(1), 2–19.

Gray, K., Keating, C., Taffe, J., Brereton, A., Eindfeld, S., & Tonge, B. (2012). Trajectory of behavior and emotional problems in autism. *American Journal on Intellectual and Developmental Disabilities, 117*(2), 121–133.

Green, V. A., Pituch, K. A., Itchon, J., Choi, A., O'Reilly, M., & Sigafoos, J. (2006). Internet survey of treatments used by parents of children with autism. *Research in Developmental Disabilities, 27*, 70–84.

Guttmann-Steinmetz, S., Gadow, K. D., & DeVincent, C. J. (2009). Oppositional defiant and conduct disorder behaviors in boys with autism spectrum disorder with and without attention-deficit hyperactivity disorder versus several comparison samples. *Journal of Autism and Developmental Disorders, 39*, 976–985. doi: 10.1007/s10803-009-0706-7

Happé, F. (1995). *Autism: An introduction to psychological theory.* Cambridge: Harvard University Press.

Happé, F., & Frith, U. (2005). The weak coherence account: Detail-focused cognitive style in autism spectrum disorders. *Journal of Autism and Developmental Disorders, 36*(1), 5–25. doi: 10.1007/s10803-005-0039-0

Hare, D.J., Gould J., Mills, R., Wing, L. (1999). A preliminary study of individuals with autistic spectrum disorders in three special hospitals in England.

Harms, M. B., Martin, A., & Wallace, G. L. (2010). Facial emotion recognition in autism spectrum disorders: A review of behavioral and neuroimaging studies. *Neuropsychology Review, 20*, 290–322.

328   Lysandra Podesta and Anna M.T. Bosman

Hartley, S. L., Sikora, D. M., & McCoy, R. (2008). Prevalence and risk factors of maladaptive behaviour in young children with Autistic Disorder. *Journal of Intellectual Disability Research, 52,* 819–829. doi: 10.1111/j.1365-2788.2008.01065.x

Haskins, B. G., & Silva, J. A. (2006). Asperger's disorder and criminal behavior: Forensic psychiatric considerations. *Journal of the American Academy of Psychiatry and the Law Online, 34*(3), 374–384.

Howlin, P. (2004). Legal issues. In P. Howlin (Ed.), *Autism and Asperger syndrome: Preparing for adulthood* (2nd ed., pp. 300–312). London/New York: Routledge.

Howlin, P. (2005). Outcomes in autism spectrum disorders. In F. R. Volkmar, R. Paul, A. Klin, & D. Cohen (Eds.), *Handbook of autism and pervasive developmental disorders* (Vol. 1, pp. 201–220). Hoboken, NJ: Wiley.

Howlin, P., Magiati, I., & Charman, T. (2009). Systematic review of early intensive behavioral interventions for children with autism. *American Journal on Intellectual and Developmental Disabilities, 114*(1), 23–41. doi: 10.1352/2009.114:23-41

Jennes-Coussens, M., Magill-Evans, J., & Koning, C. (2006). The quality of life of young men with Asperger syndrome: A brief report. *Autism, 10,* 403–414. doi: 10.1177/1362361306064432

Kaartinen, M., Puura, K., Helminen, M., Salmelin, R., Pelkonen, E., & Juujärvi, P. (2014). Reactive aggression among children with and without autism spectrum disorder. *Journal of Autism and Developmental Disorders, 44,* 2383–2391. doi: 10.1007/s10803-012-1743-1

Kanne, S. M., Gerber, A. J., Quirmbach, L. M., Sparrow, S. S., Cicchetti, D. V., & Saulnier, C. A. (2011). The role of adaptive behavior in autism spectrum disorders: Implications for functional outcome. *Journal of Autism and Developmental Disorders, 41,* 1007–1018.

Kanne, S. M., & Mazurek, M. O. (2011). Aggression in children and adolescents with ASD: Prevalence and risk factors. *Autism and Developmental Disorders, 41,* 926–937. doi: 10.1007/s10803-010-1118-4

Kapczinski, F., Lima, M. S., Souza, J. S., & Schmitt, R. (2003). Antidepressants for generalized anxiety disorder. *Cochrane Database of Systematic Reviews, 2.* doi: 10.1002/14651858.CD003592

Kasari, C., Locke, J., Gulsrud, A., & Rotheram-Fuller, E. (2011). Social networks and friendships at school: Comparing children with and without ASD. *Journal of Autism and Developmental Disorders, 41,* 533–544.

Kawakami, C., Ohnishi, M., Sugiyama, T., Someki, F., Nakamura, K., & Tsujii, M. (2012). The risk factors for criminal behaviour in high-functioning autism spectrum disorder (HFASDs): A comparison of childhood adversities between individuals with HFASDs who exhibit criminal behaviour and those with HFASD and no criminal histories. *Research in Autism Spectrum Disorders, 6*(2), 949–957.

Kessler, R. C., Petukhove, M., Sampson, N. A., Zaslavsky, A. M., & Wittchen, H. (2012). Twelve-month and lifetime prevalence and lifetime morbid risk of anxiety and mood disorders in the United States. *International Journal of Methods in Psychiatric Research, 21,* 169–184. doi: 10.1002/mpr.1359

King, C., & Murphy, G. H. (2014). A systematic review of people with Autism Spectrum Disorder and the criminal justice system. *Journal of Autism and Developmental Disorders, 44,* 2717–2733. doi: 10.1007/s10803-014-2046-5

Kirino, E. (2014). Efficacy and tolerability of pharmacotherapy options for the treatment of irritability in autistic children: Clinical medicine insights. *Pediatrics, 8,* 17–30. doi: 10.4137/CMPed.S8304

Kivisto, A. J., Moore, T. M., Elkins, S. R., & Rhatigan, D. L. (2009). The effects of PTSD symptomatology on laboratory-based aggression. *Journal of Traumatic Stress, 22*(4), 344–347. doi: 10.1002/jts.20425

Kreiser, N., & White, S. W. (2014). ASD in females: Are we overstating the gender difference in diagnosis? *Clinical Child and Family Psychology Review, 17*(1), 67–84. doi: 10.1007/s10567-013-0148-9

Kumagami, T., & Matsuura, N. (2009). Prevalence of pervasive developmental disorder in juvenile court cases in Japan. *Journal of Forensic Psychiatry & Psychology, 20*, 974–987.

Långstrøm, N., Grann, M., Ruchkin, V., Siøstedt, G., & Fazel, S. (2009). Risk factors for violent offending in autism spectrum disorders: A national study of hospitalized individuals. *Journal of Interpersonal Violence, 24*(8), 1358–1370. doi: 10.1177/0886260508322195

Lai, M. C., Lombardo, M. V., Pasco, G., Ruigrok, A. N., Wheelwright, S. J., Sadek, S. A., & Baron-Cohen, S. (2011). A behavioural comparison of male and female adults with high functioning autism spectrum conditions. *PLoS ONE, 6*(6): e20835. doi: 10.1371/journal.pone.0020835

Liss, M., Mailloux, J., & Erchull, M. J. (2008). The relationships between sensory processing sensitivity, alexithymia, autism, depression, and anxiety. *Personality and Individual Differences, 45*, 255–259. doi: 10.3923/jas.2010.570.574

Losh, M., & Capps, L. (2006). Understanding of emotional experience in autism: Insights from the personal accounts of high-functioning children with autism. *Developmental Psychology, 42*(5), 809–818. doi: 10.1037/0012-1649.42.5.809

MacEachron, A. E. (1979). Mentally retarded offenders: Prevalence and characteristics. *American Journal of Mental Deficiency, 84*, 165–176.

Magnée, M. J. C. M., de Gelder, B., van Engeland, H., & Kemner, C. (2007). Facial electromyographic responses to emotional information from faces and voices in individuals with pervasive developmental disorder. *Journal of Child Psychology and Psychiatry, 48*, 1122–1130.

Malone, R. P., Gratz, S. S., Delaney, M. A., & Hyman, S. B. (2005). Advances in durg treatments for children and adolescents with autism and other pervasive developmental disorders. *CNS Drugs, 19*, 923–934.

Malow, B. A., Crowe, C., Henderson, L., McGrew, S. G., Wang, L., Song, Y., Stone, W. L. (2009). A sleep habits questionnaire for children with autism spectrum disorders. *Journal of Child Neurology, 24*, 19–24.

Mandell, D. S., Walrath, C. M., Manteuffel, B., Sgro, G., & Pinto-Martin, J. A. (2005). The prevalence and correlates of abuse among children with autism served in comprehensive community-based mental health settings. *Child Abuse and Neglect, 29*, 1359–1372.

Markram, H., Rinaldi, T., & Markram, K. (2007). The intense world syndrome: An alternative hypothesis for autism. *Frontiers in Neuroscience, 1*(1), 77–96. doi: 10.3389/neuro.01.1.1.006.2007

Martin, A., Scahill, L., Klin, A., & Volkmar, F. R. (1999). Higher-functioning pervasive developmental disorders: Rates and patterns of psychotropic drug use. *Journal of the American Academy of Child & Adolescent Psychiatry, 38*, 923–931.

Matson, J. L., & Cervantes, P. E. (2014). Assessing aggression in persons with autism spectrum disorders: An overview. *Research in Developmental Disabilities, 35*(12), 3269–3275.

Matson, J. L., & Jang, J. (2014). Treating aggression in persons with autism spectrum disorders: A review. *Research in Developmental Disabilities, 35*(12), 3386–3391. doi: 10.1016/j.ridd.2014.08.025

Matson, J. L., Mahan, S., Hess, J. A., Fodstad, J. C., & Neal, D. (2010). Progression of challenging behaviors in children and adolescents with Autism Spectrum Disorder as measured by the Autism Spectrum Disorders-Problem Behaviors for Children (ASD-PBC). *Research in Autism Spectrum Disorders, 4*(3), 400–404. doi:10.1016/j.rasd.2009.10.010

Matson, J. L., Mahan, S., & LoVullo, S. V. (2009). Parent training: A review of methods for children with developmental disabilities. *Research in Developmental Disabilities, 30*(5), 961–968.

Matson, J. L., Sipes, M., Fodstad, J. C., Fitzgerald, M. E. (2011). Issues in the management of challenging behaviours of adults with autism spectrum disorder. *CNS drugs, 25*(7), 597–606.

Mayes, S. D., & Calhoun, S. L. (2011). Impact of IQ, age, SES, gender, and race on autistic symptoms. *Research in Autism Spectrum Disorders, 5*(2), 749–757. doi:10.1016/j.rasd.2010.09.002

Mazefsky, C. A., Herrington, J., Siegel, M., Scarpa, A., Maddox, B. B., Scahill, L., & White, S. W. (2013). The role of emotion regulation in autism spectrum disorder. *Journal of the American Academy of Child and Adolescent Psychiatry, 52*(7), 679–688. doi: 10.1016/j.jaac.2013.05.006

McLaughlin, K. A., Hatzenbuehler, M. L., Mennin, D. S., & Nolen-Hoeksema, S. (2011). Emotional dysregulation and adolescent psychopathology: A prospective study. *Behaviour Research and Therapy, 49*, 544–554. doi: 10.1016/j.brat.2011.06.003

Mehtar, M., & Mukkades, N. M. (2011). Posttraumatic Stress Disorder in individuals with diagnosis of Autistic Spectrum Disorders. *Research in Autism Spectrum Disorders, 5*(1), 539–546.

Montes, G., & Halterman, J. S. (2007). Bullying among children with autism and the influence of comorbidity with ADHD: A population-based study. *Ambulatory Pediatrics, 7*, 253–257. doi: 10.1016/j.ambp.2007.02.003

Mouridsen, S. E. (2012). Current status of research on autism spectrum disorders and offending. *Research in Autism Spectrum Disorders, 6*, 79–86. doi:10.1016/j.rasd.2011.09.003

Mouridsen, S. E., Rich, B., Isager, T., & Nedergaard, N. J. (2008). Pervasive developmental disorders and criminal behaviour. A case control study. *International Journal of Offender Therapy and Comparative Criminology, 52*, 196–205. doi: 10.1177/0306624X07302056

Murphy, D. (2003). Admission and cognitive details of male patients diagnosed with Asperger's Syndrome detained in a special hospital: Comparison with a schizophrenia and personality disorder sample. *Journal of Forensic Psychiatry and Psychology, 14*(3), 506–524.

Murphy, D. (2007). Hare Psychopathy Checklist revised profiles of male patients with Asperger's syndrome detained in high security psychiatric care. *The Journal of Forensic Psychiatry & Psychology, 18*(1), 2007. doi: 10.1080/14789940601014777

Murphy, G., Beadle-Brown, J., Wing, L., Gould, J., Shah, A., & Homes, N. (2005). Chronicity of challenging behaviors in people with severe intellectual disabilities and/or autism: A total population sample. *Journal of Autism and Developmental Disorders, 35*, 405–418.

Murrie, D. C., Warren, J. I., Kristiansson, M., & Dietz, P. E. (2002). Asperger's syndrome in forensic settings. *International Journal of Forensic Mental Health, 1*(1), 59–70. doi: 10.1080/14999013.2002.10471161

Newman, S. S., & Ghaziuddin, M. (2008). Violent crime in Asperger syndrome: The role of psychiatric comorbidity. *Journal of Autism and Developmental Disorders, 38*, 1848–1852. doi: 10.1007/s10803-008-0580-8

NICHD Early Child Care Research Network (2004). Trajectories of physical aggression from toddlerhood to middle childhood: I. Introduction. *Monographs of the Society for Research in Child Development, 69*(4), 1–25.

North, A. S., Russel, A. J., & Gudjonsson, G. H. (2008). High functioning autism spectrum disorders: An investigation of psychological vulnerabilities during interrogative interview. *Journal of Forensic Psychiatry & Psychology, 19*, 323–334.

O'Hearn, K., Asato, M., Ordaz, S., & Luna, B. (2008). Neurodevelopment and executive function in autism. *Development and Psychopathology, 20*(4), 1103–1132. doi:10.1017/S0954579408000527

Oswald, D. P., & DiSalvo, C. A. (2003). Adaptive behavior assessment. In T. H. Ollendick & C. S. Schroeder (Eds.), *The encyclopedia of pediatric and clinical child psychology*. New York: Kluwer Academic/Plenum Publishers.

Palermo, M. T. (2004). Pervasive developmental disorders, psychiatric co-morbidities, and the law. *International Journal of Offender Therapy and Comparative Criminology, 48*, 40–48.

Paterson, P. (2008). How well do young offenders with Asperger syndrome cope in custody? Two prison case studies. *British Journal of Learning Disabilities, 36*, 54–58. doi: 10.1111/j.1468-3156.2007.00466.x

Pennington, B. F., & Ozonoff, S. (1996). Executive functions and developmental psychopathology. *Journal of Child Psychology and Psychiatry, 37*(1), 51–87.

Porges, S. W. (2003). Social engagement and attachment: A phylogenetic perspective. *Annals of the New York Academy of Sciences, 1008*, 31–47. doi: 10.1196/annals.1301.004

Posey, D. J., Aman, M. G., McCracken, J. T., Scahill, L., Tierney, E., Arnold, L. E., & McDougle, C. J. (2007). Positive effects of Methylphenidate on inattention and hyperactivity in pervasive developmental disorders: An analysis of secondary measures. *Biological Psychiatry, 61*(4), 538–544. doi: 10.1016/j.biopsych.2006.09.028

Rao, P. A., & Beidel, D. C. (2009). The impact of children with high-functioning autism on parental stress, sibling adjustment, and family functioning. *Behavior Modification, 33*(4), 437–451. doi: 10.1177/0145445509336427

Reese, R. M., Richman, D. M., Belmont, J. M., & Morse, P. (2005). Functional characteristics of disruptive behavior in developmentally disabled children with and without autism. *Journal of Autism and Developmental Disorders, 35*(4), 419–428.

Research Units on Pediatric Psychopharmacology (RUPP) Autism Network (2002). Double-blind, placebo-controlled trial of risperidone in children with autism. *The New England Journal of Medicine, 347*, 314–321.

Rogers, J., Viding, E., Blair, R. J., Frith, U., & Happé, F. (2006). Autism spectrum disorder and psychopathy: Shared underlying underpinnings or double hit? *Psychological Medicine, 36*, 1789–1798.

Samson, A. C., Hardan, A. Y., Lee, I. A., Phillips, J. M., & Groos, J. J. (2015). Maladaptive behavior in autism spectrum disorder: The role of emotion experience and emotion regulation. Journal of Autism and Developmental Disorders. Advance online publication. doi: 10.1007/s10803-015-2388-7

Samson, A. C., Huber, O., & Gross, J. J. (2012). Emotional reactivity and regulation in adults with autism spectrum disorders. *Emotion, 12*(4), 659–665.

Schechtman, M. A. (2007). Scientifically unsupported therapies in the treatment of young children with Autism Spectrum Disorders. *Pediatric Annals, 36*, 497–505.

Scragg, P., & Shah, A. (1994). Prevalence of Asperger's syndrome in a secure hospital. *The British Journal of Psychiatry, 165*(5), 679–682.

Senland, A. K., & Higgins-D'Alessandro, A. (2013). Moral reasoning and empathy in adolescents with autism spectrum disorder: Implications for moral education. *Journal of Moral Education, 42*(2), 209–223. doi: 10.1080/03057240.2012.752721

Sevlever, M., Roth, M. E., & Gillis, J. M. (2013). Sexual abuse and offending in Autism Spectrum Disorders. *Sexuality and Disability, 31*(2), 189–200. doi: 10.1007/s11195-013-9286-8

Shah, N., & Ujifusa, A. (2013). Advocates worry shootings will deepen Autism's stigma: Adam Lanza reported to have Asperger's syndrome. *Education Week, 32*(15), 18.

Simonoff, E., Pickles, A., Charman, T., Chandler, S., Loucas, T., & Baird, G. (2008). Psychiatric disorders in children with autism spectrum disorders: Prevalence, comorbidity, and associated factors in a population-derived sample. *Journal of the American Academy of Child and Adolescent Psychiatry, 47*(8), 921–929.

Siponmaa, L., Kristiansson, M., Jonson, C., Nydén, A., & Gillberg, C. (2001). Juvenile and young adult mentally disordered offenders: The role of child neuropsychiatric disorders. *The Journal of the American Academy of Psychiatry and the Law, 29*, 420–426.

Singh, N. N., Lancioni, G. E., Winton, A. S. W., Fisher, B. C., Wahler, R. G., McAleavey, K., & Sabaawi, M. (2006). Mindful parenting decreases aggression, noncompliance, and self-injury in children with autism. *Journal of Emotional and Behavioral Disorders, 14*, 169–177. doi: 10.1177/10634266060140030401

Smith, A. (2009). The empathy imbalance hypothesis of autism: A theoretical approach to cognitive and emotional empathy in autistic development. *The Psychological Record, 59*, 273–294.

Soderstrom, H., Rastam, M., & Gillberg, C. (2002). Temperament and character in adults with Asperger syndrome. *Autism, 6*, 287–297. doi: 10.1177/1362361302006003006

Søndenaa, E., Helverschou, S. B., Steindal, K., Rasmussen, K., Nilson, B., & Nøttestad, J. A. (2014). Violence and sexual offending behavior in people with autism spectrum disorder who have undergone a psychiatric forensic examination. *Psychological Reports, 115*(1), 32–43. doi: 10.2466/16.15.PR0.115c16z5

Stouthamer-Loeber, M., Loeber, R., Wei, E., Farrington, D. P., & Wikstrorm, P. O. (2002). Risk and promotive effects in the explanation of persistent serious delinquency in boys. *Journal of Consulting and Clinical Psychology, 70*(1), 111–123.

Tager-Flusberg, H., & Joseph, R. (2005). How language facilitates the acquisition of false-belief understanding in children with autism. In Astington, J. and Baird, J. (Eds.), *Why language matters for theory of mind* (pp. 298–318). Oxford: Oxford University Press.

Taylor, J. L., Dove, D., Veenstra-VanderWeele, J., Sathe, N. A., McPheeters, M. L., Jerone, R. N., & Warren, Z. (2012). Interventions for adolescents and young adults with Autism Spectrum Disorders. *Comparative Effectiveness Reviews, No. 65.* Retrieved from: http://effectivehealthcare.ahrq.gov/ehc/products/271/1196/CER65_Autism-Young-Adults_20120723.pdf

Troyb, E., Rosenthal, M., Eigsti, I., Kelley, E., Tyson, K., Orinstein, A., & Fein, D. (2014). Executive functioning in individuals with a history of ASDs who have achieved optimal outcomes. *Child Neuropsychology: A Journal on Normal and Abnormal Development in Childhood and Adolescence, 20*(4), 378–397. doi: 10.1080/09297049.2013.799644

Van Dorn, R., Volavka, J., & Johnson, N. (2012). Mental disorder and violence: Is there a relationship beyond substance use? *Social Psychiatry and Psychiatric Epidemiology, 47*(3), 487–503. doi: 10.1007/s00127-011-0356-x

Vermeiren, R., Jespers, I., & Moffitt, T. E. (2006). Mental health problems in juvenile justice populations. *Child and Adolescent Psychiatry Clinics of North America, 15,* 333–351.

Vieillevoya, S., & Nader-Grosbois, N. (2008). Self-regulation during pretend play in children with intellectual disability and in normally developing children. *Research in Developmental Disabilities, 29,* 247–255.

Weissman, A. S., & Bates, M. E. (2010). Increased clinical and neurocognitive impairment in children with autism spectrum disorders and comorbid bipolar disorder. *Research in Autism spectrum disorders, 4,* 670–680.

Werner, R. S., Cassidy, K. W., & Juliano, M. (2006). The role of social–cognitive abilities in preschoolers' aggressive behavior. *The British Journal of Developmental Psychology, 24,* 775–799. doi:10.1348/026151005X78799

White, S. W., Mazefsky, C. A., Dichter, G. S., Chiu, P. H., Richey, J. A., Ollendick, T. H. (2014). Social-cognitive, physiological, and neural mechanisms underlying emotion regulation impairments: Understanding anxiety in autism spectrum disorder. *International Journal of Developmental Neuroscience, 39,* 22–36. doi: 10.1016/j.ijdevneu.2014.05.012

White, S. W., Oswald, D., Ollendick, T., & Scahill, L. (2009). Anxiety in children and adolescents with autism spectrum disorders. *Clinical Psychology Review, 29*(3), 216–229. doi: 10.1016/j.cpr.2009.01.003

Witwer, A., & Lecavalier, L. (2005). Treatment incidence and patterns in children and adolescents with Autism Spectrum Disorders. *Journal of Child and Adolescent Psychopharmacology, 15*(4), 671–681. doi:10.1089/cap.2005.15.671

Woodbury-Smith, M., Clare, I., Holland, A. J., & Kearns, A. (2006). High functioning autistic spectrum disorders, offending and other law-breaking: Findings from a community sample. *The Journal of Forensic Psychiatry & Psychology, 17*(1), 108–120. doi: 10.1080/14789940600589464

Woodbury-Smith, M., Clare, I., Holland, A. J., Watson, P. C., Bambrick, M., & Kearns, A. (2010). Circumscribed interests and 'offenders' with autism spectrum disorders: A case control study. *Journal of Forensic Psychiatry & Psychology, 21,* 366–377.

Zablotsky, B., Bradshaw, C. P., Anderson, C., & Law, P. A. (2013). The association between bullying and the psychological functioning of children with autism spectrum disorders. *Journal of Developmental and Behavioral Pediatrics, 24,* 1–8.

Part IV

Risk assessment and rehabilitation

16 Risk management in forensic psychiatry

Integrating a social network approach

Lydia ter Haar-Pomp, Stefan Bogaerts and Marinus Spreen

Introduction

Risk assessment plays an important role in forensic psychiatric treatment to determine the likelihood of violent behaviour during and/or after treatment. Risk assessments are usually conducted to support major clinical forensic decisions such as those regarding leave. Risk assessment instruments like the HKT-R (Spreen, Brand, Ter Horst, & Bogaerts, 2014) and HCR-20[V3] (De Vogel, De Vries Robbe, Bouman, Chakhssi, & de Ruiter, 2013; Douglas, Hart, Webster, & Belfrage, 2013) provide indicators to support structured professional judgement when evaluating risk factors. Risk factors are categorised as static or dynamic (Douglas, Webster, Hart, Eaves, & Ogloff, 2001). Static factors (age at first offence, prior criminal history, etc.) are useful for evaluating long-term risk, but largely unchangeable and untreatable. Dynamic risk factors (coping, self-control, etc.) are treatable and changeable over time and therefore feasible as treatment goals for interventions to minimise, monitor and control risk.

The presence of risk factors is associated with higher recidivism rates (Bonta, Law, & Hanson, 1998; Monahan et al., 2001). However, the presence of protective factors may contribute to lower recidivism rates. Protective factors have been defined as 'any characteristics of a person, his or her environment or situation which reduces the risk of future violent behaviour' (de Vogel, de Ruiter, Bouman, & de Vries Robbe, 2007, p. 23). An example of a risk assessment that focuses on protective factors is the Structured Assessment of Protective Factors for violence risk (SAPROF; de Vogel et al., 2007; English version, 2009). The SAPROF includes two historical factors (intelligence and secure attachment in childhood) and 15 dynamic factors, which consist of three internal factors (empathy, coping, self-control), seven motivational factors (work, leisure activities, financial management, etc.), and five external factors (social network, intimate relationship, professional care, etc.).

After assessing the risk and protective factors, professionals determine the level of risk management needed (how to control the risk factors). Although the essential role of risk management is noted by professionals, risk management has received far less attention than risk assessment in forensic psychiatric research.

338   *Lydia ter Haar-Pomp et al.*

This chapter reviews the current state of affairs concerning risk management procedures and risk management models in forensic psychiatry. This chapter begins with a description of different definitions of 'risk management'. Second, underlying theoretical models of risk management are explored and their effectiveness is described. Third, an overview is provided regarding the currently used risk management tools and their possibilities and limitations. Fourth, a Forensic Social Network Analysis tool is introduced as an innovative method of managing individual risk. The fifth and final part of this chapter provides a set of recommendations.

Definition of 'risk management'

Various definitions of 'risk management' exist in the forensic psychiatric literature. *For instance*, Douglas et al. (2014) stated that risk management includes 'the full breadth and range of risk reduction strategies at the disposal of agencies or persons responsible for the supervision of an individual' (p. 104). Evaluators can select or recommend risk management interventions including: (1) monitoring, (2) supervision, (3) treatment and (4) victim safety planning (Douglas et al., 2001; Webster et al., 2014). De Vogel (2005) defines violence risk management as 'all intervention strategies aimed at reducing violence risk developed on the basis of the results of violence risk assessment' (p. 45). *The Dutch* Expertise Centre of Forensic Psychiatry *(EFP, 2013)* stated that risk management includes 'conducting risk reduction interventions based on risk assessment and risk analysis in conjunction with the diagnostic findings' (EFP, 2013, p. 55). The Workgroup IFPA Risk Management (2013) defines risk management as 'a structured measurement of security and recidivism risks and targeting of these risks by individualised counselling and treatment with the aim to reduce the risks' (p. 2).

Based on the definitions above, in this chapter we consider it prudent to define forensic psychiatric risk management as: the process of controlling a forensic psychiatric patient's risk of criminal and violent behaviour using a combination of ongoing monitoring and evaluating of the high-risk behaviour and situations throughout the patient's treatment and rehabilitation.

Theoretical principles of risk management

Risk management in forensic psychiatry is driven by various theoretical models. The most influential model is the risk-need-responsivity (RNR) model based on rehabilitation theory (Andrews, Bonta, & Hoge, 1990; Andrews & Bonta, 1994; Bonta & Andrews, 2010).

Rehabilitation theories refer to 'the overall aims, values, principles, and aetiological assumptions that are used to guide the treatment of offenders, and translates how these principles should be used to guide therapists' (Ward, Melser, & Yates, 2007, p. 211).

The RNR model includes five principles, also known as the 'what works principles'.

The Risk Principle matches the intensity and level of services with the risk of the offender (*who*). Intensive treatment should be offered to moderate and high-risk offenders to ensure public safety. Low-risk offenders should receive minimal rehabilitation services. Another reason to divide moderate/high-risk offenders from low-risk offenders is to prevent low-risk offenders from learning more serious criminal behaviour from higher-risk groups.

The Need Principle targets dynamic criminogenic risk/need factors (*what*). It is important that the treatment is focused on the factors associated with recidivism. Bonta and Andrews (2010) defined eight central risk/need factors. One factor is static, namely 'criminal history'. The other seven are dynamic risk factors, namely 'antisocial personality pattern', 'pro-criminal attitudes', 'social supports for crime', 'substance abuse', 'family/marital relationships', 'school/work' and 'pro-social recreational activities'. The list of the seven dynamic risk factors is followed by four non-criminogenic minor need factors, namely 'self-esteem', 'vague feelings of personal distress', 'major mental disorder' and 'physical health' (Bonta & Andrews, 2010).

The Responsivity Principle targets risk and need factors (*how*). Interventions should be delivered in a manner that is appropriate to the individual characteristics of the offenders. It is important to employ empirically supported social learning and cognitive behavioural treatment, because these treatments have been evaluated as most effective in reducing risk behaviours in offenders (Andrews & Bonta, 1994). According to the principle of programme integrity, the programme should be conducted in practice as intended by its theory and design. This can be accomplished by providing staff with training, supervision and ethical guidelines. Guiding professionals during supervision programmes is essential for effective offender supervision (Bonta & Andrews, 2010). The last principle of professional discretion requires that staff members have the necessary skills and access to supervisory support to make appropriate decisions. Investing in professional discretion has a significant impact on crime reduction. The RNR model provides useful information regarding offender treatment and effective interventions (Bonta & Andrews, 2010). Research shows that programmes that adhere to the RNR principles are more effective at reducing recidivism (Andrews, Bonta, & Hoge, 1990; Dowden, Antonowicz, & Andrews, 2003; Hanson, Bourgon, Helmus, & Hodgson, 2009; Olver, Wong, & Nicholaichuk, 2009). For instance, Dowden, Antonowicz, and Andrews (2003) could assess during meta-analysis that relapse prevention programmes had the greatest impact in those situations in which the RNR principles were strictly followed within the programme. Hanson, Bourgon, Helmus, and Hodgson (2009) focused on the effectiveness of treatment for sexual offenders. In a meta-analysis they found that programmes that adhered to the RNR principles showed the largest reduction in sexual and general recidivism.

Despite the promising outcomes regarding the effectiveness of the RNR principles for reducing recidivism, the RNR model is subject to increasing criticism. The most important critique involves the imbalance of strengths and risks. The RNR model does not focus on core therapeutic tasks and intervention tasks,

340 *Lydia ter Haar-Pomp et al.*

such as treatment alliance and motivational issues (Kemshall, 2010; Taxman & Thanner, 2006; Ward & Maruna, 2007; Ward, Melser, & Yates, 2007). It needs to be mentioned that Bonta and Andrews are aware of this criticism; they stated: 'we also recognise that some may object to our emphasis on criminogenic needs at the expense of non-criminogenic needs that may be particularly important to an individual's happiness' (Bonta & Andrews, 2010, p. 35).

To achieve a better balance between strengths and risks, so-called 'restorative' approaches have been developed. Restorative models focus not only on deficits like risks and needs, but also on promoting specific goods or goals in offender rehabilitation (Ward & Maruna, 2007). An example of a more restorative-focused model is the 'good lives' model (GLM), which focuses on promoting human goods to provide the offender the essential ingredients for a 'good' life (Kemshall, 2010; Ward & Maruna, 2007). The GLM is based on the general assumption that offenders (in our case, forensic psychiatric patients) who have a good or fulfilling life have a lower risk of (re-)offending (Bouman, 2009; Ward & Maruna, 2007). However, the GLM has also been criticised. For instance, it has been suggested that the focus on needs may obscure attention to risks (McNeill, 2009). However, it is essential that the GLM is compared with the more traditional risk management strategies to improve its effectiveness (Ward & Maruna, 2007).

Risk management tools

De Kogel and Nagtegaal (2006) described how various countries deal with individuals with a mental disorder who have committed serious violent or sexual offences. The countries, namely Canada, England, Sweden, Germany and Belgium, applied different forms of supervision and after-care. In most countries an individual risk management plan and a relapse prevention plan are part of the patient's treatment. For example, forensic psychiatric professionals in Canada are working with risks and needs analyses, which are used to construct a correctional plan that includes the reintegration possibilities of the offender and the time path of the treatment. The theoretical foundation of most risk management tools is based on the principles of risk, need and responsivity (Andrews, Bonta, & Hoge, 1990). De Kogel and Nagtegaal (2008) showed that supervision programmes which contain elements of control and treatment are most effective. Additionally, the researchers noted that there are still very few impact studies on the results of supervision programmes (De Kogel & Nagtegaal, 2008).

The most frequently used risk management tool in Dutch forensic psychiatry is the (individual) risk management plan. This plan defines which measures are needed to prevent and decrease risks (Expertise Centre of Forensic Psychiatry, 2013). The plan is adjusted on the basis of a systematic evaluation of the patient's treatment and rehabilitation.

Next to this risk management plan is the Early Recognition Method (ERM; in Dutch: signaleringsplan; Fluttert et al., 2008). This method aims to explore and describe signs of deteriorating behaviour in situations associated with the patient's aggressive behaviour. Early signs are related to the patient's perceptions, thoughts and behaviour. The patient's active participation is needed to gain knowledge about how the precursors of aggression can be recognised at an early stage. To detect warning signs, it is crucial to evaluate the patient's behaviours and the possible occurrence of precursors of aggression at predetermined intervals. The patient is taught to monitor their behaviour themselves. The ERM (Fluttert et al., 2008) can be used to let patients score their early warning signs on a weekly basis. This method has been primarily developed for the intramural treatment phase.

The third tool is the relapse prevention plan (in Dutch: terugvalpreventieplan). This plan consists of interventions focused on controlling the patient's dynamic risk factors (EFP, 2013). The aim of the interventions is to improve the patient's self-regulation and whenever necessary, to motivate the patient to accept external interventions. The interventions empower patients to recognise early warning signs of relapse and develop appropriate response plans. In practice the relapse prevention plans are mainly used for the prevention of risky behaviour.

Research by Nagtegaal (2010) shows that risk management interventions in Dutch forensic psychiatric centres (FPCs) can be divided into four broad categories: (1) performing interventions (therapy, medication, etc.); (2) information transfer between staff members (daily reports and staff meeting, feedback for incident reporting, etc.); (3) measures aimed at security, management and control; and (4) tools aimed at risk management, such as the Structured Outcomes Assessment and Community Risk Monitoring (SORM, Grann et al., 2005).

The outcomes of the mentioned risk management tools are primarily dependent on an active involvement of the patient and the professionals. Some forensic psychiatric risk management tools also involve the patient's social network members. The most commonly used social network management intervention is the Circles of Support and Accountability (COSA) programme, which was developed in Canada (Wilson, Picheca, & Prinzo, 2005). A key feature of COSA is the involvement of the local community in offering a protected and protecting area for the sex offender to change their problem behaviours (Höing et al., 2011). COSA addresses some key factors for reoffending like social isolation and emotional loneliness (Höing et al., 2011). Two statements express the core of COSA: 'no more victims' and 'no one is disposable' (Höing, Bogaerts, & Vogelvang, 2013). COSA circles consist of three to seven trained volunteers who meet the high-risk sex offender weekly to support their integration into the community. For instance, they provide support by modelling pro-social behaviour, offering moral support and assisting with practical needs. The volunteers (inner circle) are supported by professionals (outer circle). The professionals can take appropriate measures based on the reported concerns of the volunteers to prevent the core member from reoffending (Höing et al., 2011). Studies have shown that COSA can reduce sexual,

342   *Lydia ter Haar-Pomp et al.*

violent and general recidivism, whereby the reduction of sexual offence rates is the largest (Aos, Miller, & Drake, 2006; Wilson, Cortoni, & McWhinnie, 2009; Wilson, Picheca, & Prinzo, 2005, 2007). Since 2008, COSA has been used by the Dutch Probations Organisation (Reclassering Nederland, RN). In the Dutch situation, COSA is intended for sex offenders with a moderate to high risk of reoffending and a high need for social support, who are on a conditional release with a court supervision order of at least 12 months (Höing et al., 2011; see also Chapter 14).

Another social network risk management tool is the Forensic Social Network Analysis (FSNA), which was developed in the Netherlands. This tool, used by forensic social workers, systematically charts details of the personal networks of forensic psychiatric patients and rates past, current and future relationships and network members in terms of risk (and severity) of recidivism (Pomp, Spreen, Bogaerts, & Völker, 2010). The FSNA tool has been qualitatively evaluated in a nationwide study in the Netherlands. Forensic social workers reported that compared to the conventional approach new and more specific information was obtained about high-risk contacts, network positions of the victims and offenders, and quantity and quality of the personal networks (Spreen & Pomp, 2009).

Forensic social network approach

Risk assessment and management tools need to consider the situational community context into which the offender is released (Monahan, 1981; Shapiro & diZegera, 2010; Sjöstedt & Grann, 2002), specifically concerning access to potential victims. Changing dynamic social and personal circumstances in the future may cause behavioural changes that affect the risk (and severity) of future recidivism (Kalish & Robins, 2006; Monahan et al., 2001; Ward & Beech, 2004). The FSNA method is used to systematically chart and interpret the personal networks of forensic psychiatric patients in relation to their individual risk behaviour. In FSNA a personal social network consists of the patient, their direct relationships with network members and the relationships between their network members (Wasserman & Faust, 1994). An individualised social network approach enables professionals to focus on typical individual social dynamic risk factors such as access to victims, relationship instability, 'bad friends', (a lack) of personal support, etc. FSNA is based on theories found in the sociological, criminological and psychological literature (see Pomp et al., 2010). For instance, the RNR model of Andrews, Bonta, and Hoge (1990) is integrated into the FSNA. The frequency and intensity of a FSNA intervention is adjusted to the risk level of the offender. The social network analysis focuses on the major risk/need factors related to the offender's social environment, such as network members with anti-social and pro-criminal attitudes, antisocial peer associations and isolation from anti-criminal others, pro-social recreational activities, etc. (Bonta & Andrews, 2010). After assessing the patient's risks and needs present in their

Risk management in forensic psychiatry 343

social environment, interventions are formulated that are matched with the patient's individual risk profile.

The FSNA method in practice

The FSNA method uses three steps to analyse the personal networks of forensic psychiatric patients (Bem & Funder, 1978; Monahan, 1981). Step one determines which network members had a risk-increasing and/or a risk-reducing influence on the patient in social situations related to the crime-period. Step two determines the same, but focuses on the current situation and future. The third step compares the different risk-increasing and/or risk-reducing roles the network members may have in current and future risk-increasing social situations with the 'crime' network roles in mind. Based on the results of the analysis, social network interventions for the patient's individual risk management are formulated. To illustrate these three steps, a brief case study is presented.

Step 1: Studying the patient's file

Every FSNA study starts with collecting relevant background information by studying the patient's file. Box 16.1 contains a selection of relevant background information.

Box 16.1   Forensic Social Network Analysis (FSNA) case study: background information

Background information

Brian was diagnosed with a personality disorder Not Otherwise Specified (NOS). Brian had committed severe sexual offences: multiple rapes of under-aged girls. One of these girls was also murdered by Brian. According to Brian, he had committed his offences because he was bored and unhappy due to losing the relationship with his under-aged stepdaughter. Before committing his offences, he was driving with his car near his hometown, looking for girls who had physical similarities to the young girl. After Brian found the 'right' girl, he took her against her will with him. After talking, Brian raped the girls. In one case, Brian murdered the girl.

Why was he selected for FSNA? Brian is a high-risk offender. The professionals suspect that there is a feigned adjustment and feigned change during the intramural treatment, because Brian's status as 'exemplary patient' conflicts with his severe criminal behaviour in the past and his 'high-risk label'.

(continued)

---

344   *Lydia ter Haar-Pomp et al.*

(continued)

Aim of the FSNA research: The treatment team has to decide whether Brian has shown sufficient progress to enter the next phase of the treatment. According to the Dutch TBS treatment, returning an offender to society can be achieved only by gradually granting the patient more liberties. In Brian's case, the treatment team needed to decide if supervised leave may be granted. The treatment team uses FSNA to provide a clearer view of the patient's risk profile and to define responsible risk management actions.

Step 2: Interviewing the patient and their network members

To collect personal network data, the patient and their network members are interviewed using a standardised questionnaire. The interview aims to obtain information of the dynamics within the network at the moment of the crime, and in current and future situations. Network members can provide information about the patient's whereabouts in an uncontrolled environment. Network members are selected based on their roles, network position and influence on the patient. The influence of network members on the patient depends on their roles, network position, forensic risk factors (e.g. criminal record, psychiatric support) and the degree a patient is susceptible to positive or negative support concerning risk behaviours. Box 16.2 shows an example of FSNA interview data.

Box 16.2   Forensic Social Network Analysis (FSNA) case study of 'Brian': answering the FSNA main questions based on FSNA (interview) data

Interviews with Brian, Brian's mother and his two brothers

FSNA step 1: Which network members had a risk-increasing and/or a risk-reducing (protective) influence on the patient in social situations related to the crime period?

Information from Brian (during period of offences 40 years old)	Additional information from network members	Additional information from treatment team
• Tense relationships with his partner (37 years) and his family members.	• They did not like Brian's partner because of her antisocial attitude.	• During the sexual contacts, Brian humiliated the young girls: he used both psychological and physical violence.

- Tense relationship between partner and Brian's network members.
- A close, positive and sexual relationship between Brian and his underage stepdaughter.
- No friendships.
- Unexpectedly, the young girl started a relationship with a boy of her own age. Brian was angry and disappointed. After a short period, the girl moved out of the house and was living with her boyfriend.
- The family did not know about the relationship between Brian and the young girl.
- They were not informed about the broken 'relationship'.
- It was shocking for the family to find out that Brian had committed severe (sexual) offences.
- The young girls were afraid of Brian.
- The stepdaughter was looking for ways to avoid Brian.
- Brian used a disproportional degree of violence during the murder.

FSNA step 2: Which network members have a risk-increasing and/or a risk-reducing (protective) influence on the patient in social situations for the current situation and future?

Information from Brian	Additional information from network members	Additional information from treatment team
<ul><li>There is no risk that he will reoffend.</li><li>The relationship with his family members has improved.</li><li>There are no friendships between Brian and other patients.</li><li>Brian likes his female social worker/mentor very much. He wants to continue this relation in future, especially when he re-enters society.</li><li>There are tensions between his family and the social worker.</li></ul>	<ul><li>They are interested in Brian and his treatment.</li><li>They have faith in a future without crimes, even after his release into society.</li><li>The family has difficulties 'accepting' the severe (sexual) offences of their son/brother.</li></ul>	<ul><li>The female social worker has only a professional relationship with Brian.</li></ul>

346 *Lydia ter Haar-Pomp et al.*

Step 3: Analysis and interpretation of the data

The analysis and interpretation of the data are focused on the similarities and differences in the roles of the network members in the crime-period and their current/return network (e.g. network members may be new in the current network, but their role can be similar to other network members in the crime-period). The aim of this comparison is to evaluate whether the roles of the network members are in such a degree positively changed that leave is responsible. Box 16.3 shows a summary of the analysis and interpretation phase, based on the case study.

Box 16.3 Forensic Social Network Analysis (FSNA) case study of 'Brian': analysis and interpretation of the data

Analysis and interpretation of the data

FSNA step 3: Comparing the different risk-increasing and/or risk-reducing roles the network members have in current and future risk-increasing social situations with the 'crime' network roles in mind.

Similarities:

- Brian's focus on a female social worker. According to Brian his relation with the female social worker is positive (+). The female social worker, his stepdaughter and the victims happen to share the same physical characteristics (blond hair, brown eyes, smart looking, etc.).
- The difference in perception of the content of contact between Brian and his female significant other. (Crime network: Brian to stepdaughter: positive romantic relationship/stepdaughter to Brian: negative contact → current/return network: Brian to social worker: positive friendship – in future romantic relationship?/social worker to Brian: professional relationship).
- Brian's family does not accept the female social worker like they did not accept Brian's partner in his crime period.
- No friendships.

Differences:

- Currently, Brian has positive relationships with his family members.

A helpful tool to interpret the social network dynamics in the patient's network is to graphically visualise the three time periods (see Figures 16.1 and 16.2).

Every piece of FSNA research ends with specific individual risk management interventions (see Box 16.4). To monitor the interventions, in most cases FSNA follow-ups are recommended.

Risk management in forensic psychiatry 347

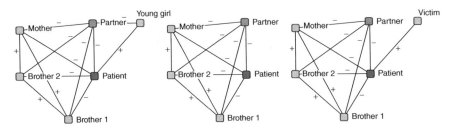

Figure 16.1 Network patterns leading up to and during the offences

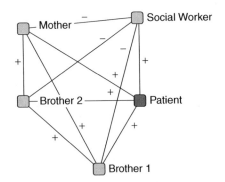

Figure 16.2 Current and return network (based on Brian's perceptions and expectations)

Box 16.4   Forensic Social Network Analysis (FSNA) case study of 'Brian': risk management implications/interventions

Risk management implications/interventions

After reading the outcomes of the FSNA, the treatment team was negatively surprised, because of the apparent similarities between the time periods. This resulted in:

- Not allowing supervised leaves.
- Replacing the female mentor with a male mentor.
- Monitoring whether changes occur in the interaction between Brian and his significant others. The next FSNA interview will be conducted prior to the next decision about allowing supervised leaves.
- Organising family therapy, also referred to as systemic therapy, with Brian and his family members.
- Encouraging Brian to participate in pro-social recreational activities.

348 *Lydia ter Haar-Pomp et al.*

Recommendations

Risk management in general

This chapter aims to provide insight into the nature of risk management within forensic psychiatry. Risk management is one of the central elements in forensic psychiatric treatment. Theoretically effective risk management is most effective when interventions are personalised based on a valid risk assessment tool and a thorough offence(s) diagnosis. In this chapter, various risk management tools were discussed. However, the effectiveness of most tools has not yet been well studied, despite their obvious importance in forensic psychiatric treatment. An important next step is to study the effectiveness of the current risk management strategies and, if necessary, improve them.

Concluding remarks

There has been a longstanding recognition that social networks play an important role in risk management. So far, social relationships and patterns have only been partially taken into account in the clinical forensic psychiatric practice of risk management. The FSNA method was introduced as a practical tool to measure positive and negative dynamic social network factors on an individual level. The case study demonstrated the potential benefits of using such an approach. Interviewing network members yields new essential risk management information about the stressors in the patient's network. Similarities in the network roles of network members between the period leading up to and during the committed offences and the period during forensic psychiatric treatment can be used to define risk management interventions.

To contribute to more effective risk management, it is important to involve the patient's network members (Shapiro & diZegera, 2010). Network members are likely to be aware of signs of deteriorating behaviour that are not readily apparent to clinical staff. Involvement of network members can contribute to better social control (RNR model), support (good lives model) and functioning of the patient during all identified phases. When the context of the risk assessment changes (e.g. when the patient goes on leave), new FSNA measurements are recommended to re-assess the patient's network.

It is essential that professionals apply effective risk management interventions specifically aimed at increasing protective social relationships during treatment. Focusing on the preventive effect of certain types of social relationships might protect society from crime (Colvin, Cullen, & Vander Ven, 2002).

Literature

Andrews, D.A., & Bonta, J. (1994). *The psychology of criminal conduct.* Cincinnati, OH: Anderson.

Andrews, D.A., Bonta, J., & Hoge, R.D. (1990). Classification for effective rehabilitation: Rediscovering psychology. *Criminal Justice and Behavior, 17,* 19–52.

Risk management in forensic psychiatry   349

Aos, S., Miller, M., & Drake, E. (2006). *Evidence-based adult corrections programs: What works and what does not.* Olympia: Washington State Institute for Public Policy.

Bem, D.J., & Funder, D.C. (1978). Predicting more of the people more of the time: Assessing the personality of situations. *Psychological Review, 85*, 485–501.

Bonta, J., Law, M., & Hanson, K. (1998). The prediction of criminal and violent recidivism among mentally disordered offenders: A Meta-analysis. *Psychological Bulletin, 123*, 123–142.

Bonta, J., & Andrews, D. (2010). Viewing offender assessment and rehabilitation through the lens of the risk–need–responsivity model. In: F. McNeill, P. Raynor, & C. Trotter (Eds.). *Offender supervision: New directions in theory, research and practice* (pp. 241–256). New York: Willan Publishing.

Borgatti, S.P., Everett, M.G., & Freeman, L.C. (2002). *Ucinet for Windows: Software for social network analysis.* Harvard, MA: Analytic Technologies.

Bouman, Y.H.A. (2009). *Quality of life and criminal recidivism in forensic outpatients with personality disorders. A Good Lives approach.* Maastricht, the Netherlands: University of Maastricht.

Colvin, M., Cullen, F.T., & Vander Ven, T. (2002). Coercion, social support, and crime: An emerging theoretical consensus. *Criminology, 40* (1), 19–42.

Douglas, K.S., Webster, C.D., Hart, S.D., Eaves, D., & Ogloff, J.R.P. (Eds.) (2001). *HCR-20: Violence risk management companion guide.* Burnaby, BC, Canada: Mental Health, Law, and Policy Institute, Simon Fraser University, and Department of Mental Health Law & Policy, University of South Florida.

Douglas, K.S., Hart, S.D., Webster, C.D., & Belfrage, H. (2013). *HCR-20V3: Assessing risk of violence: User guide.* Burnaby, Canada: Mental Health, Law, and Policy Institute, Simon Fraser University.

Douglas, K.S., Hart, S.D., Webster, C.D., Belfrage, H., Guy, L.S., & Wilson, C.M. (2014). Historical-Clinical-Risk Management-20, Version 3 (HCR-20v3): Development and Overview. *International Journal of Forensic Mental Health, 13* (2), 93–108.

Dowden, C., Antonowicz, D., & Andrews, D.A. (2003). The effectiveness of relapse prevention with offenders: A meta-analysis. *International Journal of Offender Therapy and Comparative Criminology, 47* (5), 516–528.

Expertise Centre of Forensic Psychiatry. (2013). *Basis Zorgprogramma: Landelijk zorgprogramma voor forensisch psychiatrische patiënten.* [Basic Care Program: Nationwide care program for forensic psychiatric patients.] Retrieved from: http://www.efp.nl/sites/default/files/webmasters/basiszp_laatste_versie_jan_2013.pdf

Fluttert, F., Meijel, B., van, Webster, C., Nijman, H., Bartels, A., & Grijpdonck, M. (2008). Risk management by Early Recognition of Warning Signs in Patients in Forensic Psychiatric Care. *Archives of Psychiatric Nursing, 22* (4), 208–216.

Grann, M., Sturidsson, K., Haggård-Grann, U., Hiscoke, U.L., Alm, P.O, Dernevik, M., & Woodhouse, A. (2005). Methodological development: Structured outcome assessment and community risk monitoring (SORM). *International Journal of Law and Psychiatry, 28*, 442–456.

Hanson, R.K., Bourgon, G., Helmus, L., & Hodgson, S. (2009). The principles of effective correctional treatment also apply to sexual offenders: A meta-analysis. *Criminal Justice and Behavior, 36*, 865–891.

Höing, M., et al. (2011). *European Handbook: Circles of Support and Accountability.* The Netherlands: Hertogenbosch: Circles Together for Safety/Circles NL.

Höing, M., Bogaerts, S., & Vogelvang, B. (2013). Circles of Support and Accountability: How and why they work for sex offenders. *Journal of Forensic Psychology Practice, 13*, 267–295.

350   *Lydia ter Haar-Pomp et al.*

Kalish, Y., & Robins, G.L. (2006). Psychological predispositions and network structure: The relationship between individual predispositions, structural holes and network closure. *Social Networks, 28,* 56–84.

Kemshall, H. (2010). The role of risk, needs and strengths assessment in improving the supervision of offenders. In: F. McNeill, P. Raynor, & C. Trotter (Eds.). *Offender supervision: New directions in theory, research and practice* (pp. 155–171). New York: Willan Publishing.

Kogel, C.H. de, & Nagtegaal, M.H. (2006). *Gewelds- en zedendelinquenten met psychische stoornissen – een inventarisatie van wetgeving en praktijk in het forensisch psychiatrische systeem en het gevangenissysteem in Engeland, Duitsland, Canada, Zweden en België.* [Serious violent and sexual offenders with a mental disorder: An inventory of legislation and practical experience in the forensic psychiatric systems and the prison systems in England, Germany, Canada, Sweden and Belgium.] Den Haag, Boom Juridische Uitgevers, Reeks Onderzoek en beleid, nr. 240.

Kogel, C.H., de, & Nagtegaal, M.H. (2008). *Toezichtprogramma's voor delinquenten en forensisch psychiatrische patiënten: Effectiviteit en veronderstelde werkzame mechanismen.* [Supervision programs for offenders and forensic psychiatric patients: Effectiveness and mechanisms that are assumed to be effective.] Meppel: WODC/BJU.

McNeill, F. (2009). *Towards effective practice in offender supervision.* Glasgow: Scottish Centre for Crime and Justice Research.

Monahan, J. (1981). *Predicting violent behaviour: An assessment of clinical techniques.* London: Sage Library of Social Research.

Monahan, J., Steadman, H.J., Silver, E., et al. (2001). *Rethinking risk assessment: The MacArthur Study of mental disorder and violence.* Oxford: Oxford University Press.

Nagtegaal, M.H. (2010). *Risicotaxatie- en risicomanagementmethoden: Een inventarisatie in de forensisch psychiatrische centra in Nederland.* [Risk assessment and risk management methods: An inventory in the forensic psychiatric centers in the Netherlands.] WODC projectnummer 1561. Den Haag: WODC.

Olver, M.E., Wong, S.C.P., & Nicholaichuk, T.P. (2009). Outcome evaluation of a high-intensity inpatient sex offender treatment program. *Journal of Interpersonal Violence, 24* (3), 522–536.

Pomp, L., Spreen, M., Bogaerts, S., & Völker, B. (2010). The role of personal social networks in risk assessment and management of forensic psychiatric patients. *Journal of Forensic Psychology and Practice, 4,* 267–284.

Sampson, R.J., & Laub, J.H. (1990). Crime and deviance over the life course: The salience of adult social bonds. *American Sociological Review, 55,* 609–627.

Shapiro, C., & diZegera, M. (2010). It's relational: Integrating family into community corrections. In: F. McNeill, P. Raynor, & C. Trotter (Eds.). *Offender supervision: New directions in theory, research and practice* (pp. 241–256). New York: Willan Publishing.

Sjöstedt, G., & Grann, M. (2002). Risk assessment: What is being predicted by actuarial prediction instruments? *International Journal of Forensic Mental Health, 1,* 179–183.

Spreen, M., Brand, E., Ter Horst, P., & Bogaerts, S. (2014). *Handleiding en methodologische verantwoording HKT-R. Historische, Klinische en Toekomstige – Revisie.* Stichting FPC: Dr. S. van Mesdag.

Spreen, M., & Pomp. L. (2009). *Landelijke implementatie Forensische Sociale Netwerk Analyse (FSNA): Procesevaluatie.* [Nationwide implementation of Forensic Social Network Analysis (FSNA): Process evaluation.] Utrecht, the Netherlands: The Expertise Center for Forensic Psychiatry.

Taxman, F.S., & Thanner, M. (2006). Risk, Need, and Responsivity (RNR): It all depends. *Crime & Delinquency, 52* (1), 28–51.

Vogel, V. de (2005). *Structured risk assessment of (sexual) violence in forensic clinical practice. The HCR-20 and SVR-20 in Dutch forensic psychiatric patients.* Dissertation, Amsterdam, the Netherlands.

Vogel, V., de, Ruiter, C., de, Bouman, Y., & Vries Robbe, M., de (2007). Guidelines for the assessment of protective factors for violence risk. Utrecht: Van der Hoeven Stichting.

Vogel, V., de, Vries Robbe, M., de, Bouman, Y.H.A., Chakhssi, F., & Ruiter, C. de (2013). Innovatie in risicotaxatie van geweld: De HCR-20 V3. *Gedragstherapie, 46,* 107–118.

Ward, T., & Beech, A. (2004). The etiology of risk: A preliminary model. *Sexual Abuse: A Journal of Research and Treatment, 6,* 271–284.

Ward, T., & Maruna, S. (2007). *Rehabilitation: Beyond the risk-paradigm.* London: Routledge.

Ward, T., Melser, J., & Yates, P.M. (2007). Reconstructing the Risk–Need–Responsivity model: A theoretical elaboration and evaluation. *Aggression and Violent Behavior, 12,* 208–228.

Wasserman, S., & Faust, K. (1994). *Social network analysis, methods and application.* Cambridge: Cambridge University Press.

Workgroup IFPA Risk Management (2013). *Werkgroep risicomanagement: Advies 2013 versie 10-09-1* [Workgroup risk management: Advice 2013 version 10-09-1]. Utrecht: Expertisecentrum Forensische Psychiatrie.

Wilson, R.J., Picheca, J.E., & Prinzo, M. (2005). *Circles of Support & Accountability: An evaluation of the pilot project in South-Central Ontario.* Ottawa, Canada: Correctional Service of Canada.

Wilson, R.J., Picheca, J.E., & Prinzo, M. (2007). Evaluating the effectiveness of professionally facilitated volunteerism in the community-based management of high-risk sexual offenders: Part two: Recidivism. *The Howard Journal of Criminal Justice, 46,* 327–337.

Wilson, R.J., Cortoni, F., & McWhinnie, A. (2009). Circles of Support & Accountability: A Canadian national replication of outcome findings. *Sexual Abuse: A Journal of Research and Treatment, 21,* 412–430.

17 Forensic rehabilitation

A phase of transition on a lifelong risk (and health) continuum

Sanne Verwaaijen and Marion van Binsbergen

Introduction: understanding rehabilitation

To adequately construct a model for rehabilitation of offenders, it is necessary to consider the nature of rehabilitation. Ward, Melser, and Yates (2007) found, somewhat to their surprise, that the nature of rehabilitation tends to be taken for granted in the correctional field and very little has been said as to what actually constitutes a *rehabilitation theory* as opposed to a treatment or aetiological theory. The terms 'treatment', 'therapy' and 'rehabilitation' are used interchangeably as if they refer to the same thing. Ward et al. (2007) propose to use the terms *treatment and therapy* as *local theories of change* to guide the treatment of offenders, and to use *rehabilitation* as in *rehabilitation theory*, an overarching structure of the broad aims of treatment and their relationship to offending, based on *aetiological* assumptions. As an introduction to this chapter, we sketch an overarching structure for rehabilitation in line with Ward et al. (2007), who propose a three-component rehabilitation theory: (1) general principles of rehabilitation, (2) aetiological and methodological assumptions and (3) practice implications.

We will discuss Ward's first component, e.g. general principles of rehabilitation, using the Psychology of Criminal Conduct (PCC) and the forthcoming Risk-Need-Responsivity (RNR) model of Andrews and Bonta (2012).

Second, we touch upon an aetiology of antisocial behaviour and criminal conduct in line with (a) a recent meta-analysis by Loeber, Hoeve, Slot, and Van der Laan (2012) on persisters and desisters in crime from adolescence into adulthood, and (b) recent research findings in the neurosciences, with special attention to brain maturing and an evidence-based working model, the dual-systems model (Steinberg, 2010).

Third and finally, treatment implications and pressing policy recommendations end this chapter on rehabilitation.

An overarching structure for rehabilitation

As already mentioned in Chapters 15 and 16, the RNR model of offender rehabilitation is deservedly the premier treatment model for offenders (Ward et al., 2007). It stems from the PCC, a psychology that seeks to account for variation in the criminal behaviour of individuals (Andrews and Bonta, 2012).

Forensic rehabilitation

PCC describes and accounts for the fact that not all human beings equally engage in antisocial acts or criminal conduct. People differ in the number, type and variety of antisocial acts in which they engage, and they differ in when and under what circumstances they act in harmful ways. They also differ in when and under what conditions they reduce and may even cease their antisocial activity, e.g. desistance. PCC describes how people who are more into crime differ from those who are less into it and assists in predicting who will be into it more in the future. PCC offers a structure that:

(a) thoroughly analyses the risk factors at play; these factors *do* predict future criminal behaviour and match levels of treatment services to the risk level of the offender;

(b) addresses criminal correlates; offenders have multiple needs. These needs are all problematic circumstances and are both criminogenic and non-criminogenic, the criminogenic needs are a subset of dynamic risk factors, applicable for change, and they should be target for change through treatment interventions. The noncriminogenic needs may be targeted for motivational purposes, though Andrews and Bonta emphasise the notion that addressing noncriminogenic needs is unlikely to alter future recidivism, so in PCC this is optional;

(c) addresses responsivity, e.g. offenders differ in ability and learning style, and treatment approaches should be offered in a style and mode that is consistent with these individual differences.

These three general principles of classification for effective correctional treatment, RNR, also provide us an important part of the answer on what to do in individualised risk assessment and risk management plans (Andrews & Bonta, 2012). It is under the responsivity principle that many of the psychological approaches to offender assessment and treatment may have their value. By identifying personality and cognitive styles, correctional interventions or clinical treatment can be better matched to the offender (Andrews & Bonta, 2012). Offender characteristics such as interpersonal sensitivity, anxiety, cognitive maturity and intelligence speak to the appropriateness of different models and styles of treatment service (and even different legal systems and correctional options, as we argue in this chapter).

Thus, the principles of RNR extend well beyond risk, need and strength factors. They should be guiding us on *all* levels from individualised treatment plans to overarching legal and policy structures. PCC and RNR provide a solid (science-based) psychology of human behaviour and this goes for legal measures and justice response as well. Furthermore, a psychology of criminal behaviour considers not only biological, personal, interpersonal, familial and structural or contextual factors, it also considers the individual in particular and immediate situations. Or as Andrews and Bonta put it: the broader social context. Accordingly, we would like to add a *lifelong* perspective, especially in working with children and youngsters, in such a way that it considers the

354 *Sanne Verwaaijen and Marion van Binsbergen*

individual, in particular immediate *and future* situations that enhance risk, since most adult crime occurs as a relapse in problem behaviour and recidivism.

Rehabilitation is (mostly) not just a once-in-a-lifetime intervention programme, or just evaluative to treatment results, or a single supervised transfer to society. Rehabilitation should also provide a prognosis for the future and the chance and conditions for relapse, so as to plan relapse prevention and the possible need for aftercare or means of long support and control. In this sense *long* is as long as nature e.g. brain maturing takes, as we will argue in this chapter.

An aetiology of antisocial behaviour and criminal conduct

Aetiology is the study of *origination* in medicine and behavioural sciences. The term refers to the causes of pathologies. Aetiology has evolved from uni-causation to (sometimes) chains of causation, to a framework to explain multiple (epidemiological) associations or risk factors which may or may not be causally related, to seek actual aetiology. In short: aetiology refers to the many factors coming together to cause an illness or disorder; it explains the antecedents and maintaining factors of disease and disorder and gives a basis for a prognosis (Harvard Medical Dictionary).

So, an aetiology of criminal behaviour is needed and asks for explanatory depth and external consistency. What are the antecedents of criminal behaviour?

An aetiology on persisting criminal behaviour: a developmental perspective

It is already more than two decades ago that Kazdin (1987) remarked on the serious and pervasive character of antisocial behaviour in children. Kazdin advocated for high-strength intervention, amenability-to-treatment (which can be compared to the present concept of responsivity), broad-based treatment and, most importantly, chronic-disease models. To date his call has been unanswered in a serious way.

White, Moffitt, Earls, Robins, and Silva (1990) asked *how early can we tell*, and examined the predictive power of a variety of characteristics of the preschool child for antisocial outcomes at ages 11 and 15. The subjects were 1037 members of a longitudinal investigation of a New Zealand birth cohort. A discriminant function analysis was computed with the five most promising preschool variables. The function correctly classified 81% of subjects as antisocial or not at age 11 and 66% of subjects as delinquent or not at age 15. White et al. concluded that behaviour problems are the best predictor of later antisocial outcome.

Simonoff et al. (2004) explored the independent and joint effects of childhood characteristics on the persistence of antisocial behaviour in adult life and found that childhood disruptive behaviour has powerful long-term effects on adult antisocial outcomes, which continue into middle adulthood.

Another important finding is that learning problems and low IQ also associate with crime in adulthood, but hyperactivity may be the intermediating factor in school failure and early dropout. This does not take away the importance of early intervention to prevent school dropout and act upon learning problems or disabilities.

Some risk factors enhance even earlier in life. Raine, Brennan, Sarnoff, and Mednick (1994) found that a significant interaction between birth complications and early maternal rejection indicated that those who suffered both birth complications and early child rejection were most likely to become violent offenders in adulthood. While only 4.5% of the subjects had both risk factors, this small group accounted for 18% of all violent crimes in their study. The effect was specific for violence and was not observed for nonviolent criminal offending. Injuries during birth and early physical injuries, especially repeated head injuries, in combination with maternal rejection, abusive parenting styles, alcoholic fathers, sexually stressful events during childhood, isolation and emotional abuse and neglect, are risk factors for violent crime.

So, longitudinal studies on the development of antisocial behaviour consistently indicate that chronic behaviour problems early in life predict serious delinquency and crime during adolescence and childhood. Meta-analyses conclude on a chronic course in the persistence of criminal careers in some adolescents, leading to repetitive crime during adulthood.

The risk factors at play are identified. Loeber et al. (2012) presented an extensive study on the nature and chance of youngsters who show high-risk behaviour turning into criminal offending adults. Essential information on the persistence of high-risk behaviour derives from longitudinal research and offers understanding on age normative versus delayed outgrowing of delinquency. They identified 10 explanatory processes ranging from early individual differences in self-control and brain maturation to situational contexts of specific criminal events and justice response. Loeber et al. meticulously analysed the risk factors at play, and summarised essential items for risk assessment: (early) history of violence; early onset offending; history of school suspensions or expulsions; criminality in the family; mental illness, both in the individual and in the family; (serious) parental conflict; low family income; high crime neighbourhood; impulsivity (cognitive impulsivity, behavioural impulsivity); hostility; low empathy; sensation seeking; low remorse; callousness; immaturity (longer durations to mature cognitively and behaviourally); (early onset) drug and alcohol abuse; poor parenting (or absent parenting); parent-youth conflicts; lack of family supports; and negative peer associations (antisocial or criminal friends).

Loeber et al. also summarised protective factors that are associated with desistance by known delinquents, e.g. factors that mitigate risk: prosocial attitude; good social skills; educational achievement; job stability; positive attitude towards treatment and authority; stable and cohesive surrounding or family; supportive parents; positive peer associations.

Most adolescents do not persist in violent or criminal behaviour (Moffitt, 2008; Loeber et al., 2002; Moffitt, Caspi, Harrington, & Milne, 2002; Van der Geest,

356 Sanne Verwaaijen and Marion van Binsbergen

Bijleveld, & Blokland, 2007; Fabio et al., 2008; Lynam, Loeber, & Stouthamer-Loeber, 2008; Moffitt, 2008; Salekin & Lochman 2008; Pardini & Loeber, 2008; Loeber, Hoeve, Slot, & Van der Laan, 2012). However, those who do show an accumulation of risk factors remain criminally active and often cause society the greatest harm once they reach adulthood. At least three processes may underlie divergent developmental patterns of offending during early adulthood.

First, the escalating pattern of offending may reflect individual characteristics whose negative outcomes had thus far been buffered by a supportive social environment (Thornberry & Krohn, 2005). When social support starts to wane as young people age and when young adults are increasingly left to their own devices, deficits in human capital – especially low academic competence – can quickly become deficits in social capital. As these young adults increasingly fail to make the expected transitions to adulthood, they become increasingly vulnerable to crime as a way to cope with life stressors. According to Thornberry and Krohn, individual characteristics such as low intelligence do not directly make an individual more prone to crime; it is only in interaction with shifting contextual demands that these vulnerabilities cause them to embark on criminal trajectories.

Second, Sampson and Laub's (1997) age-graded theory mentions cumulative continuity as a major force in bringing about persistence in crime during early adulthood. Criminal behaviour has an attenuating effect on an individual's social and institutional bonds, disconnecting adolescents from conventional developmental trajectories. Attenuated bonds in turn make future criminal behaviour more likely, thus setting in motion a downward spiral of cumulative disadvantage that leads to prolonged criminal involvement, making desistance from crime more difficult.

Third, transitions to adulthood also bring new opportunities and motivations for crime (e.g. access to valuable goods at work or intimate partner violence). However, transitions into adulthood may not only provide for new criminal opportunities but also carry with them new obligations and expectations that, when young adults experience trouble meeting them, can also provide new and strong incentives for criminal behaviour. The transition to parenthood has been shown to elevate criminal behaviour in those who highly value parenthood but at the same time feel that they are failing at being a good parent (Liu & Kaplan, 2001; Bijleveld, Van der Geest, & Hendriks, 2012).

In conclusion, longitudinal studies and a developmental perspective show a lifelong vulnerability to criminal behaviour that exacerbates in transitional phases and in certain high-risk environments. In the Netherlands little is known about the transition into adulthood of specific vulnerable groups. Boendermaker (1998) and Wouda (1987) illustrate that their transitions are accompanied with great difficulty. Vulnerable groups made the transition into adult domains (employment, relationship, parenthood) later and probably in the end less well than average. An exception was made for high-risk women who come into parenthood very early, but on all other aspects vulnerable

Forensic rehabilitation 357

young adults lag behind. Based on their research findings, Bijleveld et al. (2012) recommend that to reduce recidivism for high-risk groups as they transition into adulthood, all young offenders and particularly those in high-risk groups should have access to education, receive job skills training and have available employment programmes that continue after discharge from an institution.

An aetiology on persisting criminal behaviour: a neurobiological and health perspective

Recent neuroscience theory views risk-taking as the result of a competition between two neural systems: a socioemotional system (a phylogenetically older affective system) which is localised in limbic and paralimbic areas of the brain, including the amygdala, ventral striatum, orbitofrontal cortex, medial pre-frontal cortex and superior temporal sulcus, and a cognitive-control system (a phylogenetically younger deliberative system) which is mainly composed of the lateral prefrontal and parietal cortices and those parts of the anterior cingulated cortex to which they are interconnected (Steinberg, 2008; Figner, Mackinley, Wilkening, & Weber, 2009; Strang, Chein, & Steinberg, 2013). Affective processing is spontaneous and automatic, operates by principles of similarity and contiguity, and influences behaviour by affective impulses. Deliberate processing is effortful, controlled and operates according to formal rules of logic. It is the neural basis of inhibitory control, a mechanism that can block affective impulses and therefore enables deliberative decision making even in affect-charged situations. The affective and deliberate neural systems have been shown to mature at different speeds. The affective system's respon-siveness increases rapidly at puberty, whereas the deliberative cognitive-control system matures later and more gradually over the course of adolescence *and* young adulthood (Figner et al., 2009).

In recent years, a special theory on maturational brain imbalance has become increasingly popular: the dual-system explanations (Casey, Getz, & Galvan, 2008; Steinberg, 2008; Steinberg, 2010; Strang et al., 2013). Derived from developmental neurosciences and behavioural experiments, it becomes clear that age differences in reward-seeking follow a curvilinear pattern, increasing between preadolescence and mid-adolescence, and declining thereafter. In contrast, age differences in impulsivity follow a linear pattern, with impul-sivity declining steadily from age 10 on. Heightened vulnerability to risk-taking in middle adolescence may be due to the combination of relatively high inclinations to seek rewards and still maturing capacities for self-control (Steinberg, 2010).

Figner et al. (2009) investigated risk-taking and underlying information use in successive age levels, measuring differential involvement of affective versus deliberate processes of the dual-system explanation of adolescent risk-taking. First, as observed in their study, risk-taking occurs when the impulse from the affective system overrides deliberate impulses to avoid risk. Second, relying too much on deliberation can lead to increased risk-taking in adolescents in situations in which adults would never even consider the pros and cons but instinctively would avoid a risk because of a strong fear response, for example when choosing whether to play Russian roulette. The adolescent (immature) brain is more sensitive to the frequency (and probability) than to the magnitude of reward and punishment. Results are consistent with dual-system explanations of risk-taking as the result of competition between affective processes and deliberative cognitive-control processes, with adolescents' affective systems tending to override the deliberative system in states of heightened emotional arousal. The deliberate cognitive-control system matures later and more gradually over the course of adolescence and young adulthood.

According to Dadds and Rhodes (2008), the neurobiology of violence and antisocial behaviour varies according to the type of aggression; the distinction between hot and cold (or callous-unemotional) maps nicely onto distinctions between serotonergic and cortisol-dependent functions. Put simply, in both humans and animals, there is clear evidence that serotonergic dysregulation appears to be related to decreased thresholds for explosive violence, whereas low cortisol appears to be associated with colder, more predatory violence associated with a low capacity for fear, aversive conditioning (or punishment insensitivity) and probably with diminished amygdala involvement in attention and responsiveness to emotionally salient stimuli. According to Dadds and Rhodes, these relationships are unlikely to be linear; rather, complex inter-relationships between hormonal and neurobiological agents (e.g. testosterone) that occur at critical and sensitive periods for critical epigenetic and neural transcription will be the rule (e.g. early nurturance and epigenetic changes to hippocampal development or testosterone transporter at puberty).

From a health perspective, the World Health Assembly declared violence a major public health issue in 1996. The World Report on Violence and Health analyses different types of violence, including child abuse and neglect, youth violence, intimate partner violence, sexual violence, elder abuse, self-directed violence, and collective violence. For all these types of violence the report explores the magnitude of the health and social effects – both for perpetrators and victims – the risk and protective factors, and the types of prevention efforts that have been initiated. They aim to raise awareness among decision makers about social and economic costs of violence, promote the need to transcend traditional crime-fighting approaches based on control, promote approaches emphasising prevention, and point to parental training and rehabilitation programmes starting in high schools that are more effective than offender incarceration programmes, such as the three strikes law in the United States.

Health research in general asks for drastically transforming systems of imprisonment for youngsters, especially prisons without treatment or rehabilitation programmes, into effective treatment programmes on early intervention, to prevent children developing into perpetrators of violence (Krug, Dahlberg, Mercy, Zwi, & Lozano, 2002).

Neurosciences specifically press on the adverse effect of imprisonment for adolescents and young adults. Swaab (2012) summarises the findings of fundamental research over the last 50 years and emphasises the need for a drastically different approach to crime and correction, knowing the difficulties in immature brains with planning, organisation, impaired inhibition, behavioural limits and the moral framework. The immature prefrontal cortex has specific needs and asks for a specific approach such as extended parenting, adequate role modelling and risk-reducing surroundings that do not promote or facilitate drugs and alcohol. Due to their immature prefrontal cortex, adolescents are mainly preoccupied with immediate consequences and much less with threads of punishment or long-term adverse effects, which increases the risk of substance abuse and an inherent permanent damage to the brain through excessive alcohol or drug abuse.

Equally as important, Swaab (2005, 2012) explains that disruptions in the formation of the brain *during* development lead to psychiatric, neurological or neuro-endocrine illnesses, aggression or criminal behaviour later in life. During development the brain produces an exceptional number of cells and connections, the most during early infancy but development lasts well until the age of 26–28. By the functioning of the brain system, it is decided which cells and connections remain. The development – and therefore the functioning – of the brain is permanently organised by everything a child or adolescent experiences, sees and thinks. Genetic information is less important in the development of the brain. Every experience during this development is essential for the personality that is developed into adulthood once the brain is fully matured. In adulthood, there are larger restrictions to change the brain and (therefore) behaviour.

The search for the biological basis for crime has continued for over 150 years. Research into biological variables related to criminal behaviour labours under the expectation that it will reveal some variables unique to offenders and preferably causal (Sullivan & Mullen, 2012). But complex human behaviour relies not only on factors specific to the agent (*in casu* biological or hormonal influences), but also on ever-shifting situational and contextual elements, opportunities and dispositions. Sullivan and Mullen specifically point to the elusive nature of the relationship between testosterone levels and aggression, possibly violent offending, and even more tenuously, sexual offending. They respond to recent research by Kingston et al. (2012) on the role of central and peripheral hormones in sexual and violent recidivism in sex offenders, which offers greater understanding of the hormonal underpinnings of offending and recidivism (e.g. the complex role of sex hormones and gonadotrophins in sex drive, aggression, frustration tolerance, impulsivity and hospitality). They have reported subtle but significant interactions between endocrine and behavioural variables that are associated with sexual offending and recidivism. Though collection and analysis of biological data may shed some light on the complex individual and contextual factors which contribute to offending (sexual) behaviour, comprehensive understanding is (still) a long way off.

360 *Sanne Verwaaijen and Marion van Binsbergen*

Recent research has linked genetics, serotonergic function and emotion recognition using functional magnetic resonance imaging (fMRI) methods. Adults with psychopathy show reduced amygdala activation when presented with fear faces. This is consistent with most theories of psychopathy involving a core deficit in emotional responsiveness, while non-psychopathic men who have suffered early childhood abuse and violence, and have the short polymorphisms of the monoamine oxidase A gene (associated with low serotonergic function), are at risk for chronic antisocial behaviour (Caspi et al., 2002). However, these men show hyperresponsiveness of the amygdala to fear faces in fMRI studies (see Meyer-Lindenberg & Zink, 2007). These findings bring current findings about the genetics of violent aggressive behaviour into the equation relating to responsiveness of the amygdala as a marker of cold and hot forms of violent aggressive behaviour.

In conclusion, we see a vast body of evidence form multidisciplinary standpoints like psychology, criminology, psychiatry, biology, interdisciplinary neurosciences and general health sciences showing us that brain maturing is not finished at the age of 18. Both slower brain maturation and impulsivity overriding control, and cognitive dysfunctions, correlate with crime, especially in combination with well-identified risk factors and especially in high-risk surroundings or peer groups. Distressing life events during developmental phases add to this picture.

An aetiology on persisting criminal behaviour: a gender perspective

Gender differences are apparent and important in forensic risk assessment, risk prognosis and forensic treatment. But in criminal behaviour, this is as in general behavioural research findings: overall women are more risk averse than men, but on a group level we see different outcomes. Byrnes, Miller, and Schafer (1999), for instance, conducted a meta-analysis of 150 studies in which risk-taking tendencies of male and female participants were compared. Overall, women are generally more risk averse than men, but on a group level lower levels of arousal are the actual underpinnings, different situations promote more or less risk-taking in different groups, and only certain people take risks in certain situations. In addition, the authors found that (a) there were significant shifts in the size of the gender gap between successive age levels and (b) the gender gap seems to be growing smaller over time. Additional studies to clarify age trends are needed.

Painter and Farrington (2004) call criminology 'notoriously gender-blind', particularly in explaining discrepancies in offending between males and females. Most research on risk factors for offending has been based on males because they offend more than females. But despite the clear discrepancy in offending, Painter and Farrington also mention the paucity of high-quality, large-scale, community-based research that satisfactorily explains whether the risk factors that influence male offending are similar to or different from those that influence female offending. A notable exception to this is a longitudinal

Forensic rehabilitation 361

study which makes comparisons between males and females with regard to risk factors by Moffitt et al. (2001). Inadequate parenting, neurocognitive problems, temperament and behavioural problems were the risk factors at play for (childhood onset) female delinquents.

Bennet, Farrington, and Huesmann (2005) found that gender differences in the development of social cognition may help to explain gender differences in crime and violence. How an individual ultimately responds to a stressful life event or risk factor depends on how that event is perceived, which, in turn, depends on individual cognitive processes. Social information-processing skills allow individuals to encode information, interpret and consider risks and benefits of a particular action, and determine an appropriate response based on their repertoire of behavioural scripts. It is not necessarily suggested deficiencies in cognitive capabilities cause crime, but rather that certain ways of processing information and certain social cognitive memory structures help to protect the individual form personal, social, environmental or social pressures towards criminal behaviour. So, one of the reasons females have lower rates of offending is because they have better prosocial skills. The superior social cognitive skills of females are influenced by many factors, including better inter-hemisphere communication, fewer frontal lobe deficits, greater verbal ability and differential socialisation by parents and peers.

Treatment implications

Treatment from the perspective of the RNR model

According to Andrews and Bonta, criminogenic needs represent forensic clinical needs that are stipulated by the primary targets of rehabilitation. This includes individual, social and contextual or environmental factors that form the actual underpinnings of criminal behaviour. Ward et al. (2007) support this conclusion in an evaluation of different rehabilitation models in which the RNR model of Andrews and Bonta is critically compared to the others, but still comes out as an outstanding achievement and as the nowadays premier forensic treatment model in Canada, Britain, Europe, Australia and New Zealand.

The primary treatment implication of the general principles of rehabilitation, as mentioned by Ward et al., is that interventions ought to be focused on modifying or eliminating dynamic risk factors (criminogenic needs) including individual, social and environmental factors. From the standpoint of PCC, criminogenic needs represent clinical needs that are stipulated to be primary targets of rehabilitation efforts. Thus, it is recommended that the whole rehabilitation process is steered by the empirical detection of the correlates of crime, rather than deriving treatment targets in an *a priori* fashion from clinical or criminological theories, *without consideration of the facts*. So the emphasis is on the last remark: both (individualised) theory on crime and empirical research should be used when constructing intervention plans (Ward et al., 2007;

Andrews and Bonta, 2012). Addressing noncriminogenic needs is optional, but not a direct effect of recidivism.

This constitutes the three-component rehabilitation model of Ward et al. (2006) in which the general principles form the baseline and frame of intervention, the aetiological principles form the explanatory layer of risk assessment, and the treatment constitutes the individualised aims and needs of intervention, including responsivity and programming:

Treatment implications for children and adolescents

In working with children and adolescents, an important issue arises in regard to how we weigh noncriminogenic needs in forensic treatment. A moral (adult) obligation requires targeting of noncriminogenic needs next to criminogenic needs – which is the main focus for rehabilitation – and moreover, neurosciences show us that the brain is still 'under construction' and that *all* experiences during this construction are an influence on the personality outcome. In our opinion addressing noncriminogenic needs therefore is not optional, or just motivational in working with children and adolescents (or immature people otherwise). Since brain development is still incomplete, we are dealing with cognitive immaturity. Loeber, Hoeve, Slot, and Van der Laan (2012) make strong arguments for screening executive functioning and brain maturation in youngsters, and so point to the importance of *all* risk-need factors that are predictor variables in the analysis of criminal behaviour in working with youngsters. Therefore, in working with

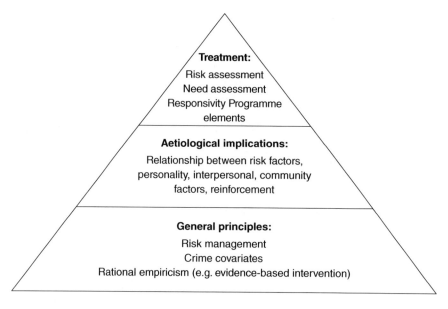

Figure 17.1 Three-component model (Ward et al., 2006)

children and adults we added aetiological aspects in brain development, in line with the second component of Ward et al. (2006) and in accordance with a vast and growing body of evidence and knowledge from neurosciences, as summarised by De Kogel (2008) and Swaab (2012). This includes treatment of mental disorders in children and youngsters as well as solving problems of a magnitude of a possibly damaging life event during development, since their brains are still 'under construction'. Studies have shown that interventions at a young age are effective in changing problem behaviour (Augimeri, Farrington, Koegl, & Day, 2007; Koegl, Farrington, Augimeri, & Day, 2008). Addressing noncriminogenic needs such as mental health issues is therefore a condition *sine qua non* in working with children and adolescents.

Therefore, we add pedagogic vital elements that stem from a growing body of empirical knowledge in neurosciences, which fit the gradual, sometimes slow biological maturing of the brain, as discussed, to this model in working with young offenders and their families:

In the general principle of *treatment* (see Fig. 17.1), as well as the risk and need assessment and responsivity, we include the diagnosis of mental health problems, e.g. maturation and cognitive dysfunctions, and programme elements are extended to caretakers and parents.

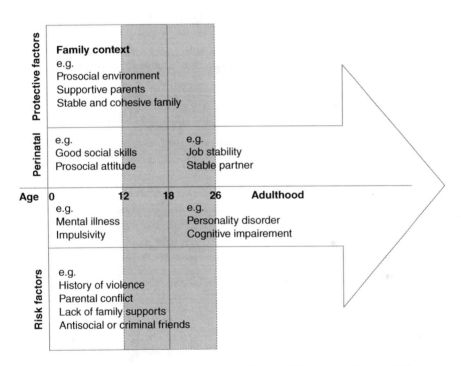

Figure 17.2 Transfer to society and aftercare planning (risk prognosis) on a lifelong continuum

364   *Sanne Verwaaijen and Marion van Binsbergen*

In the *aetiological principles* (see Fig. 17.1), under personality we include brain maturing and cognitive development; under interpersonal factors we include parental styles and attachments, as well as high-risk peer group or high-risk school group; and community factors are extended towards pedagogical environment.

Finally, for the *general principles* (see Fig. 17.1) on risk management we include a prognosis on a lifelong continuum; on crime covariates, parents or caretakers and peer group are included; and on rational empiricism, we include recent findings on brain development from neurosciences.

Treatment from the perspective of a chronic-disease model: covering the continuum

Behavioural risk is not something that can easily be avoided, treated or mitigated. But on the basis of a vast and growing body of knowledge, we believe that behavioural risk and crime should be evaluated and prognosed on a continuum: from the genetic or (early, sometimes even perinatal) biological hazards that should be mitigated, to the dynamic uncertainties that characterise most of the criminogenic needs and treatment activities and that must be managed, to, most importantly, the myriad of opportunities that are presented once watersheds between different life phases are no longer blocking the view.

The course of antisocial behaviours or conduct disorders into full-blown personality disorders or major mental disorders and criminal activities is multiform, non-linear, gender specific, unpredictable and yet evident in retrospection. This constitutes for a full phenomenology of antisocial behaviour on a continuum from (very) young childhood to adulthood.

Treatment implications for gender differences: a continuum for each gender

As mentioned before, gender differences should also be taken into account in choosing intervention techniques. Parent training and parent education techniques which target parental discipline, parental supervision, parental reinforcement of children (like praise) and parental interest in children are likely to have proportionally more impact in reducing female offending than in reducing male offending. However, the absolute number of offences reduced is likely to be greater for males than for females, because of the higher prevalence of male offending (Painter & Farrington, 2004).

Treatment implications and mental disorders or disabilities

Of course, early detection and prognosis of *all* criminal behaviour is out of reach and far from conclusive. As Sullivan and Mullen (2012) state, complex human behaviour relies not only on factors specific to the agents, but also on ever-shifting situational and contextual elements, opportunities and dispositions. Comprehensive understanding and prediction of all criminal behaviour

Forensic rehabilitation 365

is a long way off, if it will ever be fully captured. But on the continuum of early disruptive behaviour, conduct disorders, adolescent antisocial trajectories, antisocial personality disorders and adult violent crime, multidisciplinary research findings are becoming conclusive in a lifelong vulnerability to problem behaviour and crime.

Psychopathology in criminal offending is the topic here, and the emphasis in research so far mainly lies with conduct disorders growing out of severe personality disorders, mostly antisocial, though some research on women and offending offer insights into post-traumatic symptoms correlating with crime, as well as suicidal symptoms, parenting styles, absence of attachment and, of course, alcohol and drug abuse. Callous–unemotional traits in children seem very important in the development of psychopathy. Disorganised and disoriented attachments are strong predictors of deviant and hostile behaviour.

The importance of a specific diagnosis like conduct disorder, antisocial personality disorder or psychopathy is obvious, but various major mental disorders also correlate with certain types of crime, especially so in combination with known risk factors, but also with stress or isolation as mediating risk factors, for instance in disorders that carry psychotic phases. And though clinical treatment of mental disorders has little effect on recidivism – the criminogenic needs must be targeted for an effect on recidivism – mental disorders and personality disorders are important in regard to responsivity.

Treatment models from a developmental perspective

Since both 'pathology and risk' and 'circumstances and criminal conduct' are multiple-factor based and form a complex of interconnected and variable relations, it is – and maybe fortunately so, from an ethical standpoint – simply not possible to detect these groups 100% upfront. But *once* they are detected we *do* now know that they *do* have a lifelong vulnerability for high-risk behaviours or criminal conduct. Once we have seen the picture of an evident accumulation of risk factors, we should act upon the knowledge it provides and not stop intervening merely because the patient turns 18. This asks for working models that fit the full horizon and treatment models form a developmental perspective.

As mentioned, the dual-systems model states that affective and deliberate neural systems mature at different speeds, with the affective system's responsiveness increasing rapidly at puberty, and the deliberative cognitive-control system maturing later and more gradually over the course of adolescence *and* young adulthood (Figner et al., 2009). Studies and experiments with the dual-systems model are conducted on both genders and *no* special differences are reported. Increasing inhibitory control, either through treatment or supervised control, seems essential in rehabilitation and forensic treatment of impulsivity as a dynamic risk factor, for both girls and boys and (young) men and women. A dual-systems approach in forensic assessment and treatment is promising. Problems in executive functioning and slow or absent brain

366   *Sanne Verwaaijen and Marion van Binsbergen*

maturation are reported over all age groups in forensic populations, so a dual-systems approach fits the full continuum.

Prevention through early intervention

Another important implication of an aetiology that starts at the (sometimes very) young age and that grows in risk on a lifelong continuum is the need for early intervention.

Childhood disruptive behaviour has powerful long-term effects on adult antisocial outcomes, which continue into middle adulthood. The importance of a number of symptoms, the presence of disruptive disorder and high-risk intermediate experiences highlight three areas where early interventions might be targeted: (a) childhood disruptive behaviour should be a high priority for public mental health programmes, (b) reducing subsequent high-risk experiences among those with early disruptive behaviour might alter their life away from antisocial behaviour and (c) having a delinquent peer group predicts crime in both transitional early adult period and current adulthood.

Also, there is evidence that targeted training in reading emotions does lead to change. With children, it is probable that such changes would have the best impact if timed to coincide with relevant developmental changes and placed in the context of ongoing parent–child interactions. Recent work on emotion talk between children and their attachment figures has shown that children's understanding of the emotional world and their own emotions can be enhanced by training parents to regularly engage their offspring in conversational reviews of day-to-day emotional events (Reese & Newcombe, 2007). We expect that the next several years will see increasing precision brought to the specific strategies that can be used to help children and parents learn alternatives to aggression.

Dadds and Rhodes (2008) have been particularly interested in how these parental strategies work with hot versus cold variants of violent and aggressive behaviour. Their research has shown first that reward strategies are rated as effective with both variants, but timeout appears to be less effective with cold children (Hawes & Dadds, 2005). These children are insensitive to emotional stimuli and tend to be less outwardly perturbed by timeout. On the other hand, hot children become outwardly very emotional during discipline. Based on their clinical work and research findings, Dadds and Rhodes proposed the following corollaries for the use of the timeout technique. Hot children may be particularly sensitive to threat cues, and as the reason for implementing timeout is often interpersonal in nature (an argument), allowing the emotion to escalate before implementing timeout is problematic. More specifically, during the instructions for the child to go to timeout, close and direct eye contact with the parent can lead to acutely elevated stress responses and result in escalation and aggression from the child. We are careful with these children to advise parents to avoid 'getting in the child's face' too much, and especially to avoid aggressive facial emotion and eye contact. On the other hand, cold children are more likely to come into conflict due to inappropriate

Forensic rehabilitation 367

reward-seeking behaviour, and are unlikely to attend to the salient emotional aspects of the timeout procedure. Taken together, Dadds and Rhodes indicate that increasing emotional salience and indeed close eye contact should increase the chances of a positive outcome for these children. They find that getting very close to the child and calmly attempting to make direct eye contact actually has the positive and opposite effect of focusing the cold aggression in children with callous-unemotional traits.

Policy recommendations

It is essential that we acknowledge a lifelong vulnerability in certain groups *and* circumstances that are prone to high-risk behaviours or factual criminal offending. However, at the same time it is of *vital importance* not to stigmatise these groups to avoid them becoming moral or ethical outcasts or even having dangerous ideological interests. Nevertheless, nowadays we do know certain combinations of risk factors and disorders confer for high-risk or antisocial behaviour and criminal conduct. The accumulating new evidence calls for a lifelong phenomenology and prognosis that would better describe the complexity of the interrelated risk factors and clinical diagnosis of pathology, both backwards and forwards. A sharper definition of prognostic and treatment-relevant phenotypes (or risk profiles) is the first step towards aetiologically informed treatment (and rehabilitation). This will help us towards a science-based approach in legal and correctional programmes.

Dryfoos (1990) emphasised more than a decade ago that now that we know how high-risk behaviours interrelate, we gain understanding of the size and scope of the prevention interventions needed. If the risk factors and various problem areas are connected, then solutions may require a more cohesive, less fragmented approach as to what currently is practice. She calls for comprehensive strategies at different levels, institutional, local and national and federal, and especially emphasises the need to give the highest priority to integrating (1) research and practice, (2) school systems and health systems, and (3) antecedents, maintainers and consequences of criminal behaviour, in *one* timeline, leading to a focus of strategy. However, overall it seems that we still wait for high-risk children, adolescents and young adults to develop into adult offenders of serious aggression and crime before intervening in a serious and legally sufficiently overarched fashion. This asks for a change of policy in some areas concerning those with a lifelong susceptibility to high-risk behaviour.

Loeber et al. (2012) present an impressive overview with conclusions and recommendations for policy and research:

- Screening on executive functioning, delayed brain maturation, impulse control and intelligence is of the utmost importance in dealing with young offenders.
- An important conclusion is that young adult offenders are more similar to juveniles than to adults with respect to features such as their executive

functioning, impulse control, malleability, responsibility, susceptibility to peer influence and adjudicative competence.
- The focus should be on features that are typically targets of clinical treatment and rehabilitation in (youth) treatment programmes, especially in speeding up maturation, training self-control and reversing antisocial attitudes and surroundings, in prosocial behaviours and surroundings (including peers), and that are more promising than detention, especially detention without gradual treatment programmes.

We conclude that rehabilitation is a phase on a lifelong continuum. Rehabilitation as a phase of transition on a lifelong risk and (mental) health continuum provides for better options than letting adolescents at risk go at 18 or detain late adolescents i.e. early adults in high-risk surroundings, such as adult prison systems.

Considering the recent science on brain development and biological maturing, imprisonment of (children and) youngsters is probably the worst option. Forensic treatment and rehabilitation offer much better options that fit the evidence. And as far as an effect on behavioural change goes: the sooner the better, since intervention and harm reduction *during* the development of the brain influence behaviour on a deeper level than in adulthood. Gradual treatment approaches and *continuous* transfer strategies – in line with individual biological processes of maturation – offer the best structure for interventions and rehabilitation and fit the special needs underlying the biological functioning of the brain and the inherent responsivity to interventions during different lifetime phases. Brain maturation and screening of executive functioning should be added to responsivity as a leading treatment principle.

One of the most important (and hard to realise) recommendations is breaking down the watershed between juvenile and adult justice systems. Loeber et al. (2012) discuss various opportunities such as raising the age for juveniles at which the adult system becomes applicable, which prevents precarious incarceration of immature, low-intelligence and impulsive young adults in adult prisons, where they are highly exposed to adult crime behaviour and antisocial role models. For these susceptible young adults – or biological late adolescents – placement in a juvenile forensic treatment centre for rehabilitation is a much more promising option. Loeber et al. (2012) expect 10% lower rates of recidivism than currently handled by placement in adult prisons. From an economic viewpoint the long-term savings are enormous compared to the current situation.

Another option is the creation of special courts for young adult offenders, and hence specific court orders for rehabilitation in a treatment centre or programme, fit to the task of *gradual* transitions that follow *biological maturing* instead of a legal date at which a youngster is suddenly an adult. The call for transitional systems that serve as a bridge between the juvenile and adult system goes back a long way in the Netherlands (the Wiarda Committee, 1971; the Anneveldt Committee, 1982). Despite these recommendations, the legislatures

Forensic rehabilitation 369

decided to reject it. However, perhaps with the recent empirical studies and neurobiological research findings, legislatures are willing to reconsider this. It becomes difficult to ignore all the evidence pointing out the benefits of rehabilitation programmes especially focused on delayed brain maturing in accordance with the actual development and functioning of neural structures in humans, especially those who are slow in development and learning. And it is not just Loeber et al. (2012) who point out the importance of reshaping legal and correctional systems to make them fit for longer (biological) transitions rather than categorical watersheds between different age groups. The World Health Organization comes to the same conclusion in its World Report on Violence and Health, which ties child abuse and neglect, intimate partner violence, sexual violence, elder violence and self-directed violence to crime and criminal behaviour from the standpoint of victims and the damage to society as a whole.

Concluding remarks

Malfunctioning of the prefrontal cortex and slow brain development are associated with violent crime in children, adolescents and adults, both in men and women, though due weight is given to psychological and social factors. Screening of brain development and cognitive functions seems to be important in all age groups. With this 'extra' in mind, PCC offers the best structure for treatment models in working with antisocial activities and criminal behaviour and directs us to treatment targets that have long been neglected or underestimated: criminogenic needs need to be addressed first in rehabilitation. This goes for all ages, starting with the very young and their families, mostly involving inadequate parenting styles and an accumulation of risk factors, then evolving to adolescents and young adults, who are more similar in brain development to adults and who are still receptive to change on a deep biological level, and resulting in adult crime that could have been anticipated in more than half of all criminal offences, especially when recidivism occurs. This calls for covering the risk continuum on all levels. A vertical approach is more promising in lowering crime statistics than a horizontal approach: breaking down the watershed of 18, covering the full continuum of antisocial behaviour and matching services and corrections on all levels to specific (criminogenic) needs, phases of brain maturation and (executive) functions. Joy Dryfoos (1990) addressed a wide range of audiences over 20 years ago with evidence on risk factors and antisocial trajectories, and drew the same conclusions. Strong support was given by highly influential organisations such as the Carnegie Corporation of New York and Oxford University. She concluded simply that for once more research was not needed before interventions can be initiated:

> Enough is known about the lives of disadvantaged high risk youth to mount an intensive campaign to alter the trajectories of these children. Enough has been documented about the inability of fragmental programs

370 *Sanne Verwaaijen and Marion van Binsbergen*

to produce the necessary changes to proceed toward more comprehensive and holistic approaches.

(p. 268)

Recently neurosciences added even more evidence that demands a different approach in strategies to prevent aggression and crime.

There is a growing awareness of the cost-benefits derived from investing in prevention and early intervention now and saving enormous costs and immense social damage later. Still: we can't wait any longer. Changing policy and legislature takes longer than can be tolerated in the light of what we know. So we have connected child and youth care services on problem behaviour and conduct disorders to adult forensic care services. Our organisation (Conrisq Group) now vertically covers the continuum and integrates research and practice from a lifelong perspective. And if legislators will allow us, we offer rehabilitation programmes 'customised' to risk, needs and responsivity (dysfunctions), for as long as maturing of the brain takes. In the longer run, this will prevent youth at risk from becoming adult offenders of serious aggression and crime.

Literature

Andrews, D.A., & Bonta, J. (2012). *The Psychology of Criminal Conduct.* New Providence: LexisNexis Group.

Andrews, D.A., Bonta, J., & Hoge (1990). Classification for effective rehabilitation: Rediscovering psychology. *Criminal Justice and Behaviour* (17), 19–52.

Augimeri, L.K., Farrington, D.P., Koegl, C.J., & Day, D.M. (2007). The SNAP™ Under 12 Outreach Project: Effects of a community based program for children with conduct problems. *Journal of Child and Family Studies* 16, 799–807.

Bennet, S., Farrington, D.P., & Rowell Huesmann, L. (2005). Explaining gender differences in crime and violence: The importance of social cognitive skills. *Aggression and Violent Behaviour* (3), 263–288.

Bijleveld, C.J.H., Van der Geest, V., & Hendriks, J. (2012). Vulnerable youth in pathways to adulthood. In Loeber, R., Hoeve, M., Slot, W. & Van der Laan, P.H. (eds.). *Persisters and desisters in crime from adolescence into adulthood: Explanation, prevention and punishment.* Farnham: Ashgate Publishing Limited, pp. 105–125.

Boendermaker, L. (1998). Eind goed, al goed? De leefsituatie van jongeren een jaar na vertrek uit de justitiële behandelinrichting. Onderzoek en Beleid, No. 167. The Hague: WODC.

Byrnes, J.P., Miller, D.C., & Schafer, W.D. (1999). Gender differences in risk-taking: A meta-analysis. *Psychological Bulletin* 125 (3), 367–383.

Casey, B.J., Getz, S., & Galvan, A. (2008). The adolescent brain. *Developmental Review* (28), 62–77.

Caspi, A., McClay, J., Moffitt, T.E., Mill, J., Martin, J., Craig, I.W., Taylor, A., & Poulton, R. (2002). Role of genotype in the cycle of violence in maltreated children. *Science* 297, 851–854.

Dadds, M.R., & Rhodes, T. (2008). Aggression in young children with concurrent callous-unemotional traits: Can the neurosciences inform progress and innovation in treatment approaches? *Philosophical Transactions of the Royal Society B (Biological Sciences)*, 363–1503, 2567–2576.

Dryfoos, J.G. (1990). *Adolescents at risk: Prevalence and prevention*. New York: Oxford University Press.

Fabio, A., Yuan, Z., Wisniewski, S.R., Henry, D.B., Farrington, D.P., Bridge, J.A., & Loeber, R. (2008). Cohort differences in the progression of developmental pathways: Evidence for period effects on secular trends of violence in males. *Injury Prevention* 14, 311–318.

Figner, B., Mackinley, R.J., Wilkening, F., & Weber, E.U. (2009). Affective and deliberate processes in risky choice: Age differences in risk taking in the Columbia Card Task. *Journal of Experimental Psychology* 35 (3), 709–730.

Geest, V. van der, Bijleveld, C., & Blokland, A. (2007). Ontwikkelingspaden van delinquent gedrag bij hoog-risicojongeren. *Tijdschrift voor Criminologie* 49 (4), 351–369.

Hawes, D.J., & Dadds, M.R. (2005). The treatment of conduct problems in children with callous-unemotional traits. *Journal of Consulting and Clinical Psychology* 73, 737–741.

Kazdin, A.E. (1987). Treatment of antisocial behaviour in children: Current status and future directions. *Psychological Bulletin* 102 (2), 187–203.

Kingston, D.A., Seto, M.C., Ahmed, A.G., Fedoroff, P., Firestone, P., & Bradford, J.M. (2012). The role of central and peripheral hormones in sexual and violent behaviour. *The American Academic Journal for Psychiatry and Law* 40 (4), 85–476.

Koegl, C.J., Farrington, D.P., Augimeri, L.K., & Day, J. (2008). Evaluation of a targeted cognitive behavioural program for children with conduct problems: The SNAP™ Under 12 Outreach Project: Service intensity, age and gender effects on short and long term outcomes. *Clinical Child Psychology and Psychiatry* 13, 441–456.

Kogel, C.H. (2008). *De hersenen in beeld: Neurobiologisch onderzoek en vraagstukken op het gebied van verklaring, reductie en preventie van criminaliteit*. Meppel: Boom Legal Publishers, WODC.

Krug, E.G., Dahlberg, L.L., Mercy, J.A., Zwi, A.B., & Lozano, R. eds. (2002). *World report on violence and health*. Geneva: World Health Organization.

Liu, X., & Kaplan, H.B. (2001). Role strain and illicit drug use: The moderating influence of commitment to conventional values. *Journal of Drug Issues* 31, 833–856.

Loeber, R., Farrington, D.P., Stouthamer-Loeber, M., Moffitt, T.E., Caspi, A., & Lynam, D. (2002). Male mental health problems, psychopathy, and personality traits: Key findings from the first 14 years of the Pittsburgh Youth Study. *Clinical Child and Family Psychology Review* 4 (4), 273–297.

Loeber, R., Stouthamer-Loeber, M., Farrington, D., Lahey, B.B., Keenan, K., & White, H.R. (2002). Three longitudinal studies of children's development in Pittsburgh: The Developmental Trends Study, the Pittsburgh Youth Study, and the Pittsburgh Girls Study (Editorial introduction). *Criminal Behaviour and Mental Health* 12, 1–23.

Loeber, R., Hoeve, M., Slot, W., & Van der Laan, P.H. (eds.). (2012). *Persisters and desisters in crime from adolescence into adulthood: Explanation, prevention and punishment*. Farnham: Ashgate Publishing Limited.

Lynam, D.R., Loeber, R., & Stouthamer-Loeber, M. (2008). The stability of psychopathy from adolescence into adulthood: The search for moderators. *Criminal Justice and Behaviour* 35 (2) (Special Issue), 244–262.

Meyer-Lindenberg, A., & Zink, C.F. (2007). Imaging genetics for neuropsychiatric disorders. *Child Adolescence. Psychiatry Clin.N.Am.* 16, 581–597.

372   Sanne Verwaaijen and Marion van Binsbergen

Moffitt, T.E. (2008). A review of research on the taxonomy of life-course persistent versus adolescent limited antisocial behaviour. In F.T. Cullen, J.P. Wright, & K.R. Blevins (eds.), *Taking stock: The status of criminological theory. Advances in criminological theory* 15, 277–311.

Moffitt, T.E., Caspi, A., Harrington, H., & Milne, B.J. (2002). Males on the life-course-persistent and adolescence-limited antisocial pathways: Follow-up at age 26 years. *Development and Psychopathology* 14, 179–207.

Moffitt, T.E., & Avshalom, C. (2001). Childhood predictors differentiate life-course persistent and adolescence-limited pathways among males and females. *Development and Psychopathology* 13 (2), 355–375.

Painter, K., & Farrington, D.P. (2004). *Gender differences in risk factors for offending: Findings 196.* London: Research, Development and Statistics Directorate of the Home Office.

Pardini, D.A., & Loeber, R. (2008). Interpersonal callousness trajectories across adolescence: Early social influences and adult outcomes. *Criminal Justice and Behaviour* 35 (2) (Special Issue), 173–196.

Raine, A.D., Brennan, P., Sarnoff, A., & Mednick, P.D. (1994). Birth complications combined with early maternal rejection at age 1 year predispose to violent crime at age 18 years. *Archives of General Psychiatry* 51 (12), 984–988.

Reese, E., & Newcombe, R. (2007). Training mothers in elaborative reminiscing enhances children's autobiographical memory and narrative. *Child Development* 78, 1153–1170.

Salekin, R.T., & Lochman, J.E. (2008). Child and adolescent psychopathy: The search for protective factors. *Criminal Justice and Behaviour* 35 (2) (Special Issue), 159–171.

Sampson, R.J., & Laub, J.H. (1997). A life course theory of cumulative disadvantage and the stability of delinquency. In T.P. Thornberry (ed.), *Developmental theories of crime and delinquency.* New Brunswick, NJ: Transaction Publishers, pp. 133–161.

Simonoff, E., Elander, J., Holmshaw, J., Pickles, A., Murray, R., & Rutter, M. (2004). Predictors of antisocial personality: Continuities form childhood to adult life. *British Journal of Psychiatry* (27), 118–184.

Steinberg, L. (2008). A social neuroscience perspective on adolescent risk-taking. *Developmental Review* 28 (1), 78–106.

Steinberg, L. (2010). *A dual systems model of adolescent risk-taking.* New York: Wiley Interscience.

Steinberg, L., Albert, D., Banich, M., Cauffman, E., Graham, S., & Woolard, J. (2008). Age differences in sensation seeking and impulsivity as indexed by behaviour and self-report: Evidence for a dual systems model. *Developmental Psychology* 44 (6), 1764–1778.

Strang, N.M., Chein, J.M., & Steinberg, L. (2013). The value of the dual systems model of adolescent risk taking. *Frontiers of Human and Neurosciences* (27), 7–233.

Sullivan, D.H., & Mullen, P.E. (2012). Exploring hormonal influences on problem sexual behaviour. *Journal for American Academic Psychiatry and Law* (40), 486.

Swaab, D. (2005). We are our brain: Brains, consciousness and faith: Neurobiological aspects. *Academy Magazine* (3), 2–10.

Swaab, D. (2012). *Wij zijn ons brein.* Amsterdam: Atlas-Contact.

Thornberry, T.P., & Krohn, M.D. (2005). Applying interactional theory to the explanation of continuity and change in antisocial behaviour. In D.P. Farrington (ed.), *Integrated developmental and life-course theories of offending.* New Brunswick, NJ: Transaction Publishers, pp. 183–209.

Ward, T., Melser, J., & Yates, P.M. (2007). Reconstructing the Risk-Need-Responsivity model: A theoretical elaboration and evaluation. *Aggression and Violent Behaviour* 12, 208–228.

White, J.L., Moffitt, T.E., Earls, F., Robins, L., & Silva, P.A. (1990). How early can we tell? *Journal of Criminology* (28), 507–533.

Wouda, P.L. (1987). *Jongeren tussen wal en schip*. Leiden: University of Leiden (Ph.D. Dissertation).

Index

abnormal motor behaviour 256–257
abuse 4, 103, 236–237, 358, 369; Autism Spectrum Disorder 314, 321; dependent personality disorder 192; deterministic reasoning about 37; family deception 146; intellectual disability 281, 283; suggestive memory recovery techniques 41; violence risk 266, 355, 360
ad hoc hypotheses 41
adaptive calibration model (ACM) 62–63, 64
ADHD *see* attention deficit hyperactivity disorder
Adler, N. E. 4, 168
adolescence 6, 74–75, 85–86; abuse during 103; adolescence-limited offenders 3, 98–99, 100; aetiology of criminal behaviour 355, 356; affective empathy 80–82; aggression 172; Autism Spectrum Disorder 309–311, 318–319, 321–323; brain development 3, 9, 74, 357, 359, 362–363, 369; callous unemotional traits 60; cognitive distortions 124; cortisol 236; imprisonment 359; inhibition 77–79; moral behaviour 126; neurobiological heterogeneity 84–85; policy recommendations 367–368; psychopathic traits 77; reward and loss processing 79–80; risk-taking 357–358; treatment 362–364; *see also* children; juvenile offenders
adulthood, transition to 356
adversarial model 32
affective empathy 6, 80–82, 125, 318–319
affective morality 113, 119, 125, 128; *see also* moral emotions

Affective Morality Index (AMI) 119, 127, 128
aggression 1, 7, 33, 157–182; ADHD 100; antisocial personality disorder 187; Autism Spectrum Disorder 307, 309–310, 314, 315, 316–317, 322–324; biological theories 163–166; children 57, 59–60, 366–367; conduct disorder 65, 187; corpus callosum 235; definition of 157; dual hazard hypothesis 237; hormones 17, 76, 236, 359; HPA activity 63, 64; impulsivity 158–160; instinct 160–161; integrated emotion systems model 229–230, 234; integrative theories 166–168; intellectual disability 8–9, 276–291; interventions 169–172; moral behaviour 115; neurobiology of 358; parental monitoring 103; peer rejection 101; personality disorders 183, 192–193, 195–199, 200; risk assessment 21; self-esteem 130; social theories 162–163; subtypes 158; *see also* violence
Aggression Replacement Training (ART) 129, 169
Ainsworth, M. D. S. 287
Aksan, N. 122
alcohol use: adolescents 359; aetiology of criminal behaviour 355; impact of intoxication on memory 148–149; intellectual disability 282, 289, 290; parental 266, 289, 355; prenatal 131, 167; psychopathy 365; sex offenders 247; *see also* substance use
Allen, D. 319
Alpert, R. 116
AMI *see* Affective Morality Index

amnesia 145, 147–149, 151–152
amygdala 74, 227, 231–232, 234; affective
empathy 80–81, 82; aggression 159–160,
164; conduct problems 61; differential
amygdala activation model 215–216,
230, 231–232; emotion recognition
360; empathy 121; hyperreactivity
316; integrated emotion systems model
214–215, 220–221, 229–230, 231; low-
fear hypothesis 212, 228–229; moral
behaviour 125; paralimbic dysfunction
model 216–217; psychopathy 8; reward
and loss sensitivity 80; risk-taking 357;
violence 358
Anderson, C. A. 168
Andrews, B. P. 209
Andrews, D. 339–340, 342, 352, 353, 361
anecdotal evidence 42
anger: aggression and 158, 159, 173;
anger management 169, 170, 171, 285;
borderline personality disorder 188, 191;
children 57; cognitive neoassociation
theory 161; corpus callosum 235;
inability to control 102; medication 171;
provocation 126; reactive aggression
59–60; skills-based interventions 66
anticonvulsants 171
antipsychotic medication 170, 266–267,
268–270, 271, 284, 321, 322–323
antisocial behaviour 5–7, 364; adolescence
74, 83, 98, 99; aetiology of 354, 355;
attachment 120; biological studies 76;
callous unemotional traits 65; conscience
115, 130, 131; early intervention 366;
executive dysfunction 78; family risk
factors 104; fearlessness linked to 58;
heritability 165–166; hormones 236;
lifelong vulnerability 365, 367; moral
behaviour 114, 115, 126; neurobiology
of 75–76, 121, 358; parental 103; peer
rejection 101; prefrontal cortex 233;
prenatal factors 167; Psychology of
Criminal Conduct 353; psychopathy
77, 145, 207, 208, 210, 219; risk
factors 55, 57; stressful experiences 4;
temperament 118
antisocial personality disorder (APD) 17,
144, 187, 190, 227, 266; aggression
183, 196–197, 200; assessment of

195; comorbidity 193–194; diagnosis
29, 30; heritability 166; intellectual
disability 282; lifelong vulnerability 365;
malingering and deception 7; motivation
for crimes 195; offence types 193, 194;
prefrontal cortex 233; prisoners 191,
200, 228; psychopathy 145, 186, 199,
210, 217–218; risk management 339
Antonowicz, D. 339
anxiety: Autism Spectrum Disorder
314, 315, 319; avoidant personality
disorder 195; borderline personality
disorder 187; children 59, 83; cortisol
236; internalising disorders 1, 2;
pharmacotherapy 170; protective factors
104, 105; psychopathy 209; psychotic
disorders 268; schizotypal personality
disorder 185; stress response system 62
APD see antisocial personality disorder
Appelbaum, P. 263
Applied Behaviour Analysis (ABA)
321, 322
Arntz, Arnoud 157–182
arousal 9, 30, 58; aggression 164, 166;
biological studies 76; Effortful Control
119; intellectual disability 282; lack of
empathy 81; parasympathetic 63
Arseneault, L. 265
arson 194, 276, 289, 311, 312, 313, 314, 318
ART see Aggression Replacement Training
ASD see Autism Spectrum Disorder
Asperger syndrome 307, 308, 310–313,
315, 319, 321
attachment 118, 120, 130, 365; intellectual
disability 280–281; lack of empathy 81;
SAPROF 337; Schema Therapy 287;
sex offenders 245–246
attention 83, 318; attention bias 261;
differential amygdala activation model
230; psychopathy 212–213, 216, 220,
229, 237
attention deficit hyperactivity disorder
(ADHD) 2, 3, 313–314; inhibition 78;
intellectual disability 282; life-course
persistent offenders 100; peer rejection
101; protective factors 104
attention seeking 188, 283
attribution bias 62, 82, 126, 127
auditory hallucinations 256, 259, 264

376 *Index*

Australia 361

Autism Spectrum Disorder (ASD) 9, 307–333; ADHD and 313–314; anxiety and social isolation 314–315; cognitive difficulties 317–318; comorbidity 313, 315–316, 323–324; emotional reactions 316; intellectual disability 282; psychopathy compared with 318–320; sensory processing differences 317; treatment 321–324; types of offending 310–311, 312–313; victimisation 320–321; young people 309–311

autonomic reactivity 164

availability heuristic 37

avoidant personality disorder 189, 192, 194, 195

avolition 257

Baker, A. 146

Bakermans-Kranenburg, M. J. 4, 167

Bandura, A. 17, 162

Barker, E. D. 58

Baron, J. 36

Bartley, William 27

base rate neglect 38

Basic Empathy Scale (BES) 127, 128

Baskin-Sommers, A. 218

Bates, A. 251

Baumeister, R. F. 197

Baumrind, D. 102

Beail, N. 279

Beauchaine, T. P. 83

Beck, A. T. 260

Becker, H. S. 162

Beech, A. R. 121–122

behaviourism 16, 17, 19, 116

Belgium 242, 340

beliefs 35, 256, 260–261, 262

Benjamin, A. J. 197

Bennet, S. 361

benzodiazepines 170–171

Berkowitz, L. 161

Berman, M. E. 199

BES *see* Basic Empathy Scale

beta-blockers 171

Bettencourt, B. A. 197

bias blind spot 39–40

biases 35–40, 43, 261, 262; *see also* confirmation bias

Bijleveld, C. J. H. 357

Binder, R. L. 264

biology 17, 359; aggression 163–166, 277; conduct problems 61–64; conscience 121–122; dual hazard hypothesis 237; externalising disorders 75–86; maturation 368; protective factors 105; social push hypothesis 237; *see also* neurobiology

biomarkers 62

biopsychosocial model 74–75

biosocial hypotheses 236–237

bipolar disorder 263, 315

Birbaumer, N. 211

Bjork, Robert 33–34

Bjørkly, S. 317

Blair, R. J. R. 58, 80, 121, 212, 232

Blasi, A. 131

Bo, S. 266

Boccardi, M. 216–217, 232

Boendermaker, L. 356

Bogaerts, Stefan 245, 337–351

boldness 210

Bonta, J. 339–340, 342, 352, 353, 361

borderline personality disorder 3, 186, 187–188, 268; aggression 183, 198–199, 200; assessment of 195; comorbidity 193–194; diagnosis 184; dimensional structure 190; intellectual disability 282; medication 170, 171; Mentalisation-Based Treatment 286; motivation for crimes 195; offence types 193; prisoners 191–192, 200

Bornstein, R. F. 192

Bosman, Anna 307–333

Bourgon, G. 339

Bowlby, John 120, 287

Boyce, W. T. 4, 168

brain 2–3, 17, 74, 227–241, 359, 364; aggression 159–160, 163–164, 166, 277; brain-based lie detection techniques 42; conduct problems 61; corpus callosum 235; criminal responsibility 86; diagnostic scans 18–19; differential amygdala activation model 215–216, 230, 231–232; dual-systems model 357–358, 365–366; empathy 80–82, 121, 125; event-related potentials 216, 217–218; inhibition 77–78; integrated emotion systems model 213–215,

220–221, 229–230, 231, 234; limbic system 9, 231–235, 316, 357; moral development 131, 212; neuroimaging 76–77, 78, 83–84, 163–164, 216, 360; paralimbic dysfunction model 216–217, 220–221, 230–231; psychopathy 8; psychotic disorders 260; rehabilitation approaches 368, 369; reward and loss sensitivity 79–80; risk factors 355; temporal cortex 235, 236–237; treatment of young people 362–363; *see also* amygdala; neurobiology; neuroscience; prefrontal cortex
Brazil, Inti A. 206–226
Brennan, P. 355
broken homes 103–104
Bronfenbrenner, U. 170
Brylewski, J. 284
bullying 320, 321
Burke, J. M. 192
Bush, N. R. 4, 168
Bushman, B. J. 168, 197
Byrd, A. L. 65
Byrnes, J. P. 360

callous unemotional (CU) traits 6, 59–66, 77; affective morality 119, 125; aggression 172; Autism Spectrum Disorder 319; brain functions 81–82; cortisol 236; neurobiological heterogeneity 85; psychopathy 144, 208, 365; reward and loss sensitivity 80
Campbell, Donald 26
Campo, Joost A. 255–275
Canada 242, 340, 341, 361
Cane, René 183–205
Carlson, M. 4
Caspi, A. 4, 167, 265
catatonic behaviour 257
CBT *see* cognitive behavioural therapy
CD *see* conduct disorder
Chapman, J. P. 38
Chapman, L. J. 38
Chekhonin, V. P. 165
children: abused 4, 146; aetiology of criminal behaviour 354–355; aggression 172, 237; anger provocation 126; attachment 120, 280–281; Autism Spectrum Disorder 307–308, 309–311,

314, 320, 321–323; brain development 3, 362–363, 368, 369; bullying 320, 321; conduct problems 6, 55–73, 97; cortisol 236; deception 144; developmental characteristics of offenders 98–100; early intervention 366–367, 370; environmental influences 168; externalising and internalising disorders 83; extra-familial risk factors 100–101; family risk factors 102–104; individual risk factors 102; intellectual disability 283; moral behaviour 115–116, 125, 126, 130–131; neglect 4; protective factors 104–105; socialisation 119–120; temperament 118; trauma 122; treatment 105–107, 358, 362–364; *see also* adolescence; juvenile offenders
Chistiakov, D. A. 165
Cima, Maaike 1–12, 74–96, 113–140, 143–156, 157–182, 206–226
Circles of Support and Accountability (COSA) 8, 242–254, 341–342
Clare, I. C. H. 280
classical conditioning 116
Cleckley, H. 30, 38, 185–186, 206, 208, 209
clinical psychology 21
CNT *see* cognitive neoassociation theory
cognitive behavioural therapy (CBT) 80, 106; aggression 169–170, 173; effectiveness 339; intellectual disability 285, 286, 290; psychotic disorders 267
cognitive deficits: Autism Spectrum Disorder 317–318; intellectual disability 278–280; psychotic disorders 261–262
cognitive distortions 123–124, 126, 129, 131; aggression 173; measurement of 127; psychotic disorders 261; schizotypal personality disorder 185; sex offenders 146, 147, 249
cognitive empathy 125
cognitive morality 113–114, 116–118, 122–124, 126–127, 129, 130, 279–280; *see also* moral reasoning
cognitive neoassociation theory (CNT) 161
cognitive psychology 17, 19–20
Cohn, Moran D. 74–96
Coid, J. W. 193, 194, 195
common sense 33–34, 35

378 Index

comorbidity: Autism Spectrum Disorder 313, 315–316, 323–324; personality disorders 192, 193, 199, 200

conduct disorder (CD) 1, 2, 65, 75, 97, 187, 364; aggression 172; brain regions 233, 234, 235; cortisol 236; deception 144; inhibition 78; lifelong vulnerability 365; psychopathic traits 85

conduct problems 6, 55–73, 99; ADHD 100; behavioural evidence 59–60; biological evidence 61–64; brain functions 81; diagnosis 65; emotional and cognitive evidence 60–61; research 65; temperamental risk factors 56–59; treatment 66

confirmation bias 28, 31–32, 36, 39, 41, 261

connectivity 43

conscience 7, 58, 113–140; development of 115–116; measurement of 126–127, 130; neurobiological approach 121–122; socialisation 119–120; temperament 118–119; theories of 116–118, 130; treatment 129–130; *see also* moral behaviour

contingency management 287

control question technique (CQT) 21

Cooke, D. J. 207–208

corpus callosum 235

cortisol 4, 122, 164–165, 168, 236, 358

Cortoni, F. 251

COSA *see* Circles of Support and Accountability

counselling 106

courts 368

CQT *see* control question technique

crime and punishment 15–16

criminal history 339

criminal irresponsibility 16–19, 22

criminal profiling 38–39

criminal responsibility 20, 86, 143

CU traits *see* callous unemotional traits

curricular revisions 287–288

DAAM *see* differential amygdala activation model

Dadds, M. R. 58, 216, 358, 366–367

Dams, L. 146

Darwin, Charles 26, 118

Dawes, R. M. 41

De Gelder, B. 316

De Keijser, J. M. 15

De Kogel, C. H. 340, 363

De Ruiter, C. 337

De Vogel, V. 337, 338

De Vries Robbe, M. 337

De Waal, F. 118

De Wachter, D. 3

Deane, K. 281

deception 7, 143–156; antisocial personality disorder 187, 191; brain-based lie detection techniques 42; conduct disorder 187; detection of 149–152; personality disorders 194; polygraph tests 30, 43, 151; psychopathy 144–146, 208; sex offenders 146–147, 150–151; simulated amnesia 145, 147–149, 151–152

decision-making 6, 219–220, 227, 231, 233, 234

delusions 256, 262, 264, 268, 269

dependent personality disorder 189, 192, 194

depression 1, 83; Autism Spectrum Disorder 315; intellectual disability 282, 283; internalising disorders 2; MacArthur Risk Assessment Study 263; maternal 103; medication 171; prenatal 167

desistance 248, 249, 252, 353

Desmet, M. 245

developmental social neuroscience 2

deviant behaviour 158, 162

diagnosis: conduct problems 65; personality disorders 184, 190; psychopathy 199; psychotic disorders 258–259

Diagnostic and Statistical Manual of Mental Disorders (DSM) 8, 85; antisocial personality disorder 29, 145; Autism Spectrum Disorder 308, 313–314; conduct disorder 65; impulse control 159; intellectual disability 276; malingering 143; personality disorders 184, 190, 197; psychopathy 206, 210, 217; psychotic disorders 256–257, 258–259

Diathesis-Stress model 4

Dietz, P. E. 314

differential amygdala activation model (DAAM) 215–216, 230, 231–232

differential association theory 162
differential susceptibility theory 4, 167
'difficult temperament' 56, 210
disinhibition 6, 17, 210, 212, 281–282
disorganised thinking 256
divorce 103–104
Doll, H. 19
Dollard, J. 160–161
domestic violence 85, 103, 192, 196, 199,
  283, 369
Doob, L. W. 160–161
dopamine 165, 166, 260
Douglas, K. S. 338
Dowden, C. 339
drug use *see* substance use
Druyan, Anne 27
Dryfoos, Joy G. 367, 369–370
DSM *see Diagnostic and Statistical Manual of
  Mental Disorders*
dual hazard hypothesis 237
dual-systems model 357–358, 365–366
Duggan, L. 284
Duncan, L. E. 4
Duwe, G. 251

Earls, F. 4, 354
early intervention 366–367, 370
Early Recognition Method (ERM)
  340–341
Eaton, W. W. 257
ED *see* externalising disorders
Edens, J. F. 145
education 101, 104–105, 283, 357
Effortful Control 119, 120
ego-threat hypothesis 197–198
Eisenstadt, M. 146
Eisner, J. P. 264
Emde, R. N. 118
EMDR *see* Eye Movement Desensitisation
  and Reprocessing
emotion regulation 1–3, 6, 9, 60, 171;
  aggression 173; Autism Spectrum
  Disorder 315, 316; intellectual disability
  280; skills-based interventions 66;
  temperament 56–57, 58; *see also*
  self-regulation
emotional abuse 103
emotional contagion 58, 81
emotional responsiveness 60–61, 360

emotions: aggression 160, 173; amygdala
  231; Autism Spectrum Disorder 316,
  318, 319–320; early intervention 366;
  facial recognition 230, 231, 316, 318,
  360; intellectual disability 280–281;
  moral 113–114, 116, 118–119,
  124–125, 127, 128, 130–131, 219;
  non-verbal therapies 286; prosocial 65,
  85; psychopathy 219
empathy: adolescence 6, 74; aetiology of
  criminal behaviour 355; affective 6,
  80–82, 125, 318–319; Autism Spectrum
  Disorder 318–319; Basic Empathy Scale
  127, 128; brain structures 121; children
  6, 58, 59, 65, 102, 118; cognitive
  distortions 124; externalising disorders
  75; fear recognition 231–232; HPA
  activity 64; intellectual disability 279;
  moral behaviour 113, 114, 116, 125,
  126, 130; narcissistic personality disorder
  188; oxytocin 122; prosocial behaviour
  115, 118; psychopathy 186, 206, 229;
  skills-based interventions 66; temporal
  cortex 235
empiricism 26
employment 357
England and Wales 97, 157, 193, 262–263,
  313, 340
environmental enrichment programmes 85
environmental toxins 55
Equip 129
ERM *see* Early Recognition Method
Ermer, E. 217, 218
ERPs *see* event-related potentials
ethnicity 101, 265
Europe 101, 242, 361
Evenden, J. L. 159
event-related potentials (ERPs) 216,
  217–218
evidence 25, 31, 40–41, 42
evidence-based treatment 19, 105
evolutionary epistemology 26
excitation transfer theory 162, 164, 166
executive functioning 77–78, 362,
  365–366, 367–368; Autism Spectrum
  Disorder 311, 317–318; prefrontal cortex
  233; psychotic disorders 261, 262
externalising disorders (ED) 1–4, 6, 74–96,
  107; affective empathy 80–82; affective

380 *Index*

morality 119, 125; Autism Spectrum Disorder 310; cortisol 236; inhibition 77–79; intellectual disability 279; internalising disorders compared with 83–84; neurobiological heterogeneity 84–85; reward and loss sensitivity 79–80; self-esteem 130
eye contact 115, 231, 316, 366–367
Eye Movement Desensitisation and Reprocessing (EMDR) 290
eyewitness testimony 42

facial recognition 230, 231, 316, 318, 360
Faigman, David 32
falsifiability 28, 40–41
family: aetiology of criminal behaviour 355; Autism Spectrum Disorder 315; Forensic Social Network Analysis 344–345, 346–347; functional family therapy 106–107; intellectual disability 281; multisystemic therapy 106, 170; protective factors 104, 363; risk factors 102–104, 339; *see also* parenting
family therapy 106–107, 170, 347
Farrington, D. P. 360, 361
Fazel, S. 19
fear 3–4, 114; avoidant personality disorder 189; low-fear hypothesis 119, 211–212, 228–229; psychopathy 209, 210; psychotic disorders 268; recognition of 230, 231–232
fearlessness 28, 57–58, 119, 212
Felson, R. B. 163
Fergusson, D. M. 99
Festinger, D. S. 193
Feynman, Richard 27, 28, 29
fight or flight responses 161, 316
Figner, B. 357
forensic psychiatry 15, 19, 20; risk management in 337–351
forensic psychology 15, 17, 21–22; bias blind spot 39–40; naïve realism 36; pseudoscience 40–43; risk assessment 19; self-reports 18; sex offenders 252–253
forensic psychopathology 5, 15–24; confirmation bias 36; legal issues 19–20; pseudoscience 40; psychopathic personality 26, 29–30; risk assessment 20–21; risk prediction 25; science 44;

as unique discipline 21–22; *see also* psychopathology
Forensic Social Network Analysis (FSNA) 9, 342–347, 348
foster care 107
Fragile X syndrome 277, 308
Frazier, T. W. 323
free will 19, 86
Freud, Sigmund 116, 160
Frick, Paul J. 55–73, 80
Frijters, Karin 276–306
frontal lobe dysfunction theory 163
frustration–aggression hypothesis 160–161
FSNA *see* Forensic Social Network Analysis
functional family therapy (FFT) 106–107

Gacono, C. B. 145
Gadow, K. D. 314
GAM *see* General Aggression Model
gangs 100, 107
Garb, H. N. 19
gender 360–361; Autism Spectrum Disorder 308, 310; prefrontal cortex 233; sexual abuse 103; treatment implications 364; violence risk 265
General Aggression Model (GAM) 168–169
general theory of crime 166
genetics 4, 165–166, 360; aggression 167; Autism Spectrum Disorder 308; conduct problems 61; gene-environmental interaction studies 75; psychotic disorders 260; *see also* heritability
Germany 340
Gibbs, J. C. 117, 123
Gilbert, Daniel 34
Gillberg, C. 319
Gleaser, W. 281
Glenn, Andrea L. 58, 227–241
GLM *see* 'good lives' model
GoA *see* Grip on Aggression programme
Goin-Kochel, R. 321
'good lives' model (GLM) 288, 340, 348
Gorenstein, E. E. 79
Gottfredson, M. R. 166
grandiosity 188, 194, 198, 256
Grann, M. 19
Great Britain 242, 361; *see also* England and Wales

Green, V. A. 321–322
Grip on Aggression (GoA) programme 286
Gudjonsson, G. H. 148–149
guilt 58, 59, 65, 234; children 6; conscience 116, 118, 119; integrated emotion systems model 230; moral behaviour 113, 114, 124, 125, 127; psychopathy 186, 206; sex offenders 147

Haaven, J. L. 288–289
hallucinations 256, 259, 264, 268, 269
Halterman, J. S. 314
Hanson, R. K. 247, 339
Happé, F. 318
Hare, Robert D. 29–30, 207, 208, 220, 312
harm avoidance 320
Hartley, S. L. 310
Heck, C. 103
Helmus, L. 339
heritability 29, 165–166, 278; see also genetics
Hernandez-Avila, C. A. 193
Hess, Rudolf 148
heuristics 37–38
Higgins-D'Alessandro, A. 318–319
hindsight bias 37, 39
hippocampus 227, 232–233
Hirschi, T. 166
histrionic personality disorder 186, 188, 192, 194, 195
HIT see How I Think Questionnaire
Hodgson, S. 339
Hoeve, M. 352, 362
Hoffman, M. L. 117, 118
Hoge, R. D. 342
Höing, Mechtild 242–254
Holst, U. 124
homelessness 265
homicide 255, 263, 264, 307, 343
hormones 2, 4, 17, 76, 236; adolescence 74; aggression 164–165; conscience 122; puberty 3; sex offenders 359; violence 8
Horwood, L. J. 99
hostility: aetiology of criminal behaviour 355; children 57; medication 171; reactive aggression 59–60; sex offenders 247
Houssa, M. 279

Houston, R. J. 198–199
How I Think Questionnaire (HIT) 127
HPA see hypothalamic-pituitary-adrenal axis
Hudson, S. M. 245, 282
Huesmann, L. Rowell 163, 361
human capital 248–249, 356
Hume, David 124
hyperactivity 1, 76, 170, 321, 322, 324; see also attention deficit hyperactivity disorder
hyperarousal 316, 317
hyperreactivity 6, 76, 83–84, 316, 319
hypothalamic-pituitary-adrenal (HPA) axis 2, 4, 62–64, 164, 260

Iacoboni, M. 121
ID see intellectual disability
idiographic approaches 32–33
IED see intermitted explosive disorder
IES model see integrated emotion systems model
Ijzendoorn, M. H. 4, 167
illusory correlation 38–39
imprisonment 16, 311, 358–359, 368
impulse control 74, 119, 159, 163, 210, 281, 367–368
impulsivity 1, 126, 166, 360, 363; adolescence 74, 77, 86; aetiology of criminal behaviour 355; aggression and 7, 158–160; antisocial personality disorder 187, 191; borderline personality disorder 187, 192, 198; brain maturation 357; executive dysfunction 78; pharmacotherapy 170, 171; prefrontal cortex 233; protective factors 104; psychopathy 145, 146, 186, 208, 209; rehabilitation 365; sex offenders 247
inhibition 6, 75, 77–79, 119, 125, 227, 357
inhibitory control 365
instinct 160–161
integrated emotion systems (IES) model 213–215, 220–221, 229–230, 231, 232, 234
intellectual disability (ID) 8–9, 276–306, 311; behaviour 281–282; case example 289–290; cognitions 278–280; emotions 280–281; environmental/social factors 283–284; treatment 284–290, 291

382 *Index*

intelligence 353, 356, 367; as protective factor 104, 337; psychotic disorders 262; risk factors 170
intermitted explosive disorder (IED) 159
internalising disorders 1–3, 83–84, 85

Jackson, J. L. 15
Jelicic, Marco 143–156
Johnson, Alexandria K. 227–241
Johnson, J. G. 191
jumping to conclusions (JTC) bias 262
jurors 34–35, 36
juvenile offenders 6, 9, 97–112, 368; aggression 169; cognitive distortions 124; developmental characteristics 98–100; extra-familial risk factors 100–101; family risk factors 102–104; individual risk factors 102; moral reasoning 123, 219; protective factors 104–105; psychopathy 219; self-esteem 129–130; treatment 105–107, 129; *see also* adolescence; children

Kaartinen, M. 310
Kahn, R. E. 65
Kahneman, Daniel 34
Kanne, S. M. 309
Kant, Immanuel 122–123
Kawakami, C. 321
Kazdin, A. E. 354
Keeling, J. A. 282
Keeney, M. M. 193
Kemner, C. 316
Kennealy, P. J. 165
Keshavan, M. S. 257, 259
Keulen-De Vos, Marije 276–306
Kiehl, K. A. 212, 218
Kimonis, E. R. 61
King, C. 316
Kingston, D. A. 359
Kirby, K. C. 193
Kochanska, G. 58, 118, 119, 122, 130
Koenigs, M. 219–220
Kohlberg, L. 116–117, 123, 279–280
Korebrits, Andries 97–112
Kozlowski, A. M. 283
Krabbendam, L. 260
Krebs, D. L. 117, 123
Kristiansson, M. 314
Krohn, M. D. 356

labelling theory 162, 172
Laible, D. J. 120
Langdon, P. E. 280
Långström, N. 124, 316
Larden, M. 124
Large, M. M. 265
Laub, J. H. 356
learning: aggression 172; emotional 232; passive avoidance 116, 119; psychopathy 216; social fear learning 211–212; social learning theory 162, 172, 283, 339; stress response system 64
legal issues 19–20, 31
legal system 32, 33, 42, 368–369
Lehnecke, K. M. 17
Libby, Scooter 33
life-course persistent (LCP) offenders 3, 98–99, 100
Lilienfeld, Scott O. 2, 19, 25–51, 209
limbic system 9, 231–235, 316, 357
Lincoln, T. M. 262
lithium 171
Lobbestael, Jill 183–205
Loeber, R. 65, 98, 99–100, 103, 352, 355, 362, 368–369
loneliness 243, 246, 315, 320, 341
Lorenz, K. 161
low-fear hypothesis 119, 211–212, 228–229

MacArthur Risk Assessment Study 263
Magnée, M. J. C. M. 316
magnetic resonance imaging (MRI) 76–77, 78, 216, 360
Magnum, Crystal Gail 36
malingering 7, 39, 143–156; detection of 149–152; personality disorders 194; psychopathy 144–146; sex offenders 146–147, 150–151; simulated amnesia 145, 147–149, 151–152
maltreatment 103, 167
Mandell, D. S. 314
Mann, R. E. 247
Manteuffel, B. 314
Marlowe, D. B. 193
Matson, J. L. 283, 284
Mattson, S. N. 131
maturation 3, 9, 118, 131, 367–368, 369
Mazurek, M. O. 309

Mazzone, S. 279
MBT *see* Mentalisation-Based Treatment
McMahon, R. J. 65
McNiel, D. E. 264
McWhinnie, A. 251
meanness 210
media attention 22, 307
medication: aggression 170–171;
    antipsychotic 170, 266–267,
    268–270, 271, 284, 321, 322–323;
    Autism Spectrum Disorder 321–323;
    intellectual disability 284–285; *see also*
    pharmacotherapy
Mednick, P. D. 355
Meehl, Paul 33, 41–42
Mehl, S. 262
Mehtar, M. 314
Melin, L. 124
Meloy, J. R. 145
Melser, J. 338, 352
memory 33–34, 36, 41, 232; cognitive
    neoassociation theory 161; impact of
    intoxication on 148–149; psychotic
    disorders 262; simulated amnesia 145,
    147–149, 151–152
mental illness: aetiology of criminal
    behaviour 355; bullying 321; faking
    good 143–144; forensic versus general
    mental health care 267–268, 270–271;
    intellectual disability 282–283; juvenile
    offenders 107; malingering 143,
    145, 149–152; risk factors 339; sex
    offenders 147; treatment 16, 363; *see
    also* personality disorders; psychopathy;
    psychotic disorders
mentalisation 262, 286, 318
Mentalisation-Based Treatment (MBT) 286
Merton, Robert 27
metacognition 261, 262
Miller, D. C. 360
Miller, N. E. 160–161
Minnesota Multiphasic Personality
    Inventory (MMPI-2) 149–150
mirror neurons 121, 125, 130
Mitchell, I. J. 121–122
MMPI-2 *see* Minnesota Multiphasic
    Personality Inventory
Moffitt, T. E. 6, 98–99, 100, 265, 354,
    360–361

Monahan, J. 263
Montes, G. 314
mood disorders 1, 315, 321
mood stabilisers 171
Moore, G. A. 61
moral behaviour 113–115, 124, 126, 130
moral cognitions 113–114, 116–118,
    122–124, 126–127, 129, 130, 279–280;
    see also moral reasoning
moral development 7, 114, 116–118, 122,
    127, 129–131, 212, 279–280
moral emotions 113–114, 116, 118–119,
    124–125, 127, 128, 130–131, 219
Moral Judgment Interview 126, 127
Moral Judgment Sorting Task 126
moral reasoning 113–114, 123–124, 125;
    Autism Spectrum Disorder 318–319;
    intellectual disability 279–280;
    measurement of 126–127, 128;
    neurobiology of 121; psychopathy
    219; stages of 116–118, 279; treatment
    programmes 129, 130, 169; *see also*
    moral cognitions
Moral Sense Task (MST) 127
Moritz, S. 262
Morris, A. S. 57
motivation 195, 235
Moul, C. 216
Mouridsen, S. E. 312
Mowrer, O. H. 160–161
MRI *see* magnetic resonance imaging
MSI-II *see* Multiphasic Sex Inventory
MST *see* Moral Sense Task; multisystemic
    therapy
MTFC *see* Multidimensional Treatment
    Foster Care
Mukkades, N. M. 314
Mullen, P. E. 359, 364
Multidimensional Treatment Foster Care
    (MTFC) 107
Multiphasic Sex Inventory (MSI-II)
    150–151
multisystemic therapy (MST) 106, 170
Murphy, D. 319
Murphy, G. H. 280, 316
Murrie, D. C. 314

Nader-Grosbois, N. 279
Nagin, D. S. 99

384   *Index*

Nagtegaal, M. H. 340, 341
naïve realism 35–36
narcissistic personality disorder 186, 188, 192; aggression 183, 197–198, 200; assessment of 195; comorbidity 193; motivation for crimes 195; offence types 194; prisoners 200
Narcissistic Personality Inventory (NPI) 197
Nasrallah, H. A. 257, 259
Neal, D. 284
negative affect 161
negative emotional reactivity 56–57, 59, 61
neglect 4, 103, 289, 321, 355, 358, 369
Netherlands: criminal irresponsibility 16–17, 22; forensic psychology 21; intellectual disability 286, 287, 289; juvenile offenders 368; nutrition and aggression 172; psychotic disorders 255, 262, 270–271; risk management 340–341, 342; sex offenders 242, 244, 342; transition to adulthood 356
Neumann, C. S. 209
neurobiology 17, 227–241, 357–360; aggression 7, 159–160, 163–164, 171–172; biosocial hypotheses 236–237; conscience 121–122; developmental social neuroscience 2; dual hazard hypothesis 237; externalising disorders 75–86; life-course persistent and adolescence-limited offenders 98–99; limbic system 9, 231–235, 316, 357; models of criminal behaviour 228–231; psychopathy 210–217, 220–221; psychotic disorders 266; *see also* brain; neuroscience
neurocognition 261–262
neurocriminology 86
neuroimaging 76–77, 78, 83–84, 163–164, 216, 360
neuroscience 2, 18–19, 20, 85–86, 363, 364, 370; *see also* brain; neurobiology
neurotransmitters 2, 4, 121–122, 165, 236, 260, 277
New Zealand 361
Newman, J. P. 79, 82–83, 212–213
Nielssen, O. 265
Nifong, Mike 36
Nigg, J. T. 119

Nijman, Henk 255–275
nomothetic approaches 32–33
non-verbal therapies 286
Novaco, R. W. 285
NPI *see* Narcissistic Personality Inventory
Nucci, L. P. 126
nutrition 172, 173

Obradovic, J. 4, 168
O'Brien, B. S. 80
obsessive-compulsive disorder 189–190, 192, 194
ODD *see* oppositional defiant disorder
OFC *see* orbitofrontal cortex
'old me/new me' model 288–289
omega 3 fatty acids 172
operant conditioning 287
oppositional defiant disorder (ODD) 61, 75, 83, 144, 314, 322
orbitofrontal cortex (OFC) 2, 227, 231, 234–235, 357; inhibition 77–78; integrated emotion systems model 230, 231; psychopathy 8, 214–215, 220–221
organised-disorganised typology 30, 39
Ostrov, J. M. 198–199
oxytocin 121–122

Painter, K. 360
Palermo, M. T. 315
Pantus, M. 146
paralimbic dysfunction model 216–217, 220–221, 230–231
paranoid personality disorder 184, 190, 192–193, 194, 195
paraphilia 17, 146
Pardini, D. A. 59, 65
parenthood, transition to 356
parenting 85, 98, 102–103, 369; abusive 355; aetiology of criminal behaviour 355; attachment 120; biological correlates 84; conscience development 130; female delinquents 361; hostile and coercive 60, 66; multisystemic therapy 170; neurobiology of 2; protective factors 104; socialisation 119–120; timeouts 366–367; training 364, 366; *see also* family
passive avoidance learning 116, 119
Patrick, C. J. 165, 209–210

Pavlov, K. A. 165
PCC *see* Psychology of Criminal Conduct
PCL-R *see* Psychopathy Checklist Revised
pedophilia 146–147, 151, 245
peer pressure 86, 355, 366
peer rejection 2, 57, 101
peer review 42
penile plethysmography (PPG) 151
perfectionism 189–190
personality 17, 353; Autism Spectrum
   Disorder 319; psychopathic 26, 29–30,
   206–207, 209, 220
personality disorders 183–205, 206, 363,
   364, 365; aggression 7, 195–199, 200;
   assessment methods 194–195; Autism
   Spectrum Disorder 315; categorical or
   dimensional operationalisation of 190;
   cluster A 184–185, 192–193, 194; cluster
   B 7, 186–188, 191–192, 193–194,
   195, 282; cluster C 189–190, 192,
   194; comorbidity 192, 193, 199, 200;
   intellectual disability 282; MacArthur
   Risk Assessment Study 263; motivation
   for crimes 195; offence types 193–194;
   parental 103; prevalence of 191–193,
   199–200; sex offenders 245; *see also*
   antisocial personality disorder
Peters, Maarten 255–275
PFC *see* prefrontal cortex
pharmacotherapy: aggression 170–171,
   173; Autism Spectrum Disorder
   321–323; externalising disorders 85;
   intellectual disability 284–285, 289;
   psychotic disorders 266–267, 271; *see also*
   medication
Piaget, J. 116
pilot programmes 105
Pinto-Martin, J. A. 314
Pirsig, Robert 27, 29
Plato 123
Platt, J. J. 193
PMT *see* Psychomotor Therapy
Podesta, Lysandra 307–333
Point Subtraction Aggression Paradigm
   (PSAP) 196, 199
policy recommendations 367–368
polygraph tests 21, 30, 43, 151
Popma, Arne 74–96, 164–165
Popper, Karl 26, 27–28, 40–41

positive psychology 250
post-traumatic stress disorder (PTSD) 15,
   314, 317
poverty 100–101, 283
Poythress, N. G. 145
PPG *see* penile plethysmography
PPI *see* Psychopathic Personality Inventory
Prader-Willi syndrome 277
Pratt, D. 16
prefrontal cortex (PFC) 83, 227, 233–234,
   357, 359; adolescence 74; aggression
   160, 163–164, 166, 171; conscience
   121, 125; hyperreactivity 316; violent
   crime 369
prenatal factors 55, 131, 166–167
prevention 2, 16, 76, 324, 370;
   aggression 169; conduct problems
   55; early intervention 366–367;
   neurocriminology 86
Prichard, J. C. 206–207
prisoners 200, 228; personality disorders
   191–193; psychotic disorders 262–263
proactive aggression 158, 163, 168,
   172–173; Autism Spectrum Disorder
   319; community violence 237;
   differential susceptibility theory 167;
   integrated emotion systems model
   229–230; personality disorders 196,
   198–199, 200; social theories 162;
   treatment 169–170
profiling 38–39
Propper, C. B. 61
prosocial behaviour 4, 114, 115, 355,
   363, 368; cortisol reactivity 168; moral
   reasoning 118; school atmosphere 123;
   secure attachment 120
prosocial emotions 65, 85
protective factors 3–4, 97, 104–105, 337,
   348, 355, 363
pseudoscience 5, 28, 40–43
psychodynamic approaches 17, 19
psychological capital 250
Psychology of Criminal Conduct (PCC)
   352–353, 361, 369
Psychomotor Therapy (PMT) 290
Psychopathic Personality Inventory (PPI)
   18, 145, 209
psychopathology 4, 5, 15–24, 365;
   antisocial behaviour and 99; deception 7;

386   *Index*

externalising and internalising disorders 1–4; life-course persistent offenders 99; nomothetic and idiographic approaches 32–33; origins of 1; parental 103; predispositions and environment 9; *see also* forensic psychopathology

psychopathy 8, 206–226, 227, 365; *ad hoc* hypotheses 41; adolescence 77; antisocial personality disorder 186, 199, 217–218; Autism Spectrum Disorder compared with 318–320; brain structure 82, 235; cortisol 236; definition of 185–186; differential amygdala activation model 215–216, 230; emotional responsiveness 360; executive dysfunction 78; falsifiability 28; heuristics in evaluation of 37–38; hippocampus 232–233; integrated emotion systems model 213–215, 229–230; juvenile offenders 107; lack of empathy 80–81, 125, 126; low-fear hypothesis 211–212, 228; malingering 144–146; measurement of 208–209; moral behaviour 115, 124, 125, 130; neurobiological heterogeneity 85; neurocognitive models of 210–217, 220–221; oxytocin levels 122; paralimbic dysfunction model 216–217, 230–231; parental 281; prefrontal cortex 233; psychopathic personality 26, 29–30, 206–207, 209, 220; response modulation 212–213, 229; reward and loss sensitivity 79; risk of future offending 17; self-reports 18; social cognition 218–220; Triarchic model of 209–210; two-factor and three-factor models 207–208; Violent Inhibition Theory 121

Psychopathy Checklist Revised (PCL-R) 17–18, 30, 207–208, 209, 210, 220, 233

psychotic disorders 8, 17, 255–275, 365; aetiology 259–261; case-reports 268–271; cognitive deficits 261–262; definition of 256; diagnostic classification 258–259; phases 259; risk factors for violence 264–266; treatment 266–271; types of violent behaviour 263–264; *see also* antipsychotic medication

PTSD *see* post-traumatic stress disorder

puberty 3, 9, 357, 365

punishment 15–16, 60, 64, 359; frustration-aggression hypothesis 160–161; IES model 232; low-fear hypothesis 228; neurocriminology 86; parenting style 102–103; psychopathy 215, 216; reward and loss sensitivity 79

Radke, S. 220

Raine, Adrian 74–96, 121, 125, 233, 355

Ralfs, S. 279

Rassin, Eric 15–24

Rastam, M. 319

Rau, L. 116

Rawls, John 126

reactive aggression 158, 159–160; Autism Spectrum Disorder 319; biological factors 163–164, 165; children 59–60; community violence 237; differential susceptibility theory 167; disinhibition 210; excitation transfer theory 166; frustration-aggression hypothesis 160; integrated emotion systems model 229–230, 234; personality disorders 196, 198–199, 200; social theories 162; treatment 169–170, 171, 172–173

recidivism 16, 17, 20, 354; Autism Spectrum Disorder 324; deception 144; effectiveness of treatment 19; Forensic Social Network Analysis 342; high-risk groups 357; media attention 22; mental disorders 365; moral development 114; motivation for crimes 195; reward-based treatment 235; risk factors 337; RNR model 339; sex offenders 243, 246–247, 251, 341–342, 359; young people 368

rehabilitation 15, 16, 352–354, 361–366, 370; 'old me/new me' model 288–289; policy recommendations 367–369; restorative approaches 340; sex offenders 8, 151; theories 338; three-component model 362; *see also* treatment

reintegration 242, 245, 251–252, 340

rejection, fear of 189

relapse prevention 148, 340, 341, 354; Circles of Support and Accountability 244, 249, 250; intellectual disability 290; RNR model 339

remorse 187

reparenting 287

representativeness heuristic 37–38
research-based treatment 106–107
response modulation (RM) 28, 79, 83, 212–213, 216, 218, 220, 229
restorative approaches 340
reward and loss processing 6, 74, 75, 79–80, 84
reward-based treatment 235
Reynolds, N. 264
Rhodes, T. 358, 366–367
Rief, W. 262
Riley, E. P. 131
risk assessment 9, 19, 20–21, 85, 337, 348, 355; gender differences 360; MacArthur Risk Assessment Study 263; personality disorders 183; RNR model 353; sex offenders 247; three-component model 362; *see also* risk management
risk factors 6, 97, 100, 360, 363, 369; aetiology of criminal behaviour 354, 355–356; Autism Spectrum Disorder 321, 324; biological 84; conduct problems 55–66; dual hazard hypothesis 237; extra-familial 100–101; family 102–104; fear 3–4; Forensic Social Network Analysis 342; gender differences 360–361; gene-environmental interaction studies 75; individual 102; lifelong vulnerability 9, 356, 365, 367; mental disorders 365; multisystemic therapy 170; personality disorders 183; Psychology of Criminal Conduct 353; psychotic disorders 260, 264–266, 271; relapse prevention 341; sex offenders 243, 244, 247, 248, 250, 252; static and dynamic 337, 339; 'what works' principle 106
risk management 9, 337–351, 353, 364; definitions of 338; Forensic Social Network Analysis 9, 342–347, 348; theoretical principles of 338–340; three-component model 362; tools 340–342; *see also* risk assessment
risk prediction 25
risk-need-responsivity (RNR) model 9, 288, 338–340, 342, 348, 352–353, 361, 370
risk-taking behaviour 74–75, 357–358, 360
risky tests 27–28

RM *see* response modulation
RNR *see* risk-need-responsivity model
Roberts, A. D. L. 193, 194
Robins, L. 354
Robinson, Brittany A. 25–51
Rorschach ink blot test 18, 41
Rose, J. 282
Roske, A. 145
Ross, D. 17
Ross, S. A. 17
Rubia, K. 78

Sagan, Carl 27, 43
Sagarin, E. 162
Salmon, K. 58
Sampson, R. J. 356
SAPROF *see* Structured Assessment of Protective Factors
Sarnoff, A. 355
scepticism 33–34
Schachter, S. 166
Schafer, W. D. 360
Schema Therapy (ST) 287
schemata 168
schizoid personality disorder 184, 185, 193, 194, 195, 245–246
schizophrenia 29, 33, 83, 150, 255–275, 282, 312, 315; *see also* psychotic disorders
schizotypal personality disorder 184, 185, 190, 193, 194, 195, 258
Schonfeld, A. M. 131
school 57, 101, 104–105, 123, 339
science 5, 25–44; biases 35–40; complementary perspectives 27–29; confirmation bias 28, 31–32, 36; empiricism 26; evidence 25; evolutionary view 26; pseudoscience distinction 40–43; scepticism 33–34; scientific realism 25; scientific reasoning 31; scientific thinking 34–35
SCM *see* social competency model
Scragg, P. 264, 312
scripts 163, 168, 361
Sears, R. R. 116, 160–161
Sebastian, C. L. 61
selective attention 213, 220
self-control 1, 104, 158–159, 165, 166, 355, 368

self-correction 41, 44
self-esteem 129–130, 131; aggression 197; intellectual disability 280, 289; risk factors 339; sex offenders 250
self-injury 278, 307, 314, 321, 323
self-referential bias 261
self-regulation 118, 163, 164; intellectual disability 282; sex offenders 147, 245, 247, 248–249, 252; *see also* emotion regulation
Self-Report Psychopathy Scale (SRP) 209
self-serving bias 39, 126, 127, 129
Senland, A. K. 318–319
sensory processing 317
Seo, D. 165
serial killers 30
serotonin 165, 171, 358, 360
SES *see* socio-economic status
sex offenders: Autism Spectrum Disorder 313, 320, 323; Circles of Support and Accountability 8, 242–254, 341–342; Forensic Social Network Analysis 343–347; 'good lives' model 288; hormones 359; intellectual disability 276, 278–279, 281, 282, 285; juvenile offenders 107; malingering 146–147, 150–151; medication 284; psychodynamic interpretation 17; recidivism 243, 246–247, 251; risk assessment 247; subtypes 245–246; testosterone 164; treatment effectiveness 339
sexual abuse 103, 146, 266, 281, 314; *see also* abuse
Sgro, G. 314
Shah, A. 312
shame: aggression 130; avoidant personality disorder 189; conscience 116; moral behaviour 113, 114, 125
Shaw, D. S. 58
Shaw, J. 16
Sheppard, K. 145
Shirtcliff, Elizabeth A. 55–73
siblings 103
Sigurdsson, J. F. 148–149
Silva, P. A. 265, 354
Simonoff, E. 354
SIMS *see* Structured Inventory of Malingered Symptomatology

simulated amnesia 145, 147–149, 151–152
Singer, J. 166
Singh, J. P. 19
SIRS *see* Structured Interview of Reported Symptoms
SIT *see* Stress Inoculation Treatment
skills training 285, 290
Slot, W. 352, 362
Smeets, T. 170
Smith, Sarah Francis 25–51
smoking 167
SMR-SFO *see* SocioMoral Reflection Measure-Short Form Objective
social cognition 261, 262; gender differences 361; intellectual disability 278; orbitofrontal cortex 214; psychopathy 218–220
social competency model (SCM) 288, 289
social exclusion 101
social fear learning 211–212
social interaction theory of coercive action 163
social isolation 243, 248, 315, 317, 324, 341
social learning theory 162, 172, 283, 339
social network analysis 9, 342–347, 348
social norms 186, 187, 191, 206–207
social push hypothesis 237
social skills 97, 355, 363; Aggression Replacement Training 169; Autism Spectrum Disorder 308, 316, 321, 322; Equip programme 129; intellectual disability 285; peer rejection 57; psychotic disorders 267; sex offenders 248–249, 250; women 361
social support 170, 250, 284, 315, 342, 356
socialisation 57, 118, 119–120, 232; conduct problems 58; conscience and 130–131; fear recognition 230; integrated emotion systems model 230; low-fear hypothesis 211, 212, 228; oxytocin 122; women 361
socio-economic status (SES) 83, 104, 265–266, 277, 283, 309
SocioMoral Reflection Measure-Short Form Objective (SMR-SFO) 126, 127, 279–280
Soderstrom, H. 319

SORM *see* Structured Outcomes
    Assessment and Community Risk
    Monitoring
South, S. C. 194
special educational needs 101, 107
Spreen, Marinus 337–351
SRP *see* Self-Report Psychopathy Scale
SRS *see* stress response system
SS-R *see* supernormality scale – revised
Stamperdahl, J. 4, 168
Stanovich, Keith 34, 43
Steinberg, L. 86
Stouthamer-Loeber, M. 100, 103
stress 1, 4, 167, 315
Stress Inoculation Treatment (SIT)
    169–170
stress response system (SRS) 62, 64
Structured Assessment of Protective Factors
    (SAPROF) 337
Structured Interview of Reported
    Symptoms (SIRS) 150
Structured Inventory of Malingered
    Symptomatology (SIMS) 150,
    151–152
Structured Outcomes Assessment and
    Community Risk Monitoring
    (SORM) 341
Sturmey, P. 285
substance use 257, 339, 365; ADHD 100;
    adolescents 359; aetiology of criminal
    behaviour 355; antisocial personality
    disorder 191, 196; Autism Spectrum
    Disorder 315–316; HPA activity
    63–64; intellectual disability 281–282;
    juvenile offenders 107; MacArthur Risk
    Assessment Study 263; parental 103;
    psychopathy 217; psychotic disorders
    260, 271; sex offenders 247; violence
    linked to 265
suicide 16, 187, 314, 365
Sullivan, D. H. 359, 364
supernormality scale – revised (SS-R) 146
supervision 340
Sutherland, E. H. 162
SVT *see* Symptom Validity Test
Swaab, D. 359, 363
Sweden 237, 311–312, 340
Symptom Validity Test (SVT) 152
System 1 and System 2 thinking 34–35

Tabacoff, R. 146
Talley, A. 197
Tandon, R. 257, 259
Taylor, J. L. 285
Taylor, P. J. 265
TCO *see* threat/control override
Tedeschi, J. T. 163
temperament 2, 56–59, 62; Autism
    Spectrum Disorder 319; biological
    correlates 84; conscience and 118–119,
    130–131; female delinquents 361;
    protective factors 104; psychopathy 210;
    stress response system 64
temporal cortex 235, 236–237
Ter Haar-Pomp, Lydia 337–351
Terman, Lewis 277
testosterone 76, 164–165, 236, 284, 358, 359
theory of mind (ToM) 262, 279, 318
therapy 19, 106, 352; Autism Spectrum
    Disorder 321; intellectual disability
    285–286, 287, 288; psychotic disorders
    267; *see also* cognitive behavioural
    therapy; treatment
Thompson, R. A. 113, 120
Thornberry, T. P. 356
Thornton, D. 247
thought disorders 256, 257
threat/control override (TCO) 264
thrill-seeking behaviour 58, 59
timeouts 366–367
ToM *see* theory of mind
Tonnaer, Franca 157–182
Tornusciolo, G. 146
trauma 122, 314, 321, 323, 324
Travis, R. W. 285
treatment 9, 76, 352, 358, 361–366,
    368; aggression 169–172, 173;
    Autism Spectrum Disorder 321–324;
    Circles of Support and Accountability
    242–254; conduct problems 66;
    conscience 129–130; effectiveness of
    19; intellectual disability 284–290,
    291; juvenile offenders 105–107, 129;
    mentally disordered offenders 16;
    neurobiological heterogeneity 84–85;
    Psychology of Criminal Conduct 369;
    psychotic disorders 266–271; reward-
    based 235; risk management 339; *see also*
    rehabilitation; therapy

390　*Index*

Triarchic model of psychopathy 209–210
truth serums 43
Truzzi, M. 43
Turiel, E. 115
Tyrer, P. 284
Tysse, J. E. 148

Underwood, Benton 31–32
Unemotional ACM profile 63–64
unemployment 311, 320
United States 32, 101, 157, 242, 251, 307, 358

vagal regulation 83
Valentine, J. 197
valproate 171
Van Binsbergen, Marion 352–373
Van der Laan, P. H. 352, 362
Van der Leeden, R. 15
Van Engeland, H. 316
Van Oorsouw, Kim 143–156
Van Os, J. 260
Van Vugt, E. 279
Vanheule, S. 245
ventromedial frontal cortex (VMFC) 121, 212
Verona, E. 218
Verwaaijen, Sanne 352–373
victimisation 320–321
video games 34, 163
Viding, E. 76
Vigilant ACM profile 62–63, 64
violence: Autism Spectrum Disorder 307, 311–313; community 237; cortisol 236; deception as developmental marker for 144; definition of 157; domestic 85, 103, 192, 196, 199, 283, 369; externalising disorders 75; Forensic Social Network Analysis 344–345; General Aggression Model 168; HPA activity 64; intellectual disability 276–277, 278, 291; juvenile offenders 97, 99–100, 101, 107; lifelong vulnerability 365; neurobiology of 8, 358, 360; personality disorders 183, 191–194, 195–196; protective factors

104; psychopathy 227; psychotic disorders 255, 262–271; as public health problem 157, 358; risk factors 355; testosterone 164, 236; video games 34; *see also* aggression
Violent Inhibition Theory (VIT) 121
VMFC *see* ventromedial frontal cortex
Vogelvang, Bas 242–254
voices, hearing 256, 264

Wallace, Albert Russell 26
Walrath, C. M. 314
Walsh, A. 103
Walton, Reggie 33–34
Ward, T. 245, 282, 338, 352, 361, 362, 363
Warren, J. I. 194, 314
Waschbusch, D. A. 61
Watkins, M. M. 145
Watts, Ashley L. 25–51
Webb, R. 16
Werner, S. M. 262
West, Richard 34
'what works' principle 106, 252, 338–339
White, J. L. 354
White, S. F. 80
Williams, D. 251
Willoughby, M. T. 61
Wilson, C. 251
Wilson, R. J. 251
Witt, K. 264–265
women 360–361; Autism Spectrum Disorder 308, 312; offence types 194; personality disorders 191–192, 193; prefrontal cortex 233; treatment implications 364
Wood, J. M. 19
Woodward, T. S. 262
World Health Organization 157, 259, 369
Wouda, P. L. 356

Yang, Y. 77, 121, 125, 216–217
Yates, P. M. 338, 352

Ziegler, M. 262
Zillmann, D. 166